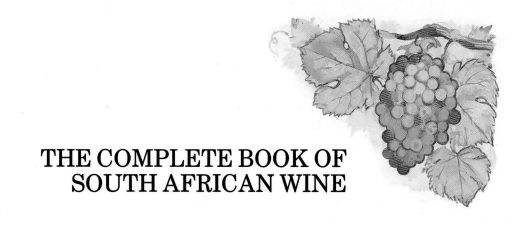

THE COMPLETE BOOK OF
SOUTH AFRICAN WINE

THE COMPLETE BOOK OF SOUTH AFRICAN

Wine

DAVID HUGHES   PHYLLIS HANDS   JOHN KENCH

Photography by CLOETE BREYTENBACH *and* GINGER ODES
Illustrations by ANGUS McBRIDE

C STRUIK PUBLISHERS CAPE TOWN

Struik Publishers Pty (Ltd) (a member of
The Struik Group (Pty) Ltd)
Struik House, Oswald Pirow Street
Foreshore, Cape Town 8001

Reg No: 63/00203/07

First Edition 1983
Second Edition 1988
Second Impression 1991

Original design by: Joanne Simpson, Cape Town
Edited by: Peter Borchert (1st Edition), Ellis
Pender and Bev Bernstone (2nd Edition)
Maps by: Institute of Cartographic Analysis,
Stellenbosch University
Map contour shading by: Margo Branch, Cape
Town
Index by: Ethleen Lastovica, Cape Town
Photosetting and reproduction by: McManus
Bros (Pty) Ltd, Cape Town
Printed and bound by: Leefung Asco Printers
(Pty) Ltd, Hong Kong

ISBN 0 86977 636 3

PHOTOGRAPHIC CREDITS

With some exceptions the photographs for this
book are by Cloete Breytenbach and Ginger
Odes. Many of those by Ginger Odes were taken
for Stellenbosch Farmers' Winery, which retains
the copyright therein. Those who kindly made
material available from their collections were:

Anglo American Corporation 218 (left)
The Bergkelder 163, 175, 177 (left)
The Cape Archives 21, 26
Andy Christowitz 119, 120, 130, 131, 132 (top),
   187(4), 215, 234, 279, 286 (bottom), 288, 297,
   302, 303, 304
Albertus De Wet 282 (right)
Bob Dickson 16 (right), 17, 18, 22 (by courtesy of
   Groot Constantia Museum)
Eikendal Vineyards 151
Patricia Fraser 203
Gilbey Distillers and Vintners 154 (top)
Hartenberg Estate 156
KWV 34 (left), 228, 230
Herman Potgieter 10, 137 (left), 209 (top), 210
André Pretorius 24 (bottom)
Simon Rappoport 247
Robertson Wine Trust 281 (right)
The South African Library 23, 27
Stellenbosch Farmers' Winery 98, 99, 100, 101,
   102, 103, 104, 105, 106, 107, 108, 109, 110, 111,
   192(2), 241 (bottom)
Stellenbosch University (P. Goussard) 65
Villiera Estate 245

Copyright for the above mentioned photographs
remains with the owners.

CAPTIONS
*Title page: Bringing in the harvest in the
Rawsonville area*
Overleaf: Delheim Estate
Pages 10 and 11: Franschhoek Valley

Acknowledgements

FIRST EDITION

John Kench

The making of this book was a unique experience in which many people were involved. In its early days it was guided by René Gordon, now continuing her career in Melbourne, Australia – I am grateful to her for much creative help and encouragement.

The knowledge and experience that lie behind this account of the Cape winelands is that of co-authors Phyllis Hands and David Hughes. Their many years of involvement in wine, in its growing, making and culture, their wealth of human contacts among the Estates, co-operatives and wine-making companies, as well as their personal kindness and encouragement, were a constant inspiration throughout.

A special debt, too, is owed to Arnold Matthews for his patient, wise and scholarly editing of a massive manuscript; at every turn of the book's progress his 'feel' for the use of good English is in evidence in a multitude of felicitous touches.

The text of the book was scrutinized by a number of people concerned with different aspects of the South African winelands. Wine writer and connoisseur Simon Rappoport made many helpful suggestions and I also freely acknowledge an indirect debt to Simon – that of his many articles in *Wynboer* magazine, particularly those on the hitherto little covered territory of the wine makers of the 'inland' region. *Wynboer* is also acknowledged in respect of the 'Vineyard Calendar' appearing in this book, as an article published by the magazine formed the basis of this month-by-month account of the vineyard manager's life. Further insights into the complexities of the modern science of wine making were given by Professor Joël van Wyk, head of the Department of Oenology at the University of Stellenbosch.

To one person in particular I would like to record a special thank you. Professor Chris Orffer, the successor of Professors Perold and Theron at the University of Stellenbosch and the doyen of present-day viticulturalists in the Cape, displayed an 'infinite capacity for taking pains' in his examination of the text, throwing fresh light not only on viticulture but on many other aspects of winelands life; and the cultivar chapter in the book is frankly in debt to Chris's definitive work, *Wine Grape Cultivars in South Africa*.

A book on this scale is made up of many parts and the putting together of these elements is a creative act in its own right. Peter Borchert of Struik Publishers has performed this creative function with a fine sympathy both for the book's overall architecture and for its multitude of details. In this he has been ably assisted by his many colleagues, especially Wim Reinders on the production of the book and Leni Martin who did the proof-reading.

And finally I record my debt of gratitude to my family, my wife Ekin and my children Paul and Nicola, for their loving support during the making of this book.

Cape Town 1983

Phyllis Hands

It would be impossible for me to acknowledge by name everyone who has contributed so much to the making of this book – to them all therefore I offer my sincere thanks, particularly my colleagues at Stellenbosch Farmers' Winery. A few, however, I must mention: David Rawdon, Bob Toms, Professor Chris Orffer and especially David Hughes, for they have provided constant inspiration and but for their encouragement I would have remained a grape grower and private wine drinker. And, of course, my thanks go to John Kench for his fine writing.

I am also grateful to Peter Borchert of Struik for his limitless capacity for work, good humour and patience. And most of all I acknowledge great debt to my family who have been so tolerant of my abiding passion for wines, especially those of South Africa.

Stellenbosch 1983

David Hughes

I find it difficult to single out people to thank as so many have parted with so much information over the years. However, thanks are sincerely due to Kathy, my wife, who has always been a source of inspiration and a willing guinea pig to try a 'new' wine. And my gratitude extends to two other women who, in their spare time, typed more pages than ever eventually made their way into this book – Cynthia Perthel and Andrea Arnold.

Bill Winshaw was fundamental in bringing me to South Africa and setting me on the South African wine trail. Thanks, too, to Stellenbosch Farmers' Winery's Ronnie Melck, in some ways my wine 'guru', and Lothar Barth for his constant encouragement, both of whom allowed me the freedom to cover the whole industry; and in particular, to wine buyers Gert Niewoudt, Jeff Wedgwood, Wouter Pienaar and Dieter Thielhelm and the wine-making staff under John Winshaw who introduced me to South African wine. Nor without the friendly reception and advice received from all Stellenbosch Farmers' Winery competitors would I have been able to test the wider horizons of the wine industry.

Then, too, all the other wine makers, viticulturists and wine-associated people in the KWV, co-operatives, Estates, farms, government institutions – especially the ever helpful people at Nietvoorbij, Stellenbosch University. Thanks go in particular to Professor Chris Orffer and his two former pupils, viticulturists Ernst le Roux and Pieter le Roux for having introduced me to their fascinating discipline, and certainly those people who provided the equipment and accessories to make it all happen – indeed, everyone mentioned in the book.

Various wine-tasting groups, in particular The Wine Swines, have always helped me to obtain a broadly based opinion on wines.

The Italians have had a considerable, yet largely unheralded, influence on the South African wine industry. Two names I must mention in this regard are Bruno Mori (retired from Monis) and Carlo Valle of Stellenbosch Farmers' Winery. John Martin of Backsberg, with his wide knowledge of the developing days, has always been a mine of information.

The book simply would not have been, without the photographs of Cloete Breytenbach and Ginger Odes, nor could it have happened without Phyllis Hands' energy, and the re-writing of John Kench and the ever-diligent, patient and painstaking Peter Borchert.

Stellenbosch 1983

SECOND EDITION

The Authors

The authors would like to thank all those involved in the production of this revised edition, particularly Ellis Pender and Bev Bernstone of Struik for their hard work. David Hughes expresses his thanks to his secretary, Cathy Kemper, for her constant help.

Cape Town and Stellenbosch 1987

The Publishers

The publishers would like to thank the many people in the winelands without whose help this major revision would not have been possible. Their patience during unexpected and lengthy telephone calls, their encouraging response to letters requesting information and their interest generally are much appreciated. Once again we are grateful to Professor Joël van Wyk and Dr Chris Orffer for sharing their knowledge. We would also like to thank Peter Bishop for his enthusiastic help, and Debbie Daniel, Cathy Kemper and Tessa Kennedy for their various valued contributions.

Cape Town 1987

CONTENTS

PREFACE

With a handful of exceptions, the wines of South Africa were for many generations regarded as the poor relations of those of Europe. This is no longer so. In the decades since the Second World War, South African wine has emerged with startling speed and vigour to find an independent voice and a clear, highly respected identity of its own. Long the passion and pleasure of South Africans, it is now also rapidly gaining recognition in international wine circles.

This has been achieved in spite of the fact that the winelands of South Africa are small by comparison with those of Europe, that their production is modest – some eight million hectolitres a year as compared, for example, to the 68 million hectolitres produced annually in Italy alone – and that historically they are a mere three centuries old compared with the vineyards of the old world whose origins are all but lost in the mists of history.

Given certain limitations and South Africa's distance from world markets, the achievements of local farmers and wine makers have been little short of heroic. They have, however, had certain advantages.

As in any flourishing wine community they have a deep rapport with their wine lovers. For South Africans, particularly the people of the western Cape region, but increasingly those of the Transvaal, the Orange Free State, and even the old whisky, gin and beer stronghold of Natal, wine is a part of life and tradition.

At the core of this tradition is the setting of the winelands, surely one of the grandest backdrops that a wine lover could desire. Soaring, rugged mountains and steep-sided valleys, images of oak trees, of whitewashed walls, the memory of the smells and sounds of summer, are readily conjured up. The visitor's camera lingers lovingly on all the myriad details of architecture, of elaborately wrought gables, of fine, glossy dark polished woodwork, of ornamental ponds, of wagons and trailers laden with grapes. And the smell and taste of summer's wealth is complemented and completed by the aroma which drifts from the doorway of the old wine cellar nearby.

This is the smell of fermenting grapes, white and red, in their vats. It is a familiar smell for wine has been one of man's most dependable companions down the ages. It has been a part of almost every major culture since the dawn of recorded history and was undoubtedly a good friend and solace to our ancestors long before then. Its wisdom has gone into many languages and the images of its growing and making have been recorded in art from the walls of the tombs of the pharoahs to the tapestries of the medieval world. For if wine was a benison to the ancient world it continued as a consolation in the Christian era, emerging like a thread from the shadows of the Dark Ages. Much of the art of its making was preserved by the monks; and as the blood of Christ it achieved sanctity. It was also given a patron, Saint Vincent, to watch over the fortunes of the vignerons of Europe, over the sturdy farmers and wine makers whose craft had been passed down from father to son since the Romans spread the culture of the vine in the wake of their conquests.

This process of colonization by the vine received a new impetus from the Renaissance onwards with the opening up of new worlds of exploration, in the Americas, in Africa. By the end of the seventeenth century the vine and its culture had taken root in a small corner of the Cape of Good Hope, from where it slowly spread, first across the coastal plain and then into the great brooding mountain ranges which stood barring the way to the vast and mysterious regions of an unknown continent.

Courage was needed in this continent, not only for the daily business of survival but for the slow development of the arts of life, of government, art and architecture, the development of language. Under the blazing sun of Africa each found a form in which many things from the inheritance of Europe were retained, but in which the

smell and taste of the new land were also powerfully present and found their way, too, into the redolence of the wine.

Over the long years man and the land grew up together. And the wine was a measure of this progress, of this subtly maturing relationship. Of course, there were setbacks. The story of wine in South Africa has its disasters, some of them of the first magnitude; one which still haunts the memory even of contemporary wine makers was that of the phylloxera epidemic. But from each setback was born a new urgency, a new determination. That determination persists today, and is paying off handsomely – the annual earnings of South African winelands exceeded R260 million in 1986, making local wines an important part of the national economy.

What exactly, shorn of all its traditional meanings and associations, its importance to the community, is this seemingly eternal liquid which has trickled through the span of human history?

At its simplest and most prosaic, wine is the fermented juice of the grape, being the fruit of the domesticated vine, *Vitis vinifera*.

Man has long domesticated the natural process of fermentation, the conversion of sugar into alcohol by the action of yeast, and has turned it to his own use. The wine maker operates as a creative midwife. At the basic level he cannot alter the reaction, nor would he wish to do so. But through his scientific training he can substantially modify it to produce a wide spectrum of wines.

He can, for example, curtail the reaction so that a high degree of natural sugar is left in the liquid, producing a sweet wine. Or he can allow the fermentation to run its course, using up more or all of the natural sugar to make a 'dry' wine.

Besides the division into sweet and dry, and all the shadings in between, there is, of course, the major distinction between red and white wines. There are two main 'types' of vine: those producing red grapes and those producing white. Within these are many individual varieties or cultivars, though a relative minority is used in the winelands. Well-known cultivars grown locally include, among the whites, Steen (Chenin Blanc), Riesling (both the local Cape Riesling and the unrelated Rhine or Weisser Riesling), Colombar, Palomino, Sauvignon Blanc, and Bukettraube; and among the reds, the noble Cabernet Sauvignon, Cinsaut, Pinotage, Shiraz and Pinot Noir. At the hands of the wine maker each cultivar produces wines of specific character.

Wine making today is a combination of craft and sophisticated technology, but for the making of fine wine a further element is necessary – a dedication on the part of the wine maker. Such dedication to their

calling has been, and continues to be, the hallmark of South Africa's makers of fine wines, both the men of the older, post-war generation who first began to put local wines on the international map, and their sons and daughters. For, as in the winelands of Europe, of France, Germany, Spain, Portugal and Italy, the threads of family tradition run strongly here. The Myburghs; the Krones and the Therons, who have been energetically populating the Tulbagh Valley for centuries; the De Villiers family of Drakenstein; the Malans, Faures, Jouberts and Bosmans: all these and many others have handed down with their ancestral lands a powerful family tradition of wine making.

But even the strongest and healthiest tradition needs new blood. And among the older families are many new ones who have brought drive and initiative to the winelands. The famous Graue family, progenitors of the Nederburg tradition which has been taken up and brought to fruition over three decades by Günter Brözel and his skilled team, the Back family of the Paarl Valley, and a host of others have all served to enrich an old tradition with new ideas. Then there are the loners who have come into the winelands from outside, gradually establishing a place for themselves. Timothy Hamilton-Russell, for example, an advertising executive with a lifelong passion for wines, both those of the Cape and of France, has planted vineyards at Walker Bay and is developing fine wines in the tradition of Burgundy and Bordeaux. A Cape Town architect, Gilbert Colyn, introduced a novel concept with his Estate of Zevenwacht, launched as a public company in which investors can buy shares, and have part of each year's vintage bottled for them under their own exclusive label.

Innovation is also evident in the Franschhoek Valley where, with the 1983 vintage, a number of small grape growers under the leadership of Michael Trull, another advertising executive, arranged with the Franschhoek Co-operative to keep their grapes separately and to have wines of origin made from them. This arrangement removes from the wine grape farmer the expense of setting up his own cellar and has the added advantage of an expert wine maker at the co-operative to make his wine but without losing its origin. It is now possible, therefore, to have wines of origin on the market from Michael Trull's farm 'La Bri' with its own special climatic and soil characters, as well as wines from several other Franschhoek farmers participating in the scheme.

In the technical field of wine making great advances have been made in recent years. Some of these have been stimulated by changes in public taste. Perhaps the most important change in South African

drinking patterns occurred from the early 1960s, with a shift from fortified wines, the Hanepoots, Jerepigos and Muscadels, towards the appreciation of natural wines. Long advocated by one of the winelands' most important historic figures, William Charles Winshaw, founder in the 1930s of the Stellenbosch Farmers' Winery, natural table wines first began to take a hold on the public imagination after the Second World War. From that time they have grown to dominate the local market, making a balance with the traditional sherries and ports and the brandies, important exports of the winelands for many years. The climax of this development was the spectacular and unexpected success of the Stellenbosch Farmers' Winery product, Lieberstein, which became for a number of years the world's largest-selling natural wine and one which still retains a devoted following.

With changes of taste and the increasing sophistication of wine-making methods has gone a marked increase in the number of wines made and these now number in excess of 1 500 individual products. Some 6 000 wine-grape farmers produced in 1986 a harvest of some one million tonnes. Only about 73 of these farmers have their properties registered as Estates, but not all are currently bottling their own wines. By far the bulk of the harvest is made by the 70 co-operative wineries who in turn supply the KWV and a number of massive producing wholesalers, led by the largest, Stellenbosch Farmers' Winery, which currently sells as much as half the wine produced in South Africa every year. Overseeing all these is the colossus of the Ko-operatieve Wijnbouwers Vereniging van Zuid-Afrika, Beperkt, the KWV, legally and administratively the controlling force in winelands life.

Until the 1970s, the KWV had almost total monopoly of South Africa's wine export sales, mostly in bulk as fortified wines and brandy, but very little natural wine in labelled bottles. However, with the introduction of the Wine of Origin legislation in 1973, major local wine merchants were at last able to exploit the potential of an overseas market and today South African wines can be found in many parts of the world bearing the familiar labels found at home. The Nederburg range is particularly successful overseas, probably as a result of prestige gained from the annual Nederburg Auction. Without doubt South African wineries are moving quietly yet impressively into the international market.

Wines and wine lovers, farmers and wine masters, vineyards in a splendid landscape enriched by memories of another age – all are the complex elements of a great and vivid canvas. And these are the subjects of this book. Many pioneer works have already been written on aspects of the emergence of South African wine, but this book is a comprehensive celebration which brings together all the many parts and provides an overview of the South African winelands and the industry as a whole.

At the heart of the book lie the winelands themselves, their many ways, their many people, the rich fabric of their wines. They are spread across three hundred years and many hundreds of kilometres of mountains and valleys. The 12 official wine-making Districts range from Constantia through to Durbanville, to Stellenbosch and Paarl, Worcester, Robertson and Swellendam, the high valley of Tulbagh, the coastal areas such as the Swartland, Overberg and Piketberg, and the irrigation-dependent schemes along the banks of the Orange and Vaal rivers comprising the Douglas District.

These are covered in geographical terms in the chapters on the winelands Districts, each producing unit of which is presented alphabetically by District. The Districts are presented spreading outwards from the Cape Peninsula, which co-incidentally reflects a roughly chronological order as well, from the oldest wine District to the youngest. The first chapters of the book supply a background of history, of the life and times of *Vitis vinifera* before and after its introduction to the vineyard, the science of the modern cellar, and, particularly important from the wine taster's point of view, the range of cultivars.

Much of this information is as old as wine making, but much is contemporary, for modern vine growing is no longer a matter of planting a row of cuttings and waiting for divine intervention to bring in a good crop. Contemporary oenology, or the science of wine making, is no longer simply a question of trampling a vat of grapes and tipping them into an ox-hide to ferment. The instinctual and 'artistic' aspects of these ancient crafts, while still there, have been brought up to date with scientific knowledge which to a great extent guarantees the purity and cleanliness of the modern product and as near to perfect a result as yet achieved.

With knowledge and insight, the experience of the many journeys of the winelands can be greatly enhanced and deepened. But at the end of the day's journey, whether it be to Hendrik Cloete's magnificent and justly famous wine cellar at Groot Constantia, a visit to the wine and brandy museums at Stellenbosch or the enormous wine-making and maturation facilities of the KWV's headquarters at Paarl, perhaps a tour of one of the popular wine routes of Stellenbosch and Paarl, or deeper inland to the vineyards of Worcester or Rawsonville, the wine lover comes home in the evening with the day's prize: the wine.

It may be a red wine or a white, rich and fortified or a fine light dry white; it may be a delicate rosé, or a sparkling wine of the kind made by the traditional *méthode Champenoise*; it may be for drinking today or at the turn of the century. But whichever it is, it will undoubtedly be a competently made wine, carefully guided through the many stages of its creation.

Such a wine needs the tribute of an understanding tasting. The final chapter of this book, 'An Approach to Wine', sums up the art of tasting as it is understood today and includes many other arcane matters such as the language of wine, suggestions on putting together a private cellar, and the many ways in which wine and food may effectively be combined.

To develop your understanding of South African wine you should ultimately go out into the sun, into the vineyards, meet the many hospitable people whose lives are bound up with this creation of man and nature in partnership. You must walk the vineyard rows, listen to the voice of the farmer, explore the cool cellar with the wine maker, then sit at a rough wooden table in the shade of oak trees and savour his wine.

This is the reality for which this book is but a prelude. All its journeys travel towards this point. They begin, however, at another point, far back in time, in the middle of the seventeenth century, at a moment on a hot and windy shore when an idea was born in the mind of the man who was to become South Africa's first wine maker.

THE HISTORICAL JOURNEY

The first wine maker in South Africa was Jan van Riebeeck. It was he who imported the first grape-vine cuttings, who was responsible for laying out the first vineyards and made the first wine – albeit in small quantity and of dubious quality. But his example was soon followed by the local farmers who were impressed by the resilient qualities of the Commander's vines and by the weight of their crops.

Thereafter, the wine and the society of the Free Burghers grew up together, gradually gaining independence and an identity of their own. This identity became established in the second half of the eighteenth century, when a new and surprising affluence came to the world of the wine farmers of the Cape. It was then that they built their splendid homesteads, the stately *opstalle* which have become a central feature of the winelands, part of the lingering nostalgia for that time.

For it was a period which came and went. It was followed by political conflicts and, for the wine farmers, increasing economic distress with the gradual loss of their overseas market and withdrawal of the protective tariffs by the Palmerston Government in Britain. All these culminated in the legendary disaster of the winelands in the late nineteenth century: the epidemic of a near microscopic plant aphid, *Phylloxera vastatrix*, which included the South African vines in its destruction of most of the world's vineyards.

Recovery in the Cape was relatively rapid; by an ironic twist, too rapid. Hardly had the winelands recovered from the grape pest than there loomed the problems of an uncontrolled over-production.

It was a testing time. Millions of litres of excess wine had to be poured away.

The beginning of a 300-year-old industry . . . Commander Van Riebeeck examines his first, long-awaited consignment of vine cuttings from Europe. Supplemented by further shipments, these 'Spaanse druyfen' flourished and in 1659 their fruits were harvested and pressed to make the first Cape wine.

Many farmers went bankrupt, many moved to the towns. Organization was needed, not least among the farmers themselves. For this was an independent and free-spirited people, not easily bound into strictures of an organizational form.

But survival was at stake, the survival of the winelands and of everything which they had stood for in the vision and tradition both of the Cape and of the country at large. A new outlook was needed, a new unity of purpose. And, in the first decades of the present century, the form of this unity was found in the co-operative movement of the winelands.

All this grew from the modest vineyard planted by the first Commander of the Cape, Jan van Riebeeck. It is a remarkable efflorescence and a triumph of a tenacious spirit in an often hard and intractable land. And this spirit and purpose was already visible in the career of the first wine maker himself.

Not that he was not human. There was, for example, the small matter of a somewhat mysterious lapse in conduct in the Far East, that had never quite been cleared up. But, still, he was a personable young man – he was in his early thirties at this time – and his report on the possibilities for settlement at the strange and rather mysterious outpost of Africa known as the Cape of Good Hope was certainly intelligent: intelligent enough to suggest him as a possibility for the position of first Commander of the post. Moreover, it would give him a chance to reinstate himself.

Such thoughts as these must have occupied the mind of Secretary van Dam on that day in 1650 when he and his fellow council members in their chamber in Amsterdam summoned Company servant Johan Anthonisz van Riebeeck, to interrogate him upon certain matters pertaining to the Company's wealth and welfare.

The Company, of course, was the Dutch East India Company, in the words of Louis Leipoldt, 'that most profitable combination of unblushing piracy and commercialized

Protestantism'. And Mr van Dam and the Council were gathered to debate a relatively minor but nevertheless important venture. This was the establishment of a halfway house on the route to the East Indies, the apparently inexhaustible source of their wealth in spice – several hundred per cent in profit on a single voyage raised no eyebrows. Dotted among the resonant Dutch accents were the magic names: Java and Batavia, Malacca and Tandjong Priok. These were the important places where the Company's senior servants were sent. But there was still a job to be done at the Cape, and this young man might be the one for it.

They took a risk and decided on Van Riebeeck. At the age of 33, he found himself no longer an assistant ship's surgeon or an assistant factor, but a fully-fledged Commander. As he mused his way through the thronged and bustling streets of Amsterdam on the way home to tell his wife, he must have been a thoughtful and somewhat nervous man. Of course, he knew the Cape. That was partly the reason he had been given the job. The year before he had spent 18 days wandering around the lower slopes of the precipitous mountain with its tablecloth of cloud, while they were rescuing the crew of the *Haarlem* which had run aground on that windy and treacherous coast. But it was a command: moreover, something might be made out of it. If nothing else, it would be an adventure . . .

They gave him three ships which together would have fitted comfortably into today's Church Square in Cape Town. His flagship was a 200-tonner, however, done up with all the trimmings, including a nicely gilded camel – the Dromedaris – and the Commander's quarters were stately, and by the hard standards of the seventeenth century, comfortable.

They had need to be, over a three-month voyage through the tropics, tacking out through a great arc of the Atlantic. And there were some nervous souls even among the old hands, while some of the few women on board were naturally apprehensive of what they were to expect.

Their anxieties, however, must soon have been forgotten in the impact of arrival. For they beheld a beautiful wilderness – and a magnificent natural monument: the vast mountain with its great buttresses on either side rose high over a deep, sandy valley which ran up from the blue edge of the ocean. After the months of speculation, this was the reality, this was the raw material of their future, of the lives they and their descendants were to make in this land of which they were to become a part.

The first boats were dropped, and the Commander and his party were rowed ashore where they scrambled out of the water onto the beach on 6 April 1652. Soon they had their belongings gathered around them. At this time of the year strong winds could be blowing, and the clouds gathered around the mountain tops might presage the coming autumn. There was urgent work to be done.

The nucleus of a small community soon sprang up at the water's edge. A rough wood-and-mud fort was a priority, and was soon built. Sailors' stories dwelt upon the terrors of the great black-maned Cape lion; and a smaller but not necessarily less malevolent threat came from those diminutive human figures that flitted among the scrub on the slopes and darted among the boulders at the end of the beach.

There were not many of these bands of Hottentots (or Khoikhoi), the only indigenous population here – about 60 all told, broken up into family-size bands. They had no settled community or agriculture, living meagrely off shellfish and fruit, including the berries of a wild vine, *Rhoicissus capensis*, later to become

popularly known as 'bobbejaanstou', or monkey creeper.

Perhaps that was what gave Van Riebeeck the idea, or perhaps he already had it. At all events, it is certain that it had crystallized within a month or so after the landing, even as the fort was being laid out and the first simple thatched houses were being built: he would introduce the cultivation of the European vine to Africa.

It was a novel idea. It might work. Van Riebeeck had spent his life in Holland and in the tropics, but he was educated enough to know something about the conditions of the Mediterranean wine-growing countries. And the Cape seemed to offer the same type of climate. The winters – their first was on its way – were wet, but without severe frosts; and the summers were long and hot, with a steady temperature. True, the earth did not appear very fertile, but he had the assurance from Hendrik Boom, his head gardener, busy laying out the Company's garden further up the valley, that the vegetables they had brought with them were taking well in this dry soil, with the help of irrigation from the Fresh River trickling down the valley.

And if the vines took, if they were successful? The possibilities were, if not infinite, at least exciting. His brief from those cautious gentlemen back in their candle-lit council chamber in Amsterdam had been to establish a station, revictualling and watering-place, as well as a repair depôt for the Company's fleets on their way around the Cape of Good Hope to the Orient. It had long been needed, and the increase of the fleet and its traffic had made it imperative. The Fresh River would supply the water, increasing flocks of sheep and cattle would supply the meat.

But the vines would supply something extra, something more than the familiar basic staples.

Sitting in his newly-built but somewhat dusty Commander's quarters down by the busy water's edge, one word must have been foremost in Van Riebeeck's mind. Wine! *De wijn!* What they had up till now had been tossed half way around the world, frozen half to death in Holland, beaten up and all but evaporated in the tropics, a pale, thin, bitter travesty of the vision which must have been in the new Commander's mind.

If all went well they would grow enough for the community, for his hundred men and their handful of sturdy wives, supplies for the passing ships, and even perhaps for a little private trading with those wine-starved Company servants in the East. But further thought was needed in an exercise of intelligence allied with cunning. Vine-cuttings must be acquired, the Company must send them out, and for that, solid reasons must be advanced to sway the minds of those sceptical old men who perpetually suspected their overseas employees of attempting to feather exotic nests at their expense.

Scratching assiduously with his quill pen, the Commander wrote eloquently to Secretary van Dam. The community was coming along, building was going forward apace, the Company's gardens were already healthily productive. Vegetables had been planted, and wheat had been sown on a fine, flat site further along the beach. But now there was a further matter which he would like to discuss. The Council did not immediately show much interest in the Commander's idea. True, many of his arguments were persuasive. The climate was promising, near enough to

A miscellany of wine artefacts spanning three centuries. From left: 'White Delft' pilgrim's bottle and an English leather bottle, both from the seventeenth century; a fine VOC glass, the lower stem and foot replaced by silver, possibly made in Newcastle during the mid-eighteenth century, but engraved in Holland; a wheel-engraved and cut VOC decanter of Silesian glass also of the 1800s; two wine bottles of the nineteenth century, probably English, the first being for Constantia wine and the second for champagne. From the late 1700s when cork gained acceptance as the material for closing bottles of wine, implements have been devised for its easy removal: from top left Samuel Pemberton's silver pocket corkscrew, Thomason's patent of 1802, Weir's 'Lazytongs' of 1884 followed by Armstrong's invention of 1902; from bottom left a plain corksrew, probably English, of the late nineteenth century, taps for drawing off champagne without removing the cork, an English invention of the latter half of the nineteenth century, and a champagne cork remover of uncertain date. These and many other exhibits are housed in the museum of Groot Constantia.

that of France or Spain. But one other argument was particularly effective, more so in view of Van Riebeeck's surgical training. This was the question of scurvy. Although the Dutch of the seventeenth century had no clear idea of what caused this disease, they were all too aware of its effects. Deficiency of the vitamins represented by fresh fruit and vegetables could cause up to a 40 per cent death rate on a long voyage (an extreme case was that of the voyage of Magellan: by the end of the journey all but 20 of his 200 sailors had died of the disease). But though the cause of scurvy was not fully understood, it had come to be general knowledge, particularly among the fleets of the wine-making countries of France, Spain and Portugal, that wine, especially young, red wine which contains some vitamins, could help to counteract the effects of the deficiency. A further advantage of wine was that though it could be chemically unstable, it generally travelled and tasted better than water kept in a leaky keg in the hold of a small wooden ship.

Compared to the fleets of the Mediterranean countries, the Dutch ships had hitherto fared badly. But by Van Riebeeck's time the advantages of carrying wine had come to be recognized by the Dutch East India Company who had written a daily ration of wine for each of their sailors into their regulations.

The response to Van Riebeeck's request was not immediate. It was, after all, an unusual one, and one which would have put the Secretary to some inconvenience. Eloquence and good sense, however, finally activated the old gentleman, who obtained some grape-vine planting material, and sent it out to Van Riebeeck 18 months after his first request.

The small vine cuttings were packed into wet earth and sewn up in sailcloth which the sailors were instructed to keep damp. Perhaps they were over-zealous, for by the time the samples arrived at the Cape and were opened, their contents had rotted. But at least his project had been approved, and within a few months the first new healthy vine plants arrived on the shores of Africa, packed in earth. It must have been a moment of intense excitement and anticipation for the Commander, as he watched the cloth wrappings fall away to reveal the small, twisted plants.

Much research has been devoted to identifying these first vine plants, and to tracing their origins. Both these and their successors appear to have come from the French vineyards, which is natural enough since these were the nearest vineyards to Holland. Van Riebeeck refers to some of them as his *Spaanse druyfen*, which reveals little. He was in fact to receive a good number of consignments of planting materials over the next few years, most of which he notes as coming from France, not Spain as his choice of name for them would imply. In 1656 two ships, the *Dordrecht* and the *Parel* both brought French vines and the following year Van Riebeeck again noted that he had received a supply of cuttings from France. It is possible that his 'Spanish grapes' were Hanepoot, otherwise known in France as Muscat d' Alexandrie (this is an early example of the kind of multiple nomenclature which still confuses South African wine lovers). Steen, the French Chenin Blanc, was also probably introduced at this time.

The exact identity of his first vine samples probably mattered less, if at all, than the simple fact that they were alive and well after their long voyage and ready

to be planted. And planted they soon were, by the Head Gardener, the appropriately named Hendrik Boom and his assistant Jacob Cloete van Kempen, the ancestor of the later aristocrats of Constantia. The new vines were introduced alongside the vegetables in the Company gardens, Mediterranean strangers among these Dutch crops.

If the Commander had any worries about their success they were soon dispelled, for the vines grew and flourished. The wind blew strongly under the great sandstone slab of mountain, but the young vines weathered its attacks. They even survived Hendrik Boom and Jacob Cloete van Kempen, for neither Boom nor his assistant had the least idea about how to run a vineyard (neither, of course, had Van Riebeeck). The Dutch were not a wine-making people, and in this wind-blown extremity of the earth they were even more sorely lacking in viticultural and oenological information, though they were to receive some help and advice on the matter of pruning from a passing German sailor with a memory of the Rhineland.

Once planted, the vines were largely left to fend for themselves, which they did, for the vine is generally an adaptable and resilient plant. The hot summers came and went, and the wet, grey Cape winters nurtured the vines, which put down ever deeper roots. In their neat rows in the Company gardens they bore each year a stronger crop of grapes, ripened to a high degree of sweetness by the rich summer sun.

Van Riebeeck was enthralled by all this. Of course, it would have been less than human not to have felt pride in his own achievement. But, though it is difficult to confirm across a three-century span of

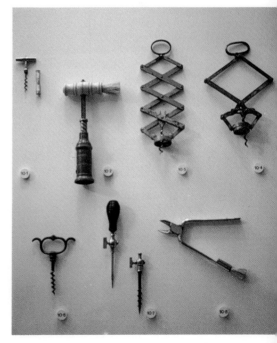

history, there seems little doubt that the vines went to his head – even before any wine was pressed.

He constantly pestered his superiors in Amsterdam for further supplies of cuttings (and this at a time when they were wondering whether the little colony would ever pay for itself). And once the nursery was well established in the Company gardens, he began casting around for larger and better sites for his vines. The first of these was in the area where attempts had been made to grow wheat – what is now Green Point – where there was a wide space of flat land with a shallow lake which should provide irrigation for the crops. Unfortunately, the wind seared the leaves off the plants, stripped the corn from its husks. And in winter the lake, which was brackish anyway, overflowed and flooded these promising-looking fields.

A new site was sought, and soon found, in the area of the present-day Liesbeek River, then called the Amstel by the colonists after the river which runs through Amsterdam. Here the ground was sheltered, and here the Company's first large-scale farm was laid out. At first named 'Wijnbergen', but later renamed 'Bosheuvel', this 101-morgen site was also

to be that of the first substantial vineyard in the Cape, though the experimental nursery in the Company's gardens was retained, supplying rooted cuttings for the new vineyard. In August 1658, for example, Van Riebeeck recorded that he 'with the aid of certain Free Burghers and some slaves, took the opportunity as the moon waned of planting a large part of Bosheuvel with young rooted vines and cuttings'. Within four days 1 200 rooted vines and cuttings were thus transported and planted.

The Commander was getting into his stride. The progress of these plantings was witnessed by a number of travellers at this time. Among them was Commissioner Rijkloff van Goens. Impressed with Van Riebeeck's efforts, he reported of the young vineyard that 'it is only one year old, but stands green and flourishes'. His enthusiasm for the venture on his return to Holland helped to overcome much of the residual resistance of the Lords Seventeen, expediting the delivery of yet more planting stock.

The vineyards were expanding, but another kind of expansion was also taking place: in the community itself. And with this went changes of structure, among

them the appearance of the first Free Burghers.

It had early become apparent to Van Riebeeck that the farming resources of the Company alone would not be enough to cover the needs of the fleet. It was therefore proposed that a number of the Company's servants be released from service to farm their own land in the neighbourhood. It was understood that this privilege would be granted only in return for good and steady service – the men were normally contracted on a five-year basis. The first nine of the Free Burgher farmers were given their formal discharge from the Company's service in February, 1657, and were installed on grants of land along the Amstel River, near to the Company's farm, from which they received supplies of planting materials and tools to help get them started. In a short while they were followed by a further 40 aspirant farmers, and soon the banks of the river became a settled network of smallholdings, few of them larger than 50 hectares in extent.

It was a sensible and, on the surface, quite casual move in response to a given situation. The last thing that probably entered Van Riebeeck's mind at that moment was that he was setting up a new society.

If the vines were one innovation, grants to the Free Burghers were another. These were men with little cultural background. In general they came from the lower ranks of the Company's service, mercenary soldiers, sailors and runaway sons, the rabble of the Dutch overseas empire: the dispossessed, the ones without land or status.

Now, if not status, they were given land. Not a great deal of land, but enough to thrust in tenacious roots. Of course, some of them gave up, for the work was hard, the returns uncertain, and there were other hazards. The Hottentot population appears belatedly to have realized that they had been elbowed away from their ancestral lands. So they took to raiding and plundering, which became part of the pioneers' way of life. Small wonder, then, that many of the Free Burghers lost heart and returned to the Company's safe bondage or drifted back to sea. But the majority set their teeth and persisted, slowly breaking the land and becoming familiar with the character and demands of farming in a hot, dry climate with a limited topsoil. They planted wheat, bred small herds of sheep and cattle, and built themselves starkly simple mud-brick dwellings thatched with the tough local reed.

At first they showed no interest in planting vines, preferring their more familiar crops. But gradually the Commander's determination began to affect them and they started introducing a few vines on their farms. They were encouraged by the evident success of the

JAN VAN RIEBEECK

Johan Anthonisz van Riebeeck was South Africa's first wine maker. A ship's surgeon by training, but later a career servant of the bustling and ambitious Dutch East India Company, he had no special enthusiasm for the Cape of Good Hope – indeed he urgently requested his superiors to remove him and put him somewhere more congenial (such as the Company's wealthy possessions in the East) within three weeks of his arrival on these magnificent, almost deserted shores. He soon got down to the business of fulfilling his brief, however, performing everything asked of him and more. Among the extras he introduced was the vine, of which neither he nor the men beneath him knew more than the sketchiest of details. With vine cuttings sent out by the Company he made a start, and was joyfully impressed with the speed with which the first vines took in this sandy and alien soil. Soon the first nursery was expanded and new vineyards laid out in the lee of the great bulk of the Tafelberg, on the Commander's own farm and the Company farm. From here, cuttings were distributed to the newly freed Burghers whose descendants were to take the vines yet further inland to lay the foundations of a future large-scale and important industry.

Of this, of course, Van Riebeeck himself

The Vereenigde Nederlandsche Ge-Octroyeerde Oost-Indische Compagnie, *or Dutch East India Company, ruled the Cape settlement from the time of Van Riebeeck to the end of the eighteenth century. Symbolising this authority, the VOC monogram is found as the central decoration to much of the Company's glass and chinaware.*

was to know nothing. After ten years of reluctantly making his way into the history books in the Cape, he departed to a comfortable obscurity in the East Indies as Governor of Malacca, ending his life far from the vines of the Cape.

vineyards at Bosheuvel, and by the hardiness of the vines – the wind was a constant threat to their exposed fields of wheat (the oak trees and stone pines which are part of the present image of this area did not exist in what was still a virgin Cape landscape).

Their vines did well, and this in spite of the fact that, as with the Company's gardeners, they knew little about their culture. Their methods were simple. The vines were set out in rows about a metre apart, with about a metre between each vine, a compact formation which must have drawn heavily on the soil's resources. The vines were not trellised; instead, the growing canes of the young plants were tied to stakes thrust into the earth. This method, commonly used in Germany, may have been shown to them by the German mercenaries who were part of the Dutch East India Company during that period.

The community by the Amstel took root, as did its vines. But the expansion of farming activity brought with it another problem. More land was being tilled, but the population had not increased. Labour was urgently needed to work these new developments and it was supplied by the Company in the form of slaves.

In the ancient world, slavery was a norm rather than an exception. In one form or another the institution of the bonded labour force had persisted through the Middle Ages – the medieval villein was little more than a serf in terms of absolute status. And if slavery had died out in Europe by the time of the Renaissance, the opening-up of new lands and colonies had revived it. From the sixteenth century onwards Africa had become a vast reservoir of slaves, exploited largely by the Arabs, and sold through European agents to the men who were building up the colonies of the New World and the Orient. In common with the other colonizing nations, the Dutch also took advantage of this supply of cheap labour in their own overseas possessions. Batavia had its slaves, and very soon so did the Cape.

There had been a few in the Cape from the beginning, a dozen or so individuals dropped off by passing ships from Batavia and Madagascar. Then, in 1658, the labour situation changed abruptly and the structure of the population altered radically, when two Dutch ships arrived bringing 200 slaves. They were drawn from a variety of sources. They included both men and women, and came from Africa, from Madagascar and from the Far East.

These people were to become crucial in the expansion and consolidation of the colony and in the development of agriculture and viticulture. At first the majority were retained by the Company. Special regulations were made concerning them, together with concerted efforts to adapt them to a European outlook. To this end Van Riebeeck's first regulation about them laid down that they were to be taught the doctrines of the Christian church (which presumably omitted any proscription on slavery). In April 1658, a school for their instruction was started in the charge of the Commander's brother-in-law, Pieter van der Stael. The slaves were given Dutch-style names and were sent to 'school' for a few hours each day. When it was first opened, Van Riebeeck made a formal visit of inspection to check that it was being properly run. As a reward for Christian diligence the slaves were given a glass of brandy and a supply of tobacco, inducements which must have warmed them to the pleasures of conversion.

In spite of all these blandishments, a fair number opted for the outback, escaping to take their chances with the mountains, the Hottentots and the Bushmen. A dangerous freedom was perhaps a fair exchange for the hardships of their present existence, the comfort of tobacco and brandy notwithstanding.

It may be as well to emphasize at the outset that the winelands were not based on an egalitarian social structure. The fact that this system worked, altered nothing of its unfairness at a human level. The principles the first slaves learned at 'school' did not for one moment square with the brute reality they encountered from one day to the next.

They were given to and later bought by

It is generally accepted that the vine was first cultivated in the Middle East during the period 6000-4000 BC and from the area south of the Caspian Sea 1 spread throughout the temperate regions of the world. In chronological order the pattern of distribution was: Egypt and Phoenicia – ±3000 BC 2; Greece and Crete – ±2000 BC 3; Sicily, Italy and Western North Africa – ±1000 BC 4; Spain, Portugal, Southern France, South-western Arabia – ±500 BC 5; Northern India and China 100 BC 6; the South of England, Northern Germany, the Rhineland, Northern France and the Balkans – 100-400 AD 7; Japan and Mexico – 1528-1545 8; Peru and Chile – 1548 9; Argentina – 1557 10; California – 1600-1610 11; South Africa – 1655 12; South-western Australia and New Zealand 1813 13.

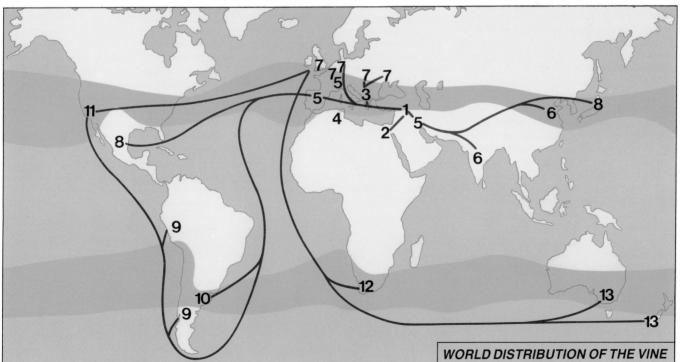

WORLD DISTRIBUTION OF THE VINE

the Free Burgher farmers, whose property they became. The farmers asked no questions. There was work to be done, land to be broken, more vines to be planted, cattle to be slaughtered, slave quarters to be built. If the sun scorched the crops in summer, or the mountain brought down floods in winter, what time or leisure, what objectivity of mind was there to debate the niceties of their moral situation? The Free Burghers were a people on the move, alone in a hostile environment, in a dangerous paradise. They had to conquer or die. Those were the only alternatives they were aware of, from one day to the next. All else was swallowed up in this central question, and by the accepted convention of the period.

They held in their hands the seed of a future society, and in the vine an element that would trigger the tremendous growth which was to sweep it to power and affluence – both economic and symbolic. It was not the vine alone, but the beautiful juice which was made from it, which performed mysterious metamorphoses, mysteries they felt known only to God.

Even with the knowledge of hindsight, and the intellectual equipment of modern science and viticulture at our command, it is still possible to feel the sense of wonder, of mystery, which the natural process of fermentation must have aroused in the early wine makers, in all parts of the world. And something of this sense of wonder lingers like a bouquet over the making of the first wine in the Cape, even over the meagre amount that Van Riebeeck made on the second day of February in 1659, at the Company's original nursery in the gardens near the fort.

The Commander's vineyards had given promise. Now, in the seventh season after the pioneers had set foot in the Bay, this promise was fulfilled. The first small crop of French grapes was harvested, and the first wine made. Given the circumstances, the method must have been very simple and straightforward.

Van Riebeeck is curiously silent about the quality of his first wine-creation. The plain fact is that it may have been almost undrinkable. But of course, this mattered neither to Van Riebeeck nor to posterity. He had made wine, and that was all that mattered. He had overcome the caution of 17 Dutchmen (in itself no easy matter), he had imported the vines, he had watched over them, he had made the first wine. His entry in his official journal for that day, scratched out at his desk by the window of his now rather elegantly appointed chamber in the fort, soberly records this small but historic moment:

'Heeden is Gode loff van de Caepse druyven d'eerste mael wijn geparst. . .'
'Today, praise be to God, wine was pressed for the first time from Cape grapes, and

from the virgin must, fresh from the vat, a sample taken – pressed from the three young vines that have been growing here for two years, yielding 12 mengels must from French and Muscadel grapes, the Hanepoot Spanish not yet ripe.'

The scratching stops. The grave figure with its long, curled seventeenth-century wig, its frilled cuffs, gazes out of the window with shadowed eyes. On the waters of the Bay the Company's ships bob, tugging at their anchor chains. On the dusty road that runs up from the newly-built jetty to the gardens, a wagon creaks, the horse urged on by a languid slave, in no hurry. On the dark, polished wood of the desk before him the sunlight catches the rim of a sightly cloudy glass of wine.

For Van Riebeeck, though he perhaps did not realize it, the adventure was over, at least for him. From now on it was to belong to others: above all, to the thickset man in a slouch hat sitting on the farm cart on the road past the fort, returning to his farm by the Amstel after delivering supplies to the fleet. His shirt lacked cuffs – neither it nor he had any frills. He smoked a clay pipe, and spat when he felt like it. His eyes were narrowed against the sun. His children, already at work on his farm, were bigger and sturdier than he had been at their age under the cloudy skies of Holland.

Growth was in the air. Within a few years a thrusting, driving expansion had taken these people from the Peninsula across the dust-blown wastes of the Cape Flats, the *Kaapse Duinen*, to the watered and fertile valleys beneath the distant, brooding mountains.

Van Riebeeck himself helped to inspire, if not the expansion, the explorations which preceded it and which began within a few years of settlement. In 1657, for example, a small party of burghers crossed the Cape Flats to the foot of the mountains in the north-east. It is thought that it was they who first named this area of the barrier of mountains the Hottentots-Holland (it was about this time that it was first mentioned). Then, early in the following year, the Commander himself commissioned a party under Sergeant Herwaarden to conduct a further and more systematic exploration. This group included the surveyor, Pieter Potter, whose job was to record and chart the journey, of which he left a vivid description, through what is now the Paarl Valley, then teeming with game, with great herds of zebra, with hippo wallowing in the mud of the Berg River. Searching for an entrance to the hinterland they eventually reached the Roodezand Pass, which looks down into what is now the valley of Tulbagh, before turning back. The journey was marred by three deaths, two from dysentery and one when a lion gnawed off the arm of a soldier almost within sight of the fort.

The following year saw the last expedition sent by Van Riebeeck, a curiously forlorn affair which throws an odd side-light on the hopes of a colonial administrator in a strange land far from home. Led by Christiaan Janssen, the party of explorers was detailed to search for the fabled land of gold, Monomotapa. Reluctant, but propelled by the Commander's passionate eloquence extended over several hours, the group trekked off to the north. With half of Africa still to traverse, they collapsed on the banks of the Great Berg River, on the edge of what is now the Piketberg district, all lust for gold expended.

There was gold further on, of course, but it was to be many decades before it was to see the light of day, and by that time Van Riebeeck's bones had long turned to dust on the island of Malacca in the East Indies, for that was where the life and career of this remarkable man ended. After his departure from the Cape in 1662, his career, if successful, was perhaps a little short on adventure. It was also saddened by the death of his first wife, Maria de la Quellerie, who had borne him seven children, four of them at the Cape. The life of a pioneer wife was not easy.

He himself died as Governor at Batavia on January 18, 1677, at the age of 58. It is to be hoped that the 17 grave but shrewd gentlemen in their candle-lit council chamber in Amsterdam offered a prayer for his soul when they heard of his death. He had, after all, turned out well, and in spite of that youthful indiscretion, whatever it was, had justified their confidence and hopes.

But the vines, they heard, lived on; the vineyards at the Cape were doing well, very well. This, in spite of the fact that some of the Free Burghers were not the most expert of farmers or wine makers at that. But the sunburnt farmer with his pipe, trundling back through the dust to his holding by the Amstel, was learning his craft. His methods were simple in the extreme. His vineyards were cultivated by hand – the close spacing of the rows precluded the use of horse and plough, which did not make their appearance in the local vineyards for a further century. No irrigation was used; in the Peninsula area the rain was generous enough. In this early period, the vines were blessedly free of the diseases which were later to cause havoc, and the main natural pest was the birds which descended in ravening flocks particularly at harvest time. The Hottentots also made periodic raids on the vineyards, and they were discouraged with musket shot, and the birds driven off by slaves with whips patrolling the vineyards.

Because of the birds the harvesting was often done too early, which affected the quality of the wine. The early crops were mostly table, rather than wine grapes, the

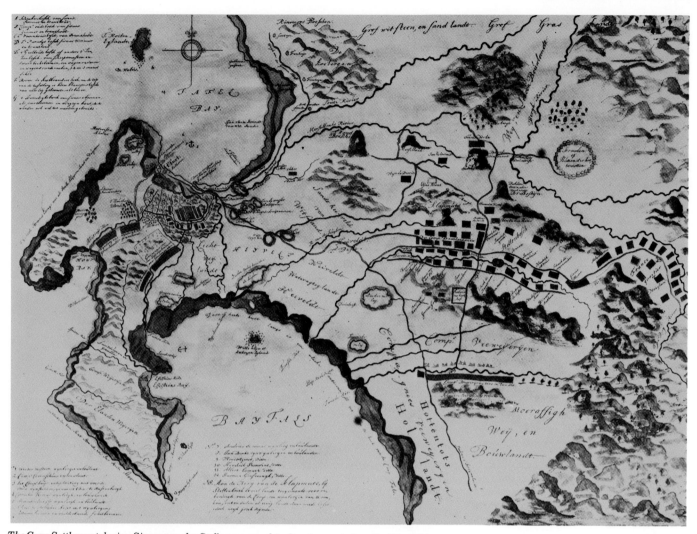

The Cape Settlement during Simon van der Stel's governorship. Development along the Eerste River, and the burgeoning town of Stellenbosch are clearly shown.

bulk of the colony's wine still being imported. Harvesting was done with crude baskets, and grapes, pips and stalks were crushed together with energetic abandon in the wooden vats. Later in the eighteenth century sizeable wooden wine presses came into use, but at first the grapes would be crushed by foot or hand (this method was used at Constantia until well into the nineteenth century). The rough juice was drained from the vat and fermented in 'velkuipe', or ox-hides suspended from four vertical wooden poles. The resulting wine contained many impurities, though it was sometimes filtered through baskets to remove most of the fragments of skin, leaves and pips which it contained.

In general the first Free Burgher wine makers were innocent of any knowledge of the importance of hygiene or cleanliness. Wines were transferred from one container to another with blithe disregard for their previous contents, whether wine, spirits or arrack.

In terms of bulk, the amount of this local wine was still small. And whatever its quality, the quantity gradually increased.

The first modest exports of the Burghers' wines were made, and the first reports on them returned to their makers.

If these reports, mostly from the Company's servants in Batavia, tended to be negative to outright hostile, this was not necessarily the fault of the wine itself. As the Burghers themselves knew, wine, whether imported or exported, fared badly through the long tropical voyages, its fragile physical and chemical structure easily disturbed by micro-organisms and by changes in temperature and humidity, as well as by the vibrations of the small wooden ships. The foreknowledge that this problem of wine transport from South Africa was to persist well into the nineteenth century would have been little consolation to the Burghers receiving biting epistles from the Orient from Company servants complaining that they were being poisoned with sulphur.

They were in sore need of help and informed advice, which they indeed were soon to receive, though not always with unmixed enthusiasm. The source of this much-needed guidance was their new

Commander, Simon van der Stel. He arrived at a propitious moment, for the 17 years since Van Riebeeck's departure had seen an increasing disorganization in the administration and a lack of direction from the Company. Van Riebeeck had been succeeded by the ailing and disgruntled Zacharias Wagenaar, and he in turn had been followed by a series of temporary commanders. One of the few positive actions in this interregnum had been the start made to the building of a new and larger stone castle to replace the old fort.

It was in this fine new castle that the fine new Commander Van der Stel now settled. There was much to be done, and he had every intention of seeing to it. Everywhere there were signs of disorganisation, the colony was losing money, the unkempt colonists perpetrated the most primitive of farming methods. However, with energy and determination perhaps something could be made from this shambles.

Van der Stel set about putting his mark upon the colony, a mark still visible. For the inhabitants of the winelands of the

Cape, the monuments to Van der Stel are still there for them to see.

Van der Stel himself made certain that they would be. He was an interesting personality and, like his son and successor Willem Adriaan, a curious mixture of altruism and self-interest. There is no doubt, however, that he did much for the growing community and its expanding but unsophisticated wine industry.

Within a few weeks of his arrival in 1679, he made one of the most important contributions to the early structure of Cape society. On the way back from a tour of inspection of the Hottentots-Holland area he turned aside from his original route to explore a long, verdant valley which he decided would make excellent farming land, and a fine spot for settlement. The area had hitherto been named the 'Wildebosch'. Resting on the banks of the river which ran through the valley, Van der Stel dreamed up what he felt would be an appropriate name for his new settlement, with its projected church and school.

It was thus that Stellenbosch was 'born' in the head of Simon van der Stel in November, 1679 – the first time that the name appeared in his journal at the Castle.

With this action, the new Commander created a centre for the growth of a new community, separate from the sea-board town under the mountain at the Cape. It was to be specifically a colonists' town, a Free Burgher town, and one in which from the beginning wine was to form a major element.

He was to have a personal effect upon the quality of this wine. On his arrival at the Cape he found the local product to be 'exceptionally harsh'. In reply to this criticism the Free Burghers bluntly maintained that the wines could not be improved – a fine and determinist excuse, perhaps, for their own ignorance. Van der Stel set out to prove them wrong by producing wine of a quality not before found at the Cape, and one which for the first time received favourable comment when exported to Holland.

At the same time he began to impose the rudiments of an administrative apparatus on the local wine industry, such as it was at the time. He also sought to find a balance between one kind of farming and another. Thus he not only encouraged the growing of grapes, but, to ensure that the main object of settling at the Cape was not forgotten, he decreed that for every morgen of grapes planted, six morgen of other crops, particularly of wheat, should be planted as well. The cultivars he introduced (or re-introduced) probably included Muscat d'Frontignan and Pontac. And of course, he was responsible for the introduction of thousands of oak trees throughout the area, lending a graceful intimacy to the grandeur of the landscape.

SIMON VAN DER STEL

Van Riebeeck had very little prior knowledge of the vine, but his most important successor in the seventeenth century, Simon van der Stel, was a cultured and well-travelled man with first-hand experience of the vine-growing countries of Europe. On his arrival at the Cape he found the vines already an integral part of the local farming system, balanced against wheat and cattle farming of the kind traditional to the Dutch-born Burghers.

There was little organization, however, and the community as a whole was generally demoralized after several years of poor management. Governor van der Stel both introduced new measures for improving local farming, including vine farming, and established Groot Constantia, one of the most famous of the surviving estates.

Among his other achievements was the settling of a new community under the distant mountains. Stellenbosch still retains, against the encroachments of modernity, much of its historical flavour, captured in its oak-lined streets which were first laid out at Van der Stel's order. This able and farsighted administrator also set the first practical 'quotas' for the growing of different crops, a conscious attempt to lay down a system of balanced agriculture in the nascent and now rapidly emerging community.

A handsomely proportioned reception room at Groot Constantia. Originally the home of Simon van der Stel, the homestead and its surrounding vineyards became the hub of wine making at the Cape in the middle to late 1700s. Now a National Monument, this fine expression of Cape Dutch architecture remains one of the most evocative symbols of South Africa's wine industry.

A painting by Kobel depicting the bustling anchorage of Table Bay in 1770. It was during these middle decades of the eighteenth century that exports of Constantia wines grew in significance as they won acclaim throughout Europe.

At the practical level he demonstrated the importance of pressing grapes only when they were fully ripe – the practice of harvesting early to avoid the attack of birds on ripe fruit gave a raw edge to the wine. He set up a committee whose duty it was to visit the vineyards and who had to be satisfied that the grapes had reached the required level of maturity: failing which a fine of 60 *rijksdaalders* was imposed. The general importance of orderliness and cleanliness, particularly with regard to the casks, was also emphasized. Fining – a method of cleaning the wine – was done with ox blood, white of egg and with imported isinglass (a gelatinous extract from a sturgeon's air bladder).

If the establishment of Stellenbosch was Van der Stel's most public memorial, it is for a more private creation that he is also remembered. This was his estate of Constantia, still one of the Cape's most gracious monuments to a past age, in the valley which bears that name. Here, in this cool valley beneath the Constantiaberg, a few hours' ride from the Castle, the Commander set up a model farm. And if the valley was cool, so was Van der Stel: he contrived to have himself granted some 891 morgen (approximately 770 hectares) of land, quite illegally, since the Company's servants were not allowed to own private property. The size of this

grant, which was made in 1685, contrasts sharply with the Burghers' usual grants of about 14 morgen (approximately 12 hectares). It was later supplemented with grazing rights amounting to a staggering 10 000 morgen (approximately 8 500 hectares), virtually the whole of the Peninsula. In the midst of all this cunningly acquired chunk of Paradise, he built the fine house to which at the end of his days in office he would gracefully retire.

He evidently had a taste for the good things of life on a grand scale, and has often been accused of serving himself with as much dedication as he devoted to the community in his charge. There is, however, no doubt that at Constantia he set an example to others in the ways of making good wine , even while turning a profit for himself.

In the year of his purchase of the Constantia land, there occurred in Europe an event which was to have a delayed effect both on the character of the colony's population, and on the quality of its wines. For it was in this year that the king of France, Louis XIV, revoked the Edict of Nantes which had guaranteed religious tolerance of the French Protestants since its promulgation by Henri IV in 1598. In the wake of this change in their circumstances some 200 Huguenots (their

name was a corruption of the word *Eedgenoot*, or 'oath-associate'), assisted by the Dutch East India Company, emigrated between the years 1688 and 1690 from France through Holland to the Cape. They were hard-working and skilled in many trades (the Huguenot weavers were particularly valued) and their loss was a blow to the French economy.

France's loss was the Cape's gain. The free population of the colony at this time did not exceed 600, so the Huguenot infusion undoubtedly made a significant change in the make-up of the burgher society. Moreover, they derived from a different stratum of society from the rough-and-ready Dutch Free Burghers and introduced a certain cultural flair.

The Huguenot farmers were readily given grants of land on the same terms as those made to the Free Burghers. The farms which they were allocated were mostly in the areas of what are now Franschhoek, Paarl and Drakenstein, the newly established farming areas beneath the mountains. One valley became their domain. Previously called De Olifants-hoek, it now acquired a number of new names, from the Fransche Quartier, to Le Coin Français, or the settlers' own name for the area, La Petite Rochelle, before coming to its present one, Franschhoek.

Many of the new settlers came from the

23

south of France, where, if not directly involved in wine making, they were at least familiar with its methods and procedures. In May, 1689, for example, the Chamber of Delft wrote to Simon van der Stel, informing him that the brothers Pierre, Abraham and Jacob de Villiers had a good knowledge of viticulture, and that he should assist them on their arrival; the brothers François and Guillaume du Toit were also noted as wine farmers.

The expertise of the Huguenot wine makers was thus added to the Free Burghers' limited store of knowledge and experience. The newcomers quickly settled down in the area, becoming absorbed in the larger community and exchanging their own language for Dutch within a generation or so – though they remembered the land of their origin in the names of their farms, from L'Ormarins to Champagne to La Provence. And if the atmosphere at first was one of suspicion from the local farmers, any resistance was soon submerged in the common antagonism felt by both groups towards the new Governor of the colony, Simon van der Stel's eldest son and successor, Willem Adriaan, or, as it was then spelt, Wilhem Adriaen.

The elder Van der Stel retired as Governor – he had been given this new title as a reward for his services – in 1699. He spent his remaining days in seclusion at Constantia until he died. The earlier distrust between the first Governor of the colony and the Burghers, a symptom of an increasing discord between the Company servants and the free landed farmers, became an open rift during the career of the able but ruthless and self-serving younger Van der Stel.

The trajectory of Willem Adriaan's career is well-known. The tendency to stretch rules, already evident in the father, becomes excessive in the son. At the same time, the intelligence and resourcefulness of the family remained. It shows in Willem Adriaan's passionate interest in the horticultural and agricultural possibilities inherent in this new land. The questing, probing mind of the scientist, of the man of reason hovering on the verge of the eighteenth century, found expression in extensive farming experiments. These were carried out at the Governor's palatial, but illegally acquired country estate of

The role of the Huguenots in the wine-making history of South Africa is often exaggerated, for few of these immigrants actually had first-hand experience of the art. But the De Villiers brothers of La Rochelle in Provence, here depicted arriving in the Drakenstein Valley with little else than a few meagre company handouts and their own determination, were exceptions, for they had a substantial knowledge of viticultural practices which was put to good use. (Illustration by Angus McBride.)

Vergelegen in the Hottentots-Holland district (600 of the Company's slaves were siphoned off to build his famous mansion) and they included meticulous investigations into viticulture. In his *Gardener's Almanack*, Van der Stel reported on the progress and care of these vines for the benefit of the community at large.

This early 'vineyard calendar' provides a fascinating glimpse into the methods of the eighteenth-century viticulturalist. In July, to which he refers as the 'second winter month', Van der Stel advised that, 'When a vineyard is intended to be planted, it is best to dig the ground to a depth of three feet and clear it of stones and weeds, and, immediately after the canes are cut, tie them into bundles of a hundred each, and so bury them until the end of September or the beginning of October, when they are to be taken up and planted in moist weather; although they will have shot while under ground, these leaves fall off, and new ones bud out.' In the same month he advised the farmer to 'Prune old Vines early this month; young Vine stalks may be planted in the place of those that have been removed. The Vine stalks or Sets intended to be planted must be fourteen or fifteen inches in length, and have at least two or three buds above soil level; those that have been slipped or torn from the stalk are the best; they should be planted regularly in a S.E. or N.W. direction. It has happened that a Young Vine has borne Fruit the same year of its being planted, and that 800 old Vines have yielded three Leaguers of good red Wine. It has also happened that a small bough of an Apple Tree, being put into the ground, has borne Fruit the following year.

'When a Vine has died, it should not be replaced by a new set; for the old Vines, having possession of the ground, would draw all the nourishment from the new one, and prevent its growing; but a hole, of about a foot deep, should be dug close to the nearest Vine, a Cane of the same laid down, and this covered, that only a couple of inches of it appears. When it is found to grow, then, the year following, it should be cut half through, closer to the Mother Vine; the second year it should be cut off quite.

'If anyone wishes to have Vines to run up by the side of Trees, they should be planted at the same time, and close together.'

In October he recommends that 'the vineyard be kept clean; and if it grows too rank, let the shoots be topped, and the ground be hoed.' In November, 'The Vineyard must now be attended to, and the long shoots tied up.'

And then, in March, 'Now is the season for gathering the Grapes and making Wine.'

The harvest that Van der Stel himself reaped was the bitter one of exile.

Though, like his father, he had begun well, encouraging further immigration and opening up for settlement the 'Land van Waveren' – now the Tulbagh Valley – he soon allowed the temptations of self-interest to overcome him. This in itself might have been tolerated by the colonists had it not been set off by an intolerant and autocratic temperament.

It was a confrontation with the wealthier and more established of the Burghers, men such as Henning Huysing and his fiery nephew Adam Tas, which led to his downfall. Van der Stel misread the tenacity of his opponents; he also misunderstood their power of organization as well as their power of protest. In the few decades since Van Riebeeck, a political nucleus, however crude, had been created among the farmers, now strengthened by the addition of the relatively articulate and sophisticated Huguenots.

Mounting tension led to open rebellion. In a furious over-reaction to this defiance, the Governor rounded up the ringleaders, first imprisoning them and then dispatching five of them to Holland for trial before the Council in Amsterdam.

It was a crucial mistake. Not only had Van der Stel misread the power of those beneath him but he had also failed to gauge the mood of those above. The Governor had been living like a lord at their expense. When the men sent for trial before them pleaded an eloquent case against Van der Stel's corruption and tyranny, a dramatic reversal took place. The Governor found his powers effectively pruned; then relieved of his post, he paid the price of his lack of human acumen and was sent in exile to Holland. Much of the benefit which his intelligence and vision could have given to local farming methods, including wine-making techniques, went into exile with him. An enigmatic personality (it is one of the curiosities of his life that no record of what he looked like, either visual or verbal, has survived), the effect of venality on the spirit of enquiry destroyed its potential for good.

With the passing of the Van der Stels – Willem Adriaan went into exile in April, 1708 and his father died on June 24, 1712 – went the larger defeat of the ambitions of the local servants of the Dutch East India Company. To an increasing degree the Cape of Good Hope came to be the land of the Free Burghers, under their control and bearing the imprint of their personality.

They were assisted in this by a number of factors, the most important of which was the fortunes of the Dutch East India Company itself during the following century. The mid-seventeenth century, the moment at which the Cape had been established, had been the high point of Dutch power. Released from the repressions of the Spanish occupation, armed with a profound knowledge of the sea and with a powerful expansionist appetite, they had thrust the Spanish and Portuguese aside and, uneasily sharing the newly charted oceans with the equally ambitious British, had begun acquiring an overseas mercantile empire.

But the eighteenth century saw the beginnings of its slow disintegration, largely from within. A series of European wars weakened Dutch resources and the administrative grip on the overseas possessions. But the European wars in which Holland became embroiled were also, if only indirectly, responsible for the first great affluence of the Free Burgher society, their first great harvest and one which was long to be remembered.

By the end of the eighteenth century, the descendants of those first pioneer farmers had become rich and prosperous beyond the wildest dreams of their forebears. The series of military entanglements between France, the Low Countries and England during this period, culminating in the French Revolutionary Wars and the succeeding Napoleonic Wars, effectively cut off the French wine trade from the opposing countries. For the first time the Cape wine farmers found a market and a large-scale demand for their products outside those of their own society and the passing fleets.

They also, for the first time, if indirectly, made the acquaintance of the English, whose drinking habits were to give them much joy: for in this period they consumed with enthusiasm all forms of alcohol. The Elizabethans had drowned themselves in raw ale and sack. Beer and gin had contested for the soul of the seventeenth- and eighteenth-century Londoner (as Hogarth had mordantly illustrated), and the middle-and upper-class drinker had discovered wine, specifically French wine. Of course, a flank attack was being mounted in the same period by an obscure oriental beverage absurdly derived from boiled leaves brought from India, but no sensible wine drinker would have taken this competition seriously or have imagined that on a steaming brown tide of tea a global empire would soon be floated.

In the late eighteenth century the British drank wine, with a prejudice in favour of very sweet wines, ports and sherries, whose high calorie content kept out the chill of the northern winters.

When the French Wars cut them off from French wines, they turned to the Cape for their supplies. A trade was established, and with it the first apparatus of wine marketing and promotion, represented by the wine dealers of London who imported the Burghers' wines.

Like the Dutch, the British knew nothing of the making of wine, but the machinery of import and marketing was of long standing, going back to the early Middle Ages (the poet Chaucer's father, for example, was a wine merchant in the Port of London in the fourteenth century).

The English demand for Cape wines was such that the precise assessment of the quality could be disregarded, at least for the time being. The British gentry sipped their newly-encountered Cape wines with perhaps the occasional delicate grimace, but were glad enough to get it.

If the English asked few questions, the Cape farmers asked none at all. British money bought their wines, and the Burghers spent their guilders.

The spending spree lasted for 50 years. With British gold they made their grand homesteads, pulling down or modifying the simple, traditional Dutch-style dwellings that had sufficed their forefathers, and built great mansions, with high, gleaming white gables fashioned to ornate shapes by Malay slaves whose temperamental subtlety inspired a rich and florid design. On either side of the gables stretched

WILLEM ADRIAAN VAN DER STEL

Willem Adriaan (more accurately Wilhem Adriaen), eldest son of Simon van der Stel and his successor in the post of Governor of the Colony, adds a nice note of villainy to the historical record of the turn of the seventeenth century.

Overwhelmingly arrogant and an administrative martinet, he was nevertheless the owner of a curious and intelligent mind, more at home with the theory of agriculture than the practice of rule. On his fine estate of Vergelegen near what is now Somerset West, he established a vast experimental farm where he tested a wide range of stock and crops, both European and Oriental. The treatment of the vine under local conditions is recorded with precision in his *Gardener's Almanack*, intended as a guide for farmers at the Cape.

Some of his own practices, however, brought his ambitions up short. Conflict with the emerging society of the Free Burghers, now acting with increasing independence from the Dutch East India Company, came to a head in open rebellion against the Governor's tyranny. A brief game of bluff and counterbluff ended in the Governor's defeat, humiliation and exile. He returned to live out the rest of his life in Holland, his researches into the farming potential of the Cape abandoned.

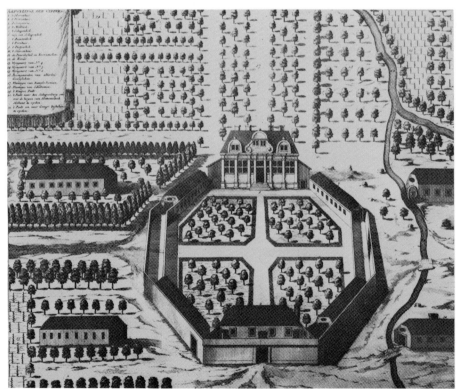

Willem Adriaan van der Stel's magnificent estate of Vergelegen as portrayed by Free Burghers incensed by the Governor's autocratic administration and corruption.

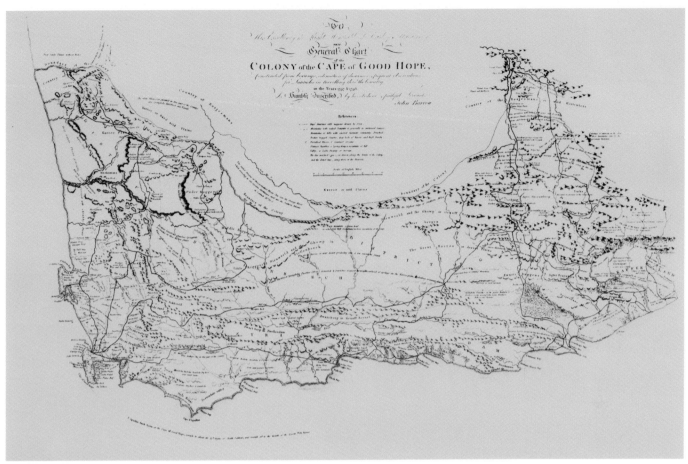

Sir John Barrow's map of 1797 was the first reasonably accurate chart of the Cape Colony, and reflects early knowledge of the area that today is largely the extent of the Cape Winelands.

smooth, tightly bound thatch. Below were green-painted teak window-frames and doors, and within was elegant yellowwood and stinkwood furniture with burnished brass handles, the finest that money could buy. Out in the fields the slaves harvested the grapes from vineyards stretching away over the rolling foothills of the great mountains.

The land had borne fruit, and for the farmers it was a time without precedent, and one which had no sequel. It was a justification and a celebration of the adventure of their forefathers, and of the generations whose lives had gone into its creation. A Cape farmer, born in 1750 and living through his appointed three score years and ten, could look back in his sunset hour on a life for which there were few parallels in terms of freedom and comfort in the old world of Europe, torn by wars and, as the century wore on, by moral and intellectual conflicts, beset by a mounting crescendo of political, social and philosophical questions.

It was at this moment that the Cape tradition was born, never to be forgotten; one in which the questions of Europe, including those of the Rights of Man, had no part. It included none of the northern currents of thought which were to lead to

the creation of a liberal vision in the nineteenth century. It had no prophets, and no analysts. Its memory survived not so much in history books, but as group consciousness, even through the upheavals of the coming decades.

Among the many famous farms and homesteads preserved from this time, one in particular stands out as a symbol. It was in this period that the wine-making *genius loci* of the Constantia Valley came into its own, represented by Simon van der Stel's historic estate of Groot Constantia.

Little had been heard of Constantia wine after 1699 when Simon van der Stel had retired there. After his death in 1712 his estates were sold by auction. The vast area of grazing land which now makes up most of the area of Bergvliet was divided into smaller farms, and the original estate of Constantia was split into two, the larger part containing the homestead becoming Groot Constantia and the remainder Klein Constantia.

The purchaser of Groot Constantia was Oloff Bergh, a former standard-bearer for the Company whom Van der Stel had once sentenced for theft and neglect of duties. As might be expected, he did little to enhance the reputation of the farm. It later passed to Johannes Colijn, who appears to

have shown a slightly more constructive interest in it. This was reflected in the first notable export of red and white Constantia wine: in 1761 and 1762 both were sold in Amsterdam, the white fetching £120 to £196 and the red £270 to £333 a leaguer.

In 1778 Groot Constantia experienced its most important change in ownership, when the Cloete family, descendants of Van Riebeeck's under-gardener, purchased it for 60 000 guilders. Under their ownership, which lasted till 1885 when it was purchased by the Colonial Government as a viticultural training centre, it was to achieve its highest renown.

The legend of Constantia wine was created against an increasingly shaky political background. Wealthy, independent, and with sophisticated tastes reflecting their increased affluence, the Burghers' world was illusory in its sense of security. Among its memories, along with white gables and the smell of dark cellars and the cool shadows of the oak trees, went the breath of freedom, of political autonomy. By this time the rambling, far-flung mercantile empire of the Dutch East India Company was in full disarray, and the farmers were wealthy, but without real political or military influence. They mistook a power vacuum for freedom.

That vacuum was soon to be filled. In 1780 war was declared between Britain and France, and the news reached the Cape in 1781. The Netherlands were in alliance at this time with the French and there was much fear that the British would attempt to take the almost defenceless Cape. Temporary relief arrived in the form of the French fleet in June 1781 under Admiral de Suffren. Among the members of the Swiss Meuron Regiment in the pay of the Dutch was the French architect Louis Michel Thibault, who abandoned military life in 1785, to make a distinctive mark on winelands architecture.

The French departed, having spent liberally on local wine. A decade later, in 1795, Europe once more returned to Africa. The first British occupation, which lasted seven years, was preceded by the invasion of General Clarke and Admiral Elphinstone. As few changes as possible were made: a Governor with supreme power replaced the Council of Policy housed in the Company's offices near the Parade, but local government and the Dutch legal system remained unchanged.

Thus, the British were somewhat casual conquerors. After all, their acquisition of the Cape had been chiefly motivated by expediency and by the need to head off French expansion at sea. They observed the local scene with interested curiosity, and for the first time had an opportunity to observe the places from which many of their imported wines came. One of the most vivid reports of the period was written by Lady Anne Barnard, wife of the Secretary to the Governor. An intelligent and observant personality, an enthusiastic letter writer and amateur artist, she appears to have struck up a friendship with Hendrik Cloete of Groot Constantia, and in her letters to Lord Macartney makes several references to him.

'Mynheer Cloete took us to the wine press hall,' she wrote, 'where the whole of our party made wry faces at the idea of drinking wine that had been pressed by three pairs of black feet; but the certainty that the fermentation would carry off every polluted article settled that objection with me. What struck me most was the beautiful antique forms, perpetually changing and perpetually graceful, of the three bronze figures, half-naked, who were dancing in the wine press beating the drum (as it were) with their feet to some other instrument in perfect time. Of these presses, there were four with three slaves in each.

'Into the first the grapes were tossed in

Lady Anne Barnard and companion with Hendrik Cloete in the wine-press hall of Groot Constantia. In her characteristic style the remarkable 'First Lady' of the Cape wrote vividly of the experience and the hospitality of 'Mijnheer Cloete'.

THE CLOETES OF CONSTANTIA

Descended from Van Riebeeck's under-gardener, Jacob Cloete van Kempen, the Cloete family emerged by the late eighteenth century as owners of Simon van der Stel's historic estate of Groot Constantia, long fallen on hard times. Here, in a fine wine-making micro-climate, and with wine-making techniques both original and meticulous, they brought the old estate back to life, and at the same time put Groot Constantia's wines on the map of Europe. In the hands of Hendrik Cloete, the massive *Bacchus Africanus* and his descendants, Constantia wine was enjoyed by an impressive list of connoisseurs: Frederick of Prussia imported it; Baudelaire included it in one of his *Fleurs du Mal;* Jane Austen mentions it.

To be sure, economic and political contingencies affected this fame (which was to echo afterwards for many decades down to the present), but at the same time there is no doubt that the Cloetes were fine wine makers, as well as careful and shrewd businessmen – they kept meticulous records of all their sales, for example, records which are still preserved, and they had a sharp eye for promotion. Modern taste has left behind this style of wine, with its extremely high concentrations of sugar and its rich flavours, but recently discovered samples brought back from England to South Africa received unanimous acclaim from those privileged to taste them after almost two centuries.

large quantities and the slaves danced on them softly, the wine running out from a hole in the bottom of the barrel, pure and clean. This was done to soft music. A quicker and stronger measure began when the same grapes were danced on again. The third process gone through was that of passing the pulp and skins through a sieve; and this produced the richest wine of the three, but the different sorts were ultimately mixed together by Mynheer Cloete, who told us that it had been the practice of the forefathers to keep them separate and sell them at different prices, but he found the wine improved by mixing them together.'

Not only did Cloete blend his wines, but he evolved other techniques, including the twisting of the branches of the vines to reduce the supply of nutrients and in this way to concentrate the flavour and sugar content of the grapes: the result being a wine of a rich, almost syrupy quality.

The first British occupation came to a close in 1802, when the Treaty of Amiens secured a break in the hostilities. But the brief Batavian Republican Government of General Janssens lasted no more than four years, a last flicker of independence before the British returned once more, this time for good.

Their century-long dominance began in January, 1806 with the Battle of Blaauwberg. Heavily outnumbered by General Baird's forces, the Dutch troops retreated in disorder (cannonballs said to be the relics of the battle are fixed on the pillars near the corner of Groot Constantia homestead); and the power vacuum in the lives of the Cape farmers was ended.

Their immediate situation suffered little change. While the European wars lasted so would a major source of their wealth, but within a few years the situation with

regard to their market in Britain was to change drastically. Trafalgar broke the French sea power, Russia broke the army, and Waterloo broke Napoleon. Half a century of wars were over, redirecting the wine market upon which much of the Free Burgher affluence had been founded. There followed a long, slow process of isolation and increasing economic hardship in the winelands, for with the end of the Napoleonic Wars the wine trade between France and Britain was gradually restored; and as it did so the supply of British revenue to the Cape dried up. The winelands became an industry without an overseas market.

At first the reality of the situation was not fully apparent. Assuming responsibility for their acquisition, the new rulers attempted to protect the local farmers. At the same time they tried to establish controls over the quality of the local vine product which had hitherto largely been left to the individual farmer who, with a booming seller's market and a high demand, had not always been to scrupulous in such matters.

On December 19, 1811, a proclamation issued by Sir John Cradock promised the Government's 'constant support and patronage to the cultivators and merchants, to give serious and lively attention to their interests as their wines are losing their reputation,' and went on 'that no means of assistance should be left unattempted to improve the cultivation and every encouragement given to honest industry and adventure to establish the success of the Cape Commerce in her great and native superiority.'

In the same month Cradock appointed an official taster, one W. Caldwell; and much advice on how to improve their product was issued to the farmers.

The moves to protect the wine trade at the Cape culminated in 1825 with the introduction by the British Government of heavy tariffs on French wines, which resulted in a rapid increase in the sale of Cape wines in Britain. These revitalised links were set up notwithstanding much opposition from many of the London wine merchants and importers whose traditional and understandable prejudice was in favour of the better quality and more accessible French wines. They instigated something of a campaign of slander against the Cape wines in an attempt to strengthen their ties with Europe. It has even been maintained that they went so far as to adulterate the Cape wine upon its arrival in England, although this may not always have been necessary – the problem of the long sea voyage and its effect on the wines was still unsolved.

But if, with these tariffs, the Government at the Cape gained favour with the farmers, one further piece of legislation was to have long-term and deep-seated effects – the emancipation of slaves in 1834.

It split the traditional Burgher society down the middle. Slavery was the base of their social structure and of their agriculture, including viticulture. As an institution it was as old as their society. The new legislation, although changing very little in practical terms, had a profound symbolic meaning for the Burghers, bringing to the surface a rebellion of spirit which had been lying dormant since the first British invasion. This was their country, and not only had it been taken away from them but the foundation of their labour force was threatened.

The reaction was mass migration. The Great Trek was to open up the interior, to see the establishment of the Boer Republics of the Transvaal and to usher in a new era in South African history. It also marked a change in the structure of Cape society.

A new kind of pioneer had been born, created as a clone from the Burgher stock. In the following decades he was to become embodied in the heroic figure of the Boer, to confront for the first time the black peoples of southern Africa, and to leave behind for ever the enclosed valleys and the vine-clad hills of his ancestors.

Those who joined the Trekkers confronted hard and unambiguous choices. Those left behind found themselves confronted with an increasingly complex economic world and a mounting sense of loss of traditional identity. Among these new uncertainties was a phenomenon not hitherto found in the early vineyards of the Cape: vine diseases.

Whatever planting stock Van Riebeeck had received had evidently been fine and healthy, and for the better part of two centuries little disease was recorded. True,

in 1819, a farmer Van Breda reported a type of 'rust' which was affecting his Hanepoot and, to a lesser degree his Steen vines, but it seems to have disappeared of its own accord.

Then in 1854, powdery mildew, a form of fungus indigenous to North America, found its way to France and devastatingly reduced the French wine crop by a quarter, in a matter of four years. It was not long before the disease was found in the Cape vineyards, but by this time it had been discovered that dusting with flowers of sulphur successfully combated the fungus. This treatment was promptly followed wherever the fungus' characteristic small spots and white, powdery, cobweb-like growth appeared, with the result that by the early 1860s it had been brought conclusively under control.

The immediate picture by the mid-century, notwithstanding these natural hazards, was hopeful. The result of the increase of the export trade during this period of protective tariffs had been the rapid expansion of the vineyards – there were some 55,3 million vines in the Cape winelands by this time. But then in 1861 an event occurred which was to prove to the wine farmers that their security was as fragile as had been their earlier prosperity, when the abolition of the preferential tariffs which had kept the trade afloat brought about the collapse of the export market.

In 1861 the Palmerston Government entered into a treaty of commerce with France which reduced the existing import duties on wine from that country to three shillings a gallon. The following year, in April, 1862, the duty was reduced still further, to one shilling a gallon on wine with less than 26 degrees proof, and to 2s 6d on wines of more than 26 but less than 42 degrees proof spirit.

This change in duties hit the Cape wine industry hard. The Cape wine makers had, of course, not been consulted by Gladstone, the Chancellor of the Exchequer, and were badly shaken by this turn of events. Protest meetings were held at which the wine industry, commerce and the professions were represented, and the Cape Parliament agreed to appoint a Select Committee to enquire into the effects of the amended tariff on the local wine industry. Their findings were brought to the attention of the Imperial Government, which, however, did not alter its tariffs; and many of the Cape farmers were forced to sell up and leave their farms.

The Cape exports dropped from 126 951 gallons (approximately 577 120 litres) in 1861 to 30 679 gallons (approximately 139 466 litres) in 1864, while French wine imports to Britain after 1860 totalled more than two million gallons (approximately 909 200 litres) annually. Notwithstanding this healthy trade, the French wine

industry was soon to face problems of its own, from which it – and the winelands of the world at large – was to be rescued by the genius of a French chemist; for it was in these mid-century years that some of the most important developments in wine-making history took place, leading to the beginnings of the modern science of viniculture. And of this science Louis Pasteur was the pioneer.

For centuries man's knowledge of the vine had been pragmatic. The processes whereby wine was made were discovered by accident. But what actually happened during the process of fermentation was unknown. Then, in 1863, the unknown became the known.

In that year the French Emperor Napoleon III asked Louis Pasteur, who had already made studies on the souring of milk, to look into the problems besetting the French wine trade which were causing a rapid loss of the newly-established links with England. The making of the famous French natural wines was accompanied by serious financial loss, owing to several ills, the most common of which was souring.

Pasteur retired to his laboratory with samples of the offending wines, and proceeded to do something which had never been done before. He looked at wine through a microscope. In doing so he made the fundamental discovery of its organic, 'living' nature. 'The wine', Pasteur wrote, 'is a sea of organisms.'

For the first time the hidden world of wine was revealed to man. For the first time, with this knowledge, the possibility of control of the wine-making process, from the vineyard to the modern bottling plant – and including Pasteur's method of 'pasteurizing' the wine by heating it to 55 degrees Centigrade to destroy unwanted souring bacteria – became feasible. Vast improvements were promised, at the level of both quality and quantity.

But the full realization of the degree of control open to the wine maker was as yet far in the future, and in the next few years was to seen even more remote. During the three decades following Pasteur's remarkable discovery occurred a salutary reminder of the power of nature and the vulnerability of human aspirations. In the years after the repeal of the protective tariffs, the wine makers of the Cape and their European counterparts were to find both their competition and their legislation brutally overshadowed: benign nature, often taken for granted, turned against them with the start of the largest disaster in the history of wine, the great *Phylloxera vastatrix* epidemic which swept the winelands of the world in the second half of the nineteenth century.

Like the powdery mildew, phylloxera originated in North America. However, it was not a fungus but an aphid and one whose life-cycle was closely and destructively bound up with that of the vine whose roots and branches it preyed upon at various stages of its life. Though not in itself bacterial, its ravages left the plant vulnerable to rot which effectively killed it.

In north-east America this near-microscopic aphid was found living in a naturally parasitic relationship with about 60 species of a locally-found form of wild grape-vine, including *Vitis riparia, V. aestivalis* and *V. rupestris*. The roots of resistant *Vitis* species generate corky layers in wounds caused by phylloxera, allowing the plant to heal itself and prevent secondary rot.

In the early 1860s specimens of these wild grape-vines were taken from America to France. Breeding experiments to incorporate resistance to powdery mildew in European grape-vines using the tough wild stock had been mooted. Unknown to the experimenters, however, the vines carried specimens of the aphid in the earth about their roots.

The more sensitive European cultivated vine lacks the inherent resistance to phylloxera of the North American species. Within a few years of its first appearance the disease had caused widespread devastation, from the point of entry in the south-west of France in 1861 to the north

and the Burgundy area, resisting all attempts at control, and eventually wiping out some 75 per cent of the European vineyards – and this in spite of the fact that its only mode of locomotion was pedestrian, from one plant to the next.

The vine growers of the Cape watched the progress of the disease from what at first appeared a safe distance – with varied reactions. The diamond magnate Cecil John Rhodes, for example, saw an opportunity to profit from the disaster in Europe and promptly became a major shareholder in a syndicate to export Cape wine. This optimistic piece of opportunism, however, was defeated by the poor quality of the local product, which had deteriorated further on its bumpy voyage through the tropics. In the meantime, the Cape Government banned the importation of grape-vine material from Europe, a move which was supported by the Austrian viticulturalist, Baron Carl von Babo, who had been invited to the Cape by the Colonial government to take over as its wine expert at the farm of Groot Constantia, then being purchased by the Government from the Cloete family as an experimental wine farm.

Von Babo's report endorsed the official ban on the importation of vines, which had kept out the phylloxera. He also suggested

as a cure for the problem one which was already being implemented in Europe – the grafting of *Vitis vinifera* onto rootstock derived from resistant American stock, the initial bearer of destruction, but now to be the main agent of its control.

His advice proved crucial to the survival of the Cape winelands, for notwithstanding the Government's measures, phylloxera found its way into the local vineyards. It was first noticed in the Mowbray area in 1885, and was then found on vines at Constantia and in the Helderberg area, two of the oldest wine-farming regions. Within a few years it had spread unchecked from its initial point of entry to lay waste most of the Cape winelands. It was a disaster of the first magnitude, and it shook the already tottering local wine industry to its foundations. Many farmers went bankrupt, long family relationships with farming areas were broken, and the vision of security, natural as well as human, sank into the ruined fields.

The first and most powerful instinct of the farmers in the face of this calamity had been to save their vines. When the disease first appeared steps were taken to combat it directly, even though no successful and economically feasible chemical remedy had been found in Europe.

It soon became clear that a complete new

Government inspectors examine phylloxera-ruined vines. The scourge of vineyards throughout the world, evidence of the microscopic aphid was first discovered at the Cape in 1885 near Mowbray from where it spread rapidly, virtually wiping out the Cape vineyards.

start would have to be made, and that the vineyards would have to be cleared and reconstructed on a basis of grafted vines, as had been done in Europe.

To this extent the Cape vine growers had the benefit of the European experience. With the backing of the Vineyards Protection Act there began the gradual replacement of all the vineyards with vines grafted onto resistant American rootstock. The Government appointed a Phylloxera Commission with powers to destroy the infested stock, for which some small compensation was paid. The dissatisfaction which this caused among the growers led to the appointment of a select committee in 1889 to investigate the complaints. It reported that although the regulations were causing tensions, there was no way in which they could be relaxed.

The Committee not only insisted upon continued strong action, but also made other recommendations which were subsequently adopted. These included restrictions on the import of any grape-vine material from abroad and more stringent quarantine regulations; it also disallowed the use of any part of the vine for packaging. More importantly for the farmers' morale, it granted larger compensation for grape vines marauded by phylloxera.

The cleared vineyards were slowly rebuilt. The enforced grafting was soon appreciated by the farmers as the only way to overcome the disease and ensure against its return, and they and the nurserymen soon mastered the art of wholesale grafting – one which is still a feature of modern vineyards.

A major crisis of winelands history was thus overcome. As Hugh Johnson aptly writes in his *Wine Atlas of the World,* the phylloxera was 'undefeated but out-manoeuvred'. Other ailments, however, were not so easily cured. In 1886 gold was discovered in the Witwatersrand. Like Van Riebeeck's gold of Monomotapa it beckoned adventurers, among whom was Cecil Rhodes. The clouds of war gathered with mounting tensions between Boer and Briton. December 20, 1895 saw the Jameson Raid as the curtain-raiser, political tensions culminating in 1899 when the Boer Republics of the Transvaal and the Orange Free State declared war on Britain.

The Anglo-Boer War and its rearguard action lasted until the Peace of Vereeniging in 1902, when the Boer Republics lost their independence and became part of the British Empire. In the years after the war the Boer Republics as such ceased to exist, and so did the traditional world of the Cape, both of which were incorporated by the Act of Union in 1910 into a new country, the Union of South Africa.

These were not easy years in the winelands. The hardships of the war were followed by uncertainty and economic stress exacerbated by the increasing problem of over-production. By 1904 the number of vines, now all grafted onto imported rootstock, had increased to some 78 million. Exports in 1905 were negligible, and a large surplus was carried over from the 1904 vintage. This was reflected in the Cape wine makers' old adage: 'Good crop bad cash; bad crop good cash.' Again it was the growers who were faced with ruin, this time of a different kind from that presented by phylloxera.

It was in response to this situation of over-production and resultant low prices for the wine that one of the most important features of the modern winelands was created – the co-operative movement.

This began in 1905 with the appointment of a government commission to examine the depression in the wine and brandy industry. It recommended the creation of the first co-operative wineries. The objective of the co-operative system was to secure the benefit of collective bargaining and marketing, as opposed to the traditional system of individual wine farmers competing with each other to market their own wine at the best prices they could obtain. A further advantage of the co-operative winery was that plant and machinery could be used more effectively with less outlay of capital investment. Unit costs of production could be reduced through the large volume of grapes being processed, and technical knowledge centralized at the co-operative. It would obviate the need for each grower to have a wine-production cellar on his farm. From now on he would be able to choose his degree of involvement with the wine-making process, making his own wine or distributing it in barrels, or simply delivering his grapes at harvest time and leaving the production of the wine to the co-operative and its chosen wine maker.

The Government made £50 000 (an enormous amount of money for those days), available for the establishment of these wineries. The first – the Drostdy in Tulbagh – came into operation in 1906. Over the next four years a further eight such pioneers were established at Helderberg, Helderfontein, Groot Drakenstein, Paarl, Wellington, Bovlei, Over Hex, and Montagu – of which, however, only four survive as originally constituted.

Most co-operatives were – as they still are – run by committees elected from the member farmers contributing grapes to them, with an elected chairman who was often the farmer who sold a part of his land as a site for the co-operative.

This system had intrinsic advantages but remained for a time somewhat limited. Power supply in these early days was apt to be a problem, often being supplied at harvest time by steam-engines or tractors. Moreover, the position with regard to over-production in the winelands continued to deteriorate owing to the limited authority of the co-operatives themselves. Not all of them survived the strain: four were soon forced to close, even though the Government wrote off the balance of their loans.

Continued over-production led to a slump in prices; 1909 saw the lowest ever received for wine – £1 17s 6d a leaguer (577 litres). Prices during the years of the First World War, particularly from 1915 to 1917, also saw extremely low levels of between £2 10s and £3 a leaguer.

The burdens of this period were only slightly alleviated by, curiously enough, the phenomenon of the ostrich boom. From 1906 to 1913 ostrich feathers were high fashion in Europe, and excessive prices were paid for them. During this period about 10 million vines were uprooted in the Oudtshoorn area to make way for fields of lucerne to feed these valuable birds. At the height of the boom the ostrich population had spread down from the Karoo to the Breede River Valley, where the lucerne (alfalfa) grown on the lime-rich soil provided a highly beneficial diet. But the boom came to an end in 1913. Whereas horse-drawn transport made little feminine flutter, the advent of the motor-car made billowing plumage disconcerting and the feather market collapsed. The ostrich population retreated to Oudtshoorn and most of the farmers went back to planting vines.

They planted far too many. By 1918 there were almost 87 million vines in the winelands, producing an annual 56 million litres of wine. Unsaleable and unsold, millions of litres were allowed to run to waste.

By hard experience the co-operative principle was being brought home to the growers. At the same time it gradually became clear that for the co-operative movement to be fully effective all farmers would have to belong to it. This was the thesis put forward by Charles W.H. Kohler, and it was a concept which was to bear fruit in 1918 with the foundation of the 'Ko-operatieve Wijnbouwers Vereniging van Zuid-Afrika, Beperkt' – the sonorous full title of what is commonly referred to as the KWV.

For several years as Chairman of the Cape Wine Farmers' and Wine Merchants' Associaton, Kohler had been involved in the mounting problems of the wine industry. This first organization collapsed in due course but he continued to refine his concept of the co-operative principle, which crystallized in 1917 when he handed a draft constitution for a new organization to a committee of growers which had been formed to draw up a memorandum.

His concept was accepted, and a new co-

THE GROWTH OF SOUTH AFRICAN VINEYARDS

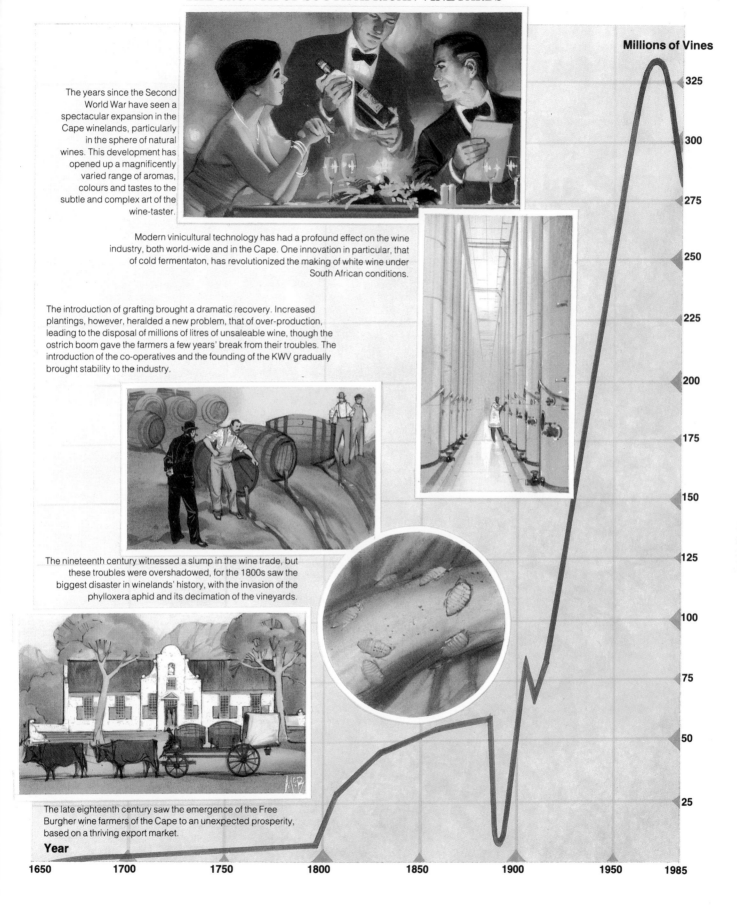

Millions of Vines

The years since the Second World War have seen a spectacular expansion in the Cape winelands, particularly in the sphere of natural wines. This development has opened up a magnificently varied range of aromas, colours and tastes to the subtle and complex art of the wine-taster.

Modern vinicultural technology has had a profound effect on the wine industry, both world-wide and in the Cape. One innovation in particular, that of cold fermentaton, has revolutionized the making of white wine under South African conditions.

The introduction of grafting brought a dramatic recovery. Increased plantings, however, heralded a new problem, that of over-production, leading to the disposal of millions of litres of unsaleable wine, though the ostrich boom gave the farmers a few years' break from their troubles. The introduction of the co-operatives and the founding of the KWV gradually brought stability to the industry.

The nineteenth century witnessed a slump in the wine trade, but these troubles were overshadowed, for the 1800s saw the biggest disaster in winelands' history, with the invasion of the phylloxera aphid and its decimation of the vineyards.

The late eighteenth century saw the emergence of the Free Burgher wine farmers of the Cape to an unexpected prosperity, based on a thriving export market.

Year

1650   1700   1750   1800   1850   1900   1950   1985

325
300
275
250
225
200
175
150
125
100
75
50
25

operative formed. Registered on January 8, 1918, it was an organization which was to alter the structure of the winelands, providing them with a new unity, an all-important bargaining power in relation to the wine merchants, and a legal and administrative machinery which provided the basis for the present system.

The main objective which the KWV set itself in 1918 was 'So to direct, control and regulate the sale and disposal by its members of their produce, being that of the grape, as shall secure or tend to secure for them a continuously adequate return for such produce'. And central to the achievement of this aim was the necessity of persuading the growers to join the new co-operative.

In due course more than 95 per cent of the wine-grape growers joined the KWV. Through this joint action they were in a position to conclude agreements with local merchants in terms of which the market price of wine was increased and stabilized. The merchants agreed to make their purchases only from members of the KWV, with the result that prices gradually rose, standing in 1919 at £10 a leaguer. A high price, however, did not necessarily mean a stable one: and when the years between 1921 and 1923 saw particularly heavy crops, the farmers once again received only £3 a leaguer. During this period 91 000 leaguers of wine were run off into the Eerste River. In these dire circumstances the farmers took matters into their own hands. Dealers succeeded in buying wine direct from them at lower prices than those of the KWV. As low prices continued some of its members lost faith in the organization and withdrew from it.

Then, in 1924, the KWV received Government ratification of its powers when the Smuts Government passed Act 5 of 1924, the Wine and Spirit Control Act which empowered the KWV to fix the minimum price to be paid to farmers for their distilling wine each year. It was the start of a progressive process of legal protection and control of the wine industry which was to be refined over the coming decades to meet a wide range of contingencies. Among its immediate effects, apart from securing for the growers a 'continuously adequate return' for their produce, was a sharp reduction in the number of wine merchants who, deprived of a manipulable market, disappeared.

The developments in scientific viniculture which had followed Pasteur's discoveries were now gaining acceptance in South Africa. In 1925 at the Stellenbosch University farm of Welgevallen there occurred an event whose significance was not to be realized for many years, when the well-known viticulturist Professor Abraham Izak Perold produced the first seedlings of the Pinotage vine. This, the first successful

locally-bred cultivar, was developed from a cross of the varieties Pinot Noir and Cinsaut, then commonly known as Hermitage. The work was later continued by Professor C.J. Theron who saved and propagated Perold's original seedlings and began the long and arduous task of evaluating the cultivar which, two decades later under the name of Pinotage, was to make its debut, achieving fame as the first successfully developed South African varietal, one which was superbly adapted to the local conditions, yet possessed a strong character of its own.

There were a number of such developments in the 1920s, but many of them remained dormant with the advent of the World Depression from the early Thirties onwards. The year 1935, however, saw the emergence into public status of an important new company, that of the Stellenbosch Farmers' Winery, the inspiration of an immigrant American, William Charles Winshaw.

Trained originally in medicine, Winshaw had arrived at the Cape in 1899 with a consignment of mules ordered by the Cape Government. A one-time acquaintance of Buffalo Bill, and a vivid personality in his own right, he stayed on in South Africa after the 'English War', and turned from medicine to wine. In 1924 he joined forces with one Gabriel Krige Jnr, whose father had purchased in 1870 a section of Adam Tas' historic farm, Libertas, on the northern bank of the Eerste River. Winshaw and Krige named their jointly-owned farm 'Oude Libertas' and began making and selling wine.

Even though the local taste at this time was largely for brandy and sweet fortified wines, as a medical man Winshaw considered a natural wine more beneficial to the public health, and so from the outset he made it his business to concentrate upon this type of wine, exemplified in his Chateau Libertas and La Gratitude wines.

In spite of the development of natural wine and improvements in quality, overseas markets remained largely closed to South African wine. Only South African sherry and port continued to enjoy a healthy market in Britain (Perold made an extensive study of their production in this period, while Professor Theron concentrated on port and Dr Niehaus on sherry). The advent of the Second World War put heavy restrictions on the import of equipment, and the co-operatives in particular marked time during this period.

But 1940 saw major new legislation extending the powers of the KWV and laying down the framework for the system of total control which now includes primary producers, wholesalers, retailers and importers.

The powers vested originally in the KWV had been limited to wine for distilling purposes only. The minimum price measures did not cover 'good' wine – wine not for distilling – as it had been assumed that once the price of distilling wine had been fixed the price of good wine would automatically become stabilized. In the event this proved false, and good wine prices had fluctuated dangerously. After investigation, the problem was resolved by also vesting in the KWV control over the production and marketing of good wine in terms of Act 23 of 1940. A minimum price was fixed for good wine; all transactions between merchants and producers had to carry the approval of the KWV; and all payments for wine had to be made through the organisation.

The Act further stipulated that no person might produce wine except under a permit issued by the KWV. Such permits would only be granted if the KWV was satisfied that the producer was in possession of the necessary cellar equipment, tanks and vats for the making of good wine. The problem of over-production was met by empowering the

Prime movers in the establishment of the South African wine industry of today: Charles Kohler,
founding chairman of the KWV; William Charles Winshaw, founder of Stellenbosch Farmers' Winery;
and Professors Theron and Perold and Dr Niehaus who placed wine making and vineyard practice on
a scientific footing.

WINE MAKING IN SOUTH AFRICA *A historical chronology of major events and influences*

1652 The Dutch East India Company, in the person of Jan van Riebeeck and his party of Company servants, establishes the first European settlement at the Cape of Good Hope

1657 First Free Burgher farmers released from Company service to work their own land

1658 First shipment of slaves arrives in the Colony

1659 February 2: Van Riebeeck records the making of the first wine at the Cape

1662 Departure of Van Riebeeck for the East Indies

1679 Appointment of Simon van der Stel as Commander of the settlement; later in the same year, his foundation of the town of Stellenbosch

1688 Arrival of the first Huguenot immigrants

1699 Simon van der Stel retires to his estate of Constantia; his place as Governor is taken by his son, Willem Adriaan van der Stel. The first modest exports of wine from the Cape take place in the same year

1708 Willem Adriaan departs to exile in Holland

1761/2 The first notable exports of red and white Constantia wine takes place

1778 Groot Constantia is acquired by the Cloete family. The following decades see the sweet Constantia wine winning acclaim throughout Europe

1795 The first British occupation of the Cape

1802 End of the first British occupation

1806 The Battle of Blaauwberg and the start of the second British occupation

1811 Quality control instituted by British authorities in the Cape on wines exported from the Colony

1825 The British Government imposes heavy tariffs on importation of French wines and sales of Cape wines in Britain increase rapidly

1834 Emancipation of the slaves and the start of the Great Trek

1860 First appearance of the phylloxera epidemic in the French vineyards

1861 Palmerston Government reduces tariffs on French wine imports to Britain which had hitherto protected the Cape wine market

1863 Louis Pasteur's investigations into diseases of wine in France

1885 Appearance of phylloxera in the Cape vineyards

1886 Discovery of gold in the Witwatersrand

1899 Start of the Second Anglo-Boer War

1906 Formation of the first South African wine co-operatives, the first being the Drostdy in Tulbagh

1909 Over-production causes a slump in wine prices to an all-time low

1910 The Union of South Africa is established

1918 Serious over-production leads to great quantities of unsaleable wine being allowed to run to waste. The KWV is formed

1924 KWV empowered to fix the minimum price for distilling wine

1925 Professor Perold crosses various vines which eventually give rise to the first specimens of the Pinotage cultivar

1935 Formation of the Stellenbosch Farmers' Winery

1940 KWV empowered to fix the minimum price for good wine

1945 Formation of Distillers Corporation. The years following the Second World War see the further development of cold fermentation, which gives impetus to the production of quality white wines

1950 Gilbeys (S.A.) formed

1955 Oenological and Viticultural Research Institute established at Nietvoorbij outside Stellenbosch

1961 First bottled Pinotage appears; first Lieberstein marketed

1965 Amalgamation of Stellenbosch Farmers' Winery, Monis of Paarl, and Nederburg

1971 Stellenbosch Wine Route opened

1973 South African Wine of Origin legislation implemented

1975 First auction of rare Cape wines at Nederburg

1979 Formation of Cape Wine and Distillers

1980 The newly-formed Cape Wine Academy begins courses for the trade and the general public

1983 The Mouton Commission recommends a less monopolistic structure for the wine industry, but this is not accepted by the Government.

KWV in terms of its constitution to fix annually the percentage of each member's vintage which was not saleable on the local market. This portion of the crop, which became known as the surplus, had to be delivered to the KWV without payment or, if the farmer could sell this fraction, he had to make an equivalent reimbursement to the KWV. The 'surplus' was (and is) processed by the KWV into wines, brandies and spirits.

The conclusion of the Second World War marked a massive hiatus in world history, not least in that of South Africa. From 1948 profound changes were to take place in the country's internal and external relationships. It was also a period which was to see increasing changes of pace in the wine industry.

These developments were both accompanied and made possible by technical advances. Perhaps the most important of these, and one which is still central to the white wine aspect of the industry, was that of the process known as 'cold fermentation'. Experiments had already been made on this process by Professor Perold in the 1920s. The KWV had made a further study of the process in the pre-war years, but had avised the farmers against it. The post-war period, however, saw renewed experiments, the most important of which came from the Graue family, an immigrant German father-and-son team who established the process on a large scale at their farm Nederburg in the Paarl Valley. At much the same time N.C. Krone was also experimenting in the Tulbagh Valley. His attempts, however, were less practical than the method of the Graues, which was to be exploited on a large scale, and permitted fine control in the making of natural white wine in the hot South African conditions. Developments both in equipment and methods accompanied this expansion.

In the period following the Second World War, the influence of producing

The sprawling headquarters of the KWV in the Paarl Valley.

wholesalers increased parallel with the enlarged role of the KWV and the co-operatives. Among them, of course, was that of the Stellenbosch Farmers' Winery, still the largest of the producing wholesalers. But there were others, too.

With the legislative control over the market introduced in the 1920s and 1930s many of the earlier wine merchants had gone out of business. A few, however, survived, often by amalgamation, to find a place in the post-war structure of the wine industry.

In spite of the 1940 controls the old problem of over-production (enhanced by streamlined modern methods) again threatened in the 1950s. This led to the introduction of the 'quota system', which provides a legal limit to the amount of vines which the farmer may grow (similar but more inspired systems than this had been of long-standing in France, providing even more rigorous control of growing). The first modern South African quotas were fixed in terms of vines growing on the farmer's property as at June 21, 1957, an allowance being made for vines uplifted immediately prior to that date in order to renew the vineyards. Increases in quota took place in subsequent years, the total available provisional quota at present being 3 million hectolitres.

No limitation was imposed on the cultivar grown or on the type of wine made, since it was accepted that the farmer would grow and produce the type of wine for which there was the greatest demand.

The 1956 Act recognized the principle of declaring the surplus each year and price fixing by the KWV, and made these provisions applicable to all producers of wine, whether members of the KWV or not. The Act further stipulated that all purchases of wine had to be made through or from the KWV and that no one might obtain or distil wine without the permission of the organization. This legislation places control of the winelands firmly in the hands of the KWV. It also provides the basic administrative machinery of the winelands as it exists today.

The Wine Industry Today

There have been many developments in the South African winelands in the past two decades, some of which fall outside the perspectives of history, for they operate within the living texture of experience. But in the stream of this experience it is possible to pick out salient features leading up to the present which will undoubtedly receive mention in future histories of the winelands.

The year 1959, for example, saw the emergence, after many years of patient development, of the first prize-winning Pinotage wine, grown by the Morkels of the farm Bellevue, which won for them the first prize at the Cape Young Wine Show. The same year also witnessed the start of the spectacular career of Lieberstein, which was introduced by Stellenbosch Farmers' Winery, and achieved a peak of some 32 million litres in 1964, making it the largest-selling bottled wine in the world at the time.

The economic curve of the 1960s and early 1970s was reflected in increasing competition between the powerful producing wholesalers, in a complex series of mergers and takeovers, and in the introduction to the market of many new ranges of wines.

The early 1970s also saw the introduction of one of the most popular innovations of recent years. This was the Stellenboch Wine Route (see also page 000), which was opened in April, 1971 and which now includes a total of 13 farms, eight of which are registered Wine Estates. Started by three local farmers, it was based on the type of wine route developed in Europe, the *Routes du Vin* of France and the *Weinstrassen* of Germany. The Stellenbosch Wine Route was followed, in the closing years of the 1970s, by the inauguration of the Paarl Wine Route, and since then by the Breë (or Breede) River and Vignerons de Franschhoek Wine Routes.

A major event took place in 1973. In September of that year the Wine of Origin legislation was introduced, providing a legal basis in the local winelands of one of the most important aspects of the relationship of wine to the land. Based on time-honoured European systems, this legislation also provided the local wine makers with a frame of reference in overseas markets. From it, by extension, derived the present-day geographical division of the winelands area into official Wine of Origin Districts, ranging from old-established areas such as Constantia, Durbanville, Stellenbosch and Paarl, through to the Tulbagh Valley, the Breede River Districts such as Worcester and Robertson, and the more recently defined areas such as those of the Orange River and Vaal River.

A booming wine industry found reflection in 1975 in the first Nederburg Wine Auction, one of the most important showcases for the Cape's wines, both in the local market and overseas. Then, in October, 1979, there occurred the most important merger of recent years, and one which represented a major restructuring of the liquor industry as a whole. The Oude Meester Group and Stellenbosch Farmers' Winery became co-subsidiaries in a new

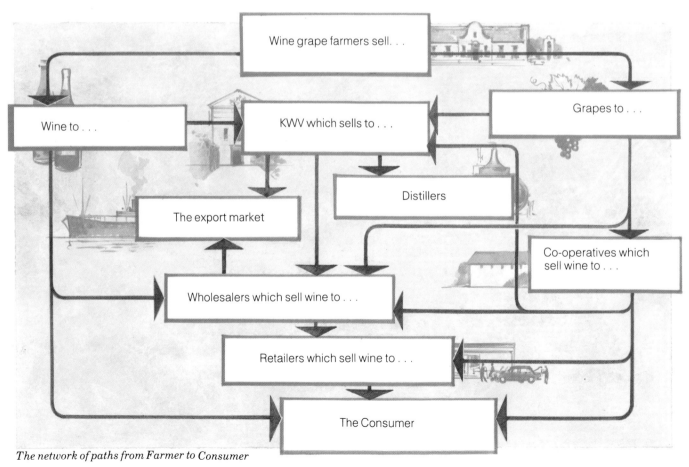

The network of paths from Farmer to Consumer

Wine events in South Africa attract a great deal of interest both locally and abroad. The Stellenbosch Food and Wine Festival (right) is a popular annual event and wine-tasting demonstrations are flourishing. The Nederburg Wine Auction which is held in the autumn each year under the auspices of Sothebys draws buyers worldwide.

holding company, Cape Wine and Distillers Limited. The Mouton Commisson, charged with investigating monopolies in South Africa, recommended in 1983 that the wine industry be ordered in a less monolithic fashion, but this was not accepted by the Government.

Together with the KWV, this new company effectively represents the guiding and governing principles of the present-day winelands, even though, for practical purposes, the companies which comprise the group retain their autonomy and compete with one another under normal market-place conditions. The shares of both co-subsidiaries are traded separately on the Johannesburg Stock Exchange.

Three hunded years ago Jan van Riebeeck had an idea. It turned out to be a good one. Many people, most of them now little more than faded names scratched on eighteenth-century land grants, picked up the idea and made from it the seeds of a new way of life. In making their wine they found purpose and identity, both for themselves and for their descendants.

But none of this, or of the massive and complex structure of the modern wine industry, would have been possible without co-operation. There have been many different kinds of partnerships in the making of the Cape winelands, but one dominates all others: the partnership between man and nature, between the farmer, wine maker and the raw material of their creation, the cultivated vine.

Structure of the South African Wine Industry

```
┌─────────────────────────┐        ┌─────────────────────────┐
│       REMBRANDT         │        │     KWV  INVESTMENTS    │
└─────────────────────────┘        └─────────────────────────┘
            50%                          50%
            └────────────┐      ┌────────────┘
                 ┌─────────────────────────┐
                 │     HOLDING COMPANY     │
                 └─────────────────────────┘
```

South African Breweries		**Public**
30%	60%	10%

Cape Wine and Distillers Ltd

100%	100%	100%
Henry Taylor and Ries[1]	**Oude Meester Group**	**Stellenbosch Farmers' Winery Group**

<table>
<tr><td rowspan="12">Major wholly-owned subsidiaries</td><td>The Bergkelder</td><td>Stellenbosch Farmers' Winery</td><td rowspan="12">Major wholly-owned subsidiaries</td></tr>
<tr><td>Castle Wine and Brandy</td><td>Monis of Paarl</td></tr>
<tr><td>Distillers Corporation</td><td>National Distillers</td></tr>
<tr><td>Drostdy Winery</td><td>Nederburg Wines</td></tr>
<tr><td>E. K. Green</td><td>Sedgwick Taylor</td></tr>
<tr><td>Henry C. Collison</td><td>J Sedgwick</td></tr>
<tr><td>James Burrough[2]</td><td>Erven Lucas Bols[2]</td></tr>
<tr><td>Paarl Wine and Brandy</td><td>Martell & Cie[2]</td></tr>
<tr><td>Richelieu et Cie</td><td></td></tr>
<tr><td>Van Ryn Wine and Spirit</td><td></td></tr>
<tr><td>Witzenberg Wynkelders</td><td></td></tr>
<tr><td>Westelike Provinsie Wynbouers-Korporasie</td><td></td></tr>
</table>

1. Importers and Wholesalers
2. Licensors

A restructuring of the liquor industry took place on October 1, 1979, with Government sanction. This resulted in the two largest producers of wine and spirits, Stellenbosch Farmers' Winery and Oude Meester, becoming co-subsidiaries in a new holding company, Cape Wine and Distillers Ltd, the shares of which are held by KWV (30%), Rembrandt (30%), South African Breweries (30%) and the remainder by the public.

In so doing, South African Breweries exchanged its 100% shareholding in Stellenbosch Farmers' Winery for the above mentioned minority interest in Cape Wine and Distillers Ltd. KWV for the first time obtained an interest in the local distribution of wine and spirits, while Rembrandt in exchange for relinquishing its share in the beer market obtained a greater interest in wines and spirits. By consolidating their shares, KWV and Rembrandt obtained effective control of Cape Wine and Distillers.

Within this new framework the Oude Meester and Stellenbosch Farmers' Winery groups continue to operate autonomously and with normal market-place competition. Although these two giants of the liquor industry have by far the greatest share of the wine market in South Africa, there are also a number of independent wholesale producers of which the W & A Gilbey and Union Wine Groups are the largest.

Gilbey Distillers & Vintners
W & A Gilbey
R Santhagens (Cape and Natal)
Francesco Cinzano
Bertrams Wines
Devon Valley Estates

Major wholly-owned subsidiaries

Union Wine Group
Culemborg Winery
Van Riebeeck Cellars
Bellingham Estates
Backs Wines
P. J. Joubert

Major wholly-owned subsidiaries

Other independent wine wholesalers

Douglas Green of Paarl

Jonkheer Farmers Winery (Pty) Ltd

Mooiuitsig Wynkelders (Edms) Bpk

Several other wine wholesalers, importers and distributors

THE MAKING OF A VINEYARD

The cultivated vine of the winelands of the world is a member of the botanical family Vitaceae. It is a family with a long traceable lineage, as is witnessed by the discovery of fossilized vine leaves (also containing traces of fossilized vine diseases).

The 12 genera of the Vitaceae embrace numerous species of wild vine as well as the type found at the Cape by Van Riebeeck, *Rhoicissus capensis*. The strain from which the modern cultivated varieties are descended is believed to have originated in the region between, and south of, the Black and Caspian seas, in the 'fertile crescent' where the first agricultural peoples settled. Its present scientific name is *Vitis vinifera – vinum* being Latin for 'wine', and *ferens* for 'bearing'.

From its first settlement at the eastern end of the Mediterranean, in about 6 000 BC, the vine slowly spread, first down the Levant as far as Egypt, and then, by about 2 000 BC, westwards to Greece. From there, during the next millenium, it spread to encompass the whole Mediterranean seaboard. It was the expansion of the Roman conquests, however, which led the vine to perhaps its most important modern homeland, France. The bulk of the early French vineyards was settled by the Romans in the wake of Julius Caesar's conquest of Gaul, completed by 51 BC. Starting from the already well-established vineyards of Provence, they spread up the Rhône Valley and thence to the Bordeaux area, generally following natural water-courses. By the second century AD vineyards were established in Burgundy; the following two centuries found them settled on the Loire, in Champagne, and on the Moselle and the Rhine, thus defining roughly the northern borders of Europe's present wine-making community. By the tenth century of the Christian era the heartland of the modern wine world had been fully laid down.

Further expansions were to follow with the opening up of new lands during the Renaissance. By the mid-sixteenth century there were already plantings of *Vitis vinifera* in Central and South America. Driven by their need for Communion wine, Jesuits introduced the vine to Mexico in 1545. In 1548 a priest by the name of Father Francisco brought the first vines to Chile from Peru, and in 1557 they were established in Argentina. By the early 1600s the grapevine had been taken to California and the first wine was made there in 1620. In the same century explorers began to discover in other countries of the southern hemisphere climatic conditions suited to the vine and similar in many respects to those of the Mediterranean basin. These new wine making countries included South Africa, and in due course Australia and New Zealand.

In all these areas *Vitis vinifera* grows to advantage. Although the wild vine is a hardy plant and flourishes under astonishingly different conditions – (there are varieties which can survive extreme cold) the classic cultivated vine is more specialized in its needs. It produces its best fruit in terms of both quality and quantity in the climatic conditions generally described as 'Mediterranean': that is, with long, fairly dry summers and wet winters without frost.

Under such conditions it grows easily – and also in variety. Indeed, over the centuries of its cultivation a wide range of different varieties of the basic red and white types of grape vine have been evolved. Known as 'varieties' in most other wine-producing countries, they are generally referred to as 'cultivars' in South Africa, a portmanteau word derived from 'cultivated varieties'.

Upwards of 2 000 of these varieties are at present known. Until the twentieth century they were generated by a process of evolution, of natural selection aided by man. Those known best in the South African vineyards were originally developed mainly in the French vineyards, and the dominant influence of the French is reflected in their traditional names – Cabernet Sauvignon, Cinsaut, Merlot, Pinot Noir, Pontac, Petit Verdot, among the red wine cultivars, and Chenin Blanc, Muscat d'Alexandrie, Clairette Blanche, Sémillon and Raisin Blanc among the white. Others, often for the making of fortified wines such as sherry and port, were developed in Spain and in Portugal. These include Tinta Barocca, Souzão, Tinta Francisca and Tinta Roriz; and in Germany wines were created well suited to the cooler conditions of the Rhineland, among them the famous white wine cultivar, Weisser Riesling, and the recently developed Bukettraube.

Together with these cultivars specific, at least originally, to one region, have been others which have come to be generally grown because of their versatility. They have tended to arise with different names in different countries, or with different versions of the same name. An extreme example of this confusing phenomenon is the Shiraz cultivar which, in one area or another, has been called Syrah, Schiras, Sirac, Syra, Sirah, Petite Sirah, Serenne, Serine, Biaune, Hignin Noir and Marsanne Noire – no less than 11 seductive titles for the same basic vine.

Some degree of such traditional confusion exists in South Africa. The early wine makers at the Cape, not always certain of the European identity of their varieties, often gave them their own local names. In time, the idea arose that these were specifically local varieties, different from those in Europe, and gradually this belief acquired the force of tradition. In

---

The propagation of virus-free vines is the keystone of the modern vineyard. These successfully grafted young vines will be planted in the nursery vineyards, uprooted when sufficiently developed and then further treated to prevent infection before being sold to the wine farmer.

Overleaf: *Situation, planting distance, trellising techniques and protection from strong wind are crucial considerations in the wine farmer's craft, and in the mature vineyard they present an eye-pleasing symmetry.*

THE VINE AND ITS ENVIRONMENT

The environment of the vine is extremely variable and this schematic illustration is intended as a general guide to growing conditions in the western Cape.

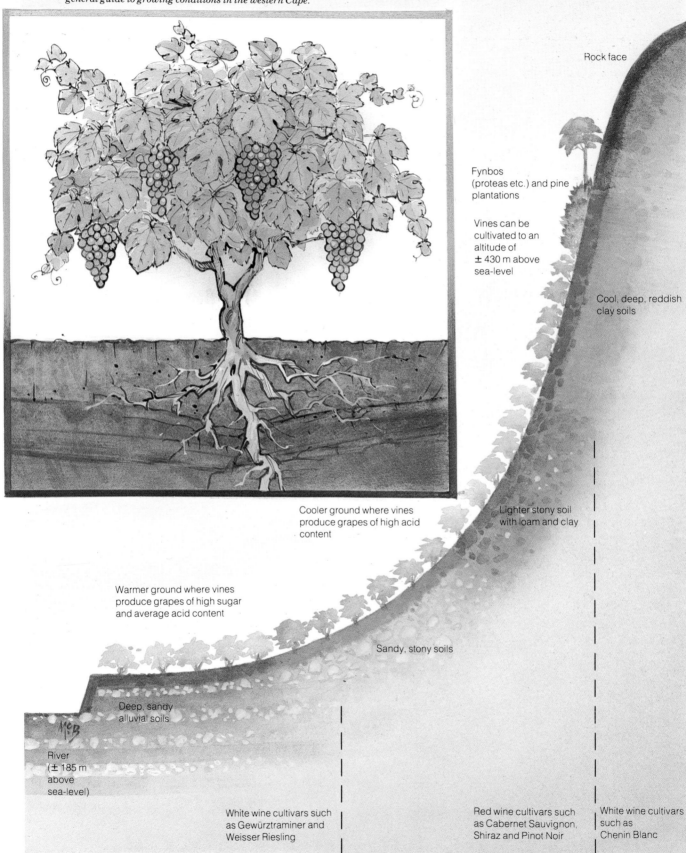

Rock face

Fynbos (proteas etc.) and pine plantations

Vines can be cultivated to an altitude of ± 430 m above sea-level

Cool, deep, reddish clay soils

Cooler ground where vines produce grapes of high acid content

Lighter stony soil with loam and clay

Warmer ground where vines produce grapes of high sugar and average acid content

Sandy, stony soils

Deep, sandy alluvial soils

River (± 185 m above sea-level)

White wine cultivars such as Gewürztraminer and Weisser Riesling

Red wine cultivars such as Cabernet Sauvignon, Shiraz and Pinot Noir

White wine cultivars such as Chenin Blanc

recent decades, however, investigations by such prominent South African viticulturists as Professors Perold, Theron and Orffer have confirmed that certain local cultivars are the same as the European varieties: for example, Steen has been identified as Chenin Blanc, Hanepoot as Muscat d'Alexandrie, White French as Palomino, and Green Grape as Sémillon, while the red wine grape Hermitage was found to be the same grape as Cinsaut (in France *Cinsault*). The South African Riesling was found to be unrelated to the German Riesling; instead it has been identified with the French vine, Cruchen Blanc.

In the wild, the evolution of a new strain of vine takes many generations of adaptation to specific conditions of soil and climate, but in the past century scientific methods of breeding new varieties have been developed, of which Pinotage and Chenel are well-known local examples. These new cultivars are generally bred from selected stock to present certain features or advantages which fit them for use in a particular area or micro-climate, or for the making of a certain kind of wine.

Each cultivar produces its own characteristic type of wine, with its own bouquet and flavour, its own private poetry. To a greater or lesser extent this inherent character can be modified or heightened by other factors, the first and most obvious of which is the way the wine is made, but others play a part at a more basic level. A common adage in the winelands holds that good wine is made in the vineyards, which is true. Good wine begins with healthy, well-tended vines and with sound vineyard practice.

The life of a vine begins before it reaches the vineyard proper – in the nursery with the propagation of the young plant. There are two main ways in which grape vines can be reproduced. One is that designed by nature, sexual reproduction by means of seeds, in this case the pips of the grapes. The flowers of the vine are mostly bisexual and formed in bunches. When they are mature, pollen is released onto the stigmas, and fertilization takes place in the ovary, after which the berry develops. If a new variety is to be bred it is necessary to cross-pollinate artificially by depositing the pollen from one strain on the stigmas of another, and the resultant seed may bear the characteristics of the parent plants.

This method is only used in the breeding of new varieties. By far the most common method of reproduction, and one that guarantees replication, is asexual. Here the large-scale reproduction of existing varieties is effected by taking cuttings and grafting them, for the *Vinifera* vine reproduces itself easily from cuttings. If a portion of cane is cut from a vine and placed in good, moist soil in protected conditions, it will quickly produce roots and shoots, eventually growing into a young vine which will almost certainly be identical to the plant from which the cutting was taken.

GRAFTING

This simple and direct method of propagation was the one used from time immemorial in the winelands of the world. It was also that of Van Riebeeck and the Free Burghers, described by Willem Adriaan van der Stel. However, since the phylloxera epidemic of the 1800s the process of reproduction has included the grafting of cuttings onto rootstocks taken from vines which are resistant to the phylloxera aphid and to other pests such as nematodes.

The cutting, or scion, of the cultivar required for fruition is grafted onto wood taken from the rootstock vine. With good contact between the cambium and living bark layers of the two vines, tissue-bridging takes place to produce what, in effect, will henceforth be a single plant. Soon this new vine puts forth roots and shoots, and when it is growing healthily can be transferred from the nursery to the vineyard.

Most vines in Europe and South Africa are grafted onto rootstock derived mainly from crosses of a number of wild vinetypes found in North America. These include Richter 99 (a cross of *Vitis berlandieri* and *V. rupestris*), Mgt 101-14 (a cross of *V. rupestris* and *V. riparia*), and Jacquez (crosses of *V. aestivalis, V. cinerea,* and *V. vinifera*).

In recent years oenological researchers have focused on these and other neglected wild vines, calling on their genetic make-up to develop a wide variety of strains suited to the exigencies of different soils and climates. Reflecting the predominant local conditions, the two most commonly used in South Africa are the Richter 99 and Mgt 101-14. Richter 99 prefers red, clayey and well-drained soils, while Mgt 101-14 favours gravelly, shallow and sandy soils which tend to be wet in spring. Others used for specific conditions include Richter 110, for heavy, fertile soils; Ramsey for poor, sandy areas under irrigation; Dogridge for poor, sandy conditions; Jacquez for deep, sandy, virgin soils; while the versatile 143-B takes to a wide range of soils where there is no threat from nematodes.

The rootstock must not only accord with its physical environment, but must remain compatible with the chosen scion. In general this is not a problem, but occasional cases of a bad marriage of scion and rootstock occur. Certain clones of Cape Riesling and Colombar, for example, are not compatible with Mgt 101-14 (it has been proved that some compatability problems are associated with certain virus combinations).

Vigour and resistance to pests and diseases are important in the rootstock but other and more complex qualities are supplied by the scion, or top-variety. Selection of good quality material for the scion part of the graft is an essential skill of the vine grower or nurseryman. Scions are obtained from producing vineyards by selection over a number of years of close observation on the progress of the established vines. The material is collected during pruning in the winter months and cut into 250-300 millimetre lengths which are bound together and stored in a cool, moist place or in cold storage until required. In choosing material for the rootstock, one-year-old canes from the mother vine are selected, cut, bound and stored in the same way as for the fruiting material.

The grafting of young vines usually takes place in winter between July and August. In the post-phylloxera era it was largely done by hand, but recent decades have seen the development of machines capable of making grafts at speed and with a fine degree of accuracy. But whether performed by hand or by machine, the basic principles remain simple.

The two elements of the fruiting material – the cultivar chosen and the cuttings of the rootstock – are prepared in such a way that they fit together. The cut is designed to present the largest growing face between one part and the other. To this end, two traditional types of cut were evolved which could be done relatively quickly by hand: the long-whip and short-whip methods.

The **long-whip graft** (see page 49) is the oldest method in South Africa, and is still very widely used. Here, both components are cut diagonally through the wood, a 'tongue' is made on the cut surface of both, and they are then fitted together. The scion in this case usually has two buds.

This is a simple method whereby a skilled grafter can complete up to 2 000 unions a day; moreover, heated rooms are not necessary for the subsequent callusing which bonds the scion to rootstock. But it has the disadvantage that the callus sometimes fails to form completely and if the graft incision is too long the tip of the incision may dry out.

The **short-whip graft** (see page 49) is similar to the long-whip except that here the incision is about half as long and usually only one-bud scions are used. The advantage of this method is that it is not necessary to tie the graft – waxing alone is sufficient – and that there is less danger of drying out. The disadvantages are that it is a difficult method which requires several years of practice before the grafter is truly proficient, and that a callusing room is necessary.

As well as these hand-cut methods a number of different machines and

47

configurations of cut are available, of which the most popular are the **Omega** and **Hengl** grafting machines (see page 49). The Omega makes matching omega-shaped cuts in the rootstock and scion which are punched in endways, from both ends of the machine. The join is automatically made. The Hengl makes a multiple saw joint to the scion and rootstock, which are pushed in endways in two different saws of the machine. The two components are then fitted together by hand.

Machine grafting has many obvious advantages over hand grafting. It is easy to operate, requiring less skill or labour, and gives good callus formation because it ensures better contact of the cambium layers.

As well as the Omega cut, a number of other configurations are possible with machine grafting. These include the **Jupiter** or **Zig-Zag** graft, and the **Heitz** or **Wedge** graft.

No matter which cut is used, once the two parts of the graft have been fitted together, the union is usually dipped in warm wax to seal it and to prevent loss of moisture from the incision. When grafting was first introduced, rootstock and scion were normally tied with raffia. The grafted vines are then placed in callus boxes and stored under ideal temperatures (24-28 °C) to ensure that the graft formed by the cuts grows together to form a strong union. This is done by packing the vines in porous material such as sand or sawdust to keep them moist. A callus box can contain about 1 000 grafted vines. The relative humidity in the plastic tunnel in which they are stored is usually kept at about 70 per cent.

Outgrowths of the respective cambium and inner bark layers bridging the gap between the scion and the stock make the primary union, and more or less simultaneously with the growth of the callus, root formation begins to take place. During this period, the callus box is placed on a moist floor to keep the lower section of the box cool. This prevents excess rooting, for if too many roots are formed they are damaged during handling of the small vines.

After root formation has taken place, the cuttings are moved from the hot-house and acclimatized to the open air, usually in a *lat-huis* or 'shade-house', which lets sun and air in but protects the young vine from excessive sunlight and strong winds.

This entire initial process usually takes about eight weeks, after which the vines are transferred to the vineyard nursery, where they remain for a year before being planted in the main vineyard for the rest of their growing and fruit-bearing lives.

Besides the propagation of young vines in the hot-house and the nursery, there are other ways in which new vineyards can be established or old ones refurbished. These are based on the principles of grafting, which are here applied directly in the field (as distinct from 'bench-grafting' or indoor methods used for vines propagated in the nursery).

There are three basic methods of such grafting: chip budding, amphi grafting and soil grafting.

Chip budding (see page 49) takes place in summer, in November and December. A small bud is grafted onto a rootstock which has been planted out during the previous winter; an incision is made about 30 millimetres above the soil level on the rootstock, and the bud is inserted and then tied with rubber or plastic tape.

Amphi grafting (see page 49), the so-called 'winter bud on green shoot' method, was developed by Professor Orffer of the University of Stellenbosch in the early 1950s. It is done in early November when the green shoot is about 450 millimetres long. The bud of the scion must be completely dormant. The rootstock in the vineyard is pruned early and severely and, when its green shoots have grown about 450 millimetres long, the strongest and straightest is chosen and trained along a stake. All the leaves on the shoot are left intact until after the graft has taken since they accelerate transpiration, thus helping to reduce excess moisture at the graft wound. An incision of about 40 millimetres is then made between the nodes on the green shoot, the scion is inserted, and the graft is tied with plastic tape and sealed with grafting wax. About two weeks after the bud has burst, the shoot is cut away at the node above the graft union. All other rootstock shoots and buds are then removed so that growth can be concentrated in the scion.

Amphi grafting has four advantages: the rootstock is not lost if the scion does not take, the percentage take is generally high, the vine can begin production almost immediately since the root system is

ERNITA

There are many excellent vine nurseries in the western Cape and one of the most progressive in the world is Ernita near Wellington. Here, under the consultancy of Ernst le Roux MSc. (Agriculture) and the management of Tossie Louw, comprehensive programmes of plant propagation and care, of grafting and plant improvement, are carried out.

The plant improvement programme in particular requires an advanced technology. It involves the selection of the best-performing clones, followed by heat therapy to rid the vine of dangerous viruses. With the growth of the vines under these conditions, together with the adverse effect of the heat on the propagation of the virus, the vines outgrow some of the viruses.

The vines are placed in a chamber for about 100 days at 38 °C in a carbon dioxide-enriched atmosphere, an artificial climate which encourages rapid growth. The first 0,5 millimetres growth is then cut off at the tip of the vine and rooted in a test tube. Thereafter the vines are stored in a growth cabinet (phytotron) at a much lower temperature. From there they are transplanted into pots. When five or six new leaves are visible, the process named 'milking' begins. One internode together with one leaf is cut off and transplanted. The process is repeated a number of times, and when the resulting plants are large enough they are propagated and indexed for viruses. Indexing can take a number of forms, but usually means grafting the plants onto indicator varieties (such as LN33, Baco 22A, Mission Seedling No. 1, and others) to show up the virus – the three main virus groups under observation being fan leaf, leaf roll, and corky bark. Further experiments are also being carried out on fan leaf, using the Elisa technique; based on serology, this method consists of injecting the virus into rabbits to produce an anti-serum.

Visitors and workers at Ernita have to pass through a disinfectant foot-bath before entering virus-free propagation areas.

GRAFTING TECHNIQUES

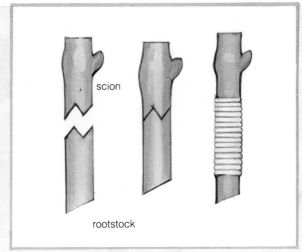

JUPITER GRAFT

CHIP BUDDING

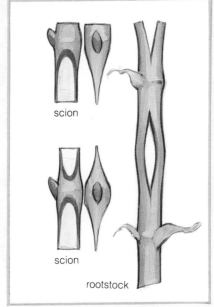

AMPHI GRAFT

CLEFT GRAFT

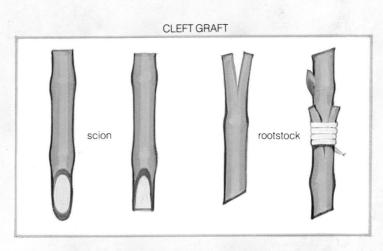

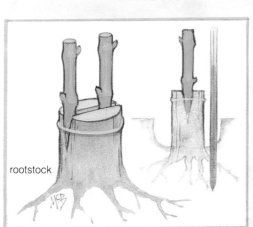

SOIL GRAFTING (Cleft)

LONG-WHIP GRAFT

SHORT-WHIP GRAFT

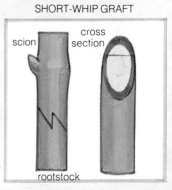

HENGL OR SAW GRAFT

OMEGA GRAFT

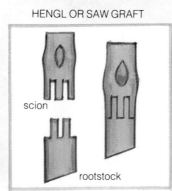

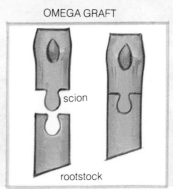

already established, and mature vines can be re-grafted to another cultivar without losing more than one harvest. The disadvantages of this method are that it is slow (a good grafter can do only 300 vines a day), and that suckers are troublesome with rootstocks such as Richter 99.

Soil grafting (see page 49) takes place from September to mid-October. A scion with two buds is grafted onto the rootstock using the cleft or whip-graft method – the rootstock here can be either in the nursery or in the vineyard. In making the graft, particular care must be paid to ensure good contact between the cambium of scion and rootstock. It is also important to make sure that the incision in the rootstock is made at right angles to the prevailing wind to prevent being dislodged by it. The graft is tied with plastic tape, which has largely replaced the raffia formerly used for this purpose. Fine soil is then piled over the graft union and packed down carefully.

After-care is important with soil grafting, and these 'molehills' must be replaced after rain. The young shoots are also susceptible to wind damage and should be staked or topped regularly to reduce that risk.

Soil grafting gives better results than bench grafting in areas with warm light soils. It is easier to perform and fits well into the farm work programme, since it is done shortly after bench grafting has been completed. Disadvantages are that weather conditions must be favourable, and that only light, well-pulverized, warm and well-aerated soils are really suitable. Moreover, if the scion does not bud the rootstock is lost for it will not bud again.

By these various methods the vine is prepared for and introduced to the vineyard, but this is not the only form of preparation, for just as the vine must be prepared for the land, so that land must be made ready to support and nurture it, to provide it with conditions for optimum growth and production.

SOIL

A balance must be found between the plant and its medium, the complex conditions in which it will live for about 30 years. They involve not only the soil and its specific effects of structural and chemical composition but also the climate.

Both the wine farmer and his vines are largely at the mercy of the elements: heavy frost in spring or a wet summer can write off the year's wine production, and in a relatively erratic climate such as that of Europe (in France the local vignerons claim God makes the wine) this can be a fairly regular occurrence, drawing heavily on human reserves of patience and resignation.

Notwithstanding the occasional act of God, the wine makers of South Africa generally have little about which to complain. Compared with the average temperatures of many other wine-making countries, those here are relatively high; the weather is commendably steady; and the summers ideal for fine, ripe grapes and good crops. And if the land is not always very fertile, this in itself is not necessarily a disadvantage. 'The worse the soil, the better the wine', is an old adage among wine farmers, for a poor soil encourages

slow growth which in turn concentrates the richness of the grape.

A combination of rich soil, high temperatures and judicious irrigation makes for large crops of grapes high in sugar content, but does not ensure complexity of character or quality. The mountain valleys of the Cape, the 'inland' areas of the Olifants River, and the Breede River districts of Worcester and Robertson, with their rich alluvial soils and high summer temperatures unrelieved by a prevailing wind from the sea (with a few notable exceptions), tend to produce such grapes. Here are many of the country's co-operatives, and from these areas large quantities of grapes for distilling wine and for making raisins have been grown from the nineteenth century onwards. Although new methods have helped to improve much of the wine made in these areas, the emphasis, with certain happy exceptions, remains upon quantity rather than quality.

Tulbagh provides a contrast. By any

agricultural standard, this seems an unattractive prospect – a high, wide and in midsummer furiously hot valley, where the river banks are relatively fertile but the slopes of the mountains little more than rock, with virtually no topsoil. Yet it is these stony slopes which yield some of South Africa's finest white wines.

The needs of the vine are therefore not always immediately predictable: indeed for the first wine pioneers, seeking to establish a crop with which they had not long been acquainted, the only guide was a kind of inspired trial and error. And if they had successes, they also had many failures, planting specific types of vines in conditions of soil and irrigation, or the lack of it, to which they were barely appropriate.

It was a hit-or-miss system. While there are still many variables in the life of the modern vine grower, however, he can operate many more conscious controls, both of the vine and the conditions under which it lives. Above all, he has a far

Workers collecting rootstock material from a mother plantation 1. The canes are bundled 2 and transported to the nursery 3 where they are trimmed for grafting to the desired 300-mm length 4 and 5 and disinfected to prevent transmission of disease 6.

Rootstock for grafting is stored in a cold room 1. Many grafting techniques are used, and though handcutting is still widely practised, mechanical devices such as that producing the omega-graft 2, produce strong, clean unions and are gaining acceptance. After grafting, the vines are placed in callus boxes 3 where the graft union between rootstock and scion forms. The callused vines 4 are then ready for planting in the nursery vineyards 5.

clearer knowledge of the way these work together, of the precise nature and influence of soil and climate than had his predecessors.

Modern viticulture, for example, informs the grower that the vine is a plant with comparatively low nutritional needs. With its long growing season of about seven months and its large root system, sometimes going down to a depth of more than seven metres (a deciduous creeper, the vine has no taproot), it can usually meet its own growth requirements, even in poor soil.

Thus almost any soil which allows conditions of mild and stable growth will provide the medium in which the well-chosen and appropriate cultivar will develop to its full potential.

The characteristics which affect its quality can be both chemical and physical. The chemical composition of the soil is vital: in particular, the degree of acidity or lack of it will influence the growth of the vine and the resultant wine. A soil with free lime present (common in the Breede River area, for example) is alkaline – in scientific terms this is referred to as a soil with a high pH. This type of soil leads to a grape juice with a high cation, or acid,

content, conducive to good quality. Lime-rich soils, however, do not automatically give high quality wine.

Soils containing an excess of potassium make for high pH grapes which tend to produce wines of uncertain stability, and in the reds, of poor colour. On the other hand, too little potassium results in poor carbohydrate production and a greater sensitivity to disease.

Nitrogen is essential for the stimulation of growth. Too much, however, causes too rapid growth, leading to high production but low quality, as well as an increased sensitivity to disease. Too little nitrogen results in poor quality.

The chemical composition of the soil is important, but so is its physical structure. In fact it is these physical properties that determine the eventual excellence of the wine. They include such characteristics as the depth of the soil, its rockiness, the degree of structural layering, the clay content, and its ability to drain well.

As far as the general physical needs of the vine are concerned, soils of good depth are better for both quality and growth. They create a more effective buffer against drought (an important consideration locally) and also against unseasonable

rain. Deep soils ensure more stable growth in both dry and wet areas.

The soil's capacity to retain moisture can have considerable effect on the vine. It is determined by its depth, texture, and the amount of organic matter it contains; it is also affected by the presence of rocks or stones. Soils with a high clay content will retain far more water than sandy soils, but this is not necessarily an advantage. Too much water can lead to rank growth or excessive moisture in the berries at ripening time, which can result in unbalanced sugar-acid ratios and mould infections. That is why in cool, moist regions, clay soils and organically rich soils are avoided for quality wine grapes.

The many different kinds of soil structure have been broken down into four broad categories which are subdivided into 'forms'. These are further classified on the basis of texture and composition into 'soil series' – soil classification is based on the morphology of topsoil, taking account of soil texture, structure and leaching potential.

Each of these different soil types has its advantages and drawbacks in relationship to the growing of vines. Many of the specific disadvantages, however, can be

4

5

Planting of grafted vines in the nursery is another critical stage in their development. Particular attention is paid to the depth of the furrow and the planting distance between the vines 1 and 2; the furrows are then filled in, the workers leaving the tops of the vines exposed to sunlight 3. A newly-planted nursery vineyard at Ernita, with Du Toit's Kloof Pass in the background 4.

removed or at least modified by the appropriate treatment of the soil, ranging from straightforward ploughing to deep ploughing, sub-soiling or trenching, or ripping ('ripping' involves the breaking-up of underlying rocky layers in the soil without disturbing the topsoil structure). With deep ploughing, chemical or organic fertilizers can be added to the soil.

Before this preparation can take place, an assessment of the soil must be made. South African soils are extremely heterogeneous – sometimes varying markedly from one part of a farm to another – and this necessitates meticulous soil screening and evaluation. A soil survey, often carried out by the technical staff of Government laboratories or those associated with the producing wholesalers, charts the various soil types present on the farm. 'Profile holes' as deep as 1,2 metres are made at points round the planned vineyard area, from which a complete 'underground map' of the land can be plotted.

The four main types of soil are 'Structureless' (further divided into Hutton and Clovelly soils and Fernwood soils), 'Duplex', 'Shallow' and 'Alluvial' soils.

Structureless may at first appear an odd name for a soil. In fact, it simply indicates that this type contains no restrictive layers in the subsoil which would impede growth, such as compacted, heavy-textured layers, hardpans, cemented layers, or layers of a generally stratified nature. Several types of these structureless soils have been recognized at the Cape, the most important being the **Hutton** and **Clovelly** and the **Fernwood** types. Hutton and Clovelly are well-drained soils of red and yellow colour respectively, while Fernwood is represented by deep, dry, sandy soils.

In general, the local Hutton and Clovelly types require little preparation. It has, however, been shown experimentally that some of them in the coastal region, which have a fairly high clay content (20-30 per cent), show compaction in the subsoil. Here it is advantageous to trench or rip up the soil to a depth of 600-750 millimetres. In areas in the interior where fine sandy types of these soils are found, sub-surface compaction takes place as a result of fine-sand fraction and prolonged cultivation. But a relatively shallow ripping or trench cultivation is an advantage here also.

It is often found that the subsoil of the Hutton and Clovelly types in the coastal areas is very acid, allowing little deep root growth, and thus resembles a shallow soil. In such cases consideration must be given to deep trenching accompanied by the addition of lime to provide a chemical balance, the determination of the requirements usually being made before the trenching.

The deep, dry and sandy Fernwood type is generally inhospitable to the vine before preparation. Deep cultivation of such soils is usually ineffectual, and the addition of straw serves little purpose. Well-rotted organic material or dung may help, for that increases the water-retaining capacity and nutritional value of the soil. But this practice is not generally economically viable, and the farmer working with this kind of soil usually prefers to give his vines frequent light irrigation.

The second major type of soil is the **Duplex.** As the name implies, these are soils which feature a marked difference of texture between the topsoil and the subsoil. There are a number of local variations, including the **Kroonstad, Sterkspruit** and **Estcourt** forms which make up a very large proportion of the soils in the western Cape coastal region. They have a relatively sandy topsoil, with an underlying clay pan. Of these three forms, Kroonstad has a sandy top layer with an iron-bearing pan of peculiar hard, nuggety forms known as *ouklip*, just above the clay. Sterkspruit has a topsoil which is relatively light-textured, changing sharply to a strongly structured, heavy-textured subsoil.

Preparation of Duplex soils is problematical. After trenching, they are often in poorer condition than before, because the clay subsoil is ploughed to the surface. The 'raw' soil is thus uppermost, inhibiting the establishment of the vines. The clay subsoil is often very acid (it can sometimes also be brackish) which compounds the problem. Moreover, these soils are inherently wet, and disturbance of the underground drainage can affect the natural balance. The general recommendation of the expert in this instance is to undertake no preparation if the top sandy layer is 900-1 200 millimetres deep: it should preferably be drained, if this is necessary. If too shallow, soils of this nature can sometimes be made deeper by ripping when in a dry condition, so that the topsoil drops into the fissures in the clay subsoil and keeps them open. The ripping operation must be carried out against the contour to promote healthy drainage. When dealing with the Kroonstad form, the iron-cemented *ouklip* just above the clay pan must also be broken to ensure effective root penetration. Large stones displaced by this method may be removed, but the gravel of the *ouklip* must be left undisturbed.

Shallow soils, the third type, feature a layer of topsoil directly over rock. These soils are known as 'Mispah' or 'Glenrosa', depending on the state of disintegration of the underlying rock, Glenrosa being at a more advanced stage of disintegration. They are not usually suitable for grape-growing unless the underlying rock can be broken or ripped. In cases where the rock can be broken and irrigation judiciously applied, great success can sometimes be achieved, particularly where the

VINEYARD COMPETITION

Sponsored by Stellenbosch Farmers' Winery and judged by a panel of experts drawn from the Oenological and Viticultural Research Institute, Elsenburg College, KWV and Stellenbosch Farmers' Winery, this annual competition seeks to encourage rigorous vineyard practices based on the common winelands maxim that 'good wine is made in the vineyard'. The entrants are judged on a regional basis, the overall winner receiving a carved wooden floating trophy and an overseas study trip to a wine area of his own choice; regional winners also receive a floating trophy and a cash prize.

Competing vineyards must be at least five years old, and a minimum of one hectare in size. Judgement is made on the basis of a number of criteria. Yield, of course, is important, and is judged in relation to the potential of the soil in the area of the vineyard. Plant material must be of a high quality; the disposal of the vines should be uniform, without gaps in the rows; there should be good affinity between rootstocks and cultivars; pruning methods, crop or yield control and the use of fertilizers and irrigation (where applicable) are also examined. General management and vineyard records are also assessed. After the final judging, the vineyard practices of the winners are analysed and discussed.

Winners of the competition to date are: **1981** – Braam van Velden of Overgaauw Estate; **1982** – Stawie Fouché, supplier to the Klawer Co-operative; **1983** – Poekel Bruwer of Uitsig in the Worcester District; **1984** – Hardy Joubert of Hooggenoeg at Kuilsrivier in the Stellenbosch District; **1985** – Pieter Hugo of Onderplaas in the Worcester District; **1986** – Tienie Louw of Diemersdal in the Durbanville District and **1987** – Stanley Louw of Opstal in the Worcester District.

When the young vines are well rooted, they are removed from the nursery and classified 1. The graft union 2 is tested for strength by twisting and bending 3, tied into bundles of 50 plants which are then dipped in a fungicide, either Kaptan or Chinosol 4. Tossie Louw, nursery manager of Ernita, in the heat therapy room 5 where the growing tips of virus-tested material 6 are nurtured in a carefully controlled environment.

underlying rock is sloping or vertical shale. For greater effectiveness the ripping action must be carried out against the vertical layering of the shale. With this method, however, steps must be taken to guard against salination of lower-lying alluvial soils. The shallow shale ground is often rich in salt, which may cause serious bracking through the rapid seepage of water through such soils and the subsequent damming against the lower alluvial soils.

The fourth main soil type is **Alluvial**. Deposited by the rivers over the ages, it is made up of alternating layers of soils of different textures. These layered alluvial soils are known as the 'Dundee' type. Alluvial soils are mostly encountered near river courses – the Eerste, Olifants, Berg and Breede rivers are the main sites in the Cape winelands for this type of soil.

With alluvial soils of the Dundee type, any intense layering, that is, sharp transitions from coarse texture layers (such as silt) to fine texture layers (such as sand), must first be corrected by deep ploughing to produce a consistent texture, since root distribution and water penetration are invariably impeded by the

layers. Intensive ripping cultivation can also be effective with this type of soil in creating channels for root and water passage.

When the type of soil in the projected vineyard has been analysed and assessed, the physical operations involved in soil preparation can begin. This procedure may involve a number of implements and machines, of which the trencher and the ripper are the most important. Each can usually cultivate to a depth of approximately 1,2 metres and the nature of the soil will to a large extent determine the choice of implement. The trencher mixes the various soil layers together, whereas the ripper breaks up the lower layers, but does not mix them with the top strata.

If there is doubt as to which will be the more effective, the choice will usually be determined by the nature of the terrain. Both trencher and ripper require powerful caterpillar tractors for their operation, but on sloping ground a trencher can often be only used downhill, while a ripper can work in both directions. For shallow cultivation, a plough is used to loosen the top layers of the soil (to a depth of some

200-300 millimetres), especially where the ground is stony.

After this preliminary treatment, the soils are left to rest for a year so that a chemical and microbiological equilibrium may re-establish itself after the trauma of cultivation.

During this rest period, green cover crops are planted, generally oats, rye or lupins. These will eventually be ploughed into the soil, together with manure. The nematode infestation of the soil is determined and, if necessary, the soil is treated against these and other organisms which attack the roots of the vine. Undesirable weeds are eradicated, and drainage and irrigation systems are installed where required.

The young vines from the nursery are introduced into this well-prepared earth. With a consistent and well-drained soil and a good supply of nutrients they are given a firm foundation for their future working life. Yet of relatively greater importance than the influence of the soil is that of the climate – the sun, wind and rainfall which from now on will to a high degree condition the quantity and quality of its crops.

2

3

4

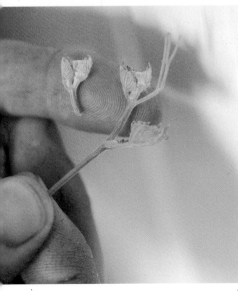

6

5

*A macro-sequence of bud development in a Steen vine: a bud sprouting in mid-September **1** (though invisible, a miniscule 'bunch' of grapes is already formed); and again at slightly more advanced stages, **2** and **3**; a further stage **4** shows a 100-mm shoot from the base bud of a short bearer, with a developing bunch of grapes clearly visible.*

CLIMATE

The optimum development of the vine and its grapes is dependent upon a balance of climatic conditions at different times during its yearly cycle of growth and dormancy.

Winter is the dormant period. For three months the vine must be allowed to rest. During this time it must receive a good supply of rainfall. At the same time, temperatures must be cold. It can endure marked drops in temperature, but severe freezing may kill arms and trunks. At the opposite extreme, temperatures must not rise too high during this dormant period – warm spells in winter induce unseasonal growth which can be killed by a subsequent drop in temperature, thus upsetting the natural growing cycle.

Spring is a particularly sensitive time in the vine's annual cycle. Severe spring frosts injure the young shoots, while strong winds can prevent good pollination at flowering time. Now, too, temperatures should not markedly fluctuate. Cold snaps during blossoming time can lead to poor setting of the young grapes – an effect referred to as millerandage – which becomes evident at the ripening stage.

During the long summer growing season the vine needs a steady supply of warmth. This is expressed both in terms of temperature and of the amount of sunshine received. Ideally, the temperature should average 18 °C: the amount of direct sunshine should be about 2 000 hours a year. Again, the 'not too much, not too

A further example of the sophisticated controlled growing environment of young vines is the mist-bed tunnel where humidity and temperature are maintained at a constant level and the sprays monitored by a time-switch.

little' principle operates. Heat and sunlight are needed to bring the grapes to fruition, for it is photosynthesis that produces the major element of sugar in the grape. Without this supply of sunshine the sugar content would be low, resulting in a light wine, high in acid and low in alcohol (it is the fermentation of the sugar which makes the alcohol).

At the opposite extreme, problems can arise in a climate with too much sunshine. In general, in a very hot climate the aromatic qualities of the grape (with the exception of Muscat flavours) are not as delicate or as rich as those which can develop in more temperate conditions. The high rate of photosynthesis which takes place results in a high sugar content in comparison to fruit acid production, yielding an unbalanced wine which is difficult to preserve.

Lack of direct sunlight is rarely a problem in South Africa; rather the reverse. Problems are often encountered with the 'burning' of flavour compounds from the grapes, especially with the heavy concentration of sunlight in the late afternoons in summer on north- and west-facing slopes. In areas where this happens ingenuity must be exercised in the siting of the vineyards, either in the shadow of a mountain, or where there is a strategically placed row of trees to block the late afternoon sun.

The effect of wind is important, too. The areas in the Cape winelands within reach of the cooling breezes from the sea are provided with a natural compensation for the effects of the heat. When accompanied by the protection of a mountain or a valley site, as in Constantia or the valleys of the Simonsberg, natural conditions prevail for the making of fine wine with a high fruit acid content, well balanced with sugar.

Together with sunlight and warmth, a continuous supply of moisture is needed throughout the summer. In the coastal region the ideal water supply to a vine during the growing season would be between 300 and 350 millimetres. Too much water can be harmful, resulting in plants and fruit with soft cell structures which become susceptible to mould. Excessive moisture can also lead to the growth of denser foliage, causing variations of the same problem. Heavy falls of rain when the grapes have almost reached their optimum ripeness can cause the berries to split and rot; the sugar content of the grape will also decline considerably owing to dilution.

Local preference tends to favour drought rather than flood, for a deficiency in natural rainfall can be made up by judicious irrigation. In very low rainfall areas, this is essential to obtain any kind of crop at all; in the coastal belt it is sometimes used as a supplement to the rainfall.

As a general principle, under South African conditions, the vine grower looks for altitude, for a cooling breeze, for a site with relatively less sunshine hours and sheltered in the late afternoons in summer, and for a good accessible supply of water – a farm with numerous dams is not exceptional in the hotter areas. He also looks for cultivars appropriate to his particular conditions. For example, certain varieties, such as Pinot Noir, are very sensitive to warm temperatures, and only achieve excellence under very specific temperatures and conditions of cultivation; Cabernet Sauvignon and Shiraz on the other hand, easily develop fine colour under hot conditions.

Assessment of these climatic influences will determine not only the type of vine to be planted but its location, the orientation of the vineyard, and the type and degree of irrigation to be used.

Once the vineyard is established, however, the farmer's focus shortens from the imponderables of sun and rain to the more mundane but equally important matter of the day-to-day running of the vineyard and the care of his vines.

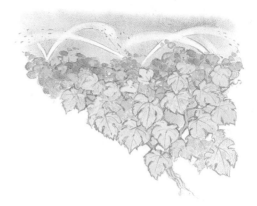

THE RUNNING OF A VINEYARD

Vines have been known to reach an impressive old age: a hundred years is not uncommon, though few come within reach of the country's oldest vine citizen, a 173-year old still going strong in Graaff-Reinet.

The average life of a commercially grown vine is about 25 to 30 years, but its productive life only begins after the first three to four years. Mature grapes for wine making are grown during the central 20 years of its life-span. At the end of its productive period it is uprooted, and the land planted with a cover crop before a new vineyard is laid out.

During its working career the vine must be given constant physical and chemical attention – physical support in the form of stakes and trellises to which it is trained; its degree and pattern of growth must be regulated and assisted by pruning; its soil must be enriched with fertilizers; irrigation applied where necessary; and a variety of vine diseases and ever-hungry pests must be kept at bay.

All this requires considerable planning. Supplies of material and tools must be ensured and fertilizers and pesticides ordered well in advance. The disposition of labour must be planned, and farm machinery, from the irrigation equipment through to the tractors and cultivators, must be kept serviced and in good repair.

All this organization reaches a climax at the time of harvest, the high point of the wine farmer's year. In a period of about two months the annual crop must be brought in. On a large farm or estate this can amount to several hundred or even

thousand tonnes of grapes, which must be delivered as quickly as possible (preferably before the days' heat starts premature fermentation) to the grower's production cellar, or to the crusher at the local co-operative or producing wholesaler.

The complexities of harvesting and delivery are increased when a range of different cultivars is concerned. Different cultivars mature at different times, some earlier than others: Pinotage, for example, early in the season, Cabernet later. Others such as Shiraz and Tinta Barocca are ready for harvesting in mid-season. To avoid uneconomic gaps in the harvest and his labour force being idle, the wine farmer plans his production to suit this. In particular, red wine producers often 'pad' their harvest programme with a white wine cultivar such as Steen to ensure a sustained level of activity throughout the vintage period. (South Africa is one of the few wine-making countries where the vineyard workers live year-round on the farm.)

At the end of the harvest, if the farmer is producing his own wine in his own cellar, much of his time and attention will be taken up with the complex mysteries, the aromatic secrets, of his wine cellar. Outside in the sun, now shadowed a little with a hint of approaching autumn, the vineyards' long rows stand lightened of their burden. In a few months the winter will come. By then the wine will have been made and been bottled or set aside in oak casks to mature. With the winter rains comes the ebb of the year, the dormant period for both the vines and the people on the farm, for the farmer and his family, the farm-manager and the workers – all bound to the cycle of nature, the slow turn of the seasons.

It is a time of regeneration in the communal life of the farm. This is not a world which is often seen or penetrated by the *stadsjapies*, the city folk who flock to the winelands in the golden height of summer: it is a secret winter world.

It is also one with a beauty of its own.

The full, ripe splendour of the summer winelands has often been celebrated, but the subtle magic of the winter in the valleys, however wind- and rain-swept, has been the subject of less frequent praise.

After the hectic days of summer, this is the wine farmer's chance to take stock, to plan ahead; a time too for renewing contacts with the many members of the extended family of the farm.

For a South African wine farm is a small community which can range from a dozen to a couple of hundred people. The bonds that operate between them, however casual on the surface, are deep, silent and powerful, of ancestral tenure in this part of the land. A South African farmer, talking to his foreman, both of whom, like their ancestors, will live and die on this piece of earth, have the language of the mountains between them, a common heritage and bond.

Theirs is largely a silent communion. And by comparison the matter on hand will appear very ordinary indeed. A casual visitor from the town might make little of this muttered debate, intent and frowning, this plucking at half-fallen leaves, this muttering of 'mildew', of 'tandpyn' and 'anthracnose', of 'dead arm' and 'snout beetle', of pruning and trellising.

TRELLISING AND PRUNING

Most vines are trellised, by one method or another, to keep them off the ground, to make the bunches of grapes more accessible and, with certain types, to provide a heavier leaf-cover for the crop.

The trellis is designed for the type of vine to be introduced to the vineyard and is erected after the vines have been growing for a year. In the course of its growth towards maturity the vine is both pruned and trained to adapt to the advantages of the specific form of trellis being used.

Not all vines are trellised, however, although all are trained in some fashion. A proportion are grown as bush or goblet

Successful management of a vineyard is a complex operation requiring careful planning and co-ordination. Vines must be pruned and trellised and they often need irrigating in the hotter, drier areas. Fertilizers are required to replenish soil nutrients, while pests and diseases that would destroy both vines and grapes must be kept at bay. Such painstaking care and attention, however, is rewarded during the harvest, usually from late January to mid-April, when healthy well-ripened grapes are gathered.

PRUNING AND TRELLISING

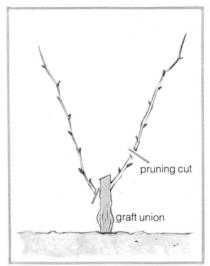

1. Pruning the rooted cutting

2. Pruning after the first growing season

3. Pruning after the second growing season

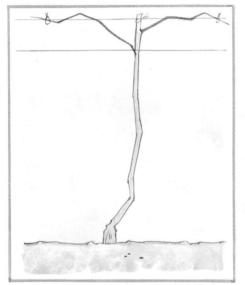

4. Pruning after the third growing season

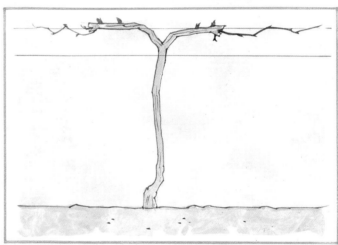

5. Pruning after the fourth growing season

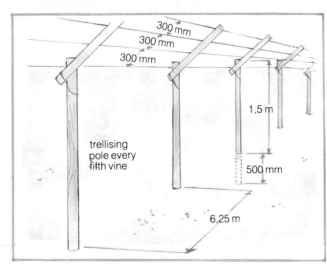

6. Trellising is a precise technology which, together with proper pruning methods, is aimed at obtaining optimum results from the vine. Among the trellising systems used in South Africa is the four-wire system shown here.

vines, generally in the more arid areas where there is nevertheless enough rainfall for the vines to grow. In this method, the simplest way of establishing a vineyard and the one largely used in the early vineyards, the vines are trained and pruned into a neat 'goblet' shape.

The main methods of trellising used locally are the three-wire system, the slanting trellis system, the fence system (a four-wire vertical trellis), and the four-wire system.

In the past table grapes were trained onto larger trellises than those used for the support of wine grapes; this was because table grapes are usually grown in fertile areas well supplied with water.

The most common method of training the vines on this variety of structures is the cordon system. By this method the trunk of the vine is trained to about 200 millimetres below the lowest wire of the trellis, the so-called 'cordon-wire', and then divided horizontally into two branches which extend in opposite directions, along the cordon. This system has the effect of disposing the growth of the vine across the full extent of the area of the wires.

But if the trellis provides the basic support for the vine, it is through the craft of pruning that its growth, development and yield of grapes is controlled.

Pruning comprises the removal of canes, shoots, leaves and other vegetative parts of the vine (the removal of flower clusters is known as thinning). By this process of selective removal, the growth of the young vine is controlled in proportion to its vigour and the depth of its root-system. A good balance between vigour and capacity to produce good quality fruit must be found. This means that weaker vines must be allowed fewer fruiting buds than vigorous vines. Pruning is therefore individual to each vine. At the same time, dead and unproductive arms, spurs and canes are removed.

The vine is also pruned according to its situation, that is, whether it is grown as a bush or 'head-pruned' vine or on one or other kind of trellis. It is also pruned according to its age, particularly in its youth – if it were not thus restrained it would develop very rapidly in the first few years of life, exhausting its growth and shortening its life-span. It would bear less fruit and the quality of its grapes would be poor.

There are a number of different styles of pruning. Spur pruning, for example, is used for grape varieties which bear large bunches and have fruitful buds at the base of their canes; of these, one to three are retained. With cane, or semi-long pruning, the principle of the system is that each arm should have one spur with one to two buds, and one semi-long cane with four to six buds. A cane will have between eight and twelve buds. In this instance the canes are for grape production, and the spurs for producing shoots to serve as canes and spurs the following year.

It is important when pruning to know which buds are fruitful. As a rule the fertile buds of the vine occur on the one year-old canes that arise from two year-old wood. The buds of vigorous water-sprouts (canes arising from three year-old wood, or older) are frequently unfruitful.

It is also necessary to know if the basal buds on a cane are fruitful or not. The most fruitful buds are situated at the fifth to the tenth node, but in most of the wine varieties the basal buds are sufficiently fruitful to allow spur pruning. With varieties whose basal buds are unfruitful, cane pruning should be practised.

Before planting, the vine is pruned as shown in fig. 1. The strongest and/or the most upright cane is retained and pruned back to two to three buds. Frequently during the first summer no training or trellising is done. During July or August of the following year the first winter pruning takes place (fig. 2). Again, the strongest cane is chosen and pruned to two to three buds, all other shoots being removed.

During early spring the two strongest of the shoots are selected and the remaining shoots are removed. The strongest is then tied loosely to the stake. The other shoot is kept as a reserve. Lateral shoots arising from the main shoot are removed, but the leaves are retained.

After the second season, the strongest shoot is tied to the second lowest wire and is cut off at this point. All the other shoots are removed, to leave one stem (fig. 3).

During the third growing season, all the bottom shoots developing from the upright stem are removed, leaving only the top four shoots below the wire – this is done at the end of September. At this time excessive bunches should also be removed, leaving only one bunch to each shoot. After the third growing season the two strongest shoots are selected, one on each side of the stem. These are pruned back to six buds, and the shoots are tied to the wire (fig. 4).

In the next dormant season, the short bearing units (spurs) are cut back to two buds, providing 16 fruit-buds on each vine. Spurs growing upright are selected (fig. 5).

In the following dormant season the cordon is lengthened and finished to leave a vine with between 10 to 12 two-bud short bearers, or spurs. The advantage of this method is that it permits the cordons to be short and sturdy.

Yearly pruning continues throughout the productive adult life of the vine. The mature plant receives its most thorough pruning during the dormant season of the winter. The first pruning usually commences in May or June, after all the leaves have dropped, and consists of removing all the canes which will not be required as spurs or canes. This is known locally as 'skoonsnoei', and is preliminary to the final pruning, which takes place at any time between mid-July and late August, depending on the variety. In areas where spring frosts are prevalent or where varieties are concerned which set their berries badly (as often in the case of Hanepoot), pruning is done as late as possible – in late August or early September.

CLIMATIC REQUIREMENTS OF VITIS VINIFERA

SPRING
Mild weather with dry spells is needed at this time when the new period of growth commences. Continuous rain makes control of fungoid diseases difficult. Mild frost can help to control insects, but very cold weather and heavy frost can be very detrimental during the flowering period, resulting in poor berry set.

SUMMER
In the summer season long, warm to hot days are needed; in particular, once the grapes have started ripening dry weather is needed. Humidity in summer causes fungus diseases and encourages insect pests. Rain at the time of full ripening causes the grapes to split and rot.

AUTUMN
Rain or irrigation after the crop has been harvested is beneficial to the vine. At this time spraying to prevent fungal diseases is important, and fertilizers should be applied to ensure the formation of healthy wood.

WINTER
In winter the vine lies dormant and during this period temperatures should remain low, without being too low, preferably not below 0 °C. There must be abundant rain. If the weather remains too warm unseasonable growth may take place, only to be killed by later drops in temperature or by frost. A lack of rain can be detrimental.

PESTS AND DISEASES

Through careful pruning and trellising, a disciplined use of the vine's resources is obtained. Against these well-ordered battalions of the vineyards, however, are ranged the armies, some visible, some invisible, of viruses, of bacteria, of rot and fungus, and their high command led by a variety of miscreants. It is for these long-standing enemies that the farmer and his assistants will be most prepared and alert.

Roses are more susceptible to disease than vines and if planted at the head of vineyards 1 these shrubs can provide the farmer with an early warning system, enabling him to take action before the vines become infected. This practice is widely used in the Bordeaux region of France and is also proving successful on some South African wine farms. Grapes showing symptoms of disease: 2 sour rot, 3 powdery mildew, or oidium, in its early stages and 4 in a more advanced stage; and 5 noble rot.

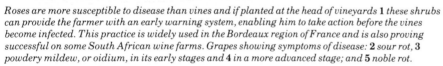

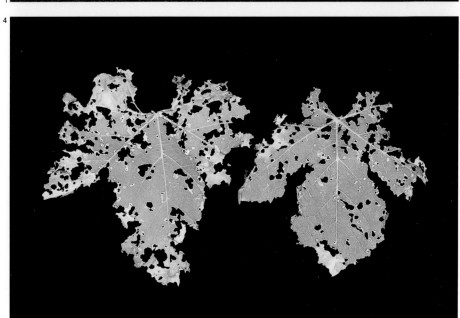

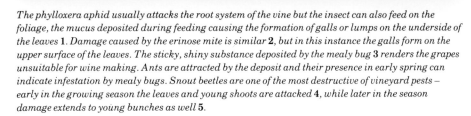

The phylloxera aphid usually attacks the root system of the vine but the insect can also feed on the foliage, the mucus deposited during feeding causing the formation of galls or lumps on the underside of the leaves 1. Damage caused by the erinose mite is similar 2, but in this instance the galls form on the upper surface of the leaves. The sticky, shiny substance deposited by the mealy bug 3 renders the grapes unsuitable for wine making. Ants are attracted by the deposit and their presence in early spring can indicate infestation by mealy bugs. Snout beetles are one of the most destructive of vineyard pests – early in the growing season the leaves and young shoots are attacked 4, while later in the season damage extends to young bunches as well 5.

There are four major pests which, when not effectively combated, cause serious damage in the local vineyards. These are phylloxera, nematodes, snout beetles, and mealy bugs. Besides these, there are a number of fungus diseases, of which five are paramount. These are, in order of importance, powdery mildew (oidium), downy mildew, rot, dead arm, and anthracnose.

Dactylosphaera vitifoliae, the current scientific name for **phylloxera,** is the most widely known of the aphid family, having caused considerable historic grief in the winelands of the world. The characteristic effects of its predations are that the affected vines stop summer growth sooner than healthy vines, that leaf colour changes to dull green and later to yellow, and that the symptoms tend to spread so that a patch of weak or of dead vines can be observed in the vineyard.

Phylloxera in this country is spread mainly by man. The insect spreads naturally by crawling slowly in the soil from vine to vine, but flood waters and man (through rooted plants, implements and boots) can distribute the pest rapidly over great distances.

The control of phylloxera is mainly a matter of prevention, since no effective chemical control has yet been found. The basic method remains the now almost universal one of grafting onto resistant rootstocks; but the planting of vines in sandy soil (generally avoided by the aphid) can have a limiting effect on the pest.

Nematodes, or **eelworms,** are microscopic worm-shaped pests which attack the roots of the vine and cause damage similar to that of phylloxera. Unlike phylloxera, however, they favour moist, sandy soils. Their control involves the use of resistant rootstock such as Richter 99, Dogridge, or Ramsey, and the fumigation of the vineyard soil before new plantings are made.

Snout beetles are insects which eat young shoots, leaf petioles, and young flower clusters, and in serious cases can lead to the destruction of all the green parts of the vine. They eat mainly at night, and hide during the day in the soil or under the bark of the vines. From October onwards they can be controlled by spraying with pesticides such as Cymbusch or Ambusch.

Mealy bugs are lice which form a sticky, sweet and shiny deposit on the shoots, leaves and on the bunches of grapes, thus making them unfit for normal wine-making purposes. This deposit also attracts ants which in turn protect the mealy bug from its natural enemies, the ladybirds. By spraying with suitable pesticides to kill the ants (traditionally, this was with Dieldrin, now made illegal and replaced by several others), and leave the field clear for the ladybirds, natural control of the mealy bugs can be obtained.

Among the prevalent diseases, **powdery mildew** (oidium), the ailment which first made its appearance in the Cape vineyards in 1859, is caused by a fungus which exhibits certain characteristic symptoms. On the lower surface of the leaves, small spots occur, and on the upper surface a white, powdery cobweb-like growth appears around the spot where the fungus begins to grow. The young shoots can be affected, but most of the damage is reserved for the grapes. Mature berries, if infected, will crack and dry up. The initial cracking of the berries provides a site for other micro-organism infections, such as *Botrytis cinerea*. A characteristic of powdery mildew is that if the normal white powderiness on the shoots and the berries is rubbed off, a brown or black discoloration shows underneath.

Powdery mildew and other forms of mildew, such as downy mildew, are easily spread in the vineyard. The fungus prefers warm, humid weather, but the spores will not germinate in wet conditions.

Oidium is best controlled with vineyard sulphur (dusting or wettable powder), or with other chemicals such as Bayleton or Karathane as well as Tilt and Rubigan.

Downy mildew *(Plasmopara viticola)* registers its appearance on the lower surface of the leaf when a white downy

mass of spores is formed. On the upper surface of the leaf an oily-looking spot, at first light yellow but later turning to a reddish colour, can be seen.

Young bunches of grapes are also infected, a white powdery covering being observed. This may cause the berries to shrivel and drop; in comparison, the shoots are little affected by the fungus.

Downy mildew is best controlled by the use of copper-containing compounds such as copper oxychloride and with organic or systemic fungicides such as Nomil, Ridomil and Mikal-M.

Besides these different types of fungi, there are two main kinds of bunch-rot found in South African vineyards. These are **botrytis,** or **grey-mould,** rot *(Botrytis cinerea),* which may develop into **noble rot** (Raisin) under favourable conditions; and **sour rot** (Rhizopus). Noble rot is advantageous to the wine maker, but sour rot is a grievous nuisance in the vineyard. Usually botrytis rot occurs first, after rains during harvest time. Sour rot is usually a secondary infection.

Chenel, Weldra, Colombar, and to a certain extent, Cabernet Sauvignon are most resistant to botrytis rot because their bunches are loose compared with those of other cultivars such as Steen, which are compact. Fungicides may aid control with susceptible varieties, which can also be

5

6

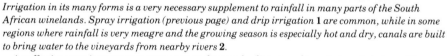

Irrigation in its many forms is a very necessary supplement to rainfall in many parts of the South African winelands. Spray irrigation (previous page) and drip irrigation 1 are common, while in some regions where rainfall is very meagre and the growing season is especially hot and dry, canals are built to bring water to the vineyards from nearby rivers 2.

An effective spraying programme to prevent damage by disease and insects is a vital element in ensuring a healthy crop 3.

Pruning during the chill winter months is a time for warm clothing, especially in areas such as Robertson 4 where snow-clad mountains ring the vineyards.

Plastic covering 5 in young vineyards helps to retain moisture and prevents the growth of weeds which would compete with the vines for both moisture and soil nutrients.

In 1983 some five per cent of the total national crop was lost as a result of bird damage. Among the many techniques of control currently being tested is the use of brightly-coloured tapes 6 suspended above the vines; wind vibrates the tape and the resultant noise and rapid colour-change frightens the birds.

helped by the removal of leaves from the inside of the vine to expose the grapes to the sun and improve ventilation.

Dead arm *(Phomopsis viticola)* is characterized by small cankers which form on the basal parts of the shoots and by small spots which appear on the leaves. These spots usually have a black centre and a yellow border. Folpan is the most effective compound for control of dead arm.

Anthracnose *(Gloeosporium*

ampelophagum) shows as small, circular, greyish-black spots on the leaves; sometimes these spots are bordered by a yellow discoloration. The spots enlarge, and often the middle portion falls out. On the shoots sunken cankers form and the bark is eventually destroyed, the shoot becoming hard and black. Organic fungicides again provide good control for anthracnose.

From planting to the first harvest some

years later, is a long and complex journey for the vine. Many people are involved in its upbringing, from the workers in the field to the farmer, the foreman, the farm-manager, to the supplier of chemicals, of fertilizers and pesticides to control the prevalent pests and diseases, to the viticultural expert giving the farmer advice on his plantings and the type of cultivar he should use, to the expert grafter and nurseryman.

The Vineyard Calendar

The climax of the wine farmer's year comes with the vintage which takes place at the height of summer, generally from February through to March and later still for certain of the vines. In a sense, everything which takes place during the remainder of the year is a preparation for this event. The arrangement of this 'vineyard calendar' therefore abandons the traditional western January to December arrangement in favour of Nature's calendar of March to February, beginning immediately after the conclusion of the harvest.

MARCH

By the end of March, most wine farmers will have brought in their crop. It is still hot in the land, but the edge of the coming autumn is now approaching. Immediately after the harvest has been brought in the vineyards are irrigated if possible, preventing early defoliation and allowing the wood to mature properly.

At this time crop seed and fertilizers for the winter cover crop are ordered to ensure an early sowing. By now, too, quick grass (fast-growing, hardy grass) on new soils and in the vineyards must be destroyed.

APRIL

New vineyards are now prepared. The farmer prepares the soils to be planted in the coming winter before the heavy winter rains begin. Advance planning of new plantings is also undertaken. Organic matter is applied during soil preparation, this being the only opportunity the farmer has to introduce it into the subsoil. Sources of organic matter include natural vegetation, which should never be removed completely when veld or bush is cleared. Sown cover crops will also supply a considerable quantity of organic matter. Before the heavy rains begin contours and stormwater ditches are constructed. Existing contours and ditches are also inspected, and repaired and cleaned where necessary. Drainage pipes are put in new soils where these tend to become waterlogged.

Argentine ants must be killed at this time to ensure biological control of mealy bug (Sanviant, Chlordaan and Dursban are sprays which have replaced Dieldrin). Vineyards which are infested with erinose or oidium receive a sulphur application after the harvest.

MAY

By this time the winter cover crops have generally been sown. By now, too, soils for new plantings are fully prepared. At the same time, preparations for pruning the vineyards are under way. All pruning equipment, particularly shears, is checked for condition – the shears should make a clean cut to prevent harm caused by bad pruning wounds. When pruning certain basic guidelines are followed. Clearing is started as soon as the leaves have fallen – the final pruning of the bearers is done later in the winter. The best time to start pruning is after a good rain. This will prevent the pruning wounds from drying out – dry wounds may give access to disease organisms. Fortunately, a sealer for large wounds is now available. Varieties which bear and grow well and are not inclined to millerandage are generally pruned early. Early pruning will also, to a certain extent, encourage the earlier ripening of the grapes. Those varieties bearing poorly and prone to millerandage are pruned late, both to delay ripening and where there is a danger of frost in the spring.

AUGUST

The farmer usually tries to complete the planting of new vineyards during this month. Orders for grafted vines for new plantings in the following years are usually placed now.

The final pruning of the vineyards is done. Those vines which do not bear so well or are prone to millerandage are left until last. Where there is a danger from frost, however, pruning should be done later.

The green manure crop (sown or natural weed growth) must be ploughed into the soil before the end of August. Some farmers prefer to kill the weed growth with herbicides, such as Gramaxone or Reglone, rather than plough it in. If weather conditions are right, the vines start growing now and competition for nutrients and water by weeds and other crops must be eliminated. This is especially important for unirrigated vineyards where growing weeds or crops will deprive the vine of valuable moisture. If the ploughing in of the green manure is delayed for too long the soil may become too hard and make cultivation difficult. The farmer should avoid working the soil too finely now. A few stalks protruding here and there will do no harm.

The spring fertilization is applied this month, or in September, depending on weather conditions. Superphosphates in pellet form are scattered, which then dissolve in the spring rain. Where anthracnose, erinose and dead arm occur the vineyards are sprayed with lime sulphur as soon as bud movement starts.

JUNE

By now decisions are made regarding the type of trellises to be used in the new vineyards. Trellising and the size of the trellis depend upon the vigour of growth, which in turn is determined by the cultivar planted, the soil fertility and depth, the water supply and the spacing between the vines, that is, the relationship of supply by the soil and demand by the vine. Trellising poles are planted. It is especially important to plant the end posts now to allow time for them to settle firmly in the soil before the wires are put up.

At the end of the month a start is made with the final pruning of varieties with moderate vigour, bearing enough or too much and showing no millerandage – Cinsaut is an example.

It must be remembered to control ants, otherwise trouble with mealy bug may occur in the coming season.

JULY

If weather permits a start can now be made on ploughing and cleaning around the vines. This may save trouble when the soil becomes hard later in the season.

The 'skoonsnoei', or clean pruning, has been completed and 'stompsnoei', or final pruning, is started with those varieties bearing well and showing no millerandage. It must be remembered to keep and to preserve properly the prunings of selected vines for grafting.

Blocks are planned and laid out for new vineyards and sometimes planting is started towards the end of the month. The drying-out of vines has to be carefully avoided, planting being done if possible directly from the nursery. It must be remembered to fill the gaps in young vineyards while planting is taking place. This replanting of missing vines is done the year after the original planting.

SEPTEMBER

If new vineyards are being planted and it is already hot and dry, the farmer generally waters the planted vines.

The cover crop will already be ploughed in by now, and the spring fertiliser is applied, if this has not been done in August. Cleaning around the vines is done at this time, before the soil becomes too hard. At this stage the soil is not worked too finely.

Where one or other of the diseases bacterial blight, anthracnose, dead arm or downy mildew occur, the farmer sprays the vines with copper oxychloride, this being done when the shoots are between 25 and 50 millimetres long. Oidium and erinose are controlled by vine sulphur. The first dusting of 15 to 20 kilograms a hectare is applied when the shoots are 150 to 250 millimetres long. Dusting is done on windless days, early in the morning. The control of oidium is of the utmost importance and the sulphur-dusting programme is neglected by the farmer at his peril.

OCTOBER

Where cultivation is practised, the second ploughing is done in this month. The soil is ploughed back towards the vines without ridging the stems.

Young vines are supported with stakes to enable them to form a straight line from the start. Dead vines can now be replaced if some grafted vines are left. Young vineyards are regularly inspected for insect damage and the insects, especially caterpillars and vine beetles, controlled where necessary.

'Tipping' is the removal of the first two to five centimetres of the growing shoot early in the season, and is done this month and in early November. It is recommended where growth is strong, temporarily curbing excessive shoot growth. This enhances the development and fertility of base eyes through improved nutritional supply. When tipping is done at the commencement of flowering the fruit sets better, particularly in the case of Hanepoot.

In trellised vineyards all the shoots are removed from the stem. Shoots growing from the rootstock are cut off below the soil surface to prevent regrowth. The removal of these rootstock shoots is important since they are mere passengers on the vine.

NOVEMBER

In unirrigated vineyards, if cultivation is practised, the second disc-cultivation is done in October while the soil is still moist. In irrigated vineyards this cultivation can be left until after the irrigation in November. Weed control is the only justification for any further summer cultivation. Here the tine-cultivator is used in preference to the disc-cultivator which makes the soil too fine. These cultivations are done only when weed growth demands, and not at predetermined times.

Irrigation, if used, must not be postponed until the soil is quite dry. Later in summer, when the soil has dried out to a considerable depth, wetting of the topsoil will be of little value, as the roots there will already be dead. The vines need moisture especially now in the early summer for sufficient growth and leaf surface. A light irrigation of 25 to 50 millimetres is therefore given now, even if the soil is still moist.

Only slight topping is done now so that the biggest possible leaf surface is maintained. 'Topping' is the removal of the first 15 to 25 cm of a young growing shoot, usually by hitting it off with a strong switch or thin stick. Sometimes a greater length, up to 60 cm, is removed, in which case it is simply cut away. There are several reasons for topping, which is usually done in November: it opens up access for implements of cultivation, allows more sunlight through, and controls fungus diseases and rot by allowing a good

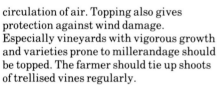

circulation of air. Topping also gives protection against wind damage. Especially vineyards with vigorous growth and varieties prone to millerandage should be topped. The farmer should tie up shoots of trellised vines regularly.

A nitrogen topdressing can still be applied early in this month to irrigated vineyards. Unirrigated vineyards should receive such topdressing in early November at the latest. Limestone ammonium nitrate is applied on acid soils and ammonium sulphate on neutral soils. Insects such as cutworms which attack the developing shoots below the soil surface must be controlled.

During this month flowering and berry set are completed. At this stage the tiny bunches are very susceptible to damage by downy mildew, which is controlled by preventative sprays. Snout beetles, too, usually appear from October onwards, and can be controlled with spray applications of Cymbusch, but only on the stems of the vines, and on trellis poles and anchor wires. For bush vines the spray must be directed to the middle of the vine, covering only the stem. By this method the beetles are prevented from reaching the aerial parts of the vine. Although damage by oidium is usually observed only in December, prevention is already started with sulphur dusting or application of soluble sulphur when the shoots are about 250 millimetres long.

DECEMBER

Summer cultivation is limited to an absolute minimum, weed control being the only justification. The disc harrow must definitely not be used at this time of the year, but only the tine-cultivator and the spade.

Ground which will be used for new plantings during the following season and is contaminated with quick grass, is sprayed with Roundup, ploughed and disc harrowed during the summer months – to date this is the only effective method of eradicating quick grass. It is, however, important to destroy this weed before the vines are planted, since it is extremely difficult to control in an established vineyard, when it can only be removed with a fork.

December is an important month for irrigation, if there has been no rain. The vine still grows at this stage and the berries begin to enlarge. Adequate moisture is needed for this.

The main shoots of young trellised vines are tied up and superfluous shoots removed. This ensures a good, strong stem. The main anchor poles of vineyards which are to be trellised next season are put in now. Topping of vineyards should only be

done slightly and must be concluded before growth stops.

Mealy bugs, snout beetles, erinose, oidium and botrytis must be well controlled now. The spray programme against downy mildew is kept up as long as weather conditions are favourable for the disease. Grapes are most susceptible to botrytis from the time when the berries begin to ripen until picking time. The nearer to picking time, the greater becomes the danger. Healthy grapes can be infected if they are wet for nine hours, whilst damaged grapes can be infected at any time. To prevent this disease the bunches must be adequately aerated so that they dry easily after rain or dew – damaging of the grapes must be avoided. The infection can be controlled to a certain extent by dusting with copper oxychloride from within six weeks before the harvest.

Hedging by machine is done this month. A common practice in France and Germany, it has only come into use locally in the last five years or so. The main advantages of hedging are that, after rain, bunches dry more quickly and the risk of fungus diseases and rot is therefore reduced; less spraying is required as sprays can be applied directly to the bunches; and, because all the bunches can be seen, there is a higher recovery of the crop and an increase in harvest speed, which in turn reduces labour costs.

JANUARY

By now the big heat of the year is intensifying in the vineyards. At this point the grapes have already been growing a few months, and some of the earlier varieties are beginning to ripen. Bearing vineyards are no longer irrigated, except in cases where soils are very shallow and where the vines are inclined to wilt or scorch. Excessive irrigation or rain especially shortly before the harvest, not only adversely affects grape quality, but also creates favourable conditions for botrytis. Where water is available, young vineyards are irrigated, as they are still growing strongly. The root systems of young vines have not yet developed strongly and deeply, and therefore suffer more readily from drought. At this stage, too, grapes vulnerable to damage have not yet developed.

In this month weeds must be eradicated, particularly those growing close to the vines. Strong weed growth near the vines impedes aeration of the bunches, creating favourable conditions for the growth of botrytis infection.

Within six weeks prior to the harvest no toxic insecticides may be applied in the vineyards. Vines which are severely infected with mealy bug maybe be treated with Chlorphos or Tukothion early in January; the stem and main arms only are sprayed to avoid contamination of the grape bunches with the insecticide, which is highly toxic. It is important, too, at this time to watch for late varieties of oidium. Judicious sulphur dusting can be done where necessary, but the chemical sulphur must never be used when it is very hot, since scorching of leaves and grapes may result. Sulphur-containing fungicides must not be applied later than six weeks prior to harvesting. Grapes become more susceptible to botrytis as harveting approaches. The disease is controllable by recently developed systemic sprays such as Rovral, Sumisclex and Ronilan. Excessive nitrogen application, as with excessive irrigation, encourages this disease.

In preparation for the pressing season, the farmer who makes his own wine will clean the cellar in readiness and make certain that all his machinery is in good order. The steel bins in which grapes are transported are thoroughly cleaned, loose rust being removed with a steel brush; they are then painted with acid-resistant paint. Sulphur dioxide, bentonite and other wine-making requirements should now be in stock in the cellar. Yeast must be ordered in time, and the containers for its propagation made clean and sterilized before use.

All possible care is taken in this hot season to improve the aeration of the grape bunches; in particular, windbreaks must allow sufficient circulation of air through the vineyards and there should not be tall weeds growing between them.

FEBRUARY

This is generally the hottest month of the year in South Africa. The vineyards (except for the younger plantings) are left unirrigated. Now, before the harvesting of the grapes, the farmer will generally take stock of the condition of his vineyards, noting aspects which may need improvement in the following season.

Vineyards or patches growing too vigorously should receive less nitrogen and be pruned longer. Where rot occurs, nitrogen and water applications are reduced. Aeration can be improved to a certain extent by the pruning method adopted. Vineyards bearing too heavily should be pruned shorter to restore the balance between growth and yield.

Note should be made of where diseases such as oidium, anthracnose, or bacterial blight, and insects such as snout beetle and mealy bug have harmed the vines; more efficient precautions can then be taken against these pests in the next season.

At this time, too, the farmer consults his fertilizer company about autumn fertilization of the vineyards, green manure crops, and new lands which are to be prepared. The fertilizer company should be allowed enough time for the analysis of the farm's soils, and to work out a fertilization programme. This enables the farmer to order the fertilizer early and to have it delivered well in time.

If the farmer does his own grafting or supplies a nursery, vines must be selected for cutting scions during the winter. This must be done before harvesting. The quantity of scions needed must be estimated and sufficient vines to supply this need must be marked.

Harvesting is only commenced when the grapes are fully ripe. Apart from a low sugar content, unripe grapes will not yet have developed a full flavour.

The grapes are harvested according to a fixed plan. Most farmers arrange their vineyards so as to dispose the ripening pattern of the different varieties, early-, middle-, or late-season ripening varieties, across the whole vintage period.

Grapes should not be left to become over-ripe. The organic acids which are essential for good quality then decrease rapidly. Furthermore, the must of over-ripe grapes has a high polyphenol content.

Grapes of good and bad quality should be kept apart in the cellar. If the farmer delivers to a local co-operative or wholesaler's cellar, a harvesting programme is decided well in advance through consultation between the supplying farmer and the cellar master. This programme, however, has to be reasonably flexible to allow for the vagaries of weather and other unforeseen factors. Good quality grapes, following the old European practice, are harvested early in the morning, the more zealous beginning before sunrise, avoiding deterioration in the quality of the grapes brought about by the heat of the day.

WHITE CULTIVARS	RED CULTIVARS
EARLY	**EARLY**
Gewürztraminer	Pinot Noir
Muscat Ottonel	
Morio Muscat	
Pinot Gris	
Pinot Blanc	
Chardonnay	
Fernão Pires	
Kerner	
Sylvaner	
EARLY-MID	**EARLY-MID**
Sémillon	Pinotage
Sauvignon Blanc	
Weisser Riesling	
Bukettraube	
Chenin Blanc	
Palomino	
MID	**MID**
Hárslevelü	Gamay
Cape Riesling	Pontac
Chenel	Merlot
	Malbec

WHITE CULTIVARS	RED CULTIVARS
LATE-MID	**LATE-MID**
Colombar(d)	Carignan
Furmint	Cinsaut
Muscat d'Alexandrie	Grenache
Weldra	Souzão
	Tinta Barocca
	Shiraz
LATE	**LATE**
Clairette Blanche	Zinfandel
Raisin Blanc	Cabernet Franc
Trebbiano	Cabernet Sauvignon

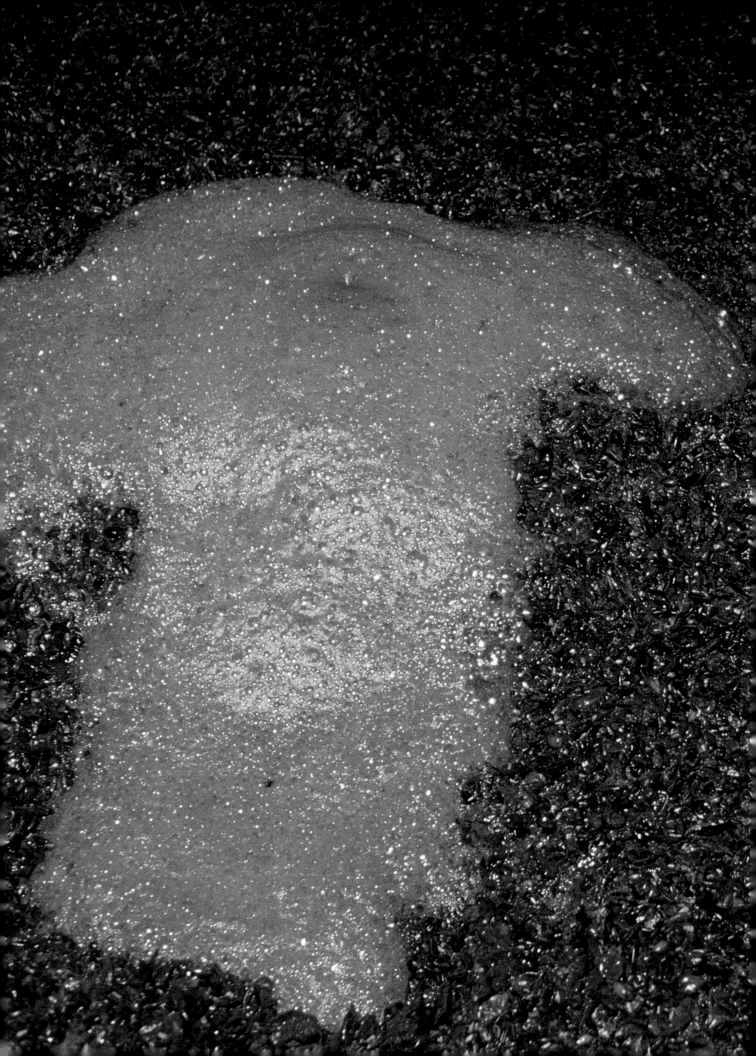

THE MAKING OF THE WINE

The technology of a modern wine cellar, with its rows of gleaming steel tanks and its rich aroma of the wine, unseen but very present, is a far cry from the simple, rough wooden vats, casks and 'velkuipe' of the pioneer wine farmers. It is far even from the nineteenth-century basket-presses, now objects of industrial archaeology, mellowed to become treasured museum pieces, their once busily clanking parts slowly welding together with time. For it is in the wine maker's cellar more than in any other area of the winelands, that the images of yesterday have more visibly given place to those of today.

But under the surface of these changes some things, of course, persist. The raw material of the vine, the grape, remains, even if it is a plumper and healthier entity than its forebears. The basic process of fermentation, the root chemical reaction of wine making, exploited for thousands of years before it came to be understood, has always been and will remain the same. The wooden casks in which the red wine (and some white wine) is matured have a familiar and traditional look too, for no modern technology could replace their subtle function in the life of the wine.

Many of the other steps in the process of wine making have been modified and streamlined to an altogether new level of efficiency. This applies particularly to some of the ancillary machinery which the modern era has introduced into the wine-making process. A tank is a tank, whether made of stone a thousand years ago, of concrete 50 years ago, or of stainless steel or glass fibre today. However decorated with dials and festooned with pipes, its basic function remains the same – to contain the wine before it is bottled. But a large-scale modern bottling machine – such as the splendid cacophonous

The lush purple of fermenting red grapes. This complex chemical process, involving the conversion of sugar into alcohol in the presence of yeast, is central to wine making.

specimens at the Bergkelder or Stellenbosch Farmers' Winery – is a far cry from the simple appliance of the nineteenth century which thrust a cork into a bottle, one bottle at a time (and still works perfectly well for a small farm with a modest output).

At the chemical level, understanding of the complexities of fermentation has led to many refinements of the process in terms of the growing of pure yeasts, of methods of effective filtering, cleaning and polishing of the wine, and of the stabilization of its chemical composition; and knowledge of the need for hygiene has swept away the haphazard methods of the past. A modern winery is a meticulously clean and well-maintained place, so that wine which comes from it is healthy and rich in its natural composition of acids, esters and many other compounds.

Indeed, one of the arts of the wine maker, of the skilled oenologist, is to strike a balance between chemical control of the wine and a respect for its natural complexity. While cleanliness and hygiene are background factors in the making of the wine, in the foreground stand the qualities which have always made wine one of the companions of mankind, its complexity and variety of sensation (wine contains over 200 different compounds), its subtle *douceur* of aroma and bouquet and flavour. The wine maker, however often he refers to his pipettes, his hydrometers, pycnometers and refractometers, his microscopes and temperature and humidity guages, must never lose sight of the life and character of the wine. It is this balance between the consciously objective and the elusive poetic and mysterious, between instinct and intelligence, which informs the modern wine-making process; a process which begins simply enough, with the image of the harvest.

It evokes, even in today's urban dweller, a sense of the past when his forebears once took part in this ancient ritual. In Europe this moment usually began on the name-day of the vignerons' patron saint, Saint

Vincent. It is reflected in the work of artists and poets from antiquity to today, from that Greek farmer-poet of old, Hesiod, celebrating the abundance of summer in his *Works and Days,* through to the *Four Seasons* of Pieter Brueghel, with their musical counterpart in the *Four Seasons* of Vivaldi, to the harvest paintings of Van Gogh, a brief but violent harvest of creation before the artist's private winter descended.

Their works reflect a sense of the self-enhancing power of the earth, of the land as 'the mother who never dies'; an image barely touched by the hand of time or technical progress in the vineyards. Though various machines have been devised to replace it, most of the world's vineyards are still harvested by the workers in the field, moving with steady rhythm along the rows of vines, cutting free the heavy bunches, transferring them to baskets or lug-boxes, to be emptied into the trucks or tractor-drawn carts which trundle away along the early morning roads – grapes are often harvested at dawn or even earlier to gather them in the best condition before the heat of the day. Picking at night has become a feature in some South African vineyards, such as Twee Jongegezellen and L'Ormarins, where the workers, like miners, wear head-mounted lamps.

At the entrance to the winery the truck is weighed together with its cargo of grapes. Then a sample of the grapes is taken and measured with a Balling hydrometer or a refractometer for its sugar content. At this point the natural fruit acid of the grapes is also determined. The truck tips the grapes into the crusher at the entrance to the winery and is then weighed empty to give the mass of the grapes. The farmer, if he is delivering to a co-operative or merchant wholesaler, is paid for his crop on the basis of its weight, and sugar content and quality. Today the producing wholesalers pay a bonus for grapes of high quality brought in at the sugar and acid levels they want. In some instances this has been almost double the minimum price set down by the KWV per tonne of grapes.

The brief independent life of the grape comes to an end at this point, with the process of crushing and possible destemming which marks the beginning of the making of the wine. During this process the stems of the grapes may be mechanically removed, where necessary, from the berries. The grapes are then gently crushed between rollers which release the juice but do not crush the pips – so as to avoid releasing the oil and tannin they contain and which would impart an acrid, biting taste to the wine. The stems, containing many phenolic compounds, undesirable because they render the wine susceptible to oxidative browning, may also give rise to a bitter taste in the wine if they are not removed.

During the crushing, sulphur dioxide (SO_2) is added to the grapes in carefully regulated small doses. This functions as an anti-oxidant and inhibits micro-organisms such as the yeasts and bacteria, which normally breed on the grapes, from reacting. Only rarely nowadays are the natural yeasts, occurring in the waxy 'bloom' on the grapes, allowed to develop spontaneously, a healthy selected yeast culture being preferred.

From the crusher the juice or the must of the grapes is run off. In the case of both red and white grapes, it is almost colourless. The colour of the red grapes is usually contained in the skin – the Pontac cultivar, which has a natural red juice, being one of the few exceptions. It is at this point that the two processes of white and red wine making, as well as those of rosé, sparkling and fortified wine, begin to diverge.

White wine

The juice of the white grapes (and in some instances of red grapes, since the juice of most red grapes is also almost colourless) is run off from the pulp through patent drainers which are, in effect, giant sieves. To inhibit the growth of micro-organisms it is cooled to 12-13 °C, and allowed to settle for periods up to 24 hours.

During the settling of the must, the suspended particles of skin, seeds and dust not removed or left behind in the crushers are allowed to sink to form a sediment at the bottom of the tank. The removal of these particles eliminates the off-odours they would otherwise produce in the wine. In the modern winery this process of settling may be aided by the use of pectolytic enzymes.

Many wineries use centrifuges to expedite the separation of the juice from its unwanted passengers. This reduces the time needed for clarification from a day to a few hours. The degree of clarification achieved, however, does not match that of proper settling. Some wineries use first the centrifuge and then settling to achieve a high degree of clarification.

When the process of clarification is completed, the must is run off into a fermentation tank, the modern equivalent of the 'velkuipe' of old. In this tank, which varies considerably in design, the process of fermentation is initiated in most instances by the addition of an active selected yeast culture.

To understand this process it is necessary to take a close-up look at the anatomy of the grape. As the seed-bearer of the vine, it is highly complex. Its three main components are the husk, or skin, the flesh, and the pip. The latter, which because of its astringency and tannin content is removed before fermentation, carries the basic woody structure of the vine.

The skin of the grape contains colour pigments, tannin, flavouring substances, fruit acid and aromatic compounds, plus innumerable other substances in minute quantities.

It is these components, mostly stored in the skin of the grape, which are released during the fermentation process and give the wine its character. The major difference, in fact, between white and red grapes lies in the skin; red grapes in particular are richly endowed with qualities which the maker of red wine aims to capture.

The flesh or pulp of the grape contains water (70-80 per cent), carbohydrates, pectins, traces of proteins, and a range of vitamins. It is the grape sugar in the flesh of the grape, produced by photosynthesis during the long summer, which is the component involved in fermentation. The element that causes the reaction is yeast.

Yeasts are forms of microscopic, unicellular plant organisms which are widely spread in nature. They are used commercially in the production of a number of commodities, including bread and pharmaceuticals, as well as wine. They occur naturally on the grape in the 'bloom', a watertight, protective layer on the skin of the berry. The bloom has a slightly waxy feel and is responsible for the characteristic dull sheen on the surface of the ripe fruit.

When the skin of the grape is broken, the yeast on the outside of the skin and the sugar in the juice (which is an almost perfect balance of nutrients for the growth of the yeast cells) meet in a reaction which converts the sugar into ethyl alcohol, or ethanol, and carbon dioxide and energy. Most of the carbon dioxide is released as a gas during the reaction, but some is retained, giving liveliness to the wine.

If the naturally occurring yeasts sufficed the world's wine makers for centuries, their modern descendants have increasingly tended to replace them with more reliable cultured strains. In the modern winery the wild yeast in the bloom is subdued by the sulphur dioxide added at the start of the wine-making process, and fermentation is started with the inoculation of a three to five per cent actively fermenting pure yeast culture to the clear juice.

From its many components the fermenting must yields a resultant wine which is broken down into 80-90 per cent water and alcohol, sugar, fruit acids (tartaric, malic and citric acids among them), colouring matter, and pigments. Varying amounts of tannin can also occur.

The amount of sugar remaining after the reaction can also vary. Left to itself, fermentation runs its natural course, that is, it proceeds until all the sugar is used up and converted to alcohol. With the assistance of the wine maker the process can be halted to give varying ratios of unfermented sugar and alcohol. The quantity of sugar in the liquid determines its sweetness or 'dryness' – a dry wine being simply one with a low sugar content (in practice, less than four grams of sugar in a litre of wine).

Energy, in the form of heat, is released during fermentation. In the white wine process the heat is removed by cooling, and fermentation temperatures are usually maintained between 14 °C and 16 °C. The innovation of this 'cold fermentation' technique during the last quarter century was a major development in enabling the making of quality white wine in warm climates. At the high temperatures prevalent in the South African summer, fermentation tends to be very fast and tumultuous if left to its own devices, and can all be over in a few hours, with carbon dioxide evolving rapidly, often sparging many of the aromatic flavour compounds from the wine: at temperatures of above 20 °C the aromatic compounds become more readily volatile. Moreover, if the heat is not removed, the fermentation temperature may rise to a level where the yeast is destroyed, thus halting further fermentation. In this condition the partly fermented must is very susceptible to bacterial spoilage.

Thus, there is both an upper and a lower temperature limit to active fermentation: above 32,2 °C (90 °F) the yeast cells are killed by the heat, while below 4,4 °C (40 °F) they are rendered dormant by cold.

Farmers try to harvest their crop in the cool of early morning **1**, thereby avoiding the sun's full heat which causes rapid deterioration in the quality of the grapes. At the winery a sample is taken **2** for analysis of sugar and acid content. Clinical steel tanks **3** are synonymous with modern white wine cellars where cold fermentation, a revolutionary process perfected in the years immediately following the Second World War to control the rate of fermentation in the hot South African climate, is essential to produce white wines of quality. After fermentation and before bottling, white wines are cold stabilized to prevent tartrate crystals from forming in the bottle. During the procedure the wine is cooled and thermostatically controlled **4** just above its freezing point for several days.

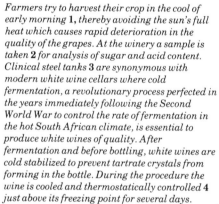

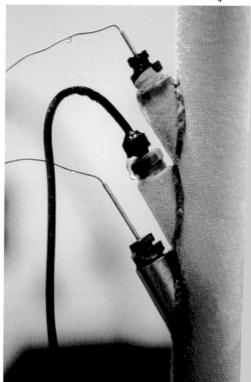

Bottling is the final step in the long and complex procedure of wine making and, as at every other stage, hygiene is critical in ensuring that a clean, healthy product reaches the consumer.

With the conclusion of fermentation, which in the case of white wines normally takes up to 15 days but can take longer at a reduced temperature, a procedure known as 'racking' takes place. This is identical for both white and red wines and involves the running off the wine from its lees. If this is not done, off-odours can arise in it as a result of yeast cell autolysis.

The first racking takes place two to four days after the completion of fermentation. At this stage the wine is usually dry, that is, there are no fermentable sugars left in it. With this first racking, sulphur dioxide, at a concentration of 50 milligrams a litre, is added to the newly-made wine, and thereafter the so-called 'free SO_2' is carefully monitored and maintained at a hygienic level of 30 milligrams a litre as a control against further oxidation. For this reason it is also important to protect the white wine from contact with air. (A distinction must be made between 'free' and 'fixed' sulphur dioxide: the 'free' SO_2 which was originally added to the crushed grapes reacts, during fermentation, with such products of the fermentation as acetaldehyde, α-ketoglutaric acid, and pyruvic acid, and becomes 'bound', or 'fixed' SO_2. The acetaldehyde-bound SO_2 has no anti-oxidant or preservative properties and is therefore of no practical use to the wine maker; it is the 'free' SO_2 which is the active assistant. Some of the remaining, loosely bound forms of SO_2 can replenish 'free' SO_2 'on demand' during oxidation. However, malic acid fermentation cannot occur if the fixed SO_2 rises above 120 parts per million.)

Some 14 to 21 days after the first racking, there is a second and sometimes even a third racking to remove further impurities which have settled down. Some wine makers use a centrifuge for this, which is quicker than racking but, as with the earlier stage of separating impurities from the must, it is not a universally accepted method.

After the final racking the young wine is filtered so that it is ready for blending and for the final stabilization procedures before it is bottled. It is then protein stabilized, usually before final filtration, with bentonite. (Some wine makers, a relative few, blend their wines at the outset of the process, mixing grapes of different cultivars at the crusher.)

The blending of wines is an almost universal practice, even when the wine maker is ostensibly dealing with a single cultivar, where a small percentage of other wines will be used to round off the character of the basic wine-type. It has developed over the years into a fine art and one central to the wine master's rôle. The wines he selects must blend harmoniously and achieve a level of excellence within the limitations imposed upon him. These include not only the specific character of the cultivar or cultivars themselves, but of area and vintage as well. Thus, for example, among white wines, the Hazendal Steen will be a blend of wines from a specific harvest from the Stellenbosch area, made from grapes of the Chenin Blanc, or Steen, variety.

After blending, the wine is stabilized, in order to restore its equilibrium after the disturbances of the blending, and to prevent it from undergoing any unwanted changes after bottling. There are four main kinds of stability which must be ensured: oxidative, protein, tartrate, and microbiological.

In white wines, unwanted oxidation leads to browning and sometimes to the formation of sediments which result in a characteristic and unpleasant odour and taste. To prevent this, contact with air is avoided as far as possible throughout the wine-making process, and sulphur dioxide is used as an anti-oxidant.

As soon as a white wine is blended it is protein stabilized. The protein content of wines can vary from a few to several hundred milligrams in a litre, but it remains one of the most important causes of white wine cloudiness. Virtually all young white wines will become cloudy if the proteins are not removed.

This is done by fining the wine with bentonite, a purified, complex, hydrated aluminium silicate, the predominant constituent of which is montmorillonite clay. A pre-determined amount is mixed with the wine whose proteins are absorbed by the clay which settles at the bottom of the tank. When the settling process is completed, the protein-stable wine is filtered off the fining lees, and is tartrate stabilized.

Tartaric acid is the most common fruit acid found naturally in wine. In young wines the concentration of bitartrate and potassium ions as well as tartrate and calcium ions, often exceeds their solubility in the wine and they separate out. In the case of potassium bitartrate (KHT), commonly known as 'cream of tartar', and calcium tartrate (CaT), a crystalline precipitation of potassium bitartrate often occurs in the wine after fermentation. If that took place after bottling, a formation of unsightly (though harmless) crystals would greet the consumer.

To make wine tartrate stable it is cooled to 1 °C above the freezing point of wine, and held at this temperature for four to eight days, after which it is filtered at this temperature to remove the crystals which have formed – at low temperatures KHT and CaT become progressively more insoluble, enhancing the process of crystallization. If the wine were to be aged for a year or more this crystallization would to some degree take place automatically; the reduced-temperature method makes it happen quickly and more reliably.

Most South African wines are marketed with a natural sugar content of between three and 30 grams a litre. To prevent micro-organisms from using this sugar in the bottle, giving rise to turbidity and off-odours, the wine must be microbiologically stabilized before and during bottling. This is usually done by one of two methods, and follows tartrate stabilization.

The most common method with lower-priced wines is to pasteurize the wine during bottling by raising it to a temperature of between 55 and 60 °C – this was the method Pasteur initiated in the 1860s during his investigations into the souring of French wines. With quality wines the usual method favoured is cold-sterile bottling. Here all micro-organisms are physically removed from the wine by extremely fine filtration, and all apparatus which comes into contact with the wine after filtration, including bottles, is sterilized.

South Africa produces far more white wine than red. Depending on the period of fermentation, different styles of white wine are made; these are characterized as dry, medium-dry or off-dry (resulting from a complete or near-complete fermentation), semi-sweet or sweet. In the case of many commercial semi-sweet and off-dry white wines the must is allowed to ferment dry and a grape juice is added to achieve the desired sweetness. (A table of sugar levels appears in the glossary, under 'Sugar level laws'.)

CORKS AND OTHER CLOSURES

A seemingly innocuous issue, the problem of the best way to seal a bottle of wine is one which causes perennial discussion in the wine industry. The traditional, and still most widely used closure for high quality wines, of course, is that of cork, derived from the bark of the cork oak, *Quercus suber,* found in Portugal, Spain and North Africa. In recent years, however, a number of other closures, metal, plastic, and combinations of these, have been developed, because of the need for convenience of opening and in an attempt to improve on the time-hallowed cork closure.

Cork has certain advantages which have stood it in good stead down the three centuries in which it has been in common use. Because of its air-filled cells containing fatty acid, each a watertight, flexible compartment, cork is an effective insulating medium against heat, cold and vibration, as well as being impervious to liquids. In addition, it is a vegetable product, free of toxic ingredients, and does not impart odour, taste or cause deterioration of the wine unless contaminated by bacteria or fungi of some kind.

But it does have a number of disadvantages. A bottle closed with a cork, once opened, is not easy to reseal effectively. Cork is prone to shrinkage under certain conditions. Corked bottles must be 'laid down'; that is, stored lying flat so that the wine remains in contact with the cork, keeping it wet. It would otherwise dry out, tend to crumble and allow air into the bottle and wine out of it. 'Laying down' is no problem in the private cellar, but is a disadvantage, for example, in supermarkets or in aeroplanes, or during transport, where there is a preference for bottles which can be stored upright.

A popular belief persists that a wine 'breathes' through its cork. In fact, if what is described as 'breathing' were to take place it would soon lead to the oxidation of the wine, and its degeneration and discoloration.

Notwithstanding the romantic prejudice in favour of the cork (like wine itself, it is a 'natural' product), most of the newly developed metal and plastic screw tops, none of which are either 'natural' or particularly alluring aesthetically, are definitely more efficient both in hermetically protecting the wine, and because they can be used to reseal the bottle. They are also non-perishable, lend no flavour to the wine, and furthermore are not susceptible to distortion or to shrinkage. They are also notably cheaper to produce. Thus, with the increased expense of cork, there appears little doubt that its use will dwindle, if not entirely die away, in the coming decades; already over the past 30 to 40 years the use of cork has been steadily reduced, to the extent that, today, it is used in less than 12 per cent of all wine bottled in South Africa.

BOXES AND OTHER PACKS

The idea of the 'wine box' originated in the 1960s in Australia as a handy way of marketing large quantities of ordinary wine of no particular distinction. It was picked up and introduced in South Africa by the Simonsig Estate, but later withdrawn because of lack of support owing to serious quality problems. These difficulties have since been resolved and in recent years the box has made a comeback. 'Chateau Cardboard' swept the country in the early eighties, with sales of almost nine million boxes annually (about half of these being marketed in the Transvaal), about 30 per cent of all wine made in South Africa. Today sales have settled down to some 10 per cent of the total wine sales.

The success of the wine box is not fortuitous. The quality of the wine, has often been of award-winning level but is usually good, dependable 'drinking' rather than 'tasting' wine. It is easily stored and carried and, since the box is unbreakable, is particularly suited to outdoor occasions where a jug or bottle would be at risk.

Moreover, the design of the box itself ingeniously preserves the wine against oxidation, allowing it to be kept safely for upwards of a month or more after being broached. Its principle is simple. A cardboard outer casing holds a laminated metallized polyester bag which is filled with wine. As the wine is dispensed through the non-drip tap at the bottom of the box, the hermetically sealed bag collapses without allowing air in, thus preventing the deterioration of its content.

After Simonsig's attempt the first box to be marketed locally was 'Cellar Cask', introduced in the Transvaal in 1979. The present range of brand names is led by Autumn Harvest, and also includes Drostdy Hof, Valley Wines, Witzenberg, Kellerprinz, Townhouse, Festival and Huguenot; the old national favourite, Tassenberg, has also appeared in a box. Nowadays many 'House-Brands' and 'No-Name' brands are available at unbelievably low 'budget' prices. The popular brands still dominate the national market but the 'House' and 'No Name' sector is the quickest growing sector of the market due to its competitive prices.

A new variation of the theme was that of the Kiesenbosch Keg; which contained a five-litre wine bag connected to a permanent dispenser in the keg, the bag being replaced when necessary. Today many hotels, public houses, clubs and fairgrounds are supplied with bags as big as 20 litres for dispensing through patent machines equipped with chilling apparatus.

Withal, the 'bag-in-a-box' is ideal for any generally jolly gathering, and has become and will remain a feature of the urban landscape.

In recent years a number of patent packs have appeared on the market with varying degrees of success. Cans, (aluminium and tin) 'Tetra Pak', 'Combibloc', 'Hypa-pack', PVC and PET bottles are all available. Maybe the future will bring 'See thru' cans and cans that will chill themselves when opened.

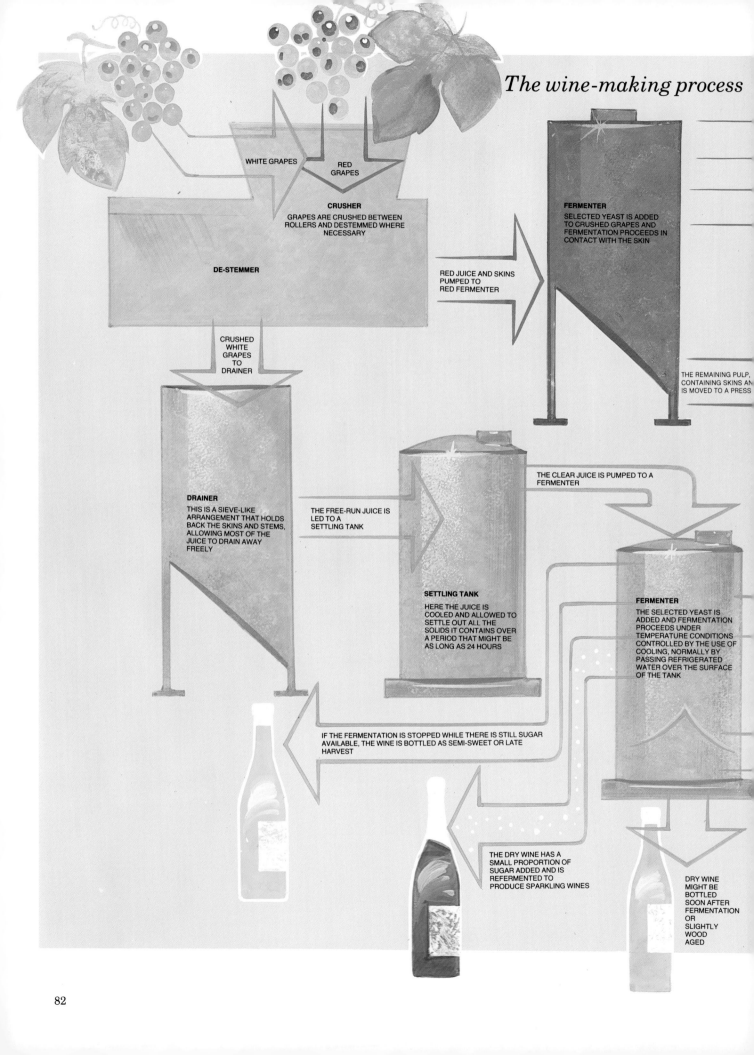

The wine-making process

WHITE GRAPES

RED GRAPES

CRUSHER
GRAPES ARE CRUSHED BETWEEN ROLLERS AND DESTEMMED WHERE NECESSARY

DE-STEMMER

FERMENTER
SELECTED YEAST IS ADDED TO CRUSHED GRAPES AND FERMENTATION PROCEEDS IN CONTACT WITH THE SKIN

RED JUICE AND SKINS PUMPED TO RED FERMENTER

THE REMAINING PULP, CONTAINING SKINS AN[D] IS MOVED TO A PRESS

CRUSHED WHITE GRAPES TO DRAINER

DRAINER
THIS IS A SIEVE-LIKE ARRANGEMENT THAT HOLDS BACK THE SKINS AND STEMS, ALLOWING MOST OF THE JUICE TO DRAIN AWAY FREELY

THE FREE-RUN JUICE IS LED TO A SETTLING TANK

THE CLEAR JUICE IS PUMPED TO A FERMENTER

SETTLING TANK
HERE THE JUICE IS COOLED AND ALLOWED TO SETTLE OUT ALL THE SOLIDS IT CONTAINS OVER A PERIOD THAT MIGHT BE AS LONG AS 24 HOURS

FERMENTER
THE SELECTED YEAST IS ADDED AND FERMENTATION PROCEEDS UNDER TEMPERATURE CONDITIONS CONTROLLED BY THE USE OF COOLING, NORMALLY BY PASSING REFRIGERATED WATER OVER THE SURFACE OF THE TANK

IF THE FERMENTATION IS STOPPED WHILE THERE IS STILL SUGAR AVAILABLE, THE WINE IS BOTTLED AS SEMI-SWEET OR LATE HARVEST

THE DRY WINE HAS A SMALL PROPORTION OF SUGAR ADDED AND IS REFERMENTED TO PRODUCE SPARKLING WINES

DRY WINE MIGHT BE BOTTLED SOON AFTER FERMENTATION OR SLIGHTLY WOOD AGED

82

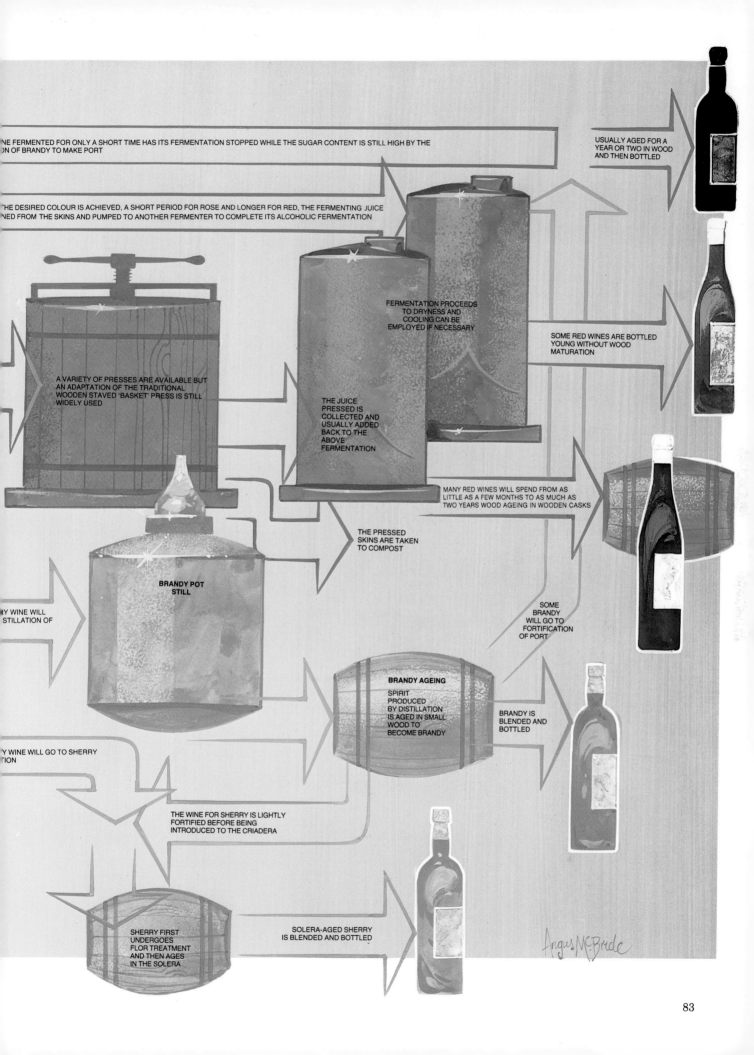

NE FERMENTED FOR ONLY A SHORT TIME HAS ITS FERMENTATION STOPPED WHILE THE SUGAR CONTENT IS STILL HIGH BY THE
ON OF BRANDY TO MAKE PORT

USUALLY AGED FOR A
YEAR OR TWO IN WOOD
AND THEN BOTTLED

HE DESIRED COLOUR IS ACHIEVED, A SHORT PERIOD FOR ROSE AND LONGER FOR RED, THE FERMENTING JUICE
NED FROM THE SKINS AND PUMPED TO ANOTHER FERMENTER TO COMPLETE ITS ALCOHOLIC FERMENTATION

FERMENTATION PROCEEDS
TO DRYNESS AND
COOLING CAN BE
EMPLOYED IF NECESSARY

SOME RED WINES ARE BOTTLED
YOUNG WITHOUT WOOD
MATURATION

A VARIETY OF PRESSES ARE AVAILABLE BUT
AN ADAPTATION OF THE TRADITIONAL
WOODEN STAVED 'BASKET' PRESS IS STILL
WIDELY USED

THE JUICE
PRESSED IS
COLLECTED AND
USUALLY ADDED
BACK TO THE
ABOVE
FERMENTATION

MANY RED WINES WILL SPEND FROM AS
LITTLE AS A FEW MONTHS TO AS MUCH AS
TWO YEARS WOOD AGEING IN WOODEN CASKS

THE PRESSED
SKINS ARE TAKEN
TO COMPOST

**BRANDY POT
STILL**

SOME
BRANDY
WILL GO TO
FORTIFICATION
OF PORT

Y WINE WILL
STILLATION OF

BRANDY AGEING

SPIRIT
PRODUCED
BY DISTILLATION
IS AGED IN SMALL
WOOD TO
BECOME BRANDY

BRANDY IS
BLENDED AND
BOTTLED

Y WINE WILL GO TO SHERRY
TION

THE WINE FOR SHERRY IS LIGHTLY
FORTIFIED BEFORE BEING
INTRODUCED TO THE CRIADERA

SHERRY FIRST
UNDERGOES
FLOR TREATMENT
AND THEN AGES
IN THE SOLERA

SOLERA-AGED SHERRY
IS BLENDED AND BOTTLED

Angus McBride

83

Red wine

The making of red wine begins as does the process for making white wine, with the crushing of the grapes. Thereafter, however, the two methods diverge. The juice of red grapes, like that of white, is almost colourless and in the making of red wine it is the pigment and other components in the skins which are leached out during fermentation to impart and influence colour, taste and flavour. Unlike in the making of white wine, skin contact during fermentation is therefore of paramount importance in the eventual composition of the wine.

Thus, after the grapes have been destemmed and crushed, the juice is not separated from the skins. A three to five per cent actively fermenting pure yeast culture is added to the crushed grapes, and a controlled fermentation on the skins takes place for a specific period, usually about four days, depending on the cellar master's desired result; the longer the skin contact, the greater the extraction of colour and flavour held in the skin. During this time the skins and must are regularly mixed as the escaping carbon dioxide (CO_2) tends to lift the skins to the surface where they form a 'head' or 'cap' on the developing wine. In earlier times this was done by hand, the head being punched down and submerged with long wooden poles. This took place every three hours, or even more frequently, and was a precarious occupation, since the worker had to balance on the edge of the concrete tank; from time to time a worker fell in and, like the Duke of Clarence, met a vinous end.

Later and less hazardous methods included pumping the juice from the bottom of the tank over the cap, but all these 'traditional' methods, though still practised in some cellars, were labour intensive and exposed the wine to the risk of excessive oxidation. With the advent of closed fermentation tanks, the problem of the skins rising remained, but at least the enclosed environment reduced the risk of oxidation. More recently, a successful system has been developed through using nets fixed below the surface of the liquid in the fermentation tanks. These nets prevent the rising skins from reaching the surface and during fermentation the juice pushes through the submerged cap. This method also reduces oxidation, fermentation is thus prevented from becoming too fierce, and good colour is achieved.

Today, even better devices such as pressure tanks, roto tanks and stirring tanks are gaining wide acceptance. In the first, CO_2 released during fermentation is prevented from escaping and pressure builds up in the tank. When the gas is released the skins and liquid are thoroughly mixed in the resultant agitation. This system prevents oxidation and as no mechanical stirring or mixing takes place, relatively little sediment is produced. The roto tank principle employs a horizontal cylindrical tank mounted on a device that rotates the tank at regular intervals. As with the previous method, thorough mixing takes place in the absence of oxygen; CO_2 is released through valves to prevent any dangerous build-up of gas during fermentation. Mixing is achieved by long metal blades welded perpendicular to the inside surface, as in a concrete-mixer. In stirring tanks various mechanical methods are used, sometimes in conjunction with pumping over, but the system produces very high sediments.

During the course of the mixing the colour and flavour compounds are extracted from the skins, the process being facilitated by the high fermentation temperature of between 20 and 25 °C. Heat actually breaks down the colour cells, resulting in the effective release of their colour but excess heat would destroy the yeast. Cooling is therefore essential to keep the temperature during fermentation within the required parameters.

The period of fermentation on the skins is critically important; if too long, too many tannins (polymers of phenolic compounds which are responsible for the astringent taste in wine) are released along with colour and flavour compounds; too short, and the colour of the wine will be too light. In both cases the character of the final wine will be unbalanced.

In addition to the methods of colour extraction already outlined, further methods make use of heat without fermentation. This procedure involves heating the must in hot-water/wine-exchange units and holding the temperature at a required level for a short time. However, rising temperature not only increases colour extraction but also promotes the activities of polyphenol oxidative enzymes which can cause the wine to brown. To prevent this the liquid is quickly heated to 55 °C, a temperature at which the enzymes become inactive. The temperature is then usually raised to between 60 and 75 °C for best results. Above 85 °C the wine develops a 'boiled' flavour as a result of partial caramelisation of sugars, especially if held at that temperature for any length of time.

Irrespective of the method used, when the right degree of extraction has taken place the wine maker separates the juice from the skins, which are usually given a final light press; and the press-juice is added back to the must, which is allowed to continue fermenting until dry.

When fermentation is complete, the wine is racked a number of times in the same way as for white wine.

After racking and filtration, the young red wine is ready for ageing in wood. Not that all red wines are matured in wood; the light, fruity young red wines are often stored in stainless steel tanks until needed for blending and/or bottling purposes. Wines which have not been aged in wood are sometimes blended with wood-matured wines, in the combination desired by the wine maker.

The word 'wood' is the wine maker's vernacular for a wooden barrel or cask. Such were originally used simply for transport or storage until it was realized that the period in the wood added something to the flavour and the character of the wine, which was also thus given a chance to 'mature', that is, to evolve its latent characteristics.

The barrel can be made from various types of wood, but oak is probably the most frequently used for better quality wines – most of the oak used for casks in South Africa being imported from France, though some now comes from Germany and, with increasing importance, from North America.

The most important physical aspect in maturation is the size of the container, for the surface-to-volume ratio affects the rate at which certain exchanges take place and the degree to which these influence the character of the wine. Containers can range in size from as little as five to as much as a hundred thousand litres, but the most commonly used size is a barrel of between 225 and 250 litres. This size appears to provide optimum conditions for maturation, and has been used empirically in many different areas in the past. In general, smaller barrels were developed for holding wines for topping up and for transport, while larger fixed vessels were made for storage and for use over many years.

The most obvious physical action involved in maturation is the absorption by the wood of some of the wine, and the leaching out of flavour from the wood by the wine. Besides this, five general factors influence maturation: the relative humidity, temperature, air movements around the cask, the physical characteristics of the wood, and the frequency of the topping up.

The first three factors are self-evident, while flavour pick-up will be greatly affected by the type, porosity, and thickness of the wood from which the cask is made. Topping up of the wine at regular intervals is important, for as the level of the liquid drops in the cask so the wood becomes drier and slightly more porous owing to shrinkage of the wood tissue. This may not only lead to increased loss of wine

*Activity on a wine farm reaches a climax during the harvest **1** when grapes are picked over the shortest possible time to ensure that they reach the winery in optimum condition. At the receiving bin **2** the grapes are fed to the crusher and then fermented with their skins.*

(through evaporation) but also allow more air in. As a result excessive oxidation, and therefore browning of the wine, may occur. The presence of oxygen also stimulates the growth of bacteria which produce acetic acid. This could increase the volatile acidity to levels which would spoil the wine. Frequent topping, done from an enclosed wine reservoir, is therefore necessary.

At the same time oxygen trapped in the cask on filling leads to certain chemical reactions. These include the extraction and development of tannic and related compounds from the wood. On the interior surface of the cask a layer develops with a high concentration of tannic compounds extracted from the wood by the wine. The minute amounts of oxygen present react with the phenols. These compounds slowly diffuse and are replaced by fresh wine; the process is thus continuous.

On the inner surface, besides the tannins, there is present a certain amount of colour, of resinous substances, and of some bitter compounds which occur in wood and which will affect the eventual

taste of the wine. These vary with the type of wood, and with the manner in which it has been treated. In particular, aromatic substances exist in the wood and contribute to the wines' bouquet. In the presence of minute amounts of oxygen certain slow reactions also occur and are not necessarily influenced by the flavour of the wood; and aldehydes, carboxyl acids and acetyls are also formed.

Most of these complex reactions will occur in a cask of any size, but more quickly in smaller ones as the surface-to-volume ratio decreases. But if the cask is too small the reaction becomes relatively quick, with a too heavy absorption of the flavour of the wood at the expense of that of the wine. At the opposite extreme, in very large containers the change is so slow that it is rarely feasible to leave the wine for the length of time required for these reactions to take place.

Biochemical or biological reactions take place as well, of which the most important during maturation is malo-lactic fermentation.

There are no precise rules as to the

length of time a red wine should be allowed to mature in wood. This will depend upon various considerations, including the style of wine for which the wine maker is aiming. He must take into account the specific properties of the wine, its particular vintage characteristics, the cultivar from which it is derived, the biological and chemical make-up, and its eventual destiny. He must also take into account the nature of the wood, including its porosity, as well as the size of the container.

Equitable conditions of temperature and humidity are of great importance during maturation in the wood. A cool, slightly humid cellar with little temperature variation will allow for a long, slow maturation which can vary from two months to two years: wine is seldom aged in wood longer than this.

Once the red wines have been matured to the wine master's satisfaction they are blended (some blends comprise matured and unmatured wines) and tartrate stabilized before bottling. It is interesting to note that red wines seldom have problems with protein instability. Phenols

85

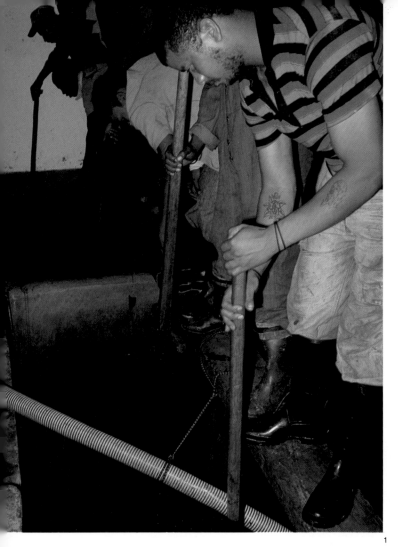

1 2

and polyphenols have a negative electrical charge in wine, and proteins a positive charge. With the excess of phenolic compounds in red wines, the proteins are 'neutralized' and removed from the wine naturally.

Young red wines are filtered and stored in stainless steel tanks, where they are allowed to 'rest' for a period of three to eight months. The rest period is necessary to ensure that they will be sufficiently

stable before bottling and to allow the desired complexity of flavour to develop.

After this rest period, the wine is sterile-filtered and cold-sterile bottled. Some of the lower-priced red wines, especially those which are semi-sweet, might be pasteurized during bottling. As with white wine, oxidation is to be avoided: it results in a loss of colour as well as a change from red to brown, accompanied by a deterioration of aroma and taste.

Red wines are described as being either full- (or heavy-) bodied, medium-bodied or light-bodied. The degree of body depends largely upon the selection of the cultivar from which the wine is made, and the wine-making process used.

Besides the basic type of white and red natural wines, other forms of wine have been developed, including the rosé wines, sparkling wines, and fortified wines such as sherry and port.

Rosé, Blanc de Noir and Blush wines

Rosé wines can be made by blending red and white grape must, but most wine makers make their rosé by leaving the red grape skins on the must during fermentation in the same way as for a red wine, but only until the desired amount of colour has been extracted to produce its clear, delicate, characteristic hue – usually no more than 24 hours, as opposed to the four days or more which give the red wines their full colour. The juice is then run off the skins and treated for the remainder of the process in the same way as white. The grape cultivar used in making rosé wines is optional; the result can be either dry, medium, off dry or semi-sweet.

A variation on the theme is the current fashion for Blanc de Noir, literally white from black, which is in fact an almost white wine made from red grapes. The method of its making differs from that of rosé wines, for the skins are not kept for long in contact with the juice. Instead the juice is drained away immediately, but in the process small quantities of pigment are released, sufficient to give the faintest blush of colour. The wine is then made as if it were white.

Blanc de Noir as a colour-term almost certainly derives from the Champagne area of France where wines made in this style have been blended with Chardonnay

wine to produce the really great Champagnes. These wines lose their Blanc de Noir colour during ageing but some (where the proportion of white wine made from red grapes is greater) retain their youthful colour described as 'Oeil de Perdrix', 'The Eye of the Partridge'.

Blanc de Noir wines made for marketing as such rather than for blending in Champagne were given real impetus in California a little more than 20 years ago. In this wine-making region of the United States there were excessive plantings of Pinot Noir and cellar masters were having little success in producing wines of good colour from these grapes. Rosé wine from

Pinot Noir was a possible answer but was considered too risky because of the poor market image such wines had in California at the time. And so Blanc de Noir wines were made and enjoyed considerable success.

Although these wines have taken a long time to reach South Africa (they were first introduced by Boschendal Estate), many are now available from local cellars. Some are very good, with a number having achieved superior rating, and many are certified with the cultivar from which they have been made.

Because of the manner of its making all Blanc de Noir wine in South Africa has to be certified by the Wine and Spirit Board. However the Board will not yet certify any wine marketed in a container larger than two litres, and so Blanc de Noir is only available in bottles and two-litre 'Bag-in-the-Box' packs or two litre jugs. To overcome this restriction the term 'blush' is being applied to some wines made in the Blanc de Noir manner. These can then be packed in a container of any size allowed by Weights and Measures without reference to the Wine and Spirit Board. However, such wines cannot be guaranteed as having been made by the usual Blanc de Noir process, although most of them are. There is nothing to stop a marketer calling his rosé wine, for example, by the term 'blush'. In any event it is the wine that counts and not the terminology.

During fermentation the 'cap' that forms on the surface of the must is constantly mixed with the liquid to aid colour extraction. In some cellars where open concrete tanks, or kuipe are used, the cap is 'punched down' with long wooden paddles 1, but more effective mechanical procedures are gaining acceptance. When fermentation is complete the skins are separated from the young wines by draining and then by pressing either in a basket press (above) or in a more modern device such as the bladder or membrane press 2. The wine and skins are fed into the long, cylindrical press; the bladder inside the cylinder is then inflated and this forces the contents against the sieve-like sides of the press, trapping the skins but allowing the wine to drain through.

BOTTLES

As with the cask, the wine bottle was originally used simply for transport. By the end of the eighteenth century, however, the enhancing effect of storing wines in the bottle came to be appreciated, encouraged by the discovery of the cork and its ally, the corkscrew. The traditional squat, flat-bottomed bottle came to be superseded by a design which could be easily stored for the period of time needed for the magic of softening, maturing and 'rounding' of the wine's qualities to take place.

Modern wine bottles come in a number of shapes, sizes and colours, depending on the type of wine. The following are some of the main styles encountered (though idiosyncratic variations, such as the Bellingham flask, enliven these basic categories).

Burgundy. A sloping-shouldered bottle of 750 ml capacity with a punt (the 'punt' is the indentation in the bottom of the bottle), this is the ubiquitous red and white wine bottle used around the world. It is usually green or amber in colour; the colour acts as a filter for ultra-violet rays in sunshine which can spoil the wine.

Hock. The name 'Hock', from Hochheim, was given by Queen Victoria to the white wines of the Rhine Valley in general. These 750 and 375 ml bottles hold both white and rosé wines; the colour ranges from amber for sweet white wines to dark green for the dry white and flint, or natural glass, for the rosés.

Claret. This is the usual shouldered bottle with a punt, used for red wines of the kind normally laid down for bottle maturation; it is available in 750 and 375 ml capacity.

Sparkling wine. This is a sloping-shouldered bottle with a punt. 750 ml in capacity, it is thicker and more heavily built than the still wine bottles, to withstand an internal pressure of about 18 atmospheres. (The pressure of Champagne and similar sparkling wines inside the bottle at room temperature is about six atmospheres.)

Sherry and Port. These dark green bottles with a marked shoulder have a 30 mm extra deep drawn seal to replace the traditional cork; this closure allows the bottle to be stored upright, as against the traditional port bottle with a long cork

which had to be stored on its side.

Jug. Usually containing 'house wines', the jug can be 1,5 or 2 litre capacity.

Jar. This is a 4,5 litre container used for natural and fortified wines of lesser quality.

250 ml bottle. This has a twist-off metal cap, and it is both easy to open and can be stored upright. It is particularly useful for the practice of tasting, since each bottle yields approximately eight 'tastes'. It is also known as a 'Wynette' or 'Dinky', but these are trade names registered by producing wholesalers in the Cape Wine and Distillers Limited group of companies.

Besides these common containers various large sizes of bottle, for display or ostentation, are made, often for champagne. Compared to a standard 750 ml bottle they are:

Magnum, 2 bottles.
Jereboam, 4 bottles.
Rheboam, 6 bottles.
Methuselah, 8 bottles.
Salmanazar, 12 bottles.
Balthazar, 16 bottles.
Nebuchadnezzar, 20 bottles.

Sparkling wines

Before corking, bottles of sparkling wine are 'topped' to an even ullage level. In cellars with small production the process is done by hand, but in large wineries it is highly mechanized.

Sparkling wines as we know them today are a relatively new phenomenon, emerging in France in the late Seventeenth Century. Before that, certain wines were sold with a slight bubble in them. This effect was called *spritzig* in Germany, and *pétillance* and, later *perlé* in France. They were due to the vagaries of the European climate: if the winter began early and the newly made wine had not completely fermented then it became dormant and still, since the low temperatures inhibited further yeast activity. It was then bottled with its slight yeast content and sealed with waxed hemp. When the weather warmed in the spring, the yeast became active once more. Since there was little sugar left in the wine, the activity was not vigorous but just enough to create bubbles, to the extent that when the stopper was removed and the wine was poured it was sparkling, *spritzig,* or *pétillant.*

Wines of this kind still exist today (the best-known examples are probably the slightly bubbly Vinho Verdes of Portugal, although these owe their bubbles to malic fermentation and not to alcoholic fermentation). The *perlé* wine of today is a natural development of this type. What would otherwise be a straightforward table wine is given a slight lift by adding bubbles to it. In South Africa, as in most other wine-making countries, if the pressure of the bubbles is less than two

atmospheres it is not considered sparkling but *perlé* – if the pressure exceeds that amount the wine would be liable for champagne duty, which is normally at the luxury tax level.

Champagne is, of course, the most famous of all sparkling wines. Its development is generally accredited to the Benedictine monk, Dom Perignon, who was appointed chief cellarer at the Monastery of Hautvillers in 1668. Before his time all the wine of Champagne had been still, but he experimented for some 20 years to produce a sparkling wine. His early efforts were further developed by his successors until today's refined product was perfected.

The production of *le vin chantant* – the singing wine – of Champagne is the most intricate of all wine-making procedures and is known as *méthode champenoise*. The grapes are picked, weighed and then pressed in broad, shallow presses. The must is settled, and the clear juice is drawn off for fermentation with selected yeasts under temperature-controlled conditions at 12 to 16 °C. The wine is fermented to complete dryness in modern tanks – very few French Champagne-makers still employ the traditional small casks for fermentation.

At least three rackings take place to remove the sediment from the wine, after which the selection of the wines takes place: those to be kept for future years are put away in vats. The current wines are blended with older ones and it is this blend which is called the *cuvée.*

After fining and clarification, the clear wine has a measured amount of cane syrup added to it, together with a special yeast which will ferment under pressure. It is then bottled and closed with a temporary cap. Thereafter, the bottles are stacked to undergo their second fermentation – it is this fermentation which will introduce the bubbles into the wine.

The bottles are stored until they are ready to be released onto the market. For non-vintage champagne, the wine must be at least one year old before this takes place; for vintage champagne the minimum is three years, although most reputable houses exceed both these legal minima.

When the wine is required for sale, the bottles are removed from their stacks and placed in racks, neck down, for *remuage*, or riddling, which is done by hand. (Riddling is so labour intensive, though, that nowadays automatic riddling is being

introduced in many countries.) The bottle is given a sharp, oscillating spin before being dropped back into the rack. Initially the bottle will be in a near horizontal position in the rack, and each time it is jolted and rotated the position of the rack alters, so that eventually the bottle rests in a vertical position, neck down. This procedure causes the sediment to collect in the neck of the bottle against the crown cork which is used as a temporary closure during champagne making. When *remuage* is complete, the bottles are placed neck down in a refrigerated bath so that a quantity of champagne in the neck of the bottle, enough to lock in the sediment, is frozen solid. The bottle is then turned upright and the closure removed, taking with it the frozen sediment and leaving behind sparkling clear wine.

The champagne then has a predetermined amount of sugar syrup added to it to bring it to the required degree of sweetness, and is closed with the familiar cork, dressed and packaged for sale.

The local Estate of Simonsig in the Stellenbosch District was the first to use the *méthode champenoise* in preference to the tank method, to make the Estate's 'Kaapse Vonkel'. Other wine makers have begun to follow suit, for example, the Estates of Boschendal, Villiera, Clos Cabrière, Boplaas and Spier, as well as the Bergkelder.

Most South African quality sparkling wines are produced by the tank fermentation method. In this process the wine is fermented in sealed tanks to capture the carbon dioxide resulting from the reaction; it is then filtered and bottled under pressure directly from these tanks. This has great advantages in cost saving, and produces excellent wines, particularly if allowed to bottle age.

Some of the local sparkling wines are produced by tank carbonation. Here syrup is added to the wine as is the case with all methods of making sparkling wines, but in this process it is added for sweetness and not for the process of fermentation. The wine is then refrigerated and carbon dioxide is passed through it by means of a carbonator. These modern machines are extremely effective and give the wine an incredibly fine bubble. Then it is stored in pressurized tanks to allow the carbon dioxide to be thoroughly absorbed before being filtered and bottled under pressure. This results in an inexpensive product of good quality.

COOPERAGE

Coopering, or the making of wooden casks, is an ancient craft. Records of early wine casks survive on the walls of Egyptian tombs from the third millennium BC. By the time of the classic period of Greece and Rome, however, wine tended to be carried in clay *amphoarae,* rather than in the more perishable wooden containers. But by 100 AD casks had generally replaced clay in the Roman wine world.

By the time of the Roman withdrawal from Britain, the use of coopered vessels was general throughout Europe. But the cooper's trade as we know it today emerged clearly about the time of the Norman Conquest, when new words entered the wine maker's vocabulary, including the word barrel, from the French *baril,* and butt from the old French *bot.*

Eventually, three main types of cooperage were recognized: wet, dry and white. The wet cooper was the most skilled, and could carry out any type of cooperage; he made casks with a bulge to hold liquids – the great strength of, and the difficulty of

making, a wooden cask comes from the principle of the double arch (the cask has the properties of a wheel in that it is easily moved and not easily damaged). The dry cooper made a similar kind of container, but for holding dry materials. The 'white' cooper made straightsided, splayed vessels, such as milk pails. Within these broad categories were others; barrels for wine, spirit and beer required greater precision than those for oils, tar and the like.

Since the First World War, traditional wood containers have been increasingly replaced by cheaper and more effective materials, from metal to plasticized hessian. Wooden beer casks, too, have yielded to ones of aluminium and stainless steel. The wine and spirit coopers, however, survive, the last representatives of their ancient *métier,* because the properties possessed by oak are not only necessary for certain styles of wine, but are essential for the ageing of most spirits.

The desired characteristics derive from a particular kind of oak. Wood for the

earliest casks came from palms. Since then many other types have been used, but wine coopering is basically concerned with oak casks. Of the 500 odd species of *Quercus,* the oaks, only a few find their way into the wine industry and the most famous of these used for wine is that from the French province once known as Limousin. Today it comes mainly from the Department of Haute-Vienne, near the city of Limoges, also famous for its ceramics. The trees originally planted were *Quercus robur,* and every effort is made to utilize this kind of oak for wine casks. They grow tall comparatively rapidly, with very little lateral growth, making for a fine-grained timber.

Though oaks are a familiar feature of the Cape landscape, the local species does not produce timber with the qualities required for wine-maturation. Most of the oak used locally to make barrels is imported from Limousin and Nevers (although more now comes from other areas, including North America and Yugoslavia), and is made up locally by skilled coopers.

Oaken casks, product of the time-honoured craft of the cooper, are crucial in the ageing of red wines, fortified wines and spirits.

Fortified wines

A further important category of wine is that of fortified wines – wines strengthened by the addition of spirits to bring their alcohol content to a level higher than that produced naturally by fermentation. Until the 1950s, most wines were fortified. This had the advantage of increasing their longevity – the alcohol acting as a preservative and stabilizer. The development of natural wines in the last century, itself dependent upon increased technical controls, has reduced the proportion of fortified wines produced, the increased popularity of one being at the expense of the other.

Of the range of fortified wines, two retain their importance: sherry and port, both prominent in the South African wine maker's canon in that they represent an important element in the country's wine exports.

SHERRY

The different styles in which sherry can be made include dry (or *fino*), medium, and full sweet (or *oloroso*). Grapes with a high sugar content and a good total acidity are normally chosen. They are crushed in the usual way, and the juice separated. Those musts which are to be matured into dry sherries, or *finos*, are inoculated with selected strains of yeast which will, under the right conditions, develop the special *flor* yeasts which are essential to the making of sherry.

The wine is fermented dry, and after one or more rackings, is subjected to chemical analysis and testing. It should be sound, fairly delicate, and have a low tannin content (since tannin inhibits *flor* growth in *finos*).

On the basis of this examination it is passed for the further stages of production, and pumped into stainless steel or concrete tanks. Here it is fortified by the addition of pure wine spirit to a 14,5 per cent alcohol level, at which vinegar-forming bacteria are killed, but the *flor* yeast can still grow. The young wine is then pumped into 500-litre vats in the *criadera* (the 'nursery'), which are filled leaving approximately 10 per cent ullage, and loosely bunged. This ensures that air can reach the wine, since oxygen is essential for the existence of the *flor* yeast.

Under these conditions, a film of *flor* starts to develop within two to three weeks on the surface of the wine. It can be left at this stage for as long as two years; after which the best of the *criadera* wine is transferred to the *solera*. The *criadera* is not cleaned after the wine has been removed, but merely refilled with the new vintage. The barrels may be washed after about four years, but they are never sterilized.

The *solera* is traditionally a three-tier or more stack of casks. When it is established the lowest one is filled from that year's production, the second tier from the next year, and the third from the third year's production. When the annual sherry blend is required, a proportion, seldom more than a third, is drawn from the bottom cask which is then topped from the one above; this in turn is topped from the top cask. The top cask is refilled from the *criadera*. On this basis it takes about seven years for a wine to pass from the *criadera* through the *solera*.

The wines leaving the bottom of the *solera* are blended according to the taste and characteristics desired. They are adjusted for sweetness by the addition of a small percentage of jerepigo matured in wood, and for colour with the addition of *shermos*, grape juice concentrated and caramelised by boiling in open pans. Blended with *oloroso* wine, they are then fortified to 17-18 per cent by volume and matured in wood.

This final blending is carried out in blending vats. Should the alcohol level need adjusting, wine spirit is added to increase it, or well-aged sherry of a lower alcohol content to reduce it.

After wood maturation the sherry is then fined with gelatine and bentonite, racked, analysed chemically, and cold stabilized for tartrates at -7 °C for 10 to 14 days. Before bottling a light filtration is carried out.

The making of the sweet *oloroso* sherries is similar to that of the *finos,* but with certain important differences. The must of the initial fermentation is inoculated with a strain of yeast different from the *flor*-producing yeast used for the *finos*. In this case the yeast used is one which does not develop *flor*. The selected *oloroso* wines are fortified with an addition of pure wine spirit to between 17,5 and 18 per cent by

volume – this alcohol content further inhibits any growth of *flor*.

The young wines are then clarified by fining with gelatine and bentonite, racked and filtered. They are then adjusted for sulphur dioxide level, and transferred into 500-litre barrels which, unlike those used for the *fino* wines, are completely filled, leaving no room for ullage. The sherries are allowed to mature for up to ten years, during which time they are checked at least once a year. Also unlike the *finos* at a similar stage, they are not topped or racked during this time.

In South Africa, *finos* are produced mainly in the Boberg region, and *olorosos* are made both there and in the Little Karoo. The main cultivars used locally are Steen (Chenin Blanc), Palomino (White French), Sémillon (Green Grape), and Pedro.

PORT WINE

The second major form of fortified wine is port, which is usually made from selected red grapes, by means of an art demanding considerable time and expense, and also long experience. Besides the apéritif-type white port, there are three main types of red port: Tawny, Ruby and Vintage Port. Tawny, as its name would suggest, is an amber-coloured wine, the colour arising from long wood ageing – a Tawny Port spends about ten years in wooden barrels. Ruby is much brighter in colour, and fruitier on the palate. It is aged for about five years in wood before being bottled. Both types are ready for consumption when bottled.

The basic difference between sherry production and port is that sherry is fortified at the end of its fermentation and then sweetened with sweetish wine. Port obtains its sweetness from the actual grape sugar with the fermentation being stopped at the required level by the addition of pure grape alcohol in sufficient quantities to inhibit further yeast action.

Vintage Port is the classic port of the type made in the Douro region of Portugal, selected from years of exceptional quality. Before bottle maturation it should be deep in colour and full-bodied. These properties are obtained, partly, by storing the young wine in wooden barrels called 'pipes' for two years; it is then bottled, after which it should be aged further for up to 20 years or more. As most of the ageing takes place in the bottle, there may be a natural sedimentation, and it is therefore often necessary to decant a Vinage Port before drinking.

The principal problem in the making of port is the extraction of sufficient colour from the skin during the restricted period of fermentation: the particular method depends upon the grape cultivars used as well as upon the optimum temperature of fermentation. Included in the Cape cultivars used are Pontac, Shiraz, Mataro, Tinta Barocca, Souzão, Cinsaut and Grenache; it is also possible to use Chenin Blanc (Steen) for the production of white port. Port should be a combination of several different cultivars, some providing richness of colour, others aroma, fruit acid and sugar, resulting in complex and many-faceted blends.

Grapes for port wines should be harvested at full maturity to over-ripe. As with red wines, the skins tend to rise during fermentation and the 'cap' so formed must be constantly mixed by various methods with the liquid to obtain maximum contact for colour and flavour extraction. The wine maker allows the must to ferment to the point where, with the fortification – usually with good quality brandy – the fermentation will cease. Hereafter, the basic port undergoes further maturation and is blended.

At Monis' of Paarl flor *sherry is made according to the traditional Spanish method of* criadera *and* solera. *A glass-fronted cask in the winery provides a fascinating glimpse of sherry in the making – the film of yeast is clearly visible on the surface of the developing wine.*

Brandy

While not strictly belonging to the family of wine, brandy is nevertheless a close relative. Moreover, particularly in South Africa, its production has considerable bearing upon the workings of the industry as a whole.

Brandy is a distillate of natural wine – its name is a corruption of the Dutch *brande-wijn,* or 'burnt-wine'. In the process of distillation the wine is heated until the alcohol, which boils at a lower temperature than the other liquid components of the wine, is driven off in the form of a vapour, which is then led away to be cooled and condensed again as a liquid. This retains much of the flavour and aroma of the original wine, though it is now very much higher in alcohol content.

Traditionally, this process took place in simple but highly effective copper brandy-stills, or pot-stills. These copper pot-stills, modelled on those of the Cognac region of France, are used in South Africa by all the South African distilleries as a requirement of the law. All brandy must contain a minimum of 25 per cent of pot-still brandy, usually referred to as 'rebate' brandy, aged a minimum of three years in approved 'small wood'. A contemporary distillery includes equipment not only for the making of rebate brandy, but for the production of pure wine spirit. Separated off by fractional distillation in modern column stills, this is a purified form of wine alcohol which does not include the flavour components which are of prime importance

in the making of brandy. This spirit is usually aged for a short time in wood and is then blended with the pot-still product to the formula of the particular brand.

Palomino, Steen, Sémillon and Cinsaut are the grape varieties most commonly used for the making of wine for distilling in South Africa, though others include Ugni Blanc (Trebbiano) and Colombar, which are important varieties prescribed in the Charente region of France for the production of Cognac.

The chief aim in the making of distilling wine is to produce a clean wine, with a high acid content relative to the alcohol, and without any off-flavour. In South Africa therefore, after a light crushing of the grapes, the juice is immediately

separated from the skins and fermented without the otherwise usual addition of sulphur dioxide.

The distillation begins as soon as the wines have been fermented dry (that is, they no longer contain fermentable sugar), the wine being stored for as short a time as possible. In South Africa's hot climate this is a necessity, since wines unprotected by the antiseptic action of sulphur dioxide would soon deteriorate.

The wine at this stage comprises some 10-12 per cent of alcohol, the balance being water. With the first distillation (or the first series of distillations) this concentration is increased to a strength of about 50 ° proof spirit, equal to 28 per cent alcohol by volume. Besides the alcohol and a reduced amount of water, this liquid contains volatile substances such as aldehydes and esters, carried over from the wine. The residue contains most of the water and the non-volatile constituents such as mineral salts, sugar, colouring matter and fruit acids.

Not yet technically a brandy, this first distillate is called a 'low-wine'. It is then further distilled and the resultant distillate is put into wood for ageing. In the pot distillation the 'heads' or 'foreshot', are 'cut away', and only the succeeding product of the distillation, the 'heart' or 'cream' of the wine, is collected in a separate vessel. When the heart has been condensed, the last vapour, the 'tails', is also 'cut off'. It is the heart which is used for ageing.

This is an extremely delicate operation, the judgement of the brandy maker being crucial in determining when the heart must be separated from the heads and tails. It is also one in which a high consumption of wine is involved: from an original 1 136 litres of wine, only about 159 litres of brandy at a strength of about 70 per cent by volume of alcohol are produced after the wine has undergone the two distillations.

The young brandy as collected in the brandy receiver is clear as water, an aromatic liquid but still far from ready for consumption. Its strength is reduced to 60 per cent alcohol by the addition of distilled water, and it is transferred into imported Limousin oak casks of about 300 litres capacity where it is matured for not less than three full years. During this period the brandy extracts colour from the wood, becoming tea-coloured. The somewhat raw character of the liquid is slowly mellowed, its 'rough edges' rounded off, and a pleasant, slightly woody smell is derived from the cask.

At the end of three years, the brandy is blended, the blender sampling from each cask to decide how they may be combined, before being bottled.

Brandy, which was first distilled about 20 years after Van Riebeeck's arrival, has a strong separate tradition of its own in South Africa. 'Dop', 'Witblits' ('White Lightning'), 'Boerblits', and 'Cape Smoke' (a corruption of *Kaapse Smaak,* literally Cape Taste'), were some of the names by which local brandy was known in earlier years. The precursor of the modern South African brandies required an iron constitution for its consumption.

Cape Smoke was made from the wet mash of husks, pips and stalks which remained after the fermented must of the grapes had been run off in the traditional process of wine making. Probably similar to the French 'Marc' or the Italian 'Grappa', it was not considered necessary to distil it more than once. In spite of its fiery potency and roughness it continued to have its devotees long after the more modern product had emerged – it is said that Barney Barnato, one of the hard-driving pioneers of the diamond industry in the late nineteenth century, continued to prefer it long after his wealth had put him within reach of imported Cognac.

Much of the improvement in the local brandy followed the arrival of the French brandy maker, René Santhagens, who shipped his own copper stills from Cognac in the 1890s. After his death in 1937, his name was perpetuated in those of his famous brandies; but perhaps his most enduring monuments resides in the design of the South African pot-stills, all of which by law must operate on the principles of his original Cognac model.

Brandy has been a long-time favourite with South Africans, and accounts for over 48 per cent of all spirit sales. The quantity of wine flowing through South African distilleries amounts at present to some 250 million litres annually.

Such is the variety of methods by which the different kinds of wine, white wine and red wine, dry and sweet, rosé, sparkling and perlé, sherry, port and brandy, are produced in the modern wineries and distilleries. These are the main classes of vine product, but the complete family of wines has a vastly wider spectrum and complexity, comprising within each of the main types many further subdivisions of type and character. And these finer distinctions are based on the qualities brought to the wine, both singly and in blended form, by the many different grape varieties, by the character, strengths and limitations of the individual cultivars.

Wood, slanting light and measured movement capture the ambience of the maturaton cellar. Reminding passers-by of a 300-year-old wine heritage, the intricately carved centre cask is inscribed with Jan van Riebeeck's famous words 'Today praise be to God, wine was pressed for the first time from Cape grapes . . .'

THE CULTIVARS

The cultivars, or wine-grape varieties, are the building blocks of the wine masters' crafts, the colours of his art. And like a true artist, he must know the strengths and limitations of his medium, what it can or cannot be made to do. Respect for the essential character of each cultivar must be rigorously observed through the procedures of wine making.

For the wine lover, a knowledge of the cultivars is central to the assessment and comparison of wines.

The most obvious and major division of the cultivars is between those which go to make white wines and those for red wine making. There are others which specifically favour the making of fortified or dessert wines such as sherry and port. Within the main classes are further divisions between those cultivars which are generally termed 'noble', that is, cultivars which are 'shy' bearers and produce a relatively small yield of high-quality grapes, and those which are more suited for high-quantity production, giving large crops of high sugar content. Others are more versatile, being adaptable to bulk or quality production under certain conditions of climate and soil, or of style of growing or of wine production.

The extent to which a particular cultivar is grown depends upon a number of factors. These include the traditions of the area – even when these traditions have not always matched the appropriate cultivar to the local conditions. They also include the pressures of public demand, and the changes in popular taste (not easily predictable) which are particularly evident in the increased plantings in recent decades of cultivars suitable to quality

natural wines, and the post-Second World War reduction of fortified wine varieties.

The dominant factors remain those of the land, the climate and the specific qualities of the individual cultivars in terms of weight of crop, resistance to disease and extremes of heat and cold and, above all, of their qualities of taste and fragrance, body and character, their inherent uniqueness. Thus each cultivar

has its own definite character, which the wine master must recognize, preserve and enhance throughout the technical process of making the wine.

The following is a 'portrait gallery' of a selection of the most important cultivars in the local vineyards, the order of the descriptions being based on the contribution of each in terms of quantity and quality.

CULTIVAR TRENDS 1965-87

Percentage of total vines

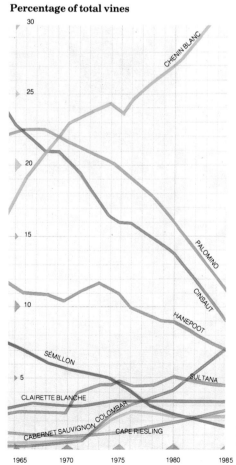

More than 300 million vines are grown in South Africa, covering some 100 000 hectares. Of these approximately 92 per cent comprise wine cultivars, with table grapes accounting for a further five per cent. The balance comprises rootstock and currant cultivars.

In all about 80 wine-grape varieties are cultivated, but of these relatively few are grown to any meaningful extent. This is well illustrated by the accompanying graph which shows ten varieties making up over 80 per cent of all vines cultivated in the winelands of South Africa.

Also interesting is that one white cultivar, Chenin Blanc or Steen, alone accounts for 32,41 per cent of the total surface area given to vines. More than any other cultivar it has grown in popularity over the past decades; and not surprisingly, for this prolific bearer will yield, depending on the skill of the cellar master, virtually any wine of quality asked of it, from dry to sweet, from sparkling to fortified, to wines of superb botrytis character.

Among the red wine cultivars, Cinsaut remains the most widely grown and at some nine per cent of the total number of vines is ahead of rival varieties such as Cabernet Sauvignon. Unlike Chenin Blanc, however, Cinsaut's star is waning, having decreased in popularity by more than 50 per cent over the 27 years between 1960 and 1987.

Chenel, a relative newcomer to the range of white wine cultivars, was developed between the 1950s and the early 1970s by Professor Chris Orffer of Stellenbosch University. A cross between Chenin Blanc (Steen) and Trebbiano, the variety has prospered under widely varying conditions in South Africa, producing grapes which are resistant to berry split, botrytis and sour rot.

White Wine Cultivars

Chenin Blanc (Steen)

being a good friend of the farmer, it is also responsive to the wine maker, who uses the grapes of high sugar and rich flavour to make wines possessing a particularly recognizable aroma.

Chenin Blanc is also very versatile. The source of many high-quality products, including grape juice, it produces the full range of natural wines: dry, off-dry, semi-sweet, rich late harvest, sparkling wines, fortified wines, sherry, white port, and brandy – an impressive list. The advent of Lieberstein, a semi-sweet natural table wine, and its spectacular burst of popularity in the 1960s, led to the planting of Chenin Blanc in even greater quantities. Depending on the area, Chenin Blanc ripens early in mid-season; in France it is inclined to be a very late ripener, sometimes being harvested as late as November. In the winelands of the Cape, Chenin Blanc adapts well to various soils and meso-climates and is also resistant to wind. It is susceptible to oidium, fairly resistant to downy mildew and very resistant to anthracnose. When planted in rich soils it is also susceptible to botrytis and sour rot. Care should be taken to prevent young trellised vines from overproducing, which they tend to do, as this would be to the detriment of the vine.

CHENIN BLANC, OR STEEN

For years this cultivar was known as Steen in South Africa and was believed to be unique to the Cape. In 1965, however, after extensive tests, it was established that the Steen cultivar was identical to the French variety, Chenin Blanc – since then, both names have been recognized.

It hailed originally from France and Jan van Riebeeck is known to have received cuttings from that country. Chenin Blanc dominates the Anjou-Touraine area where it is the only grape permitted for the making of white wine. There it covers a large vineyard area on the slopes west of Touraine and rising from the left bank of the River Loire. In the Loire Valley lies the town of Vouvray, where a popular French sparkling wine is produced from the Chenin Blanc grape. Away from its place of origin, it still produces some extremely good wines, as it does here, where it forms the backbone of the South African wine industry, to the extent that it has become

the most planted cultivar in the country. It amounts to over 32 per cent of the national crop, represented by some 92 million vines distributed throughout the wine-producing districts.

As in France, Chenin Blanc wines reach their greatest heights as sweeter wines: the Special and Noble Late Harvest wines of the Cape, such as Nederburg Edelkeur, clearly illustrate this.

Chenin Blanc is also extensively planted in California, and there are plantings in Australia (where it has several different names), Argentina, Chile and New Zealand. It is interesting to note that South Africa has more than three times the area planted to Chenin Blanc (nearly 30 000 hectares) than is planted to this variety in its home country, France.

There is good reason for this popularity. Chenin Blanc is a prolific, reliable yielder, which grows strongly and is resistant to wind and to several vine diseases. Besides

Palomino (White French)

PALOMINO, OR WHITE FRENCH

This cultivar is one of the oldest known to have been grown at the Cape. In the local vineyards it was traditionally known as White French, or Fransdruif, but was identified by Perold in 1926 not with a French grape but with one of the famous sherry cultivars of Spain, Palomino Fino – a name derived from the Spanish word for a dove. Some confusion lingers over this provenance, however, since the local performance of the grape as a basis for sherry has not matched its record in Spain and Portugal. Nevertheless, in South Africa it remains a cultivar used for sherry. In Spain itself Palomino is known by no less than ten names: it is Horgazuela in Puerto de Santa Maria and Listan in Sanlucar (as it is, too, in the Midi region of France); other names include Alban, Tempranilla, Temprana and Ojo de Liebra.

In South Africa Palomino made its home naturally on fertile soil in low-rainfall areas. It was particularly successful in the Vredendal area, where it was grown on its own roots prior to the phylloxera invasion, producing an interesting wine. (The Vredendal area remained free of phylloxera for some 60 years after it had devastated most of the rest of the vineyards in the Cape, succumbing only in the mid-1950s.) Today of course Palomino is grown on grafted rootstock and produces a light, unexciting wine which is mainly used for distillation.

The vine itself is easily identified by its dark green leaves, which are deeply lobed, showing a whitish felted covering, or tomentum, below. It is an early ripening variety, being fully ripe at about 19 ° to 20 ° Balling, and rarely reaching a higher sugar content than this; its modest sugar production and low fixed acid do not give the wine maker much scope. It needs good leaf development to allow for a slower ripening and a higher sugar content, as well as for protection from sunburn in the hotter areas. Although the must tends to oxidize very rapidly and browning can ensue, unwanted oxidation can be reduced by preventing sunburn. The young bunches are also very susceptible to downy mildew. Against this litany of disadvantages Palomino has a number of important strengths which account for its continued popularity with growers. Above all it is a robust, vigorous and heavy producer, giving crops of as much as 80 tonnes from a single hectare. Its large, loose bunches of pale green grapes, ripening to a translucent golden ochre, are easily harvested, and it adapts well to a range of training and trellising systems; its outstanding vigour allows it to be successfully cultivated on a trellis with a wide top.

Because of its vulnerability to anthracnose, Palomino has all but disappeared from the Cape's coastal districts where rainfall is relatively high. It is, however, still grown in the Paarl, Montagu, Worcester and Robertson areas, but the best results are probably obtained in the areas around De Wet, Over-Hex, Aan-de-Doorns and Nuy, where it is pruned to yield less, producing a higher fruit acid and thus a fuller, fruitier wine.

In general, Palomino table wines tend to be on the soft side, lacking in delicacy and bouquet. The cultivar plays an important part in brandy production and much of its wine goes to the distilleries, but its major use, and one for which it is well suited, is in blended wines. In this role, as a subsidiary element in the blend, it can provide a softening complement to a more acidic white wine.

Some 34 million vines are planted in South Africa which represent approximately 11 per cent of the total plantings.

CLAIRETTE BLANCHE

In the late 1940s and up to the mid-1950s, Clairette Blanche gained popularity as a vine eminently suited to the production of sparkling wines, and it still plays the rôle. Used on its own as a natural wine it gives a delicate, fruity aroma, very pronounced and distinctive when young. Unfortunately, this tends to disappear when the wine is about a year to 18 months old. When blended with other varieties, however, this pleasant aroma holds for longer, and the combination of this variety with others can lead to an extremely pleasant wine.

The wine maker has to use all his skill with Clairette Blanche since the must and the young wine have a tendency to oxidise fairly rapidly. The use of stainless steel tanks and the controls available to the modern wine maker have helped to limit this traditional problem and enhance the making of the cultivar's fine, flowery, low-acid wines.

How and when this cultivar first reached South Africa is uncertain. Grown along almost the entire Mediterranean coastline from Spain to France (where it has been known since ancient times as Blanquette) Clairette Blanche makes up some ten per cent of the blend which goes into the still and sparkling wines of Limoux. Blended with Ugni Blanc (similar to St Emilion and Trebbiano), it makes a significant contribution to many of the everyday drinking wines in this area, where it is also used as a table grape in many of the local households.

In France Clairette Blanche is considered to be somewhat subsceptible to botrytis rot, but this has not been the case in South Africa. Because of this it has been grown in summer-rainfall areas with considerable success. The grape, which tends to be low both in sugar and in acid, matures relatively late in the season and so can help the farmer to 'stretch the harvest time'. It thus fits well into the harvesting programme, an important practical consideration in the winelands, particularly in areas such as Stellenbosch. In the warmer regions further inland it may present problems, making demands on irrigation because of its late-ripening character. It is not a markedly drought-resistant cultivar and in the drier seasons the quality of the grapes may be affected. It is in general a sturdy plant but does not stand up well to wind damage. It grows best in fairly deep, cool soil and must be well pruned to give good quality fruit.

At present some 10 million Clairette Blanche vines are grown in South Africa on 3 200 hectares of vineyard, making up about 3,2 per cent of the total national crop. The occurrence of a red variation named Clairette Rose has been reported from France, but is not yet known in South Africa. In Australia the cultivar is well known as Blanquette and wines made from it are considered of reasonable quality.

Clairette Blanche

MUSCAT d'ALEXANDRIE, OR HANEPOOT

Thought to have been cultivated by the ancient Egyptians as well as by the Greeks and Romans, Muscat d'Alexandrie, known locally as Hanepoot, is believed to be one of the earliest cultivated plants. Since it was propagated asexually, that is, from cuttings rather than seeds, it is probably one of the oldest living plants on earth with an unchanged genetic make-up. Its French name, Muscat d'Alexandrie, suggests that it may have originated in the region of the ancient North African port of Alexandria. It is also known in France as Muscat Romain, as Moscatel Gordo Blanco in Spain, and as Muscat Gordo Blanco in Australia.

Muscat d'Alexandrie requires considerable heat to bring it to full maturity and so tends to be found in the warmer wine regions of the world. An early immigrant to the Cape winelands, it is thought to be the cultivar to which Van Riebeeck referred as his *Spaanse Druyfen* – his 'Spanish grapes'. The vine found a natural habitat in the warmer inland regions, though in earlier years it also thrived in Constantia and was grown with success in many of the cooler coastal areas where it produced a slightly higher acid content than inland, yielding a natural wine of a slightly different style.

The name Hanepoot was attached to the vine at some time in the course of its local history. Professor Perold held that it was an intentional corruption of the Dutch word *Hanekloot* or cock's testicles which, according to those competent to make the comparison, bear a strong resemblance to the berries of the Hanepoot vine. The identification of the local plant with the ancient French Muscat d'Alexandrie was established in the 1920s by Professor Perold, who imported Muscat d'Alexandrie from Montpellier in the south of France and determined conclusively that the existing local variety and the imported strain were the same plant.

Hanepoot is not an easy vine to grow, being very demanding in soil type and compatible with a limited number of rootstock cultivars; nor is it a particularly vigorous grower, being happy as a bush vine or on a low trellis. It is a prolific producer, a factor which may account for its lack of vigour in growth. Along with the majority of the Muscat varieties it is susceptible to anthracnose, oidium, and downy mildew, the latter being particularly damaging to the young bunches. It also sets its berries badly, unless pruned late.

Nevertheless it remains one of South Africa's most planted vines. It gives mellow, sweet wines of low acidity, but possessing an unmistakable 'muscat' flavour. By percentage, more Muscat d'Alexandrie is grown here than anywhere else in the world – its contribution to the national crop being some seven per cent represented by almost 21 million vines on about 6 000 hectares of vineyard. Most are in the Worcester area, though the grape reaches its highest quality in the Robertson and Klein Karoo regions. Here it is a multi-purpose vine, being used for table grapes, raisin production, grape juice, concentrated grape syrup and, of course, table wine and some liqueur wines. Its full-flavoured, luscious, sweet grape has long been popular among Cape gardeners, who have traditionally grown their own Hanepoot grapes for the table: indeed its distinctive flavour and rich sweetness have led many a newcomer to the country to mistake the name of the grape for 'honeypot'. Its versatility was reflected, too, in its traditional use on a large scale for raisins and for the production of *moskonfyt* (grape syrup) and even jam, particularly in the Breede River area.

More recently Hanepoot growers have begun to use their grapes for natural wine. This is not only more lucrative but less risky commercially than drying for raisins. Even more recently Hanepoot has found itself under the varietal name of Muscat d'Alexandrie as a premium table wine.

In the Cape a number of mutations of the Hanepoot variety are known, of which three are grown on a modest commercial scale. Le Roux Hanepoot was named after the first farmer to grow it on its own. It has smaller bunches than the original variety and looser berries which do not require thinning; it is generally grown more as a table grape than for wine. Red Hanepoot grows well in the cooler regions and was derived from the white as a bud variation which is now constant and which retains its distinctive characteristics. Of this red mutation some 230 000 vines are known to exist. There is also a longer-berried Hanepoot strain which dries rapidly and is therefore suitable for making raisins.

CAPE RIESLING, OR SOUTH AFRICAN RIESLING

Like so many cultivars, Cape (or South African) Riesling originated in the far south-west of France, where it is known as Cruchen Blanc. In South Africa it has also been known as Paarl Riesling. For many years it was mistakenly thought to be the same cultivar as Weisser or Rhine Riesling because it looks so similar. Extremely good wines with their own different and distinctive character are made from this cultivar.

A delicate cultivar, it is choosey about soil and climate: it only tolerates cool climates and soils having a medium yield potential. If planted in very rich and fertile soil it is susceptible to sour rot and botrytis (or noble rot). Botrytis, while necessary in grapes intended for certain sweet dessert wines, is most undesirable in grapes intended for a dry table wine. Plantings of this temperamental cultivar, which is susceptible to sunburn, oidium and downy mildew (although reasonably tolerant to strong wind) are few – even in France plantings have dwindled dramatically.

Locally, the Stellenbosch and Paarl Districts have the greatest plantings of Cape Riesling, which amount to fewer than eight million vines as against the most popular cultivar, Chenin Blanc (Steen), which accounts for about 92 million vines.

The grapes and the juice of Cape Riesling have to be carefully handled, as this cultivar is particularly prone to oxidation which causes a slight browning of the wine. However, with good grapes and an excellent wine maker, Cape Riesling can produce a wine of rare quality with a distinctive forthcoming bouquet which, when the wine is young, is quite fruity but never overpowering or cloying. It is at its best when steely dry. Not only are Cape Riesling wines delightful to drink when young, but with selected plant material, fruit of optimum ripeness, and expert wine making, wines of special quality, which have good ageing potential, can be produced. The Nederburg 1974 Riesling, for example, made excellent drinking eight years later. Some subsequent vintages have also been worth ageing. Nederburg is the only producer to have aged some Rieslings in wood. The wood, subtly used, adds an interesting flavour dimension.

Cape (South African) Riesling

WEISSER RIESLING, OR RHINE RIESLING

The Weisser Riesling vine is the most noble of the German varieties, producing a good deal of the classic Spätlesen, Auslesen and Trockenbeerenauslesen styles of wine for which Germany is famous. It can also produce very good dry white wines.

Most authorities agree that this cultivar is indigenous to the Rhine Valley and was used by the Romans for wine making when they occupied that area. It is thought to be a descendant of a wild vine found there, which was of the *Vitis vinifera* family. In Germany the existence of Weisser Riesling is recorded as far back as 1435. Because of its late-ripening characteristics, a problem in the cooler, northerly German vineyards, Weisser Riesling has been superseded over the last 50 years by Müller-Thurgau as the most widely cultivated vine in Germany. Although Müller-Thurgau is a cross of Riesling and Sylvaner it does not have the noble character of Riesling, being a producer of quantity rather than quality. Weisser Riesling remains the dominant variety in certain areas, though, such as the mid-Moselle, the Saar-Ruwer,

Rheingau and Mittelrhein, and is still grown throughout the country.

Weisser Riesling is considered by many to be one of the world's great cultivars. In spite of this, however, it is the only one of the famous, noble cultivars that is not planted in France, except in Alsace, which, for historical reasons, is more German than French in character. In France, for some reason known only to the French, Weisser Riesling is not allowed to be grown more than 50 kilometres from the German border. Outside Europe, it has travelled as far as Australia, California, Chile and South Africa, adapting almost as well as Cabernet Sauvignon has to the new and varied environments in which it is now grown.

While still retaining its identity, Weisser Riesling reflects the differences of climate and soil in which it is grown. In hot climates it is inclined to become a fatter wine and lose some of its elegance, but remains distinctive with a honeyed, spicey nose and hints of a certain flowery sweetness. It is described by French wine

makers as '*le petit aromatique*' or 'the small, fragrant' grape.

In South Africa Weisser Riesling has only really become known in the last decade. Now that the vines are more mature, and the Cape wine makers have come to terms with the idiosyncracies of the cultivar, some fine wines have been produced, particularly since 1984. Weisser Riesling produces a full-flavoured wine noted for its good acids; generally, it ages well and develops a distinctive nose. On the palate it gains complexity with age.

About 2,4 million Weisser Riesling vines are planted, mainly in the Stellenbosch and Paarl districts, about 0,8 per cent of total vine plantings in South Africa. Well-adapted to various soils, it prefers the coolest areas of our winelands, although these are still warmer than its German homeland. It is a shy bearer, fairly resistant to wind damage, oidium and downy mildew, but susceptible to botrytis due to the compact structure of its bunches. It also has a good affinity for most well-known rootstock cultivars.

SÉMILLON, OR GREEN GRAPE

The local name of this cultivar derives from the colour of its foliage, not from that of its berries. Most green growth in South Africa is duller than that of the European vineyards. The leaves of the Green Grape, however, are in the early growing season much lighter in colour than those of most other vines. In the vineyard, a verdant, almost vivid mass of green makes it easily

identifiable to the newcomer to the winelands.

The Green Grape cultivar of the Cape has been identified with the Sémillon variety of Europe and current legislation allows the use of both names for the same vine. Many experts, however, consider the old and popular Green Grape plant to be slightly different from Sémillon, in that it

Muscat d'Alexandrie (Hanepoot)

Sémillon (Green Grape)

Weisser (Rhine) Riesling

is more productive, its bunches are longer, and its berries smaller. Since these differences are due only to bud mutations, as a general principle the two are accepted as the same plant today.

In the early days of wine making at the Cape the cultivar was the most popular for the production of wine – records reveal that in 1822, 93 per cent of the vineyards were planted to the 'Wyndruif' or 'Wine Grape' as it was then known.

The Sémillon grape is used in western France for such famous wines as Graves and the magnificent sweet liqueur wines of Sauternes and Barsac. In the Cape, Green Grape traditionally produced a good wine of a distinctive character; its earlier popularity was enhanced by the fact that it was a reasonable yielder and was resistant to anthracnose. It has a reputation for growing and yielding to a ripe old age, and many of the older farms have the odd

Green Grape bush vine of respectable antiquity, retained for sentimental reasons. Green Grape vines of up to 80 years of age can still be found making a contribution to the crop.

It is argued that this cultivar gives a better wine with a longer life when grown as a bush vine than when trained on a trellis. It is very much at home in the deep, fertile soils of the Paarl, Wellington and Franschhoek valleys, especially where the site is sheltered, since it tends to be prone to wind damage. On the credit side, it is almost immune to anthracnose and seldom suffers from sunburn. Since the introduction of cold fermentation, some extremely fine and delicate wines have been made from this grape.

Besides its more usual name, the cultivar has been known locally as Wine Grape. An unusual and contradictory name crops up in a local mutation which

has a red-skinned berry and is called Red Green Grape!

Under the name of Hunter River Riesling, the cultivar is widely grown in Australia (the curious alias used there appears to argue a confusion over nomenclature similar to that once found at the Cape). There it is regarded as one of the country's most important dry white varieties, with a total of almost 2 000 hectares under cultivation. In California, on the other hand, its distribution is skimpy, covering only a few hundred hectares. Among the more recently developed wine-making countries only the Argentine, with some 5 500 hectares of Sémillon, compares with the massive 24 000-hectare plantings found in the Bordeaux region.

Some five million Sémillon vines cover 1,6 per cent of the total national vineyard area in South Africa.

COLOMBAR

Once one of the most important cultivars used in the making of Cognac, Colombar has all but, disappeared from the European vineyards in recent years, to be replaced largely by St Emilion (Trebbiano) in the vineyards of Cognac. In South Africa, it began its career as a brandy and fortified wine grape. It remained almost unheard of by the local wine lover until the early 1970s, when a serendipitous accident resulted in its sudden emergence with a new career as a natural wine.

In 1954 Wouter de Wet, a farmer in the Robertson district, was mistakenly supplied with Colombar vines instead of the St Emilion he had ordered. Since they

were equally suited to the making of rebate wine for brandy, he proceeded to cultivate the variety, which he supplied to the Robertson Co-operative Winery.

The vines did very well in the local Breede River conditions and other farmers began to follow suit. It was the manager and wine maker of the Robertson Co-operative, Pon van Zyl, who was the first to realize the potential of this new cultivar for the making of a natural wine.

Colombar's ability to produce an aristocratic wine under the hot conditions of the inland areas was quickly appreciated. At first the authorities were wary of this new development, since recent

data showed Colombar wine to be very prone to oxidation. But modern wine making has more or less dispelled this fear, and its public acceptance was signalled by a series of first prizes in the late 1970s for this hitherto unknown wine at the Cape Championship Wine Show.

Thus, while Colombar has not lost favour in South Africa as a brandy-producing grape, it has gained it as a natural wine producer. It is a vigorous grower, particularly on high potential soils in warmer climates, and has a comparatively longer life than most other varieties. This is probably due to the particularly hard-wood character of its trunks and canes; a quality which also makes it resistant to dead arm and other wood-rotting fungi. In fact it is reasonably resistant to disease generally, but is susceptible to wind damage early in the season.

When grown in the hotter regions it produces a high natural fruit acid content and a highly characteristic and fragrant aroma – variously and lyrically described by Pon van Zyl as 'rose-garden' or as resembling the scent of the koekemakranka flower – of a quality which few other varieties can achieve under these conditions. Grown in the cooler coastal regions it produces its unmistakably aromatic wine, but one which is somewhat softer than its inland sibling. The qualities of the wine are very prominent when young, but it remains an interesting wine when aged, and lends itself well to blending, adding a refreshing fruitiness – it is the backbone of the better Premier Grand Cru wines.

Some 19 million Colombar vines, representing about seven per cent of total vineyard area, are now planted, with the

Colombar

Gewürztraminer

highest concentrations in the Tulbagh, Malmesbury, Olifants River, Worcester and Robertson areas. Being a late mid-season variety, it is generally harvested about the second week of March, thus helping to 'spread the vintage'. The grapes must be fully ripe at harvesting time to achieve the special aroma which is the hallmark of this cultivar.

GEWÜRZTRAMINER

Gewürztraminer is grown in most winemaking countries to a greater or lesser extent. It is an important grape in the winelands of Alsace, where it makes up some 22 per cent of plantings. Elsewhere its distribution is limited, though its reputation stands relatively high. With its full, flowery, highly spiced taste, it is considered essentially a sipping wine, and for general purposes tends to take second place to the rounder flavour of the Weisser Riesling.

The German word *gewürzt* means 'spicy'. The Gewürztraminer vine is ampelographically identical to the Traminer cultivar. There are, however, selected clones which perform better than others, and these sought-after spicy clones are those normally referred to as 'Gewürztraminer'.

Deriving from and adapted to a cold climate, the Gewürztraminer does not always do well when transported to a warmer one and its success in the newer wine areas of the world has usually been in very localised cool conditions. In South Africa the percentage grown to date has barely made the statistics; the bulk is cultivated in the Tulbagh region, with token quantities elsewhere, particularly in the Paarl and Stellenbosch areas.

The cultivar yields bunches which are medium-to-small and fairly compact; the berries are usually pinkish but occasionally almost reddish-brown. It is not highly productive, though yields of up to seven tonnes to a hectare have been achieved while still maintaining reasonable quality.

The problems of obtaining above-average growth are compounded by those of making the wine itself. Some wine makers maintain that the precise moment of picking is important, the grape only developing its fullest and most characteristic spiciness in the last stages of maturity. The disadvantage of awaiting this crucial moment is that the acid tends to be lost, and wines of a very low acid content may result. Nevertheless, some outstanding Gewürztraminer wines have been made in the Cape.

Susceptible to oidium and, because of the compact bunches, to botrytis rot, this cultivar is also threatened by birds, which particularly like its grapes. Given these drawbacks and difficulties it is doubtful whether the Gewürztraminer vine will ever account for large volumes. Just over half a million vines are currently planted, a mere 0,2 per cent of total plantings.

FALSE PEDRO

This quaintly-named cultivar, otherwise known as Pedro Luis, and not to be confused with Pedro Ximinez, is of more viticultural than oenological interest. It is useful, however for sherry production, and, to a limited degree, for blending. Originally imported to the Cape as Pedro Ximinez, it turned out to be an altogether different cultivar, but the stigma of the impersonation lingers in its present name.

False Pedro shares a number of characteristics with the Pedro Luis of the Jerez region of southern Spain. It is also found in Australia, where it is called the Common Palomino. In fact, it probably more closely resembles the Palomino than any of the other Pedro cultivars.

In South Africa, False Pedro is grown almost exclusively in the Paarl and Malmesbury districts, where it has adapted better than other varieties to sandy soils; it is also considerably more drought- and sunburn-resistant and produces grapes which mature without wilting. The vine and its bunches suffer little from wind damage. The grapes are ready for harvesting in early mid-season. False Pedro vines in South Africa number about two and a half million, only one per cent of the total national vineyard area.

KERNER

This white grape is unusual in that it has as one of its parents the red grape Trollinger, the other being Rhine Riesling. The cross was produced at Weinsberg in Germany in the early 1960s and registered there in 1969 as a cultivar. It is planted in quantity in seven of the 11 German wine-producing regions, with the largest plantings being in the Rheinfalz. Unlike the Rhine Riesling, it has good frost resistance and bears about 10 per cent more than the noble Riesling.

Some authorities say that it was named after the poet and physician Justinus Kerner (1786-1862), who 'cured his patients by the use of wine', others that its name derives from the German *kernig*, meaning not only that the cultivar is strong and resistant, but also that the grape has a taste of the kernel, or pip. As a result of this latter quality, wine made from Kerner sometimes tastes as though it has spent some time in wood, thereby acquiring a distinctive savour of tannin. It ages well.

Kerner prefers cooler regions. Its bunches are medium to big, and very compact, which tends to lead to problems of rot. This is exacerbated by the deep shade provided by the dense foliage of this vigorous cultivar. There are about 364 000 Kerner vines planted in South African vineyards, approximately 0,13 of total vineyard area.

False Pedro

Kerner

BUKETTRAUBE

Developed from unknown parents in the winelands of Germany, this is a fairly recent addition to the family of local vines, being first imported in 1967. Since the first wines from these grapes were made at Nietvoorbij, it has been adopted by a number of prominent wine makers and just over a million vines have been planted, about 0,4 per cent of total vineyard area.

Bukettraube is a vigorous grower and bears well when heavily pruned, yielding pyramidal bunches of big, round berries with reasonably strong skins. In appearance it somewhat resembles Green Grape. It has adapted well and gives its best wine in the cooler coastal area, where the ripening of its grapes coincides with that of the local Steen. It must be watched closely for powdery and downy mildew, to which it is most susceptible – and it is also a favourite target for birds.

Bukettraube (*bukett* is German for bouquet) makes a highly characteristic wine and one, as its name suggests, with a prominent bouquet. Besides making a fine and individual wine on its own, it works well in partnership, adding a complementary bouquet to a slightly sweeter white wine.

Bukettraube

SAUVIGNON BLANC

Mistakenly, Sauvignon Blanc is considered to be a new variety in the Cape winelands, but it was extensively planted here in the eighteenth century. It lost favour earlier this century because it produced poor crops, the reason for this being the propagation of inferior plant material. It is also very sensitive to dead arm (tandpyn). In the last decade Sauvignon Blanc vines have been grown in ever-increasing quantities, mainly in the districts of Paarl and Stellenbsch. About seven-and-a-half million vines have been planted, which is some two-and-a-half per cent of total plantings.

Sauvignon Blanc has been grown in France for centuries and is found in the Loire and Bordeaux regions. In the Loire the Sauvignon Blanc wines are unblended, the best-known being Pouilly-Fumé and Sancerre. In the Bordeaux region Sauvignon Blanc is usually blended with Sémillon and Muscadelle. From the end of the 1960s to 1979, about half of the Sauvignon Blanc and Sémillon vines in the Gironde were uprooted because of the good prices being realised for red wines. In Sauterne, Sauvignon Blanc is a less important part of the blend of the lush wines of this region but is nevertheless necessary, as it increases the acid and adds interest to the aroma of the wine.

Sauvignon Blanc is also planted in Italy and Eastern Europe and fairly extensively in Argentina and California. To a lesser extent it is planted in New Zealand, where it is producing some particularly good wines, and in Australia.

At the Cape it ripens in early mid-season and is found to perform well on medium potential soils in the cooler climates. It is a high quality cultivar with a good yield potential. On fertile soils the bunches become compact and are extremely susceptible to botrytis rot, and fairly susceptible to oidium and downy mildew. Nonetheless, some fine wines have been produced, (several of which have been matured in wood), and Sauvignon Blanc is considered to have an exciting future in South Africa.

CHARDONNAY

Chardonnay is a cultivar which, in good years, and if properly used, can yield superb dry white wines. Its home is France, and there it is as versatile as Chenin Blanc is here. Many legendary French wines are made from Chardonnay, either on its own or blended with other cultivars. It holds the distinction of being the only white grape permitted for the making of champagne. In the officially delimited region known as Champagne, from which the wine takes its name,

Chardonnay is blended with the black grapes of Pinot Noir and Pinot Meunier to produce the famous sparkling magic. In the best years some Champagne houses blend a particular Cuveé called 'Blanc de Blanc', which is made entirely from Chardonnay grapes.

The tiny, but renowned, region of Chablis to the south-west of Champagne gives another interpretation to the style of Chardonnay wines. Further south and slightly east from the two regions already

mentioned is Burgundy, and there Chardonnay's personality changes from a rather delicate but elegant northerner to a more lively and opulent wine which still has a definite subtleness but also a seductive charm. Part of the Burgundy region is the Cote d'Or and some of the finest Chardonnay wines come from its southerly townships: Meursault, Puligny, Montrachet and Chassagne. The wines of Meursault are soft, dry and elegant; those of Montrachet are luscious and rich with layer upon layer of flavour impressions. Famous individual Burgundy wines like Le Montrachet or Chevalier-Montrachet, which in great years are masterpieces, are considered by some, particularly the Burgundians, to be incomparable and utterly beyond criticism, and it is the ambition of many talented wine-makers to emulate these great dry wines.

Chardonnay is planted in other regions of France, such as the Loire Valley and Alsace, where it lends its acidity and noble character to certain blends. Outside France the first country to cultivate this cultivar was the United States. The majority of American plantings are in California, and it is often difficult to distinguish the best Chardonnay wines of California from the good wines of the Côte d'Or. Today outstanding Chardonnays are also produced in Australia.

In South Africa one of the first wine makers to plant Chardonnay was Sidney Back of Backsberg. Unfortunately the plant material was not of the best, but in recent years new plant material has been acquired. Backsberg has been producing progressively better, subtly wood-matured Chardonnays for the last five years. Since the 1985 vintage, Backsberg has been using the more classic French approach of partly fermenting the wine in wood as well. This Chardonnay subsequently won the Diners Club award in 1986 for the best wood-matured white wine.

There are now about a dozen Chardonnays on the South African market with the addition of a couple of new producers each year, and there is no doubt that this cultivar will go from strength to strength as determined wine makers persevere to produce a very special wine

from this most noble of noble varieties.

If the plant material is free of harmful viruses, Chardonnay is an easy variety to grow. In South African conditions it is found to prefer medium to high potential soils and cooler areas: most plantings are in the Stellenbosch and Paarl Districts with some plantings in Constantia, Tulbagh, Worcester and the Overberg. In the Cape winelands Chardonnay is found to be only moderately susceptible to downy mildew and botrytis rot but most susceptible to virus diseases. It ripens in early mid-season and because of the small bunches and high percentage of seedless berries, it has a low yield potential. To date just over a million vines have been planted, representing some 0,4 per cent of total vineyard area, so it will take at least another decade or two before South African Chardonnay exists in any quantity.

CHENEL

This is a South African-bred cultivar, specifically developed to respond to the local conditions of soil and climate. The creation of Professor Chris Orffer, of the Faculty of Viticulture at Stellenbosch University (now retired), it was developed from crosses first made in 1950.

This new cultivar, derived from a cross of Chenin Blanc and Trebbiano, was released in the early 1970s, after some two decades of patient testing and research. Some debate attended the christening of the cultivar (new Australian varieties are

generally given Aboriginal names). The final choice was Orffer's own, and was derived from the name of Chenin Blanc and the first syllable of the teaching and research establishment of Elsenburg, where much of the work was done.

Since its introduction, Chenel has proved very successful on a wide variety of soils under intensive irrigation and if trained on a high trellis. With such treatment it has prospered both in the Karoo region and in the coastal belt. Its vigorous growth and high production

under intensive cultivation – not Orffer's initial aim in the development of the vine – have been an unexpected bonus for this variety.

Chenel was bred to be highly resistant to berry split, botrytis and sour rot, to obviate the need for expensive sprays to control these ailments. Withal, it yields a pleasant, light wine, ideally suited for consumption in a hot climate. It is also suitable for blending. There are just over two million chenel vines, planted on about 0,8 per cent of total vineyard area.

Sauvignon Blanc

Chardonnay

Chenel

Red Wine Cultivars

Cabernet Sauvignon

CABERNET SAUVIGNON

By general consensus, Cabernet Sauvignon is the finest of the red wine cultivars. It has a long and illustrious tradition in Europe – it has been speculatively identified with the *Biturica* mentioned by the Roman writer Pliny. In the Gironde region it is the oldest continuously grown variety.

It supplies much of the essence of the aroma and the flavour of the fine Médocs of Bordeaux, where it is one of the five cultivars allowed for the production of red wine, the others being Cabernet Franc, Merlot, Petit Merlot, and Malbec.

Cabernet Sauvignon produces a small crop in Bordeaux, compared to other areas. Larger crops are obtained from this cultivar beyond the borders of France, particularly in Australia, California, Chile

and South Africa. The French do not consider this small crop a disadvantage, however, as their Appellation Contrôlée law limits the production per hectare of quality wines. The planting of Cabernet Sauvignon in France nearly doubled between 1968 and 1979 and now exceeds 22 000 hectares. Three-quarters of the vines are in Bordeaux and the balance mainly in the Loire area, with some in the Midi and the Languedoc-Rousillon vineyards. Merlot, however, remains the most planted vine in the Bordeaux region.

The best French Cabernet Sauvignon wines come from the Bordeaux districts of the Médoc and Graves, where they are usually blended with Cabernet Franc and Merlot. Cabernet Sauvignon berries are almost black and can produce extremely

rich dark wines, which when not blended, are inclined to be rather austere. They need long ageing. The addition of Merlot and Cabernet Franc not only softens the austerity and gives complexity but also makes the wines accessible sooner.

After France, Bulgaria has the most extensive plantings of Cabernet Sauvignon (nearly 18 000 hectares) and California is next (about 9 000 hectares). Italy also has extensive plantings of this cultivar. Where the climate is suitable, most wine-producing countries, in fact, have planted Cabernet Sauvignon, even if it is known by another name. In South Africa there are about six-and-a-half million Cabernet Sauvignon vines.

It is not known precisely when the cultivar was first introduced to the Cape, but it has been grown locally for a considerable time: by the 1920s it was regarded as one of the local varieties of quality. In the early days it was not uncommon to find Cabernet being blended with Cinsaut at the crusher, a method still practised at Rustenberg. When pressed on its own, however, a beautifully coloured red wine is obtained, with a very dominant, characteristic flavour of green walnuts. Because of its astringent nature and high fruit acid content Cabernet Sauvignon needs a fairly long period of wood maturation and bottle ageing before the wine can produce its rich rewards.

A shy bearer, the cultivar grows long, loose cylindrical bunches, with small, big-pipped grapes which ripen late in the season, and it does not do well, therefore, in areas with low summer temperatures. Cabernet Sauvignon has good resistance to botrytis rot, but is fairly susceptible to oidium and downy mildew. It is also resistant to wind. It makes up 2,3 per cent of the total plantings and is grown predominantly in the Stellenbosch District.

CABERNET FRANC

Though somewhat austere in character, wines made from Cabernet Franc are nevertheless softer than those made from its cousin Cabernet Sauvignon, which is generally considered the nobler cultivar. Wines containing a high proportion of both cultivars are hard and rigorous when young and need ample time in which to develop their mature complexities of rich bouquet and flavour.

Both Cabernets blended together always produce a harmonious wine, particularly if, as is usually the case in Bordeaux, Merlot is also used. Unlike Cabernet Sauvignon, Cabernet Franc seems to be well-suited to both hot and cooler regions, producing its most typical wines in the latter. In such cooler areas it ripens early, whereas Cabernet Sauvignon might, in the same micro-climate, not ripen properly. This is one of the reasons Cabernet Franc is more popular than the nobler cultivar in St Emilion. It is also found in the Midi and the Anjou-Saumur region of the Loire Valley where about 10 000 hectares are planted, much the same area as in Bordeaux. Cabernet Franc is a more prolific bearer than Cabernet Sauvignon, one of the reasons for its popularity in Italy and Chile. It is also extensively planted in Bulgaria, Hungary, Romania and Yugoslavia.

In South Africa only about 200 000 vines are planted, mainly in the Stellenbosch area. Rot seldom occurs in this noble cultivar, which is a vigorous grower, but oidium can be a serious problem, attacking the leaves late in the season. It is fairly resistant to wind.

PINOT NOIR

The finest wines made from Pinot Noir have been produced in France, in the Department of Burgundy known as the Côte d'Or (the slope of gold), a thin, 60-kilometre north-to-south strip of superb vineyards beginning just south of the city of Dijon and sloping down to the charming village of Chagny. This ideal southern slope provides everything that Pinot Noir needs – the required sunlight exposure, climatic conditions and well-drained soils for this temperamental, early-ripening variety.

Botanists recorded accurate descriptions of Pinot Noir as far back as the first century. Even the invading Romans wrote of the luxuriant wines that were produced from the grape and in the fifteenth century the reigning Duke of Burgundy ensured its supremacy by banning the Gamay cultivar from the northern Burgundy district, even though it was hardier and more prolific than Pinot Noir.

Two-thirds of all champagne is made from Pinot Noir, which has a 'black' skin but a white pulp – the must is drained off immediately after pressing to ensure that it is not coloured. Its reputation for quality has led to its being planted in many other countries – northern Italy, Switzerland, Austria, Germany, Hungary, North and South America and South Africa, but in all these countries it has yet to demonstrate the greatness it has achieved in France. A sensitive and rather temperamental vine, which prefers the cooler regions, it remains a great challenge to wine makers outside France.

The exact date of the original introduction of Pinot Noir to South Africa is unknown, although by the late 1920s it was grown by an immigrant German painter-turned-wine maker, Georg Canitz, at Ou Muratie, his Estate in the Stellenbosch District. The bunches of Pinot Noir are normally small and compact and its berries are small, sweet and juicy with a thick tough skin which, when fully ripe, turns to a deep violet-blue or black. Under the right conditions, it ripens in the early mid-season, giving a good sugar content and excellent acids when the climate is not too warm. A noble variety, it is a medium-to-low volume producer and is reasonably resistant to disease, excluding downy mildew. In this country plantings are still small – less than one per cent of the total. After a rather shaky start, the improvement in the local Pinot Noir has been most encouraging considering that the oldest vines, using new improved plant material, are not even ten years old. (Older South African clones of the cultivar often proved unsatisfactory and have mostly been replaced. They were prone to millerandage, that is, to the formation of small berries among the larger, making for a looser bunch of grapes.) There are 17 South African Pinot Noir wines available at present. There are about three-quarters of a million Pinot Noir vines planted, making up a mere 0,25 per cent of total vineyard area.

Cabernet Franc

Pinot Noir

CINSAUT

The Cinsaut cultivar (previously known in South Africa as Hermitage) originated in France, in the vineyards around the small town of Tain-l'Hermitage on the banks of the Rhône. The town takes its name from the sharply rising hill which towers over it and on which once stood a hermitage of great renown. For it was to this spot in the thirteenth century that a French knight named Gaspard de Sterinburg retired from a life of war and crusades to become a hermit, dividing his time between religious meditation and the cultivation of his vineyards on the slopes of the hill. His wine soon became famous and acquired the name of the hill on which it was grown.

Its renown lasted through to the nineteenth century. Along with most of the European vineyards, however, those of the Hermitage hill were destroyed by phylloxera. After the epidemic they were replanted on resistant rootstock, but according to contemporary wine lovers something of the original quality of the wine had been lost, never to be recaptured.

Today little remains of the Hermitage or Cinsaut vine in the area, and the vines which now cover the hill are predominantly Syrah rather than Cinsaut. In South Africa, on the other hand, it has become one of the Cape's most planted red cultivars with an annual crop of 15,36 per cent of the total cultivated.

First introduced here in the 1850s, it was generally known within the industry as Hermitage, though the name was more commonly rendered in the Cape as 'Hermitake'. The name Cinsaut, however, was virtually unknown outside wine-making circles, although Professor Perold had identified Cinsaut and Hermitage as being one and the same. In terms of the so-called 'Crayfish Agreement', made with France in 1935, the local winemakers agreed to refrain from using French place-names such as Hermitage on their labels, although Hermitage was used up to the introduction of the Wine of Origin legislation in 1973, when the name

Cinsaut

Cinsaut began to appear on many of the local labels.

Under South African conditions Cinsaut is a heavy bearer and is also the most profitable of the local wines, both of which considerations – together with its high sugar content – made it popular with early growers. Unfortunately, when grown for bulk, Cinsaut makes a wine which is thin and light in colour, as well as somewhat lacking in character. Only when grown correctly does it give the palate-pleasing smooth wines of varying fullness of body. On trellises in the irrigation areas it produces insufficient colour and can be used for light wine which must be drunk early or distilled for brandy-making. In the cooler coastal regions, grown as a bush vine with an average yield, it makes an interesting red wine. It is also used for the making of rosé wine.

Owing to its relatively poor colour a percentage of the juice is often drained away at time of crushing so that the skins are concentrated in a lesser amount of juice, resulting, with fermentation, in a

deeper colour. When fermented for a longer time on the skins a very pleasant, fragrant and soft early drinking light red wine is produced. If the vine is pruned to give a much smaller crop and the fruit allowed to generate a higher sugar content, medium-full to very dark and full-bodied wines can be made; these stand well on their own, but can also be used for blending with other high-quality red wines. Some good ports have also been made entirely from Cinsaut.

Thus in general, though they can be grown for bulk, the best Cinsaut wines are made from grapes grown on bush vines on unirrigated hillsides and pruned to prevent excessive yields. Many a palate prefers the almost sweetish character (although the wines are dry) of these well-made Cinsauts to the stronger-flavoured Cabernet; it also functions well as a supporter in Cabernet blends or in partnership with Shiraz.

Over 25 million Cinsaut vines are planted in all areas of the Cape, making up nine per cent of total plantings compared to about 16 per cent nine years ago.

PINOTAGE

This famous cultivar, the first grape developed in South Africa to prove a commercial success, originated from a cross made in 1925 by Professor Abraham Perold. In that year he bred crosses of two cultivars, Pinot Noir and Cinsaut, or Hermitage (as it was then called), to produce a new vine which he named Pinotage, taking an element from the names of each of the newcomer's parents.

The choice of two such parents was based on consideration of their qualities, which Perold hoped to bring together in the new

vine. The Cinsaut, a relatively well-established and trustworthy cultivar in the local vineyards, would bring its high productivity to the match, while the Pinot Noir, one of the great traditional noble vines of Burgundy, would contribute its complexity, richness of flavour and bouquet and colour – and this notwithstanding its none-too-steady performance in the local vineyards at the time: a newcomer to the country, it was prone to non-setting, or millerandage, and old clones of the variety were susceptible to leaf-roll virus.

Perold himself could hardly have anticipated the future success of his creation. The new vine proved to be an earlier-ripening variety than most other cultivars, and so had much in its favour from the outset. Its ability to mature early in the vintage meant that it could be harvested before the other varieties, thus stretching the period of the vintage. It gave good colour, high sugar, and a reasonable if not outstanding acid content. Depending upon its pruning and trellising, it could also be a good yielder, a factor generally approved by early growers when volume seemed more important than quality. Today, however, it has been established that if stringently pruned, Pinotage will give a smaller crop, but one which, if allowed to mature fully on the vine, will yield a truly remarkable wine, with a unique and immediately recognizable personality of its own.

Being generally a light-to medium-bodied wine, a quality Pinotage is ready for drinking sooner than a quality Cabernet Sauvignon, for example. On the other hand, it can develop into a very interesting wine if aged in bottle. When young it possesses a very definite nose which, while intriguing to some, is strange to others; it disappears with time, leaving a delightfully fruity and full-flavoured wine.

Developed in 1925, Pinotage today makes up some two-and-a-half per cent of the vines grown in the country. About six-and-a-half million Pinotage vines are planted. It is grown to a greater or lesser extent in almost every area, but the bulk of almost half the crop comes from the Stellenbosch district.

Although Pinotage was developed in South Africa, it has not remained confined entirely to the local vineyards. Cuttings have found their way to many experimental plots as widely spread as Zimbabwe, Germany, California and New Zealand – in recent years New Zealand Pinotage wines have found a small market in the United States.

SHIRAZ

The origins of the Shiraz cultivar are obscure, though it is believed that they were in the ancient Persian town of that name. It was mentioned frequently by classical writers, who often conferred legendary qualities upon it, and it was encountered by Marco Polo on his travels to the Far East. He described how the vine was grown over the Persian houses, the buildings being used, in effect, as a kind of trellis. Following the prohibition by Mohammed on the making of or drinking of alcohol, the cultivation of Shiraz for this purpose fell away. Thereafter, grapes were grown only on a small scale for consumption as fresh fruit; today viniculture in Iran concentrates on a large table grape production and growing Sultana grapes.

From ancient Persia the vine set out on its travels, gathering on its way a rich harvest of synonyms, including Syrah, Schiras, Sirac, Syra, Sirah, Petite Sirah, Serenne, Serine, Biaune, Hignin Noir, and Marsanne Noir. Its establishment in France came early, when the Roman Emperor Probus made the planting of Syrah compulsory in the province of Gaul, though later legends gave the credit for its introduction to France to the returning Crusaders, or even laid it at the dusty door of the hermit of Hermitage himself.

Shiraz was brought to the Cape at an early stage, but it was never widely cultivated, although excellent dessert and red table wines could be made from it. It proved very susceptible to 'Shiraz disease', a disorder similar to corky bark which killed thousands of the vines. It was also prone to wind damage and therefore needed costly trellising and cane pruning.

It has never been a dominant cultivar, but the development of selected, virus-tested clones of Shiraz has to a degree improved its status, an advance reflected in its use in blends with Cabernet and Cinsaut. With the move towards specific varietal wines, matured Shiraz has become a sought-after wine in its own right.

With its long, loose, medium-sized bunches of small, oval berries, ripening about mid-season, its quality depends to a degree upon where it is grown. In the cool climate near the coast this cultivar yields very agreeable, well-coloured, medium-full wines, with a typical smoky, scented bouquet which makes them easy to identify.

The cooler areas of Constantia, Durbanville and Firgrove are well known for their outstanding, rich, deep-coloured Shiraz wine with a fruity character and fairly high acidity.

The amount of Shiraz grown in South Africa is still small, with the little more than 700 hectares currently under production yielding 0,75 per cent of the total national crop. More than half the total of just over two million vines is grown in the Stellenbosch District. Perhaps its greatest percentage concentration today is in Australia, where it is also known as Red Hermitage.

Pinotage

Shiraz

107

PONTAC

Many early references in the literature of Cape wine speak of Pontac as a vine peculiar to South Africa. This claim has since proved to be false, but the cultivar nevertheless retains the distinction of being one of the first to be found on local shores, if not during Van Riebeeck's time, then certainly by the time of the Van der Stels. As early as 1772 the ship *De Hoop*, after depositing a corps of militia at the Cape, returned to the Netherlands with a cargo which included an oddly named Red Steen and a leaguer of Pontac (which fetched a substantial 166 guilders as compared with a low 88 guilders for the same amount of Cape brandy).

Since the making of this Pontac coincided with the advent of the Huguenot immigration during Simon van der Stel's governorship, it has been speculated that they may have brought cuttings of the vine with them, perhaps naming it after the famous Pontac family, who were important vineyard owners in the Médoc.

In the local vineyards this cultivar came to be valued as a producer of high quality grapes and in the days of Constantia's hegemony it formed an important component of the estate's famous wines. The Cloete family sold a rich red dessert wine under the name of Pontac, which by the mid-nineteenth century was regularly considered the best of the Cape wines –

according to one local newspaper of the day, the *South African Commercial Advertiser*, it was '. . . almost, if not altogether, equal to European wine'.

Its prestige lasted into the present century and within living memory. Many old-timers nostalgically remember the Pontacs of 50 years ago: and it was also considered indispensable in giving body and superb colour to Karoo port. Remembered too are the magnificent matured dessert wines in which Pontac was the principal element and which left the legacy of a long, lingering after-taste.

Pontac has now all but disappeared from the Cape's vineyards, only 39 000 vines existing at present. A shy and light bearer, its vines have tended in recent decades to develop problems, which were not known previously, particularly in the more humid areas such as Constantia and Stellenbosch. A virulent form of the vinegar fly found its way into the pedicel end of the tightly-packed bunches, souring the grapes and making them unsuitable for red wines of high quality. Because of the wine's high volatile acidity it was also unsuitable for rebate brandy distillation, and thus tended to end up as distilling wine, a poor fate for a noble grape.

In an attempt to save one of the Cape's oldest and now most neglected cultivars, Professor C.H. Theron stressed the need for

Pontac

strict selection. During the past two decades this has resulted in clones superior to those which featured in the old commercial vineyards. Professor C.J. Orffer also produced an interesting new cross of Pontac and Cabernet which has scored well with the experimental wines made from it. Thus even if the Pontac cultivar itself does not survive into the future, perhaps some of its character may be preserved through its descendants.

MERLOT

Merlot is one of the very old varieties in Europe, and one that gives soft, full-bodied wines of a distinct character which mature quickly. It ripens earlier than either Cabernet Sauvignon or Cabernet Franc, and its thick, blue-black skin results in a wine of a good, deep colour.

It is found in most grape-growing

countries, but rarely to any significant extent although it is very important in Bordeaux. It is certainly not held in the same esteem as the Cabernets with which it is often blended to soften the steely edge of the Cabernet and to reduce its ageing time.

About 650 000 vines are currently grown

in the Cape, mostly in the Stellenbosch and Paarl areas. Like Cabernet Franc and Malbec, Merlot is one of the few Bordeaux grapes that is pleasant to eat – as is evidenced by the local grape pickers in the heat of the vintage time. Quite a prolific bearer, its quality suffers dramatically if it is allowed to bear too large a crop.

MALBEC

Malbec, one of the old traditional varieties, is one of the lesser grapes of Bordeaux, but one which contributes good colour and bouquet. It is normally included in a blend only in small quantities. It has settled in many of the world's winelands, particularly in Argentina, where it has

become the most extensively grown variety and is the backbone of their considerable wine production.

It is not yet available in the Cape in any appreciable quantity, but as more vines come into production it is being blended with Cabernet Sauvignon to complement

that variety with its colour, bouquet and taste. It also makes a pleasant wine in its own right.

In the local vineyards the largest concentration of the few thousand existing Malbec vines are found around Stellenbosch and particularly in the Paarl District.

GAMAY

A number of Europe's classic cultivars which are grown in South Africa have not excelled as they have in their homelands or in other wine-making countries. Among these reluctant travellers is Gamay.

It is a native of Burgundy where, traditionally, Pinot Noir is grown on the

hillsides for quality and Gamay on the lower slopes for quantity: but where it is grown on the hill slopes, as in the Beaujolais region, it responds with a better-quality wine.

In the Cape, Gamay experienced mixed fortunes, having been planted by

numerous growers from the 1920s onwards, only to be removed to make way for the heavier bearing and more consistent Cinsaut. Odd plantings survived, but the only winery to bottle a wine under the name Gamay was Verdun, which has since ceased to bottle any wine.

Merlot

Malbec

Gamay

However, when Günter Brözel of Nederburg launched a nouveau-style Gamay at the 1985 Nederburg Auction lunch, only 55 days after it was harvested, he revived the interest in this cultivar. The following year there was a scramble for fruit from existing vines and a sprinkling of Gamay labels appeared on the market. New vines have now been planted in the Districts of Constantia, Durbanville, Stellenbosch and Paarl, boosting the population to over 40 000 vines, and Gamay continues to be planted to meet the increasing demand for nouveau-style wines in general, and from this cultivar in particular.

GRENACHE

Spanish in origin Grenache migrated around the world in the wake of the Spanish conquistadors – one of their gentler gifts to mankind. Today it has spread not only to Argentina and Chile, but also to Australia, California, North Africa and South Africa, where it is still used in sweet, fortified wines.

In France its clear pink colour has made it one of her most sought-after rosés, and when chilled it makes a light, refreshing and thirst-quenching wine. In the Cape, as on the Alto Douro of Portugal, Grenache was used traditionally for port, even before Professor Perold imported Grenache vines from Spain and France in 1910 to establish the provenance of the local variety.

The cultivar was never particularly popular among local wine makers. It ripens in mid-season and gives a substantial quantity of wine, but it lacks the vigour demonstrated by its relatives in Europe and the New World. Its wines, moreover, lack colour, as well as acidity and tannin, and their flavour generally lacks distinction. These drawbacks are compounded in the vineyard where it is choosey about its site, and by a susceptibility to downy mildew and mealy bug, though on the credit side it is reasonably resistant to oidium, anthracnose, wind and drought.

Thus, Grenache is grown to a very limited extent in the Cape, making up only 0,1 per cent of the local plantings – just over a quarter of a million vines, almost half of which are in the Paarl District, and a quarter in the Olifants River District, with even less in the Malmesbury and Worcester areas.

Grenache

Cultivars used in the production of port

In South Africa, port-style wines have been made from early times. In the nineteenth century their production was encouraged by that enthusiastic port-drinking nation, the British, and the demand continued through to the years before the Second World War, when a number of new varieties were imported from the Douro region of Portugal in an attempt to enhance the quality of the local ports. They included such varieties as Alvarelhão, the prolific Bastardo, Donzellinho do Castello, and Tourigo, which, as both a reasonable producer and giving good colour and aroma, is the best all-rounder among the Douro varieties.

Since 1945, further attempts have been made to improve the local ports, in particular by Professors Perold and Theron, who imported further cultivars together with better selections of existing varieties. Extensive experiments were made with these vines, which included such exotically titled types as Mourisco Tinto, Tinta Barocca, Cornifesto, Tinta Francisca, Tinto Roriz, Souzão and Malvasia Rey.

Most of the cultivars introduced continue to be grown, but on a much reduced scale – they now amount to less than 0,5 per cent of the total vines in the Cape winelands.

Moreover, many of them are no longer used for port, but instead are blended with dry red wines to add a touch of the unusual. Among them are a number which make the statistics and manage to have their voices heard above the crowd.

Recently, however, the production of good port along the lines of Portuguese vintage port is enjoying something of a revival in the Cape, albeit on a small scale. With the more relaxed attitude of the authorities regarding the importation of new cultivars, fresh vine stocks are being introduced to the Cape vineyards, which should encourage the increase in port production.

SOUZÃO

Only about 80 000 Souzão vines are still grown locally, mainly in the Stellenbosch, Paarl and Swartland Districts. A traditional port cultivar deriving from the Douro and Minho regions of Portugal, it makes a natural wine of an intense dark colour, a deep red bordering on black, and with a high fruit acid content which gives it good potential for maturation. Though Souzão still has a limited use for port, its main use is in blends with other red wines.

TINTA BAROCCA

When the Stellenbosch-Elsenburg College of Agriculture and the KWV conducted a series of experiments over a decade or more to find the most promising port varieties, Tinta Barocca proved to be one of the best under local conditions. This resulted in a great deal more Tinta Barocca being planted than almost all the other rival varieties put together.

With the decline of the port market, the cultivar was diverted for the making of a dry red wine, though, when over-ripe and shrivelled, it continues to make an

Tinta Barocca

Souzão

excellent port, and one which matures with great benefit. Its natural cultivar wines are well-coloured, medium-full and characteristic in style, with an average maturation potential.

Tinta Barocca is grown mainly in the Stellenbosch, Paarl, and Malmesbury areas, with a total of 1,7 million vines making up 0,6 per cent of the total plantings.

Other cultivars

DISTILLING WINE CULTIVARS

While many white wine cultivars are grown both for their varietal wine potential and for the more traditional use of distilling wine, a number of others are retained in the winelands specifically for distilling wine purposes. The following are some of the most important of these.

Raisin Blanc, which totals more than 6,5 million vines, is an old South African grape which has been identified with the Servan Blanc of the French vineyards; its light and generally straightforward wine is largely used for brandy distilling. Canaan, which yields very large bunches of grapes, is used for the same purpose. This cultivar has reduced from about 5,2 million vines in 1983 to 2,6 million vines in 1987. Trebbiano, called Ugni Blanc in the

Canaan

Raisin Blanc

south of France, is also a copious producer, mostly used for distilling but also occasionally for blending. Some 1,7 million Trebbiano vines are now grown, mostly in the Breede River area. Sultana, or

Thompson's Seedless, is a famous raisin grape, widely grown from the early nineteenth century onwards; much of the wine made from the 13 million vines currently in production goes for distilling.

White Muscadel

THE MUSCAT GROUP

The Muscat vines are subgenera of the *Vitis* group. Their best-known and most versatile member is Muscat d'Alexandrie, better known locally as Hanepoot. Others include White Muscadel, with 1,3 million vines planted, and Red Muscadel, an important component of the old Constantia wines, originating as a mutation of White Muscadel. It is grown in much larger quantities than its progenitor, with a total of 2,3 million vines, going to make a characteristic, often sweet wine.

Old cultivars, long established in Europe and other vine-growing areas, are being tried out in the Cape vineyards. At the same time new and experimental varieties, both from home and abroad, are systematically tested, though only a few are likely to become commercially viable.

The entire procedure regarding the importation of new vines from other parts of the world to revitalize South African vineyards is undergoing scrutiny by the Commission of Inquiry headed by Mr Chris Kloppers, retired president of the Northern Transvaal Regional Court, assisted by Professor Chris Orffer, retired from Stellenbosch University. The present lengthy procedure of quarantine and eventual propagation and distribution of the approved material through the various official bodies is sure to be improved and streamlined, as long as the overseas source is an acceptable one. This should bring dramatic developments in the Cape vineyards.

The Klopper Commission of Inquiry was originally set up to investigate the alleged illegal importation of the cultivars Chardonnay, Olasz Riesling, Pinot Gris and Auxerrois, and the varietal purity of the illegal material.

Many hectares of established Auxerrois vines, originally thought to be Chardonnay, had to be uprooted. This is deplorable as the vine produced an excellent wine which had already been accepted by the South African consumer, albeit not under its own name. The vast

expense of this operation will eventually find its way through to the consumer.

Locally developed cultivars produced by Professor Chris Orffer such as Weldra, are being planted in various areas to test their acceptability. Some of the more recently introduced cultivars from Europe have proved their worth and have become acceptable to the South African wine drinker, but some are still not all that readily available. These include Nemes Furmint, a new clone of Furmint, a well-known Hungarian cultivar used to make Tokay wines; and also from Hungary, Hárslevelü, which has proved a reliable all-rounder locally and is now commercially planted in both the coastal and inland regions. From Portugal, Fernão Pires has made its mark as a cultivar of interest (especially in the Nederburg Auction wine Private Bin D207).

Minority red cultivars include Alicante Bouschet (one of the rare red grapes with red juice), Carignan, a much-grown vine in the south of France, where it contributes a high percentage of the *vin ordinaire* of the region, and Zinfandel, a leading Californian variety which gives a good, medium-coloured red wine when handled carefully. A recent cross from Germany, Heroldrebe, is still experimental and to date it has yielded a wine of only average quality. Small numbers of other varieties such as Ruby Cabernet and Emerald Riesling are to be found scattered across the vineyards of the Cape.

The Winelands of South Africa

Wine is a product of the land and its people. It brings together in its complex make-up all the qualities of soil and climate, the personalities of the individual cultivars, the specific effects of each year's contribution of sun and rain, and the brooding creativity of the individual wine master. For the wine lover it is these qualities, as they are reflected in all the colours and odours of the wine, which provide its intellectual and emotional richness over and above the sensuous pleasures of tasting and drinking.

Each individual wine fits into a larger picture, which is that of the reality of winelands life. This life, of course, is as multifarious and colourful as that of any human society. In South Africa it has, however, been formalized and organized both in theory and in practice in the Wine of Origin legislation.

This came about during the early 1970s, and was developed in the local context from systems of long standing in the winelands of Europe where the relationship of wine to the land and its human society has been a profound part of the culture of countries such as France and Germany. In regions such as Bordeaux and Burgundy such systems have become highly developed, the contrasts of individual vineyards and *crus* being ramified by the vagaries of the French climate.

South Africa's Wine of Origin legislation divided the winelands into a number of official 'Areas', now called 'Districts'. To a great extent these reflected traditional divisions. From the early days of settlement different areas of the western Cape came to acquire their own character, both social and topographical, and to a

remarkable degree these divisions survive today, not only in Divisional Council boundaries, but in the formal divisions of the winelands as well.

There are at present 12 Districts. To an extent the list follows the order of historic settlement, from Constantia to Durbanville, from Stellenbosch and Paarl to Tulbagh, the Swartland, Piketberg, Worcester, Robertson, Swellendam, Overberg and Douglas.

A number of the Districts have further subdivisions called Wards: Simonsberg-Stellenbosch in the Stellenbosch District, Franschhoek in Paarl, and the Walker Bay Ward of the Overberg District are examples of these.

All these individual areas make up the modern map of the South African winelands (see overleaf), and the concept of Origin, as it can be followed 'from soil to glass', relates both to each area and to their sum. A number of groupings of the Districts, however, are important both to the wine maker and the wine lover. These 'Regions' are based on climate and geography.

The first of these groupings, usually called the **Coastal Region,** includes the Districts of Constantia, Durbanville, Stellenbosch, Paarl, Tulbagh and Swartland, which together make up the long crescent of land between the Atlantic Ocean and False Bay and the Cape folded mountains. Over much of this area the prevailing wind from the sea helps to cool the vines in this generally hot climate, leading to a better quality of grape and, of course, a better wine. The rainfall here, too, is relatively high, so that many of the vineyards may be grown with either a minimum of irrigation or with none at all, thereby promoting a rich, slow-growing crop. Thus, in general, much of the local high-quality natural wines are made from grapes grown in the Coastal Region.

The **Breëriviervallei** (or Breede River Valley) **Region** embraces the great run of the Breede River valley, from Worcester through to Robertson. Here, and throughout other wine-farming areas of the hinterland, hot conditions prevail in which grapes will generally not grow at all without some irrigation to supplement the generally meagre rainfall. With such irrigation, however, vines grow extremely well in the lime-rich soil; sometimes too well, for the speed of growth makes for a grape of high sugar content but with a sacrifice of the flavour constituents needed for the best kinds of wine. Thus, much of the country's distilling wine and fortified wine comes from this Region, though, increasingly, the inland wine makers are finding ways of making good quality natural wines in what were traditionally regarded as adverse conditions.

The **Boberg Region** covers the catchment areas of the Berg River and the Klein Berg River, and comprises the Districts of Paarl and Tulbagh, but only with regard to fortified wines. As far as natural wines are concerned, the Paarl and Tulbagh Districts fall in the Coastal Region.

The **Klein-Karroo Region** has no Districts and only one Ward, that of Montagu. It includes the towns of Oudtshoorn and Calitzdorp.

The **Olifantsrivier Region** also has no Districts but does have Wards. These are the Wards of Spuitdrift, Koekenaap, Lutzville-vallei and Vredendal.

The Districts of Swellendam, Piketberg, Overberg and Douglas are not included in any Regions, and while the Overberg has a

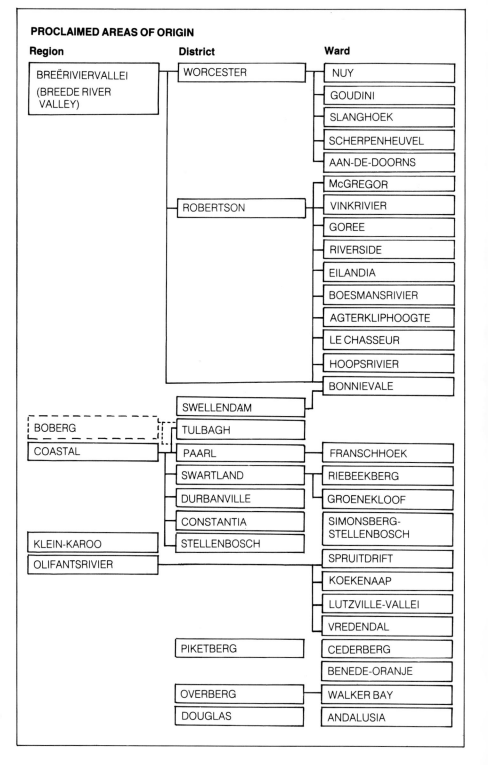

PROCLAIMED AREAS OF ORIGIN

Region	District	Ward
BREËRIVIERVALLEI (BREEDE RIVER VALLEY)	WORCESTER	NUY
		GOUDINI
		SLANGHOEK
		SCHERPENHEUVEL
		AAN-DE-DOORNS
	ROBERTSON	McGREGOR
		VINKRIVIER
		GOREE
		RIVERSIDE
		EILANDIA
		BOESMANSRIVIER
		AGTERKLIPHOOGTE
		LE CHASSEUR
		HOOPSRIVIER
		BONNIEVALE
	SWELLENDAM	
BOBERG	TULBAGH	
COASTAL	PAARL	FRANSCHHOEK
	SWARTLAND	RIEBEEKBERG
	DURBANVILLE	GROENEKLOOF
	CONSTANTIA	SIMONSBERG-STELLENBOSCH
KLEIN-KAROO	STELLENBOSCH	
OLIFANTSRIVIER		SPRUITDRIFT
		KOEKENAAP
		LUTZVILLE-VALLEI
		VREDENDAL
	PIKETBERG	CEDERBERG
		BENEDE-ORANJE
	OVERBERG	WALKER BAY
	DOUGLAS	ANDALUSIA

Ward, Walker Bay, there are Wards which stand on their own, without relation to either District or Region. These are the Wards of Cederberg, Benede-Oranje and Andalusia.

Notes
- The Ward of Bonnievale lies mostly in the Robertson District, but part of the Ward lies in the Swellendam District.

- Simonsberg-Stellenbosch is so named to identify it as being the Stellenbosch side of the Simonsberg.
- Boberg Region is only recognized for fortified wines.
- The Wolseley part of the Tulbagh District is included in the Breëriviervallei Region and the rest of the Tulbagh District in the Coastal Region. (In the case of fortified wines, though, Tulbagh District falls in the Boberg Region.)

The Estate principle and the Wine of origin seal

The concept of Origin as it was legally applied in the local winelands found form in the principle of the Estate. At its simplest, this means that the farmer both grows his own grapes, and makes his own wine from them. These two activities must take place within the boundaries of the Estate; in other words, the relationship between wine and land must be direct. Together with this provision went a number of others regarding cellar equipment and procedures, which had to be up to a rigorous standard before a farm could be granted Estate status. The regulations did not cover bottling or distribution, which many Estate farmers prefer to leave in the hands of a large wholesaler; nor did they in any way limit the number or type of cultivars grown or the kind of wine made. At present there are 73 registered Estate farmers in South Africa, out of a total of about 6 000 wine grape growers.

The Wine of Origin Seal is the aspect of the Wine of Origin legislation most familiar to the 'wine buyer in the street', and most likely to baffle him. The responsibility of the Wine and Spirit Board, it is affixed to some wines that are marketed. Its purpose is to provide a guarantee of those aspects of the wine related to the Origin concept. These are the area of Origin, the vintage year, the cultivar, and whether or not the farm concerned has Estate status.

Where applicable all this information is included by the wine maker, with all appropriate flourish, on the main label on the bottle. The official seal simply confirms the veracity of the information by means of coloured bands.

It is interesting that wines with the Wine of Origin Seal, important as they are, account for only some ten per cent of good wine made in South Africa. Many of the most popular blended wines, therefore, do not carry the seal.

COLOUR-KEY TO MAPS

Throughout the following chapters the maps for each District are graded in as many as five colours, from light green to mauve, to give an indication of altitude. Shading has also been used to enhance the effect of contour.

The Wine of Origin Seal

This guarantees that claims made on the label relating to origin, vintage and/or cultivar are certifiably true.

Origin (Blue Band) – certifies that 100% of the wine derives from the indicated Region, District or Ward, in this instance from the Constantia District.

Vintage (Red Band) – certifies that at least 75% of the wine is made from the grapes harvested in the indicated year, in this instance 1979.

Cultivar (Green Band) – certifies that the wine contains the required legal minimum percentage of the cultivar claimed, in this instance Shiraz, and is characteristic of that cultivar in appearance, smell and taste.

Estate – certifies that the wine is made on the Estate claimed, in this instance Groot Constantia, and from grapes grown on the Estate. Bottling may take place elsewhere.

Superior – as from March 1982 wines certified as Wine of Origin Superior (WOS) by the Wine and Spirit Board have been given a distinctive gold-backed seal (prior to this date Superior certified wines carried the plain Wine of Origin Seal). Superior certification may only be given for wines of origin and is the only quality grading that may be claimed for a South African wine. Originally in the case of WOS, 100% cultivar was required if a cultivar claim was made. In December 1977, however, this was reduced to 75%. A non-cultivar wine can also be certified WOS.

The vertical number is an official identification number and has little relevance for the consumer.

The Label

For Wine of Origin certification the producer of the wine has to provide certain information on the label.

A Region, District or Ward of Origin.

B Vintage year.

C Name of the producer, i.e. Estate or Co-operative.

D Cultivar.

A
B

C

D

ROGGEVELD MTS

Vanrhynsdorp

Vredendal
22
Klawer

O
L
I
F
A
N
T
S
R
I
V
I
E
R

Clanwilliam

C
E
D
A
R
B
E
R
G

Doring River

Citrusdal
21

P
I
K
E
B
E
R
G

Aurora

N7

Velddrif

Vredenburg

Piketberg

Olifants River

Saldanha

Langebaan

Porterville

Moorreesburg

Berg River

S W A R T L A N D

Gouda

TULBAGH

TULBAGH

Ceres

Touws River

Voëlvlei Dam
20

Wolseley

Riebeek Kasteel

MALMESBURY
19

De Doorns

K

W O R C E S T E R

Wellington

Rawsonville
4

L A N G E B E R G

Montagu

PAARL

PAARL

5
6
7

ROBBEN ISLAND

DURBANVILLE

N1

8
15

Robertson

9
10
11

Durbanville

CAPE TOWN

STELLENBOSCH

Franschhoek

13
12

ROBERTSON

Barrydale

STELLENBOSCH

14

McGregor

18

Bonnievale

L A N G

CONSTANTIA

Villiersdorp

16
17

SWELLENDAM

Theewaterskloof Dam

Riviersonderend

Breede River

FALSE BAY

Somerset West

Grabouw

S W E L L E N D A M

Bot River

Riviersonderend

CAPE POINT

N2

Caledon

O V E R B E R G

Hermanus
3

Bredasdorp

Cap

A
T
L
A
N
T
I
C

O
C
E
A
N

Gansbaai

I

40   0   20   40   60   80
Km

114

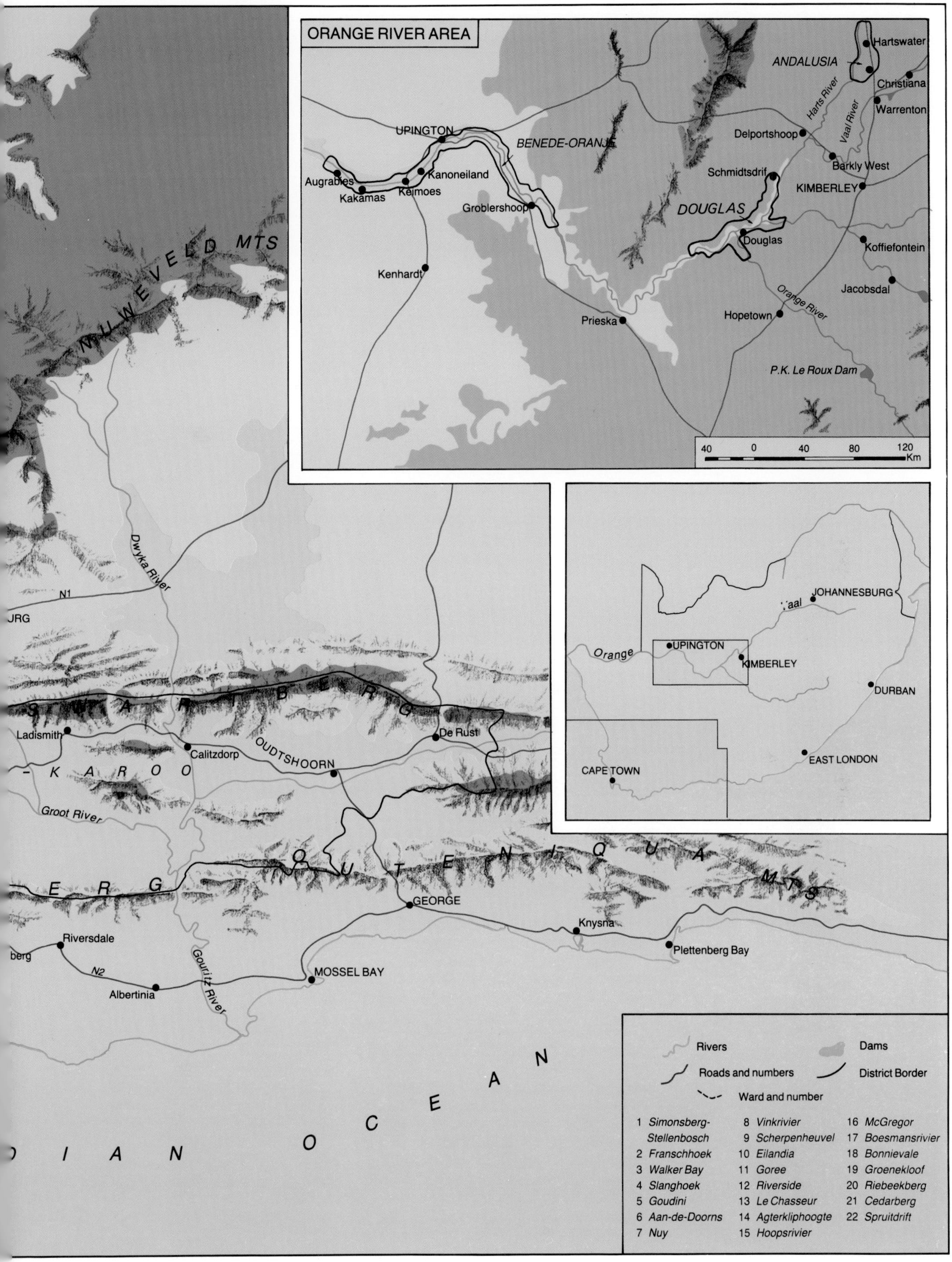

ORANGE RIVER AREA

ANDALUSIA
Hartswater
Christiana
Warrenton
BENEDE-ORANJE
UPINGTON
Delportshoop
Barkly West
Augrabies
Kanoneiland
Schmidtsdrif
KIMBERLEY
Kakamas
Keimoes
DOUGLAS
Groblershoop
Douglas
Koffiefontein
Kenhardt
Jacobsdal
Prieska
Hopetown
P.K. Le Roux Dam

Harts River
Vaal River
Orange River

40 0 40 80 120
Km

JOHANNESBURG
Vaal
Orange
UPINGTON
KIMBERLEY
DURBAN
CAPE TOWN
EAST LONDON

NUWEVELD MTS
Dwyka River
N1
JRG
SWARTBERG
Ladismith
De Rust
KAROO
Calitzdorp
OUDTSHOORN
Groot River
OUTENIQUA MTS
ERG
GEORGE
Knysna
Riversdale
Plettenberg Bay
berg
N2
Gouritz River
Albertinia
MOSSEL BAY

INDIAN OCEAN

Rivers		Dams
Roads and numbers		District Border
Ward and number		

1 Simonsberg-   8 Vinkrivier   16 McGregor
   Stellenbosch   9 Scherpenheuvel   17 Boesmansrivier
2 Franschhoek   10 Eilandia   18 Bonnievale
3 Walker Bay   11 Goree   19 Groenekloof
4 Slanghoek   12 Riverside   20 Riebeekberg
5 Goudini   13 Le Chasseur   21 Cedarberg
6 Aan-de-Doorns   14 Agterkliphoogte   22 Spruitdrift
7 Nuy   15 Hoopsrivier

115

CONSTANTIA

CONSTANTIA DISTRICT

V an Riebeeck's first modest vineyard, his nursery near the shores of Table Bay and the Company vineyards at Rondebosch and on the *Wijnbergen*, have long since vanished, engulfed by time and the expanding city of Cape Town. In the Peninsula, only one wine-making area, Constantia, survives into the late twentieth century, an island in the midst of encroaching urban development. Although the vineyards of Constantia are today much reduced, it is most gratifying that, in the last decade, the new owners of two old farms that were badly neglected and run down have spent vast sums of money on revitalizing them and making them model wine farms (see Buitenverwachting and Klein Constantia).

Constantia District is ideally situated as it has a mild climate which is regarded by wine makers as one of the most suitable of its kind in the Cape winelands. The vineyards are bounded on the west by the 600 metre-high Constantiaberg which

Grande Dame of the Cape winelands, the Groot Constantia homestead presides over the autumn-hued vineyards of the valley where a proud wine-making tradition reaches back to the late 1600s.

rises behind the vineyards, and to the south-east by the waters of the Indian Ocean in False Bay less than eight kilometres away. The vineyards face the warmth of the morning sun and enjoy the shade of the mountain in the late afternoon. The average temperature during the growing season, which is between September and March, is 18 - 19 °C. In this setting the dry summers of the Mediterranean-type climate of the Cape are softened by the influence of two oceans, the Indian and the Atlantic which is just behind the Constantiaberg. During the dormant winter season the vines receive most of their rainfall of about 900 millimetres; some of this does, however, fall during the summer months.

After the death in 1712 of Simon van der Stel, the first Governor of the new Dutch colony at the southern tip of Africa, the Constantia Estate was divided into three large areas: Groot Constantia, Klein Constantia and Bergvliet. Groot Constantia was later further subdivided, the subdivision, confusingly, being called Klein Constantia. The property originally called Klein Constantia later came to be called Hoop op Constantia, the name it retains to this day. Bergvliet was also later subdivided, a portion becoming Buitenverwachting.

Van der Stel had created the Estate of Constantia as the place to which he intended to retire at the end of his working days. Shrewd and acquisitive, he built up the farm piecemeal during his years in office, developing it into the largest single private vineyard in the area. Bought in 1695, at 770 hectares it was vastly out of proportion to the average grant of 12 hectares accorded to the local Free Burgher farmers. Later, he contrived to have himself granted a further 8 500 hectares of grazing rights, an area which amounted to virtually the whole of the Peninsula. The creation of the farm was crowned by the building of a palatial mansion, two storeys high and approached by a majestic avenue of trees – enough to arouse the envy of many a European prince, let alone a struggling Free Burgher farmer.

While he took advantage of his position to acquire all this property and land, Van der Stel soon proved that he had a clear idea of what he wanted to do with it. Within the limits of contemporary farming techniques, he set out to create a model farm, and in particular model vineyards, which were managed strictly in accordance with the rules laid down in the *Gardener's Manual*.

Even before making a move to secure the land for his Estate, he had baskets of soil dug up from a variety of points for analysis, and only after receiving favourable reports did he make his bid for the land. In laying out the Estate he employed the expert help of the Dutch East India Company's gardeners, including a certain Oldenland, who was reputed to be skilled in agriculture and to have a good knowledge of botany. The Governor planted oaks and other trees to act as windbreaks to shield his growing crops, including the newly planted vines. He took a close personal interest in the farm, to the extent that it finally became a distraction from his official duties at the Castle.

He personally supervised the bringing-in of the harvest, allowing the grapes to be cut only when they were fully ripe. The vines were grown mainly in bush form rather than upon trellises, so the bunches were often coated with soil and dust, and he instructed the slaves to brush this away before they took the grapes off the stalks for pressing. In an attempt to keep the grapes off the ground he introduced the use of palings on which to grow some of his vines.

All this meticulous and patient handling of the vineyards was matched by care and attention in the wine cellar, particularly in the matter of general hygiene and cleanliness – a sharp contrast to the often somewhat slovenly practices of some of the Free Burgher wine makers. The result was a wine of an aristocratic quality which presaged its future fame. When the Constantia wine was sent to Batavia it was reckoned as the highest quality yet received there (the Company's wine from the Cape had been severely criticized in the East). The 'Governor's Wine' became much sought-after, the only complaint being the limited quantities available.

As far as can be determined, these wines were made from a range of cultivars which included Palomino (White French), Hanepoot and Pontac. Having mastered the art of making natural wines in a number of different styles from these grapes, he extended his ambitions and set about the making of a sweet fortified wine similar to those which were coming into fashion in Holland and England at this time – James the Second of England had set the trend towards this full-flavoured, very sweet style of wine. In this area too, Van der Stel succeeded in making a wine which compared more than favourably with the contemporary European product. Thought to have been made from Red and White Muscadel together with some Frontignac, it was this wine to which the Governor gave the name of 'Constantia'.

The success of the wine brought visitors. One of the first of these, a vivid observer of the Colony as a whole at this period, was the Reverend Mr Valentijn, whose account of life at the Cape was published after his return to Holland. The advantage of a colonial career must have been brought home to his readers when they read his description of Van der Stel's domain and his palatial home.

'On approaching the princely mansion', he wrote, 'one first sees in front of it a large open area with 7 or 8 avenues of oak trees, widely spaced, about 200 yards long, leading up to the house. Then one comes to a very fine dwelling of two storeys . . .' Valentijn continues to described a house that was impressive by any standard, with two entrance halls, costly marble floors, galleries with high ceilings, and 18 other elegantly furnished rooms. The view from the homestead complimented its elegance. Valentijn described it as being 'matchless with its rare trees, colourful vines and other crops, plants and shrubs'. His report on the wine was equally enthusiastic.

In 1699 Van der Stel retired from public life and withdrew to his Estate. In the years after his death in 1712 (which took place not at Constantia, but in the home of a friend), little further is heard of Constantia wine. The Estate was divided into three sections originally, Groot Constantia, Bergvliet and Klein Constantia. The grazing rights to the surrounding land expired, and it was split up eventually into eight separate properties. Groot Constantia now covered an extent of some 100 hectares. A variety of owners during the course of the early eighteenth century failed to improve its fortunes or enhance its reputation. With the improvement of the general economy in the second half of the eighteenth

CONSTANTIA

Streams	Estates
Dams	Vineyards
Roads and numbers	Urban area

An aerial view of the Constantia Valley. Several new vineyards have been planted in recent years.

century, however, a new phase began. Indeed, in 1771 Bernardin de Saint-Pierre (whose most famous work, *Paul et Virginie*, was Napoleon's favourite book) paid a visit to the farm, then owned by a certain Jan Serrurier, and described the cellar with its rows of vats as 'very neat', noticing little neglect in the condition of the place.

But it was the next owner who was to recreate the legend of Constantia in all its splendour. In 1778, Serrurier sold the farm for 60 000 guilders to Hendrik Cloete. A direct descendant of Jacob Cloete van Kempen, Van Riebeeck's under-gardener at Table Bay, he took over a farm which (for all the French writer's approval) still appeared in poor condition. Fifty years later, in evidence before a commission of inquiry, Hendrik's son Pieter Lourens Cloete maintained that the farm was 'in a most ruinous state' when his father bought it, and that 'the buildings were all destroyed, and scarcely a vineyard was in bearing'. Whatever the condition of Groot

Constantia may have been when Hendrik took it over, he was to take a firm grip on its fortunes within a few years. Under Hendrik Cloete, Constantia's European reputation expanded rapidly. By 1783 he had begun exporting his wines – to the extent of 15 tons (13,6 tonnes) annually – to Europe, including to a number of its monarchs. The King of Prussia was a favourite customer, not only because of his praise of the wine, but probably because of his prompt payment for each shipment.

Few travellers visiting the Cape during this period failed to include Groot Constantia on their itineraries, the first of the steady flow of visitors which continues unabated to the present day. The flamboyant French explorer, Le Vaillant, for example, called on Cloete in 1783, referring to him as *'le prince vigneron'* – the prince of vine-dressers. The first invasion by the British occured in 1795 and the following year Percival visited the 'village' of Constantia, where he enjoyed

the 'sweet, luscious and excellent wines'. Lady Anne Barnard left a record in letter form of her visit to Cloete's domain, which includes a charming description of the crushing of the grapes in the 'wine-press hall' and also mentions Cloete's innovation of mixing and blending his wines: 'he found the wine improved by mixing them together'.

Cloete certainly appears to have had a developed instinct for the arts of life: he chose two of the most prominent designers of the day in the Cape to enlarge and beautify his homestead and decorate his great new double-storey cellar, built in the outstanding vintage year of 1791. Between them the immigrant French architect Louis Thibault and the German master carver Anton Anreith blended their neo-classical and baroque styles into the cool and tranquil atmosphere of Constantia.

In the course of the alterations the basic fabric of Van der Stel's main house was transformed into the image which is seen

Model vineyards at Klein Constantia.

today. The original ground floor was turned into an extensive series of cellars, the first floor becoming the present ground floor by means of raising and levelling the land in front of the house. The magnificent 'halsgewel', a rarity amongst the local gable designs, was adapted by Thibault from a similar design on Newlands House. As this gable was blown down in a gale in the 1820s, its outline survives only in a drawing by Barrow.

The decorations on the triangular pediment over the entrance to the massive Constantia wine cellar featured a central figure representing Ganymede, cup-bearer to Zeus, seated on an eagle – one of the attributes of the god – pouring wine from a cup. He is flanked by plaster panthers – attributes of Bacchus – and by energetically sportive bacchantes holding bunches of grapes. The background to this allegorical fantasy is made up of the outlines of wine casks.

This seemingly innocuous Mediterranean symbolism, which must have come naturally to artists hailing from two of the main wine areas of Europe, was not always appreciated. It was described by one prurient Dutch visitor, Teenstra, as 'a naked goddess who, astride an eagle in a manner calculated to give offence to one's chaster feelings, is pouring nectar to the

gods, surrounded by a multitude of bacchantes in equal nudity and lascivious postures' – the antics of plaster bacchantes were evidently taken seriously in those neo-classical days.

The prosperous Cloete certainly had an eye for good design but he also kept a clear head for business – as did his descendants, several volumes of the family accounts being preserved in the Archives. His son, also Hendrik, continued the making of his father's fine, rich, sweet wines, usually a blend of red and white grapes, often of Red and White Muscadels, with the addition of Frontignac and occasionally Pontac. John Burchell, the famous explorer, visited the farm in 1811, during the ownership of the younger Cloete. Like others before him, he commented on the 'dwarf vines' and on the fact that the grapes were left on them so long that they shrivelled and their juice turned to syrup. Both the Cloetes and their neighbours, the Colijns, employed a technique of twisting the grape bunches on the vine, so arresting the flow of sap and turning the grapes into semi-raisins.

Much comment was thus being made about Constantia, its owners and its wines. Given this wealth of curious and thirsty visitors, it seems a pity that the literary activities of the Cloete family members ended with their accounts and receipts. A

sharp eye and a sharp pen among them might have left a splendid vision of this vast gallery of humanity, from all nations and walks of life, that drifted through the cool rooms of their house and sipped the rich, warming wines in the dark and sweet-smelling chambers of the great wine cellar.

In spite of the recessions of the early nineteenth century, the farm continued to flourish on the whole and its flow of visitors remained unabated. They included the Prince of Orange, who visited the Cape in 1838 and was taken to Constantia.

But the halcyon days of Groot Constantia were almost over. Many changes were taking place in the society of the Free Burghers which cast their shadows over Constantia. Amongst them, of course, was the permanent presence of the British – the cannonballs on top of the pillars at the corner of the house are said to have been collected after the Battle of Blaauwberg which heralded the second British invasion in 1806. From the wine farmer's point of view, however, other changes had a deeper meaning and effect. The repeal of the protective tariffs by the Palmerston Government in 1861 was followed two decades later by the start of the phylloxera epidemic – the disease was first noticed a few kilometres away, near Mowbray, in 1885. As for so many of the other local farms, the epidemic marked a change in Constantia's fortunes. In 1885, after 100 years of continuous ownership, the Cloete family sold its Estate to the Colonial Government.

After the epidemic the farm became a Government experimental wine farm under the supervision of an Austrian, Baron von Babo, and the old homestead was converted into a hostel for the viticultural students.

During the present century Constantia, slowly encroached upon by the expanding suburbs of Cape Town, has continued in this educational and experimental role, only one incident marring the even passage of its days.

In 1925 the fragility of even the best-kept tradition was brutally demonstrated. In December of that year a spark from the kitchen chimney set alight the old building with its thick, thatched roof. In half an hour Constantia had shared the fate of many of the old Cape Dutch homesteads, the fire destroying most of the house and its precious collection of furniture and mementoes.

The house as it stands today is an architectural phoenix, a meticulous restoration. This complex and demanding work was entrusted by the Historic Monuments Commisson to the architect, F.K. Kendall, formerly an associate of Sir Herbert Baker. After completion of the work the homestead was refurnished through the gift of a Cape Town shipping magnate, Alfred Aaron de Pass, and opened as a museum to the public in 1927.

Some of the outstanding ancient dessert wines could well have originated on the part of the Constantia Estate which was given, in 1819, to Johan Gerard Cloete by his mother, Anna Catherina Cloete, widow of Hendrik Cloete, junior. This portion of the land, 228 morgen in extent and planted with about 33 000 vines, which produced some of the famous dessert wines enjoyed by Napoleon, Bismarck, Longfellow and Jane Austen, was named Klein Constantia by Johan Cloete. He probably began building the house immediately, though transfer only took place in 1823.

Klein Constantia passed through the hands of two other owners before returning to the Cloete family in 1870 when it was bought by Dirk Gysbert Cloete as a simple wine farm. He, like several other members of the original Groot Constantia branch of the family in the nineteenth century, became insolvent and was forced to surrender everything he possessed. This misfortune was largely a result of phylloxera in his vines and the lack of protection for Cape wines, which led finally to his selling of the farm in 1873 for £1 600 to William Brading, who remained there for 17 years. The next owner was William Adrian van der Byl from Witteboomen farm, who began to develop the true potential of Klein Constantia, planting orchards of figs and peaches, as well as vineyards.

Although the Van der Byls worked hard on the farm, it was certainly not all work and no play in nineteenth-century Constantia as there were continual picnics, luncheons, and all-day shooting parties in the nearby mountains where there was plenty of pheasant, guinea fowl and buck. The whole emphasis at Klein Constantia changed from farming to lavish entertainment when Abraham Lochner de Villiers, who had owned a fashionable millinery shop in Paarl, took possession in 1913 with his American steel millionairess wife, Clara Hussey, whom he met at a fashion show in Paris.

Her stylish way of life came as quite a shock and revelation to the staid inhabitants of the rather sleepy Constantia valley for Clara drove a beautiful car, of a sort that had never been seen before in Cape Town, she dressed in the height of fashion, and entertained with flair and style. The first reaction of the local residents was distinct disapproval, but it did not take long for them to realize what they were missing and they started flocking to the picnics, lunches and dinners at Klein Constantia. When the mailships called at Cape Town, the officers and guests were invited by Mr and Mrs de Villiers to a garden party, where elegant ladies in long flowing gowns drifted around the lawns, with strutting peacocks, to the

music of an orchestra. On these occasions there were often up to 600 guests.

It was Abraham Lochner de Villiers and his wife who built a whole new wing on to Klein Constantia, including a baronial hall with a minstrels' gallery and a private chapel, and who acquired some beautiful old doors, including those for the cellar, and pieces of antique furniture, all from Abraham's home town of Paarl. They had no children so their nephew, Jan de Villiers, inherited the farm after Clara's death in 1955. Although he had studied viticulture at Davis University, his heart was not in farming and within a few years he returned to the mines to work.

In 1963 Diana and Ian Austin took over this property and it reverted to a genuine farm. Ian, as chairman of the Constantia Heritage Group, supported its request that adequate facilities be made available to private farmers for the making and distribution of Constantia wine. However, partly because of urban development encroaching upon Klein Constantia over some decades, the farm, which consisted of 146 hectares with only 35 under vines, was in a derelict condition when it was bought and saved by Dougie Jooste, whose family had controlled the producing wine and spirit company, Sedgwick Taylor Limited, for three generations. Dougie had been chairman when the company merged with Stellenbosch Farmers' Winery in 1970.

The third of the subdivisions of the original Constantia Estate was named Bergvliet, 200 morgen of which was bought in 1793 by Cornelis Brink. He sold most of the farm a year later to his brother Arend, a soldier, who then built a house and called the property 'Buitenverwachting' – 'Beyond expectation'. Although he had obviously planned to bring up a large family there, only two of his ten children were born in the house as he sold the property in 1797 to Ryk Arnoldus Cloete, brother of the famous Hendrik of Constantia. He was eventually declared bankrupt as a result of the abolition of the slave trade, in which he had invested too much of his wealth, and a public sale of slaves was held at Buitenverwachting. Despite Ryk's over-spending on slaves instead of diversifying and ploughing his profits back into the upkeep of the land, Buitenverwachting reached its heyday as a wine farm in 1825, when there were 90 000 vines planted in its vineyards. The next owner was Ryk's nephew, Pieter Lourens Cloete, who bought it in 1827 and changed its name to Plumstead. Five years later, however, Pieter had sold the farm to his brother Johan Gerhard who, like their uncle, also went insolvent, although he managed to remain at Buitenverwachting for a full 20 years while the property was mortgaged again and again.

In 1852 Buitenverwachting was bought by Abraham de Smidt from the insolvent

estate for £15 000, but sold a year later to Jacob Willem Brunt whose brother owned the adjoining farm of Klein Constantia. In 1866 it was sold yet again, this time to Johannes Wynand Louw who had come to Constantia from Wellington. Through the female line of this family, the Lategans arrived in the valley, taking over no less than five farms, including Nova Constantia. Buitenverwachting was eventually inherited by Stephanus Petrus Lategan and later by his son Daniel (Oom Danie), whose daughter Olivia then lived there with her husband George Louw. His nephew Willem Lategan (Oom Willempie) owned the neighbouring farm Constantia Uitsig, owned and run by his son Stephen since his death a few years ago.

The great Constantia Estate suffered many vicissitudes after the death in 1712 of Simon van der Stel, when it was divided into three parts. Groot Constantia remained comparatively steady under the Cloete family for over 100 years until it was bought by the Colonial Government in 1885, but the other farms that had emerged from the subdivision had many different owners, several of whom went insolvent and were forced to sell both their moveable and immoveable property to appease their creditors.

As a result, these farms gradually went into a decline, affecting both their buildings and their wine, and excacerbated by encroaching urbanisation. Only very recently have two of the farms started to produce high-quality wines again, bottled on the premises. In addition to the Groot Constantia wines which have been fairly constant over the years, Buitenverwachting and Klein Constantia can now also boast wines of a quality to match those produced by Simon van der Stel and Hendrik Cloete hundreds of years ago. The Constantia wine makers of today can be proud of maintaining the tradition of this valley, the cradle of South African wines and wine making.

This introduction to the Constantia District would be incomplete without a reference to Alphen. The Alphen Estate is no more, and Alphen wines are no longer made in Constantia, but Alphen is one of the oldest names in the Cape wine story. Originally granted to a Free Burgher in the late seventeenth century, the property of Alphen was transferred to Simon van der Stel who, however, never incorporated it into his own estate of Constantia. After Van der Stel's death, the Dutch East India Company refused his heirs their claim of Alphen as a part of Constantia and it was regranted instead to Theunis Dirkz van Schalkwyk in 1714. There followed several changes of ownership, till Abraham Lever came into possession of the five morgen property in 1748, and it was he who began building the magnificent homestead which today forms a part of the Alphen Hotel.

The present owner of the hotel, Peter Bairnsfather Cloete, is a descendant of the first Cloete of Groot Constantia. In 1792 Hendrik Cloete's seventh son, Dirk, was married at the tender age of sixteen to Sophia Margaretha Myburgh. When she died young, Dirk Cloete remarried, this time to Anna Elizabeth van der Byl. Between these two wives he sired thirteen children; one of his multitude of grandsons married Reiniera Johanna Oosterzee, and moved onto the farm Alphen. It was thus that the tenacious Cloetes, even after the loss of Groot Constantia in the late 1800s, kept their roots in the land.

Wine was made at Alphen from the early days but by the late 1960s wine making had ceased on this historic site as the vineyards gave way before expanding urban development. Foreseeing the pressures of these changes, Peter Bairnsfather Cloete purchased land on the slopes of the Helderberg near Stellenbosch and planted vines there. This became known as Alphen Farm. On October 1, 1972 the exclusive distribution of Alphen wines was taken over by Gilbey Distillers and Vintners. The grapes from Alphen Farm were supplied to the nearby Gilbeys winery at Kleine Zalze for making into fine

wines under the Alphen label. Today Alphen Farm belongs to Hans-Joachim Schreiber, owner of Neethlingshof, and no longer has any connection with the Alphen Hotel in Constantia or Alphen wines. With regard to wine, Alphen is now merely a brand name for some of the wines distributed by Gilbeys. The old winery at Alphen in Contantia was taken over by the Cape Divisional Council for conversion into a library. Thus the only remaining atmosphere of the past is to be found at the hotel, focussed round the dignity of the old Cape Georgian homestead and its gracious outbuildings.

Buitenverwachting

New capital and new energy, together with careful planning, have brought this ancient farm back to life in recent years. Originally part of Simon van der Stel's huge Constantia Estate, Buitenverwachting was sold as a subdivision to Cornelis Brink in 1793, comprising 200 morgen of what was then called Bergvliet. Since then this perfect wine-producing property has had no less than 16 owners, several of whom were plagued with insolvency. Despite this unsettled background, it flourished as a wine farm, 90 000 vines having been planted by 1825, under the ownership of Ryk Arnoldus Cloete, brother of the famous Hendrik of Constantia.

From 1866, the fortunes of Buitenverwachting were inextricably linked to those of the Louw and Lategan families, one of the most colourful characters being Oom Danie Lategan whose trademark was the camellia he picked for his button-hole each morning. It was his daughter, Olivia Lategan, who was to forge the link between the Lategans and the Louws. Born at Buitenverwachting, she returned as mistress of the house when she married George Louw. The property later passed on to their children, from whom it was rented by André Badenhorst, the present general manager and viticulturist whose father, Japie, was general manager of Groot Constantia for 40 years. With its purchase by Richard Müller, an international businessman, in 1981, Buitenverwachting took a new direction, extending its area to 105 hectares at the same time. Now owned by

Buitenverwachting

Cultivars Planted	Size of Vineyards (Hectares)	Training Practice
Sauvignon Blanc	10	
Rhine Riesling	10	
Cabernet Sauvignon	10	
Pinot Noir	6	Extended Perold trellis
Pinot Gris	4	
Merlot	3	
Hanepoot*	3	
Cabernet Franc	2	
Gamay	1	

*This is a block of 100-year-old vines still bearing table grapes.

Total area under vines in 1987: 49 ha (24 still to be planted)
Irrigation: The Buitenverwachting vineyards are not irrigated.
Temperatures: Average maximum 25 °C; average minimum 10 °C
Average annual rainfall: 1 000 mm
Stock: Rooted vines are purchased from a nursery.
Envisaged new cultivar: Chardonnay
First wines bottled under the Buitenverwachting label: Buiten Blanc, Pinot Gris, Blanc Fumé, Blanc de Noir (Gamay) and Rhine Riesling (all 1985 wines)
Wines currently bottled under the Buitenverwachting label: Buiten Blanc (blend), Blanc Fumé, Rhine Riesling, Blanc de Noir (Gamay), L'Arrivée and Pinot Gris. (Future bottlings: Bordeaux blend and Pinot Noir.)
Wood ageing: Wine is aged in wood on the farm.
Capacity of the Buitenverwachting cellar: 7 000 hectolitres

Wine tastings are now available at Buitenverwachting from 09h00 to 17h00 on weekdays and from 09h00 to 13h00 on Saturdays. Cellar tours are at 11h00 and 15h00 on weekdays and 11h00 on Saturdays.

the Buitenverwachting Trust, this historic farm has been lovingly restored to its former splendour, under André Badenhorst's expert eye, and the vineyards

have been gradually replanted with the most select of cultivars – Cabernet Sauvignon, Merlot, Cabernet Franc and Pinot Noir for the reds and Rhine Riesling,

Sauvignon Blanc, Chardonnay and Pinot Gris for the whites.

Planting began in 1981 and covers 70 hectares of painstakingly prepared land which underwent costly and time-consuming three-directional ploughing. The clay and top soils have been mixed to a depth of one metre, ensuring that a regular supply of moisture is maintained in the soil and providing the depth necessary for good root development. Buitenverwachting does not irrigate at all, relying instead on the composition of the soils and the natural rainfall. The vineyards have been thoroughly planned with regard to soil types and micro-climates and the first two vintages have certainly proved the French saying that 'a good wine must be able to see the sea' – one can do so from the higher slopes.

The maiden harvest of 100 tonnes in 1985 was the first Buitenverwachting had seen for 30 years and exceeded all expectations, although relatively small in overall terms because of the strict control exercised to prevent the new vines overbearing in their first year of production. The 1985 Rhine Riesling obtained a Superior rating and the cellarmaster at Buitenverwachting, Jean Daneel, attributes the excellent balance of this wine largely to its habitat, for the Constantia valley has long been regarded as one of the finest wine-growing areas in the country and one particularly suited to this cultivar.

The white wines were the first to be produced in the enormous new cellar designed in an ultra-modern style with the most up-to-date wine-making equipment, yet with the traditional high semi-gables, white walls and lofty thatched roof so typical of the Cape. This was completed in

The magnificent Buitenverwachting homestead.

1984 and features a refrigerated bottle maturation area which has a capacity of 3 000 small French oak barrels, hewn from Limosin and Nevers oak. The old cellar, which has been restored along with all the other farm buildings and the homestead, is used for special wine tastings. Sadly, the converted kraal, which had been turned into one of the most successful gourmet restaurants in the country, burned down in February 1987. It is being rebuilt, though, and will be functional again early in 1988.

Wine lovers will have to wait for the first of the Buitenverwachting reds in the range, the classic Bordeaux blend and the rich Burgundy-style Pinot Noir. However, one of the Cape's first nouveau-style Gamays in the Beaujolais tradition, which was made using the traditional carbonic

maceration process, was released in April 1986 under the label L'Arrivée.

Jean Daneel was restrained with the second harvest, selecting his juice carefully, which meant that the yield per tonne was considerably lower than in 1985, but he maintains it has been most worthwhile as the 1986 vintage shows a distinct improvement on the high standard set by the popular maiden wines. The future of Buitenverwachting as a flourishing wine farm seems assured and its achievements so far have been *'Buitenverwachting'* – beyond expectation.

One memento of the past will be kept as part of the Buitenverwachting vineyards: a small block of Hanepoot table grapes which is about 100 years old but still bears magnificently.

Groot Constantia

Groot Constantia Estate, in particular, powerfully retains its historic aura and the popular memory of its near-legendary wines of the seventeenth and eighteenth centuries: the rich, sweet wines which kept the crowned heads of Europe – and the poets and writers who celebrated them – warm on the cold nights of winter. This Estate still makes wines – and fine wines too.

This section of the ancient Estate of

Simon van der Stel is a great symbol of the past – a past preserved. It is this which draws, from all parts of the world, many thousands of visitors each year, to wander along its tree-lined avenues and explore the beautifully restored homestead with its mysterious cellars and underground slave-quarters. The works of man have been lovingly preserved here: the majestic two-storey wine cellar of Hendrik Cloete, with its allegorical plaster figures designed by

Louis Thibault and executed by Anton Anreith, is a tribute to those immigrant artists and craftsmen who lent lightness and grace of design to the soberly symmetrical Cape Dutch architecture.

In addition to one of the most ideal climates of all the Cape wine districts, Groot Constantia also has good soil, derived from Table Mountain sandstone. Some of its lower-lying fields are sandy as distinct from the Hutton and Clovelly

Built in 1791, the old wine cellar survives as a tribute to wine making at Constantia and to the architectural and sculpting genius of Louis Thibault and Anton Anreith.

forms on the rest of the farm. The bulk of the soils in their natural state are deep and cool with a good water-holding capacity, so irrigation is not used.

It is these general conditions which, for over three centuries, have given birth to Constantia's fine wines, from the early sweet wine for which the Estate first became famous to the Cabernet Sauvignon, Shiraz and Pinotage made today by the Estate's wine maker, Pieter Daniel du Toit. He is a graduate of Stellenbosch University who spent a number of years at Nederburg and the Robertson Co-operative before coming to Constantia.

In spite of the weight of its history and the overtones of the past which linger around the house itself, the Estate of Groot Constantia still operates very much as a living farm. Though still owned by the Government, its general activities are now supervised by a Board of Control. It is run on a free enterprise basis and should show a profit. The possibility of returning it to private ownership, however, is being investigated and a report will be tabled in Parliament in 1988.

A registered Estate, its wines are entirely grown, pressed, matured, bottled and sold to the public on the Estate itself. Of the varieties grown in the earlier days, only Steen and Hanepoot are now grown, but new and more effective clones of those varieties. The 150 hectares of the area at present under vines are planted mainly with Shiraz, Steen, Cabernet Sauvignon, Weisser Riesling, Gewürztraminer, Sauvignon Blanc and Pinotage. Production is now at an annual 780 tonnes of grapes,

Groot Constantia Estate

Cultivars Planted	Size of Vineyards (Number of vines)	Training Practice
Steen	54 000	
Shiraz	53 000	
Cabernet Sauvignon	38 000	
Sauvignon Blanc	38 000	
Weisser Riesling	36 000	
Gewürztraminer	19 500	
Pinotage	15 500	
Cabernet Franc	14 500	All vines grown
Pinot Noir	12 500	on vertical
Pinot Gris	11 000	3-wire trelisses
Chardonnay	10 000	
Merlot	10 000	
Morio Muscat	10 000	
Hanepoot	7 000	
Fernão Pires	3 200	
Tinta Barocca	3 000	
Nemes Furmint	2 200	
Hárslevelü	2 000	

Total area under vines in 1987: 150 ha (5 ha still to be planted)
Irrigation: The vineyards of Groot Constantia are not irrigated.
Temperatures: Average maximum 20,8 °C; average minimum 12,7 °C
Average annual rainfall: Approximately 1 100 mm
Stock: Rooted vines are purchased from a nursery.
First wines bottled under the Groot Constantia Estate label: Cabernet Sauvignon 1963 and Shiraz 1963
Wines currently bottled under the Groot Constantia Estate label: Pinotage, Shiraz, Cabernet Sauvignon, Stein, Pinot Noir, Bouquet Blanc, Blanc de Blanc, Weisser Riesling, Heerenrood, Constantia Rood, Pinotage Rosé, Sauvignon Blanc, Rooi Dessert, Constantia Blanc, Gewürztraminer and Late Harvest
Wood ageing: Wines are aged in wood on the Estate.
Capacity of the Groot Constantia cellar: 9 600 hectolitres

Groot Constantia Estate is open to visitors and for the sale of wine on weekdays and weekends between 09h30 and 17h00. Besides the restored homestead and the wine cellar, attractions include two restaurants and the wine museum at the rear of the cellar; laid out with exemplary style, this little museum provides an ideal introduction both to Constantia and the culture of wine in general.

A recent view of the famous Groot Constantia homestead, showing the formerly-varnished shutters painted green, as the original practice is now thought to have been.

which will be progressively increased to an eventual 1 200 tonnes.

Problems have been experienced with troupes of baboons from the neighbouring mountain, making periodic raids on the vineyards. They appeared particularly to favour the Weisser Riesling which is planted on the higher ground; on one occasion so much damage was done to the crop that it had to be harvested early, with a comparatively low sugar content of 19 ° Balling. In spite of this the resultant wine turned out to be as good as ever.

Recent events in Groot Constantia's story have included the opening of a wine museum in part of the old cellar. Initiated in 1971, it was enlarged in 1980. A modern and much larger cellar has been completed in which the 1983 harvest was the first to be processed.

Recently, too, an historic encounter with the wines of the past took place. A number of precious bottles of old Constantia wine were discovered in the cellar of the Duke of Northumberland at Alnwick Castle in the north of England, some of which were brought back to South Africa, where they were opened and tasted with all due ceremony. Made from Cloete's famous 1791 vintage, the wine proved to be a magnificent deep amber in colour, with a tinge of yellow-gold round the edge. When poured into tasting glasses it greeted the twentieth century with a sweet and fruity bouquet, typical of the classic Muscadel-type dessert wine. There were no off-odours, a remarkable achievement in itself after almost two centuries in bottle. Its flavour proved to be fine and delicate, surprisingly balanced although slightly

lacking in acid, and some maderization was present. A little tannin was detected, but the general consensus was that this was a wine of great richness and character which fully lived up to its legend. Traces of the bouquet of the wine lingered in the glass for many hours after the tasting; surviving as it has through the decades both as a symbol and as a living reality, like Groot Constantia itself.

After this romantic taste of the past a more objective and sober assessment of the wine was made when, on an accepted judging scale, it scored a decisive 18,7 out of 20. It was also subjected to analysis at Nietvoorbij, where it was discovered that it had an alcohol content of 15,03 per cent, a total acidity of 7,1 (remarkable in a wine of this age) and a spectacular sugar content of 128,3 grams a litre.

Klein Constantia

After its separation from Groot Constantia in 1819, Klein Constantia was farmed by a succession of owners, until 1913 when the emphasis was put on lavish entertainment rather than farming. As a result of this and the encroaching urban development, the old farm gradually fell into a decline, from which it has only recently been rescued by a Cape Town businessman, Dougie Jooste, who bought the 146 hectares in 1980. He had been searching for a farm for ten years and had no hesitation in buying Klein Constantia, in spite of its dilapidated state. The land was almost completely overgrown with bush and Port Jackson trees, among which were dotted numerous wrecks of lorries and old cars. The buildings were also badly neglected, a daunting prospect for anyone without the foresight, knowledge and tenacity of Dougie Jooste.

He had always known that Constantia, with its cool meso-climate six kilometres from the cold South Atlantic and overlooking False Bay, could produce quality wines. He consulted Professor Chris Orffer of Stellenbosch University, a viticulturist, and Ernst le Roux, chief viticulturist at Nederburg and oenologist who, after extensive testing of the soil, endorsed the great potential for prime wines at Klein Constantia. As far as natural resources and location are concerned this Estate is richly endowed. Distinctive meso-climatological variations

exist, attributable to the variance in elevation above sea level, starting from 72 metres on the north-facing slopes and rising to 440 metres on the south-facing slopes. This enables the successful cultivation of later-ripening cultivars such as Cabernet Sauvignon on the lower slopes and Rhine Riesling and Chardonnay on the higher slopes, where the latter reach full potential under cool growing conditions.

Ernst le Roux, now general manager and viticulturist at Klein Constantia, was asked to draw up a development plan for the farm. An even more intensive soil survey was done which showed that the soils were mainly of granitic origin and were deep, red, fertile and well-drained, mainly Hutton types with sufficient water-holding capacity to facilitate dry land cultivation. Even the virgin soils were found to be high in pH and rich in calcium. The soil had been prepared and was finally ready for planting by mid-1982. The very best clonal propagation material from Ernita nursery is used at Klein Constantia, and the planting of new vineyards has proceeded at the rate of approximately 15 hectares per year and should be completed by 1989.

The homestead at Klein Constantia has had its thatch roof renewed and the old wine cellar has also been thatched, and will not be used again for pressing. Wine had not been made on this Estate for

nearly 50 years when, in 1986, the first grapes since 1937 were crushed in the new cellar, which was completed in the same year. Consulting the wine maker, Ross Gower, about the practical aspects of such a cellar, the well-known Cape Town architect Gawie Fagan designed it partially below ground-level to reduce the impact of a large building on the beautiful natural surroundings. The underground cellar provides ideal maturation conditions and impressive barrel-vaulted ceilings lend a unique atmosphere.

In the first vintage of the renovated Estate, when Sauvignon Blanc, Rhine Riesling, Cabernet Sauvignon and Shiraz (the reds are still being aged) were made, wine maker Ross Gower's talent was proved immediately: Klein Constantia won the Johann Graue Memorial Trophy for the champion South African dry white wine, with his 1986 Sauvignon Blanc. Ross is no newcomer to wine making: he has had 13 years' experience in Germany, New Zealand, France, and at Nederburg where he worked under Günter Brözel. The two white wines, the Sauvignon Blanc and Rhine Riesling, were released in mid-March 1987 to an eager wine public, and are being sold on the Estate as well as being marketed by Stellenbosch Farmers' Winery. In 1987 the same four cultivars were crushed for wine making and the first Chardonnay grapes came into the cellar.

It has taken over 300 years, but immaculate vineyards now stretch well up the mountainside where vines have never been planted before. The build-up of humus in this virgin soil, together with its inherently good water-retaining capacity, enable the vines to be grown without irrigation. Such is the gradient that the higher vineyards have had to be contoured to prevent soil erosion, but one problem Klein Constantia never has is the presence of grape-eating birds, thanks to the preying Steppe Buzzards which migrate from the steppes of Russia and frequent the Constantia valley between October and March. As soon as they migrate north in April, hundreds of starlings descend on the vineyards but by then there are only a few grapes left.

Another delight of the Constantia winegrowing area is the cooler climate which allows grapes to ripen slowly without losing volatile flavour compounds. That is why Klein Constantia's crop is picked two to three weeks later than most other areas in South Africa and at a higher sugar level than most. The wines are left on the lees for at least two months, in the French style, and are filtered as little as possible. As a result of the long skin contact (whites have between 18 and 24 hours), the wines are slightly deeper in colour and more fully flavoured than normal. Only the best wines are bottled under the Estate's label and the rest is sold in bulk.

Cultivation practices followed are aimed at producing premium quality grapes for noble wines of distinction. With his experience as viticulturist and oenologist, Ernst le Roux knows exactly what a wine maker is looking for, which is a tremendous help to Ross. There is much to look forward to from Klein Constantia, as Ross and Ernst make a formidable team, and in Dougie Jooste it has the benefit of a far-sighted and dedicated owner.

Klein Constantia Estate

Cultivars Planted	Size of Vineyards (Hectares)	Training Practice
Sauvignon Blanc	17,0	
Cabernet Sauvignon	10,6	
Chardonnay	9,24	
Rhine Riesling	6,5	5-wire hedge
Chenin Blanc	6,4	
Merlot	4,3	
Shiraz	4,2	
Muscat de Frontignan	2,4	

Total area under vines in 1987: 61 ha (18 ha still to be planted)
Irrigation: 95 per cent of the Klein Constantia vineyards are not irrigated.
Temperatures: No records available yet.
Average annual rainfall: 1 017 mm (over the last ten years)
Stock: Rooted vines are purchased from Ernita.
Envisaged new cultivar: Cabernet Franc
First wines bottled under the Klein Constantia Estate label: Sauvignon Blanc 1986 (WOS) and Rhine Riesling 1986
Wines currently bottled under the Klein Constantia Estate label: Sauvignon Blanc and Rhine Riesling (future bottling: Chardonnay 1989; red wines 1990)
Wood ageing: The wine is wood aged on the Estate.
Capacity of the Klein Constantia cellar 12 360 hectolitres (+ 150 000 ageing bottles)

Klein Constantia is open to the public for tours and wine tastings by appointment. Wine is sold on the Estate on weekdays from 09h00 to 13h00 and 14h00 to 17h00 and on Saturdays from 09h00 to 13h00.

The beautifully restored homestead at Klein Constantia is the home of Lowell Jooste, son of Dougie Jooste, the owner of the Estate.

DURBANVILLE

The tiny hamlet of Pampoenkraal, or 'Pumpkin Kraal', was established within a few years of the first settlement at the Cape. In those days the hills in the area were mostly devoted to wheat and cattle farming, later to be shared with the vine. In 1836 the then Governor of the Colony, Sir Benjamin D'Urban, was petitioned by the Pampoenkraalers to be allowed to call their village D'Urban. Subsequent confusion with the growing Natal city of Durban led to a further change to the present name of Durbanville.

Like that of Constantia, the arable area of Durbanville is rapidly dwindling, and for the same reason: the expansion of metropolitan Cape Town. The Southern Suburbs have swallowed much of what was once Van der Stel's leisurely domain; in the same way the thrust of the Northern Suburbs has enclosed the Tygerberg Hills, leaving an enclave of wheat farmland and a handful of wine farms, including the Estates of Meerendal and Diemersdal.

As with Constantia, the location of the Durbanville vineyards suits them particularly to the making of high-quality wines, with an emphasis upon fine reds. Lying mainly on the slopes, they receive the benefit of any cool wind off the Atlantic 15 kilometres to the south, and of south-easterly breezes off False Bay. These strong winds prevent the moist conditions in which many vine diseases flourish. The annual rainfall is modest, being some 357 millimetres annually. During the growing season, that is, between September and March, the average temperature is approximately 19 °C.

The soils in the area are predominantly of the Hutton and Clovelly type, deep, cool and well-drained, but with a good water-holding capacity. Notwithstanding the low rainfall the vineyards here, as in Constantia, are cultivated without irrigation – heavy dew and the water-retaining properties of the well-weathered red soils make irrigation unnecessary.

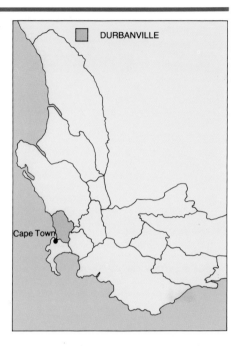

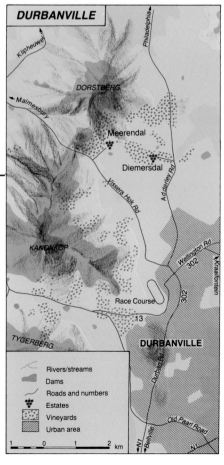

Altydgedacht

Although this picturesque Estate, lying on the fertile slopes of the Tygerberg Hills, is one of the oldest wine farms in the Cape, boasting an unbroken tradition of wine making over the last 280 years, it was only in 1985 that it was registered as an Estate and had wine bottled under its own label. The cellar was built in 1705 and there are inventories showing that wine was sold on the farm to wholesalers in 1730. Until the mid-1960s the entire grape crop was made into wine in the cellar and sold in bulk to merchants (notably to Monis of Paarl), but in more recent years the grapes have been sold directly to Nederburg and Stellenbosch Farmers' Winery.

Unusually, women have played an important role in shaping the destiny of Altydgedacht, starting with Elsje van Suurwaarde after whom the Elsieskraal

River is named, commonly known by the shorter name of Elsies River. As her husband was an official of the Dutch East India Company, he was not allowed to own land, which is why the farm was officially granted to her in 1698, under the name 'de Tygerbergen' – it was renamed 'Altydgedacht' in 1936, although the name has been spelt 'Altijd Gedacht' in some documents. The title deeds, which were signed by Simon van der Stel himself, can be seen on the Estate. Elsje, in fact, outlived two husbands who were high officials of the Dutch East India Company, namely Andries de Man, the *Secunde*, and Henricus Munkerus, the Treasurer.

The second woman to have strong influence was the present owner's mother-in-law, Daisy Parker, who, as a widow, courageously ran the farm while her three

Altydgedacht Estate

Cultivars Planted	Size of Vineyards (Hectares)	Training Practice
Chenin Blanc	35,7	Bush vine
Cabernet Sauvignon	13,6	Perold trellis and bush vine
Bukettraube	8,3	
Shiraz	7,2	
SA Riesling	6,7	
Chardonnay	6,1	
Sauvignon Blanc	5,9	5-wire trellis
Gewürztraminer	3,6	
Gamay	2,6	
Merlot	1,6	
Pinotage	1,1	
Barbera	1,0	

Total area under vines in 1987: 104 ha (approximately 50 ha still to be planted out of 450 ha)
Irrigation: The vineyards of Altydgedacht are not irrigated.
Temperatures: Records are not kept.
Average annual rainfall: 550 mm
Stock: Some parent stock is used for grafting and rooted vines are purchased from a nursery.
Envisaged new cultivars: Cabernet Franc, Pinot Noir and Rhine Riesling
First wines bottled under the Altydgedacht Estate label: Cabernet Sauvignon 1982, Bukettraube 1985 and Chenin Blanc 1985
Wines currently bottled under the Altydgedacht Estate label (in order of volume): Bukettraube, Cabernet Sauvignon, Tintoretto, Tygerberg Wood Aged White, Gewürztraminer, Pinotage and Chenin Blanc. These wines are bottled by Stellenbosse Botteleringskoöperasie Beperk (Lynedoch).
Wood ageing: Altydgedacht wines are aged in wood on the Estate.
Capacity of the Altydgedacht cellar: Only ten per cent of the crop is made into wine on the Estate, but the old cellar is being renovated.

Visits to Altydgedacht Estate are by appointment only, although plans are being made for wine tastings in the future.

sons were away during the Second World War. Earlier, during the Depression of the 1930s, she had started a tearoom there which had proved to be extremely popular, providing an income which Daisy put towards her sons' education.

For the last three decades the farm has been owned and run by Jean Parker, who was widowed in 1954 when her sons, John and Oliver, were both under four years old. Running a farm is a formidable task, but especially for a woman as young as Jean was when her husband, Dennis, died. Her family and her attorneys tried to persuade her to sell the farm, but she would not hear of it, as Altydgedacht had belonged to the Parker family for over 100 years – or five generations – and she was determined to keep it as a legacy for her sons. In the meantime Jean, who had graduated from Rhodes University with a degree in fine art and languages, started attending courses at Elsenburg Agricultural College and with the help of her farm staff and neighbours managed on her own for a few years until she was able to hire a farm manager, Hennie Heydenrych.

Altydgedacht has had an interesting history over the last 300 years, and Jean tells of one particular period when the farm was used as a 'prison' for Napoleon's secretary, Count de Las Cases, who was held there for four months by the British. He had arrived in the Cape on his way from St Helena to Europe with his invalid son and it was considered wise to keep a close eye on this associate of the exiled emperor. The Count wrote in his diary: 'We left Newlands about the middle of the day on 6 April and at night reached Tygerberg. At De Tygerbergen we found ourselves situated at the very extremity of the civilised world'.

As Jean had hoped, John and Oliver studied viticulture and oenology at Stellenbosch University, followed by some years' experience in the Napa Valley in California. Oliver also spent a year in Australia and New Zealand, where the wine-making conditions are similar to those in South Africa. Now these two young men are managing the vineyard and

As with Constantia, the winelands of Durbanville are much diminished and hemmed in by urban sprawl. But rural order prevails in isolated pockets such as this vineyard on Meerendal Estate where sheep graze the winter cover crop.

wine division of this old Cape farm, which also produces fruit, grain and sileage for the beef herd. Until recently there was also a dairy herd and some sheep.

The vine plantings cover 104 of the 450 hectares at Altydgedacht and comprise Cabernet Sauvignon, Shiraz, Pinotage, Steen, Cape Riesling and the only plantings of Barbera in the country. This is Italy's most popular cultivar, and is also grown in America, particularly in California where it makes up 10 per cent of the local red wine production. Cooler climates bring out the best in Barbera, a high acid level and good fruit, and although the wine can be drunk immediately, it can also be aged for a few years which makes it smooth and

flavourful. Altydgedacht's Barbera Tintoretto is a blend of Barbera and Shiraz, and was originally called Barberaz. The Wine and Spirit Board forbade the use of this name, however, as being too close to the names of the cultivars. Production of this wine dropped dramatically because of the age of the vines, which Jean maintains was 80 years. Originally planted on the recommendation of Italian friends of the Parkers, these old vines have been uprooted and replaced with new ones of the same variety.

Other grape varieties planted are Weisser Riesling, Gewürztraminer, Bukettraube and Muscat d'Alexandrie, with young vineyards of Sauvignon Blanc, Chardonnay and Merlot now in their third

and fourth years. The growing of noble cultivars is facilitated by the cool winds from the Atlantic Ocean, the deep soils and the varied aspects of the slopes.

Until recently, Altydgedacht was the only Estate in the Durbanville District to bottle white wine. The Parkers have also upheld the reputation of this area for producing excellent red wine grapes, established by the nearby Meerendal Estate, which specialised originally in port cultivars. Indeed, Jean Parker still owns a bottle of 1938 port made by Oom Willie Starke of Meerendal who is now over 90 years old. The Parker family can justly be proud of their début into Estate wines, but as they bottle only a small proportion of their crop, demand may soon exceed supply.

Bloemendal Estate

Jackie Coetzee, the wine maker at Bloemendal, in front of his cellar.

Bloemendal Estate

Cultivars Planted	Size of Vineyards (Number of vines)	Training Practice
Chenin Blanc	124 000	
Chardonnay	33 000	Bush vines
Shiraz	19 000	
Cabernet Sauvignon	89 000	
Sauvignon Blanc	78 000	
Weisser Riesling	47 000	Perold trellises
Merlot	25 000	
SA Riesling	25 000	

Total area under vines in 1987: 145 ha
Irrigation: The vineyards of Bloemendal are irrigated.
Temperature: Records not available
Average annual rainfall: Records not available
Stock: Rooted vines are purchased from a nursery.
First wine bottled under the Bloemendal Estate label: Sauvignon Blanc (1987)
Wines currently bottled under the Bloemendal Estate label: Sauvignon Blanc and Bloemen Blanc.

Bloemendal Estate is open to the public on Wednesdays from 13h00 to 18h00 and on Saturdays from 09h00 to 12h00.

In 1987 the first wines were released from this 280-hectare Estate, now being farmed by Jackie Coetzee, an Elsenburg-trained wine maker. However, rebate wine for brandy was being made at Bloemendal at

the beginning of the century, so vineyards have been planted there for many decades and possibly longer.

About twenty years ago, under the direction of Koos Coetzee, False Pedro and

Cinsaut vines were replaced by Cabernet Sauvignon, while additions of Chardonnay, Merlot and Weisser Riesling have been made in recent years. Jackie's first vintage, a Sauvignon Blanc, was awarded a gold medal at the Championship Wine Show and his Cabernet Sauvignon, at present being aged in sixteen new Bordeaux barriques, was judged the best in the 20 hectolitre class of wooded Cabernet Sauvignon wines. After further bottle maturation, it will be available to the public in 1990. An off-dry white wine, Bloemen Blanc, is also produced on the Estate. The Bloemendal wine labels depict water lilies of various colours, a large pond of these beautiful flowers being a striking feature near the homestead and cellar.

For the moment, wine making at Bloemendal remains rather more of a hobby than a business, as production will be limited to about 2 000 cases annually.

Diemersdal

Diemersdal was originally granted to Hendrik Sneewind in 1698. His widow married a Captain Diemer, after whom the property was then named. Diemer was at one time 'fire chief' of the settlement at the Cape and Master of the Artillery, and was a son of Jan van Riebeeck's table waiter.

In the 1920s the great-grandfather of the present owners, Tienie and Beyers Louw, converted the property from a wheat farm to a largely wine-making concern, and today, nestling among rolling tracts of wheat and excellent vineyards, there is a large and most impressive complex of farm buildings with the old Cape Dutch homestead at its hub. Tienie Louw and his wife live there and his brother, Beyers, lives on the nearby farm Maastricht, which they bought in 1982. Maastricht is named after an area in The Netherlands where a particularly fine type of clay is found. The subsoil under the Hutton and Clovelly soils of this part of Durbanville is mostly clay, so that the soil generally retains moisture well, and this no doubt reminded the early settlers of Maastricht in their country of origin. Mixed farming is practised on Maastricht; wine is not made there, but the grapes are delivered to the KWV.

Diemersdal is one of two farms, the other being Vergenoegd in the Stellenbosch District, which have marketing agreements with the KWV going back to 1920. Vergenoegd bottles a fairly small percentage of the wines they make, the rest being sold to the KWV. Diemersdal sold all its wines to the KWV until recently but in 1986 and 1987 retained a total of about 100 hectolitres (roughly 100 cases) of red wine which is being aged in wood on the Estate and will be released for sale in 1989. This wine will be a blend of Cabernet Sauvignon, Cabernet Franc and Merlot. Otherwise, the red wine of Diemersdal is sold under the Estate's own label on overseas markets by the KWV, and a small quantity is released to KWV members. A Pinot Noir from Diemersdal won the Alfa

Tienie Louw.

Diemersdal Estate

Cultivars Planted	Size of Vineyards (Hectares)	Training Practice
Chenin Blanc	38,0	
Cabernet Sauvignon	19,8	
Sauvignon Blanc	19,0	
Gewürztraminer	15,7	
Weisser Riesling	13,5	Perold trellis
Pinot Noir	11,2	
Chardonnay	7,5	
Cabernet Franc	7,0	
Pinot Gris	4,0	
Merlot	3,0	
Ferdinand de Lesseps	2,0	
Kerner	14,0	One-wire trellis
Pinotage	10,5	
Shiraz	14,0	Perold and one-wire trellis

Total area under vines in 1987: 179,2 ha
Irrigation: The Diemersdal vineyards are not irrigated.
Temperatures: Records are not kept.
Average annual rainfall: Records are not kept.
Stock: Rooted vines are purchased from a nursery.
Envisaged new cultivars: None
First wine bottled under the Diemersdal label: Dry Red
Wines currently bottled under the Diemersdal label: Cabernet Sauvignon, Cabernet Franc, Shiraz and Merlot. Diemersdal wines are bottled by the KWV.
Wood ageing: Wine is aged on the Estate and at the KWV.
Capacity of the Diemersdal cellar: 6 000 hectolitres

Diemersdal is not open to the public.

The impressive complex of the homestead and wine-making facilities at Diemersdal.

Laval Trophy for the champion new-cultivar wine at the 1979 Cape Championship Wine Show and a Cabernet Franc from the Estate won the award in 1981.

Although the climate and soil of this area are eminently suited to red wine cultivars, white grapes are also grown at Diemersdal, and wine is made from them, which is then sold in bulk to the KWV. All the Kerner and Weisser Riesling bottled under the KWV label comes from this Estate. In fact 60 per cent of the area under vines is given over to white cultivars, all suitable for making wine of excellent quality. Tienie includes the ubiquitous Steen among these, as he maintains, rightly, that outstanding wines can be made from Steen grapes. The first crop for wine making from the 40 000 Chardonnay and 20 000 Pinot Gris wines on the Estate will be harvested in 1988.

Diemersdal produces a large wheat crop annually and Tienie also keeps German Merino sheep and beef cattle. His wife, Joanita, also a wine enthusiast, has started a small Red Poll stud at Diemersdal. The presence of these beautiful, richly hued cattle on the rolling pastures adds to the pleasantness of the place.

Kosie Starke, Meerendal's present owner and wine maker.

Meerendal

The first Estate in the Durbanville area to produce wine under its own label, Meerendal is an old farm which for many years produced wheat, as did many of the Durbanville farms before the development of wine making in the district. Wheat remains an important crop in that area. As early as 1716, however, there were vines on the farm, 60 000 of them, according to the records of the *Veldkornet* who acted as tax-collector that year. They were planted and tended by the widow of Jan Meerland, to whom the farm was granted by Willem Adriaan van der Stel in 1702. Meerland, in spite of this munificence, was involved, along with Henning Huysing of Meerlust and others, in the movement to unseat Van der Stel. He sailed to Holland as part of the deputation which put the complaints of the Free Burghers to the Chamber of

Seventeen, the directors of the Dutch East India Company, but died on the outward voyage, leaving his widow to run the farm. His original grant was about 50 morgen and his widow acquired a further 50, so that her farm extended over 85 hectares in today's measurements. Nonetheless the tax-collector's count of 60 000 vines seems inordinately high.

Meerendal changed hands many times over the years until it was bought by William Starke, whose son Kosie now owns and runs the farm. Kosie Starke's son, also named William, has now joined his father as wine maker at Meerendal. William Starke the elder, generally known as Oom Willie, is now over 90 years old and lives in Durbanville, though not on the Estate. His wife, Kosie's mother, was a Faure of Vergenoegd (see page 196). There are

Harvest of a different sort . . . Contrasting sharply, wheatfields and vineyards on Meerendal.

several Starkes in the Durbanville District, descended from those Starkes who emigrated from the Wash in England in the middle of the nineteenth century. The family had its origins in Germany but had later settled in England. The well-known Cape garden nurseries, Starke Ayres, were started by one of the sons of the first Starkes to arrive in South Africa.

When Oom Willie bought Meerendal it was purely a wheat farm, but, inspired by the advice of Professor Perold, he set about planting and developing a range of red wine varieties with an emphasis on port cultivars in the years before the Second World War. They included such quality varieties as Shiraz, Tinta Barocca, Cornifesto, Souzão, and Cinsaut. Post-war changes in taste and the decline of the port market, together with the dramatic advent of Pinotage in the 1950s, persuaded Kosie Starke when he took over the farm in 1952 to make a change in policy.

Extending the existing Shiraz vineyards, he also introduced Pinotage vines from which he set about making fine, dry red wines, concentrating upon them but retaining a minority of some 15 per cent of his vineyards for Chenin Blanc grapes. Grown largely to fill out the harvesting programme, these are not pressed on the Estate.

The first Pinotage and Shiraz vintages appearing in 1969 were bottled by the KWV as 100 per cent varietal wines under the Estate's own label. They were, however, not available to the general public, being reserved for export or for sale to members of the KWV. Kosie was, incidentally, a member of the Board of the KWV for many years.

Kosie soon decided that he wanted to age and bottle his own wines and sell them through retail outlets. But when he investigated the economics of doing so he found that it would not be a viable proposition, given the amount of wine he would be able to produce. He thus became one of the earliest of the Estates to form an association with the Bergkelder, which now matures, bottles and markets for him.

The first wine to come from this partnership and to be made available to the public was the 1974 Meerendal Pinotage (awarded a Superior rating); and the first Shiraz was from the 1974 vintage.

The early 1970s, a period when there was a sudden shortage of red wine, saw a brief diversificaton when, as did many others, Kosie Starke planted Cabernet Sauvignon. But apart from this excursion, the emphasis at Meerendal has remained firmly upon Shiraz and Pinotage, the pride of the Estate and still the only wines sold under its label.

Meerendal Estate

Cultivars Planted	Size of Vineyards (Number of vines)	Training Practice
Cabernet Sauvignon	65 000	
Shiraz*	39 000	Perold trellis
Sauvignon Blanc	27 000	
Pinotage	45 000	Bush vines
Cinsaut	18 000	
Chenin Blanc	24 000	Perold trellis and bush vines
Chardonnay	60 000	Split cordon,
Gewürztraminer	34 000	2-wire trellis

*The oldest commercial vineyard on the Estate is a 10-ha Shiraz vineyard which was planted 55 years ago.

Total area under vines in 1987: 115 ha (20 ha still to be planted)
Irrigation: The vineyards of Meerendal are not irrigated.
Temperatures: Records are not kept.
Average annual rainfall: Approximately 600 mm
Stock: Rooted vines are purchased from a nursery.
Envisaged new cultivar: Merlot
First wines bottled under the Meerendal Estate label: Pinotage 1969 and Shiraz 1969
Wines currently bottled under the Meerendal Estate label: Pinotage and Shiraz. Both wines are bottled by the Bergkelder.
Wood ageing: Meerendal wines are aged in wood at the Bergkelder.
Capacity of the Meerendal cellar: 5 875 hectolitres

Meerendal Estate is not open to the public.

STELLENBOSCH

A fter the Constantia Valley, Stellenbosch is the oldest wine-making centre in South Africa. Its foundation goes back to that day in

November 1679, when Simon van der Stel, still in the first flush of excitement and enthusiasm with both his new appointment and his new country, turned aside on his return from a visit of inspection to the Hottentots-Holland area to explore the broad and fertile valley of the Eerste River, and to conceive it as an ideal spot for a pioneer settlement, to be named most appropriately after himself.

The small town thus founded grew rapidly, fed by incoming settlers eager for land and independence. From the start, though wheat and stock-raising were staples of the local economy, wine and its making were an integral part of the burgeoning community's life and culture – as they still are. For while Stellenbosch has contemporary rivals among the other wine-producing districts of the Cape, it still retains its position of *primus inter pares*.

On the official viticultural map, the District of Stellenbosch includes the Divisional Council area of Stellenbosch itself, as well as those of Somerset West and Sir Lowry's Pass; and it also encloses the Ward of Simonsberg-Stellenbosch. Topographically, the district is dominated

The craggy profile of the Helderberg dominates many vineyards of the Stellenbosch District, which together with the town is the hub of South Africa's wine industry, challenged only by neighbouring Paarl.

Two landmarks of tranquil Dorp Street in Stellenbosch are La Gratitude (above), home of the Winshaw family (see page 190), and Oom Samie's General Store (below), which has been in business for almost a hundred years.

by the complex of high ranges of the Hottentots-Holland mountains, the Helderberg, the Stellenbosch mountains, and the Simonsberg, which reach around the town and its valley from east to north-east. A lower and gentler bastion for the town and its adjacent farms is provided on the west by low hills, including those following the course of the Eerste River, the Papegaai hill hard by the town (an eighteenth-century shooting range on the crest of this hill featured clay parrots as targets: hence the name), and those of the Stellenbosch Kloof area. Further to the west the area gradually flattens and merges with the infertile dunes of the Cape Flats, which together with the waters of False Bay to the south form natural boundaries to the arable land. The Eerste River, which rises in the east high in the Jonkershoek mountains, meanders down through the Stellenbosch Valley to debouche into False Bay near Macassar Beach.

At the heart of this broad stretch of land, the modern town of Stellenbosch flourishes as a university and agricultural centre where the quickening rhythms of contemporary life – the university, in particular, provides a lively forum for political and cultural debate – are disguised beneath a carefully preserved historic atmosphere. This is expressed in the formal beauty and dignity of the local eighteenth-century architecture, especially in the region of the central square, the *Braak*, and in the rows of 'senior citizens', the old oak trees, many planted in Van der Stel's day and now declared National Monuments (the ruling on the preservation of National Monuments in perpetuity virtually ensures the town against the pressures of change).

As befits its farming and academic role Stellenbosch is notable for its viticultural institutions. These include the Department of Viticulture and Oenology at the University of Stellenbosch, the only one of its kind in the country, and the Oenological and Viticultural Research Institute, whose headquarters are at the farm Nietvoorbij on the outskirts of the town. Ten kilometres to the north is a further important grape and wine education centre, the experimental farm and campus of the Elsenburg School of Agriculture, once one of the many farms belonging to the redoubtable Martin Melck.

But while these institutions have made a major contribution to local viticulture – not least through creative reseachers and wine scientists, both of past and present, men such as Professors Abraham Perold, Christiaan Theron, Christiaan Orffer (viticulture) and Joël van Wyk (oenology), to name but a few – the roots of wine culture are in the land. This area provides

Stellenbosch is graced by many fine buildings such as the Lutheran Church (left) which overlooks Die Braak, *the town square.* De Akker *is more than an ordinary pub: visitors can taste local wines and enjoy a wholesome meal while their purchases are being assembled.*

a fertile earth and a variety of micro-climates for growing most of the outstanding quality cultivars. The soils tend to be of the Hutton and Clovelly types, with Kroonstad types on the lower lands, and alluvial forms along the banks of the Eerste River – one of the main water sources for vine irrigation. The granitic soils, mostly against the mountain slopes in the east, are well suited to the growing of quality red wines, whereas the vineyards towards the west are located on sandy soils of Table Mountain Sandstone origin, which favour the production of white wines. Along the Eerste River a small number of vineyards are found on alluvial soils, most of which are acidic and require deep ploughing and applications of agricultural lime in the subsoil to achieve a balanced medium for good growth.

The Stellenbosch District in general has a moderate and fairly cool climate, with rain largely confined to the winter months, and with fairly hot, dry summers. The average rainfall ranges from 600 to 800 millimetres annually, while the average temperature during the summer growing season is between 18 and 19 °C, depending on the location. The temperature in the Stellenbosch District varies considerably from one Estate to another, depending on the influence of the south-easterly and southerly winds on the respective properties. Vineyards set against the slopes on Hutton and Clovelly soils, and within reach of the cooling wind from the sea, do not normally require irrigation.

Other sites with different soil types require supplementary irrigation, particularly during the hot months of December and January.

The organization of wine farming to exploit this wealth and variety of resources falls into a number of categories, divisions which are reflected in the structure of the winelands as a whole. The first is that of the primary producers, that is, the farms themselves, of which a certain number have been granted, in terms of the Wine of Origin legislation of September 1973, official recognition as Wine Estates. To achieve this recognition the farms concerned must both grow and make their own wine within the fixed boundaries of the Estate (these boundaries must be continuous, that is, the Estate must constitute a single unit). The general condition of the cellar and its technology must be to a certain standard, though bottling and distribution can be done elsewhere, often through one of the producing wholesalers. The general aim of this classification is to ensure that as far as possible the specific qualities of the land of the Estate shall be captured in its wine. At present, some 32 farms in the Stellenbosch area, the largest concentration of such Estates in South Africa, have been accorded this prized status.

Those farms not classified as Estates operate largely as wine growers, supplying their grapes to one of the Co-operatives, to the KWV, or to one of the producing wholesalers. The wine made from their grapes will be included in the range of products put out by the Co-operative or company, which will decide itself on the style and quality of the wine.

In terms of bulk, the Estate wine farms make a relatively small amount of wine. By far the larger quantity is made by the Co-operatives, then bought, blended, processed and aged by the producing wholesalers, such as the Stellenbosch Farmers' Winery, the Bergkelder and Gilbeys, the three organizations that dominate the Stellenbosch District. If some of the romanticism connected in the popular mind with the making of Estate wine can sometimes be lost in this large-scale production, it is to a great extent compensated by a high degree of expertise, and by skills which are available if desired to the Estate farmers, many of whom have links at the bottling and marketing levels with these larger organizations.

One further feature of the District calls for mention – the Stellenbosch Wine Route (see also page 207). Since its inception largely at the instigation of Estate owners Spatz Sperling, Niel Joubert and Frans Malan, the Stellenbosch Wine Route has been an immense success with the public and with wine lovers, old and new. Its success has encouraged the inception of several other Wine Routes. Indeed, there can be no better beginning for a neophyte wine lover than a visit to these farms, providing as they do both a rich pattern of history and architecture, and an intimate glimpse of the world of the wine maker.

Alto

Since 1974 this has been one the Estates linked in partnership with the Bergkelder. Situated on the slopes of the Helderberg mountain, Alto was once part of a larger farm named Groenrivier, the land for which was first granted in 1693. In 1919 the then owner of Groenrivier, Hennie Malan, divided the farm vertically in order to sell half to his brother-in-law.

The development of Malan's share was a co-operative venture between himself and his son, Manie. In the next few years they set about converting this partial wilderness into a wine farm, to which they gave the Latin name, Alto, a reference both to the altitude of the vineyards and the loftiness of their own aspirations. They built a homestead and a cellar, and planted the lower slopes with vines. On the higher they had grazing and grew oats as fodder, and onion seed (one of the outbuildings is still known as Die Saad Saal).

His choice of cultivars was based on a shrewd assessment of the nature of his land, its strengths and limitations. The vineyards were limited in extent – at present they comprise no more than 100 cultivated hectares – but the granitic soils found here were well suited to noble vines,

situated where both the sea breeze from False Bay and the warmth of the late afternoon sun could reach them.

The main cultivar planted was Cabernet Sauvignon. But the Malans were not wealthy, and the maturation of Cabernet is a long and expensive business. So Manie planted Shiraz and Cinsaut, which make an earlier maturing wine, to blend with the Cabernet. Without the benefit of sophisticated modern soil or suitability tests, he balanced the quantities of these cultivars planted to suit the wine he wished to produce. In the resultant blend, the Cinsaut and Shiraz added smoothness to a dry red wine that could be drunk after only a couple of years' maturation.

The Malans called their new creation Alto Rouge. Almost immediately it began to make its mark, and in an unexpected quarter. In 1923 the elder Malan sent samples of the wine to the reputable firm of wine merchants, Burgoyne's, in London, and received an immediate and enthusiastic order for a supply for five years. A link was thus set up which continued unbroken for over 30 years, Alto being one of the two ruby red wines which reached the British public in this period

(the other was Zonnebloem); both were exported in small casks. With a healthy demand for the wine from overseas, it was some years before the Alto Rouge was released on the local market in 1933.

Manie Malan continued to supply Burgoyne's until 1956, when he left Alto. Thereafter, the farm went through a number of owners, including Advocate Broeksma and Piet du Toit who was part-owner and wine maker from 1959 to 1983 when he retired, and was succeeded by his son Hempies, a well-known rugby Springbok. When he first arrived, neither Piet nor the experts he called in for analysis and advice could fault the planting or the wine created by the Malans. Thus he has continued the fine red wine-making tradition of his predecessors, while developing and streamlining the farm's vineyard methods. A 100 per cent Cabernet Sauvignon has been added to the Estate's output, but the focus remains the famous Alto Rouge: it continues in demand and is now being sold again in London, this time through Henry C. Collison & Sons of St James. It is now a blend of Cabernet Sauvignon, Shiraz, Cabernet Franc and Merlot.

Alto Estate

Cultivars Planted	Size of Vineyards (Number of vines)	Training Practice
Cabernet Sauvignon	76 000	
Shiraz	56 000	
Merlot	55 000	All cultivars are
Pinot Noir	55 000	grown on vertical
Cabernet Franc	25 296	4-wire trellises
Carignan	12 840	

Total area under vines in 1987: 100 ha
Irrigation: The vineyards of Alto are not irrigated.
Temperatures: Records are not kept.
Average annual rainfall: 750 mm
Stock: Root stock and parent stock are supplied to a nursery from which grafted vines are purchased.
Envisaged new cultivars: None
First wine bottled under the Alto Estate label: Alto Rouge 1933
Wines currently bottled under the Alto Estate label (in order of volume): Alto Rouge and Cabernet Sauvignon (both wines are bottled by the Bergkelder)
Wood ageing: Wine is aged on the Estate in both big and small wood.
Capacity of the Alto cellar: 4 700 hectolitres

Alto is not open to the public.

Alto Rouge is one of South Africa's truly great wines, but is not widely known as it has always been made in relatively small quantities. The wine was first made by the Malans, then owners of the Estate, in the early decades of this century and it remains a sought-after blend both locally and abroad. It is now made by Hempies du Toit (above).

Bellevue

Bellevue Estate

Cultivars Planted	Size of Vineyards (Hectares)	Training Practice
Chenin Blanc	53,11	
Pinotage	27,66	
Cinsaut	11,44	
Hárslevelü	9,02	Bush vine
Merlot	8,75	
SA Riesling	5,97	
Fernão Pires	0,63	
Colombar	23,21	Bush vine and Perold trellis
Sauvignon Blanc	12,70	Bush vine and
Weisser Riesling	7,11	5-wire vertical
Gewürztraminer	6,75	trellis
Cabernet Sauvignon	11,73	Bush vine, Perold trellis and 5-wire vertical trellis
Clairette Blanche	3,75	Perold trellis
Hanepoot	2,84	Trellis system

Total area under vines in 1987: 184,65 ha
Irrigation: The vineyards of the Bellevue Estate are not irrigated.
Temperatures: Average maximum: approximately 37 °C; average minimum: approximately 4 °C
Average annual rainfall: 553 mm
Stock: Rooted vines are purchased from a recognized nursery.
Envisaged new cultivar: Pinot Noir

Bellevue Estate is not open to the public.

Bellevue's owner Danie Morkel inspects the Estate's vineyards, where his father was one of the first wine farmers to experiment with the Pinotage cultivar.

This farm, once known as 'Houd de Mond', has been owned since the 1860s by four generations of the Morkel family, and is now run by Dirk Cloete Morkel. In a long history of wine making the farm's finest hour was its dramatic appearance at the 1959 Cape Wine Show with the then almost unknown new varietal, Pinotage.

In 1951 the then owner of Bellevue, Pieter Krige Morkel, having failed to obtain Gamay from a nursery, approached the Stellenbosch Agricultural College at Elsenburg for advice as to what other varieties he could plant. Dr Piet Venter suggested that he should try Pinotage, the variety developed almost two decades earlier by Professor Perold. To that date this new cultivar had been grown at Elsenburg, under the supervision of

Professor Theron, on a trial basis only. Morkel accepted the advice and, together with Cabinet Minister Paul Sauer, owner of Kanonkop, became one of the first farmers to develop a commercial Pinotage vineyard – a move which bore fruit in the prize for the best wine on show at the Cape Wine Show almost a decade later.

Today Bellevue covers 308 hectares, of which 185 hectares are under grapes, and from which an annual crop of over 1 400 tonnes of grapes is delivered to the farm's old wine cellar. Here the fermentation of the red wines still takes place in open cement tanks, the 'cap' formed by the husks of the grapes being submerged by cellar workers using long wooden paddles.

The soil in this area, which overlooks the Bellville district, varies from pure, clean

Kraaifontein sand to a variety of gravel-based soils, to pure clay, a range which makes farming both interesting and difficult. The average rainfall over the past 40 years has been a little over 600 millimetres annually. In general, dry land farming is practised, with only 15 per cent of the vines receiving irrigation from the two farm dams – those concerned being Cabernet Sauvignon and young plants. Bellevue had its own nursery to provide its own planting stock, and also sold plant material to other local farmers, but this has ceased.

All the good wine produced at Bellevue is delivered to the Stellenbosch Farmers' Winery, the distilling wine going to the KWV. A very small amount is bottled by Dirkie Morkel for his own use.

Blaauwklippen

Originally known as Blaauwklip – it is situated on the Blaauwklip River, which runs into the Eerste River – this farm at the foot of the Stellenbosch mountains was first granted by Simon van der Stel in 1692 to a skilled craftsman named Gerrit Visser. The present cool, tree-shaded homestead was built by a later owner in the high days of the late eighteenth century, by which time vine growing was well established here.

It continued into the nineteenth century as a wine farm – in 1840 wine was sold from Blaauwklippen to Groot Constantia.

But by the middle of the present century the farm's fortunes had declined. Converted into a fruit farm at the time of Cecil Rhodes's attempts to find viable alternatives to wine farming in the wake of phylloxera, it had seen no effective wine making in many decades.

Then, in 1971, it was acquired by a new owner, Graham Boonzaier, an industrialist much of whose career had been associated with mining in the Orange Free State but who now returned to the Cape to pursue a long-standing ambition to farm.

Boonzaier's original intention was to

start a dairy and cheese farm based on his Jersey herd. He soon turned his attention, however, to rebuilding the wine farm as well.

The land was in a sad condition. There was only about half a hectare of open ground out of a total of some 70 hectares. The rest was bush, apart from a neglected orchard of 10 000 apple trees. The soil had been devitalised by heavy afforestation, and in all the place was badly run-down.

The bush was cleared, the existing dams enlarged, with well points set up on the river. The irrigation was replanned. An organic manuring programme was introduced to revitalize the soil. Extra land was bought from the municipality to make a total present area of 220 hectares, of which some 92 hectares are now under vines.

In 1975 Graham was joined by Walter Finlayson, previously a very successful winemaker at Montagne, later called Hartenberg. Walter brought with him a pedigree herd of Ayrshire cows (he had originally trained as a dairy farmer), to add to Blaauwklippen's Jersey herd. Soon the existing wine cellar was enlarged and modernized, with complete wine-making facilities as well as new casks for maturing red wines.

The soils on Blaauwklippen are generally alluvial, with Hutton and Clovelly soils on the higher ground. The latter are ideal for vineyards, having good water retention properties. The vineyards on these soils are not irrigated, though micro-spraying or sprinkler irrigation is used on the rest of the farm. Cultivation is purely by herbicide; since much of the alluvial soil is stony and hard on implements, Graham and Walter aerate the soil on alternate years by putting a ripper through it.

A broad range of noble cultivars is now planted. These include Cabernet

The harsh steel of the Blaauwklippen wine cellar is softened by warm wooden beams and a reed ceiling.

Sauvignon, Pinot Noir, Shiraz, Merlot, Pontac, Sauvignon Blanc and Weisser Riesling. Also included are substantial blocks of Zinfandel.

Great attention is paid to detail throughout the whole wine-making process; during vintage time, for example, the pickers, wearing mine-lamps, work on shift from about 03h00 until noon to bring the grapes to the cellar before premature fermentation can occur.

To date their hard work and enthusiasm for the venture have put a substantial range of new wines on the market under the Blaauwklippen label. There are five white wines now bottled as well as five reds, including a Cabernet Sauvignon given Superior status for the 1978 vintage, and a Zinfandel for which Walter won the Diners' Club award in 1981 for the best and most innovative red wine; the following year he won the same award for his 1980 Cabernet Sauvignon. He continues to experiment further, particularly with Chardonnay and some of the more unusual cultivars such as Pinot Blanc, as well as other varieties, to make more interesting blends.

Blaauwklippen Estate

Cultivars Planted	Size of Vineyards (Hectares)	Training Practice
Chenin Blanc	21,02	Untrellised, grown as bush vines
Zinfandel	7,28	
Clairette Blanche	1,67	
Pontac	1,35	
Cabernet Sauvignon	21,37	3-wire vertical trellis
Weisser Riesling	7,20	
Merlot	5,39	
Sauvignon Blanc	5,26	
Pinotage	4,97	
Colombar	3,09	
Muscat Ottonel	2,10	
Pinot Noir	6,30	Grown as untrellised bush vines and on 3-wire trellis
Shiraz	2,86	Perold trellis
Chardonnay	0,5	Trellised

Total area under vines in 1987: 92 ha
Irrigation: About a third of the Blaauwklippen vineyards is irrigated.
Temperatures: Records are not kept.
Average annual rainfall: Records are not kept.
Stock: Parent stock is used for grafting; rooted vines are also purchased from a nursery.
First wines bottled under the Blaauwklippen Estate label: White Landau, Red Landau and Late Vintage (all 1976 vintage)
Wines currently bottled under the Blaauwklippen label: White Landau, Red Landau, Cabernet Sauvignon, Zinfandel, Rhine Riesling; Sauvignon Blanc, Muscat Ottonel, Special Late Vintage, Blanc de Noir, Pinot Noir and Shiraz. A fortified wine, Zinfandel Port, is also made and bottled on the farm.
Wood ageing: Wines are kept in wood on the farm.
Capacity of the Blaauwklippen cellar: 5 387 hectolitres

Besides the 200 000 bottles of wine produced annually, the farm also features an added attraction in the form of a coach museum, and collections of well-preserved and displayed wine-making and farming equipment – a private interest of the owner shared with his visitors. The collection includes Cape carts, 'plaasbakkies', gigs, a horse-drawn omnibus which last ran between Kuils River and Cape Town in 1905, and two graceful landaus, built in 1833 and 1834, which have given a name to two of the farm's most popular blended wines, the White and the Red Landau.

There is also a 'Cape Kitchen', and besides the Blaauwklippen wines a Coachman's Lunch is available to visitors in the summer months. On the Stellenbosch Wine Route, Blaauwklippen is open on weekdays between 08h30 and 12h00, and from 14h00 to 17h00, and on Saturdays from 08h30 to 12h30.

Walter Finlayson 1 has gathered a number of accolades for Blaauwklippen and his innovative approach to wine making was rewarded in 1981 and 1982 when he won the Diners' Club award. The farm is well attended by visitors to the Stellenbosch Wine Route 2 and 3, and especially popular is its fine collection of old coaches.

Bonfoi

Bonfoi lies on the southern slopes of the Bottelary Hills, in the Stellenbosch Kloof. Here the late Christoff van der Westhuizen, who had owned Bonfoi (an old French Huguenot name meaning 'Good faith') since 1958, made both white and red wines. His widow, Jessie, now runs the Estate. The emphasis is still mainly upon the making of white wines such as Steen (which its maker markets as Chenin Blanc in deference to the Estate's French traditions). The fine balance between sugar and acidity in this semi-sweet Chenin Blanc wine helps it to achieve a longer bottle maturation – in competitions this particular product has done consistently well as a bottled wine.

On two occasions in the past Bonfoi's owners have witnessed the capricious power of nature in this low-lying area. In 1933 and again in 1970 the entire crop of grapes on the farm was destroyed in a violent hailstorm. But the memory of either of these disasters beyond the control of the farmer has not prevented the resilient wine makers of Bonfoi from persisting in their chosen vocation.

Bonfoi Estate

Cultivars Planted	Size of Vineyards (Hectares)	Training Practice
Steen	63	
Clairette Blanche	15,95	
Sauvignon Blanc	10,67	All cultivars
Palomino	10	are grown on
Pinotage	7,50	Perold trellises
SA Riesling	7,14	
Pinot Gris	4	
Weisser Riesling	3,03	

Total area under vines in 1987: 120 ha
Irrigation: The vineyards of Bonfoi are not irrigated.
Temperatures: Average maximum 33 °C; average minimum 12 °C
Average annual rainfall: Records are not kept.
Stock: Rooted vines are purchased from a nursery.
Envisaged new cultivar: Chardonnay
First wine bottled under the Bonfoi Estate label: Chenin Blanc 1976
Wines currently bottled under the Bonfoi Estate label: Chenin Blanc (bottled by Bergkelder) and Cuvée Agée (wood-matured Chenin Blanc)
Capacity of the Bonfoi cellar: 8 500 hectolitres

Bonfoi is not open to the public.

Bottelary CO-OPERATIVE WINERY

In the ships of the Dutch East India Company in its seventeenth-century heyday, the store-room for the ship's provisions which contained supplies for men and animals alike was called the *bottelary*, the word (as was its English equivalent 'buttery') being a corruption of the French *bouteillerie*, literally, a place for the storage of bottles. In the days of the Company's first establishment at the Cape, the area now known as Bottelary supplied the fodder for horses. A memory of this origin of the name survives on the labels of the wines made by the Bottelary Co-operative Winery, which feature a design of a pantry on an old sailing ship.

Now a flourishing and well-equipped modern enterprise, the Co-operative began life in the immediate post-Second World War period with limited facilities and support. Formed in 1946 by eight farmers in the area under the chairmanship of Mr F.W. Ninow, the cellar was built on a portion of the farm Welgelegen, purchased from Mr J. Bonthuys. With all the machinery belt-driven from a single tractor, and with the building still open to the sky, the Co-operative's first wine maker, Sakkie Uytenbogaardt, extemporized with considerable ingenuity to produce the first wine from the 1947 vintage – not surprisingly, however, it ended up as distilling wine.

Since those early days of hectic improvisation, the Bottelary Co-operative has matured into a respected winery under its present wine maker Danie Zeeman, who took over the Co-operative in 1972,

Bottelary Co-operative

Wines bottled and marketed by the Bottelary Co-operative

Red wines: Cabernet Sauvignon, Shiraz, Pinotage and Adelroodt
White wines: Sauvignon Blanc, Riesling, Chenin Blanc, Blanc de Blanc, Colombar, Bukettraube, Gewürztraminer, Weisser Riesling, Late Harvest and Noble Late Harvest, and a sparkling wine
A Blanc de Noir and a Goue Muskaat (Hanepoot) are also available.

The Bottelary Co-operative is on the Stellenbosch Wine Route and is open to the public on weekdays from 09h00 to 17h00, and on Saturdays from 08h30 to 13h00.

and has since seen it through many developments. These include the replacement of the old concrete tanks with stainless steel systems, and the introduction of cold fermentation for white wines.

Since 1981 the cellar has modernized tremendously with the implementation of a Vaslin press, a Bucher separator and Roto tanks mainly for red wines, but also used for white varieties where skin contact is needed.

The 37-member Co-operative under the present chairman, Mr Piet Carinus, draws its annual 11 000 tonnes of grapes from within the Bottelary district. Of the wine made, only two per cent is bottled and sold under the winery's own label, the balance of the good wine going to Stellenbosch Farmers' Winery and Distillers Corporation, and the distilling wine to Distillers Corporation and the KWV.

Of the good wine produced, 84 per cent is white and 16 per cent is red. The most important white cultivars are Steen, Riesling, Sauvignon Blanc, Colombar, Weisser Riesling, Bukettraube and Gewürztraminer. The Gewürztraminer and Sauvignon Blanc were released on international S.A.A. flights in 1985. The reds are Cabernet Sauvignon, Shiraz and Pinotage.

In 1983 the cellar initiated a 'Harvest Day' which is open to the public. This annual event involves grape picking in the vineyards and further activities, involving all aspects of wine making, at the cellar for the day. Pickers receive their self-made wine later in the year.

Delaire

Delaire was bought by John and Erica Platter in 1982. It is situated in most magnificent surroundings at the crest of the Helshoogte Pass between Stellenbosch and Franschhoek, facing the stately Simonsberg. From the highest point on the farm can be seen the Groot Drakenstein Valley to the east, and to the west, in the distance, Table Mountain and the hazy sweep of False Bay. The name Delaire is derived from the French for an eyrie, and on the distinctive labels of the Delaire wine bottles, the work of the artist Cecil Skotnes and his daughter Pippa, appear the words 'Vineyards in the Sky' and various bird motifs. One of them is, appropriately, an eagle.

John Platter was born in Hungary, a country which has produced choice wines for centuries. His Austrian father and Scottish mother moved to the Italian Tyrol, where they had relatives, when John was very young, and then in 1950 to Kenya. There they had a cattle farm, grew some vines and made wine. The wine was 'pretty awful', but his father felt, no doubt, that it was better than no wine at all. After he left school, John attended an agricultural college for a while, but when he realised that his true instinct lay in politics he studied history, and eventually became a journalist. He joined United Press International and worked in many African countries, was transferred to London, then the Middle East, and finally to Johannesburg in 1974 as the southern African correspondent for U.P.I. He met Erica, also a journalist, in Johannesburg, they married in 1977 and moved to the Cape the following year, where John began writing his popular wine column for the Rand Daily Mail and other periodicals.

They first settled in Franschhoek, on one of the subdivisions of La Provence, and planted fruit trees. There were Sémillon, Steen and Hanepoot vines on the farm and the grapes were delivered to the Franschhoek Co-operative. John soon realised, however, that the soil on this small farm was not suitable for the growing of grapes for the particular styles of wine he wanted to make. Deeper soils and a cooler climate were necessary for his purposes. In looking for a different site he inspected 51 farms over a long period, until he bought the lofty farm of Avonduur, as Delaire was then called, which provided his requirements and in addition had north- and south-facing slopes and good drainage. The mainly Hutton soils do not require irrigation as there is, usually, ample rainfall.

During their first two years at Delaire the Platters made no wine. They sold their grapes, and spent the time preparing the farm for its future rôle, among other things converting a shed, which had been used for packing fruit, into a practical cellar. In 1985 the first Delaire wines were produced, a Rhine Riesling and a Blanc de

Delaire Vineyards

Cultivars Planted	Size of Vineyards (Hectares)	Training Practice
Cabernet Sauvignon	5	
Rhine Riesling	4,5	
Merlot	3	Modified Guyot trellis
Pinotage	3	
Chardonnay	2,5	

Total area under vines in 1987: 18 ha (4 ha still to be planted)
Irrigation: The Delaire vineyards are not irrigated.
Temperatures: Average maximum 22,5 °C; average minimum 13,7 °C
Average annual rainfall: Approximately 900 to 1 000 mm
Stock: Rooted vines are bought from a nursery.
Envisaged new cultivars: None; however, more Chardonnay will be planted.
First wines bottled under the Delaire Vineyards label: Rhine Riesling and Blanc de Noir, 1985
Wines currently bottled under the Delaire Vineyards label: Rhine Riesling, Cabernet Sauvignon, Chardonnay, Grànde Cuvée, Blanc de Blanc, Blanc de Noir and Cuvée Rouge. Vintage blends are bottled by Stellenbosse Botteleringskoöperasie Beperk.
Wood ageing: The wines are wood aged at the Delaire Vineyards.
Capacity of the Delaire Vineyards cellar: 1 000 hectolitres

Delaire is open to the public on weekdays from 09h00 to 13h00 and from 14h00 to 16h00; on Saturdays from 09h00 to 13h00, or by appointment.

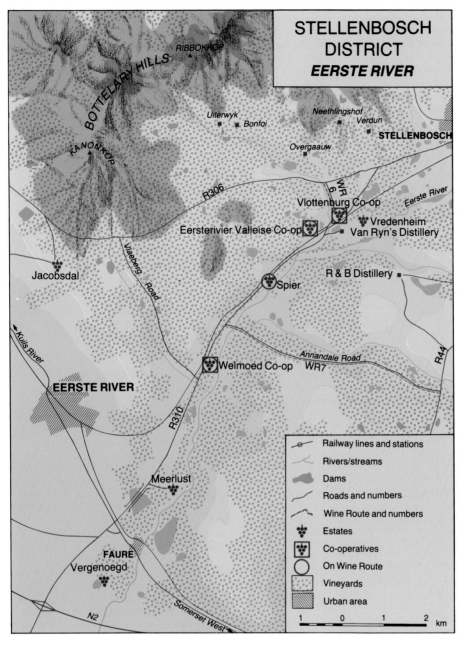

STELLENBOSCH DISTRICT
EERSTE RIVER

Railway lines and stations
Rivers/streams
Dams
Roads and numbers
Wine Route and numbers
Estates
Co-operatives
On Wine Route
Vineyards
Urban area

Noir, followed in 1986 by three new wines, two dry whites and a red. Grande Cuvée is a dry blend of Rhine Riesling and Sauvignon Blanc matured in French oak casks, Blanc de Blanc is a blend of the same two cultivars but in different proportions, and not matured in wood, and Cuvée Rouge is a blend of Cabernet Sauvignon and Pinotage.

John Platter finds wine making a challenge and enjoys its strong element of the unexpected. From the first steps in the vineyard to the bottling of the wine everything can be done 'by the book' and yet each year will yield different results and, sometimes, surprises. He has always been a Burgundy enthusiast and has long cherished the ambition to produce a good Chardonnay. This ambition began to be fulfilled in 1987, when Delaire's first Chardonnay was released, although in small volume. Having spent some time in Burgundy and California observing wine makers at work, he now experiments with different styles of Chardonnay. He has, for example, a batch to which no sulphur at all has been added, a batch which is being left on the lees for a whole winter, and so on. He has planted three different clones of Chardonnay on three different rootstocks, just as in Burgundy most vineyards are planted to several clones. He was one of the unfortunate farmers supplied with Auxerrois instead of Chardonnay, and, having tried regrafting, without success, he has had to uproot and replant the vineyards. These replanted Chardonnay vineyards will only bear properly in 1991, and the financial loss incurred due to this whole exercise is enormous.

Delaire is 38 hectares in extent, 18 of which are under vines. John intends to plant another seven hectares, mostly Merlot, but also some Cabernet Sauvignon. As is the case with a number of well-known independent wine farms, Delaire is not registered as an Estate, as John wants to have the freedom to buy grapes from selected sites elsewhere when required, or simply when he feels like it, which is largely the practice in Australia, California and Burgundy.

The Platters work closely as a team, both on the farm and in the production of *John Platter's South African Wine Guide*, a comprehensive pocket book which is revised annually. The appearance of 'the new John Platter' about November each year is eagerly awaited by thousands of wine lovers.

Publisher's Note: As this edition was going to press it was established that Delaire had just been sold to Storm and Ruth Quinan of Somerset West, and the Platters are moving to a smaller farm on the slopes of the Helderberg, where John will concentrate on producing Chardonnay only.

Delaire's 'Vineyards in the Sky'.

Delheim

In 1938, a retired builder, Mr H. Hoheisen, purchased the 177-hectare property of De Driesprongh for £5 000 from Charles Nelson (a grand-nephew of the hero of Trafalgar, Lord Nelson). With no experience in farming, Hoheisen looked around for someone to help him in the task of making a going concern of his newly acquired land. With the arrival of his wife's nephew, Michael Sperling, he finally discovered the ideal partner.

Ironically enough, neither Hoheisen nor his new assistant 'Spatz' knew anything about wine farming, though Sperling's family had farmed in Poland for 150 years and he himself had been trained as a farmer. The only workable idea that they had between them was that of making wines of quality – and this at a time when the general level of local wine making was far from high.

But enthusiasm and intelligent trial and error soon paid off. Recognition of Sperling's growing skills came in 1957, when Spatz and his uncle came to an arrangement whereby the younger man would run the farm and pay Mr Hoheisen a portion of the profits – if there were any. So, with an injection of £1 500 from Hoheisen's private capital, Spatz began farming on his own, although his aunt gave him much help growing and selling flowers during the leaner times.

The improvement in the quality of Spatz's wines came slowly, but steadily. At this time there were numerous young German wine makers in the Cape, and many of them would visit Driesprongh for the weekend, and, in return for hospitality, would assist and advise Spatz with his wine making. It was at this time that one of the estate's most popular wines, the Spatzendreck, originated. When Spatz was struggling with the making of this wine, he gave a sample to a friend who described it bluntly in somewhat agricultural terms. Since *Sperling* is the German word for a sparrow and Michael's nickname is a more colloquial name for the bird, the wine inevitably became 'Spatzen-dreck'. Spatz vowed he would make his friend eat his words, and with determination went on to develop and refine this fine Late Harvest wine, the label of which shows a cheerful sparrow perched over a barrel, its droppings – the *Dreck* – falling through the bung-hole into the wine.

If the high reputation of the Delheim wines is a relatively modern phenomenon,

the land from which they come goes back to the time of the earliest grants in this area. De Driesprongh was the name of the property originally granted to Lourens Campher by Willem Adriaan van der Stel in February, 1699 – the name Driesprongh is thought to have meant 'where three roads join'. Above the homestead and wine

cellar, set among magnificent old oaks, are the ruins of the ancient house once inhabited by the Dutch East India Company servant whose job it was to fire the cannon on top of the Kanonkop to alert the local farmers to the arrival in Table Bay of a ship bringing provisions. This cannon was the third in a relay, the other

Delheim Estate

Cultivars Planted	Size of Vineyards (Number of vines)	Training Practice
Cabernet Sauvignon	42 000	
Pinotage	32 000	Bush vines
White Muscadel	15 500	
Hárslevelü	7 000	
Sauvignon Blanc	42 000	
Weisser Riesling	20 000	
Pinot Noir	18 500	5-wire vertical
Gewürztraminer	14 300	trellis
Chardonnay	13 500	
Merlot	10 000	
Colombar	15 900	3-wire vertical
Clairette Blanche	8 100	trellis
Chenin Blanc	102 000	3-wire vertical
Shiraz	16 700	trellis and bush vines
Bukettraube	8 900	5-wire vertical trellis and bush vines
Cape Riesling	42 000	3- and 5-wire vertical trellis

Total area under vines in 1987: 118 ha
Irrigation: Most vineyards can be irrigated when necessary.
Temperatures: Records are not kept.
Average annual rainfall: Approximately 850 mm (Driesprongh); approximately 628 mm (Veracruz)
Stock: Parent stock is used for grafting; rooted vines are purchased from a nursery.
Envisaged new cultivars: Ruby Cabernet and Morio Muscat
First wines bottled under the Delheim label: H.O.H. Muscat (dessert), Delheim Cabernet and Delheim Riesling (all in 1949)
Wines currently bottled under the Delheim label: Edelspatz Noble Late Harvest, Special Late Harvest, Spatzendreck Late Harvest, Gewürztraminer, Blanc Fumé, Goldspatz, Stein, Rhine Riesling, Riesling Sec, Heerenwijn Extra Dry, Pinot Noir, Cabernet Sauvignon, Pinotage, Shiraz, Delheim Dry Red, Pinotage Rosé, Riesling Brut and Grand Reserve. A port is also made.
Wood ageing: Wine is aged in wood at Delheim.
Capacity of the Delheim cellar: 9 000 hectolitres

Driesprongh is on the Stellenbosch Wine Route and is open to the public between 08h00 and 17h00 on weekdays and on Saturdays from 08h30 to 12h00. Cellar tours are laid on, and a Vintner's Platter is available from the beginning of October to the end of April.

A vineyard on Delheim's Driesprongh farm on the slopes of the Simonsberg.

Delheim's owner 'Spatz' Sperling is always on hand to talk to and advise visitors to his cellar.

this point limits the amount of available sunshine. Looking back over several decades of experience, Spatz estimates that his vines receive some 10 to 12 days less sunshine (an advantage in the general South African conditions) at Driesprongh, compared with farms lower down the Simonsberg. The high rainfall here, on the other hand, makes it difficult to produce very full-bodied red wines. Although in most years he can make excellent white wines, Spatz maintains that he can only produce top quality red wines when there is a drought. Except for one three-hectare block of Pinot Noir, all red varieties have now been shifted from Driesprongh to Veracruz, the warmer farm, where Delheim's latest red wines such as the Grand Reserve (Bordeaux blend), are produced.

Spatz believes that white wine making is a specific technical skill which can be acquired by training, whereas the making of red wine is more of an art, less of a science. This, he feels, is why the technically acute German wine makers in South Africa make much of the best white wine, and why the locals, who in some cases may not be quite so formally technical, turn out the better reds. Be this as it may, Driesprongh makes very good red wines as well as high-quality whites, especially the sweeter ones.

In view of the farm's inauspicious start, current standards are impressive. A keen Cape Wine Show entrant (subsequently the South African Championship Wine Show) since 1959, when he first emerged with quality wines, Spatz has seldom failed to win a trophy, and has twice been runner-up to the Grand Champion of the Show. Among the wines now made under the Delheim label (the name, in memory of Mrs Hoheisen, is coined from her name, Deli, and the German word for 'Home', *Heim*) are the Delheim Spatzendreck Late Harvest, the Delheim Gewürztraminer, the Delheim Goldspatz (featuring another sparrow, this time continent), the Riesling Sec, and the 'quaffing wine', Heerenwijn.

Delheim's extensive cellar is modern in all its aspects, from grape crushing through to the final bottling and labelling, and can accommodate up to 1 000 tonnes of grapes, of which 400 come from the vineyards of Driesprongh, and the balance from Veracruz, down the valley, with its drier conditions and more generous supply of sunshine.

Since 1973 Spatz has been assisted in his expanded production by a number of young wine makers. The first of these was Otto Helmer, who was succeeded in 1980 by Kevin Arnold, who made wine at Delheim until July 1987. Kevin had had as his assistant Jeff Grier, who subsequently acquired his own Estate, Villiera, and thereafter he was assisted by the present wine maker, Philip Costandius.

two being in Cape Town and on Koeberg. Today this beautiful spot makes a tranquil setting for the cemetery of the farm Driesprongh.

Most of the land which comprised Campher's grant now falls within the boundaries of the farms of Muratie and Nieuwetuin, which lie lower down the valley. The land which today carries the name Driesprongh was first registered when it was transferred to G.A. Berry from William van der Byl in 1903.

Delheim wines are made from grapes grown on two farms: Driesprongh was first planted commercially in the 1940s (the oldest still drinkable wine is the 1949 Muscat-Dessert of which there are a few bottles remaining); and Veracruz, three kilometres away at the foot of Klapmutskop, which was purchased in 1975 (the oldest wine from this farm dates from the early 1960s). Apart from the vineyards, Delheim owns 150 hectares of forest on the steep mountain slopes which enclose the valley. The soil on the farms varies slightly, most of the vines being grown on red granite and on a rocky black turf. The enclosed nature of the valley at

The Departments of Viticulture and Oenology,

FACULTY OF AGRICULTURAL SCIENCES, UNIVERSITY OF STELLENBOSCH

The Departments of Viticulture and Oenology at Stellenbosch University have played a pioneer rôle in the development of scientific vine growing and wine making to South Africa since 1917. In that year the Department of Viticulture and Oenology was formed under its first Professor, Abraham Izak Perold. It was he who began the scientific examination of the local vines, research into their origins (he was responsible for the identification of many of the local varieties with their European counterparts), and the study of their behaviour under many different conditions of soil and climate. Together with these studies went the crossing of standard vine varieties to breed new types, the most famous of these being the creation of Pinotage from Pinot Noir and Cinsaut, or Hermitage as it was then generally known. Besides these practical contributions, Perold made many theoretical advances, summed up in his *Treatise on Viticulture,* published in the 1920s and the first major local work of its kind.

His work was further developed by his successor, Christiaan Jacobus Theron, who succeeded to the post in 1930. Theron (who hailed from the Tulbagh Valley, and where he is now contentedly retired) was responsible for much of the patient spade-work of testing which ensured the survival of the Pinotage vine and its commercial emergence after the Second World War.

Professor Theron held the post at the University for 32 years, until his retirement in 1962. His successor as Head of the Department was one of his former students, Chris Orffer. Appointed Professor in 1965, Chris Orffer made extensive contributions to local viticulture, including many published articles on his subject, and was editor of the book *Wine Grape Cultivars in South Africa.* In the practical sphere he has been responsible, among other innovations, for the introduction of two new scion cultivars designed for the local environment, those of Chenel and Weldra, as well as ten new rootstock varieties. Professor Orffer retired at the end of 1986 and his post has been filled by Pieter Goussard, his assistant for many years. Professor Goussard's place has in turn been taken by Eben Archer from the VORI.

Until the 1960s the Department had been known simply as that of 'Wynbou', a handy word which covers all aspects of wine agriculture. After the foundation of

the Research Institute of the VORI at Nietvoorbij in 1967, however, the Department was split at Orffer's suggestion, to create a separate Chair of Oenology, or the science of wine making. Joël van Wyk was appointed Professor of this new Department; among his specialist interests are the identification and determination of the aromatic substances

'Test-tube vines' . . . A fascinating sequence of photographs reveals the stages in development of a vine from a single-cell culture to a viable plant. This study into the propagation of virus-free root-stock material is led by Prof. Pieter Goussard of Stellenbosch University.

in grapes and wine and their evaluation as they emerge in the wine's bouquet, and the study of malo-lactic fermentation in local red table wines. In addition attention is also focussed on phenols of wine and their relationship to wine quality and stability.

Though technically separate, the two Departments are closely linked in their work, sharing premises in the University's

Agriculture building, where both teaching and research take place. Much of the Viticulture Department's work, however, takes place out in the open, at Welgevallen, one of the University's two experimental farms on the outskirts of the town. It is here that students can both observe the Department's test-programmes in action in the vineyards and conduct experiments of their own.

If the ultimate end of vine growing and wine making is largely practical, the viticultural and oenological courses provided here are well rooted in theory. All students begin their courses with a first year of the standard BSc course before beginning viticultural and oenological studies in their second year. The full BSc-Agric. course, majoring in both viticulture and oenology, takes four years – many of the prominent local wine makers possess this qualification. A BSc Honours course of one year in viticulture or oenology is also offered. And upon submission of a thesis on research conducted under the guidance of the teaching staff of either Department, an MSc-Agric. degree can be obtained. Advanced students may go on to take a PhD in specialist aspects of their subject. At present some 50 students are enrolled in the two Departments.

The complexities of contemporary wine-making theory are well evidenced in Joël van Wyk's Department of Oenology. Here the students all work on an individual basis, studying all aspects of cellar technology 'in miniature' in the laboratory, performing small-scale vinifications to make their own individual wines which are then rigorously analysed and assessed – only in their final year do the students become directly involved in the outside world of the winelands, usually spending a term at the beginning of the year at work in a Co-operative winery.

At the higher student level of MSc and PhD, as well as among the staff, active research is an important part of the calendar. Under Orffer, the Department of Viticulture built up a broad base of studies. These include ampelography, or the study of grape varieties, the breeding of new scion and rootstock cultivars, and studies on the compatibility of scions and rootstocks. Carried out at Welgevallen, these are protracted experiments, calling for careful control and patience of a high order: it is rare for a new cross to be released in less than 20 years (there are still a few patches of Perold's original Pinotage vines on the sun-warmed slopes of Welgevallen).

Further studies examine the resistance of the plants to pests and diseases, and assessment of different ways of treating these – a few vines are grown ungrafted to allow the students to witness the effect of the phylloxera aphid. Heat treatment of vine propagating material to reduce viruses and virus-like infections was one of Orffer's special interests, as was the development of new training and trellising systems.

The study of the rapid reproduction of new vine cuttings and their development *in vitro* in an agar medium, carried out by Pieter Goussard, has been of great benefit to the industry. He works in a small forest of test tubes, each containing a tiny plant, in a temperature-controlled culture room.

In the Department of Oenology, research includes micro-vinifications of grapes from the crosses developed by the Department of Viticulture. Particular attention is paid to the separation and analysis of the wine's components, which are recorded in graph form by a mass spectrophotometer and then computer-stored; these spectra are then compared with many thousands of the records which have been compiled from the literature to make a rapidly expanding library of the myriad possible tastes and aromas of the wines. An even more recent development has been the introduction of oak wood chips into white wine during fermentation, in comparison with the traditional ageing of such wines in small barrels, adding further ramifications to the sensuous spectrum of wine. The flavour substances of oak wood and their significance to wine quality are at present also being investigated.

Behind the meticulous rows of vines on Welgevallen and behind the sober front of the Agriculture Department building lurks a new wine world in the making; if its raw material, that of the vine and the wine, is immemorial, its guiding spirit is contemporary, that of the scientist whose passion is to reach into and understand the inner molecular world of nature.

Devonvale

The development of the modern Estate of Devonvale began with its purchase in the late 1950s by Simeon Blumberg. Almost concurrently he also acquired the firm of Bertrams of Constantia and in 1959 combined his two acquisitions by moving the Bertrams headquarters to the Devon Valley, where he established new and expanded cellars. The enterprise was subsequently taken over by the Gooderson family who severed the connection with Constantia, moving the complete wine-making and merchandising operation to Stellenbosch. In 1972, in their turn, the Goodersons were bought out by Gilbey Distillers and Vintners, for whom the farm is today an impressive showplace, built up over 16 years by its well-known and highly respected former Technical Director, Dr Arnold Schickerling, who retired in March 1986.

Brought up on a wine farm in Constantia, Arnold's interest in wine began early. An interest in chemistry intervened, however, leading him to the University of Cape Town and a Masters Degree followed by a Doctorate. During a two-year period of lecturing at Rhodes University he was invited to join the company then known as South African Distilleries and Wines, returning to the Western Cape to take up his new appointment in 1953.

Having thus come full circle back to the world of wine, he set about applying his knowledge of organic chemistry to the problems of wine making, studying many facets of production both locally and overseas in France, Italy, Germany and California. Then, in 1970, he joined Bertrams Wines to run the Devon Valley Estate for the then owners, the Gooderson family. At present Martin van der Merwe is in charge of wine making at Devonvale, with the designation of Technical Manager. He is no newcomer to the Estate, having worked there since 1978.

The Devonvale Estate, its olive-lined vineyards reminiscent of a typical Tuscan scene, is ideally suited for the making of both red and white wines of high quality. Situated on the southern edge of the Bottelary Hills in one of the most beautiful of the wineland valleys, it has good, deep, rich soil in some areas and in others is relatively sandy. The 160 hectares of vines are almost without exception laid out on slopes receiving the benefit of a tamed Southeaster. When the wind is howling over the rest of the Peninsula it is rarely more than a stiff breeze in the shelter of the Devon Valley.

The variety of soils and micro-climates here provide a challenge to the wine maker and the inspiration for a broad range of fine wines. Martin van der Merwe leads a

Towards the west and the neighbouring District of Paarl, the mountains of Stellenbosch give way to the gentler slopes of the Bottelary Hills.

Devonvale Estate

Cultivars Planted	Size of Vineyards (Hectares)	Training Practice
Weisser Riesling	5	
Grenache	4	2-wire
Merlot	3	
Cabernet Sauvignon	18	Bush vine and
Sémillon	14	Y-trellis
Chenin Blanc	15	Bush vine and
Clairette Blanche	15	2-wire
Muscat d'Alexandrie	18	Bush vine, 2-wire
Shiraz	14	and Y-trellis
SA Riesling	21	2-wire and Y-trellis

Total area under vines in 1987: Approximately 150 ha (8 ha still to be planted)
Irrigation: The vineyards at Devonvale are not irrigated.
Temperatures: Average maximum 25 °C; average minimum 11 °C
Average annual rainfall: 934 mm
Stock: Rooted vines are purchased from a recognized nursery.
Devonvale wines currently bottled by Gilbeys (see page 000): Cinzano Spumante, Bertrams Cabernet Sauvignon, Bertrams Shiraz, Bertrams Pinotage, Bertrams Zinfandel, Alphen Riesling, Alphen Pinotage Blanc de Noir, Alphen Premier Grand Crû, Alphen Rosé and Alphen Cabernet Sauvignon
Wood ageing: Wine is aged in wood on the Devonvale Estate.
Capacity of the Devonvale cellar: 62 000 hectolitres

small team of dedicated wine makers who place considerable emphasis on the importance of good vineyard practices. Irrigation is not employed so as to keep the yield low and concentrate the quality of the grapes. About 40 per cent of the vineyards are devoted to red varieties, including relatively large quantities of Cabernet Sauvignon, Shiraz and Pinotage. During the vintage period selective picking of some of the noble cultivars is done, and this, while labour intensive, helps to guarantee a high quality in the wine.

The Devonvale winery crushes grapes only from its own vineyards; and if the vineyard is important, cellar procedures receive equal attention. In particular, much emphasis is given to blending, regarded by Martin as one of the wine maker's most effective tools. The blended red wines produced at Devonvale are marketed under the Bertrams label, and the white wines mostly under the Alphen label, thus perpetuating two famous old Constantia names, now transplanted to Stellenbosch.

Eersterivier Valleise
CO-OPERATIVE WINERY

This Co-operative, which receives grapes from 19 wine farmer members in the vicinity, was built on a subdivision of the Vlottenburg farm. The farm dates back to 1687, when two French refugees, Pierre Rochefort and Gerard Hanseret (who has posthumously given his name to a number of Eersterivier's products), worked the land, planting the first vines in 1689. In 1709 it was purchased by Antoine Vlotman, who had apparently either rented it previously or had worked on it as foreman, for it was already known as Vlottenburg at the time of his purchase. In 1716 Johannes Wessels bought the adjoining property of Vredenburg, and later in the same year that of Vlottenburg from Vlotman. Thereafter the two farms were run as a single unit for more than a hundred years. In the early 1950s Vlottenburg was owned by Paul Roux, whose family, still owners of the farm, has lived here for over two hundred years. It was from him that the land for the Eersterivier Valleise Co-operative was purchased.

Established in August 1953, the Co-operative pressed its first vintage in the Deciduous Fruit Board's building in Stellenbosch. At this early stage only distilling wine was made, but building was already under way on the selected site, and in 1954 the first vintage was handled in the newly completed cellars by the Co-operative's first dedicated wine maker,

Malherbe Rossouw, who developed the Eersterivier Valleise Co-operative during the next 15 years into one of the leading local wineries. An innovator and designer, he produced a system of static drainers which in their time were far ahead of anything comparable in the Cape wine industry. Their outstanding features were that they drained well, filled and emptied well, and could be easily cleaned. A number of other wineries were not slow to follow suit, employing very similar methods. By the standards of today, Rossouw's invention drained too rapidly, gave a high lees content, and perhaps allowed for insufficient skin contact, but in its time it was an important contribution to local wine technology.

After Rossouw's death in 1970 the running of the Co-operative was taken over by its present wine maker and manager, Hermanus Albertus Coetzee Rossouw, generally abbreviated to Manie. A young wine maker of distinction, he combines the hearty, jovial air traditionally associated with wine makers with an extensive knowledge of his art. He started his career as an assistant wine maker to Oom Sarel Rossouw at the Simonsvlei Co-operative in 1962, and was impressed by both Oom Sarel's hard taskmastership and his attention to hygiene. With this experience behind him, he left in 1966 to be wine maker at the Rooiberg Co-operative in the Robertson

District. Here he set about raising the performance of the Co-operative from the average level at which he found it to that of one of the top prize winners at the Cape Wine Show.

This sure touch in the making of quality wines has been further reflected in Manie's career with the Eersterivier Co-operative. He receives grapes from the farms of the Co-operative's members, all in the Stellenbosch District but widely spread across the area, with crops coming in for processing from the foot of the Helderberg, and from throughout the Eersterivier and Devon valleys, Stellenbosch Kloof and Kuilsrivier.

Great changes have been brought about at this winery in recent years, and it is now certainly one of the most modern and technically most advanced in the country. In 1954 the Co-operative had 17 members who delivered 4 731 tonnes of grapes to the newly completed cellars. Today, with only two more members, the cellars receive between 13 000 and 14 000 tonnes annually.

The Co-operative is on the Stellenbosch Wine Route and receives many visitors. A small percentage of the output is bottled for these customers, but the majority of Eersterivier Valleise Co-operative's good wine is supplied to the Stellenbosch Farmers' Winery, while their distilling wine goes to Distillers Corporation. Except for the popular Hanseret range, which consists of blended wines, all the Co-operative's wines sold to the public are fully certified for vintage, cultivar and origin.

The modern premises of the Eersterivier Valleise Co-operative.

Eikendal Vineyards

Although the land on which Eikendal stands was first granted in 1793 (to Jacobus Carolus van Graan), the first building which the visitor to the farm sees today is decidedly and arrestingly modern.

This is the large cellar, which has become something of a landmark on the road between Stellenbosch and Somerset West. It was designed, by an architect who spent some time in California, to combine the best elements of traditional Cape and modern Californian architecture.

Eikendal consists of two old farms on the lower slopes of the Helderberg, Longridge and Mietjiesvlei. It is said that the site of what was to become the farm Mietjiesvlei was originally called Moddergat, meaning mudhole, by Simon van der Stel, whose wagon stuck fast in a mudhole there, while he and his entourage were heading for the coast on a fishing expedition. There are the ruins of an old homestead and other farm buildings on the Mietjiesvlei part of Eikendal, and plans are afoot to restore them.

A Swiss public company, AG für Plantagen, owns Eikendal Vineyards. This company had extensive rubber and coffee plantations in Indonesia and Tanzania, but after nationalization of its interests in Tanzania in 1976, it was decided to invest in South Africa. The company bought the two old farms in 1982 and set up Eikendal Vineyards. The managing director of Eikendal is Professor R. Saager, who is based in Zürich, but visits South Africa regularly.

Jan 'Boland' Coetzee is a director of Eikendal and acts as consultant wine maker. Trained locally and in Europe, he is well known and highly respected in the South African wine industry, and acts as a consultant to several new Estates and private cellars. Having been wine maker at Kanonkop for some years, he bought the farm Vriesenhof (see page 201) in 1980 and produces excellent wines there. It was with his aid and advice that the winery at Eikendal was set up. The original vineyards were mainly Cinsaut and Chenin Blanc, but on the advice of 'Boland' Coetzee, there have been extensive new plantings of Cabernet Sauvignon, Merlot, Pinot Noir, Sauvignon Blanc, Pinot Blanc and Chardonnay. As these vines are still young, grapes are still bought in to supplement the crop.

The general manager and wine maker of Eikendal is Josef Krammer, who learned his skills in his homeland, Austria. He first came to South Africa in 1971 to gain experience, intending to stay for a year. He stayed for 18 months, working at Delheim. At the time he intended to go on to Australia for further experience in the wine industry, but as it happened he hitchhiked across Africa and finally returned to Austria. There he met Helmut Ratz, who wanted to buy a wine farm in South Africa,

Eikendal's general manager and wine maker, Josef Krammer.

Eikendal Vineyards

Cultivars Planted	Size of Vineyards (Hectares)	Training Practice
Chenin Blanc	27	Some bush vines and 2-wire trellis
Cinsaut	9	
Sauvignon Blanc	7,4	
Cabernet Sauvignon	5,7	2-wire trellis
Chardonnay	4	
Merlot	3	
Pinot Noir	3	

Total area under vines in 1987: 59 ha (8 ha still to be planted)
Irrigation: Overhead irrigation when necessary.
Temperatures: Records are not kept.
Average annual rainfall: Records are not kept.
Stock: Rooted vines are purchased from a recognized nursery.
Envisaged new cultivars: Cabernet Franc, Rhine Riesling and Gewürztraminer
First wines bottled under the Eikendal Vineyards label: Duc de Berry Rouge, Premier Grand Crû, Stein and Late Harvest (all of the 1984 vintage)
Wines currently bottled under the Eikendal Vineyards label: Eikendal Blanc de Blanc, Eikendal Special Late Harvest, Eikendal Cabernet Sauvignon, Duc de Berry Rouge, Duc de Berry Premier Grand Crû, Duc de Berry Stein and Duc de Berry Late Harvest
Wood ageing: The wines are wood aged at Eikendal.
Capacity of the Eikendal cellar: 6 500 hectolitres

Eikendal is open to the public for wine tasting and purchasing on weekdays from 09h00 to 17h00, and on Saturdays from 09h00 to 12h00. A 'Swiss country lunch' (bockwurst, ham, various Swiss cheeses) is served from November to February. During the winter months cheese fondues are a speciality on Friday evenings.

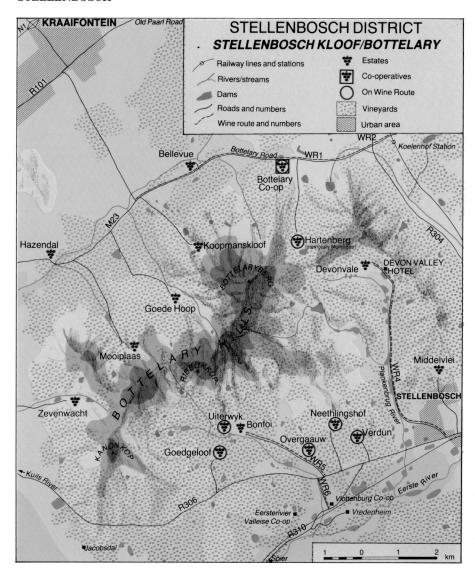

STELLENBOSCH DISTRICT
STELLENBOSCH KLOOF/BOTTELARY

Railway lines and stations   Estates
Rivers/streams   Co-operatives
Dams   On Wine Route
Roads and numbers   Vineyards
Wine route and numbers   Urban area

management of Eikendal Vineyards, and the wine making, from Abraham Beukes.

There are five white wines available from Eikendal – two under the Eikendal label and three under the Duc de Berry label – and two red wines, Duc de Berry Rouge, and a 1984 Eikendal Cabernet Sauvignon, which was their first Cabernet vintage.

The first Merlot and Pinot Noir grapes were picked in 1987, and Josef Krammer is confident that these will make very good red wines, when blended with Cabernet Sauvignon. He is also keen to plant Gewürztraminer and Rhine Riesling and to have special releases of these wines when he feels the quality is exceptional.

The label 'Duc de Berry' is used in honour of the third son of King Jean II of France, 'John the Good'. This son, Jean de France (1340-1416), was duke of, among others, the province of Berry, hence the title 'Duc de Berry'. Although his oppressive policies once led to a peasants' revolt, he is also known as a peace negotiator (with, for example John of Gaunt, Duke of Lancaster) and as a patron of the arts. He spent lavishly on the treasures that remain as his monument, on paintings, tapestries, jewellery and illuminated manuscripts (to such an extent that there was not enough money to pay for his funeral). He commissioned from the Limburg brothers the world-famous *Très riches heures du duc de Berry*, the 'Book of Hours', poetry beautifully illuminated and handwritten in Gothic script. A rare facsimile of this book passed into the hands of the Saagers, and they decided to display it at Eikendal and to use the name as a wine label. The Duc de Berry label is a print of one of the pictures in the book. In future, most of the wines will be marketed under the Eikendal label and the Duc de Berry label will be used mainly for special releases, or wines available only at the farm.

and so Josef found himself back in the Cape winelands in 1975 as wine maker at Villiera, the Estate which Helmut Ratz bought (see page 244). In 1983 the Grier brothers bought Villiera and Josef stayed on as wine maker for a while before returning to Austria. Finally, he returned in 1986 to take over the general

Elsenburg School of Agriculture

This college, which includes an important wine-making course in its curriculum, is situated 11 kilometres from Stellenbosch, on the farm of Elsenburg, once one of the grand total of 10 farms owned by Martin Melck in the late eighteenth century. Its origins go back to 1887, when a miniscule College of Agriculture was established in the Victoria College (the precursor of Stellenbosch University). Its human resources were one principal and five students, while its agricultural resources were limited to half a hectare of rented land near the Stellenbosch railway station.

In 1898 the Elsenburg farm was purchased by the Colonial Government, and the College, now with a complement of 30 lecturers and 193 students, moved out to its new quarters in the same year. When in 1918 the Victoria College became the University of Stellenbosch it was endowed with a Faculty of Agriculture; in 1926 this was amalgamated with the Elsenburg College to form the Stellenbosch-Elsenburg School of Agriculture of the University of Stellenbosch, which in the 1960s was brought under the auspices of the Department of Agriculture and Fisheries.

Today the College is the immediate responsibility of the Director of the Winter Rainfall Region, Dr Johan Burger, the former head of the VORI. He has two deputy directors, Alex Kriel in charge of extension services and Mike Walters in charge of research and responsible for the Elsenburg Agricultural College. One of five Assistant Directors, Mr L.S. Erasmus, is the head of the college.

The viticulture and wine-making course now consists of two years of viticulture with a third optional year of Cellar Technology. Theoretical studies in chemistry and physics, in plant physiology and microbiology, accompany study of vineyard practices such as pruning, grafting and trellising, cellar methods, including cellar hygiene, wine analysis and fining, and practical exercises in wine making. Micro-vinifications of all the major types of wine are followed by experimental wine making on a commercial scale. The students have excelled in recent years, winning many medals and occasional trophies for their wines on the young wine shows especially at the South African Championships at Goodwood.

There are usually about 100 entrants each year on the viticultural and wine-making side with between 50 and 70 going through to do the final year of cellar technology. There is accommodation for some 200 single students. A feature of recent years has been the enrolment of female students and about half a dozen young women each year are embarking on the courses of study to become wine makers.

Elsenburg's contribution to the industry can be seen in the number of highly successful viticulturists and wine makers among its graduates, such as Kevin Arnold, the Champion South African wine maker in 1986, and Martin van der Merwe who has succeeded Dr Schickerling at Bertrams, to name but two.

The Elsenburg vineyards are now planted to a total of some 50 000 vines, representing 22 cultivars.

Gilbey Distillers and Vintners

Typical of those early wine firms which have survived in a larger capacity as modern producing wholesalers, is the big Stellenbosch-based company of Gilbey Distillers and Vintners, commonly referred to simply as 'Gilbeys'.

In 1857, two London wine importers, Walter and Alfred Gilbey, became associated with Cape wines, importing the local port and sherry, Madeira Bucellas and Marsala – an advertisement placed by them in a contemporary London newspaper priced the wines at 20 shillings a dozen, with brandy at 30 shillings per dozen. Within five years the Gilbeys had established a healthy two-way trade between England and the Cape.

It was almost a century later, however, that the company became involved directly in the local production. In July 1950, W. & A. Gilbey, the holding company of Gilbey Distillers and Vintners, was founded in Pietermaritzburg with the opening of a distillery originally designed only to produce gin – the first of the London gins to be made locally.

A decade later the company made a move to include not only spirits but wine in its range of interests. In 1962 Gilbeys acquired R. Santhagens Cape Limited, one of the country's oldest established brandy producers and leading wine merchants. Reinier von Eibergen Santhagens, otherwise known as René Santhagens, or 'Santy', had imported the refined French methods of brandy making to the Cape in the 1890s. Among his innovations had been the maturation of brandy in Cognac

Wines distributed by the Gilbeys Group

Alphen Range
Red Wines: Cabernet Sauvignon, Pinotage, Smooth Old Vintage and Dry Red
White Wines: Riesling, Stein, Premier Grand Crû and Late Harvest
A rosé wine is also produced

Bertrams Range
Red Wines: Cabernet Sauvignon, Shiraz, Pinotage, Stellenrood and Zinfandel Director's Reserve
White Wines: Riesling, Premier Grand Crû, Dry Steen, Chenin Blanc, Stein, Late Harvest and Hochheimer

Carafino Range
Rouge, Dry White, Blanc, Late Harvest and Rosé

Sparkling Wines
Chamblanc Demi Sec and Vin Doux, and Cinzano Spumante

Festival Range
Smooth Red, Grand Crû, Dry White, Stein and Late Harvest

Malamed's Range (Kosher)
Fine Muscat and Fine Vintage Port (both fortified)

Santys Range
Old Ruby Port and Invalid Port (both fortified)

Valley Range
Red Wines: Selected Pinotage, Smooth Red and Selected Dry Red
White Wines: Dry White Premier Grand Crû, Laté Harvest and Stein
A rosé wine is also made

Vredenburg Range
Vintage Red, Blanc de Blanc, Crystal Blanc, Rosé Blanc, Late Harvest and Stein

Bill Husband, chief executive officer of Gilbeys.

oak, the introduction of an improved design of brandy-still (which is still the basis for the modern equipment), the production of light Hermitage wine, a form of cold stabilization of the local wine, and the marketing of sparkling grape juice.

The Santhagens company was based on the old property of De Oude Molen, near the Plankenbrug; and it was here that the new company of Gilbey-Santhagens Limited made its headquarters in the Cape. The amalgamated company began to expand rapidly. It retained the title of

Gilbey-Santhagens till 1970, when, to provide a clearer indication of the company's activities, it was changed to the present name of Gilbey Distillers and Vintners.

In 1968 the company bought a wine farm, De Kleine Zalze, which is situated opposite Blaauwklippen on the road between Stellenbosch and Somerset West. The following year their first wine was made there, and incorporated into ranges such as the Alphen Dry Red and Valley. The first Zinfandel to be bottled under its varietal name, made from the 1975 vintage, was marketed by the company under the Kleine Zalze label, and proved an interesting and unusual wine. It is interesting to note that Gilbeys have indicated that one or two wines may well be marketed under the Kleine Zalze label again in the near future. The present wine maker on this farm is Marinus Bredell, South African Champion Wine Maker in 1983, and formerly of the Helderberg Co-operative. The comtemporary homestead on Kleine Zalze was the home of Allan Bell, who was chairman of Gilbeys South Africa from 1963 to 1987, until his retirement. The present chief executive officer of the company is Bill Husband.

The most important take-over in Gilbey's recent history, the acquisition of Bertrams Wines Limited, occurred in 1972. The Bertrams company had come into being towards the end of the last century, when Robertson Fuller Bertram purchased the Constantia Estate, famous for the quality of its wines for over 200 years. He extended and modernized the Constantia cellars, and conducted his wine and spirit business from the Estate. During the early part of the present century, Bertrams acquired a high reputation for the quality of its wines and other products, including

the internationally known Bertrams Van Der Hum, a naartjie (tangerine)-based liqueur.

The Bertram family continued to control the business until 1939, when it was bought by G.N. Maskell who, in 1940, introduced a complete range of wine and spirits to the South African market under the name of 'Bertrams of Constantia'. New cellars were built adjacent to Groot Constantia, and the company extended its operations into the Transvaal and Natal. In 1943 it also acquired control of Groot Constantia vineyards. A few years later Maskell brought together the various companies under his banner under the name of Bertrams Wines Limited.

In the post-Second World War years, the traditional farming structure of Constantia life began to break down under increasing pressures from urban expansion. In 1959, Bertrams Wines passed into the hands of Simeon Blumberg, who had previously purchased a large wine estate in the Devon Valley, outside Stellenbosch (see Devonvale Estate, page 148). Shortly after taking over his new company, Blumberg moved both its head office and its cellar activities to the Devonvale farm.

The early 1970s saw the brief ownership of the Devon Valley concern by Gooderson Hotels Limited, and a new emphasis on the making of top quality table wines. After the merger with Gilbeys, further rationalization took place, the Devonvale winery concentrating on the making of the Estate's own wines, as well as upon the blending, maturation and bottling of the Gilbey Group's other quality table wines.

Besides the production of its own wines, Gilbeys markets and distributes N.C. Krone's Twee Jongegezellen range of white wines.

The Goede Hoop homestead.

Goede Hoop

Once predominantly a white wine farm growing largely Palomino, Sémillon and Steen, the vineyards of Goede Hoop have been progressively modified by their present owner and wine maker, Johann Bestbier, to the making of fine, red blended wines, the emphasis now being on the planting of Cinsaut, Shiraz, Tinta Barocca and Pinotage.

The Estate was purchased in 1928 by Johann's father, Petrus Johannes Bestbier, and the qualities of the Estate's soil have since been exploited for high quality production. The steep, gravelly slopes high on the hills of Bottelary are ideally suited for the growing of shy-bearing red varieties of the kind introduced by the elder Bestbier at a time when the demand for such wines still lagged behind the public taste for sweet, white fortified wines.

In recent years, however, this taste has moved towards full red wines though, as is the practice with most red wine makers, Johann maintains substantial Steen plantings to balance the work programme in his vineyard calendar.

Goede Hoop Estate

Cultivars Planted	Size of Vineyards (Hectares)	Training Practice
Steen	36,0	
Sauvignon Blanc	17,7	
Cabernet Sauvignon	4,0	
Pinotage	3,25	
Chardonnay	2,7	All cultivars
Carignan	2,6	grown on 3-wire
Cinsaut	2,0	vertical trellises
Shiraz	2,0	
Tinta Barocca	1,0	
Clairette Blanche	0,47	

Total areas under vines in 1987: 80 ha
Irrigation: The vineyards of Goede Hoop are not irrigated.
Temperatures: Records are not kept.
Average annual rainfall: Approximately 630 mm
Stock: Rooted vines are purchased from a nursery.
Envisaged new cultivars: None
First wine bottled under the Goede Hoop Estate label: Vintage Red 1974
Wine currently bottled under the Goede Hoop Estate label: Vintage Rouge (bottled by Bergkelder)
Wood ageing: Goede Hoop wines are aged in wood at the Bergkelder.
Capacity of the Goede Hoop cellar: 4 050 hectolitres

Goede Hoop is not open to the public.

Hartenberg

Hartenberg Estate, which for many years was known as Montagne, was originally incorporated in Nooitgedacht, granted to an ancestor of the Esterhuizen family named Christoffel Estreux, or L'Estreux, in 1704. The name Estreux is now used for the Estate's late harvest wine.

Since those early days the farm has passed through many hands. A famous elephant hunter, Paulus Keyser, owned Hartenberg during the 1720s; Ari Lekkerwyn was in residence for a while; a freed slave, Aron van Ceylon, owned it for a few years; and in 1838, the Bosman brothers took over the farm. Johannes Bosman constructed the existing square-gabled manor house in 1849. There being no Bosman heir to the farm, it was eventually sold to a Swiss immigrant with the magical name of Doctor Hampf. He is the first recorded wine maker on the Estate, though he played safe and only produced distilling wine. The farm's record remained modestly undistinguished until the advent of a Cape Town pathologist, Dr Maurice Finlayson, who bought it in 1949.

Though wine was being made on the premises, he and his wife concentrated, at first, on the development of a chicken hatchery, and later of a dairy herd. No wine of any distinction was made until the Finlaysons' eldest son, Walter, came onto the farm in 1959. At this time, dry red wines, including quantities of Cabernet Sauvignon, and sherries were produced for the Castle Wine and Brandy Company, which incorporated the Cabernet and Pontac into their very popular range of Vlottenheimer wines.

Walter Finlayson had begun his agricultural career by studying to become a dairyman at the West of Scotland Agricultural College. On his return to Hartenberg he was put in charge of the Ayrshire herd, until Dr Finlayson, a veteran lover of good wines, set his son the task of improving the Estate's wine production.

The square-gabled manor house of Hartenberg, built in 1849.

Walter took up the challenge with alacrity, and with encouragement from the Castle Wine and Brandy Company and advice from the Wine Institute, quality soon improved: and with better techniques went an upgrading of equipment. The original cellar dates back many years, but it was substantially modernized in the early 1960s, when Walter and an agricultural engineer, Johan Murray, collaborated to design a compact crushing and draining plant, which was erected on higher ground alongside the old cellar. The wines produced were sold under the Montagne label and developed a high reputation, particularly the reds.

In 1975 Walter, having set his mark upon the wines of Hartenberg, moved off to new pastures, becoming the wine maker at Blaauwklippen, and his younger brother, Peter, took his place.

After Gilbey Distillers and Vintners bought the property a few years later Peter also moved on, to become wine maker at Hamilton Russell Vineyards, and was succeeded, in 1982, by Danie Truter, the present wine maker. Gilbeys changed the name back from Montagne to Hartenberg, a name previously only used by them for a range of inexpensive wines.

The range of modern Hartenberg wines was launched in 1985 and immediately found favour, especially the red wines. The style of these showed a distinct similarity to that of the Gilbeys/Bertrams red wines. The Cabernet and Shiraz will be released not earlier than six years after their vintage, and the Zinfandel not until four years after vintage.

Today Hartenberg belongs to a businessman, Ken Mackenzie, who bought it from Gilbeys in 1986 and who now controls it directly, together with his partner, Graham Elliot. Ken Mackenzie was born in the Cape and educated in South Africa. After serving throughout the Second World War as a fighter pilot, he started a business which grew into a very successful international enterprise. He is domiciled abroad but has always maintained a keen interest in South Africa. He has, over the past 40 years, put together an enviable private cellar in which are represented some of the top quality wines from vineyards all over the world. He and his partner, because of a mutual interest in fine wines, sought to purchase one of the finest vineyards in the country, and, when the opportunity to buy Hartenberg arose, they seized it.

The Estate is now some 180 hectares in extent, of which 98 are under vines. The soil here is mainly of decomposed granite, varying from one to 1,5 metres of deep red loam on the higher southern sections to a shallower topsoil of about 0,5 metres on the lower areas. Steen, Sémillon, Palomino and Cape Riesling are grown, together with small quantities of Bukettraube, Muscat Ottonel and Weisser Riesling, but the Estate is predominantly a red wine producer, with the greater area given to Cabernet Sauvignon, Shiraz, Pontac, Pinotage and Cinsaut. A Swiss clone of a heavy-bearing Pinot Noir as well as Zinfandel are grown in lesser quantities but are being developed. The average rainfall is 750 millimetres which allows for dry land farming, but certain of the white cultivars, mainly Steen, are irrigated when necessary.

Hartenberg Estate

Cultivars Planted	Size of Vineyards (Number of vines)	Training Practice
Cape Riesling	28 100	
Weisser Riesling	18 300	
Sauvignon Blanc	16 150	4-wire vertical
Pinot Blanc	4 600	trellis
Morio Muscat	3 000	
Schönberger	3 000	
Gewürztraminer	18 000	
Zinfandel	12 500	3-wire vertical
Chardonnay	11 200	trellis
Shiraz	46 600	
Cabernet Sauvignon	32 400	2-wire vertical
Tinta Barocca	5 400	trellis
Pontac	4 600	
Chenin Blanc	37 300	Perold trellis
Sémillon	9 000	

Total area under vines in 1987: 98 ha
Irrigation: The vineyards of Hartenberg are not usually irrigated.
Temperatures: Average maximum 24 °C; average minimum 12 °C
Average annual rainfall: 750 mm
Stock: Rooted vines are purchased from a nursery.
Envisaged new cultivar: Merlot
Wines currently bottled under the Hartenberg label: Blanc de Noir, Cabernet Sauvignon, Chatillon, L'Estreux, Shiraz, Weisser Riesling and Zinfandel
Wood ageing: Wines are aged in wood at Hartenberg.
Capacity of the Hartenberg cellar: 5 272 hectolitres

Hartenberg is open to the public on weekdays from 08h00 to 17h00, and on Saturdays from 09h00 to 12h00. Cellar tours are available on weekdays at 10h00 and 15h00, and on Saturdays at 10h00; vintner's lunches are served from November 1 until March 31.

Hazendal

Situated between Stellenbosch and Kuils River on the sandy fringes of the Stellenbosch wine-making region, Hazendal has been the home of the Bosman family for over a hundred and fifty years. The farm itself dates back to a grant of 1704, and features a very fine late eighteenth-century Cape Dutch homestead named after the farm's first owner, Christoffel Hazenwinkel. It was taken over by the Bosmans from the widow Wilhelmina de Waal in 1831. Already well-established in the Cape, they were descended from one Hermanus Lambertus Bosman, the *sieketrooster*, or sick-comforter, to the Drakenstein congregation in the early Eighteenth Century. The modern farm of Hazendal emerged, however, with Piet Bosman, owner and wine maker from 1941 until his death in 1982.

Although Hazendal is particularly well-known for one of its white wines, the prize-winning Steen, the plantings that Piet established were predominantly of red varieties. Most of the red cultivars were trellised while the whites were left as bush vines, the exception being in the low-lying alluvial soils where the white cultivars, particularly the Steen, grow vigorously and therefore need the support of trellises to keep them clear of the ground. Piet never irrigated his vineyards, feeling that the soil retained sufficient moisture for their needs, leading to a smaller crop of better quality. Apart from Steen, Cinsaut is the most important of Hazendal's present varieties.

A traditionalist, Piet Bosman felt that it was important that there should be contact between the must of the white grapes and their skins during fermentation, if only for a few hours. It was on this basis that the Steen was made. A semi-sweet wine, it is both elegant and versatile, since it can be drunk immediately or matured in the bottle for up to five years.

The fifth generation of the Bosmans has now taken over the running of the farm. Piet's son Michael is the owner and wine maker while his wife Carita looks after the dairy herd.

Hazendal has been in the Bosman family since 1831, but it was the late Piet Bosman 1, father of the present owner, Michael, who established the farm as a modern Estate and commenced the restoration of the lovely farm buildings. An intricately carved wine barrel lid 2 graces a wall in the Hazendal cellar.

Hazendal Estate

Cultivars Planted	Size of Vineyards (Hectares)	Training Practice
Steen	60	
Sauvignon Blanc	14	Bush vines
Cape Riesling	8	
Cabernet Sauvignon	20	Split cordon
Shiraz	20	trellises

Total area under vines in 1987: Approximately 130 ha
Irrigation: The vines at Hazendal are not irrigated.
Temperatures: Average maximum 22 °C; average minimum 12 °C
Average annual rainfall: Records are not kept.
Stock: Rooted vines are purchased from a nursery.
Envisaged new cultivars: None
First wines bottled under the Hazendal Estate label: Steen 1974
Wines currently bottled under the Hazendal Estate label: Freudenlese (bottled by the Bergkelder)
Capacity of the Hazendal cellar: 3 000 hectolitres

Hazendal is not open to the public.

De Helderberg

KOÖPERATIEVE WIJNMAKERIJ BEPERKT

Of the nine original co-operative wineries established with government support in the years immediately after 1905 this is one of the four still extant.

At the turn of the century, with the recovery of the local winelands from the phylloxera epidemic and the improvement of wine making and viticultural methods, over-production had brought economic crisis to the wine farmers. The law of 'the higher the quantity, the lower the price'

drastically reduced the earnings of most of them, and drove many to bankruptcy.

In this critical situation a proposal to create a co-operative winery system was put forward, and during 1905 a number of farmers in the Helderberg district came together for discussions with a view to rationalizing their activities and making wine co-operatively (the going price then was the equivalent of R3 for 577 litres). With little prospect of change in the

immediate situation, and with no other available solution to the problem, the decision for co-operation was taken. It was agreed to take up a loan for the erection of a cellar, and a portion of the farm Vredenburg was acquired for the purpose from one of the founder members.

Building commenced towards the end of 1905. Since there were no transport facilities the eighteen founder members turned out to help in conveying bricks and sand from Faure, and cement from the Firgrove railway station, in horse-drawn wagons. The pressing cellar was completed in time to receive the 1906 crop, with an expected yield of 3 000 leaguers (17 310 hectolitres). Mr Dawie de Villiers was appointed the first wine maker at the co-operative.

Power to drive the machinery was supplied in the early days by a steam engine of the type used to drive threshing machines. By 1927, however, it was replaced by a diesel machine; which in its turn became obsolete when ESCOM made electricity available in 1932.

The early years of the co-operative's life were far from easy, and there were a number of defections by members during the difficult time of the Depression years in the early 1930s. Advances in legislation protecting the co-operative movement as a whole, together with the determination of the remaining members, kept it afloat, if sometimes precariously, over the years.

The emergence of the Helderberg winery in recent decades has been largely the work of its former manager and wine

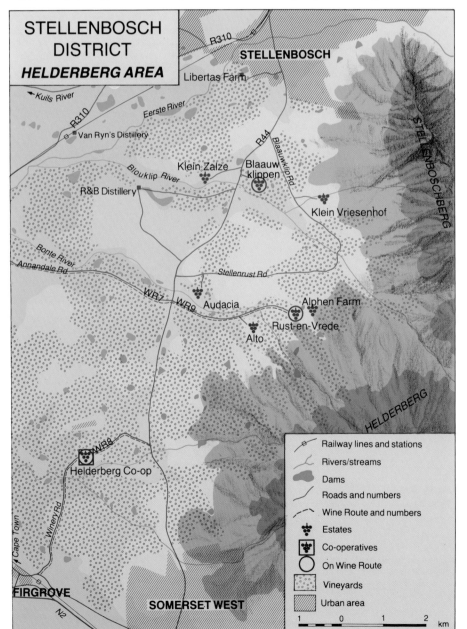

De Helderberg Co-operative

Wines bottled and marketed by De Helderberg Co-operative

Red wines: Shiraz, Pinotage, Pinor Noir, Dry Red and Cabernet Sauvignon
White wines: Dry White, Colombard, Sauvignon Blanc, Cape Riesling, Semi Sweet and Chenin Blanc
Fortified wines: Jerepigo

One of the four co-operatives on the Stellenbosch Wine Route, Helderberg at present bottles its comprehensive range of wines for sale both to members and direct to the public. It is open on weekdays from 09h00 to 13h00 and from 14h00 to 17h30, and on Saturdays from 09h00 to 12h00.

In 1905 nine co-operative wine cellars were established with Government assistance to provide the wine industry with stability at a time when over-production problems beset the Cape winelands. Only four remain in production today; one is the flourishing De Helderberg Co-operative which is a popular venue for visitors to the Stellenbosch Wine Route.

maker, J.C. (Christo) Herrer, whose roots lie not far from the Helderberg. Born on the old farm of Bo Rustenberg about a kilometre from the cellar, he began work at the winery as a learner wine maker under L.T. Sparks in 1945. After attending the annual viticultural courses held at Elsenburg Agricultural College he was appointed assistant wine maker in 1952, and when Sparks retired in 1964, he took over as manager and wine maker.

Christo's speciality was the making of the co-operative's red wines, that of the white being the responsibility of his assistant, Michael Titley. On Herrer's retirement in 1983, after 37 years of energetic wine making, his place was taken by the present manager and wine maker, Inus Muller, previously of the Weltevrede Estate, just outside Bonnievale.

Jacobsdal

This Estate is an example of the ingenious exploitation of limited resources. Situated on the extreme southern edge of the wine-producing area of Stellenbosch, facing the sea less than ten kilometres distant, Jacobsdal combines deep, predominantly sandy soil with a dearth of water supply. Without the advantages of a natural reservoir such as that of the Eerste River, the Estate relies on the 600-millimetre annual winter rainfall.

Given these unpromising conditions the owner and wine maker of Jacobsdal, Cornelis Dumas, has adapted his vineyard procedures with the use of extensive pruning. With a minimum of plant nutrition and moisture available in the soil, it has been necessary to concentrate the strength of the growing vines by cutting back their bearing capacity, and by growing them as bush vines rather than on trellises.

The result of this approach is that though the farm features what are generally regarded as prolific cultivars, the crop, small by comparison with those of other local farms, is of a high quality, the pruning techniques giving fine, rich colour to such wines as Jacobsdal's award-winning 'Superior' Pinotage, to date the only one of the Estate's products to be bottled under its own label.

Of the total 500 hectares of generally low-lying land, about 100 are given to the vineyards. The bulk of these are shared equally between Pinotage, Cinsaut and Steen while smaller blocks are planted to Sauvignon Blanc, Cabernet Sauvignon and Merlot. The remaining 400 hectares are mostly used as grazing for Cornelis's large flocks of Merino sheep.

Jacobsdal Estate

Cultivars Planted	Size of Vineyards (Hectares)	Training Practice
Pinotage	30	
Steen*	30	
Cinsaut	20	Bush vines
Sauvignon Blanc	15	
Merlot	5	
Cabernet Sauvignon	2	

*includes the oldest vine on the Estate (60 years)

Total area under vines in 1987: 102 ha
Irrigation: The vineyards at Jacobsdal are not irrigated.
Temperatures: Average maximum 30 °C; average minimum 5 °C
Average annual rainfall: 600 mm
Stock: Rooted vines are purchased from a nursery.
Envisaged new cultivars: Cabernet Franc
First wines bottled under the Jacobsdal Estate label: Pinotage 1974 (awarded 'Superior' certification)
Wine currently bottled under the Jacobsdal Estate label: Pinotage 1982 (bottled by the Bergkelder)
Wood ageing: Wines are aged in wood at the Bergkelder.
Capacity of the Jacobsdal cellar: 4 800 hectolitres

Jacobsdal is not open to the public.

Kaapzicht

The farm Rozendal was bought by Major D.C. Steytler in 1946 when he and his two sons, David and George, returned from Italy after the war. George, the younger of the brothers, ran the farm for his father, building up grape production from 250 tonnes in the 1940s to 1 100 tonnes in the

1970s. He formed a company in 1969 called Steytdal-Farm (Pty) Ltd, and bought the farm from his father.

George's son, Danie joined the family company in 1976 as farm manager after finishing his studies in agriculture, and in 1982 Danie tried to register the farm as an

Estate. He was unable to do so as a company had registered the name 'Rosenthaler', and the well-known farm of Hazendal was already registered as an Estate. It was felt that 'Rozendal' was too similar to these names, which meant an alternative name had to be found. As the

farm is situated in the Bottelary hills and has a breathtaking view of Cape Town and its mountains, the name 'Kaapzicht' was considered appropriate and the Estate was registered in 1984 under this name.
In the same year, George Steytler Junior joined the company and with his brother Danie formed a company, Kaapzicht-Landgoed (Pty) Ltd, drawing up a lease contract to hire the farm Rozendal from Steytdal-Farm (Pty) Ltd for a period of six years from February 1985.

As a result of a large vineyard renewal programme, the production of the Estate dropped to 750 tonnes in 1986 but there is a KWV quota of 1 600 tonnes, which should be reached by 1992. The wine is bottled by Stellenbosse Botteleringskoöperasie Beperk, but the family wants to keep its bottling venture small and exclusive, with quality and individuality as its main aims, increasing the range to five wines but not letting it exceed 10 per cent of the total production, so that they can manage their own marketing.

Kaapzicht's first wine was bottled in 1984, an off-dry Weisser Riesling. 1985 saw a better vintage, and a more delicate Weisser Riesling with a lower alcohol level was produced, in the same style. In 1986 the Steytlers changed the style of the wine to completely dry, as well as introducing night picking, which improved the bouquet of this vintage.

Kaapzicht Estate

Cultivars Planted	Size of Vineyards (Hectares)	Training Practice
Chenin Blanc	77,7	Bush vine
Hanepoot	18,5	Bush vine and 3-wire trellis
Cinsaut	17,2	
Colombar	3,2	
SA Riesling	3,4	Perold trellis
Pinotage	1,8	3-wire trellis
Weisser Riesling	1,6	
Clairette Blanche	0,6	

The oldest vineyard comprises 2,4 hectares, containing 5 354 Steen/Jacquez vines planted in 1929.

Total area under vines in 1987: 124 ha (36 ha still to be planted)
Irrigation: The Kaapzicht vineyards are not irrigated.
Temperatures: Records are not kept.
Average annual rainfall: 572 mm
Stock: Kaapzicht used its own parent stock for grafting until 1977; it now purchases from a nursery in Wellington.
Envisaged new cultivars: Sauvignon Blanc, Gewürztraminer, Cabernet Sauvignon and Merlot
First wines bottled under the Kaapzicht Estate label: Weisser Riesling, 1984, 1985 and 1986
Wines currently bottled under the Kaapzicht Estate label: Weisser Riesling (all bottling is done by the Stellenbosse Botteleringskoöperasie Beperk.
Wood ageing: No wood ageing is done on the Estate.
Capacity of the Kaapzicht cellar: 5 422 hectolitres

Kanonkop

Originally the land of Kanonkop was part of the farm Uitkyk, the property of the late Senator J.H. Sauer. Then, in 1930, the larger portion of Uitkyk was sold to Baron von Carlowitz, while the lower section was renamed Kanonkop – in the days of the Dutch East India Company, sightings of the approach of the Company's fleet were signalled by a cannon on a nearby hill. It was on this newly created farm that J.H.'s son, the former Minister of Transport, the Honourable P.O. Sauer (respectfully known as 'Oom Paul') began wine farming,

together with Danie Rossouw, in the early 1930s.

Since Oom Paul's death in 1975, the farm has been run by his son-in-law, Jannie Krige. The making of its high-quality wines, however, was the responsibility of Jan 'Boland' Coetzee. A renowned rugby Springbok, Jan has since retired from the game, converting his career to that of a dedicated wine maker. A quietly spoken man, Jan Coetzee, who left Kanonkop in 1980 to farm on his own account (see 'Vriesenhof', page 201), put his mark on the wine-making style of this farm, concentrating upon two cultivars in particular, upon Cabernet Sauvignon and Pinotage.

Beyers Truter, the innovative wine maker at Kanonkop.

Kanonkop Estate

Cultivars Planted	Size of Vineyards (Hectares)	Training Practice
Weisser Riesling	9	
Pinot Noir	8	Perold trellis
Cabernet Franc	6	
Merlot	6	
Sauvignon Blanc	9	
Pinotage	13	Bush vines and Perold trellis
Steen	3,7	Bush vines and 5-wire trellis
Cabernet Sauvignon	30	2-wire vertical trellis
Chardonnay	6	
Cape Riesling	3	2-wire vertical trellis

Total area under vines in 1987: 140 ha
Irrigation: The vineyards of Kanonkop are not irrigated.
Temperatures: Records are not kept.
Average annual rainfall: Records are not kept.
Stock: Rooted vines are purchased from a nursery.
Envisaged new cultivars: None
First wine bottled under the Kanonkop Estate label: Cabernet Sauvignon 1973
Wines currently bottled under the Kanonkop Estate label: Cabernet Sauvignon, Pinotage, Pinot Noir, Paul Sauer Fleur, Weisser Riesling, Sauvignon Blanc, Kadette Rooiwyn and Witwyn
Wood ageing: Wines are aged in wood on the Estate.
Capacity of the Kanonkop cellar: 7 000 hectolitres

Kanonkop is open to the public by appointment only.

These two vines were eminently suited, to the soil and climate of Kanonkop, which was one of the first of the local Estates to plant Pinotage. Of the three main soil types found on the Estate, the most important is the pebbly, granitic soil found on the high, sloping western side of the farm. It is in this area that the farm's Pinotage and Cabernet plantings are concentrated. In the lower areas of the property, where the soil is sandy, white varieties such as Steen, Colombar and Clairette Blanche are planted. In an Estate where the main emphasis has been placed upon a small number of high-quality red wines, the white wines are used to fill out the distribution of labour during the picking season – always a consideration for the wine farmer.

The present wine maker on Kanonkop is Beyers Truter, who has continued to work more or less within the style of his predecessor, while putting his own individual stamp on the excellent wines produced there. In his first seven years on the Estate he has achieved great success.

One of his aims is to restore Pinotage to the important position in the South African market which he thinks it deserves. To this end Beyers makes sure that the grapes are picked at optimum ripeness and that the correct wood contact is given to the wine. He has purchased a large quantity of new barrels of French, American and Yugoslavian oak and is experimenting to ascertain the influence on his wines of each different type.

He has also been experimenting in his wine making with cultivars such as Pinot Noir, Sauvignon Blanc and Weisser Riesling, varying such factors as degree of ripeness of the grapes at picking, duration of skin contact, and so on. He also experiments with Cabernet and Cabernet blends, varying fermentation temperatures and the extent and style of wood contact. A modern bottling-plant was installed on the Estate in 1981, enabling bottling to be done under the most sterile conditions. All these developments have yielded gratifying results: in recent years Kanonkop wines have won an impressive array of awards and medals at wine shows, strengthening the already sound reputation of this fine Estate.

Koelenhof

Established in August 1941, this Co-operative began as a family concern, involving J.W.S. de Villiers, four of his sons, and Nico de Kock. They had their own wine maker, Hugo de Vries, whose son, Helmie, succeeded him as wine maker and is now manager of the Co-operative. The present wine maker is Herman du Preez.

Today the Co-operative has 65 members, mostly in the Stellenbosch District, but some as far away as Constantia, Durbanville, Wellington and even Clanwilliam. The bulk of the wine produced at Koelenhof is sold to Stellenbosch Farmers' Winery and a relatively small amount is bottled for sale on the premises. This winery boasts most modern and technologically advanced wine-making equipment, and was the first to install a fully automatic pressing cellar, operated from a one-man control panel.

Koelenhof Co-operative

Wines bottled and marketed by the Koelenhof Co-operative

Red wines: Cabernet Sauvignon, Pinotage and Koelenberg Dry Red
White wines: Riesling, Chenin Blanc, Bukettraube, Sauvignon Blanc, Koelenhoffer Dry and Koelenheimer Semi-Sweet
A Pinotage Rosé, Steen Jerepiko, Sweet Hanepoot and a Port are also available.

Koelenhof Co-operative is open on weekdays from 08h30 to 13h00 and from 14h00 to 17h00, and on Saturdays from 08h30 to 12h30.

Koopmanskloof

This 750-hectare farm on the northern slopes of the Bottelary Hills is one of the largest wine Estates in South Africa. Once seven separate farms, it has been amalgamated under the ownership of Stevie Smit, the third generation of his family to own Koopmanskloof.

They were preceded by a full seven generations of the Bosman family, beginning with Izaak, who purchased a subdivision of the original farm 'Bottelary' from a certain Jan Rotterdam in 1777. When Stevie's grandfather bought it in 1898 it was run as a mixed farm, with wheat and vines side-by-side. The present owner took over the property in 1956, and has since expanded its production, building extensive new cellars and installing 36 stainless steel tanks, each holding 15 000 litres of wine. He has also split the running of the practical aspects of the farm between two farm managers and his son, Stefan, who has returned from wine studies in Europe to work in his father's cellar.

In Koopmanskloof's rich, granite-and-shale-based soil, Stevie grows a representative range of cultivars. White wine cultivars account for about two-thirds of the vineyards, Chenin Blanc alone making up some 40 per cent of plantings. Other white cultivars include Weisser Riesling (he grows no Cape Riesling), Colombar and Clairette Blanche. Red varieties include Pinotage and Shiraz, together with good quantities of Cinsaut. All the vines are grown as bush vines, using organic fertilizer only.

At present only two of Koopmanskloof's wines, the Blanc de Marbonne and the Rhine Riesling are marketed (by the Bergkelder) under the Estate's label. Made from Chenin Blanc, the Blanc de Marbonne is a superb wine and the pride of the Estate. First marketed in 1979, it received the Gold Medal at the International Club Oenologique Wine and Spirit Competition in London in its début year.

Following the success of the Blanc de Marbonne, the first Koopmanskloof Rhine Riesling, the 1984 vintage, was released to great acclaim. The 1986 vintage of this wine carries a neck label depicting a species of fynbos, *Erica mammosa ericaccae*, one of the splendid ericas found on Koopmanskloof, and subsequent vintages will depict a different species each year. Similarly, other species of fynbos will appear on the neck labels of the Blanc de Marbonne from the 1987 vintage onwards. The delicate drawings are by the talented Cape illustrator Drexler Kyzer. Stevie Smit's interest in the wealth of flora in his part of the world has led him to establish a 60-hectare fynbos reserve on Koopmanskloof.

Between running his Estate and his involvement in the public affairs of the Stellenbosch area (he has been, among other things, a Divisional Councillor), Stevie seeks peace and relaxation in the beautiful mountains which surround him. At the highest point of the Vineyard Trail, the 24-kilometre hiking trail along the crest of the Bottelary Hills which he was instrumental in establishing, he has built a stone rondavel, and makes energetic dashes up the hill from the farm to this peaceful retreat. This dynamic, tireless farmer can also be seen every year among the runners in the 'Winelands Fun Run' on the slopes of the Papegaaiberg at Stellenbosch, and on Sundays jogging up Table Mountain before breakfast.

Koopmanskloof Estate

Cultivars Planted	Size of Vineyards (Hectares)	Training Practice
Chenin Blanc	300	
Cinsaut Blanc	20	
Furmint	15	
Sauvignon Blanc	35	
Pinotage	10	
Tinta Barocca	18	
Cinsaut	10	Bush vines
Pinot Gris	20	
Carignan	10	
Cabernet Sauvignon	8	
Sémillon	5	
Raisin Blanc, Ugni Blanc, Pedro, Hanepoot, Braakland	60	
Colombar	30	
Weisser Riesling	30	Vertical trellis
Shiraz	22	

Total area under vines in 1987: 650 ha
Irrigation: About 50 ha of the Koopmanskloof vineyards are irrigated.
Temperatures: Records are not kept
Average annual rainfall: Approximately 600 mm
Stock: Rooted vines are purchased from a nursery
Envisaged new cultivars: Sauvignon Blanc, Chardonnay, Pinot Noir and Merlot
First wine bottled under the Koopmanskloof Estate label: Blanc de Marbonne 1979
Wines currently bottled under the Koopmanskloof Estate label: Blanc de Marbonne and Rhine Riesling (bottled by the Bergkelder)
Capacity of the Koopmanskloof cellar: 42 000 hectolitres

Koopmanskloof is not open to the public.

Stevie Smit.

Le Bonheur

Le Bonheur Estate

Cultivars Planted	Size of Vineyards (Number of vines)	Training Practice
Steen	30 000	Perold trellis
Shiraz	25 800	3-wire vertical
Cabernet Sauvignon	39 000	trellis
Chardonnay	40 000	
Sauvignon Blanc	37 400	5-wire modified
Merlot	17 000	Perold trellis
Carignan	7 200	Bush vines

Total area under vines in 1987: 70 ha
Irrigation: The vineyards of Le Bonheur are not irrigated.
Temperatures: Records are not kept.
Average annual rainfall: Approximately 800 mm
Stock: Parent stock is used for grafting; rooted vines are also purchased from a nursery.
Envisaged new cultivars: Pinot Noir
First wines bottled under the Le Bonheur label: Rosé Sec 1979, Cabernet Sauvignon Rosé 1981/82 and Blanc Fumé (Sauvignon Blanc) 1981/82
Wines currently bottled under the Le Bonheur label: Cabernet Sauvignon, Blanc Fumé and Chardonnay (all bottled by Bergkelder)
Wood ageing: Wines are aged at the Bergkelder.
Capacity of the Le Bonheur cellar: 4 000 hectolitres

Le Bonheur is not open to the public.

Previously known as Oude Weltevreden, this 163-hectare Estate with the optimistic name of Le Bonheur – 'Happiness' – is situated along the slopes of the Klapmuts Hill on the northern point of the Simonsberg.

In earlier decades the original road between Stellenbosch and Paarl crossed the farm, and there was a public outspan by the vlei on the property. The first owner of the Estate was a Jacob Isak de Villiers, to whom it was issued by Lord Charles Somerset. It was he who built the H-shaped Cape Dutch homestead, developing it from a building believed once to have been an outbuilding of the farm Natte Vallei. The roof of the homestead was destroyed by fire some seventy years ago; when it was rebuilt the characteristic gables of the period were covered by a corrugated iron roof.

The farm was bought by Michael Woodhead in the early 1970s. Born in Johannesburg, he studied Tropical Agriculture and Soil Science at a university in Holland. Before becoming a wine farmer he held a variety of positions in agriculture in different parts of the world, working in South America on sugar plantations, raising beef, tobacco and maize in Swaziland, and running a cattle ranch in the Knysna area. He was also once an agricultural adviser to the President of Tanzania, Julius Nyerere.

When Michael acquired Oude Weltevreden, both lands and house were considerably dilapidated, and wine had not been made on the farm for 50 years. He found that the soils here were relatively poor. The lower-lying areas were sandy, with a clay sub-soil, while those on the higher areas, running from Klapmuts Hill to Klapmuts Nek, though of granite origin and deep and well-drained, were also poor in quality.

Enrichment of the soil was obviously a priority and large quantities of compost were introduced to improve the organic matter content. Michael has a dairy which produces about half his compost needs; a small stud farm on the property also makes its contribution. Grape husks added to the soil, a regular practice on most farms, have also helped to improve its quality. He has

Since his arrival at Le Bonheur, owner and wine maker Michael Woodhead has placed great emphasis on improving soil quality on the Estate and has completely replanted the vineyards.

generally been very active in attempting to restructure the composition of his soils as far as possible along the lines of some of the better vineyard soils of France.

Complete replanting of the vineyards was undertaken. Red cultivars introduced include Cabernet Sauvignon, Shiraz and Carignan; white include Steen, Sauvignon Blanc and Chardonnay. Michael is one of the few local farmers to grow Carignan, an important grape in the South of France but rare here, which he intends to use in blending – with a full-bodied Shiraz, for example. Because he has difficulty in obtaining the rootstocks he prefers – Richter 110 on the clay soil and Richter 99 on the other soils – he has started his own nursery and mother plantation, now numbering about 20 000 vines.

The Estate launched a 1981 vintage dry rosé which was made in the traditional manner for this kind of wine, and exclusively from Cabernet Sauvignon grapes. The 1982 vintage was even better, yet, incredibly, neither of these excellent wines, which were fresh and fruity with unmistakeable Cabernet character and delightful colour, took the fancy of the consumers to any extent, and have now been discontinued. The Le Bonheur Blanc Fumé, which followed, has become a bench mark for wines of its type. It is made from Sauvignon Blanc, a selectively cultivated variety which gives a very dry but full wine with a flowery aroma. More recently magnificent Cabernets from the 1982 and 1983 vintages have been released. Made entirely from Cabernet Sauvignon, and well aged in small wood, they show promise of being truly great in the 1990s. The Le Bonheur Chardonnay also promises to be an exceptional wine.

Lievland

The tiny eastern European state of Lievland, which since the Second World War has disappeared from the map, gave its name posthumously to this Estate. In the early 1930s, the Baron von Stiernhielm of Lievland came to South Africa and bought land at the Cape. The Baron, however, died before he could bring his family to the country he had decided to make his home, leaving his widow to bring her four children out alone in 1936.

The farm her husband had purchased, Beyers Kloof, had, until 1820, been part of the property of Natte Vallei. The Dutch-born Baroness promptly renamed it Lievland, in honour of her husband's fatherland. She also set out to make it a paying proposition. An indomitable woman, she took up the study of viticulture under Dr A.I. Perold, and within four years was making her own wine. At first she was assisted by a wine maker, but soon decided she could do the job better and more cheaply herself, and therefore boldly took on the running of the whole operation.

The wines she made in those early days were an 'Uitgesoekte Riesling' made from Cape Riesling, a Burgundy-type red, various sherries and ports (including a 'volbloed' vintage port) and a red Jeripigo which cost 12 shillings a gallon in 1960. These wines were marketed under the names of Santa Monica and Beyerskloof. This remarkable and enterprising lady retired to a flat in Cape Town in 1964, where she lived until her death in 1982. After an interregnum of nine years during which no wine was made on the farm, it was bought in 1973 by Dan Benadé and Gert van der Merwe.

The new owners took Lievland in hand, planting a range of new cultivars, including Bukettraube, Kerner, Weisser Riesling, Sauvignon Blanc and Merlot. Then, in 1982, a new cellar was completed and Lievland was once again equipped to make and bottle its own wine.

One of the most enterprising newcomers to the winelands, Janey Muller, was approached to become wine maker at Lievland. In a wine milieu largely dominated by men, Janey has staked out a

Lievland Estate

Cultivars Planted	Size of Vineyards (Number of vines)	Training Practice
Chenin Blanc	47 000	Bush vines and 3-wire vertical trellises
Cinsaut	7 000	Bush vine
Cabernet Sauvignon	29 000	
Cape Riesling	25 000	
Weisser Riesling	12 500	
Shiraz	9 000	3-wire vertical trellis
Bukettraube	8 500	
Kerner	7 000	
Sauvignon Blanc	7 000	
Merlot	6 000	
Clairette Blanche	4 000	

Total area under vines in 1987: 55 ha (10 ha still to be planted)
Irrigation: The vineyards of Lievland are not irrigated.
Temperatures: Records are not kept.
Average annual rainfall: Approximately 875 mm
Stock: Rooted vines are purchased from a nursery.
Envisaged new cultivars: Cabernet Franc, Ruby Cabernet, Gewürztraminer and Chardonnay (grafted onto existing Muscadel root stock)
First wines bottled under the Lievland Estate label: Cape Riesling, Riesling, Chenin Blanc, Stein, Cellar Master's Private Reserve, Director's Private Stock and Lievland Rood (all in 1982)
Wines currently bottled under the Lievland Estate label: Bukettraube, Cabernet Sauvignon, Cheandrie, Kerner, Noble Late Harvest, Rood, Sauvignon Blanc, Shiraz and Weisser Riesling
Wood ageing: Wines are aged in wood on the Estate.
Capacity of the Lievland cellar: 2 100 hectolitres

The Lievland Estate is open to the public on weekdays from 09h00 to 17h00 and on Saturdays from 09h00 to 13h00.

The beautiful vineyards of Lievland, like those of Uitkyk, came into being through the efforts of a European nobleman, Baron von Stiernhielm. Today the owner is Paul Benadé and the wine maker is Abraham Beukes.

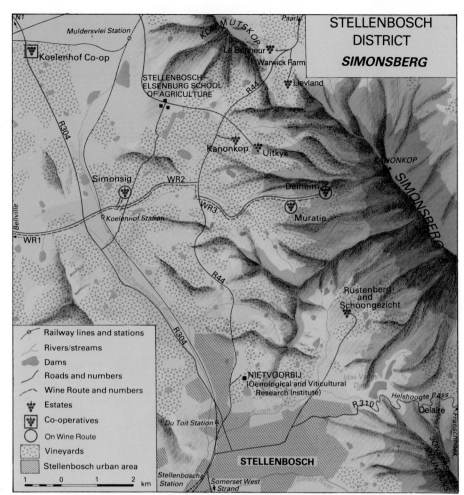

claim for herself, all the more impressive for the fact that she does not come from a wine-making family or even directly from the winelands. Brought up in Sea Point, she picked up a love of wine from her father, an enthusiasm which gradually became an *idée fixe*, finally leading her to study viticulture and oenology at Stellenbosch University. With her husband, Jan Muller, she started a small wine Estate, that of Lémberg, in the Tulbagh Valley (see page 258). While working to consolidate this new farm the couple met Gert van der Merwe, with whom they worked out a double-sided arrangement, Janey making wine both at Lievland and at Lemberg – differences of ripening times in the two areas allow for this kind of 'shuttle wine making' between the two farms. After two years of hard but successful work Janey left Lievland to concentrate on wine making at Lemberg.

In 1984 Paul Benadé, Dan's son, took over the management of the Estate. A B.Comm. graduate from the University of Port Elizabeth, Paul had previously worked at Stellenbosch Farmers' Winery in the marketing division. Jako Smit joined the Estate as wine maker that year, and on his departure in 1987 was succeeded by Abraham Beukes who had previously worked as wine maker at Eikendal and Simonsig. Having bought his father's interest in Lievland, Paul Benadé

is now sole owner of the Estate, and has embarked on a vigorous planting programme, adding some 24 000 new wines in the last four years. In addition to

the cellar built in 1982 a new underground cellar for maturation and storage was completed in 1987, further strengthening the infrastructure of this sound Estate.

Meerlust

Situated on the Eerste River near the old Companiesdrift Road to Somerset West, the Estate of Meerlust has a long and fascinating history, reaching back to the turn of the Eighteenth Century. It was then that the first owner of the land, Henning Huysing, built the basic T-shaped house around which the rest of the complex was subsequently developed. An ambitious and enterprising Free Burgher, he amassed vast wealth through obtaining the monopoly on the meat trade, supplying

the passing ships of the Dutch East India Company's fleet on their way to the Orient. Besides the land at Meerlust, he also secured extensive grazing rights in the Eerste River area on which his enormous herds, reputed to number 20 000 cattle and 60 000 sheep, were fattened.

All this wealth and abundance appears to have aroused the ire of the then Governor of the Colony, Willem Adriaan van der Stel. Among the many enemies made by the younger Van der Stel,

Huysing was the most powerful. He became the natural leader for the insurgence of the Free Burghers against the tyranny of the Company's servants. Arrested and sent with a number of the other rebels to Holland to appear before the Council, he made out a convincing case both for the Governor's guilt and his own innocence: and when Van der Stel went into exile Huysing returned, a free man, to Meerlust.

He died in 1713, without leaving an heir.

Bringing in the harvest at Meerlust.

The present owner of Meerlust, Nico Myburgh (left), here discussing the Estate's products with his wine maker Giorgio Dalla Cia.

Hannes Myburgh.

Meerlust Estate

Cultivars Planted	Size of Vineyards (Number of vines)	Training Practice
Cabernet Sauvignon	160 000	
Merlot	120 000	
Cabernet Franc	70 000	
Pinot Noir	65 000	4-wire vertical
Steen	65 000	trellis
Pinotage	15 000	
Sauvignon Blanc	15 000	
Hanepoot	5 000	
Chardonnay	1 000	

Total area under vines in 1987: 235 ha
Irrigation: All the vineyards can be irrigated.
Temperatures: Records are not kept.
Average annual rainfall: Approximately 650 mm
Stock: Rooted vines are purchased from a nursery.
Envisaged new cultivars: None
First wine bottled under the Meerlust Estate label: Cabernet Sauvignon 1975
Wines currently bottled under the Meerlust Estate label: Cabernet Sauvignon, Rubicon, Pinot Noir and Merlot (all Meerlust wines are bottled by the Bergkelder)
Wood ageing: Wines are aged in wood on the Estate, but not at the Bergkelder.
Capacity of the Meerlust cellar: 12 000 hectolitres

Meerlust Estate is not open to the public.

Thereafter, the farm passed through a number of hands until, in 1756, it came into the possession of Johannes Albertus Myburgh.

By this date wine making was already well established, both in the locality and at Meerlust. Myburgh and his son expanded the farm to its present extent, building the complex of cellars, stables and slave workshops, each with its insignia over the door of the trade carried on within, and of the columbarium, or pigeon-house, a rare and beautiful example of its kind. They also made additions to the homestead itself, adding a further T-shape to the front of Huysing's original design to create the present unique and eccentric variant of the local H-shaped Cape Dutch ground plan.

By the time Nicolaas Myburgh, the present owner and eighth generation of this family to own the farm, took it over in 1950, the condition of the property had declined sadly from its late eighteenth-century splendour. Its wines, too, were not generally of exceptional quality. Based mainly on two grape varieties, the Steen and Green Grape (Sémillon), they were mostly of the sweet fortified type which appealed to the taste of the earlier part of the century.

Nicolaas (better known as Nico) set out

both to repair and restore the time-worn homestead and to replant the vineyards, introducing new and better vines and developing a range of fine wines, including a number of red wines of exceptional quality. During the last three and a half decades both these activities have been carried out concurrently, improvements in the wine making to a large extent financing a superb restoration of the farm complex, one of the largest of its kind.

Crucial to this change to a better quality product was the introduction of adequate water supplies. Nico built a large dam on the Estate. Water reserves for the summer season are pumped into them from the Eerste River, and they supply the spray irrigation used. Nico's approach to his

Cabernet Sauvignon and Pinot Noir vines has been to prune the shy-bearing varieties so as to give a relatively high yield, but to support the extra burden on the plant with irrigation (an exception being the prolific Cinsaut, which loses colour and flavour in the wine with excessive irrigation). Further moisture in this area comes from the mists which are a feature of the coastal belt.

The area under cultivation has been expanded from its previous 85 hectares to its present 235 hectares. Though the Estate is close to the sea and benefits from the breeze which reaches across the dunes from False Bay, there are few sandy areas. Two main soils are found: the deep-draining alluvial types which flank the

river well support the farm's white wine cultivars – as with most red wine growers, these varieties are used to keep production continuous throughout the harvesting season. On the higher ground is the pebbly loam soil on which are grown the red varieties which are Meerlust's speciality, the Cabernet Sauvignon, Pinot Noir, Cabernet Franc and Merlot vines.

The white wine grapes are supplied direct to a wine merchant for the making of blended wines: the red are processed and fermented at Meerlust. This activity is shared between Nico, his son Hannes and Giorgio Dalla Cia, the skilled wine master; the three men work together in balancing the colour and flavour of their wines to make the Estate's prize-winning blends.

The vineyards and the gracious homestead of Meerlust, which have belonged to the Myburgh family for eight successive generations.

'Stil Jan' Momberg, owner and wine maker of the Middelvlei Estate.

Middelvlei

Middelvlei Estate

Cultivars Planted	Size of Vineyards (Number of vines)	Training Practice
Pinotage	62 200	Bush vines
Cinsaut	46 900	
Chenin Blanc	92 900	
Cabernet Sauvignon	62 000	2-wire vertical trellis
Clairette Blanche	28 500	
Sauvignon Blanc	45 200	
Chardonnay	33 550	
Shiraz	19 700	4-wire vertical trellis
Tinta Barocca	15 000	
Hárslevelü	4 500	

Total area under vines in 1987: 130 ha
Irrigation: Only the Tinta Barocca and Clairette Blanche vineyards are irrigated.
Temperatures: Records are not kept.
Average annual rainfall: 596 mm
Stock: Rooted vines are purchased from a nursery.
First wines bottled under the Middelvlei Estate label: Pinotage 1973
Wines currently bottled under the Middelvlei Estate label: Pinotage and Cabernet Sauvignon (bottled by the Bergkelder)
Wood ageing: Wines are aged in wood at the Bergkelder.
Capacity of the Middelvlei cellar: 12 000 hectolitres

Middelvlei is not open to the public.

The neat, carefully tended vineyards of Middelvlei are bounded on one side by houses, gardens and tarred streets. The suburbs of Stellenbosch now extend to the front gate of this lovely Estate, where the emphasis has always been on the making of red wines. The wine maker and owner of the farm is 'Stil Jan' Momberg, to be distinguished from his cousin 'Jan Bek' Momberg formerly of Neethlingshof (see page 173).

The two Jan Mombergs jointly inherited the farm of Middelvlei (their fathers, who were brothers, had worked the farm together for many years previously). Then in 1963 Jan Bek sold his share of Middelvlei to Stil Jan, and purchased the nearby Estate of Neethlingshof, leaving Stil Jan as the sole owner of Middelvlei Estate.

Since those days Jan has done much to develop Middelvlei's potential. In the course of extensive replantings, he has altered the inherited 80:20 ratio of red to white cultivars to equal amounts of each.

To secure registration of Middelvlei as an officially recognized wine Estate he rebuilt and re-equipped the farm's antiquated cellar, installing cold fermentation equipment for the white wines as well as cooling equipment to control the fermentation of the red wines.

The rich granite soil of this area of the Bottelary Hills favours the making of Middelvlei's Pinotage, which has been a consistently fine example of this cultivar wine for many years. Jan prunes his Pinotage vines to reduce their otherwise prolific bearing capacity, adding the press-juice to the free-run juice and maturing the

wine in wood before bottling. The success of his Pinotage has led him to expand his plantings of this cultivar and to plant Cabernet Sauvignon, from which the first wine was pressed in 1981, in almost equal quantities. This Middelvlei Cabernet Sauvignon was released in 1985 and has proved to be an excellent wine, gaining gold medals at the Stellenbosch and South African Championship shows. Nonetheless, the proportion of wine marketed under the Estate's own label remains fairly small, the bulk of production being supplied to the Bergkelder.

Morgenhof

The early history of Morgenhof is somewhat chequered. This is reflected not only in the number of times the farm changed hands, but also in its different

names. The original farm (granted in 1680) was known as Harmony, but the good will inherent in the name seems to have been lost in later years, when it was renamed

Onrus, after a water rights dispute among the family members who owned the farm.

When 'Stil Jan' Momberg, of Middelvlei, took over the farm it was known as

Morgenhof. In a most neglected state when he bought it, the farm thrived on Jan's expertise. Previous owners had taken much from the land without putting anything back, but Jan set about remedying the situation by improving the existing vineyards and developing new ones. He did not concern himself with the restoration of the buildings, however, as his home is at Middelvlei.

In 1981 Morgenhof was bought by three German businessmen. Gert Grobe, the managing director of Schenk Filters (a subsidiary of Rhine Ruhr Holdings (Pty) Ltd) and his associates have committed themselves not only to improving the vineyards and the farm in general, but also to investing much money in restoring the dilapidated homestead and outbuildings, which were erected in 1820. The chicken house, built in 1770, has received particular attention. Plans are afoot to renovate it as a tasting room, featuring a traditional floor, nowadays rare, made of peach pips arranged in a special pattern, with a protective wax covering. A building shown on old drawings of the farm, is to be rebuilt and will be used as a restaurant.

The hilly terrain at Morgenhof provides ideal sites for the various needs of different cultivars (the highest ground, for example, is reserved for Chardonnay), and the first vintage was a 1984 Cabernet Sauvignon made under the direction of Pieter Theron, who, having retired after 40 years at the KWV, joined Morgenhof as wine maker. A replanting programme is in progress with new virus-free plant material replacing the old vineyards (to date Cinsaut has been

removed in favour of Rhine Riesling), and the completion of a new cellar, with a capacity of 500 tonnes of grapes, is envisaged by 1991.

As Gert Grobe is resident in Johannesburg, the farm is in the capable hands of Lorene Thompson, who is both public relations officer for Morgenhof and

represents Schenk Filters in Cape Town. Lorene oversees most of the activities of the farm, as diverse as the laying of the peach pip floor and catering for Gert's house guests.

All renovations should be complete by 1991, when Morgenhof will be a proud addition to the Stellenbosch Wine Route.

Morgenhof

Cultivars Planted	Size of Vineyards (Hectares)	Training Practice
Sauvignon Blanc	9,24	
Chenin Blanc	8,83	
Cabernet Sauvignon	4,25	All cultivars are on vertical trellises
Rhine Riesling	4,05	
Tinta Barocca	3,18	
Colombar	3,10	
Pinotage	2,43	
Chardonnay	1,10	

Total area under vines in 1987: 36,18 ha (approximately 12 ha to be planted)
Irrigation: The vineyards of Morgenhof are not irrigated.
Temperatures: Average maximum approximately 34 °C; average minimum approximately 8 °C
Average annual rainfall: 630 mm
Stock: Rooted vines are purchased from a nursery.
Envisaged new cultivars: Merlot
First wines bottled under the Morgenhof label: Cabernet Sauvignon 1984
Wines currently bottled under the Morgenhof label: Sauvignon Blanc, Cabernet Sauvignon, Cabernet Sauvignon Blanc de Noir, Blanc de Blanc and Rhine Riesling. Morgenhof wines are bottled by the Stellenbosse Botteleringskoöperasie Beperk.
Wood ageing: Wines are aged in wood on the farm.
Capacity of the Morgenhof cellar: 630 hectolitres

Visits to Morgenhof are by appointment only.

Muratie

The name of Muratie is synonymous with that of the Canitz family. Georg Paul Canitz was an immigrant German artist who first came to South Africa largely for reasons of health. His creative imagination stirred by the wealth of the African landscape, he stayed on in the country, opening a small art school in Stellenbosch.

Then in 1925, while riding on horseback with his two daughters to a party in this valley under the Simonsberg, he mistook

the way and came upon the old and then almost derelict farm of Muratie – appropriately enough, its name was a corruption of the Dutch word *murasie*, meaning 'ruins'. With this encounter began a lifelong romance between Canitz and the farm, and with the wines he made.

At first little more than an inspired and enthusiastic amateur, he was lucky to include among a wide circle of convivial companions (Canitz's parties were

legendary) a key figure in the modern history of South African wine, Professor Perold of Stellenbosch University. An innovative wine scientist, Perold took the aspiring wine farmer under his wing, advising him to introduce a number of red wine varieties for which he felt the climate and soil of the farm were eminently suitable. Among these proposed cultivars was Pinot Noir, then a hardly-known cultivar in the local vineyards.

Muratie Estate

Cultivars Planted	Size of Vineyards (Number of vines)	Training Practice
Cabernet Sauvignon	27 500	
Pinot Noir	21 000	
Cinsaut	16 150	
Steen	13 100	
Hanepoot	8 600	All cultivars are grown on Perold trellises
Riesling	8 000	
Clairette Blanche	8 000	
Shiraz	7 250	
Port Varieties	6 100	
Pinotage	4 500	

Total area under vines in 1987: 50 ha (5 ha still to be planted)
Irrigation: The vineyards of Muratie are not irrigated.
Temperatures: Records are not kept.
Average annual rainfall: Records are not kept.
Stock: Rooted vines are purchased from a nursery.
First wines bottled under the Muratie Estate label: Pinot Noir 1927, Cabernet Sauvignon, Claret, Amber and Port (vintage dates not available)
Wines currently bottled under the Muratie Estate label: Pinot Noir, Claret, Cabernet Sauvignon, Red Velvet, Riesling, Special Dry Red, Dry White, Dry White No. 2, Stein, Amber and Port are bottled on the Estate.
Wood ageing: Wines are aged in wood on the Estate.
Capacity of the Muratie cellar: 3 000 hectolitres

Muratie is on the Stellenbosch Wine Route and is open to the public on weekdays from 08h00 to 12h00 and from 14h00 to 17h00, and on Saturdays from 08h00 to 12h00.

Within a few years, with Perold's encouragement (the professor spent most of his spare time for two years on the farm) and with the assistance of Wynand Viljoen, Muratie's first wine maker, Canitz was able to introduce the first of the now famous Muratie Pinot Noir wines.

Viljoen was soon to leave the valley to begin farming on his own account in the Karoo and Georg Canitz continued on his own in his adopted métier, with unabated enthusiasm. But his death in 1959 left his elder daughter, Annemarie, with a decision as to the future course of the farm – female wine makers were uncommon in the winelands. With the determination characteristic of her family, however, Miss Canitz continued to run the Estate and to make her father's wines, with the assistance of a new wine maker, Ben Prins.

The partnership between Miss Canitz and Ben Prins continues, three decades later. There is about this charming old tree-enclosed early nineteenth-century farm an air of defiance of time. A rich sense of atmosphere, intensified by the wealth of trees which surround the house and shadow its neo-classical façade and gable, of a refusal to be hurried, lingers about the house and in the wine cellar on the other side of the dusty farm road. Here in the cellar the original concrete fermentation tanks, installed by Canitz half a century ago on the advice of Roberto Moni, are still well in use. And other traditions have been retained, in the face of fashion and the developments of scientific viticulture. Ben Prins is very much an instinctive wine maker, living with his wine, aiming for quality above quantity, working with natural yeasts rather than the now almost universal cultured varieties, employing a minimum of machinery (his disdain for the constraints of urban footwear have given him the unofficial title of the 'barefoot wine maker').

The result is a sense of the humanity of wine. This is reflected in the abiding relationship between Muratie and its clients, always happy to make the trip to secure a bottle of the estate's distinctive Pinot Noir, its Cabernet Sauvignon or port.

Old world charm and a sense of romance pervade the Muratie Estate, especially the cellar where wine maker Ben Prins prepares for a tasting.

Neethlingshof

Neethlingshof was originally granted by Simon van der Stel to Willem Barend Lubbe (Adam Tas makes a reference to him in his diary, in 1699), who named the farm 'De Wolwedans' – The Dance of the Wolves – a name probably referring to the packs of jackals which ranged the area and no doubt harassed the flock of about 100 sheep which Lubbe kept. He later married Jacoba Brandenberg and was succeeded by Joost Hendriks van Reenen as owner of the farm in 1716. After six further changes of ownership, the farm was bought in 1788 by Charles Marais, great grandson of one of the original Huguenot settlers. In 1814 he began the building of the present homestead, with its fine 'Cape Flemish' façade and gable. He died soon afterwards, however, leaving his wife, Magdalena Maria de Villiers, to complete the house in 1816. This beautiful example of the local domestic architecture features a painted 'dado' on the gable depicting grape vines and bunches of grapes. Magdalena sold the completed house and the farm to her son-in-law, Johannes Neethling, in 1816 (the Deed of Sale for January 2, 1816, is signed by Lord Charles Somerset). In the same year the farm was extended by a 200 hectare grant. Neethling, after whom the farm came to be named, was a colourful and eccentric character, something of a dandy, whose flamboyant dress and lifestyle earned him the nickname the 'Lord' of Neethlingshof, or simply 'Lord Neethling'. Although Neethling had three sons, he sold Neethlingshof in 1871, the year before his death, to his son-in-law, Jacobus Louw, and the farm stayed in the hands of the Louw family for almost a hundred years. In 1963 the Momberg cousins bought Neethlingshof from Nico Louw. Jannie Momberg, a public figure with wide-ranging interests and activities, and popularly known in the winelands as 'Jan Bek', is the son of a wine farmer, born and brought up with the language of wine and its making. At school he became interested in history, which he intended to study further, with the ambition of eventually becoming a lecturer. The death of his father in 1959, however, diverted the course of his life. He returned to the family farm of Middelvlei, which he shared with his cousin, also Jan Momberg, but distinguished from him as 'Stil Jan'.

At the time the Mombergs purchased Neethlingshof it had the reputation of being one of the best wine farms in the

district, but closer inspection revealed that the cellar facilities were somewhat primitive. In the first few years, until 1970, Jan made no wine, instead selling his grapes to the Stellenbosch Farmers' Winery. Soon, however, he set about modernizing the cellar. In due course, he and his cousin came to an arrangement whereby Jan sold his share in Middelvlei to Stil Jan and bought Stil Jan's share in Neethlingshof. After 22 years of successful farming at Neethlingshof, Jan sold the Estate to Hans-Joachim Schreiber in March 1985. Towards the end of his time at Neethlingshof he was the patron and protector of the athlete, Zola Budd. The Estate became her refuge when she was

being hounded by the media and there she was able to train unseen by the curious eyes of the reporters.

The present owner of Neethlingshof, Hans-Joachim Schreiber, also owns the farms of Alphen near Stellenbosch and Klein Welmoed (not to be confused with the Welmoed Co-operative, which it adjoins). He is an international financier, a German citizen based in Singapore, and a former managing director of the Dresdner Bank AG of Frankfurt. No sooner was the purchase of the Estate finalised than he proceeded to implement a comprehensive and significant development programme comprising not only new farm buildings but also an extended vineyard replanting

---

Neethlingshof Estate

Cultivars Planted	Size of Vineyards (Hectares)	Training Practice
Chenin Blanc	22	Perold trellis
Clairette Blanche	21	and bush vines
Colombar	20,4	
Pinotage	10,5	
Riesling	7,4	
Sauvignon Blanc	7,4	
Cabernet Sauvignon	7,4	Perold trellis
Weisser Riesling	3,9	
Tinta Barocca	3,3	
Kerner	3,3	
Bukettraube	1,9	
Gewürztraminer	1,5	

All old and redundant vineyards are being replaced and 30 hectares a year will be replanted with more of the same cultivars, for example Cabernet Sauvignon, Gewürztraminer, Weisser Riesling and Sauvignon Blanc, as well as new cultivars (see below).

Total area under vines in 1987: 110 ha (40 ha still to be planted)
Irrigation: The Neethlingshof vineyards are not irrigated.
Temperatures: Records are not kept.
Average annual rainfall: Records are not kept.
Stock: Rooted vines are purchased from a nursery.
Envisaged new cultivars: Cabernet Franc, Merlot, Shiraz, Chardonnay, Sémillon and Morio Muscat
First wines bottled under the Neethlingshof Estate label: Clairette Blanche 1971 and Chenin Blanc 1971
Wines currently bottled under the Neethlingshof Estate label (in order of volume): Colombard, Blanc de Noir, Cabernet Sauvignon, Weisser Riesling, Bukettraube, Riesling, Sauvignon Blanc, Gewürztraminer and Lord Neethling Rouge (all bottled by Stellenbosse Botteleringskoöperasie Beperk).
Wood ageing: The wines are aged in wood on the Estate.
Capacity of the Neethlingshof cellar: 12 000 hectolitres

Neethlingshof is open to the public during the week from 08h30 to 12h30 and from 13h30 to 17h00, and on Saturdays from 09h00 to 12h00.

The restored wine cellar at Neethlingshof.

Chardonnay, Pinot Noir and Gewürztraminer. To make the most of these advantages and establish Neethlingshof as one of the leading Cape wine Estates, the vineyard programme includes scientific soil classification, the uprooting of old, redundant vineyards and the planting of new or additional vines of the noble cultivars (Chardonnay, Pinot Noir, Merlot, Cabernet Franc and Cabernet Sauvignon).

The Neethlingshof wine-making team consists of Schalk van der Westhuizen in charge of the vineyards, Nico van der Merwe as wine maker and Pieter de Bruyn as general manager. Between the three of them, the team boasts considerable vinicultural knowledge and experience. Schalk was born on the Estate, where his father was Estate manager for over 30 years, grew up in the wine industry and has a certificate in viniculture. Pieter, who specialised in viticulture at Stellenbosch University, has supervised vineyard programmes at Nietvoorbij and Gilbeys. Nico is a graduate of both Stellenbosch University and the Geisenheim Wine Institute in the Rhineland. From 1983 to 1985, this team had the benefit of the assistance of Giles Webb as consultant wine maker. Some of the Neethlingshof red wines which are enjoying such high praise at present were made by him. A chartered accountant, he also holds a B.Sc. degree in viticulture and oenology and has done experimental wine making at Stellenbosch Farmers' Winery and in the winelands of California.

scheme. Within ten years all standard cultivars will probably have been replaced by noble varieties. Vast and costly renovations and extensions to the office complex and wine cellar provided the latest in wine-making facilities, and a host of features for visitors and tourists. The developments also included the building of an attractive new extensively equipped staff housing complex, housing 26 families, as well as the restoration of the homestead, which is now a large restaurant, 'The Lord Neethling'.

Most importantly, however, is the comprehensive new vineyard programme now under way. Neethlingshof is situated five and a half kilometres out of Stellenbosch on the Kuils River road, on the eastern slopes of the Bottelary hills and the ridge of the famous Polkadraai basin, enjoying a prime position with optimum growing conditions. The fact that the vineyards run north to south, and rise to 300 metres above sea level on the northern boundary benefits varieties which enjoy cooler temperatures, such as

Neil Ellis Vineyard Selection

The source of fine wines is top quality grapes and thus the vintner's work begins in the fields. Throughout the world it has been a centuries-old practice to designate the very best wines by the individual vineyards from which they originate. Vines vary greatly, however, in their soil and climatic requirements and no single vineyard can satisfy the needs of all the different grape varieties.

With this in mind, Neil Ellis, former wine maker at Groot Constantia and now the consultant wine maker at Zevenwacht, searched the winelands to find where individual varieties excel and to build up associations with grape growers who would cultivate, under his direction, the high quality grapes he required for his vineyard selection wines. He was given permission for this venture by Gilbert Colyn,

chairman of the publicly owned farm Zevenwacht, where Neil produces a very creditable range of wines.

Neil Ellis is not the first wine maker to produce, independently, his own range of wines, while employed as wine maker by a particular farm. Achim von Arnim, cellarmaster at Boschendal, bought his own Estate, Clos Cabrieré in Franschhoek. There he produces a sparkling wine, by the *méthode Champenoise*, from the classic varieties of Chardonnay and Pinot Noir.

At present the Neil Ellis Vineyard Selection range comprises a Cabernet Sauvignon, a Rhine Riesling and a Sauvignon Blanc. The Cabernet Sauvignon, the first wine in the series, was made from grapes grown in two very different vineyards: the first, on a north-western slope in the Banhoek valley high

above Stellenbosch, gives a round, elegant, plummy wine; the second vineyard, situated near Firgrove close to False Bay, yields a wine with the type of structure that is suitable for maturation. The blend is matured for 12 months in small French oak, followed by further ageing in large French oak vats.

Similarly, the Sauvignon Blanc and the Rhine Riesling are blends of grapes from a selection of vineyards, three in the case of the Sauvignon Blanc. Neil would eventually like to identify the individual vineyards on his labels, as is the growing trend in California, where these wines are often termed 'boutique' wines. Neil's wines are produced in small quantities, because of the limited selection of the crop, but this does emphasize the personal touch to this venture.

The Oude Meester Group
THE BERGKELDER

Like the Stellenbosch Farmers' Winery, this large company is a producing co-subsidiary of Cape Wine and Distillers. Its historical growth begins, however, with the emergence after the Second World War of the Distillers Corporation.

Distillers Corporation (SA) Limited was registered in June, 1945, and, early in 1946, the first of its cellars was completed, the first pot-still installed, and a modern wine laboratory, the first of its kind in South Africa, was established. Combining this modern technology and equipment with traditional processes, the company launched a full range of vine products – the most famous being Oude Meester Brandy.

The following years saw an energetic expansion. Marketing relationships were set up with local estates, Alto and Theuniskraal being the first to enter into this now familiar kind of partnership, in 1947. The early 1960s saw the absorption of the largest privately owned sherry-maturation cellars in the country, those of the Drostdy Co-operative Cellars at Tulbagh. The following year the mother company of Oude Meester Kelders, Distilleerders en Brouerskorporasie, was established.

In 1968, at the instigation of Dr Anton Rupert, chairman of the Oude Meester Group, occurred one of the most important of the company's innovations, with the building of the Bergkelder. These are maturation cellars, tunnelled into the flank of the mountain on the southern slopes of the Papegaaiberg. Here red wines can be matured at ideal temperatures, even in the fierce heat of the Cape summer. Here also are made the well-known Fleur du Cap wines, the Stellenryck 'Collection' and, probably the best known of all the Oude Meester wines, the Grünberger range.

The Oude Meester Group proper was formed in 1970, when the mother company of Distillers Corporation, Oude Meester Kelders, Distilleerders en Brouerskorporasie, merged with another company, South African Distilleries and Wines Limited, the latter consisting of upwards of some 40 wine merchants, including many of nineteenth-century provenance such as Castle Wine and Brandy Company, E.K. Green, Collisons (now revived in London with an injection of capital from the Oude Meester Group to distribute and market the Group's products in the United Kingdom) and the Van Ryn Wine and Spirit Company.

A further ramification of the Group's structure occurred in August, 1974, when it was announced that a number of leading private wine Estates had entered into a marketing partnership with the Bergkelder; a fitting tribute to the efforts of Dr Rupert who some two decades earlier had laid the foundation to such partnership with the marketing agreements he had concluded with Alto and Theuniskraal. This meant that independent farmers would continue to make their own individual wines in their own personal style from grapes grown on their Estates, but that they would now have the advanced technology of the Bergkelder (much of this in the persons of the Bergkelder's wine makers, Dr Piet Venter and, more recently, Dr Julius Laszlo) at their disposal, and that henceforth they would be able to leave the increasingly complicated bottling and marketing of their wines to the company. Since 1974 the number of Estates in partnership with the Bergkelder has increased from nine to 19; in the

'Walls' of maturing bottled wines in the Bergkelder's underground cellar where visitors are treated to a tasting of the company's products.

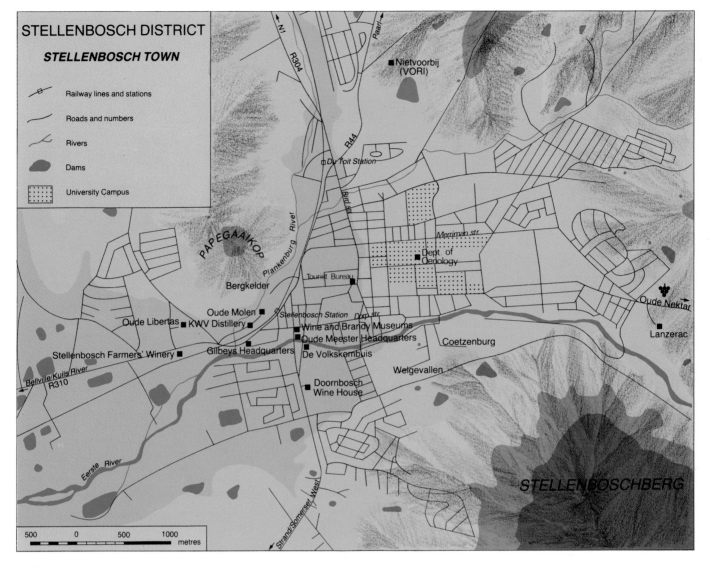

Stellenbosch District they include
Meerlust, Alto, Jacobsdal, Bonfoi, Goede
Hoop, Middelvlei, Hazendal,
Koopmanskloof, Uitkyk and Le Bonheur;
Durbanville is represented by Meerendal;
the Swartland by Allesverloren; Tulbagh
by Theuniskraal; and the Robertson area
by four Estates, those of De Wetshof (the
first Estate to be registered there), Mont
Blois, Zandvliet, Rietvallei; and
L'Ormarins and La Motte in Franschhoek.

The head office of the Oude Meester
Group is off Dorp Street in Stellenbosch.
The Bergkelder organizes public tours of
its underground cellars; these begin at the
giant door which opens directly into the
side of the hill and continue down dim
corridors tunnelled into the earth and
lined with thousands of bottles of maturing
red wine. To these cellars has now been
added a magnificent, air-conditioned wood
maturation cellar where the wines are
aged in 225-litre oak casks. Further into
the hillside are rooms housing hand-carved
maturation vats, the tour being completed
in the tasting room where visitors may
sample a selection of the cellar's wines.

The Bergkelder Vinotèque

The Bergkelder has also introduced an
innovative system which gives the
individual wine lover the opportunity of
maturing wines in the Bergkelder
Vinotèque. This is one of the several
underground cellars in which the temperature, humidity, light and noise levels
are carefully controlled, providing ideal
conditions for the maturation of wine.

Each year small quantities of rare and
special vintage Bergkelder wines are
offered for sale by tender. In terms of the
Liquor Act, individuals may not tender
directly, but many wine merchants are
happy to tender on the individual's behalf.
If his tender has been successful, the
purchaser can decide to have his wine
delivered immediately or further matured
in the Vinotèque.

The progress of the wine is monitored by
the cellarmaster, who sends the owner
regular reports on the maturation progress

of his wine, advising him when the wine is
approaching optimum maturity.

'Buying forward' – that is, the
purchasing of young wines while they are
still maturing in the producers' cellars – is
common practice in Europe and has been
introduced in South Africa by the
Bergkelder. Once a year, the cellar offers
small quantities of young wines that are
still maturing in the bottle and are
therefore not available to the wine
merchant.

After purchase these young wines are
left to mature in the Vinotèque, but only
on the condition that they remain there
until the wine is officially released. Again,
the owner of the wine is advised when his
wine will be available and he is given the
option to leave the wine for further
maturation. Not only does the wine
improve in character in this way, but also
increases in value.

Dr Piet Venter, production director at the Bergkelder.

Dr Julius Laszlo in one of the wood-maturation cellars at the Bergkelder.

Wines distributed by the Oude Meester Group Bergkelder (Estates)

Bergkelder (Estates)
Allesverloren: Cabernet Sauvignon, Swartland Rood and Tinta Barocca
Alto: Cabernet Sauvignon and Alto Rouge
Bonfoi: Chenin Blanc and Cuvée Agée
De Wetshof: Chardonnay, Edeloes, Rhine Riesling and Sauvignon Blanc
Goede Hoop Vintage Rood
Hazendal Freudenlese
Jacobsdal Pinotage
Koopmanskloof: Blanc de Marbonne and Rhine Riesling
La Motte: Blanc de Noir and Légère
Le Bonheur: Blanc Fumé, Cabernet Sauvignon and Chardonnay
L'Ormarins: Sauvignon Blanc, Blanc Fumé, Riesling, Rhine Riesling, Cabernet Sauvignon, Shiraz, Chardonnay, Noble Late Harvest and Pinot Gris
Meerendal: Pinotage and Shiraz
Meerlust: Cabernet Sauvignon, Rubicon, Pinot Noir and Merlot
Middelvlei: Pinotage and Cabernet Sauvignon
Theuniskraal: Gewürztraminer, Riesling and Sémillon
Uitkyk: Carlonet, Carlsheim and Riesling
Zandvliet: Pinot Noir and Shiraz

Other Bergkelder wines
Fleur du Cap: Emerald Stein, Riesling, Pinotage, Cabernet Sauvignon, Shiraz, Premier Grand Crû, Natural Light, Natural Light Rosé, Gewürztraminer, and Sauvignon Blanc

Grünberger: Blanc de Blanc, Stein and Spritziger
Here XVII (Dry Sparkling Wine)
J C le Roux Le Domaine
J C le Roux Pinot Noir
J C le Roux Sparkling Sauvignon Blanc
Kupferberger Auslese
Stellenryck Blanc Fumé
Stellenryck Cabernet Sauvignon
Stellenryck Rhine Riesling
Stellenryck Gewürztraminer

Cellar cask vineyards
Cellar Cask (boxed wines): Grand Crû, Semi-Sweet, Smooth Dry Red and Late Harvest

Western Province Cellars
Rooderust

Drostdy-Hof
Stein Select, Premier Grand Crû, Claret Select, Late Harvest, Adelpracht Special Late Harvest, Extra Light, Ruby Light, Pinot Gris, Vin Noir and Sémillon

Witzenberg
Stein, Grand Crû, Late Harvest and Perlé White

Fortified wines
Sherries
Drostdy Pale Dry, Full Cream and Medium Cream

Port
Allesverloren Port

Muscadel
Mont Blois White Muscadel
Rietvallei Rooi Muskadel

THE WINE MUSEUMS

Adjacent to the Oude Meester headquarters in Stellenbosch and within a few metres of each other are the Stellenryk Wine Museum and the Oude Meester Brandy museum, which are models of their kind, compact but comprehensive, well designed and entertainingly informative.

STELLENRYCK WINE MUSEUM. This museum draws its exhibits both from local and overseas sources, ranging from clay amphorae, both elongated and spherical, from the classic period of Greece and Rome, to early modern wine-making equipment. There are glasses and goblets from Holland to England to China; there is an early model of the type of machine used for putting the wire on champagne bottles; there is a nineteenth-century wine cooler and a miniature French wine press once used to make samples of wines. In the rear of the museum, which is designed in imitation of a wine cellar, are different types of oak cask for maturing wines, a flor sherry display and a magnificent nineteenth-century Italian oak wine cart. Outside in the sunshine is an enormous German wine press built in the late eighteenth century and last used in 1936.

The Stellenryck Wine Museum.

THE OUDE MEESTER BRANDY MUSEUM. Featuring some 1 000 exhibits, this collection is housed in a cluster of labourers' cottages designed in 1904 by Sir Herbert Baker for the farm then owned by his friend, Cecil Rhodes, on the Eerste River. Baker's only known contribution to Stellenbosch architecture, they were rescued from the bulldozers and restored by the Oude Meester Group, to be opened as a museum of the *Eau de Vie du Vin* – the 'Water of Life from Wine' – in 1977.

The museum contains sections on the general history of brandy (exhibits include a Dutch miniature of an early brandy distillery, and a cognac brandy-still dating from 1818 and on loan from Richelieu et

Cie of Cognac), modern methods of production, displays on the early nineteenth-century local brandy houses such as Collisons, Greens and Van Ryns, a beautifully reconstructed Victorian period room, a maturation cellar, and fine photographic displays of cask making and *witblits* making in the mountains.

Both museums are open at the following times: From Monday to Friday, from 09h00 to 12h45, and from 14h00 to 17h00; on Saturdays and public holidays, from 10h00 to 13h00, and from 14h00 to 17h00; and on Sundays from 14h30 to 17h30. The museums are closed on Good Friday, Ascension Day, the Day of the Covenant and Christmas Day.

177

Oude Nektar

The history of this farm in the beautiful Jonkershoek Valley, some five kilometres from Stellenbosch, can be traced back to 1692. It was given its evocative name in 1814 by a certain Gertrude de Villiers. Over the years it changed hands and was subdivided several times, until in 1942 the main homestead and about six hectares of adjacent ground were bought by Major General Kenneth Van der Spuy – it was his wife, Una, who established the now famous Oude Nektar gardens.

A variety of wines, including Claret, Cabernet, Riesling, Sauterne and Frontignac, were made and bottled under the Oude Nektar label in the old cellar near the homestead until 1956. Then in 1970, after a lull of several years, the main part of the farm, including the cellar, was bought by a Transvaal farmer and businessman, Derrick Peck. Since then Derrick has redesigned the vineyards with the intention of producing good quality wines. In this he has the assistance of the micro-climate and soils of the Jonkershoek Valley. With the farm's proximity to the mountains, the vineyards receive fewer sun-hours than in more exposed areas, allowing slow and concentrated growth. The valley has considerably higher rainfall than most of the Stellenbosch District, so irrigation is not needed. With limitations of quota, only 32 hectares of the farm's total 232 hectares are at present planted with vines, some of the balance being given to proteas and lemons.

Until 1983 the grapes grown on Oude Nektar were delivered to the Bergkelder. In that year a new cellar was completed and under the management of Derrick's son, Gregory (who has a number of years' experience in the Bergkelder behind him), the first wines under the Oude Nektar label were released in November, 1983, and are sold from the Estate.

Oude Nektar Estate

Cultivars Planted	Size of Vineyards (Number of vines)	Training Practice
Cabernet Sauvignon	23 000	
Chenin Blanc	17 000	
Riesling	17 000	
Shiraz	12 000	4-wire vertical
Sauvignon Blanc	10 000	trellis
Pinotage	7 000	
Nemes Furmint	5 000	
Muscat d'Alexandrie	4 000	

Total area under vines in 1987: 32 ha
Irrigation: The vineyards of Oude Nektar are not irrigated.
Temperatures: Average maximum 24 °C; average minimum 16 °C
Average annual rainfall: 1 000 mm
Stock: Parent stock is used for grafting; rooted vines are also purchased from a nursery.
Envisaged new cultivar: Merlot
First wines bottled under the Oude Nektar Estate label: Chenin Blanc, Nemes Furmint, Olasz Riesling, Cabernet Sauvignon, Shiraz, Pinotage (all in 1983), Blanc de Noir, Late Vintage and Muscat d'Alexandrie
Wines currently bottled under the Oude Nektar Estate label: Blanc de Noir, Cabernet Sauvignon, Furmint, Late Vintage, Muscat d'Alexandrie, Pinotage, Riesling, Rosé and Shiraz
Wood ageing: Wines are aged in wood on the Estate.
Capacity of the Oude Nektar cellar: 1 500 hectolitres

The Estate is open to the public on weekdays from 09h30 to 16h30, and on Saturdays from 09h30 to 12h30.

The new cellar where wine maker Gregory Peck has led Oude Nektar's re-emergence as a producing Estate.

Overgaauw

This Estate originally formed part of the historic farm By-den-Weg, granted by Simon van der Stel to Hendrik Elbertz in 1704. In 1784, By-den-Weg was purchased by Daniël Joubert, of Huguenot origin, and it remained in possession of the Joubert family for five generations.

In 1906, Abraham Julius van Velden bought a portion of By-den-Weg from his maternal grandfather, Willem Joubert, and named it Overgaauw, after the maiden name of the wife of Dirk, the first Van Velden to emigrate to the Cape from Holland. Abraham built a wine cellar on the farm in 1909 and his home the following year.

His son, David van Velden, worked for his father before taking over the farm in 1945. The area under vines comprised about 40 hectares of the more traditional varieties such as Steen, Green Grape, Cinsaut and Hanepoot and also some Shiraz and Cabernet Sauvignon. To these basic cultivars he added further plantings of Cabernet, and blocks of new cultivars such as Clairette Blanche, Colombar and Riesling. He also introduced Sylvaner, well known in Alsace, Austria and Germany and also a popular cultivar in California, but hardly known in South Africa. It was planted as an experimental plot by the

Viticultural Research Station on a neighbouring farm. Of this stock, David planted a vineyard in 1959. Almost unique to Overgaauw, this distinctive dry white wine was first bottled on the Estate in 1971, and when it reached the market it brought an immediate response. The range of cultivars was further enhanced and expanded by plantings of Pinotage, Merlot, Cabernet Franc, Sauvignon Blanc and Chardonnay, and a selection of five Portuguese cultivars for Port production.

They were Tinta Barocca, Tinta Francisca, Malvasia Rey, Cornifesto and Souzão.

In 1974, David was joined by his son Braam, who returned in 1973 to Overgaauw after oenological studies at Geisenheim in Germany. Taking increasing responsibility in the wine making, Braam was the instigator of the building of a large underground maturation cellar with a capacity of over 100 000 bottles, as well as a vinotèque for all the Overgaauw wines. Bottling of some

The owner of Overgaauw, David van Velden, and his son, Braam.

Overgaauw Estate

Cultivars Planted	Size of Vineyards (Hectares)	Training Practice
Steen	14	Y trellis and bush vines
Cabernet Sauvignon	9	Y and 4-wire trellises
Sylvaner	7	Perold and vertical trellises
Clairette Blanche	5	Slanting and Perold trellises
Colombar	7	Perold trellis
Pinotage	4	
Merlot	6	
Chardonnay	4	4-wire vertical trellis
Sauvignon Blanc	4	
Cabernet Franc	3	
Kerner	3	
Cinsaut	4	Bush vines
Port varieties	1,5	

Total area under vines in 1987: 71,5 ha
Irrigation: 60 per cent of the Overgaauw vineyards are irrigated.
Temperatures: Records are not kept.
Average annual rainfall: 670 mm
Stock: Grafted vines are purchased from a nursery.
Envisaged new cultivars: None
First wines bottled under the Overgaauw Estate label: Selected Cabernet 1970, Selected Pinotage 1970, Cinsaut 1970, Dry Port 1970 and Sylvaner 1971
Wines currently bottled under the Overgaauw Estate label: Cabernet Sauvignon, Tria Cordia, Sylvaner, Sauvignon Blanc, Merlot, Overtinto, and Chardonnay. A port is also made and bottled on the Estate.
Wood ageing: Wines are aged in wood on the Estate.
Capacity of the Overgaauw cellar: 6 500 hectolitres

Overgaauw is open to the public at the following times: Cellar tours – Wednesdays from 14h30 to 16h30; Wine sales – weekdays from 08h30 to 12h00 and on Wednesdays from 14h00 to 17h00. Otherwise by appointment.

Oaken maturation casks redolent of wine-making tradition contrast sharply with modern stainless steel tanks in the Overgaauw cellar.

of the Overgaauw wines on the Estate, started by David in 1971, necessitated the building of these adequate storage facilities. Subsequent expansion and modernising of equipment has made the Overgaauw cellars an interesting blend of both traditional and modern building styles. There is also a quaint Victorian reception and tasting room.

The Estate produces excellent wines in the proportion of 55 per cent white to 45 per cent red. The red wine range includes a vintage port, a dry port, a blend of Cabernet Sauvignon, Cabernet Franc and Merlot, as well as wines made entirely from two classic varieties, a Cabernet Sauvignon and a Merlot. All reds are matured in new and old oak for at least two years before being bottled. The whites are the aforementioned Sylvaner, a Sauvignon Blanc and, since 1986, a Chardonnay.

Braam has also achieved success in the Vineyard Block Competition (see page 55).

Rozendal Farm

Kurt Ammann, the owner of Rozendal Farm, was born in Switzerland where he trained as a chef and then worked for a time in restaurants in Germany and France. Already fluent in French, German and Italian, he wished to live a year in an English-speaking country to improve his English. England did not appeal to him, and he was considering Australia when a friend, already in South Africa, persuaded him to come to Johannesburg. He has been in South Africa ever since. In fact it was eight years before he again saw his native Switzerland.

In Johannesburg he first worked at the Zoo Lake Restaurant but soon opened his own, the 'La Rotisserie' in Emmerentia. This was well patronised by personnel of the S.A.B.C. and through them he learned about the restaurant in the top of the Hertzog Tower, the television tower in Brixton, Johannesburg. He eventually took over this restaurant, and it was here that his keen interest in wine manifested itself. During 1979 the restaurant was closed for eight months for additions and alterations, and Kurt spent that time working on various wine farms. It was then that he was fired with the desire to make his own wines one day. Among those who inspired him was Jan 'Boland' Coetzee.

Back in Johannesburg, on completion of the refurbishment of his restaurant, he amassed one of the best wine cellars in the country before, by a cruel turn of fate, he was forced to give up the business. Just as it was really making its mark it was closed by the authorities on the grounds that the television tower was a 'key point' and the restaurant was a security risk. Expecting considerable compensation for the 13 years his lease still had to run, Kurt searched for a suitable farm in the Cape where he could fulfil his ambition to make his own wine. All his requirements he found in the 25-hectare farm Rozendal, which he purchased in December 1981.

Immediately he set about improving the property which had originally been part of Lanzerac and had on it a homestead and cellar built in 1864. Wine had been made up until 1955, with Hermitage, Steen and a fortified wine being delivered to the famous old firm of R. Santhagens Limited. Kurt's first step was to plant one-and-a-half hectares of Merlot and Cabernet Franc and to build a modern wine cellar. He and his family moved onto the property in December 1982 and he set about making his own wine.

Blissfully ignorant of all the ramifications of KWV registration, excise requirements and KWV grape buying contracts, he bought grapes and made his first wine, breaking a host of regulations in the process. All these problems were eventually solved, however, and the first remarkable Rozendal wine emerged from the 1983 vintage. A blend of Cabernet and Cinsaut, it drew severe criticism when young and yet it developed into a fine wine, and was sold at the first Auction of the Cape Independent Wine Makers Guild held in Johannesburg in 1985. The first few vintages were called simply 'Rozendal', but from the 1986 vintage, with the introduction of Merlot to the blend, a new label, 'Val de Lyn', is being used (Lyn is Kurt's wife). Those Rozendal wines that are exported to Switzerland appear under the label 'Konstanz'.

Kurt has increased his plantings of Merlot and Cabernet Franc to nearly five hectares and improved his wine-making techniques. He is now accepted as one of the new and innovative wine makers.

Initially Kurt applied for registration of his property as an Estate but later dropped his application, preferring to purchase good quality grapes from other farms when necessary, as is common practice in some of the other wine-producing countries. He buys, for instance, Cabernet Sauvignon from the vineyards of his neighbour, the Lanzerac Hotel, and also occasionally buys in Cinsaut. He had the contract to tend the vineyards of the Lanzerac Hotel, but found it too time-consuming, and they are now farmed by Guy Chennells of nearby Navarre, famed for its magnificent Cape Dutch homestead.

The vagaries of the law saw to it that

Rozendal Farm

Cultivars Planted	Size of Vineyards (Number of vines)	Training Practice
Merlot	12 000	Perold trellis
Hanepoot	3 000	
Cabernet Franc	3 000	Bush vines

Total area under vines in 1987: Approximately 5 ha
Irrigation: The Rozendal vineyards are not irrigated.
Stock: Rooted vines are bought from a nursery.
First wine bottled under the Rozendal label: 1983 Rozendal (a blend of Cabernet and Cinsaut)
Wines currently bottled under the Rozendal label: Rozendal and Konstanz (which is exported to Switzerland)
Wood ageing: Wines are aged in small new wood and in some large casks on the farm.
Capacity of the Rozendal cellar: 60 tonnes of grapes

Rozendal is not open to the public.

Doornbosch, the charming restaurant which Kurt Ammann took over from the KWV, and where his wines are for sale.

Kurt did not get the compensation he expected from the closing of the television tower restaurant and so he has had to earn a living while he builds up his winery. He took over the KWV's Doornbosch Wine House and has turned it into one of the finest haute cuisine restaurants of Stellenbosch.

Rustenberg and Schoongezicht

These two farms, which operate as a single wine-making and administrative unit, occupy a special place in the regard of the wine lovers of the Cape. Situated on the foothills of the Simonsberg, looking away to the south beyond woods of sun-dusted oak trees to False Bay in the distance, and approached by a winding, shaded road intersected by the valley's streams, this is one of the most beautiful of the Cape's traditional wineries – it is in the old cellar at Schoongezicht that the Estate's fine natural wines are made.

The property has a long history, dating back to 1682, when Roelof Pasman

A champion dairy herd complements the vineyards of Schoongezicht which commands one of the most picturesque settings in the Cape winelands.

Schoongezicht/Rustenberg

Cultivars Planted	Size of Vineyards (Hectares)	Training Practice
Cabernet Sauvignon	31	
Weisser Riesling	12	
Merlot	9	
Pinot Noir	9	3-wire vertical
Chardonnay	5	trellis
Sauvignon Blanc	3	
Cabernet Franc	2	
Souzão	1	
Clairette Blanche	5	Bush vines
Cinsaut	3	

Total area under vines in 1987: Approximately 80 ha
Irrigation: Only 6 ha of Schoongezicht/Rustenberg can be irrigated when necessary.
Temperatures: Average maximum 23,6 °C; average minimum 9,1 °C
Average annual rainfall: Approximately 810 mm
Stock: Rooted vines are purchased from a nursery.
First wines bottled under the Schoongezicht/Rustenberg labels: Schoongezicht Dry Red, Schoongezicht Hock and Schoongezicht Frontignac, ± 1906
Wines currently bottled under the Schoongezicht/Rustenberg labels: Rustenberg (red), Rustenberg Cabernet Sauvignon, Rustenberg Cabernet Dry Rosé, Rustenberg Pinot Noir, Schoongezicht (white), Schoongezicht Rhine Riesling, Schoongezicht Chardonnay and a vintage port. All these wines are made and bottled on the Estate.
Wood ageing: Wines are aged in wood on the Estate.
Capacity of the Schoongezicht/Rustenberg cellar: 1 600 hectolitres

Schoongezicht/Rustenberg is not on the Stellenbosch Wine Route, but is open to the public by appointment on weekdays and Saturday mornings.

obtained a grant of land of nearly 93 morgen (80 hectares) from Willem Adriaan van der Stel, always a prolific giver of land grants. Situated on the slopes of the Simonsberg above Ida's Valley, the farm was named Rustenberg. In 1783 this became the property of Jacob Eksteen, who, in 1810, deducted nearly 61 morgen to form the new farm of Schoongezicht, which he gave to his newly-acquired son-in-law, Arend Brink.

Schoongezicht was transferred from Brink to Pieter Lourens Cloete, a scion of the Cloete family of Constantia, in 1813; it was he who added the present classically Cape Dutch frontage to the existing homestead – the view up the meadows to the high gable of Schoongezicht has become one of the archetypal images of the winelands setting, and one much reproduced.

Almost 80 years after Cloete's purchase, and in very different economic circumstances from the confident affluence of Cloete's day, the farm was bought by John X. Merriman. Later to become the last Prime Minister of the old Cape Colony, Merriman was at this time the Minister of Agriculture. Concerned at the poor condition of the local farming, he decided that the most effective way of gaining an insight into the problems concerned would be to become a farmer himself.

Soon after his purchase of Schoongezicht in 1892, Merriman was joined by a young English immigrant named Alfred

Nicholson, whose job was to oversee the practical aspects of running the almost derelict farm, recovering, as were so many of the local estates, from the destruction of the phylloxera epidemic. Together Merriman and Nicholson (who was later to marry Merriman's niece) set about replanting the vineyards on the hillsides and establishing fruit orchards where the vines had been killed by the phylloxera. With the gradual recovery of the vineyards, Nicholson began making wine in the old cellar, built in 1770.

After Merriman's death, Nicholson became the owner of Schoongezicht. The early decades of the century, however, were an unstable time for the local wine industry, and for all the quality of his products, Nicholson's lack of capital told against him.

Then, in 1945, the capital was supplied. In that year Peter Barlow bought the farm. This was his second purchase in the valley for, five years earlier, he had bought the neighbouring farm of Rustenberg as a family home. Now Peter reunited the two estates after a century of separation, to complete the original but now slightly larger property, and restoring both the homestead and the old cellar. Today the farm of Glenbawn has also been added, but is restricted to fruit production rather than wine. Since Peter Barlow's death in 1975, the Estate has been owned by his widow, Pamela.

Nicholson continued to live at Schoongezicht and to manage the running of the farm. After his retirement his son, Reg, continued his work. Reg Nicholson in turn retired after the 1975 vintage, but for a while continued to act in an advisory capacity to the new wine maker, Etienne le Riche.

Reg Nicholson held to traditional views in his wine making, and, while he was duly impressed by the changes taking place in wine-making technology in recent years, he insisted on making his wines by the more traditional methods. Refrigeration, he claimed, is needed only to provide sufficient cooling to prevent the fermentation from killing itself, rather than for the whole process to be reduced to very low temperatures. He also looked askance at the use of cultured rather than natural yeasts, those found in the 'bloom' on the skin of the grapes. The cellar at Schoongezicht still contains few of the new-fangled innovations which would disturb the peace and quiet of its restful atmosphere, though it does now include efficient modern machinery and a handsome new maturation cellar well stocked with Bordeaux barrels.

Etienne le Riche, a graduate in Viticulture, Oenology and Agricultural Economics from Stellenbosch University, joined Nicholson in 1974, taking over on his retirement the following year. He has followed his predecessor in his insistence upon the use of natural yeast but on red wines only. In recent years, too, he has experimented with the maturation of batches of Chardonnay in wood for up to three months, thus giving the wine a more complex character. This is a procedure adopted in France and in many other wine-making countries, and increasingly used in South Africa today.

This individual approach and willingness to experiment with new ideas as well as to respect old ones, has resulted in a fine range of natural wines. But if the wine master's skill is important, no less important is the co-operation of climate and setting. And in these respects Schoongezicht has been singularly fortunate. In South Africa many wine farmers face a problem not shared by their counterparts in Europe. This is the excessive heat to which their vineyards are subjected in the late summer. In its high, cool, sheltered valley under the Simonsberg, Schoongezicht receives as much as 19 days less sunlight a year than the majority of farms in the Stellenbosch and Paarl areas. The soil here, which is highly fertile, red granite-based soil, gives the grapes a further natural advantage. The farm receives some 810 millimetres of rain annually, though this can be variable – the three years leading up to 1974, for example, gave as little as 500 millimetres each year.

The Schoongezicht vineyards are located at an altitude ranging from 270 to 330 metres. At present 80 hectares are in full bearing. The established vineyards consist of 31 hectares of Cabernet Sauvignon, the next most planted variety being Pinot Noir, on nine hectares.

Rustenberg bottles a 100 per cent Cabernet Sauvignon, as well as the popular Rustenberg, previously called Dry Red. This is made up of approximately 66 per cent Cabernet Sauvignon and 34 per cent Cinsaut, and is not made in the usual way for a blend of this kind, that is, by crushing the grapes separately before blending. Here the grapes are blended together at the crusher in the required proportions. There are only three hectares of Cinsaut, but since this cultivar is a prolific bearer compared to Cabernet, the crop is sufficient for the blend, which makes up the major part of the farm's red wine output. 1985 was also the first vintage of a Bordeaux blend using Cabernet Sauvignon, Cabernet Franc, and Merlot, which is being aged in small new oak barrels.

The Rustenberg red wines are matured in large vats for about 18 months, then for a further three to six months in the classic Bordeaux-type vat. Of the farm's total production, 70 per cent is red wine, 25 per cent white; the balance includes a vintage port and an innovation in the form of the first rosé to be made from 100 per cent Cabernet Sauvignon.

Besides wine, the farm Schoongezicht is famous for its magnificent Jersey herd, one of the first to be established in the country. The flat, low-lying land of the two farms, where lush kikuyu grass, rye and clover grow in profusion, is reserved for this herd. As with most of the older-style farms on the Stellenbosch side of the Simonsberg, the herd's manure is used on the vineyards and is considered an integral part of the farming cycle.

Since the reuniting of the two halves of the original farm it has been a tradition to sell the red wines under the name of Rustenberg, and the white wines under that of Schoongezicht (the labels of each feature the respective gables of the contrasting homesteads, the flowing Cape Dutch of Schoongezicht and the more restrained neo-classical of Rustenberg). In terms of the Wine of Origin legislation, by which, to receive the appellation of 'Estate', wine must come from a single property, the combined Schoongezicht and Rustenberg concern fails to qualify for estate status – though in all other respects its wines comply with the Wine and Spirit Board's requirements. Its lack of the customary label, however, has hardly hindered the farm's excellent reputation, its rating in the wine shows, or the demand for its finely-made wines.

Etienne le Riche, wine maker of Rustenberg/Schoongezicht.

Rust-en-Vrede

The homestead and the wine farm of Rust-en-Vrede have both been brought back from a virtually derelict condition by the former rugby Springbok, Jannie Engelbrecht. Born in Namaqualand, he went to senior school and university in Stellenbosch, where, through his schoolfriends who were the sons of wine farmers, he first came into contact with the making of wine and its lore. A developing interest crystallized in practical form with his purchase in 1978 of the old farm of Rust-en-Vrede lying at the foot of the Helderberg at Stellenbosch.

Once part of a much larger property named Bonte Rivier, which was granted by Simon van der Stel in 1694 to Willem van der Wêreld, the first vines were planted here in 1730, wine being made and sold, as was the custom in those days, in casks. Round about 1780 a plain building was erected which comprised living quarters, a small wine cellar and a coach house. By 1790 the existing old wine cellar was completed, and as the wine making flourished, the main house was built and completed in 1825. The three historical buildings form a unique unit. In later years the property was divided, and in the mid-nineteenth century one of the subdivisions became Rust-en-Vrede.

By the 1920s wine making had died out on the farm, though grapes continued to be grown. When Jannie moved onto his newly acquired farm he found the old wine cellar being used as a stable for horses and cows. Some of the original open cement fermentation tanks still survived but were of no practical use. In the vineyards were blocks of Cabernet Sauvignon, Shiraz, Tinta Barocca, Cinsaut and some Chenin Blanc.

He set about bringing new life to the property. With the architects, Gabriel Fagan and his wife Gwen, well known for many other restorations in the winelands, he restored the old buildings to their original glory.

The old vineyards were largely replanted with new stock, to the extent that of the 40 hectares about half are new plantings. The emphasis here is strongly upon red varieties, which are particularly suited to the situation of the farm, with good Hutton and Clovelly soils on well-drained slopes at the foot of the Helderberg. Before making these plantings, Jannie consulted the prominent viticulturalist, Desiderius Pongrácz, who stressed that he would produce excellent Shiraz wines from grapes grown on the higher slopes of the farm.

The old cellar was renovated, and Jannie made his first wine in 1979, working against time and in response to a sporting challenge from friends, the last equipment for the cellar arriving at the same time as the first load of grapes.

His wines were an immediate success – Rust-en-Vrede's fruity, medium-bodied Tinta Barocca is a gold medal winner. Jannie himself considers Cabernet Sauvignon to be the 'king of the wines', and an ideal wine for keeping. His ambition to be purely a red wine producer has been achieved, for since 1981 Rust-en-Vrede has been an exclusively red wine Estate. This is both a matter of soil and climate and of temperament, too. The relationship of the wine maker and his red wines is longer and more complex than with white wines. From the time the white grapes are brought in to the moment when the wine is marketed can be less than a year, whereas the making of red wine is more protracted, a more lingering and contemplative activity and, Jannie feels, more rewarding.

Jannie Engelbrecht has owned Rust-en-Vrede since 1978; his first wines were made the following year and won him immediate success.

Rust-en-Vrede Estate

Cultivars Planted	Size of Vineyards (Number of vines)	Training Practice
Cabernet Sauvignon	60 000	
Shiraz	45 000	
Pinot Noir	20 000	Vertical trellises
Merlot	15 000	
Tinta Barocca	15 000	
Cabernet Franc	5 000	

Total area under vines in 1987: 40 ha
Irrigation: The vineyards at Rust-en-Vrede are not irrigated.
Temperatures: Records are not kept.
Average annual rainfall: 650 mm
Stock: Rooted vines are purchased from a nursery.
First wines bottled under the Rust-en-Vrede Estate label: Cabernet Sauvignon, Shiraz, Tinta Barocca, Cinsaut and Chenin Blanc (all 1979 vintage)
Wines currently bottled under the Rust-en-Vrede Estate label: Cabernet Sauvignon, Shiraz, Tinta Barocca, Pinot Noir and a blended wine using Merlot.
Wood ageing: Wines are aged in wood on the Estate.
Capacity of the Rust-en-Vrede cellar: 2 000 hectolitres.

Rust-en-Vrede is on the Stellenbosch Wine Route and is open to the public on weekdays from 09h00 to 16h30; during December and January the Estate is also open on Saturdays from 09h00 to 12h00.

Six red cultivars are produced at Rust-en-Vrede and outstanding results have been achieved at the various wine shows in a relatively short period of time, including numerous gold medals. The 1983 Cabernet Sauvignon was chosen as the South African Red Wine Champion and many Superior awards have also been received, including the first ever for the Tinta Barocca cultivar, in 1980.

Besides the restored original cellar, a new modern cellar, capable of handling 300 tonnes of grapes, has been designed. Its pressing and working cellar is on the ground floor and there are two floors underground. The first of these is for bottle maturation, accommodating 500 000 bottles, and the second for use as a private vinotèque and public wine-tasting area. Now that this building is complete, the old

cellar will be used only for the ageing of the red wines in Nevers oak vats.

In October 1987, Kevin Arnold accepted a post as wine maker and cellarmaster at Rust-en-Vrede. Formerly wine maker at Delheim, Kevin was South African Champion Wine Maker in 1986. The combined talents of Kevin and Jannie will ensure the continued eminence of Rust-en-Vrede as a red wine Estate.

Saxenburg

A venture into wine making today requires business expertise, capital and good marketing. It is not surprising, then, that a trend has developed in some wine-producing countries, including France, Australia and the United States, for large, well-established industrial companies to buy wine farms. Seemingly, most of these companies have little to do with wine making, yet a number of them have widely diversified interests, which include the wine industry: the major shareholder of Anglo Alpha Limited, for example, is Holderbank of Switzerland, owned by the Schmidheiny family, which has its own wine estate in Switzerland and another in the Napa Valley of California.

Anglo Alpha, established in 1935 and today one of South Africa's largest industrial companies, bought Saxenburg in 1980. Originally the land had been granted by Governor Simon van der Stel to a Free Burgher, one Joachim Sax (hence the name of the farm) in 1693. The farm was sold to two Swedes, Oloff and Albertus Bergh in 1705 and changed hands again a decade later when Oloff sold both Saxenburg and the adjoining farm De Kuijlen, in order to acquire one of the most beautiful farms of the time, Groot Constantia.

The Saxenburg homestead was built around 1701, the style being a simple farmhouse typical of that era. It was so badly damaged by fire in 1945, however, that it had to be demolished. Fortunately, the inner doors, made of stinkwood and yellowwood, and a built-in cupboard, which is the oldest of its type in South Africa, were saved. In the same year the present homestead was built in almost the same position as the original and in the

Saxenburg

Cultivars Planted	Size of Vineyards (Hectares)	Training Practice
Steen	31	
Sauvignon Blanc	5	
Rhine Riesling	5	Hedge trellis
Gewürztraminer	5	
Cape Riesling	5	
Hanepoot	5	
Clairette Blanche	9	Perold trellis
Cinsaut	5	Bush vines

Total area under vines in 1987: 70 ha (50 ha still to be planted)
Irrigation: The vineyards at Saxenburg are not irrigated.
Temperatures: Average maximum 27 °C; average minimum 10 °C
Average annual rainfall: Approximately 900-1 000 mm
Stock: Rooted vines are purchased from a recognised nursery.
Envisaged new cultivars: Cabernet Sauvignon, Merlot, Chardonnay and Pinotage
First wines bottled under the Saxenheim label: Blanc de Blanc 1986, Chenin Blanc 1986 and Pinotage 1985
Wines currently bottled under the Saxenheim label: Chenin Blanc, Blanc de Blanc, Blanc de Noir, Special Late Vintage, Pinotage, Rosé and Noble Late Harvest (all wines are bottled by Stellenbosse Botteleringskoöperasie Beperk.)
Wood ageing: Wines are aged in wood on the farm.
Capacity of the Saxenburg cellar: 3 500 hectolitres

Saxenburg is open to the public on weekdays from 08h00 to 17h00, and on Saturdays from 08h00 to 13h00 from the beginning of December to the end of January.

same style, although with an additional bedroom wing, giving the house the present H-shape.

The farm manager and wine maker is Ernst Gouws, who joined Anglo Alpha in 1984 and who was born and bred on a wine farm. After completing a two-year course

at the West German Wine School, Weinsberg, he spent a year at Stellenbosch Farmers' Winery, before returning to Weinsberg for a year of practical work. In 1974 Ernst joined Du Toitskloof Co-operative Winery as wine maker and manager, producing some most successful wines. In 1983 he went to France, where he stayed for nearly a year, working for a few months in the Champagne region, followed by an exciting period in Bordeaux making wines for Château Peyreau and Château L'Oratoire, after the French vigneron had been taken ill.

At present there are 70 hectares planted to vines at Saxenburg and the adjoining farm Uitsig and this will be increased to 120 hectares. The cultivars planted are Chenin Blanc, Cape Riesling, Clairette Blanche and Cinsaut with young plantings of Sauvignon Blanc, Weisser Riesling, Gewürztraminer, and Muscat d'Alexandrie to follow. Ernst takes advantage of the fact that Saxenburg is not classified as an Estate by buying in grapes, for example Pinotage, that he cannot supply himself.

The wines are bottled and distributed under the Saxenheim label, the range consisting of Blanc de Blanc, Blanc de Noir, Rosé, Chenin Blanc, Noble Late Harvest, Special Late Harvest, and Pinotage.

Simonsig

Simonsig Estate

Cultivars Planted	Size of Vineyards (Hectares)	Training Practice
Chenin Blanc	32,24	
Pinotage	18,20	
Sauvignon Blanc	15,94	
Palomino	15,55	
Cabernet Sauvignon	14,18	
Bukettraube	12,20	
Shiraz	11,83	All cultivars are
Chardonnay	10,55	grown on Perold or
Weisser Riesling	10,54	extended Perold
Gewürztraminer	10,40	trellises
Kerner	6,62	
Colombard	5,43	
Clairette Blanche	4,22	
SA Riesling	3,75	
Pinot Noir	3,18	
Hanepoot	3,06	
Merlot	2,62	
Schönberger	1,84	
Muscat Ottonel	1,82	
Morio Muscat	1,80	
Cabernet Franc	1,00	

Total area under vines in 1987: 187 ha
Irrigation: 85 per cent of the vineyards can be irrigated if necessary.
Temperatures: Records are not kept.
Average annual rainfall: Approximately 540 mm
Stock: Rooted vines are purchased from a nursery; clonal material supplied by the KWV.
Envisaged new cultivars: Merlot
First wines bottled under the Simonsig Estate label: Clairette Blanche, Steen and Riesling (all 1968 vintage)
Wines currently bottled under the Simonsig Estate label: Adelberg, Cabernet Sauvignon, Chardonnay, Chenin Blanc, Colombard, Franciskaner Special Late Harvest, Gewürztraminer, Kaapse Vonkel, Mustique, Noble Late Harvest, Pinotage, Pinot Noir, Riesling, Rosé, Sauvignon Blanc, Shiraz, Sonstein, Vin Fumé, Vin Gris and Weisser Riesling
Wood ageing: Wines are aged in wood on the Estate.
Capacity of the Simonsig cellar: 230 000 hectolitres

Simonsig is open to the public on weekdays from 08h00 to 13h00 and from 14h00 to 17h00, and on Saturdays between 08h30 and 12h30.

This is one of the largest of the Cape's private wine Estates. It comprises two original land grants, those of the farms De Hoop and Simonsig, separated by three kilometres but unified under a single ownership and organization, that of Frans Malan. One of the originators, in the early 1970s, of the idea for the Stellenbosch Wine Route, Frans is a determined and independent man who has concentrated upon establishing a broad foundation of both white and red wines – some 18 cultivars are grown on the Simonsig Estate, 70 per cent of the total of 180 hectares being given to white wine varieties.

Included in the Simonsig range is the first South African Estate sparkling wine produced by the *méthode champenoise*, the Simonsig Kaapse Vonkel (since the 'crayfish deal' made in the 1930s with the French Government, the Cape wine makers agreed not to use French place-names, including that of Champagne, for their wines). Though made in the same way as champagne, Kaapse Vonkel is derived from grape cultivars different from those used in making the French wine, and of course, differences in soil and climate also have an effect. As young vineyards of Chardonnay and Pinot Noir come into production during the course of 1988, the *cuvée* will be similar to the wines of champagne.

In earlier days in the Cape, all sparkling wines were made by this method, but with the perfection of tank fermentation, bottle fermentation all but disappeared, the little that was made being either experimental or purely for own use. Frans has led the modern re-introduction of *méthode champenoise* sparkling wines with his Kaapse Vonkel. From 1971 he produced it every second vintage but since 1977 it has been made every year.

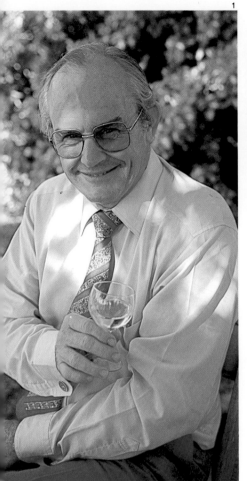

Simonsig's Kaapse Vonkel is a sparkling wine made according to the traditional méthode champenoise. *Here a bottle is checked for the clearly visible sediment which is deposited during bottle fermentation* **2**. *Bottles of Kaapse Vonkel are temporarily closed and placed neck down so that sediment is drawn towards the cap. The small amount of wine in the neck is then frozen to lock in the sediment; the frozen wine and sediment are removed* **3** *and the bottles closed with the traditional 'champagne' corks. Frans Malan* **1** *wine maker and owner of Simonsig was largely responsible for the re-introduction to the Cape of sparkling wine made by the traditional method. Frans's son, Johan,* **4**, *is now the wine maker at Simonsig.*

The scale of enterprise at Simonsig is a relatively recent development in the Estate's history. Originally, Simonsig formed part of the farm Nooitgedacht, the grant for which dates back to 1682. Its companion-farm, De Hoop, is of even earlier origin, being part of the old property of Koelenhof, granted to Simon de Groott in 1682.

The first wine to be made on De Hoop was bottled as recently as 1941, and the farm which Frans Malan took over from his father-in-law in 1953 still largely featured mixed farming. With his MSc in oenology from Stellenbosch University, Frans set about enlarging and streamlining the cellar facilities on De Hoop, planting larger quantities of better vines. Further expansion led him in 1964 to purchase the nearby farm of Simonsig and to consolidate the two farms,

registering them as a wine Estate – since De Hoop was not available for the Estate name, that of Simonsig, named for its sweeping view of the Simonsberg which appears in miniature on many of the Estate's labels, was used instead. The first wine under a Simonsig label appeared in 1968.

The soils in the area are predominantly Hutton and Clovelly types. Though relatively poor, Frans maintains that they encourage the production of quality over quantity. For this reason only light applications of fertilizer are used, though careful analyses of soil and leaves are regularly made in case of sudden or unexpected deficiency.

Though traditional staples such as Steen and Cape Riesling are grown on Simonsig and De Hoop (where the cellar is situated), Frans's interest in building up high-

quality wines has led to a constant broadening of the range of cultivars grown. Eight different clones of Chardonnay are planted at Simonsig, as well as Weisser Riesling, Gewürztraminer and Bukettraube, the last two producing particularly notable wines.

Frans's three sons have joined him on the farm and now Pieter does the marketing and administration, while Francois, a qualified viticulturist, manages the vineyards. Johan, the youngest son, became the wine maker after completing his studies at Stellenbosch University majoring in oenology and viticulture.

A visit to Simonsig and in particular to the Kaapse Vonkel cellar, with its inverted bottles undergoing *remuage* in wooden racks or *pupitres*, is a fascinating experience.

Spier

This is an old Cape wine farm run by an old Cape family. The present owner of the Spier complex (which includes some five farms in all) is Niel Joubert, descendant of a Huguenot immigrant who first put down tenacious roots in the Cape at the turn of the eighteenth century. Pierre Joubert was a wine farmer from the Loire Valley of France, who joined the 1688 Huguenot emigration to the VOC's colony at the Cape in search of political and religious freedom. Once arrived, he soon settled down to ply his trade, buying a property in the Drakenstein district.

Two centuries later his descendants were established in the Vlaeberg-Polkadraai area. It was here that the father of the present Joubert was born. He was Christiaan Joubert, and it was he who, in 1918, bought the farm Goedgeloof; his son Niel bought the historic Spier in 1965, making it the centre of the present flourishing wine-making concern.

One of the oldest wine farms in the Stellenbosch area, Spier was first granted by the Governor Simon van der Stel in September 1692, to one Arnout Tamboer Jansz (the original title-deed, a treasured possession, is preserved by the present owners). In 1712 Jansz disposed of the property to Hans Hendrik Hattingh (who hailed from Speyer in Germany, hence Spier), and in the following decades it changed hands a number of times. Rhodes farmed here, as did families such as the Cartwrights and the Keppels before its purchase by the present generation of Jouberts.

With the assistance of his son Chris, who now manages the Estate, Niel Joubert built up a thriving organization which includes three other vineyards – Olives, Goedgelegen, and Goedgevonden – besides Spier and Goedgeloof.

The making of the wide range of the Spier wines is done in the extensive cellars at Goedgeloof. Here an annual crop of between 2 000 and 2 500 tonnes of grapes is processed. The Estate's red wines are matured in casks in a special maturation cellar which also contains up to 250 000 bottles for ageing. During its first ten years of Estate bottling, the talented Arthur Boulle was responsible for the wine making at Spier, with Chris taking an active interest. Since June 1982, Jan Smit has assisted Chris in the cellars as wine maker.

Earlier in the present century the farm specialized in the production of export fruit; and a certain amount is still grown here, but the remaining orchards are being steadily replaced by vines, the emphasis being on the establishment of quality cultivars. Considerable care is taken to match the type of cultivar to the conditions prevailing in the different areas of the Estate. Among the red wine vines currently grown, the most important is

Spier Jonkershuis (above). Tea and luncheon are served both inside the wine house and outside under the oaks.

Goedgeloof, one of the five vineyards of Spier, which together produce a yearly harvest of 2 000 to 2 500 tonnes of grapes.

Spier Estate

Cultivars Planted	Size of Vineyards (Number of vines)	Training Practice
Steen	135 744	
Pinotage	83 530	
Cabernet Sauvignon	67 870	
Shiraz	32 170	
Clairette Blanche	26 932	Perold trellises
Colombar	25 124	
Hárslevelü	5 000	
Pinot Gris	5 000	
Hanepoot	3 700	
Pontac	1 875	
Sauvignon Blanc	54 034	
Cape Riesling	34 340	
Gewürztraminer	22 500	Fence trellises
Bukettraube	8 250	
Weisser Riesling	8 150	

Total area under vines in 1987: 350 ha
Irrigation: All Spier vineyards are irrigated.
Temperatures: Records are not kept.
Average annual rainfall: Approximately 600 mm
Stock: Rooted vines are purchased from a nursery.
First wines bottled under the Spier Estate label: Pinotage 1969 and Colombar 1972
Wines currently bottled under the Spier Estate label: Premier Grand Crû, Pinotage, Vin Rouge, Chenin Blanc, Late Harvest, Special Late Harvest, Chenin Blanc Special Late Harvest, Noble Late Harvest, Colombar, Shiraz, Rosé, Blanc de Noir, Durendal Rosé, Blanc de Blanc, Bouquet Blanc, Cabernet Sauvignon, Dry Red, Sauvignon Blanc, Dry Steen, Riesling and two sparkling wines, Vin Brut and Vin Sec. Two fortified wines, a Port and Mistelle, are also made and bottled on the Estate.
Wood ageing: Wines are aged in wood on the Estate.
Capacity of the Spier cellar: 21 800 hectolitres

Spier is on the Stellenbosch Wine Route and is open to the public on weekdays from 08h30 to 13h00 and from 14h00 to 17h00, and on Saturdays from 08h30 to 13h00. Meals are served at both the Jonkershuis wine house and the Spier Restaurant.

As are so many Cape wine farms, Spier is owned and managed by a father and son team, Niel and Chris Joubert.

Pinotage, while others include Cabernet Sauvignon, Pontac and Shiraz. Among the white cultivars are Sauvignon Blanc, Chenin Blanc, Bukettraube, Colombar and Riesling. Since the Estate's inception its most popular and consistently good wines have been Special Late Harvest Colombar, Pinotage and Port.

The old homestead of Spier has been meticulously restored by the Jouberts; its Jonkershuis has been converted into a charming wine house where meals are also served, while the slave-quarters have been developed into the Spier Restaurant. The cellar building (no longer used for its original purpose) is one of the oldest of its kind in the country, dating back to the early eighteenth century. Attractive tasting facilities are also included on the premises.

Stellenbosch Farmers' Winery

Situated on the Eerste River approaches to the town of Stellenbosch is the headquarters of the Stellenbosch Farmers' Winery. Since its merger in October, 1979, with the Oude Meester Group to form part of Cape Wine and Distillers Limited, this huge company – it makes over half the wine drunk in South Africa – has retained its operational autonomy. More importantly, it has kept its own style and identity, exemplified in a broad spectrum of wine products.

The spectacular rise and expansion of the Stellenbosch Farmers' Winery is very much a twentieth-century phenomenon. Its agile response, both in terms of advancing wine technology and in the changing patterns of consumer demand, has kept the company well in the forefront

of the modern industry. Although this is a winery with a contemporary style, echoes of the past still linger in the brisk and efficient corridors of the company's headquarters, in its large modern cellars and laboratories, for the land on which the Stellenbosch Farmers' Winery stands is that of the historic farm of Oude Libertas, once the property of the inflammable Adam Tas. It is often forgotten that Tas, besides being a diarist, agitator and polemicist of some talent (he left a vivid portrait of the first society in South Africa, spiced with much malicious gossip) was also a wine farmer.

Legend has it that the farm was named by Tas (Liber + Tas) to commemorate his release from the Castle where he had been held by Willem Adriaan van der Stel on

charges of sedition. But Tas was not the first owner of the land. It was first granted by Simon van der Stel in 1689 to Jan Cornelis van Oudenlingenland and, contrary to popular belief, it was he, not Tas, who gave his new property the name of Libertas, meaning 'liberty'. In 1692 Libertas was merged by a subsequent owner with a number of other areas of land, though the original name was retained. This farmer was Hans Jurgen Grimp; after his death Adam Tas married the widow Grimp, and thus gained title to the land – this was a common way in which a presentable but impecunious young man could acquire land of his own in those days.

After Tas' death in 1722, the farm changed hands several times, being eventually divided into two, the properties

Ronnie Melck, managing director of Stellenbosch Farmers' Winery.

The Adam Tas Cellar at the centre of the vast Stellenbosch Farmers' Winery headquarters.

of Libertas and Oude Libertas. After many vicissitudes, the Oude Libertas portion of the land was bought by the Krige family in 1867. The first of the Kriges on Oude Libertas, Gideon Johannes, was an effective enough wine farmer. His son and namesake, however, tried his hand at a number of kinds of farming, from breeding ostriches to growing mushrooms, all with equal lack of success. The early years of the present century saw the Kriges, father and son, attempting to establish a small private winery and distillery on Oude

Libertas. Notwithstanding their enthusiasm for the venture, and their motto – 'Hours of Business – Sunrise to Sunset' – they soon ran into difficulties.

It was at this point, in 1924, that William Charles Winshaw made his appearance on the scene. Winshaw is one of the great characters of modern winelands history, and a personality remembered with affection and respect by the people of the Stellenbosch Farmers' Winery, one of the grander adventures in a life well filled with adventure.

His career up till this point had been nothing if not chequered. An American immigrant to the Cape, Winshaw had been born in Kentucky, the son of an eccentric doctor. At the age of 12 he ran away from home to begin a wandering life, living by the wits with which he appears to have been well endowed. He tumbled through a series of adventures which included gold prospecting, a spell as a Texas ranger, encounters with Wild West types such as Buffalo Bill, gambling at faro, and fighting in a campaign on the Mexican border. More dignified ambitions crystallized, and he returned to the life of a gambler to finance medical studies at Tulane. After a visit to Germany to study tropical diseases, he returned to New Mexico, where, in the intervals of treating gunshot wounds, he met a hitherto unencountered species in the person of a British army officer named McGuiness. This man was buying mules for the army engaged in the Anglo-Boer War, and it was not long before the wanderlusting Winshaw had agreed to organize the transportation of 4 500 mules to Cape Town.

Winshaw and his mules arrived in the Cape in 1899. The mules were taken to Stellenbosch, where they were quartered on the hillside behind Koelenhof and tended by British officers who had been 'Stellenbosched' – withdrawn from combat for reasons of incompetence and dumped in camp at Stellenbosch where they could do no further harm. Winshaw himself spent the war as an army doctor, returning to Stellenbosch after the hostilities to the start of a more settled way of life.

He married an English Boer-War nurse named Ada Day and in 1904 he became the tenant of a Cape Town dentist, Dr Lindup, who owned a small farm called Patrys Vlei, some 21 hectares in extent, outside Stellenbosch. Here Winshaw began to

---

Wines marketed and distributed by Stellenbosch Farmers' Winery Group

Autumn Harvest Range
Crackling (bottled wine)
Grand Crû, Late Vintage, Ausberger,
Country Claret and Blanc de Noir (boxed wines)

Kellerprinz Range
Stein, Grand Crû, Dry Red, Rosanne, Late Harvest and Blanc de Noir (available in bottles or as boxed wines)

Nederburg Range (see Nederburg, page 238)

Taskelder Range
Claret, Premier Grand Crû, Late Vintage and Blanc de Noir (available in bottles or as boxed wines)

Zonnebloem Range
Cabernet Sauvignon, Special Late Harvest, Riesling, Grand Crû, Pinotage, Shiraz, Rhine Riesling, Cabernet Blanc de Noir, Blanc de Blanc and Sauvignon Blanc

Individual Labels
Tasheimer Goldtröpfchen
La Gratitude
Lieberstein

Roodendal Cabernet Sauvignon
Casa de Ouro Graça
Roma White
Virginia
Zonnheimer
Chateau Libertas
Tassenberg (available in bottles or as boxed wine)
Capenheimer
Oom Tas
Lanzerac: Rosé, Muscat d'Alexandrie Light

Sparkling Wines
Grand Mousseaux: Extra Brut, Vin Doux, Vin Sec and Spumante
5th Avenue Cold Duck

Fortified Wines
Monis: Full Cream, Medium Cream and Dry Sherries, Moscato, Marsala, Very Old Port and Collector's Port

Sedgwick: Old Brown Sherry and Government House Port
Libertas White and Red Muscadel
Ship Sherry
Soetendal Hanepoot

experiment with the making of wine, mostly from Hermitage and Pontac. His first attempts (cooked up on his wife's kitchen stove) were not a great success, but he soon discovered ways of improving his humble product. In a short while he began selling his 'raisin wine', or 'processed Hermitage', to Fred Green of the wine merchants E.K. Green and Company. Encouraged by a current shortage of wine owing to a bad harvest, his products soon gained in popularity.

Then, in February, 1909, Winshaw went into business on a serious scale. With a capital of £1 000 he opened his Stellenbosch Grape Juice Works, from which he sold both wine and unfermented grape juice. This was complemented in 1913 by a part-ownership in the Stellenbosch Distillery.

William Charles Winshaw was finding his feet. He was also beginning to make his personality felt in a more general way in the local wine-making milieu. In the years before the First World War, he began shrewdly buying up good unsold wine from the local growers, at double its normal price of £2 a leaguer, thus outbidding the other merchants who were manipulating a depressed post-war market to their advantage and at the expense of the growers.

In this tactic Winshaw found support from Charles Kohler, the most active proponent of the budding co-operative movement. Kohler was a dentist who, like Winshaw himself, had been involved in mining before moving to the vineyards.

In return Winshaw gave Kohler much support (particularly against the wine merchants) in the formation of the KWV in 1918.

Winshaw's first adventure in the wine trade lasted little more than a decade. With 'too many irons in the fire', his company ran into financial trouble, followed by insolvency, a process hastened by the KWV which (momentarily forgetting previous loyalties and any principle of co-operation) advised the growers who were supplying Winshaw to insist on their payments in advance. The *coup de grâce*, however, was delivered by the merchants who raised their prices to the farmers (as Winshaw himself had once done to them), forcing him to bid beyond his financial strength. The value of Winshaw's wine stocks slumped from £670 000 to £230 000, and then to even less. On January 12, 1921, he was declared insolvent, the KWV moving quickly in to buy up his company, its stocks and its fustage, its extensive cellar and wine-making equipment.

Now over fifty years of age, Winshaw returned to the United States for a brief spell as a doctor. But within a few years, ever dogged, he was back in the Cape, and on March 3, 1924, at the age of 53, he was formally rehabilitated from his insolvency,

the court pointedly noting, 'in a measure the applicant has been misled by the farmers themselves'.

Winshaw's *wandeljahre* were now finally over. Looking for a new point of entry into the local wine market, he soon discovered Gideon Johannes Krige Jnr and his faltering distillery on the northern banks of the Eerste River. With an entrepreneurial instinct for a 'good thing', and with many years of wine-making and trading experience behind him, Winshaw first entered into partnership with the Kriges of Oude Libertas, then later bought them out for the modest sum of £5 500.

Back in business with a vengeance, Winshaw brought his two sons, Bill, who was at university, and later Jack, into his new concern. Soon they were making and selling their own wine on a rapidly expanding scale. They were also making changes in the type and style of this wine, making radical departures from the prevailing norm.

During this period very little natural wine was drunk in South Africa; almost all was sweet fortified wine, such as Muscadel, sweet ports, brown sherries, and jerepigos with colourful names such as Worcester Hock, Polly Hock and Paarl Rock. Not only were these wines strengthened with the addition of wine spirit or brandy, but the addition of cane sugar, in the event of a poor summer, was common practice – to an almost absurd degree: one Cape Town company had purchased 1 000 000 pounds of sugar in one year for this purpose.

Either sensing an impending change of taste or feeling that he might be able to help make it himself, Winshaw had long argued both economically and qualitatively against this practice, finally bringing the Prime Minister, General Smuts (whose wife was related to the Kriges of Oude Libertas) around to his viewpoint. One result of this lobbying was Act 15 of 1924, which forbade the use of cane sugar in the flavouring and fermenting of wine.

A further element in Winshaw's reasoning was medical. As a doctor, he felt that a natural wine, with its relatively low sugar and alcohol content would be better for the public health than the rich and powerful concoctions of old. From the beginning, therefore, the Winshaws concentrated upon making natural wines.

The company expanded steadily, its growing strength reflected in new wines. Among the most famous of these were the Château Libertas and La Gratitude wines – the latter named after the beautiful old house in Dorp Street in Stellenbosch, now a National Monument, which was (and still is) the Winshaw family home. In other wine ranges the name of Adam Tas is remembered, in Tasheimer, Oom Tas, Taskelder and Tassenberg, to the extent that 'Tassies' has gone into the vernacular.

Wine appreciation class held by the Cape Wine Academy, which is sponsored solely by S.F.W.

As in many wine making organizations, tradition and modern technology exist side-by-side at Stellenbosch Farmers' Winery. Huge Limosin-oak casks **1**, *many of them crafted on the premises by skilled coopers, contrast sharply with the winery* **2** *where red wine maker Jan de Waal studies 'cap' formation through the inspection hatch of a closed fermentation tank. The company is also heavily committed to research into developing better wine making methods* **3**.

Winshaw attached great importance to names and labels, defending them ardently against plagiarism by other wine makers. He also continued to make it a fixed policy to buy only good wines from the growers, and only at good prices.

In these years the younger William Winshaw (universally known as 'Bill') began to take a larger share in the emerging character of the firm, following study of modern wine-making methods in Europe; in 1930 he introduced Grand Mousseaux, still one of the most famous and best-selling of the Cape's sparkling wines.

The business operation at Oude Libertas remained a private concern until 1935, when it was converted into a public company. With this move, the basic structure of the present-day Stellenbosch Farmers' Winery was laid down. With further expansion came mergers with other companies, one of the more important of these being the amalgamation in November, 1950, with the old firm of V.H. Matterson, first established in Pietermaritzburg in 1851; this merger led to the establishment of the Stellenbosch Farmers' Wine Trust. Further large mergers took place in 1966 and 1970. In the first of these Stellenbosch Farmers' Winery merged with Monis Wineries of Paarl, of which the now famous Nederburg Estate formed a part. With the creation of this big new company the paths of two other pioneers of the local wine industry, of Roberto Moni and Johann Georg Graue, were linked with the Stellenbosch Farmers' Wine Trust. After Nederburg's inclusion in the Trust, large sums were allocated for the further development of the Estate, which is today fully equipped in all respects for the making of high-quality wine (see Nederburg, page 238). With a heavy investment in the natural wine industry, the Trust achieved a bigger share of the spirits and fortified wine market with their 1970 take-over of Sedgwick-Taylor, a company with origins dating back to the middle of the last century.

Together with these expansions into new areas went major developments both in marketing – the Winery allocated R2 million in 1962 for advertising their products – and in production and research facilities, reflected in the 1964 purchase of two farms for viticultural research.

The most spectacular expression of this new thrust was in the meteoric career of a Stellenbosch Farmers' Winery product which first appeared in 1959. In that year a semi-sweet natural table wine, largely made from Chenin Blanc, was launched with the name of Lieberstein. Three decades later, the following table still brings a misty look to the eyes of Stellenbosch Farmers' Winery executives:

Year	Amount of Lieberstein sold (litres)
1959	30 000
1960	700 000
1961	4 500 000
1962	12 700 000
1963	22 300 000
1964	31 200 000

The peak achieved in 1964 made this the largest selling bottled wine in the world at the time, and though public taste has moved on, Lieberstein retains a devoted, if diminished, following.

During all these developments, William

Charles Winshaw remained at the head of his company. Seemingly immortal, it was only at the indomitable old age of 92 that the founder retired from his creation, handing over the running of the company to his son, Bill Winshaw. Still a cunning hand with a deck of cards, rich in anecdotes and the pleasure of a long, maverick life, a living proof of the medicinal value of his own wine, the elder Winshaw died in 1968 at the age of 96, many miles and much achievement away from Pulaski County, Kentucky.

His memorial on the northern banks of the Eerste River is an impressive one. The extensive cellars and winery produce a quantity of wine which gives the company turnover in excess of R600 million a year. Public tours of the premises are laid on; these include not only a view of the winery itself, from the enormous steel tanks of the cold fermentation process to the teams of skilled coopers assembling the red wine maturation vats from staves of imported Limousin oak, but also films on wine and a tasting of the company's products in the elegant tasting-rooms. More sophisticated educational courses are also housed in the complex.

One further attraction of Oude Libertas needs mention. This is the Oude Libertas complex, comprising an underground cellar-restaurant and the Amphitheatre, built in 1977 on the slopes of the Papegaaisberg, and opened with a performance by the famous Russian pianist, Vladimir Ashkenazy. Based on the design of the ancient Greek theatres of Athens and Epidauros, it seats some 430 theatre-goers – the arrangement of the theatre being cunningly calculated to protect them from the prevailing Southeaster wind – and is open during the summer from December to March.

Bill Winshaw, who ran Stellenbosch Farmers' Winery after his father retired in 1966, retired as chairman of the company in 1980, but remains on the Board of Directors. His son John is the cellarmaster, assisted by a former wine buyer, Wouter Pienaar. The fine wine-making team is well supported by experienced wine buyers. The head wine buyer is Jeff Wedgwood, who, with his colleagues Dieter Thielhelm and Colin Frith, not only liaises with the Co-operatives, Estates and farms which supply wines in bulk to Stellenbosch Farmers' Winery, but also advises them in their wine making. Lothar Barth, who had been managing director since 1970, succeeded Bill Winshaw as chairman. He retired in 1986, but also remains on the Board of Directors. Frans Davin is the present chairman and Ronnie Melck is the managing director. Ronnie joined the company in 1956, became an executive director in charge of production in 1963, deputy managing director in 1978, and managing director in 1981. The director in charge of production is Duimpie Bayly, a graduate of Stellenbosch University and the University of California.

Uiterwyk

One of the oldest Estates in the Stellenbosch area, Uiterwyk was once on the main road from Cape Town to Stellenbosch which wound through this panoramic valley. Originally named after an area of old Holland, the land was first settled in 1682 by Dirk Coetzee, and formally granted to him by Willem Adriaan van der Stel in 1699.

It began to make a mark as a wine farm in the late eighteenth century, with the advent of the Krige family. It was they who built the present homestead – a beautiful example of the Cape Dutch type – in 1791. An adjacent cellar was added in 1798, and the stables in 1812. A further smaller house was added at the back to complete the complex in 1822.

In the present century Uiterwyk came into the ownership of another old South African family, the De Waals. The first De Waal to be born in the country farmed vines in what is now Wale (or Waal) Street in Cape Town. His son, Pieter, moved away to farm at Alphen, and subsequent generations crossed the Cape Flats to the

The gracious herehuis *of Uiterwyk, built in 1791, in its harmonious garden setting.*

Stellenbosch area. After various further moves the family finally settled at Uiterwyk when it was bought by Jan Christoffel de Waal in 1912. When he retired in 1946 his son, Danie, the present owner, took over. Danie's son Chris, who studied overseas, is the winemaker of Uiterwyk. Pieter, the second son, studied Economics at the University of Stellenbosch and worked in the Napa Valley, California, to gain experience in the marketing of wine. He is responsible for the marketing and sales of Uiterwyk wines.

The Estate's impressive new cellar was opened in 1979. Danie designed it so that it can be enlarged and it incorporates a reception, tasting and selling area, an office, laboratory and a cellar for ageing bottled wines. But for the visitor to Uiterwyk the old wine cellar remains rich in atmosphere; with many of its massive oak casks still intact (they were erected with the building), it has seen continuous yearly production of wine since it was built in 1798.

The Estate covers 150 hectares, of which about 110 are presently under vines. Here Danie de Waal concentrates about two thirds of his production on Steen and Clairette Blanche, followed by Pinotage, Colombar, Cinsaut and Cabernet Sauvignon. The balance is made up of relatively small quantities of Cape Riesling, Müller-Thurgau, Bukettraube, Sauvignon Blanc, Weisser Riesling, Merlot and Cabernet Franc. Of these, nine wines are bottled and sold under the Estate's own label.

Uiterwyk Estate

Cultivars Planted	Size of Vineyards (Number of vines)	Training Practice
Chenin Blanc	124 000	
Pinotage	28 600	
Cabernet Sauvignon	13 800	
Müller-Thurgau	9 900	
Sauvignon Blanc	9 100	
Rhine Riesling	6 200	One-wire trellis
Cape Riesling	5 700	
Merlot	5 100	
Bukettraube	4 900	
Cabernet Franc	3 200	
Clairette Blanche	85 500	One-wire trellis
Cinsaut	10 000	and bush vines
Colombar	28 500	High slanting and one-wire vertical trellis

The oldest vineyard is over 40 years old and is still bearing well.

Total area under vines in 1987: 110 ha
Irrigation: All Uiterwyk vineyards are irrigated.
Temperatures: Records are not kept.
Average annual rainfall: Approximately 780 mm
Stock: Parent stock used for grafting; rooted vines are also purchased from a nursery.
First wines bottled under the Uiterwyk Estate label: Colombar 1972, Cabernet Sauvignon 1973 and Riesling 1974
Wines currently bottled under the Uiterwyk Estate label: Cabernet Sauvignon, Colombar, Kromhout, Riesling, Rhine Riesling, Blanc de Noir, Pinotage, Müller-Thurgau and Merlot.
Wood ageing: Uiterwyk wines are aged in wood on the Estate.
Capacity of the Uiterwyk cellar: 10 000 hectolitres

One of the Estates on the Stellenbosch Wine Route, Uiterwyk is open to the public on weekdays from 09h00 to 12h00 and from 14h00 to 16h30, and on Saturdays from 10h00 to 12h00.

Uitkyk

This is a wine farm which has made a come-back under new management in recent years. Once the domain of an enterprising German immigrant wine maker renowned for the Estate's original Carlonet, a dry red wine, the production of quality red wines has been resurrected by its present wine master, Harvey Illing, son-in-law of the former owner, the late Gerry Bouwer. Between them, these two men gave new life to a farm which fell on hard times in the post-war period.

The renewal of Uitkyk has taken place on two fronts, with the rebuilding of the vineyards and their expansion, and with

the restoration of the striking and beautiful homestead, a neo-classical masterpiece and one of the rare architect-designed homesteads in the winelands. The designer in this instance was almost certainly the French immigrant, Louis Michel Thibault, who abandoned a career as a designer of military fortifications to devote himself to the graceful embellishment of the local Burgher architecture. He often collaborated with the German sculptor and designer, Anton Anreith, here responsible for the carving of Uitkyk's monumental front door.

First granted to Jan Oberholzer in 1712

and largely used for grazing in the early years, by the late eighteenth century the farm had become the property of one of the most successful self-made immigrants of his day, the redoubtable Martin Melck. By hard work and shrewd investment he had accumulated a large number of farms, including the area of the present Estates of Uitkyk, Kanonkop and Elsenburg. Then, in 1776, Melck ceded the land of Uitkyk to his son-in-law, Johan David Beyers, as a wedding gift. It was Beyers who built the present splendid townhouse-style mansion for himself and his large family. During the following century the farm continued to be used mainly for grazing or as a country seat for various wealthy families. In 1929, however, it was purchased by an immigrant Prussian nobleman, Hans von Carlowitz. It was Von Carlowitz who recognized the wine-making possibilities inherent in the high slopes of the farm, with their good soil and drainage. With his two sons, Hans and Georg, he divided his land between vines, timber on the steeper slopes, and wheat on the lower-lying areas. Responsibility for the different kinds of farming was shared by Von Carlowitz between his sons, with Hans attending to the wheat and timber and Georg being in sole charge of the vineyards.

In 1939 the elder son returned to Germany, leaving Georg in full control of the Estate's operations. In the following years Georg developed the vineyards, planting predominantly Steen, Riesling, Cinsaut, and Cabernet; it was a blend made from the last-mentioned two cultivars for which the family is still remembered. This was the famous Carlonet (the few remaining bottles of this blend are prized collector's items), which was complemented by a fine white blend of Steen and Riesling, the sweet and fruity Carlsheim.

In the post-Second World War period these outstanding wines gained for Georg von Carlowitz a secure reputation among Cape Town's discerning wine lovers. Unfortunately, this reputation was not accompanied by financial security. The area of the vineyards was small; its 35 hectares provided quality, but not the quantity to ensure a working profit, or the capital needed for expensive developments such as the cooling equipment introduced to the country in the 1950s, or the planting of new vines to replace Uitkyk's now ageing vineyards.

In 1963, in the face of these pressures, Von Carlowitz was forced to sell. The man who bought the farm at this juncture in its fortunes, Gerry Bouwer, was at least as interested in the old homestead as in the farm which went with it. Moreover, business commitments in the Transvaal prevented full-time involvement in its activities. Gerry's daughter, however, was married to a Durban dentist named Harvey Illing, and the new owner of Uitkyk soon persuaded his son-in-law to abandon a life of drilling and filling to devote himself to the art of viticulture.

Harvey responded to this invitation, moved to Uitkyk, and set about learning his new craft. At first he picked up and continued the tradition of his predecessor, supplying Carlonet and Carlsheim to their long-time devotees. The economic disadvantages, as well as the drawbacks in the person-to-person deliveries which were involved, however, soon persuaded Harvey and Gerry to change their approach. Their new tactics included rapid expansion of the

The beautiful, neo-classical Uitkyk homestead.

Uitkyk Estate

Cultivars Planted	Size of Vineyards (Hectares)	Training Practice
Steen	34,06	Perold trellis
Clairette Blanche	16,04	
Cape Riesling	16,32	
Sauvignon Blanc	14,30	
Chardonnay	12,00	3-wire vertical trellis
Pinot Gris	8,8	
Shiraz	7,63	
Pinot Noir	6,5	
Cabernet Sauvignon	23,00	2-wire vertical trellis
Cinsaut	4,5	Bush vines

Uitkyk has 8 ha of Steen planted on the slopes of the Skurweberg, the north-western extension of the Simonsberg. Year after year it invariably produces the best Chenin Blanc on Uitkyk and is blended with Riesling to produce Carlsheim.

Total area under vines in 1987: 189,15 ha
Irrigation: About two-thirds of the Uitkyk vineyards can be irrigated when necessary.
Temperatures: Records are not kept.
Average annual rainfall: The rainfall varies considerably, depending on the altitude: the lower vineyards receive approximately 630 mm, while the upper regions as much as 1 000 mm.
Stock: Rooted vines are purchased from a nursery.
Envisaged new cultivars: Merlot
First wines bottled under the Uitkyk Estate label: Carlonet and Carlsheim, 1946
Wines currently bottled under the Uitkyk Estate label: Riesling, Carlonet, Carlsheim and Shiraz. All the wines are bottled by the Bergkelder.
Wood ageing: Wines are aged in wood at the Bergkelder.
Capacity of the Uitkyk cellar: 7 737 hectolitres (excluding 640 hectolitres in the new cellar)

Uitkyk is not open to the public, but can be visited by appointment with the Bergkelder.

2 3

The modern roto-tanks 1 for the fermentation of wine at Uitkyk are a far cry from the equipment used by the aristocratic Hans von Carlowitz 2, erstwhile owner and wine maker of the Estate who created the famous Carlonet and Carlsheim wines. Technical innovations, however, have not altered the Estate's commitment to the production of fine wines and present wine maker Harvey Illing 3 continues to make the 'famous two'.

farm, and substantial cash injections to install modern equipment in the cellar, which was needed for the large-scale processing of both red and white wines.

By 1969 this radical process of modernization had been completed, and the new cellar (discreetly lower down the hill, at a distance from the sight-lines of the main house) was in energetic production. By this time, too, the original

35 hectares under cultivation had been expanded to a substantial 120; further expansion has since taken place and the Estate presently comprises some 190 hectares under vines. The upper slopes of the farm were bulldozed and planted, care being taken in the choice of site, both with regard to soil and to the wind direction – easterly gales are prevalent in this exposed sector of the Simonsberg. Another cellar

has recently been completed, the first phase of a two-phase construction which will cost several million rands. Extensive use of glass in the roof and walls of this magnificent structure allows illumination largely by natural light, and with its unique and ingenious design and technologically advanced equipment it is one of the most impressive complexes of its kind in the world.

Vergenoegd

Situated on the lower reaches of the Eerste River, the Estate of Vergenoegd, like Groot Constantia, enjoys the cooling winds of False Bay (even if it does not have the 1 000 metre-high Constantiaberg to lend it shade in the late afternoon). And this well-chosen site has undoubtedly had an influence on the growing of the vines and the making of the extremely good wines of Vergenoegd, now produced by the brothers

Jac and Brand Faure, the fifth generation of the family to live here.

Since the late 1900s, their red wines have come decisively into their own, featuring prominently in the local wine shows. For four years in succession, 1971 to 1974, their Cabernet Sauvignon carried off the General Smuts Trophy for the most outstanding wine at the Cape Young Wine Show at Goodwood, an achievement

remembered as a local wine maker's record. In 1981 their Cabernet-Shiraz blend won the National Red Wine Championship trophy. This wine was not marketed, however.

One of the oldest farms in the Eerste River area, the land of Vergenoegd was originally granted to Pieter de Vos in 1696. After a series of changes it became in 1772 the property of Johannes Nicolaas Colijn,

Jac Faure, renowned wine maker of Vergenoegd and joint owner of the Estate with his brother Brand, who is responsible for the vineyards.

Vergenoegd Estate

Cultivars Planted	Size of Vineyards (Hectares)	Training Practice
Steen	32	Bush vines and 4-wire trellis
Cinsaut	15	Bush vines
Tinta Barocca	9	
Pinotage	6	
SA Riesling	1	
Sauvignon Blanc	5	
Merlot	2	4-wire trellis
Cabernet Franc	2	
Cabernet Sauvignon	25	Perold trellis
Shiraz	22	

The original Hermitage vineyard was planted *circa* 1896. In 1932 alternate rows were removed to allow tractor cultivation. In 1956 the vineyard was removed and replaced with Shiraz vines. Cabernet Sauvignon was planted in 1962, began bearing in 1965, and has won the Vergenoegd Estate all its honours.

Total area under vines in 1987: 125 ha
Irrigation: All vineyards can be irrigated if necessary.
Temperatures: Records are not kept.
Average annual rainfall: 400-450 mm
Stock: Rooted vines are purchased from a nursery.
First wines bottled under the Vergenoegd Estate label: Cabernet Sauvignon 1969 and Shiraz 1969 (bottled by KWV); Cabernet Sauvignon 1972 (bottled on the Estate)
Wines currently bottled under the Vergenoegd Estate label: Cabernet Sauvignon, Shiraz, Pinotage, Tinta Barocca, Sauvignon Blanc and Cinsaut (all bottled on the Estate)
Wood ageing: Wines are aged in wood on the Estate. (Some Vergenoegd wines are also aged in wood and bottled at the KWV, but this is a completely separate venture.)
Capacity of the Vergenoegd cellar: 5 000 hectolitres

Vergenoegd Estate is not on the Stellenbosch Wine Route, but it is open to the public every Wednesday between 14h00 to 17h00 and by appointment on other days.

the son of the Colijn who had acquired Groot Constantia in 1720. It was he who built the present gable, dated at 1773, onto the already existing homestead (it is believed that one of his slaves was responsible for the curious spelling of the name Vergenoegd on this gable).

In 1820 the farm was sold to the first of the Faure family, Johannes Gysbertus Faure – the local proliferation of the Faures gave their name to the area at large. Johannes Faure continued the making of wine which had begun here in the eighteenth century. But the course of the nineteenth century saw a diversification of the farm's activities, particularly in the breeding of race-horses for which numerous stables were added. During the Anglo-Boer War a thriving horse-dealing business was run from here, to the extent of exporting horses to India – a groom was sent out to look after the horses on the boat during their voyage from the Cape.

But it was during the present century that Vergenoegd began to establish its own marked identity as a wine farm, under the guidance of John Faure, the father of the present owners. A committed wine farmer, he set about building up the vineyards, and in doing so concentrated, at the suggestion of Dr Charles Niehaus, upon two specific areas of development.

Niehaus is an important figure in modern South African wine history. He 'fathered' the sherry industry in the 1920s and 1930s, making a study of the distribution in the local vineyards of the naturally-occurring 'flor' yeasts of the kind traditionally associated with the making of the fine, dry Spanish *fino* sherries. Vergenoegd was among the first of the 18 local farms where he discovered this yeast. His advice to plant cultivars for sherry production was adopted by John Faure, whose sons have continued their cultivation.

The second piece of advice given by Niehaus was to plant Cabernet Sauvignon. Though it was not taken up immediately, on Niehaus' further insistence vineyards of Cabernet were laid out, replacing many of the old Shiraz vines. The foundation for the excellent Vergenoegd Cabernet of today, one of the most respected wines of its kind in the country, was thus laid.

The soil on the Estate varies considerably, from deep alluvial alongside the Eerste River, through all types of sandy soil to deep, yellow pot-clay types. It is on this latter, water-retaining type that the Cabernet vines are grown, and most of the other noble red varieties are also planted in soil with a high clay content.

The summers are hot but tempered by the South-Easter wind, which appears to live up to its title of the 'Cape Doctor', for the vineyards suffer little from disease, and only light dusting is needed to counteract oidium and downy mildew. The rainfall here is lower than in most of the other areas which fall under the Stellenbosch Wine of Origin District, particularly those which are close to the mountains, but most of the grapes are given only one irrigation. Vergenoegd is situated on the irrigation canal which emerges from the Eerste River in Stellenbosch and runs down the length of the valley. During winter, heavy rainfall in Jonkershoek causes the Eerste River to run very full, and with its shallow fall from Faure to the sea – Vergenoegd itself is only ten to 13 metres above sea-level – this last meandering stretch of the river tended in the past to silt up, causing it to burst its banks and flood the adjacent vineyards. Today a good deal of the silt has been removed, and flooding reduced with the construction of artificial banks, or levées, along the river. With heavy winter rains, however, the possibility of flooding still causes the Faure brothers some anxiety – in some parts of the farm it is not unusual

The farm of Vergenoegd dates back to a land grant in 1696. The lovely homestead and its outbuildings have been painstakingly restored.

to find the odd patch of poor growth among the vines owing to lack of drainage.

Originally the property covered an extent of about 736 hectares, but it was reduced by 51 hectares to allow for the big Cape Town to Strand motorway and the road to Stellenbosch which leads from it. Of the remaining 685 hectares some 125 are currently under wine-grapes, though the planted area is being extended yearly. The main varieties are Steen, which makes up a third of the area under vines, with the remainder being red cultivars. Besides the Cabernet Sauvignon, these include Shiraz vines, Cinsaut, Tinta Barocca and Pinotage. In the old days Vergenoegd also produced a quality Steen wine which was

supplied to the KWV; but with the development of the KWV's extensive modern white wine cellars the organization has handled the farm's output of Steen leaving the Faures to concentrate on the production of their red wines. Steen grapes are sold to the KWV. Some white wine is made from the free-run juice which is taken off the Cinsaut before the skins are allowed to ferment in the smaller quantity of juice needed for a darker and fuller red wine.

Since the death of John Faure in 1969 the activities of Vergenoegd have been divided between his two sons. The younger, Brand Faure, is responsible for the vineyards, while the elder brother, Jac Faure, concentrates upon the making of the wine. Jac's son, John, joined them in 1983, after graduating in Cellar Technology from Elsenburg Agricultural

College. In recent years the fine old buildings of Vergenoegd have been renovated and restored (including the charmingly florid gateway, bearing the same date as the main homestead, which leads to the courtyard at the rear of the house). The outbuildings, too, have been refurbished, and converted to offices, wine sales rooms, and maturation stores for the Estate's wine – the Cabernet Sauvignon receives a minimum of three years in wood and a further six months in bottle before being sold. The old homestead itself is occupied by Jac Faure and his family. Filled with paintings of and trophies won by magnificent horses, its atmosphere is a legacy from the late nineteenth-century days of horse-breeding and racing. But it is the making of Vergenoegd's splendid red wines which remains the consuming interest of the twentieth-century Faures.

The Viticultural and Oenological Research Institute

ONE OF FOUR HORTICULTURAL INSTITUTES OF THE DEPARTMENT OF AGRICULTURE AND WATER SUPPLY

The headquarters of the Viticultural and Oenological Research Institute is situated on 200 hectares of the farm Nietvoorbij, on the northern outskirts of the Stellenbosch municipal area. Here are performed a

number of important functions which have a bearing on general viticultural and oenological research.

The Institute was founded in 1955, in response to a long-felt need for exact

research into the local conditions of viticulture and its allied disciplines. Launched with a R1 million state grant, it began as a scattered collection of offices and laboratories in Stellenbosch,

Elsenburg, Paarl and Cape Town. Since this state of decentralisation seriously hampered its activities, the present complex was built. Completed in 1968, it was officially inaugurated by the then Minister of Agriculture, Mr D.C.H. Uys.

The present resources of the VORI include its main building, consisting of offices, laboratories, and an experimental distillery and winery, one of the most modern of its kind in the world. There are also extensive nursery facilities, and a *glashuis* and *lathuis* where young vines are propagated and established before being transferred to the vineyards of the experimental farm. The soil and climate at Nietvoorbij are fairly typical of those found in the Boland region in general; research, however, requires close study of vine performance under specific local conditions across the winelands as a whole. The Institute therefore runs a number of further experimental farms at Robertson (to serve the Breede River area) and at Lutzville (for the Olifants River region), as well as the farms Bellevue in Paarl and Hexvallei in De Doorns, both of which produce table grapes. Trial plots are also maintained on the experimental farms of other Departmental institutions at Oudtshoorn (Klein Karoo), Upington (for the Lower Orange River Irrigation Scheme), Jan Kempdorp (for the Northern Cape and Orange Free State areas) and at Roodeplaat (north of Pretoria) and Messina, both specialising in table grapes, (for the northern Transvaal area). Much of the experimental work takes place directly on these farms – it is not unusual at certain times of the year to find the Institute's main building almost deserted.

There is little in the culture of the vine that is not included in the VORI's investigations. One area of particular concern is that of the improvement of the country's grape cultivars (the rising cost of energy and the competing demand for the water supply by the expanding towns make the development of better quality and more economical cultivars a priority). The Institute's grape improvement programme is based on the evaluation of imported cultivars and the selection of the most promising vines in existing vineyards. The imported varieties begin with a period of quarantine at the Research Institute for Plant Protection (the days when the phylloxera aphid was a free-loading international traveller are long over). Upon release from quarantine, the immigrant vine stocks are planted on a small scale at Nietvoorbij, and their growth and bearing characteristics evaluated in the first phase of screening.

In the second phase of screening the most promising clones are planted on a larger scale in statistically planned experiments on all the farms of the VORI.

Together with the development of scion

INTERNATIONAL CO-OPERATION

International co-operation amongst viticultural and oenological scientists has had a great deal to do with South African wines attaining gold-medal recognition overseas. The Cape's close relationship with the University of California's Davis Campus – in particular Professors Hod Berg, Corney Ough, Vernon Singleton, Mark Kliever and Harold Olmo has helped local wine makers to improve the quality, longevity and marketability of their wines. Sabbatical students and visitors of the stature of Professor Emeritus Maynard of the United States also bring to our winelands their knowledge and suggestions. The list is impressive: Dr Helmut Becker, Hans Ambrosi, Dr Adolf Rapp and Dr Franc from Germany; Alain Bertran from France and Israel's Ben ami Bravdo. Many South African wine makers and Estate owners also travel overseas regularly to broaden their knowledge.

It is a two-way process, however, and the opinions and knowledge of many local wine scientists and makers are highly valued throughout the world. Bearing witness to this is the fact that a number of prestigious international conferences have been held in South Africa, including the Symposium on the Quality of the Harvest in 1977 and the 1982 Federation Internationale Vinical. Probably the greatest tribute of all was the decision of the Organisation Internationale Vinical, with its membership of 30 countries, making up 90 per cent of the world's wine producers, to hold its eighteenth congress in Cape Town in October 1983.

cultivars goes the development of suitable rootstock cultivars, Successful growth and bearing depends upon the grafting of the top cultivar onto a rootstock cultivar with which affinity problems do not occur; the resulting plant must also adapt well to soil and climate conditions. To determine the adaptability of the various rootstock cultivars in the many viticultural regions, series of experiments are carried out both on the Institute's farms, and on private farms on a co-operative basis.

Research is also done into soil and its preparation, into general vineyard practices, trellising and spacing (the relationship between the number of vines and the quality changes with the density of the vines), pruning and crop control, the effect of fertilizers, methods of cultivation and of irrigation, and into the control of diseases and pests (tested in special 'disease gardens').

And together with viticultural research goes oenological research. This includes investigations into wine chemistry and microbiology, as well as into the full gamut of cellar technology – the grapes from the experimental vineyards are fermented in rows of 20-litre steel tanks.

Besides all its other departments, the VORI also administers a National Oenothèque, a wine library where samples of wines made and marketed in South Africa are kept. Wine producers partake in this venture on a voluntary basis, and after every vintage 24 bottles of wines selected by the producer are delivered to the Oenothèque. All relevant information

The Viticultural and Oenological Research Institute at Nietvoorbij.

regarding these wines is stored in a computer. The Oenothéque has accommodation for 84 000 bottles of wine, and at present there are 21 622 bottles of 1 283 different wines in storage, including their most precious possessions, a number of bottles of Constantia wine dating from 1793 and 1823, donated to the Institute.

The dissemination of information about new developments is regarded by the VORI as one of its most important functions. To this end well-attended courses on all aspects of vine growing and wine making are held throughout the year and scientific as well as popular publications are issued on a regular basis. The present Director of the VORI is Dr Jakob Deist and its Liaison Officer is Eugene Booysen.

Vlottenburg CO-OPERATIVE WINERY

Vlottenburg Co-operative

Wines bottled and marketed by the Vlottenburg Co-operative

Red wines: Cabernet Sauvignon, Pinotage, Gamay and Claret
White wines: Riesling, Steen, Premier Grand Crû, Gewürztraminer, Chenin Blanc, Sauvignon Blanc, Weisser Riesling, Blanc de Blanc, Special Late Harvest, Hanepoot (dessert), Muscat de Hambourg and a port

The Vlottenburg winery is on the Stellenbosch Wine Route and is open to the public on weekdays from 08h30 to 12h30, and from 13h30 to 17h00, and on Saturdays between 08h30 and 12h00.

Much of the process of wine making is slow and patient, but there are moments when considerable dispatch is needed: one of which is that of the delivery of the freshly harvested grapes to the winery. It was the inordinate congestion of grape deliveries in the mid-1940s that led to the establishment of the Vlottenburg Co-operative Winery. In this period the KWV's Stellenbosch depot was regularly besieged at harvest time by farmers who had gathered their grapes at dawn, only to find themselves waiting through the following night to deliver loads of already fermenting grapes.

To relieve the pressure on these inadequate facilities the Vlottenburg Co-operative was built, after being launched at a meeting in September, 1945. The cellar, completed in time for the 1947 harvest, was built on part of the farm of Vlottenburg (on which the Eersterivier Winery also stands). Its first few seasons' activities were supervised by Charlie Sparks, of the Castle Wine and Brandy Company, before the appointment of a full-time wine maker and manager.

The present incumbent is Kowie du Toit, who took over the winery in 1973, after the death of the then wine maker, Nico Mostert. Mostert had trained under Oom Sarel Rossouw at the Simonsvlei Co-operative in the Paarl District, and had built up Vlottenburg's range of wines, achieving a reputation for steady good quality. Kowie, who also received his first wine-making experience at Simonsvlei, has followed this example in his own style as a wine maker, producing an interesting and good range of wines.

The winery's up-to-date cellar is equipped with two grape crushers, eight static drainers, two tank presses and a dejuicer. Fermentation is carried out for the white wines in stainless steel tanks, and in concrete ones for the red wines: the final pressing being done on two presses.

Today the Co-operative has 30 members distributed around the Lynedoch, Stellenbosch Kloof and Kuils River areas. Of the 11 000 tonnes of grapes received annually, 60 per cent is Steen, 10 per cent Clairette Blanche. The remaining 30 per cent is mainly made up of Riesling, Weisser Riesling, Sauvignon Blanc, Cabernet Sauvignon, Pinotage, Cinsaut, Colombar and Hanepoot. The first Cabernet Sauvignon was added in 1977, when plantings in the Stellenbosch Kloof area by the Co-operative's chairman, Mr E.P. Andrag, began to yield. All the good wine made here is sold to the Stellenbosch Farmers' Winery, while the distilling wine goes to Oude Meester.

Modern equipment and efficiency are the order of the day at Vlottenburg Co-operative, but redolent of former days are such artefacts as the basket press which greets visitors to the winery.

Vredenheim

Situated along the Eerste River immediately below Stellenbosch, this Estate was previously known by its original name of Vredenburgh. Under this name it supplied good quality sherries to the Santhagens Company, but with the merger of Santhagens and Gilbey Distillers and Vintners in 1962 the name became attached to a range of the new company's wines. When the former owner of Vredenburgh, Johann Neethling, subsequently applied for registration of his farm as an official wine Estate, he found that the prior use of the name on a marketed wine product effectively vitiated his application. The answer was a new name – hence the range of Vredenheim wines, made on the Vredenburgh farm.

One of the first local wine makers both to plant Cabernet Sauvignon in the late 1950s, and to instal cold fermentation equipment, Johan bottled a small number of his best wines under the Estate's own label, and supplied the balance to the Stellenbosch Farmer's Winery.

The present owner, Coen Bezuidenhout, formerly from Natal, took over the farm in July 1986. He and his family live in the lovely old homestead, which has baroque-style gables dated 1789. Coen's daughter, Elzabé, has bravely taken on the task of wine making at Vredenburgh. During the 1987 vintage she was assisted by the Stellenbosch Farmers' Winery wine-making team, as many cellars have been over the years, and is also assisted by

Vredenheim Estate		
Cultivars Planted	Size of Vineyards (Number of vines)	Training Practice
Chenin Blanc	153 364	
Cabernet Sauvignon	42 693	
Colombar	35 787	
Pinotage	18 337	
Sauvignon Blanc	13 684	3-wire vertical
SA Riesling	11 000	trellis
Weisser Riesling	4 857	
Tinta Barocca	1 712	
Shiraz	959	
Carignan	476	

Total area under vines: 86 ha
Irrigation: Micro-irrigation and overhead irrigation are used when necessary.
Temperatures: Records are not kept.
Average annual rainfall: Approximately 700 mm
Stock: Rooted vines are bought from a nursery.
Envisaged new cultivar: Chardonnay
First wines bottled under the Vredenheim Estate label: Blanc de Noir, Chenin Blanc and Colombar (all 1987 vintage)
Wines currently bottled under the Vredenheim Estate label: Blanc de Noir, Chenin Blanc, Colombar, Debuut and Cabernet Sauvignon
Wood ageing: Wines are aged in wood on the Estate.
Capacity of the Vredenheim cellar: 800 tonnes of grapes are being pressed at present.

The Estate is open to the public on weekdays from 09h00 to 16h00, and during December and January on Saturdays as well from 09h00 to 12h00.

Denzil Weitz, who was previously with Oude Meester. Initially only a limited number of wines will be available to the public but the Bezuidenhouts are keen to release more in due course, and to make their mark in the winelands.

Vriesenhof

Towards the end of the Paradyskloof Road at the foothills of the Helderberg and almost on the outskirts of Stellenbosch is the 25 hectares of Vriesenhof. Little is known of its earlier wine-making history, though previous owners, Mr and Mrs G. Gerryts, found a good Steen being made on the farm when they bought it in 1946. In subsequent years grapes were delivered at harvest time to a local winery.

Then, in 1980, the farm was bought by Jan 'Boland' Coetzee, the famous Western Province and Springbok rugby player, who during his rugby-playing career also made a name for himself as a wine maker. He began the active practice of his craft at Kanonkop, quickly making his presence felt, particularly with fine red wines. He spent ten years at Kanonkop.

For Jan the purchase of Vriesenhof represented a strong desire to strike out on

Apart from his duties as consultant wine maker to several Estates and farms, Jan (Boland) Coetzee also produces excellent wines on his own small farm, Vriesenhof.

Vriesenhof

Cultivars Planted	Size of Vineyards (Hectares)	Training Practice
Cabernet Sauvignon	4	
Chardonnay	3	Perold trellis
Merlot	3	

Total area under vines in 1987: 10 ha
Irrigation: The vineyards of Vriesenhof are not irrigated.
Temperatures: Records are not kept.
Average annual rainfall: Records are not kept.
Stock: Rooted vines are purchased from a nursery.
First wines bottled under the Vriesenhof label: Cabernet Sauvignon (1981), and Chardonnay (1986)
Wines currently bottled under the Vriesenhof label: Chardonnay, Cabernet Sauvignon and Kallista (a blend of Cabernet Sauvignon and Merlot). Wines not qualifying for the Vriesenhof label are marketed under the Paradyskloof label at a lower price.
Wood ageing: Wines are aged in wood on the farm.
Capacity of the Vriesenhof cellar: Temporary facilities are presently being used as the cellar is still under construction, but should be completed during 1988.

Vriesenhof is open to the public by appointment only.

his own. Within a few months of his settling at the farm he had made a first 26 000 litres of Cabernet Sauvignon wine, which after being aged in wood was further aged in the bottle and released in 1984. His first priority on arrival was to get his cellar in order; in due course he intends to renovate the old homestead, built at the beginning of the nineteenth century.

At present the bulk of the vineyards are planted with Cabernet Sauvignon, but he has introduced other noble cultivars such as Merlot, Pinot Noir, Sauvignon Blanc and Chardonnay. All the vines here are trellised and no irrigation is used.

Jan feels very strongly about the importance of the use of wood in the production of the best red wines, in combination with the factors of cultivars, soil and the local climate. A major expense in the setting up of the Vriesenhof cellar was the purchase of wooden vats made to his specifications by the well-known French cooper, Jean Demptos; other, smaller casks (barriques) of varying sizes were also acquired. Jan feels that casks should be renewed reasonably often and not, as is often the case in the Cape, used for decades on end. The barriques are used for the first period of maturation and then

the wine is put into big wood for further maturation. To date 1981, 1982, 1983 and 1984 vintages of Vriesenhof Cabernet Sauvignon have been released. The 1984 and 1985 vintages are blends of Cabernet Sauvignon and Merlot. Only the pick of Jan's wine is used in these blends and the rest is bottled under the Paradyskloof label.

Jan's reputation at Kanonkop was for wines of robust quality; this has changed, as the micro-climate of Vriesenhof is considerably cooler than that at Kanonkop. With the benefit of cooling breezes off the Indian Ocean as well as the effect of the relatively fewer sunshine-hours at the foot of the Helderberg, Vriesenhof wines are lighter wines, both elegant and complex in character.

At Kanonkop and at Vriesenhof Jan has never submitted his wines for Superior rating as he has never believed in the system. His wines sell well because of their quality. As he puts it, 'The wines must fight their own battles in the market place and not with The Wine and Spirit Board!'. He has also chosen not to register Vriesenhof as an Estate. He is a member of The Cape Independent Wine Makers Guild, which holds an auction, conducted by Sotheby's, in Johannesburg on the first Saturday in September each year. The first auction was held in 1985. For these auctions Jan and the other 17 members of the Guild choose some specially selected barrels of wine which differ completely from the usual wines offered for sale. The wines are tasted blind by all the members of the Guild and a wine that is not approved as being of a particularly high standard will be withdrawn and not considered for the auction. The Vriesenhof 1982 Cabernet Sauvignon, Vintners Private Reserve, was auctioned by Sotheby's in 1985 and is only available for collectors in very small quantities at specialised liquor outlets. To avoid confusion all the wines sold at the auction have an additional special seal. Jan also acts as a consultant for numerous wineries and farms and gives invaluable assistance to those concerned, such as Buiten-verwachting and Eikendal Vineyards.

During the European 1981 vintage Jan, his wife Anette, two small daughters and baby son went to France where Jan spent time in the famous cellars of Joseph Drouhin in Beaune, adding to the spectrum of his knowledge and experience. One of France's most respected *négociants*, Drouhin owns numerous vineyards in Burgundy, and also buys wines from selected vineyards in the region and blends, ages and bottles them. In time, Jan hopes to be able to emulate, though in his own personal style, the great wines of France, particularly those of Burgundy, and many knowledgeable wine drinkers feel that he is already beginning to fulfil this ambition.

Warwick Estate

In the valley enclosed by the Simonsberg, Kanonkop and Klapmutskop lies Warwick Estate, originally part of 'Good Success', a vast, eighteenth century farm that extended over most of the catchment area. The founder of Warwick farm was one Colonel William Alexander Gordon, who named his portion of 'Good Success' in honour of the Warwickshire Regiment, which he commanded during the South African War. Like so many of his compatriots, Gordon decided to stay in South Africa and so settled on Warwick farm, raising livestock and growing fruit trees.

The serious business of wine making, however, lies mostly in the hands of one of the two 'Ladies of Warwick': Norma Ratcliffe. Norma's husband, Stan, bought Warwick in 1964, planted vines and produced Steen of such high quality, that it was soon much sought after by other wineries and wholesalers. It was with Norma's arrival in 1971, that the Ratcliffes made a few experimental wines from Cabernet, with encouraging results.

After many trips to Bordeaux, and investigation of all possibilities, Stan and Norma decided to build their own cellar and to make wines in a Bordeaux style. Norma began to study wine making in earnest and by 1984 launched the Ratcliffe's pilot project. The classic cultivars of Merlot and Cabernet Franc were planted; one of the historical buildings, which had, very likely, been a winery, was restored, and Stan transformed second-hand equipment into working items, and acquired new open drainers. By 1985 the Ratcliffes were in full production.

Norma prefers traditional methods of red wine production, one of which is pushing the 'cap' of the wine down manually, using a wooden pole with a flat piece of wood at the end, which acts as a type of plunger. At Chateau Sénéjac, she learned the natural methods of red wine making. Without artificial fining agents or filtration and through careful racking, the wine gradually settles and clarifies itself. Several egg white finings (three egg whites to every hectolitre of wine) are used to assist the settling without stripping colour, flavour or tannin. After the wine is finally racked into 225-litre Bordeaux barriques, in temperature-controlled maturation cellars, wood and time complete the rounding and maturation of the red wine.

Warwick Estate

Cultivars Planted	Size of Vineyards (Number of vines)	Training Practice
Cabernet Sauvignon	50 000	
Merlot	28 000	4-wire trellis
Cabernet Franc	6 000	

Total area under vines in 1987: 58 ha (20 ha still to be planted)
Irrigation: The Warwick vineyards are not irrigated.
Temperatures: Records are not kept.
Average annual rainfall: Approximately 300 mm
Stock: Rooted vines are purchased from a nursery in Wellington.
First wines bottled under the Warwick Estate label: The 1985 Cabernet will be released in 1988.
Wood ageing: The wines are wood aged on the Estate.
Capacity of the Warwick cellar: 4 000 hectolitres

The Ratcliffes' ultimate goal is to specialize in superb red wines. Their first official vintage (1985) is entirely Cabernet Sauvignon – only 1 500 cases will be released – and, from 1987, their first Bordeaux blend will be produced. Consisting of Merlot, Cabernet Franc and Cabernet Sauvignon, the wine will be called the 'Warwick Trilogy', aptly emphasising the importance of each cultivar in this classic blend, which will vary slightly every year to illustrate the difference in the vintages. Norma claims that consciousness of the vintage is magnified tremendously when you are making your own wine.

Norma Ratcliffe inspecting her maturing red wine.

The newly designed label for the Cabernet Sauvignon with its striking blue border sets off the second 'Warwick Lady'. She is the gold image of the original quaint drinking vessel that has pride of place on the Ratcliffes' dining table. Called a marriage or wager cup, it was used originally for toasting a marriage or waging a bet. The 'Warwick Lady' is in Elizabethan costume, and holds a small swivel cup in her outstretched arms. The skirt of her dress forms a second cup, which, like the smaller one she holds, is made of silver on copper and is gilt-lined. When the figure is inverted, both cups can be filled with wine, but the utmost care must be taken when drinking from the larger vessel not to spill the contents of the smaller one, and not to put the cup down until all the wine is finished. If preliminary tastings of the young Warwick Estate wines are any indication of what is to follow, no-one will want to put down the 'Warwick Lady' until it is quite empty.

Welmoed CO-OPERATIVE WINE CELLARS

This is the first co-operative on the road from Cape Town to Stellenbosch through Faure, and is built on a site between the road and the Eerste River. As with the Estates in the vicinity, the wines of Welmoed reflect the felicity of the local climate and the moderating influence in the summer months of the wind from False Bay.

The farm of Welmoed was granted to Henning Huysing by Simon van der Stel in 1690, though Huysing had already occupied the land for a decade previously. Three years later, in 1693, van der Stel also granted Meerlust, adjoining Welmoed, to Huysing. In 1696 Huysing sold Welmoed to his friend Jacobus van der Heyden who put up the buildings and the bell-tower which are now part of the nursery of Rosarium, adjacent to the winery which retains the right to use the image of the bell-tower on its labels. Van der Heyden was one of those who, with Huysing and his nephew Adam Tas, were responsible for the unseating of Willem Adriaan van der Stel. During the course of events leading up to this Van der Heyden was arrested by Van der Stel and sentenced to death. Van der Stel was relieved of his post before the sentence could be carried out, but not before the unfortunate Van der Heyden had spent twenty-seven miserable days in the *Donker Gat* ('Black Hole') at the Castle.

Pieter Gerhard van der Bijl acquired Welmoed in 1797 and on his death in 1831 it was divided between his two sons, Philipus Johannes calling his portion Klein Welmoed and Pieter Voltelen retaining the original name, Welmoed, for his larger portion.

Many years later the Castle Wine and Brandy Company built a winery at Welmoed, where farmers from the surrounding areas delivered their grapes, but in 1940 the company decided to close down the operation. Eight of the farmers who had delivered grapes there then bought the property and founded Welmoed Koöperatiewe Wynkelders Beperk on 15 October 1941. The following season 500 tonnes of grapes were pressed. Today there are 44 members with 55 different farms and 10 000 tonnes of grapes are pressed and made into wine annually. The Co-operative had a somewhat lack-lustre period in the early 1960s but its organization and wine making were much improved and overhauled with the advent of Jassie Coetzee in 1966. Previously at the Stellenbosch Farmers' Winery, when he arrived at Welmoed he found himself in charge of a run-down wine cellar and a set of books in decidedly precarious condition.

The entire cellar layout was redesigned by Jassie for greater ease in handling the annual crop. A major change took place to cope with the 1975 vintage with a full-scale clear-out of old concrete tanks and their replacement with stainless steel. Besides other equipment in the cellar, there is a patent dejuicer for producing white wine from red grapes and concentrating the red skins in a smaller quantity of juice to produce deeper-coloured red wine. This was designed and built by Jassie, who also carried out all his other engineering work during his tenure. A keen horseman and Chairman of the South Cape American Saddle Horse Sub Union, he was wont to ride through the members' vineyards on horseback, armed with a saccharometer to see how the grapes were ripening.

Jassie Coetzee was succeeded in 1980 by Kobus Rossouw, who achieved great success for Welmoed, with more awards being won at wine shows than ever before in the Co-operative's history, including South African Champion Co-operative Winery in 1985. Kobus took over as wine maker at Simonsvlei from his father, Oom Sarel Rossouw, in December 1985, and when Oom Sarel retired at the end of April 1986, Kobus became manager of Simonsvlei as well. Nicky Versveld, an Elsenburg graduate, succeeded him as wine maker at Welmoed. Co-incidentally, after leaving Elsenburg, Nicky received further training at Simonsvlei, under the tutelage of Oom Sarel and Johan Rossouw.

The bulk of the good wine made at Welmoed goes to the Stellenbosch Farmers' Winery, with some going to Gilbeys, and the distilling wine to Oude Meester and the KWV. A small amount of the production is bottled for the co-operative's members and for the public. The winery includes a well-appointed tasting room and a vinotéque containing a comprehensive collection of 20 000 bottles of red and white wines.

Welmoed Co-operative Wine Cellars

Red Wines: Cabernet Sauvignon, Pinotage, Shiraz, Rouge Sec and Zinfandel
White wines: Weisser Riesling, Sauvignon Blanc, Riesling, Steen, Chenin Blanc, Premier Grand Crû, Noble Late Harvest, Late Vintage, Special Late Harvest, Blankenzee, a Rosé, a Blanc de Noir, two dessert wines, Sweet Hanepoot and Red Jerepiko and a port

Welmoed Co-operative is on the Stellenbosch Wine Route and is open to the public on weekdays from 08h00 to 17h00.

Zevenwacht

In 1974 a Cape Town architect, Gilbert Colyn, bought a small 39-hectare farm named Avonduur in the Banghoek Valley, with the intention of using it both as a private retreat and for farming on a modest scale. This farm later became Delaire (see page 143). Involvement with Avonduur sparked a larger ambition to start an Estate wine farm. To this end Colyn acquired a further two farms, beginning with Zevenfontein in 1978, and increased by the addition of the adjacent property of Langverwacht; together they cover some 353 hectares, between Kuils River and Stellenbosch, spread over the Bottelary Hills.

At the time of purchase the land was in a neglected condition. The existing vineyards were replaced and extended with plantings of a range of cultivars, including Cabernet Sauvignon, Merlot, Shiraz, Steen, Weisser Riesling, Cape Riesling, Gewürztraminer, Pinot Gris, Pinot Noir and Sauvignon Blanc.

The soils on the two farms – registered as a limited company and known collectively as Zevenwacht – are varied and of good quality, with a mix of Clovelly and Glenrosa forms, well suited to the growing of quality grapes. Most of the vineyards are located on south- or southwest-facing slopes, towards the prevailing wind from the sea.

Gilbert (who is descended from the Colijn family with long connections with the Constantia Valley, and, for a period, with Groot Constantia itself) has built compact modern housing for his farm workers and manager, and has restored the fine old late eighteenth-century homestead on Zevenfontein. As an architect he was responsible for the design of the new Groot Constantia cellar, and has built a new cellar not far from the Zevenwacht homestead. In establishing his cellar he has worked closely with his wine maker, Neil Ellis, who came to the farm having proved his talents at Groot Constantia; Gilbert's first wines were released at the end of 1983. Neil Ellis is also known for his own range of 'boutique' wines, the Neil Ellis Vineyard Selection (see page 174). A novel aspect of Gilbert's plans for Zevenwacht was his offer of shares in the farm, which is a registered company, to the public.

The prime soils and situation of Zevenwacht are well suited to growing high-quality cultivars.

Zevenwacht

Cultivars Planted	Size of Vineyards (Number of vines)	Training Practice
Chenin Blanc	120 000	
Cabernet Sauvignon	30 000	
Sauvignon Blanc	30 000	
Cape Riesling	25 000	
Chardonnay	25 000	
Rhine Riesling	25 000	Extended Perold trellises
Merlot	20 000	
Shiraz	20 000	
Gewürztraminer	15 000	
Pinot Noir	12 000	
Cabernet Franc	10 000	
Pinot Gris	8 000	

Total area under vines in 1987: 142 ha (80 ha to be planted over the next five years)
Irrigation: The vineyards of Zevenwacht can be irrigated if necessary.
Temperatures: Average maximum 24 °C; average minimum 16 °C
Average annual rainfall: 700-750 mm
Stock: Rooted vines are purchased from a nursery.
First wines bottled under the Zevenwacht label: Rhine Riesling (1983), Cabernet Sauvignon, Chenin Blanc, Blanc de Blanc and Bouquet Blanc
Wines currently bottled under the Zevenwacht label: Blanc de Blanc, Sauvignon Blanc, Rhine Riesling, Gewürztraminer, Bouquet Blanc, Blanc de Noir, Zevenwacht (Blended Red), Cabernet Sauvignon, Shiraz, Pinotage, Pinot Noir and red and white house wines
Wood ageing: Wines are aged in wood on the farm.
Capacity of the Zevenwacht cellar: 700 tonnes of grapes are being processed at present, but the cellar is being enlarged to accommodate up to 1 400 tonnes.

Zevenwacht is not open to the public, but its shareholders and friends enjoy a private wine farm and its facilities. Wine is sold to the public, however, from the wine cellar on the lower farm, Langverwacht.

THE WINE ROUTES

There are six wine routes in the local winelands, those of Stellenbosch, Paarl, Franschhoek, Worcester, Robertson and Klein-Karoo. The Constantia District is soon to have its own wine route, as will the Olifants River Region. Inspired initially by the *Routes du Vin* of France and the *Weinstrassen* of Germany, they have become immensely popular with the general public. Away from the pressures of city life, surrounded by fields of vines, in the shadow of homestead and cellar, the urban dweller can feel himself close to the source of the

wine and its meaning. He can also witness its making as a living experience, talking to the farmer or wine master, prowling cool cellars with their magically evocative smells of wine and wood, their stately rows of casks and their bottling and labelling machinery. In the tasting-room or out in the open, under the trees, he can taste and compare and assess the Estate's produce at leisure. And even for those of whom wine is less of a priority, a wine route tour is memorable alone for the majesty of the landscape, for the lingering echoes

of history and a hardy tradition reaching from the seventeenth to the twentieth century.

The wine routes are well organized for public convenience and pleasure. Many of the farms, Estates and Co-operatives involved have tasting facilities on their premises; some have further attractions such as cellar tours, restaurants, historic homesteads, gift shops and the occasional small private museum. Entrance to each of the places concerned is indicated by a roadside emblem and the routes are all clearly signposted.

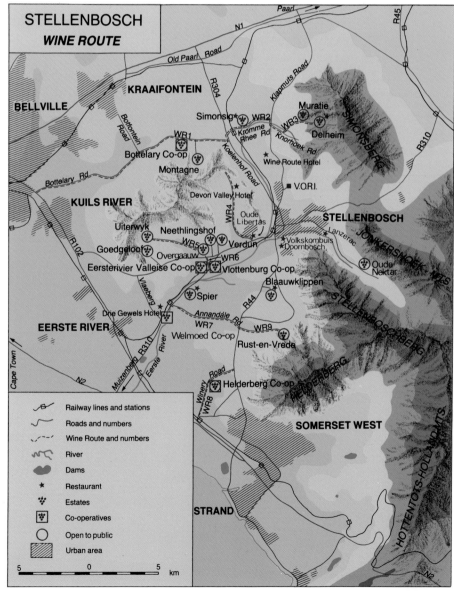

STELLENBOSCH WINE ROUTE

The first of the Cape wine routes, this was started by a small group of local farmers in April 1971. It currently comprises eight Estate wine cellars, six private cellars and five co-operative wineries. These are: Blaauwklippen

Inspiration for the first of the western Cape's wine routes, that of Stellenbosch, came from three of the region's best known vignerons (from left) 'Spatz' Sperling, Frans Malan and Niel Joubert. Attractions for the many thousands of visitors to the wine routes each year include wine tastings, superb restaurants, buying wine directly from the Estates and Co-operatives, cellar tours and not the least, relaxing rides through an incomparable landscape of patchwork vineyards, valleys and rugged peaks.

(page 140), Bottelary Co-operative Winery (page 142), Delaire (page 143), De Helderberg Co-operative Winery (page 158), Delheim (page 145), Eersterivier Valleise Co-operative Winery (page 150), Eikendal Vineyards (page 151), Hartenberg Vineyards (page 155), Muratie Estate (page 171), Neethlingshof Estate (page 173), Oude Nektar Estate (page 178), Overgaauw Estate (page 179), Rust-en-Vrede Estate (page 184), Simonsig Estate (page 186), Spier Estate (page 188), Uiterwyk Estate (page 193), Vlottenburg Co-operative Winery (page 200), Welmoed Co-operative Winery (page 204), and Saxenburg (page 185).

Wine is available at all these places at fixed hours, throughout the year. Besides facilities for the tasting and purchase of wine, a number of Estates and private cellars have further attractions. Spier, for example, has two restaurants, one of them in the old

Jonkershuis. Blaauwklippen features a coach museum (and trips in the farm's elegant landaus), as well as displays of wine-making and farming equipment. Other farms provide cheese luncheons, terrace luncheons, and a host of other attractions.

Detailed information on the Stellenbosch Wine Route may be obtained from the Wine Route's offices on the Strand Road on the outskirts of the town of Stellenbosch.

PAARL WINE ROUTE

Following the example of Stellenbosch, the Paarl Wine Route was opened in 1978 at the instigation of Sydney Back of Backsberg. It comprises five prominent Estates in the District, together with three co-operative wineries and one registered producing merchant.

These are: Backsberg Estate (page 214), Bolandse Co-operative Wine Cellar (page 216), Drakenstein Co-operative Wine Cellar (page 223), Fairview Estate (page 223), Laborie Estate (page 231), Landskroon Estate (page 233), Nederburg (page 238), Simonsvlei Co-operative Wine Cellar (page 243), and Villiera Estate (page 245). The KWV is also on the Paarl Wine Route.

Tasting facilities and cellar tours are provided at these various ports of call along the Wine Route, as well as other attractions. At Fairview, for example, a variety of the Estate's own goats-milk cheeses can be bought. Besides its tasting parlour, Backsberg runs self-guided tours of the cellar, accompanied by closed-circuit television demonstrations of the stages of the making of the Estate's wine; there is also a small museum of wine-making equipment. In summer, Villiera provides a terrace lunch under the oaks, where visitors can sample Cathy Grier's delicious fare. Cathy trained in London under the famous cookery writer and restaurateur, Prue Leith, who is originally from the Cape. Landskroon has fine new tasting facilities and also offers wholesome cheese lunches, and

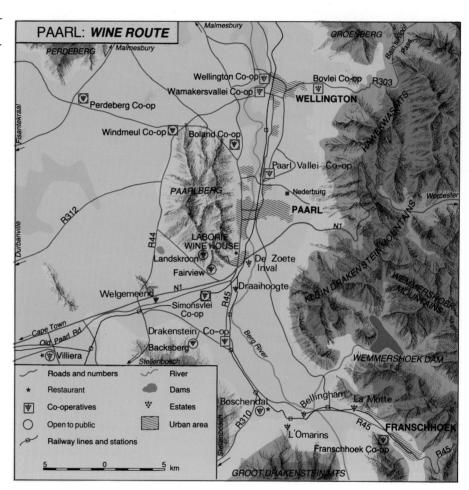

there are similar extra facilities at some of the other places on this wine route. Further information can be obtained

from the Wine Route's offices at the Paarl Publicity Association in Main Street.

THE ROBERTSON AND WORCESTER WINE ROUTES

These were formerly one route, known as the Breede River Wine Route, but are now two separate routes, administered by the Robertson Wine Trust and the Worcester Winelands Association respectively.

The Robertson Wine Trust was founded in 1983 and represents nine Estates, 11 co-operative cellars, and seven private producers in the Ashton,

Bonnievale, McGregor and Robertson areas. To promote the wines of the Region it organizes a Young Wine Show, a Bottled Wine Show, and a Food and Wine Festival every year. The following members of the Trust are on the Robertson Wine Route and open to the public at specified times: Agterkliphoogte Co-operative Cellar (page 278), Ashton Co-operative Cellar

(page 278), Bon Courage Estate (page 279), Bonnievale Co-operative Cellar (page 291), Clairvaux Co-operative Cellar (page 280), De Wetshof Estate (page 280), Jonkheer Boerewynmakery (page 291), Langverwacht Co-operative Winery (page 292), Merwespont Co-operative Winery (page 292), Mon Don Estate (page 284), Nordale Co-operative Winery (page 293), Robertson Co-

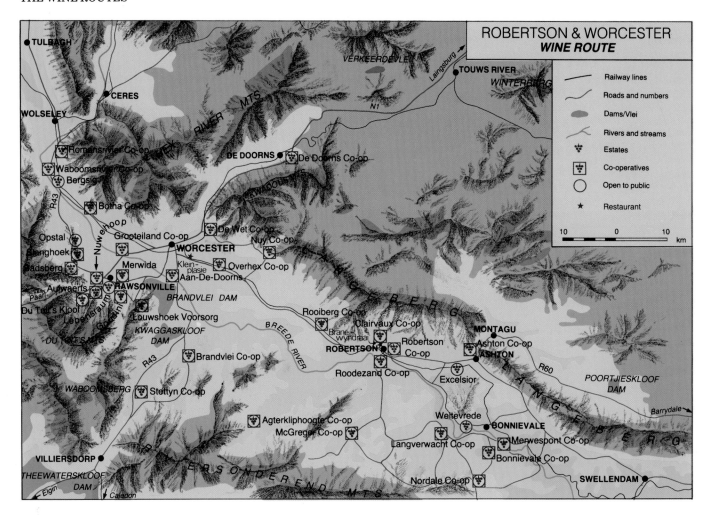

operative Winery (page 285),
Roodezandt Co-operative Winery (page
286), Rooiberg Co-operative Winery
(page 287), Van Loveren (page 287),
Weltevrede Estate (page 289) and
Zandvliet Estate (page 290).

The Worcester Winelands Association
was formed in 1985, with the well-
known Kleinplasie, with its open-air

farm museum, as its headquarters. Due
to the long distances on this route, a
kind of 'miniature wine route' is
available at Kleinplasie – the wines
from all 26 members of the Association
can be tasted and bought at Kleinplasie,
as well as all sorts of other farm products
such as cheese, honey, jams, preserves,
home-baked confectionery and many

other items. Every wine producer in the
Worcester District featured in this book
is a member of the Association and are
all signposted as being on the Wine
Route, but several do not have tasting
facilities and are not open to the public.
Further details are available from the
Worcester Winelands Association at
Kleinplasie on the outskirts of the town.

THE VIGNERONS DE FRANSCHHOEK WINE ROUTE

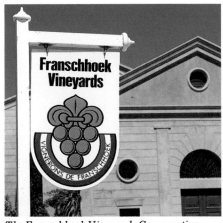

The Franschhoek Vineyards Co-operative

In 1984, under the leadership of Michael
Trull of La Bri Vineyards, the
association known as Vignerons de
Franschhoek was constituted to promote
the wines of the beautiful Franschhoek
Valley and also as a tribute to the first
Huguenot wine makers of the area. At
present there are twelve members, all on
a 'wine route' in the sense that they are
signposted as members of the Vignerons
de Franschhoek, but not all open to the
public at specified hours. In the case of
several, wine tastings and cellar tours
are by appointment only.

The members of the association are
Bellingham (page 215), Boschendal
Estate (page 217), Chamonix (page 219),

Clos Cabrière (page 220), Franschhoek
Vineyards Co-operative (page 225), Haut
Provence (page 226), La Bri Vineyards
(page 231), La Motte Estate (page 232), La
Provence (page 234), Les Chênes (page
235), L'Ormarins Estate (page 235), and
Mouton-Excelsior (page 237).

There are several attractions on this
wine route other than tastings and cellar
tours. Boschendal is well known for its
magnificent restaurant and also its
taphouse, gift shop, and in summer Le
Pique-nique, a hamper of bread, pâte,
cheeses and wines, to be enjoyed on the
lawns in the shade of the tall pine trees.
At Bellingham there is a 90-seat natural
amphitheatre where lectures and

muscial performances are given and other types of entertainment offered. Chamonix has a lovely scenic drive, and Haut Provence offers interesting pottery for sale, made on the premises. A particularly interesting cellar tour, showing the intricacies of the **méthode champenoise**, is offered at Clos Cabrière, and a farm tour as well as a cellar tour at beautiful La Provence. And, of course, several of these farms boast splendid historic homesteads which alone are worth the trip to see them.

Wine tastings are offered at most venues on the wine routes, and visitors can buy wine directly from the farms.

KLEIN KAROO WINE ROUTE

This wine route developed from the small Calitzdorp wine route, which still exists, with its separate logo and sign posts, as part of the larger Klein Karoo route. The Calitzdorp route was started in 1984 with Karel Nel of Boplaas Estate as the prime organizer, and enlarged to the Klein Karoo route in 1986. There are 14 wine producers on the route: three Estates, four private producers and seven Co-operatives, but only ten of these bottle wine and are open to the public. They are Barrydale Co-operative (page 295), Boplaas Estate (page 295), Calitzdorp Co-operative Cellar (page 296), Die Krans Estate (page 296), Domein Doornkraal (page 298), Kango Co-operative Cellar (page 298), Ladismith Co-operative (page 299), Montagu Soetwynboere Co-operative (page 299), and Rietrivier Co-operative (page 299). Boplaas and Die Krans offer cheese lunches in summer. Further details are available from Karel Nel.

Wine Shows

Each year the wines of the vintage are judged at a number of 'young wine' shows, organized by the KWV on both a regional and a national basis. The regional shows are held in Stellenbosch, Paarl, Robertson, Worcester, Olifants River and Klein-Karoo Districts; from these the best of the wines go forward to compete in the South African Champion Wine Show, held at the Goodwood Show Ground annually in October. Here, with much fanfare from the media, the year's champion wines are selected, and the champion wine-maker awards made.

These shows judge the abilities of individual wine makers on the basis of their young wines of the season, which often bear little direct resemblance to the wines eventually marketed. The red wines will need a period of maturation, and the whites will usually be blended before bottling. In addition to the 'young wine' shows, Stellenbosch and Robertson hold bottled wine shows at which wines are judged as they will greet the consumer in the bottle-store, restaurant or hotel – a more meaningful event as far as buyers and the wine lover are concerned.

Besides the local shows, many South African wines are submitted to shows and exhibitions overseas. Important among these are the Monde Sélection, administered from Brussels but held in a different country each year, the Club Oenologique in Great Britain and Vinexpo in Bordeaux. Judging at these competitions includes chemical as well as organoleptic analysis. Gold, silver and bronze medals are awarded, depending upon the judges' consensus or upon average scores.

At the Club Oenologique wines are first judged on a regional basis; for example, the South African wines are judged as a group as are those from Germany, France, Spain and so on. Winners of gold medals in these regions then compete internationally for top honours in specific categories. These winners are awarded double gold medals. South African successes in recent years have included three 'double golds' in a row.

Sydney Back (left) and Dassie Smit, champion wine makers in 1982.

PAARL

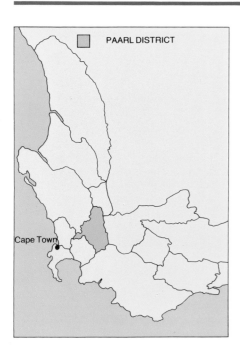

On a clear, windless morning in February 1658, a party of 15 explorers authorized by the Commander, Jan van Riebeeck, set out from the Dutch East India Company's fort at the Cape. They were led by Sergeant Jan van Herwaarden, and included a surveyor named Pieter Potter whose job was to record and map the journey. Accompanied by several Hottentots, and their equipment, food and weapons carried by oxen, they followed the route taken six months earlier by Abraham Gabbema, travelling north and east towards a large hill which Gabbema had named Klapmuts Koppie – a landmark still known by this name. Van Herwaarden's expedition passed the koppie on the third day (the pace of an ox being about five kilometres an hour on easy terrain, and time off for rest and

Ordered with almost military precision, the vineyards of a Paarl wine farm provide a verdant aisle amid the town's growing suburbs.

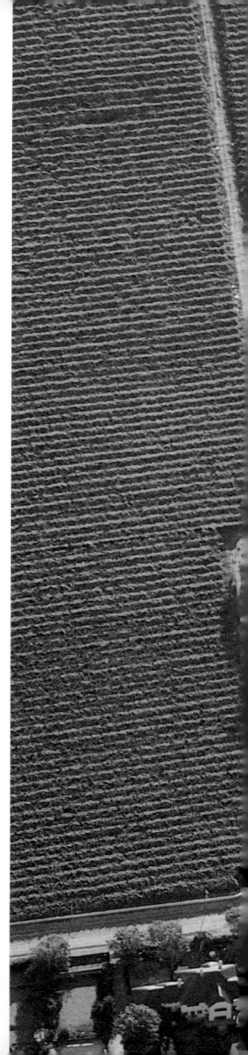

Vines in the rich russet of their autumn dress sprawl at the foot of the Du Toit's mountains.

grazing being needed during the heat of noon). The following day at the foot of a chain of seemingly impassable mountains they came to a stream running north, which they named the Berg River. It seemed an ideal place to pass the night and they were able to have a welcome change of diet by catching fish in the river pools.

On the fifth day the party continued its journey along the river, passing on the left a low mountain whose crest was domed with bare granite rocks, previously christened Paarl and Diamant from the way they shone in the morning light after a night of rain. The only sign of life on this still, brilliant morning as they walked along, the long dry grass brushing their horses' hooves, were the herds of sleek zebra which warily studied these intruders to their ancestral domain. At a certain point of the visitors' approach, as if at a silent signal, the herd would break and canter away snorting, only settling down

to graze again at a safe distance. Later that day they saw many rhinoceros, which took off at a lumbering trot, shy unless provoked. There were also many hippopotami, which never strayed far from the large pools in the river, shaded by the magnificent trees which filled the valley.

The Sergeant and his party had wandered into a natural Paradise, known hitherto only to the Hottentots who grazed their cattle here. But within the next few decades this valley beneath the shining rocks was to become a settled farming community – the first 23 farms, each of 52 hectares, were marked out along the Berg River in October, 1687 – and within a century to be a wine-making centre second only to Stellenbosch in importance.

The soil, climate and setting here were ideally suited to the making of wine. Rising in the south, the Berg River flows through the length of the valley, supplying a ready source of irrigation. To the south, south-east and east the area is bordered by the ranges of the Groot Drakenstein, the Franschhoek and the Klein Drakenstein

mountains. In the west the valley broadens into a plain which allows cool breezes from the Atlantic some 60 km distant to penetrate and influence the Paarl climate which, typically Mediterranean in character, features a good winter rainfall and comparatively long, hot summers. The average rainfall here is some 650 millimetres compared with the generous 1 000 millimetres of Constantia, the low 357 millimetres of Durbanville, and the similar 600 to 800 millimetres in the Stellenbosch area. The average temperature is between 19 and 21 °C compared with a maximum of 19 °C in Constantia in the growing season alone, to an average of 19 °C in Durbanville and between 18 and 19 °C in Stellenbosch.

The vineyards of Paarl are distributed across three main types of soil. In the area along the Berg River they are grown on the sandy soils of Table Mountain Sandstone origin; in the town of Paarl and its immediate vicinity, they are located on granitic soils; and along the slopes of the mountains to the south-east they are also

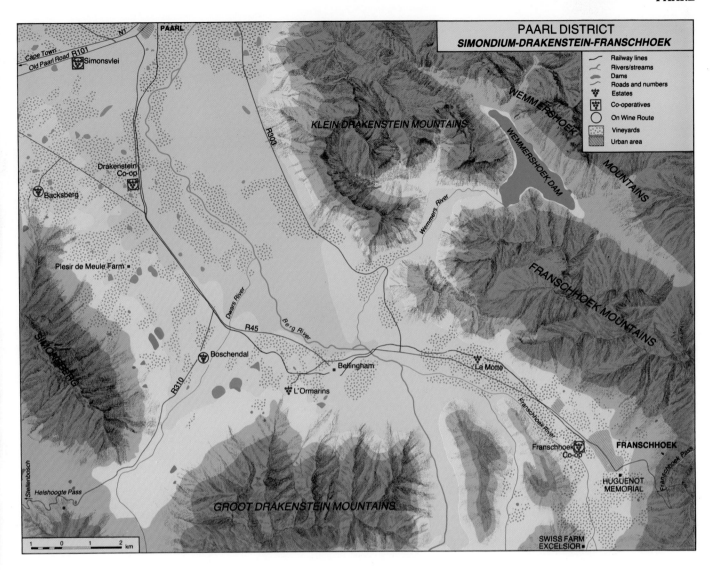

found on this type of granite-based soil, while to the north-east they are mainly on soils of Malmesbury Shale origin.

The lower-lying lands in the valley often require mechanical drainage by the laying of underground pipes, as well as supplementary irrigation during December and January. Deep ploughing and the application of agricultural lime is generally needed during soil preparation (the soils of both the Paarl and Stellenbosch areas lack naturally-occurring lime). The cooler soils against the eastern slopes normally require higher lime applications during preparation but, because of their greater water-holding capacity, are not usually irrigated.

The dominant cultivars in the Paarl area include Steen, Palomino, Sémillon and Cinsaut, generally grown untrellised and without irrigation. Red quality cultivars, such as Cabernet Sauvignon and Pinotage, are also grown.

Besides the Paarl Valley itself, the officially delimited Paarl wine-making district which includes the Drakenstein

and Wellington areas, also incorporates the Ward of Franschhoek, a relatively small area, but one with a marked character and tradition of its own.

In the two-year period between 1688 and 1690, some two hundred Protestant Huguenot immigrants arrived at the Cape. They were mainly settled by the then Governor, Simon van der Stel, at the upper end of the Groot Drakenstein valley, an enclave to which they at first gave the name of *Le Quartier Français* – the French Quarter. Here they introduced to the skills of wine making refinements as yet unknown to the local Free Burgher population. Becoming socially and culturally integrated within a couple of generations, they established farms, many of which are still worked by their descendants. And the legacy of their names survives – Lombard, Marais, Malan, Fouché, De Villiers, Du Plessis, Joubert, Rousseau, Nel, Nortier, Malherbe, Fourie, Vivier, Roux and Du Toit (literally 'of the roof': the thatcher) to name only a few – even if with altered pronunciation; while

the names of their farms – L'Ormarins, Picardie, Rhône, La Provence, La Dauphine, La Motte, Bourgogne, and many others – are a nostalgic memory of the distant French countryside.

The general topography of the Franschhoek Valley resembles that of Paarl, though the average rainfall here is higher, at an annual 900 millimetres (Wellington, by contrast, is lower, at 500 millimetres annually, than either Paarl or Franschhoek).

The wine-making life of the Paarl District is dominated by two organizations, the first being the KWV, whose headquarters are at Suider-Paarl, and the other is Nederburg, under the aegis of the Stellenbosch Farmers' Winery. Further up the valley, in Wellington, is situated the important nursery and research station of Ernita (see page 50) as well as a number of other nurseries.

The Paarl Wine Way (see page 207) is modelled, as are its counterparts in other Districts, on the *Routes du Vin* of France and the *Weinstrassen* of the Rhineland.

Backsberg

The modern history of the Backsberg Estate is a three-generation success story. In a few decades the Back family have put this Estate and its wines firmly on the map of the Paarl winelands. The achievement is all the more remarkable in that the Estate had virtually no historical or viticultural tradition when it was bought by Charles Back, an immigrant from Lithuania, in 1916. In those days it was called 'Klein Babylonstoren', and the farm's first wines were made and sold under this name. They were either supplied in barrels to the KWV, or exported to Britain.

In 1938 the elder Back was joined by his son, Sydney, now the owner of the farm. In the post-war years the two men worked hard to expand and improve the vineyards, and at the same time to adapt to coming trends in wine-making technology. By 1970, when the farm was registered as the Backsberg Estate Winery, the emphasis in its production was firmly upon the making of quality red wines, the cultivars for which had been planted by Sydney Back with shrewd prognosis of the advent of public interest in the mid-1970s in this kind of wine.

The reward for this industry and expertise has been an impressive range of wine awards and Superior certifications by the Wine and Spirit Board, including no less than twelve such for the Estate's outstanding Cabernet Sauvignon. The climax of a wine maker's career came in 1978, when Sydney Back was voted

Backsberg Estate

Cultivars Planted	Size of Vineyards (Hectares)	Training Practice
Cabernet Sauvignon	40	
Pinotage	15	
Bukettraube	10	
Pinot Noir	10	
Shiraz	7	Perold trellis
Cape Riesling	3	
Hanepoot	3	
Kerner	2	
Chardonnay	15	
Weisser Riesling	14	
Sauvignon Blanc	12	Extended Perold trellis
Merlot	10	
Gewürztraminer	7	
Chenin Blanc	32	Perold and extended Perold trellises

Total area under vines in 1987: 180 ha
Irrigation: All Backsberg vineyards are irrigated only if necessary.
Temperatures: Records are not kept.
Average annual rainfall: 800 mm
Stock: Parent stock used for grafting.
First wines bottled under the Backsberg Estate label: Late Harvest, Steen, Clairette Blanche, Rosé, Perlé, Pinotage and Hanepoot, all in 1970
Wines currently bottled under the Backsberg Estate label: Cabernet Sauvignon, Shiraz, Pinotage, Dry Red, Rosé Chenin Blanc, Blanc Fumé, Pinot Noir, Riesling, Klein Babylonstoren, John Martin (wood-aged dry white), Sauvignon Blanc, Chardonnay, Bukettraube, Kerner, Rhine Riesling, Special Late Harvest and Hanepoot
Wood ageing: Wines are aged in wood on the Estate.

A member of the Paarl Wine Way, Backsberg is open to the public between 08h30 and 17h00 on weekdays, and from 08h30 to 13h00 on Saturdays and public holidays. There is a small wine museum on the premises and an added attraction is the self-guided tour aided by closed-circuit television, demonstrating vineyard practices and wine making on the Estate.

The cheerful, unassuming Sydney Back of Backsberg Estate, who in 1978 and again in 1982 was honoured as South Africa's 'Champion Wine Maker of the Year'.

champion wine maker of the year at the Cape Championship Wine Show. He repeated this outstanding achievement in 1982 when he shared the award with Dassie Smit of the Rooiberg Co-operative of the Robertson District.

The Backsberg vineyards now cover 180 hectares, predominantly of Cabernet Sauvignon, Shiraz and Pinotage, grown in soils on the northern slopes of the Simonsberg which are largely of decomposed granite. The cellars on the Estate are a model of their kind, and include a beautifully designed cave-cellar where much of the farm's produce is stored for bottle maturation before sale.

In 1971 Sydney Back's son, Michael, returned from studying viticulture and oenology at the University of Stellenbosch.

He now tends to the vineyards, while the bulk of the cellar work is in the hands of the wine master, Wynand Hamman, and John Martin handles the extensive administration of the farm. John Martin is a household name in the winelands, and has been at Backsberg for many years as the Estate's administrator, bottling supervisor, persuasive salesman and even wine maker on occasion. John has always been against wood-aged or wood-treated white wine, so, with a fine sense of irony, Sydney Back has honoured John by naming one of his more recent white wines, a wood-fermented and further wood-aged Sauvignon Blanc, 'Backsberg John Martin'. It is to be hoped that John is learning to like this full-flavoured and complex wine.

Bellingham

The original grant for this 37-hectare farm in the Groot Drakenstein district was made for Gerritt Jansz van Vuuren in October, 1693. During the late nineteenth century the estate was expanded, but by the Depression years of the 1930s it had declined into a near derelict condition. It was in this state that it was purchased by Bernard and Fredagh Podlashuk in 1943. Invalided out of the Air Force, Bernard had come to the Cape with a vague but powerful desire to become a farmer.

The raw material of Bellingham – the name is surmised to be a corruption of the French *Bellinchamp*, or 'beautiful fields' – was unpromising in the extreme, nor for his chosen occupation had Podlashuk any professional training. But he was a man of determination and ingenuity; and supported, too, by a wife who fully shared his aspirations. In the post-war years they began an extensive overhaul and re-creation of the Bellingham farm and its beautiful though somewhat Victorianised homestead. He replanted the farm's decayed vineyards with new, high-quality cultivars, cheerfully mortgaging himself to the hilt in the process. To provide himself with the necessary technical and theoretical background to his work he made extensive visits to the French winelands, penetrating with his enthusiasm and charisma their wine makers' reserve to gather advice and insights for the kind of wines he planned to make, especially the fine dry white wines which appealed to his own palate but which at that time had little influence on local South African taste.

Within a few years, in their characteristically-designed Bellingham flask, the first of Podlashuk's wines, his Johannisberger, Shiraz and Premier Grand Crû, began to appear. This last in particular was to make the Bellingham name, opening up a new wine category in the local market, that of extra dry, Grand Crû wines. Although the number of cellars making this type of wine has increased rapidly in recent years, the Bellingham Premier Grand Crû remained alone in its field for two decades.

Bellingham draws grapes for the making of its blends from a number of sources in

The entrance to Bellingham Estate, on the Vignerons de Franschhoek Wine Route.

Bellingham

Cultivars Planted	Size of Vineyards (Hectares)	Training Practice
Cape Riesling	42	
Shiraz	20	
Chenin Blanc	20	
Rhine Riesling	7	4-wire vertical
Chardonnay	6	trellis
Pinotage	6	
Bukettraube	5	
Gewürztraminer	4	

Total area under vines in 1987: 110 ha
Irrigation: The vineyards of Bellingham are irrigated.
Temperatures: Average maximum 23 °C; average minimum 11,1 °C
Average annual rainfall: Approximately 630 mm
Stock: Rooted vines are purchased from a nursery.
Envisaged new cultivars: Pinot Noir
First wines bottled under the Bellingham label: Riesling 1950, Premier Grand Crû 1951, Rosé 1951, Johannisberger 1955 and Shiraz 1957
Wines currently bottled under the Bellingham label: Almeida Rosé, Blanc de Noir, Brut, Bukettraube, Cabernet Sauvignon, Classic Thirteen, Grand Provence, Grand Trinité, Johannisberger, Pinotage, Premier Grand Crû, Rhine Riesling, Riesling, Rosé Sec, Sauvignon Blanc, Shiraz, Special Late Harvest, Stein and Vin Gris (All Bellingham wines are bottled by Union Wine Limited.)
Wood ageing: Wines are aged in wood by Union Wine Limited.
Capacity of the Bellingham cellar: 21 000 hectolitres

Bellingham is open to the public on weekdays from 08h00 to 12h30 and from 14h00 to 17h00, with wine tastings at 09h30, 10h30, 14h30 and 15h30 during the summer months.

Bernard Podlashuk, who purchased Bellingham in 1943 and created the famous Bellingham Johannisberger, Shiraz and Premier Grand Crû.

the Groot Drakenstein and Franschhoek areas, and for this reason is not classified as an Estate. Since 1970 the farm has been under the management of the Union Wine Company, which uses the Bellingham label for its successful range of wines blended and bottled on its premises at Wellington. But the spirit of the farm, of its garden and homestead with its extensive collections of classic French furniture and artefacts, remains that of the couple whose life's creation it has been.

Bellingham has taken on a new lease of life under the management of Henry Kempen of the Union Wine Company. In 1985 a centre was opened by Jan Pickard, chairman of Union Wine, where visitors to Bellingham can be received and entertained. A 90-seat natural amphitheatre surrounded by age-old oaks is the venue for lectures, musical performances and many other different types of entertainment during the summer. The Bellingham railway siding has become a feature, with groups of

visitors to the winery arriving by steam train from Cape Town.

Bellingham was one of the founder members of the Vignerons de Franschhoek Wine Route, established as a tribute to the French Huguenots who settled in the valley of Franschhoek three centuries ago.

In 1986, Bellingham almost doubled in extent with the purchase of an additional 100 hectares of virgin soil. This ground has been cleared, and, when planting is finally completed on it, 220 hectares of the total 329 hectares will be under vines.

In recent years the painstaking attention to high quality on the part of the cellarmaster, Johan Schreuder, has brought about an improvement to the wines of Bellingham, the old favourites and the interesting newcomers alike. Two of the more recent wines, for example, are Bellingham Classic Thirteen, a base of Shiraz and Cabernet blended with 10 other red varieties and one white, and Grand Trinité, a blend of wood-aged white cultivars.

Bolandse CO-OPERATIVE WINE CELLAR

This is one of the biggest and best known of the coastal co-operatives and was recently further enlarged when it incorporated the Paarl Vallei Wine Co-operative which itself had been formed in 1976 by the merger of the Pêrelse Wine Cellars and Bergrivier Co-operative. Situated on the slopes of the Paarl mountain, this huge concern now has over 160 members who supply some 24 000 tons of grapes from a wide area, reaching as far afield as Durbanville, Klipheuwel and Malmesbury.

The Bolandse Co-operative winery pressed its first grapes, some 3 000 tonnes, in 1948. Built on a section of the farm Nieuwedrift on the outskirts of Noorder-Paarl, the co-operative served an initial 18 members under its first chairman, Willie de Waal.

'Vollie' de Vries first joined the organisation as assistant wine maker in 1954, armed with a BSc in viticulture and oenology from Stellenbosch University. After a spell at the Badsberg Co-operative, Vollie returned as manager and wine maker to the Bolandse Co-operative, and is now the general manager. The winemaker, Abe Rossouw, and the assistant winemaker, Altus le Roux, are responsible to him for the Co-operative's production.

The Co-operative has an excellent reputation, particularly for red wines, with its Cabernet frequently being judged better than those from some of the Cape's top red wine Estates at wine shows. The Co-operative's prestige is reflected in its splendid collection of awards over the years – over 100 medals in all.

Apart from making wine it also runs its own experimental vineyard, developing new clones and varieties.

Bolandse Co-operative Wine Cellar makes a wide range of wines, of which only a proportion is bottled under its own label, the bulk being sold to merchants.

Bolandse Co-operative

Wines bottled and marketed by the Bolandse Co-operative

Red Wines: Cabernet Sauvignon, Cinsaut and Pinotage.
White wines: Bouquet Blanc, Bukettraube, Chenin Blanc, Late Vintage, Premier Grand Crû, Riesling, Sauvignon Blanc, Stein and Weisser Riesling. A Rosé, a Hanepoot Jerepigo, and a port.

Boschendal

Granted in 1685 and originally named 'Bossendaal' by its first owner, a Huguenot immigrant named Jean le Long, the farm was sold in 1715 to another Huguenot, Abraham de Villiers, in whose family it was to remain for a further 160 years. He was one of three brothers who had arrived in 1689 bearing a letter from the *Here XVII* of the Dutch East India Company's council in Amsterdam to the Governor of the Cape, Simon van der Stel, recommending the brothers for their knowledge of viticulture.

It was a knowledge which was to find full expression in the coming decades in this dramatically beautiful valley of Groot Drakenstein, with its wide flow of land and soaring mountains. Through the eighteenth century the generations of the De Villiers family built up one of the finest farm complexes of its kind in the area, completed in 1812 with the Cape Flemish-style manor house built for his wife, Anna Susanna Louw, by the then owner, Paul de Villiers.

The sumptuous style of those early days of affluence crumbled during the nineteenth century before the increasing economic difficulties which affected the wine-farming world of the Cape. In 1879, the last of the De Villiers family was forced to sell his home (a scion of the family, Paul de Villiers, bought the Paarlberg farm of Landskroon in the same period, however, thus keeping alive the De Villiers' wine-making tradition to the present).

Hereafter Boschendal passed, like Groot Constantia, out of family ownership. Within a few years of the sale of the farm it was acquired as one of the Rhodes Fruit Farms, the thirty-odd farms in the district which were brought together in a project devised by Cecil John Rhodes. His intention was to provide the farmers of the region with alternative crops to the devastated vines which they were forced to destroy by the million in the wake of the phylloxera. An export fruit trade to Britain, Rhodes argued, would provide a more secure market than that of the vulnerable grapes. Moreover, the recent introduction of refrigeration on cargo ships made the move now practically feasible (it was also suggested by Harry Pickstone, Rhodes's fruit-growing expert, that the scheme might have been motivated by Rhodes's need to restore himself to favour in the eyes of the farmers after the *débâcle* of the Jameson Raid).

Whatever the motive, altruistic or

Boschendal Estate

Cultivars Planted	Size of Vineyards (Hectares)	Training Practice
Chardonnay Chenin Blanc Gewürztraminer Pinot Gris Sauvignon Blanc Sémillon SA Riesling Weisser Riesling	White cultivars extend over approximately 274 ha	Extended Perold trellises
Cabernet Sauvignon Merlot Pinotage Pinot Noir Shiraz Tinta Barocca	Red cultivars extend over approximately 76 ha	Extended Perold trellises

Total area under vines in 1987: 350 ha
Irrigation: The vineyards of Boschendal are irrigated if necessary.
Temperatures: Average maximum 21,8 °C; average minimum 12,6 °C
Average annual rainfall: 1 090 mm
Stock: Parent stock is used for grafting; rooted vines are purchased from a nursery.
Envisaged new cultivars: None
First wines bottled under the Boschendal Estate label: Chenin Blanc 1976, Steen 1976, Blanc de Blanc 1978, Riesling 1978, Vintage Steen 1978, Bouquet des Fleurs 1978, Le Mirador 1979, Le Pavillon 1979 and Vin d'Or 1979
Wines currently bottled under the Boschendal Estate label: Blanc de Blanc, Blanc de Noir, Brut, Cabernet Sauvignon, Chenin Blanc, Grand Vin Blanc, Lanoy, Le Bouquet, Riesling, Gewürztraminer, Rhine Riesling, Chardonnay, Sauvignon, and a Bordeaux Blend
Wood ageing: Wines are aged in wood on the Estate.
Capacity of the Boschendal cellar: 2 000 – 3 000 tonnes of grapes

Boschendal is open to the public on weekdays from 08h30 to 17h00, and on Saturdays from 08h30 to 12h30. There is an audio-visual presentation on weekdays at 11h00 and 15h00, or upon request. Attractions for the visitor include the restored Boschendal Manor House, the Restaurant housed in the original farm cellar, the Waenhuiswinkel and 'Le Pique-Nique', a lunch hamper available in Boschendal's spacious gardens between December and April.

At Boschendal great care and attention is paid to the living standards of employees, and these labourers' cottages are a model for the industry.

Under the direction of wine maker Achim von Arnim (right), the wines of the Estate have improved remarkably in recent years and the vineyards dominated by the Groot Drakenstein mountains (above) have been progressively restructured by Herman Hanekom.

otherwise – and Rhodes was an inherently secretive personality – he invested large amounts of his fortune in the purchase of these farms, including Lekkerwyn, Papiermolen, Welgegund, and old Huguenot farms such as La Motte, Languedoc, Champagne and La Rhone – and of course, Boschendal itself.

He died in 1902, and in the coming decades his dreams of extended Empire were to fade. His modest fruit farm scheme, however, has survived, given a

new lease of life in recent years by its take-over in 1969 by the Anglo American Corporation, which has assumed management for the Rhodes Fruit Farms, and restored both the farms and their old homesteads; the restoration of the buildings of Boschendal being undertaken by the architect, Gabriel Fagan. The complex as it stands today consists of the Manor House itself, the *Waenhuis* (now a gift shop), the *Taphuis*, one of the oldest buildings on the Estate, and the modern

winery. The Manor House, meticulously restored to reflect the transitional period in local taste from Dutch to English influence at the turn of the nineteenth century, has among its treasures a fine collection of Ming porcelain – dubbed *Kraakporselein* by the Dutch since they had first encountered it in the hold of a captured Portuguese carrack, or *kraak*.

Recent developments in the wine-making side of the Estate have been spectacular: the structure of the vineyards has been extensively revised, with new varieties carefully matched to soil and conditions on the farm. The vineyards are managed by Herman Hanekom, while the wines are the province of Achim von Arnim, his assistant Hilko Hegewisch and the quality controller, Mynhardt Theron. They have at their disposal one of the most modern of the local cellar systems and a fine range of predominantly white wines is made. Their Blanc de Noir (literally, 'White from Black'), is a full-bodied, dry wine, pale pink in colour, made from four different red grape varieties.

Among the many other innovations introduced by the Anglo American Group both here at Boschendal and at other farms belonging to Rhodes Fruit Farms, have been improved conditions of employment, amenities and health services for their staff. The housing scheme for workers on the Estate is a model of its kind.

Bovlei CO-OPERATIVE WINERY

One of the earliest-established of the Co-operatives (it was founded with Government support in 1907), Bovlei was also one of the few to survive the rigorous early years before the advent of the KWV and the ensuing legislation which stabilized the struggling co-operative movement. During these early years it was known as the Boven Vallei Co-operative Winery.

Today, under its manager and wine maker, 'Tokkie' Marais, the Bovlei Winery

handles 11 500 tonnes of grapes a year, produced by 66 members – a far cry from the 350 tonnes pressed at the 1907 vintage.

Although wine has been made at Bovlei Co-operative since 1908, it was only with the 1982 vintage that its range of wines was made available to the public, including its particularly good Cabernet and Pinotage. The bulk of its production is sold to the KWV, the Union Wine Company, Distillers Corporation, Stellenbosch Farmers' Winery and Bertrams Wines.

Bovlei Co-operative

Red wines: Pinotage and Grand Rouge.
White wines: Riesling, Premier Grand Crû, Colombard, Stein, Sauvignon Blanc and Bukettraube.

The Co-operative is open to the public on weekdays from 08h00 to 12h30 and from 13h30 to 17h30.

Chamonix

Chamonix

Cultivars Planted	Size of Vineyards (Hectares)	Training Practice
Clairette Blanche	11,4	Perold trellis
Cabernet Sauvignon	4,2	
Rhine Riesling	3,8	Vertical trellis
Pinotage	1,6	
Chenin Blanc	9,0	Perold and vertical trellis

Total area under vines in 1987: 30 ha (14 ha still to be planted to vines)
Irrigation: The vineyards of Chamonix are not irrigated.
Temperature: Records are not kept.
Average annual rainfall: Approximately 900 mm
Stock: Rooted vines are purchased from a nursery.
Envisaged new cultivars: Chardonnay and Pinot Noir
First wines bottled under the Chamonix label: Vin Blanc and Blanc de Rouge (1983 vintage)
Wines currently bottled under the Chamonix label: Bouquet Blanc, Rhine Riesling, Blanc de Noir, Cabernet Sauvignon (to be released during 1988), Courchevel Cuvée Brut, and Courchevel Demi Sec (These wines are bottled by the Stellenbosse Botteleringskoöperasie Beperk.)
Wood ageing: Wines are aged in wood at the Franschhoek Vineyards.

Chamonix is open, by appointment, seven days a week for scenic farm drives; wine tasting and sales at the Franschhoek Vineyards.

The farm Waterval, now called Chamonix, was originally part of La Cotte, one of the first farms granted to the French Huguenots in 1688. One of the largest farms in the Franschhoek Valley, it was fairly undeveloped for many years. This is probably due to the hilly topography: Chamonix, which covers 270 hectares, has some of the highest vineyards in the Cape. In 1947, Judge Malan bought the farm, built the main homestead and began developing the land. After his death, the farm was bought by the Pickering family in 1965, and they continued to develop it on the excellent infrastructure created by its former owner.

Since 1980 the farm has been run as a partnership by Michael and Timothy Pickering. Michael and his wife, Bronwen, handle the administration of the farm and the marketing of the wine, while Timothy runs the agricultural side. Although Chamonix is planted mainly to fruit (plums, nectarines, canning peaches, pears and apples) and timber, the cool south-eastern slopes are ideal for the growing of grapes. The vineyards comprise some 33 per cent of the cultivated area: the cultivars planted are Clairette Blanche, Chenin Blanc, Cabernet Sauvignon, Rhine Riesling and Pinotage; Chardonnay and Pinot Noir are planned for the future. The deep, cool Hutton soil, the wide range of micro-climates and the prevailing south-easterly breezes allow for a lengthy ripening period, and the grapes of Chamonix are the last to be harvested in the area.

In 1983 the Franschhoek Vineyards Co-operative agreed to keep the grapes of Chamonix and of Michael Trull's farm, La Bri, separate from those of all the other members of the Co-operative, thereby ensuring that Wines of Origin would be made from them. In this way the grape farmer can avoid the expense of providing his own cellar, and have his wine made by an expert wine maker at the Co-operative. Other farmers in the Franschhoek area have since come to the same agreement with the Co-operative, and several different Wines of Origin are now made under one roof at the Franschhoek Vineyards Co-operative and then sent back to their farms of origin, from where they are sold.

Towards the end of 1983 Chamonix marketed its first wines, a Vin Blanc and a Blanc de Rouge. In 1985 a Rhine Riesling was added to the range, and the name Blanc de Rouge was changed to Blanc de Noir due to an objection by the Liquor Board. The combination of the talents of the Pickerings as wine growers and the favourable geography of the vineyards has been successful: the first two Chamonix wines submitted to the Vignerons of Franschhoek received the Vignerons Controlée seal and the Chamonix Vin Blanc was awarded the Gold medal at the Paarl Wine Show in 1985.

In 1986, the Pickering brothers commissioned Robbie de Villiers of Janice Ashby Design Partnership to design a new range of labels, which would reflect the contemporary orientation of the Chamonix wines. These labels won a Laurie Award and have been nominated for the International Cleo award in New York. The entire range is now bottled in Claret bottles to increase range recognition among consumers. Mark Tanner has been appointed as Public Relations Officer (Mark successfully ran the Binnehof for the Swiss Farm Excelsior for its first year), and he will be working closely with Gilbeys International, distributors of Chamonix wines, to conduct wine tastings and arrange promotions.

Clos Cabrière

Pierre Jourdan, a Huguenot settler, was granted a farm in 1694 at Olifantshoek, so called because elephants had been encountered there. He named his farm Cabrière, after the French village of his birth, Cabrières-d'Aigues. Other Huguenots settled in Olifantshoek, which soon became known as *Le Coin Français* or *Le Quartier Français*, then *Het Fransche Quartier* and eventually Franschhoek.

During the three centuries that have passed since then, Pierre Jourdan's farm has changed hands, and been subdivided, many times. One of those subdivisions is today called Clos Cabrière, and is owned by the well-known wine maker of Boschendal, Achim von Arnim. The homestead on Clos Cabrière, although undoubtedly very old, is not the original dwelling on Pierre Jourdan's Cabrière – that is now thought to be the restored home a few hundred metres away in Cabrière Street, known as Klein Cabrière.

Achim von Arnim specializes at Clos Cabrière in producing sparkling wine made in the true *méthode champenoise* and using only the classic Champagne varieties, Chardonnay and Pinot Noir. Although the property is a mere 17 hectares in extent, the situation and soils are ideal for the production of the style of wine Achim has chosen to make there. Chardonnay has been planted in the alluvial river soils, and more Chardonnay and Pinot Noir in the loamy and clayey soils on the slope on the side of the Franschhoek River opposite to the farm buildings. A modern cellar has been installed in the picturesque old outbuildings without spoiling their outward appearance.

The first release from the cellar came from the 1984 vintage, but this wine was made from grapes bought in, as the vines on Clos Cabrière are not yet sufficiently mature. For this reason the wine is not called Clos Cabrière, but has been named Pierre Jourdan. Although this was not the first sparkling wine made in South Africa by the *méthode champenoise*, it was the first made in this traditional manner to contain the classic Champagne varieties of Chardonnay and Pinot Noir. Subsequent releases, in bottles with labels of a different colour to those on the original wine, have been universally acclaimed and command high prices. Having seen the level of expertise and artistry which Achim and his assistant, Pieter Ferreira, have achieved in making *méthode champenoise* wines, the first sparkling wine made entirely from grapes grown on the Estate is eagerly awaited by 'bubbly'-drinkers.

When not making sparkling wine at Clos Cabrière, and when Achim's considerable responsibilities at Boschendal allow him, he and Pieter devote time and effort to the re-introduction of indigenious flora to their beautiful riverside farm. They have removed much of the exotic vegetation and have planted trees such as yellowwood and white stinkwood. As this programme develops they will eventually remove most of the exotic species such as pines, poplars and oaks.

Clos Cabrière Estate

Cultivars Planted	Size of Vineyards (Hectares)	Training Practice
Chardonnay	24 000	
Pinot Noir	16 000	Cordon trellising

Total area under vines in 1987: 10 ha (2 ha still to be planted)
Irrigation: The vineyards of Clos Cabrière are irrigated.
Temperatures: Records are not kept.
Average annual rainfall: 1 561 mm
Stock: Clone-grafting on Chardonnay vines is practised on the Estate.
First wine bottled by the Clos Cabrière Estate: Pierre Jourdan (from the 1984 vintage)
Wines currently bottled by the Clos Cabrière Estate: Pierre Jourdan Cuvée Brut, Cuvée Extra Brut and Cuvée Reserve
Wood ageing: Wood ageing is not practised on the Estate.
Capacity of the Clos Cabrière cellar: 1 000 hectolitres

Clos Cabrière is open to the public by appointment only.

De Zoete Inval

Den Zoeten Inval, the old Dutch name for this farm, can be roughly translated as 'Happy event', or 'Welcome arrival'. The land was first granted by Simon van der Stel in 1688 to Hercule des Prés (or du Preez), literally 'Hercules of the Meadows', a felicitous name for a farmer. The lower portion of the farm adjacent to the Berg River changed hands regularly in the early years because of the almost annual flooding of the river. But its modern history began with its purchase, in 1878, by the first member of the Frater family in South Africa.

Robert Frater was one of three brothers born in the lowlands of Scotland who grew up to make their living from sheep and wool. About 1870 they emigrated to North America. But Robert did not settle; instead he came to South Africa, hoping to make his fortune in diamonds at Kimberley. He soon decided to return to the business he knew best, however, and moving to Cape Town, entered into partnership with Thomas Mossop, founder of the Rondebosch tannery, with the intention of starting a woolwashery.

He chose Paarl as the most suitable site, since it was within easy reach of the wool-producing areas and yet close enough to Cape Town to make export relatively easy. The decisive factor, however, was the good supply of soft water from the Berg River. To obtain the necessary water rights, the farm De Zoete Inval was purchased from the then owner, Jac de Villiers, together with two neighbouring farms which were then added to the main property. This not only gave a large frontage along the Berg River itself but incorporated the supply from Van Wyk's River which joined the main river within the new farm's boundaries.

A fine supply of water was thus secured and the washery was soon built and in operation. But the farm was not neglected, for while the acquisition of the land had been almost incidental to the main business of woolwashing, the farm itself had been productive and had included a modest amount of wine making. The new owners therefore decided to keep it as a sideline.

And the sideline turned out a success. Soon Mossop and Frater had extended the wine cellar to cope with increased production, and when Mossop died in 1918

De Zoete Inval Estate		
Cultivars Planted	**Size of Vineyards** (Hectares)	**Training Practice**
Cabernet Sauvignon	41,5	
Cinsaut	11,0	
Sauvignon Blanc	7,0	One-wire vertical
Steen	7,0	trellis
Chardonnay	3,0	
Pinot Noir	1,0	

Total area under vines in 1987: Approximately 70,5 ha
Irrigation: The vineyards of De Zoete Inval are irrigated.
Temperatures: Records are not kept.
Average annual rainfall: Records are not kept.
Stock: Parent stock is used for grafting.
First wine bottled under the De Zoete Inval Estate label: Cabernet Sauvignon 1976
Wines currently bottled under the De Zoete Inval Estate label: Cabernet Sauvignon, Cinsaut, Capri Bianco Secco (Steen), Pinot Noir, Blanc de Blanc, Grand Crû and Blanc de Noir
Capacity of the De Zoete Inval cellar: 6 300 hectolitres

De Zoete Inval is open to the public by appointment only. Wine can be purchased at the farm.

and the partnership was dissolved, Frater found himself in possession of both wool and wine.

In the following years wine gradually prevailed, the Scottish wool-farming family becoming South African wine farmers. Adrian Robert Frater, the current owner of De Zoete Inval, is the fourth generation to farm the land. A science graduate from the University of Cape Town, he has further developed the farm, building wine grapes into its most important crop.

Today De Zoete Inval has some 71 hectares under vines, including a few hectares planted to table grape varieties. At one stage over 15 hectares supported table grape cultivars but these are gradually being replaced by white wine

cultivars – Sauvignon Blanc has already replaced all the Waltham Cross and Chardonnay has replaced most of the Alphonse Lavalle and New Cross. Cabernet Sauvignon is the major wine cultivar grown, but a moderate quantity of good quality Cinsaut is also grown, together with some Steen. The ground not used for vines is used for fruit.

Some 3 500 hectolitres of dry red wine are made annually in De Zoete Inval's cellar. Prior to concentrating on dry wines, the Estate produced excellent port which was sold to the KWV (in 1955 a port from the farm was judged 'Grand Champion' of the Cape Wine Show). But the decline in the English port market in the post-war years forced the Fraters to cut back this branch of their production.

Dieu Donné et De Lucque Vineyards

The two farms of Dieu Donné and De Lucque lie within the municipal area of the picturesque village of Franschhoek, and are owned and run as one venture by John Smeddle.

Unlike so many of the other wine farms in the Franschhoek valley, this winery does not have its wines made at the local Co-operative, but produces them on its own property. Twelve wine enthusiasts, with a

particular interest in French wine, have invested in Dieu Donné et De Lucque Vineyards and with their capital, advice and assistance John Smeddle has built a winery consisting of four buildings against the north-eastern slopes of the Franschhoek mountains, where he makes wine very much in the French manner and style. The four winery buildings have been carefully designed to blend in with the

atmosphere of the Franschhoek valley, and were modelled on some 200-year-old buildings in the Cape Flemish style. The five-gabled Cape Dutch homestead has also been restored.

Nine different cultivars are grown on the farms from which nine blended wines are made, all carrying fascinating, very French names. Only small quantities of these various wines are made and it is

Dieu Donne et De Lucque Vineyards

Cultivars Planted	Size of Vineyards (Hectares)	Training Practice
Colombar	10	
Cabernet Sauvignon	7	
Sémillon	6	
Tinta Barocca	4	
Chenin Blanc	3,5	Vertical trellis
Rhine Riesling	2	
Merlot	1,5	
Sauvignon Blanc	1,5	
Gewürztraminer	1	

Total area under vines in 1987: 42,5 ha
Irrigation: Only young vines are under irrigation.
Temperatures: Records are not kept.
Average annual rainfall: 1 280 mm
First wines bottled by the Dieu Donne and De Lucque Vineyards: Chiara de Lucque and Fait de Foi (1986)
Wines currently bottled by the Dieu Donne and De Lucque Vineyards: Grand Saint-Marc, Saint-Jo, Chiara de Lucque, Fait de Foi, Piquant Rouge, Fait de Complis, Beauvillage, Jean de Lucque and Chiara
Wood ageing: Wine is aged in wood on the farms.
Capacity of the cellar: 1 900 hectolitres

Dieu Donne and De Lucque Vineyards are open to the public by appointment only.

John's intention to keep it that way – his aim is always quality, not quantity. The well-known wine maker at Zevenwacht, Neil Ellis, who also makes his own 'boutique' wines (see page 174), is retained by John as a consultant, assisting him in the wine making.

Neil Ellis.

Douglas Green of Paarl

Shortly after the turn of the century, a wine farmer named Piet le Roux sold wine to customers who brought their own containers – bottles, cans, or even buckets – to his address at 360 Main Street, Paarl (now long associated with the headquarters of the KWV). Evidently his wine was palatable, for his business prospered, being expanded in 1930 after its acquisition by the Forrer brothers of Paarl. The new owners started a bottling line and opened a retail outlet which still survives as a local landmark today, the Stukvat Bottle Store.

Then in 1942 the Forrer brothers sold their company to a young man named Douglas Green. The son of a well-known local wine merchant, he had been brought up in close contact with the liquor trade, and had spent some time in France studying wine farming and making. On his return to South Africa, and with the help of a loan from his mother, he bought up the Forrers' concern, changing its name to Douglas Green of Paarl. With his new company well situated near the centre of town, he soon began to expand the

operation, extending the office block and building new premises for Stukvat. Soon the company's reputation was expanding too, owing to its good and moderately priced wines, matured brandies, ports and high-quality sherries.

In the post-war years Douglas Green of Paarl changed hands, being bought by Mr 'Cappy' Sinclair in 1973, though it retained both its name and the style of its wines. Then, in March 1976, a new chapter in its fortunes began, when it was bought by Rennies to form a new merchant and national liquor distributor, also under the name of Douglas Green of Paarl. Rennies, the then Johannesburg-based subsidiary of the Jardine Matheson Group of Hong Kong, took over two further wine companies, those of J.D. Bosman & Company of Johannesburg and Avrons Limited of Cape Town.

The three companies then amalgamated into a single large operation, but within a few years increased demand for Douglas Green wines and subsequent growth in its market shares over-taxed the capacity of the original Paarl bottling and

Douglas Green of Paarl

Wines distributed by Douglas Green of Paarl

Red wines: Cabernet Sauvignon, Pinotage, Shiraz, Pinot Noir, St Augustine and St Raphael
White wines: Blanc de Blanc, Chenin Blanc, Premier Grand Crû, Riesling, Bukettraube, Selected Stein, Late Harvest, Sauvignon Blanc, Pinotage Blanc de Noir, Rhine Riesling, Gewürztraminer, St Vincent of Saragossa, St Anna Schloss and St Morand
Rare releases: Kerner and Rhine Riesling 1983
Sherry: Douglas Green Flor Range: Extra Dry, Medium, Medium Cream, Cream, and Clorosa. Aspen Range: Full Cream, Medium Cream and Medium Dry

warehousing organization: since July 1980, the company has been largely transferred to a new large-scale depot at Montagu Gardens, on a three-acre site near Milnerton Racecourse. The depot includes a bottling plant, warehousing, and a sales, marketing, distribution and administration centre controlling a network of outlets throughout Southern Africa. The company also distributes the full ranges of Delheim and Blaauwklippen wines and is the largest importer of liquor, except for whisky, into South Africa.

The Jardine Matheson Group sold Rennies, the then holding company of Douglas Green, to Old Mutual. In December 1984 Rennies merged with

Safmarine to form a new company, Safren, which then became the holding company of Douglas Green of Paarl. In April 1985 Douglas Green was sold to Kersaf Liquor Holdings, part of Kersaf, the giant group formerly controlled by Sol Kerzner which also includes the Sun International Group. Douglas Green is thus now a wholly-owned subsidiary of Kersaf, which is owned by Safren, which is controlled by Old Mutual.

Douglas Green do not actually make any of their own wines, relying largely on the KWV as a source of their regular ranges

and their special releases, but blend, bottle and market them. Every season they select quality wines, skilfully blending them to their vintners' requirements and according to continuous research undertaken to test consumers' tastes. The company's cellar of wines currently features more than 30 products, including many which have become familiar household names over the years, such as Douglas Green Premier Grand Crû, St Augustine, St Raphael, Douglas Green Blanc de Blanc, St Morand and St Anna Schloss.

Drakenstein

The oldest Co-operative in the area, the Drakenstein Winery, was founded by a group of eight local farmers in October, 1906. Those were uncertain days for the local wine industry, and an air of improvisation lingers over the record of the Co-operative's first two pressing seasons, when two of the winery's directors were appointed as wine makers at a fee of £15 each. The grapes were taken to the winery by two labourers with a wagon drawn by four horses, at the rate of a shilling a day. Another of the directors was responsible for the racking of the wine.

In the first decades, between 1909 and 1948, brandy was distilled at the Co-operative. The first Hanepoot Jerepigo was made in 1909 and long remained one of its best-known products. In the early days,

too, fine Cabernet, Pontac and Cinsaut wines were made here. The first official wine maker was a Mr Boettgen, succeeded in 1921 by Wolfram Wagener, whose son took over from him in 1950. The winery's present manager and wine maker is Mr L. Vlok. The Co-operative has been successful in direct marketing to the public and through some retailers and has made extensive use of modern packaging: its wines are marketed in soft packs and patent plastic bottles.

Visitors to the winery will be able to see the many-gabled façade of the building which houses the Co-operative, as well as the two well-preserved brandy-stills from which the early brandy was made, and a number of the first cork-sealed bottles of brandy.

Fairview

At the turn of the century a large area of the Paarl mountain belonged to a certain Mr Hugo, owner of the farm Bloemkoolfontein. Short on water and with soil which was largely sand, it made an unprepossessing property, but it supplied enough nutrition to support a limited quantity of Cinsaut from which Hugo made dry red wine which he purveyed to the public and the wine merchants in small wooden barrels.

When he died in 1937 his farm was bought by an immigrant from Lithuania named Charles Back, who had bought the Drakenstein farm now known as Backsberg in 1916. Reduced in extent (Hugo had sold off the highest part of the farm in 1917), his new acquisition

nevertheless had a working cellar and, Back realized, considerable potential for the production of shy-bearing, high quality vines for which the poor nature of the soil and the limited water supply would be relatively less of a disadvantage.

He set about rooting out the old Cinsaut vineyards and replanting them with quality cultivars. After his death in 1954, his son, Cyril, continued this process of replacement with noble vines such as Cabernet Sauvignon, Pinotage, Shiraz, Pinot Noir and Steen. Over the next 20 years Cyril Back consolidated his father's efforts, winning numerous awards for his red wines at the Boberg Show where in 1974, 1976 and 1978 he won the KWV trophy for the Champion Red Wine.

The Backs have always worked as a team. From the early years Cyril's wife, Beryl, has been very involved in everything to do with Fairview. Cyril's eldest son, Charles, has been cellarmaster since 1978 although Cyril still helps in the winery during the vintage. Charles was trained at Elsenburg, where he also did an extra cellarmaster's course. He is not only an extremely talented wine maker but also has a natural innovative flair for marketing. In 1986 Charles was the first to make a Gamay Nouveau by the traditional method of carbonic maceration. In 1987 he produced a similar wine but used mostly Pinotage as the Gamay crop had suffered severe hail damage. A fortified sweet Shiraz is also one of Charles's innovations.

Two of the Swiss Saanen goats imported in 1981. Fairview has become almost as well known for its goat's milk cheese as for its wine.

Cyril Back and his son Charles have produced a range of wines of which they can be justifiably proud.

Fairview Estate

Cultivars Planted	Size of Vineyards (Number of vines)	Training Practice
Cabernet Sauvignon	79 698	
Shiraz	45 128	
Merlot	20 000	
Pinot Noir	15 605	4-wire vertical trellis
Bukettraube	12 536	
Sauvignon Blanc	12 136	
Weisser Riesling	9 000	
Gewürztraminer	6 000	
Pinotage	57 645	
Pinot Gris	15 000	Bush vines
Sémillon	14 720	
Chardonnay	12 000	
Gamay	30 000	Perold trellis
Hanepoot	3 000	
Cabernet Franc	30 000	Bush vines and Perold trellis

Total area under vines in 1987: 120 ha (10 still to be planted)
Irrigation: The vineyards of Fairview are not irrigated.
Temperatures: Records are not kept.
Average annual rainfall: Approximately 600 mm
Stock: Rooted vines are purchased from the KWV.
First wines bottled under the Fairview Estate label: Cabernet, Shiraz, Pinotage (all 1974 vintage)
Wines currently bottled under the Fairview Estate label: Bukettraube, Cabernet Sauvignon, Blanc de Noir, Charles Gerard Blended White, Charles Gerard Estate Red, Chenin Blanc, Bouquet Fair, Full Sweet Sémillon, Gamay, Hanepoot, Pinotage, Pinot Noir, Port, Rosé d'une Nuit, Sauvignon Blanc, Shiraz, Special Late Harvest, Sweet Red, Tinta Barocca and Weisser Riesling
Wood ageing: Wines are aged in wood and bottled on the Estate.
Capacity of the Fairview cellar: 7 500 hectolitres

Fairview is open to the public on weekdays from 09h00 to 18h00 and on Saturdays from 08h30 to 13h00.

White cultivars are well represented at Fairview (a Sauvignon Blanc fermented and aged in wood will be released during 1988 under the label Charles Gerard Dry White), but there are more red wine cultivars than white. Situated against the southern slopes of the Paarlberg, Fairview's soils range from the decomposed granite of the upper slopes – derived from the mountain itself – through the middle section of the farm made up mostly of sandy loam, down to the lower reaches which are too poor to support vines. Further still to the south the land rises again to present a very good, clay-based soil, well suited to shy-bearing cultivars.

None of these soils is fertile enough to give high production. Of the 200 hectares of Fairview, 120 are currently devoted to vineyards. The remainder of the land, mostly comprising the areas of poorer soil, is occupied by 12 000 laying hens and 8 000 pigs and goats. In 1981 Fairview imported Swiss Saanen goats and became the only commercial goat's milk cheese producing unit in South Africa. The herd has now increased to 600 and Fairview produces a range of excellent cheeses, as well as yoghurt, in their modern factory on the Estate. Mr Giovanni Agnostinelli is responsible for the making of the cheeses, which include picorino, ricotta, chevin, feta and serra. The Backs also have a flock of special milk-yielding sheep from Germany and will be making a popular Portuguese cheese called 'Cesa de Serra', or Cheese of the Mountains. The poultry and animals produce enough organic fertilizer to enrich the vineyards – an impressive 4 000 tonnes a year. Virtually no inorganic fertilizer is used at Fairview, other than the lime needed to supply a common deficiency in the districts of Paarl and Stellenbosch.

In 1974 the Estate scored a notable 'first' in the industry with the highly successful private auction of its wines, the first of its kind for the general public in South Africa. One and a half thousand cases of wine were auctioned.

Fairview offers a comprehensive range of wines, which includes a Port and a Red Jerepigo both of which are made entirely from Shiraz, and a fortified Hanepoot. A *méthode champenoise* sparkling wine made from the traditional Pinot Noir grape will be released by 1988. Although Fairview has, of late, been better known for its red wines, Charles denies any preference for either white or red wines. Like most other Estates, Fairview has made a considerable investment in new Bordeaux barriques, although large vats are still used, and Charles is ageing some red wines to be released when ready.

Franschhoek Vineyards
CO-OPERATIVE

The Franschhoek Vineyards Co-operative was founded in 1945, with its winery built in a commanding position at the head of this beautiful and historic valley, on La Cotte, one of the original Huguenot farms. Its first wine master was an immigrant from Italy, Alberto Agostinis, who developed the winery which receives its grapes from most of the farmers in the valley, and experimented with new cellar methods. In particular, he worked on the

problems of controlling fermentation in the heat of the summer (this, of course, was before the advent of cold fermentation). One method he devised involved adding sulphur to the must to halt the fermentation during the summer, and then desulphuring it again in winter when the cool temperatures would permit a slower fermentation rate.

On his death in 1969, Agostinis' place was taken by Johan Theron. Son of a

Tulbagh wine farmer and a graduate in viticulture and oenology from the University of Stellenbosch, he guided the fortunes of the Co-operative for 15 years. On his departure in 1984 his assistant, Deon Truter, who has a diploma in cellar technology from Elsenburg Agricultural College, took over as wine maker. Deon, too, has wine making in the blood, as his father, Bennie Truter, was also a wine maker. He has been assisted by Driaan van

Vines and trees stand winter-bare in the sheltered valley of Franschhoek, where soils rising from the banks of the Berg River to high mountain slopes have supported wine making since Huguenot times.

Franschhoek Vineyards Co-operative

Wines bottled and marketed by the Franschhoek Vineyards Co-operative

Red wine: Claret
White wines: Sauvignon Blanc, Premier Grand Crû, Sémillon, Sémillon (Semi-Sweet), Hárslevelü, Rhine Riesling, Chenin Blanc, and Stein

A Pinotage Blanc de Noir, a sparkling wine, a Sweet Hanepoot and a Red Port are also available.

The Franschhoek Vineyards Co-operative is open to the public on weekdays from 08h30 to 13h00 and from 14h00 to 17h30, and on Saturdays from 09h00 to 13h00.

der Merwe since 1984 and between them they have further developed and refined the wines characteristic of this area, with its high winter rainfall and relatively mild summers, favouring the making of light dry and semi-sweet wines such as Sémillon and Chenin Blanc.

Deon has been fundamental in the successful development of the scheme – unique, so far, to Franschhoek – whereby certain members of the Co-operative request that their grapes be kept separate from the bulk of the members' contributions. Wine is then made from these separate lots of grapes, bottled separately, and the individual members of the scheme then market their own wines from their premises. In this way fairly small farmers, and in some cases relatively inexperienced

ones, can enjoy the benefits of a well-equipped cellar and the expertise of Deon and Driaan, and still have the satisfaction and pride of marketing their own wines.

The Franschhoek Vineyards Co-operative receives annually approximately 12 000 tonnes of grapes from its 123 members. About two per cent of the total is selected to be bottled under the La Cotte label, a further small percentage goes back to the members who have their wines made separately in terms of the scheme previously mentioned, and the rest is made into wines which are sold to the large wholesalers. During 1986 over R1 million was spent in renovating and re-equipping the cellar, greatly improving the wine-making facilities to meet the specific requirements of its members.

Haut Provence

When Michael Guassardo settled in the beautiful cool valley of Franschhoek in 1982, he was determined to make a top quality French-styled wine. He called the farm he bought (it once belonged to John Platter, see page 143) Haut Provence. It is a portion of the original farm La Provence, which was granted to Pierre Joubert, a Huguenot, in 1694 by Governor Simon van der Stel.

One of the first things Michael did was to establish a laboratory and experimental wine cellar. With the help and guidance of Johan Theron, Franschhoek Vineyards' wine maker, he set about mastering the art of wine blending. At the same time the vineyards were reorganized, some being replanted. More recently fruit orchards have been replaced with more plantings of Sauvignon Blanc vines. After two years of hard work, Haut Provence was ready to announce its 'Grand Vin'.

The farm produces this wine in limited quantities. It is a blend of three cultivars, Sauvignon Blanc, Sémillon and Chenin Blanc. Each cultivar is pruned, thinned and grown with the final blend in mind. As the grapes ripen, the vineyards are monitored daily for acid and sugar, while careful note is taken of the pH levels. Harvesting takes place in the late afternoon and early morning, all grapes being kept in 20 kilogram baskets and bins. This ensures delivery of cool, firm bunches to the press.

The grapes are pressed in a pneumatic horizontal press, to ensure clear juices and

Haut Provence

Cultivars Planted	Size of Vineyards (Number of vines)	Training Practice
Sauvignon Blanc	13 000	
Chenin Blanc	7 500	
Chardonnay	6 500	Perold trellises
Hanepoot	2 500	
Sémillon	19 000	Bush vines

Total area under vines in 1987: 9 ha
Irrigation: The vineyards of Haut Provence are irrigated.
Temperatures: Records are not kept.
Average annual rainfall: Approximately 1 080 mm
Stock: Rooted vines are purchased from a recognized nursery.
Envisaged new cultivars: None
First wines bottled under the Haut Provence label: Haut Provence Grand Vin H4 Series, Haut Provence Grand H5 Series, Haut Provence Grand Vin Doux
Wines currently bottled under the Haut Provence label: Grand Vin, Grand Vin Doux, Grand Crû and Sparkling Maxine (These wines are bottled by the Stellenbosse Botteleringskoöperasie Beperk.)
Wood ageing and cellar capacity: Wines are aged at the Franschhoek Vineyards cellars.

Haut Provence is open to the public from 1 December to 15 April, on Wednesdays and Fridays from 14h00 to 16h00 and on Saturdays from 09h30 to 12h00. Visits at other times by appointment. The pottery shop is open on weekdays from 09h00 to 17h00 and on Saturdays from 09h30 to 12h00.

little tannin, as well as minimum oxidation. The must is then fermented with special imported yeasts selected for their ability to ensure complete

fermentation, thus giving a good alcohol yield. Once the controlled cold fermentation is complete, the wines are tested and tasted, and only those tanks whose wine is ideal for the Grand Vin blend are selected.

Haut Provence also produces a Grand Vin Doux, which is a blend of two cultivars, Chenin Blanc and Muscat d'Alexandrie in equal proportions, resulting in a semi-sweet wine. The yield of the Chenin Blanc is kept to an absolute minimum, and just ten tonnes are harvested from two hectares. Only 940 cases have been produced. Michael has also made a sparkling wine named after his daughter, Maxine. Apparently he was going to make just enough for Maxine's wedding, but he was so pleased with the result that Sparkling Maxine has gone into full production.

When not making wine, Michael edits the quarterly magazine *The Cape Potter* – he and his wife, Norma, are enthusiastic and talented potters. They have a studio on the farm, where visitors can purchase items made by the Guassardos.

At the moment all Haut Provence's wines are made at the Franschhoek Vineyards Co-operative. Michael has experimented with making his own wine, however, and it is not unlikely that the results could entice him to produce his own wines in the future.

KWV
(KO-OPERATIEVE WIJNBOUWERS VERENIGING VAN ZUID-AFRIKA BEPERKT)

The dominant organization of the winelands, the KWV is very much a twentieth-century phenomenon, and one which has emerged in response to a number of powerful stimuli. Of these, perhaps the most important has been that of over-production. Market problems attendant upon over-production dogged the nineteenth-century Cape wine farmers, particularly after the repeal of the protective tariffs in 1861. But they attained near critical dimensions in the period after the control of the phylloxera epidemic towards the turn of the century. New methods of viticulture led to a population explosion among the vines, resulting in a vast quantity of unsaleable wine. The depression in the aftermath of the Anglo-Boer war took further toll: and by the early years of the present century the winelands of the Cape were in an advanced state of crisis.

Not only was the industry suffering from over-production, but to an extreme degree it lacked organization. Every farmer acted for himself, and the local wine merchants, many of them of English origin and equally pressed by a hard economy, played the market in an attempt to keep their earnings at a healthy level.

Thus, although there was plenty of wine in the winelands, the financial return was poor. At the turn of the century the bulk of the surplus grown was distilled into brandy, but even this brought only partial relief. Further inflation and a rise in the excise duty on alcohol once more brought the industry to a crisis.

Then in 1904 the first sign of forthcoming organizational unity emerged. The sturdy farmers of the Cape were offered an alternative to their traditional but now increasingly costly independence. For in that year a Government commission

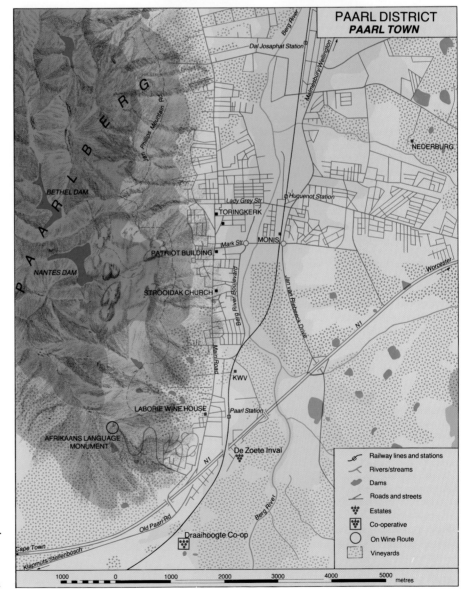

Mr P.B.B. Hugo, the present chairman of the KWV.

of inquiry into their problems recommended the establishment of co-operative wineries – it was from this innovation of the co-operative system that the KWV was eventually to evolve.

The Government set aside £50 000 to start the scheme, and with this assistance nine co-operatives were established between 1905 and 1909 with the object of providing the farmers with increased leverage in collective bargaining as well as money saving by pooling cellar facilities and technical resources. In spite of its evident advantages, however, the co-operative movement remained small, exercising little effect in countering over-production because the majority of the farmers remained outside the system.

Continued over-production resulted in an acute depression in prices. 1909 witnessed the lowest price ever received for wine on the local market, at £1 17s 6d a leaguer. The unexpected ostrich boom relieved some of the pressure on the market between 1906 and 1913, when a number of farmers turned from wine to birds, but the years of the First World War, particularly from 1915 to 1917, saw further poor returns at £2 10s and £3 a leaguer. By 1918 there were almost 87 million healthily producing vines in the Cape, making an annual 96 750 leaguers of wine. Millions of litres of unsaleable wine had to be thrown away (old-timers in Stellenbosch remember the dusty streets running with wine!).

To be effective in controlling prices and stabilizing the market, the farmers had to present a united front; they needed a body to represent them and to bargain on their behalf, and at the same time to handle the increasing bulk of excess wine. It was from these two requirements that the basic idea for the structure of the KWV was developed.

To a great extent the inspiration for this new system was that of one man, Dr Charles William Henry Kohler. A dentist by training, he was born in 1862 at Calvinia in the northern Cape, and after qualifying in Cape Town settled in Paarl for a while before moving to the Transvaal to become involved in mining investments. But in 1909 he returned to the Cape, bought the farm Riverside in the Paarl district, and settled down to become a wine farmer.

As a farmer he shared in the problems and concerns of his time; and he soon became aware that only a centralized body would be able to deal with them. At a meeting of the Paarl Wine Farmers' Association on December 13, 1916, convened by Kohler himself, it was decided to form a Co-operative Viticultural Union of South Africa. Financed by voluntary contributions from the farmers, the Union held its first meeting in Paarl in December 1917, and on January 8, 1918, it was converted into a co-operative and registered under the Companies Act of 1892 as the Ko-operatieve Wijnbouwers Vereniging van Zuid-Afrika Beperkt (it still retains this Dutch form of the title).

The two-fold aims of the new organization were set out in its constitution. With regard to the market, the KWV was 'So to direct, control and regulate the sale and disposal by its members of their produce, being that of the grape, as shall secure or tend to secure for them a continously adequate return for such produce.' At the same time, the organization undertook to dispose of its members' surplus produce – at this stage powers vested in the company by law were limited to wine for distilling purposes only.

For the KWV to be fully effective both in terms of dealing with over-production and in controlling prices, it had to ensure that all the wine farmers joined its ranks. Given the straitened economic circumstances and Kohler's energy, determination and persuasiveness, it was not long before the great majority – up to 95 per cent – had joined.

The result of this unity of purpose was that, at least as far as distilling wine was concerned, minimum prices could be fixed, though there was some initial confusion about the rights of the remaining growers who were not members of the KWV to sell directly to the merchants. Since they did not have to deduct any surplus, they received better prices than if they had sold their wine to the KWV, while at the same time the merchants could buy more cheaply from these growers than from the Co-operative. Notwithstanding this manipulation, however, the immediate effect of the new organization's presence was a sharp rise in prices, reaching £10 a leaguer in 1919.

In these early years, short of staff and funds, the KWV converted all its surplus into distilled ethyl alcohol. In the same period considerable quantities of this alcohol were being distilled from unsaleable molasses by the sugar farmers of Natal. Collaboration between the two industries led to the development of a petrol substitute named 'Natalite', the KWV's first product. Unfortunately, it was more expensive than petrol, the return of which to the market after the blockade of the war years caused Natalite to fade away. Further problems came in the early 1920s with particularly heavy crops in the years 1921 and 1923; and a recurrence of the earlier pattern took place, with a price drop to £3 a leaguer and the destroying of over 50 million litres of unsaleable wine.

But 1924 saw an important turning-point in the KWV's fortunes: the Government ratified its powers with Act 5 of 1924, the Wine and Spirit Control Act, which empowered the KWV to fix on a yearly basis the minimum price to be paid to farmers for their distilling wine. That same year, too, saw the organization begin its second major project for the disposal of excess wine by making mature brandy; and round this main product the Co-operative's range was gradually expanded to include dry table wines, fortified wines and liqueurs. This was well-timed, for the following year saw the introduction by Britain of a preferential tariff in respect of high-strength wines imported from Commonwealth countries; which had a marked effect in reviving the local industry by providing a protected outlet for the KWV's growing export produce (by its constitution, the Co-operative had agreed to share its markets abroad with the producing wholesalers, selling its wares in Africa only in countries north of the Equator).

With increased quantity came improved quality. In these years the KWV began a concerted programme of technical improvement aimed at every level of the wine-making process. In 1927 one of the most important of South Africa's viticultural pioneers, Dr Izak Abraham Perold, became the organization's principal research scientist. A decade later he was joined by another eminent wine scientist, Dr Charles Niehaus, who as his assistant, investigated local sherry production, before turning to the improvement of table wines.

Subsequent decades have seen a progressive enlargement of the KWV's scope and power. By Act 23 of 1940, the organization's control was extended to cover not only distilling wine but also good wine (it had originally been assumed, erroneously, that the stabilization of

The KWV plays an important rôle in the education of visitors to the Cape winelands and some 45 000 tourists are conducted through the organization's huge cellars each year.

Laborie homestead, where overseas guests of the KWV are entertained and accommodated.

distilling wine prices would lead to a similar stability in good wine prices as well). Control was extended to include the whole wine industry. All transactions between merchants and producers had to be approved by the KWV, and all payments made through the organization. The Act further stipulated that no person might produce wine except under a permit issued by the KWV, such permits only being granted if the Co-operative was satisfied that the producer was in possession of the necessary cellar facilities and fustage. The legislation concerning the annual surplus to be delivered to the KWV was further expanded and refined.

The post-war years saw an accelerating pace in the local wine industry. And, stimulated by new methods and despite the controls introduced in 1940, the old problem of over-production now returned, as fresh as ever. In response, new legislation was devised. In 1957, after over half a century, controls were put on production at source. A detailed scheme, known as the Quota System, was introduced for the limitation of production; the first of these quotas was fixed in terms of the vines growing on the farmer's

property on June 21, 1957 (allowance being made for vines removed earlier pending renewal of the vineyards). Increases in the total quota occurred in 1963 and 1970 to the extent that the total quota volume at present amounts to nearly 13 million hectolitres of wine, at 10 per cent alcohol by volume.

The present structure and policy of the KWV continues to reflect its legal and administrative evolution, though now, of course, on a vastly increased scale. The co-operative principle with which it began remains firmly at its centre. Membership is not compulsory, although wine control is applicable to all producers, currently amounting to about 6 000 wine farmers and 70 co-operative cellars. Members are represented by a Board of Directors elected by the farmers themselves – in theory at least, the farmers have the power to dissolve the organization at any time they may wish. For the purposes of election the winelands are divided into eight geographic regions without any specific 'Wine of Origin' connotation. The 12 Directors who represent these districts, generally known as the 'KWV districts', are headed by the present Chairman of the

KWV (the fourth to hold office in the organization's history), Mr P.B.B. Hugo.

Some 900 highly qualified personnel run the many aspects of the KWV's life, which is centred around its Head Office at Suider-Paarl. Here, on a site covering nine

---

Wines distributed by the KWV

(All KWV wines are for export, except the Laborie range which is available locally.)

Red wines: Roodeberg, Cabernet, Pinotage, Cinsaut, Shiraz, Bonne Esperance and Laborie Red
White wines: Riesling, Steen, Chenin Blanc, Bonne Esperance Dry White and Stein, Weisser Riesling, Kerner, Late Vintage, Noble Late Harvest Superior, Cape Forêt, Cape Bouquet, Cape Nouveau Blanc and Laborie White
Sparkling wines: Petillant Blanc and Rosé, Mousseux Blanc Brut, Blanc Demi Sec and Rouge, Musanté and Laborie Blanc de Noir

A Bonne Esperance Rosé, a Cabernet Sauvignon Blanc de Noir and a range of Muscadels, Ports, Sherries and Liqueurs are also made.

hectares, are extensive administrative and research buildings, as well as one of the biggest wine storage facilities in the world. With a total storage capacity of 2,3 million hectolitres of wine, it includes maturation facilities for a stock of almost 33 000 hectolitres of port-type liqueur wines, brandies and sherries.

KWV products are not generally available on the local market since, by agreement, the organization sells only minimum amounts for domestic consumption to merchants and distillers. The major emphasis remains upon production for export. Of the four to five per cent of the national production which is exported, the KWV handles 95 per cent of the fortified wines and a small percentage of the natural wines – the remainder being divided largely between the Stellenbosch Farmers' Winery and the Oude Meester Group, with important contributions also from Gilbeys, Union Wine and many other producers.

Considerable research is undertaken by the KWV, and liaison takes place with other research centres such as the Viticultural and Oenological Research Institute at Stellenbosch. In the late 1970s it instituted a levy on good wine and on the unsaleable part of the distilling wine crop to raise funds for research and for extension services to farmers, a move which netted R1,2 million in the first year.

A further important responsibility of the KWV is that of publicity and image-building for the industry in general, in particular with the creation of overseas markets. On home ground, the headquar-

ters at Paarl – the target of over 45 000 visitors every year – is the scene of conducted tours, film shows and wine-tastings.

In 1972 the KWV bought the eighteenth-century Cape Dutch homestead of Laborie in Paarl and since then has restored the manor house, and developed the farm into a flourishing wine estate, where the cellarmaster, Willi Hacker, supervises the making of the KWV's own Laborie range of wines. The old cellar is used as a training centre, where the popular KWV wine education courses are held.

Visibly or invisibly, the KWV is everywhere in the modern Cape winelands. Born of a series of defensive gestures, this vast organization provides both a controlling and a mediatory rôle between the different divisions of the winelands, between producers, co-operatives, wholesalers and retailers: indeed, on a larger scale, through its export function, this rôle extends beyond the Cape to the wine world in general.

La Bri

The small, 18-hectare farm known as La Bri Vineyards, owned by Michael and Cheryl Trull, is situated at the top end of the Franschhoek valley where, in 1694, a French Huguenot called Jacques de Villiers first planted vines. The vines which thrive there today are Rhine Riesling, Sauvignon Blanc and Sémillon, and the grapes harvested from these are delivered to the Franschhoek Vineyards Co-operative where they are vinified and bottled separately, so that Michael can sell them from the farm under his own label.

It was Michael Trull and two other Michaels, Michael Pickering of Chamonix and Michael Guassardo of Haut Provence, who first approached the Franschhoek Vineyards Co-operative with the idea for this novel scheme. Several other farms now also follow this procedure in collaboration with the Co-operative.

The Vignerons de Franschhoek Wine Route is also mainly Michael Trull's brainchild.

His first wine, released in 1983, was the 'Blanc de La Bri', a wood-aged blend of Sémillon and Sauvignon Blanc along the lines of the white blends of Bordeaux. The Sémillon grapes used in Blanc de La Bri

La Bri

Cultivars Planted	Size of Vineyards (Hectares)	Training Practice
Sauvignon Blanc	10,3	Extended Perold
Rhine Riesling	3,4	trellis
Sémillon	5,2	Bush vines

Total area under vines in 1987: 18,9 ha
Irrigation: The vineyards of La Bri are not irrigated.
Temperatures: Records are not kept.
Average annual rainfall: 1 300 mm
Stock: Parent stock is used for grafting; rooted vines are purchased from a recognized nursery.
First wine bottled under the La Bri label: Blanc de La Bri (1983)
Wines currently bottled under the La Bri label: Blanc de La Bri, Weisser La Bri, Sauvage de La Bri and Blanc de Fumé
Wood ageing: Wines are aged in wood at the Franschhoek Vineyards Co-operative.

La Bri is open to the public by appointment only.

are from 70-year-old vines, of the special small-bunch clone which is cultivated at the top end of the Franschhoek valley. There is now also a sweetish Rhine

Riesling from the 1986 vintage called 'Weisser La Bri', sold under a colourful, rather Germanic label, and a Sauvignon Blanc called 'Sauvage de La Bri'.

La Motte

La Motte Estate

Cultivars Planted	Size of Vineyards (Hectares)	Training Practice
Cabernet Sauvignon	27	
Sauvignon Blanc	20	
Shiraz	11	
Merlot	8	Extended Perold
Chenin Blanc	7	trellis
Chardonnay	4	
Pinot Noir	4	
Cabernet Franc	3	

Total area under vines in 1987: 84 ha
Irrigation: Only the vineyards planted to white cultivars are irrigated at La Motte.
Temperatures: Average maximum 23 °C; average minimum 16 °C
Average annual rainfall: 810 mm
First wine bottled under the La Motte Estate label: Chateau la Motte Cabernet Sauvignon (vintage uncertain – approximately 1969)
Wines currently bottled under the La Motte Estate label: Cabernet Sauvignon, Shiraz and Pinot Noir. La Motte also produces two wines under the L'Etiole label: Légère and Blanc de Noir.
Wood ageing: Wines are aged in wood on the Estate.
Capacity of the La Motte cellar: 6 000 hectolitres

La Motte is not open to the public.

The Huguenot Pierre Joubert, progenitor of the family of that name, owned a number of farms in the Franschhoek valley, one of which he called La Motte d'Aigues, a part of France which had once been his home. He bought the land in 1709 from a German called Hans Heinrich Hattingh who had been granted it in 1695 and used it merely for grazing his cattle. Joubert's widow sold the farm to Jan Hendrik Hop, and he in turn was succeeded by Gabriel du Toit who erected the original house which is incorporated in the present beautiful homestead. Du Toit was a wealthy man, who planted about 20 000 vines on La Motte. Ownership of the property reverted to the Jouberts when Gideon Joubert, great-grandson of Pierre, bought it in 1815, enlarging the homestead and improving the farm during the 43 years he lived there.

In 1897 Cecil Rhodes bought La Motte from his friend, Lewis Lloyd Michell, then chairman of De Beers, and it later became part of Rhodes Fruit Farms. Some thirty years later it once more passed into private ownership. In 1970 the Rupert family bought the farm, and extensively restored the outbuildings and the old homestead, which has been altered from a T-shape to a more spacious H-plan. Noble cultivars, such as Chardonnay, Rhine Riesling, Chenin Blanc, Sauvignon Blanc, Shiraz, Cabernet Sauvignon, Pinot Noir and Merlot were planted over about half of the extensive property, one of the largest in the Franschhoek area. A modern pressing cellar was built in 1985 while the old cellar, suitably converted, continues to be used for maturation purposes.

Dr Anton Rupert's daughter, Hanneli Neethling, and her husband, Paul, live in the gracious homestead. Paul Neethling is manager of the Estate and Jacques Borman is the cellarmaster. This team's first two wines were L'Etiole Légère, a low-alcohol, light wine made from Sauvignon Blanc, and a Blanc de Noir made from Shiraz and Cabernet Sauvignon.

Top quality Cabernet Sauvignon, Pinot Noir and Shiraz are maturing in the Estate's cellars and are scheduled for release late in 1988.

Once owned by Cecil Rhodes, La Motte is now the home of Paul and Hanneli Neethling.

Landskroon

Located on the southern slopes of the Paarlberg, this farm was named by its first owner, Jan Holsmit, a Swede, in 1692. It continued in the hands of a series of Free Burgher farmers throughout the eighteenth century, but in 1872 a subdivision of the property, under the name of Weltevreden, was bought by a member of the De Villiers family which still owns the farm.

They were of Huguenot descent from one Abraham de Villiers who, early in the eighteenth century, had established himself at the Groot Drakenstein farm of Boschendal (see page 217). The family continued to farm there until the onslaught of the phylloxera in the 1880s, when they were forced to sell their two-century-old property, leaving Paul de Villiers, newly established on the slopes of the Paarl mountain, to continue the dynasty.

He soon set about enlarging and consolidating the family's new base, within a few years acquiring the rest of Landskroon farm and further adding to it the neighbouring property of Schoongezicht (not to be confused with the farm of the same name in the Stellenbosch District).

Settled on their substantial piece of land, the new branch of the De Villiers family steadily developed the wine-making side of the farm. These developments in the present century can be traced through a series of De Villiers owners all, with a fine sense of dynastic continuity, named Paul de Villiers – the present owner is the fourth Landskroon patriarch of this name, and the fifth Paul de Villiers has been in charge of the wine making since 1980.

The first Paul de Villiers, of the 1872 vintage, found an area of the farm planted with vines, though there is no record of their type. In the next few years he planted Steen, Cinsaut and Muscadel vines and built a cellar where he made the sweet fortified wines of the type popular at that time. Borne by oxwagon to Cape Town and sold in small wooden casks, these luscious wines fetched good prices both for local consumption and for export.

The second Paul de Villiers brought the farm into the twentieth century and to the period of the inception of the KWV in 1918. From then until 1973, almost all Landskroon wine was sold to the KWV, a system which, with its price controls, protected the farmers against the vagaries

of public taste and secured them adequate return for their produce.

The third Paul de Villiers developed the cultivar side of the farm and, in a period when the bulk of the local wine was white, began producing dry red table wine. He also planted a variety of port wine cultivars, including a number such as Tinta Barocca, Souzão and Tinta Roriz still grown on Landskroon. In this enterprise he was encouraged by the KWV and by Dr Charles Niehaus who, often described as the 'father of the South African sherry industry', was at this time investigating the occurrence in the local vineyards of 'flor' type yeasts, of the kind found in the vineyards of Spain and associated with the making of the traditional 'fino' styles of sherry. Landskroon was among the 18 or so

farms in the Cape where this naturally-occurring yeast was found.

Paul de Villiers senior, together with his brother Hugo, inherited the farm in 1963. Since then they have divided the running of the Estate between them. Part of the property has been developed as a Jersey stud farm and dairy farm (as at nearby Fairview, the animals provide the organic fertilizer for the vineyards). The running of the dairy farm is the responsibility of Hugo, while Paul concentrates on the vineyards and cellar.

In the past two decades the vineyards of Landskroon have seen radical change. The port- and sherry-type cultivars have been retained, but extensive new plantings of high-quality red varieties, such as Cabernet Sauvignon, Pinotage, Pinot Noir

Landskroon Estate

Cultivars Planted	Size of Vineyards (Number of vines)	Training Practice
Cinsaut	256 000	
Pinotage	63 000	
Chenin Blanc	61 800	
Port Varieties	40 000	
Pinot Noir	34 800	
Cabernet Sauvignon	34 000	
Sauvignon Blanc	33 000	
Shiraz	25 000	All cultivars grown
Alicante Bouschet	25 000	untrellised as bush
Pedro	23 000	vines
Merlot	22 500	
Cabernet Franc	20 000	
Other	18 000	
Morio Muscat	10 000	
Pinot Gris	9 000	
Pinot Blanc	8 800	
Palomino	3 000	

Total area under vines in 1987: 250 ha
Irrigation: The vineyards of Landskroon are irrigated.
Temperatures: Records are not kept.
Average annual rainfall: 660 mm
Stock: Rooted vines are purchased from a nursery.
First wine bottled under the Landskroon Estate label: Cinsaut 1974
Wines currently bottled under the Landskroon Estate label: Cinsaut, Chenin Blanc Dry, Bouquet Blanc, Cabernet Sauvignon, Blanc de Noir, Chenin Blanc (semi-sweet), Pinotage, Sauvignon Blanc, Bouquet Rouge, Pinot Noir, Shiraz, Tinta Barocca and Cabernet Franc. A port is also made and bottled on the Estate.
Wood ageing: Wine is aged in wood on the Estate.
Capacity of the Landskroon cellar: 10 500 hectolitres

Landskroon Estate is open to the public on weekdays from 08h00 to 12h30 and from 14h00 to 18h00, and on Saturdays from 08h00 to 12h30. Cheese lunches are served from November to April, between 11h00 and 14h30.

The untrellised Landskroon vineyards on the lower slopes of the Paarlberg.

and Shiraz, have been made. Since 1973 the wines made from these quality cultivars have been progressively bottled under the Estate's own label, though the bulk of the production is still delivered to the KWV. Since 1918 the KWV has used Landskroon port in the blending of its own ports. A limited quantity bottled under the Landskroon label is now sold at two years old for further laying down. This vintage port is made from Tinta Barocca, Cinsaut and Alicante Bouschet.

The majority of Landskroon's vineyards are found on the lower slopes of Paarl mountain. The sun rises behind the granite domes here, so that the farm receives very little early morning warmth and this permits the high-quality grapes to mature slowly – out of a total of 326 hectares of vines, about 75 per cent are of these high-quality varieties.

The new departures of recent years have paid off and the Estate has been a consistent prize winner at the annual wine shows; the 1978 Cabernet Sauvignon won the Championship Wine Trophy at the South African Championship wine show.

When Abraham de Villiers and his two brothers first arrived at the Cape in 1689 on the packetboat *Zion*, they carried a letter from the *Here XVII* recommending their skill in the art of wine making to Governor Simon van der Stel. A prophetic assessment, it has been borne out across three centuries.

La Provence

In 1694, La Provence was granted to the French Huguenot, Pierre Joubert, who came from Provence in south-eastern France. The homestead is one of the most beautiful historic homes in the Franschhoek valley. Its early neo-classical east gable bears the intriguing inscription 'ANNO 1800 D3MD 13D'. The code-like part stands for *de derde maand, den dertiende dag*, the whole inscription meaning 13 March 1800. The building of the homestead was started by Pieter de Villiers in about 1756 and completed by his widow, Elizabeth Anna Kriel. She later married Pieter Joubert, a great-grandson of the original owner of the farm. On 29 September 1969 the homestead was severely damaged by the earthquake which wrought much havoc over large areas of the south-western part of the country, but was faithfully restored by Gabriel Fagan, an architect known particularly for this sort of work.

John Rudd, of Trelew Investments Limited, the company that owns the farm,

La Provence

Cultivars Planted	Size of Vineyards (Number of vines)	Training Practice
Sauvignon Blanc	25 954	
Weisser Riesling	13 876	
Chenin Blanc	13 096	
Chardonnay	5 666	All cultivars are grown on hedge rows
Sémillon	3 000	
Cabernet Sauvignon	1 750	
S.A. Riesling	461	

Total area under vines in 1987: 20 ha
Irrigation: The vineyards of La Provence can be irrigated when neccessary.
Temperatures: Records are not kept.
Average annual rainfall: 834 mm
Stock: Some parent stock is used for grafting; rooted vines are purchased from a nursery.
First wine bottled under the La Provence label: Cuvée Blanche (1985)
Wines currently bottled under the La Provence label: Cuvée Blanche and Blanc Fleuri
Wood ageing: Wine is aged in wood on the farm.

La Provence is open to the public by appointment only on Wednesdays, Fridays and Saturdays from 09h30 to 12h30.

lives in the homestead, and Freddie Steytler, the farm manager, lives in the nearby Jonkershuis. Freddie is a graduate of Stellenbosch University, with a degree in oenology and viticulture. As the farm was formerly owned by his parents, Freddie has an added, and personal, incentive to produce high-quality wines there.

The farm has considerable plantings of Sauvignon Blanc, Weisser Riesling and Chenin Blanc as well as Chardonnay, Sémillon, Cabernet Sauvignon and South African Riesling, 63 800 vines in all. The first wine released was Cuvée Blanche, a dry white blend of predominantly wooded Sémillon (60 per cent) and Sauvignon Blanc and Weisser Riesling (20 per cent

each). The latest release is a dry, unwooded Sauvignon Blanc, called Blanc Fleuri.

At present the harvest of grapes from La Provence is delivered to the Franschhoek Vineyards Co-operative, where the wines are made and bottled, but the cellar on the farm has been restored and equipped with a view to the future production of the wines at La Provence.

Les Chênes

The vineyards of Les Chênes ('The Oaks') are among the highest in the Cape and this, together with the shadow from their mountain backdrop, makes them some of the coolest. These cool conditions make for slow-ripening crops, producing grapes of distinctive character. The vines on the farm are of fair age with most being more than 20 years old and one vineyard of Sémillon is over 80 years old. However, a replanting scheme is in progress including nearly 11 000 Sauvignon Blanc vines planted in a new vineyard high up on very steep slopes which will probably give their fruit even greater character.

Sarel van Vuuren purchased the property in 1983 after successful careers as a mining engineer and an estate agent. Now totally dedicated to wine he has taken to his new occupation with great enthusiasm and, to ensure he learns every aspect of his chosen craft, has personally trellised and pruned his newly-planted Sauvignon Blanc vineyard on its precipitous slope.

Sarel is a participant in the scheme whereby the Franschhoek Vineyards Co-operative makes the wine of certain individual members separately for them (see page 225), and his off-dry Chenin Blanc has been particularly well received.

Les Chênes

Cultivars Planted	Size of Vineyards (Number of vines)	Training Practice
Sauvignon Blanc	10 800	Extended Perold
Weisser Riesling	5 400	trellis
Chenin Blanc	15 000	
Pinotage	2 000	Bush vines
Sémillon	2 000	

Total area under vines in 1987: 7,5 ha
Irrigation: The vineyards of Les Chênes are not irrigated.
Temperatures: Records are not kept.
Average annual rainfall: Approximately 900 mm
Stock: Rooted vines are purchased from a nursery.
Envisaged new cultivar: Chardonnay
First wines bottled under the Les Chênes label: Chenin Blanc, Sémillon and Blanc de Noir (all 1986 vintage)
Wines currently bottled under the Les Chênes label: Chenin Blanc, Sémillon and Blanc de Noir
Wood ageing: Les Chênes wines are aged in wood at the Franschhoek Vineyards Co-operative.

Les Chênes is open to the public by appointment only.

He also sells a Sémillon and a Blanc de Noir.

The 7,5 hectares of vineyards at Les Chênes are planted with Sémillon, Chenin

Blanc, Sauvignon Blanc, Pinotage and Weisser Riesling, and as the older vines are replaced other cultivars, particularly Chardonnay, will be added.

L'Ormarins

Mountains tower behind the particularly beautiful homestead of L'Ormarins. Its perfect proportions and dignified neo-classical gable, dated 1811, are reflected in

a willow-fringed ornamental lake in front of it, which shimmers in the sunlight. This lovely old Huguenot farm was acquired in 1969 by Dr Anton Rupert and is now

owned by his younger son, Anthonij. The farm has been modified for the production of good red wines such as Cabernet Sauvignon, Merlot, Pinot Noir, and Shiraz,

together with white wine cultivars such as Sauvignon Blanc, Rhine Riesling, Chenin Blanc, Chardonnay and Cape Riesling. The wines are made by Anthonij Rupert and Nico Vermeulen and bottling and marketing are done by the Bergkelder from their well-equipped cellar.

Now some 167 hectares of vineyards in extent (it will eventually be expanded to 200), L'Ormarins was initially granted in 1694 to a Huguenot refugee, Jean Roi. It later passed into the ownership of the De Villiers family, one of whom built the oldest surviving structure on the property, a T-shaped dwelling now occupied by a farm manager. The farm's cellar, now used only for storage, dates from 1799, while the H-shaped main house was completed in 1811. In the early years of the nineteenth century L'Ormarins appears to have thrived. By 1825 its then owner, Izaak Jacob Marais, could number an impressive 114 000 vines on his land, and an equally impressive array of prizes in the contemporary wine shows – after the Cape of Good Hope Agricultural Society's show of 1833, for example, he rode home with a prize of 100 rixdollars (for his Cape Madeira) and a silver trophy.

The gracious L'Ormarins homestead, completed in 1811 and now the home of Antonij Rupert, is reflected in the waters of the ornamental lake. Nico Vermeulen (below), who shares the wine-making responsibilities with Antonij Rupert, in the new cellar at L'Ormarins. Completed in 1981, the cellar is one of the most sophisticated of its kind.

L'Ormarins Estate

Cultivars Planted	Size of Vineyards (Hectares)	Training Practice
Sauvignon Blanc	35	
Chardonnay	30	
Cabernet Sauvignon	20	
Cape Riesling	20	
Chenin Blanc	20	
Rhine Riesling	15	
Pinot Gris	10	
Pinot Noir	10	Perold trellises
Merlot	7	
Gewürztraminer	6	
Shiraz	5	
Souzão	3	
Bukettraube	2	
Cabernet Franc	1	
Colombar	1	

Total area under vines in 1987: 167 ha
Irrigation: All L'Ormarins vines are irrigated.
Temperatures: Records are not kept.
Average annual rainfall: Approximately 1 200 – 1 500 mm
First wines bottled under the L'Ormarins Estate label: SA Riesling, Rhine Riesling and Sauvignon Blanc (all 1982)
Wines currently bottled under the L'Ormarins Estate label: Sauvignon Blanc, Franschhoek Riesling, Rhine Riesling, Cabernet Sauvignon, Shiraz, Chardonnay, Rulander (Pinot Gris) and a Noble Late Harvest. All L'Ormarins wines are bottled by the Bergkelder.
Wood ageing: Wines are aged in wood on the Estate.
Capacity of the L'Ormarins cellar: 15 000 hectolitres

L'Ormarins is open to the public on weekdays from 09h00 to 13h00 and from14h00 to 17h00, and on Saturdays from 09h00 to 13h00.

Monis of Paarl

Now part of the Stellenbosch Farmers' Winery Group and a subsidiary of Cape Wine and Distillers, Monis of Paarl was founded in the early years of the century by Roberto Moni, one of three immigrant sons of a prominent Tuscan wine-making and merchandizing family.

Applying their inherited skills in the local context, the brothers began making wine, concentrating in the early years on fortified dessert wines. With experience came innovation. The hot South African summers complicated the making of the delicate noble wines; to overcome this problem Roberto Moni imported large-scale refrigeration equipment from Europe – the first of its kind on the local scene and an important development in the improvement of the Cape wines.

With post-war expansion, Monis took over the Nederburg farm in 1956, with a subsequent shift of emphasis towards the making of the kind of natural wines for which Nederburg was already well known. A new market was opened in 1962 when the company became the first in South Africa successfully to market a *perlé* wine, Capenheimer (now marketed by Stellenbosch Farmers' Winery).

Roberto Moni was quick to appreciate the excellence of fortified wines made at Montagu and he brought them to his own cellar where they were matured and blended. In so doing he established a tremendously popular and high-quality range of sweet fortified wines of which Marsala and Moscato were perhaps the best known.

Moni also began producing *flor* sherry by the traditional Spanish method and today the winery boasts one of the finest private *soleras* in the country.

In recent years Monis have released a series of 'Collectors' Ports' with interesting labels. Some have depicted rare South African stamps, and for the Johannesburg Centenary the labels were sketches of the 'Randlords'. The latest 'Collectors' Port', to commemorate the three hundredth anniversary of the arrival of the Huguenots and the founding of Paarl, is contained in most attractive replicas of a ship's decanter, which cannot tip over.

Monis have always been producers of high-quality grape juice and following the modern trend have entered the growing market for health-giving, natural fruit juices, producing juices such as citrus, apricot, peach and litchi.

A full list of Monis products appears together with others of the Stellenbosch Farmers' Winery Group on page 189.

Mouton-Excelsior

Ben Mouton, a descendant of the Huguenot Jacques Mouton who settled in the Franschhoek valley in 1699, bought the well-known hotel Swiss Farm Excelsior in 1984. The hotel is situated on a farm, where Ben is rapidly reviving and replanting the vineyards, with the intention of producing high-quality wines, mostly red.

His first wines were a Cabernet Sauvignon, a Blanc de Noir and a Sémillon. The attractive labels on the bottles won a Clio award in 1986.

His most recent plantings have been eight hectares each of Chardonnay and Merlot. Other cultivars planted are Sauvignon Blanc, Sémillon, Cabernet Franc, Cabernet Sauvignon and a small quantity of Pinot Noir.

Mouton-Excelsior

Cultivars Planted	Size of Vineyards (Number of Vines)	Training Practice
Chardonnay	18 000	
Merlot	17 000	
Cabernet Sauvignon	16 000	5-wire Perold
Sauvignon Blanc	6 000	trellis
Sémillon	6 000	
Cabernet Franc	6 000	

Total area under vines: 25 ha
Irrigation: Dryland
Average temperature: 17 °C
Average annual rainfall: 800 mm
Stock: Rooted vines are purchased from a nursery.
First wines bottled under Mouton-Excelsior label: Lemoutonne Sémillon and Cabernet Sauvignon (1985)
Wines currently bottled under Mouton-Excelsior label: Lemoutonne Sémillon, Cabernet Sauvignon and Die Binnehof
Wood ageing: Mouton-Excelsior wines are wood-aged in Nevers oak.
Capacity of Mouton-Excelsior cellar: 820 hectolitres

Mouton-Excelsior is open for tours and wine tasting from Tuesdays to Sundays from 09h00 to 18h00.

Nederburg

Situated in the Klein Drakenstein area of the District of Paarl, the land of Nederburg was first granted, relatively late for this area, in 1792. In that year the Dutch East India Company sent out one of its officials, the Commissioner-General Sebastian Nederburgh, to perform one of its periodic checks on the behaviour and probity of its servants at the Cape – though by now the Colony's days as a Dutch possession were numbered. In the course of his stay, he granted a piece of land to a German immigrant named Philip Wolvaart, who gratefully remembered his debt to the Commissioner in the name of his new property.

It was he who in 1800 built the fine Cape Flemish homestead, based on the classic 'inland' ground-plan of an H-shape. Thereafter, the farm continued in the nineteenth century in the hands of a succession of owners, few of whom showed more than a minimal interest in wine farming: indeed, Nederburg remained generally undistinguished until 1937 when, with the advent of a new owner, Johann Graue, the real life of the Estate began.

A German immigrant, he had begun his working life in a prominent German brewery, and by the early 1930s had achieved a secure position as a managing director of the firm. But although his personal security seemed assured, the shadow of uncertainty loomed in the days after the collapse of the Weimar Republic. The coming of Hitler precipitated a choice for Graue and his family; and in particular, he wished to find a secure future for his only son, Arnold.

There were shadows over Europe, but South Africa, a young country, appeared to offer a refuge from the mounting tensions at home and, from the point of view of the Graue family, something more. For notwithstanding the elder Graue's many years in the brewery, both father and son were possessed by the wine-making spirit. For Johann, South Africa appeared the ideal creative opportunity for an ambitious wine maker searching for something new. With its dependable soil and climate, its steady sunshine and mild winters, it offered conditions of stability rarely to be found in the erratic climate of northern Europe.

So for the Graues the acquisition of Nederburg was the start of a great wine-making adventure. Not that the immediate prospects were prepossessing; the farm taken over by the newly-arrived immigrants in 1937, though enchanting in aspect with its beautiful old homestead and its stately setting of mountains, was undeveloped and limited in extent with 93 hectares of ill-tended vines. But fired with a sense of new opportunities, Graue remained undaunted, immediately beginning his first task – planting new vineyards.

To this task he brought a degree of knowledge and thoroughness not always found locally. His motto was simple and direct. 'Good wine', he maintained, 'starts in the vineyards.' He kept the fullest possible records of all plantings made, and of the lineage and performance of every vine on the farm. Setting the highest standards for his vines, he ruthlessly culled those which fell short. At the same time he made a close study of the cultivars themselves, making a number of important discoveries about them. At the time of his purchase of the farm, the vineyards contained limited amounts of Steen, Cape Riesling, Clairette Blanche, Cinsaut and Cabernet Sauvignon; he found, though, that the Cape Riesling, Cinsaut and Steen types varied appreciably from one part of the farm to another. In particular, the Steen was found to exhibit great variation. Graue considered that the Cape Steen was a superior variety and set about selecting and developing it as the basis for a high-quality white wine.

So the foundation of Nederburg's future vineyards was laid during these early years, but little large-scale technical progress was possible during the Second World War. It was only with the end of the war that the Graues began to emerge, not only as vine growers, but as wine makers, and in little short of a spectacular manner.

It was based on an innovation, and a stroke of genius, of Johann's – the perfecting of the process now known as 'cold fermentation', a method which was to revolutionize the whole structure of the South African wine industry.

A wine tasting at the Nederburg cellars.

The solitude of the Nederburg Maturation cellar contrasts sharply with the frenetic activity surrounding the winery at the time of the annual auction of rare Cape wines.

If there is a major fault in the local climate it lies in the high summer temperatures, reaching a peak at harvest time, which , particularly in the case of white wines, can have an adverse effect. The natural reaction of fermentation is speeded up to an alarming degree, to the extent that the high temperature can stop the process altogether. With the knowledge of German white wine making behind him, Graue's instinct told him that only cool conditions, even if artificially created, would give the precision of control in the wine making which he had already obtained in the Nederburg vineyards.

In the exciting years of expansion after the war, Graue and his son developed the technique of cooling with refrigerated water the tanks in which the white wine fermentation took place. The equipment required was installed, and the farm's facilities enlarged and modernized. While the elder Graue concentrated upon these innovations, the son returned to Europe for periods of study at the famous Geisenheim Wine Institute in the Rhineland, at Wadenswiel in Switzerland, and in the Château wineries of Bordeaux; for the Graues had realized that if cold fermentation could help them perfect their white wines, the optimum use of the soils and climate of the Cape could do the same for their reds.

With well-rationalized vineyard procedures and controlled and technically sophisticated methods for the production of both white and red wines, the ground-plan for the future success of Nederburg was laid. In 1951 Arnold returned to South Africa, to be put in charge of the technical control of the winery. A year later, at the 1952 annual Cape Wine Show, the first wines made by the younger Graue achieved recognition with a spectacular array of prizes.

It was a success which appeared to mark the beginning of a fine career, and the consummation of the father's work. The dream, however, was brutally ended, almost at the moment when it had begun: for in September 1953, Arnold was killed when his private aeroplane was involved in a collision with a military training aircraft at Young's Field in Cape Town.

For Johann it was both a personal tragedy and the end of his life's adventure. Though he took control of the winery again for a while, the burden of its rapid expansion soon proved too heavy. Within a few years of his son's death he had merged his company with that of Monis of Paarl. Johann Graue died in April, 1959, a broken man, having withdrawn increasingly from active wine making.

But although his personal life ended in tragedy, his creation and his wine-making ideas have survived him, largely in the person of the man who took over the role of wine master at Nederburg after the death of Arnold Graue, Günter Brözel.

Since his arrival at Nederburg from Germany in 1956, Günter has exploited and developed all the elements inherited from the Graues, building up a broad and varied spectrum of wines, made at a remarkably high level of quality and consistency. The meticulous control of vineyard standards is a part of this quality, as is the extensive and streamlined modern technology of the large Nederburg cellars, including the massive cold fermentation complex for the white wines. Together with these goes a further aspect, based upon a practice originated by the elder Graue, that of blending and using grapes grown in different areas, but well suited to his particular needs.

As the demand for Nederburg wines increased rapidly in the early 1950s,

Günter Brözel of Nederburg, doyen of wine makers in South Africa.

Johann Graue had begun supplying vines for farmers in many different parts of the western Cape to grow grapes in optimum conditions for use in making Nederburg wines. In doing so he maintained the strictest control over quality, taking advantage of the range of different soils and micro-climates available to select the best possible quality of grapes of each specific cultivar. Many of the vines grown by these other farmers came from the Nederburg nurseries. By this method the problems attendant upon making wine from grapes grown on a limited area of land were greatly reduced.

A good deal of Nederburg's wines are still made on this basis, with grape deliveries at harvest time being made from across a wide area from specially selected farms. Günter has remained a creative constant and the dominant figure in the style of Nederburg, but the organization itself has expanded. In 1966, together with Monis of Paarl, it was merged with the massive Stellenbosch Farmers' Winery, which in turn was latterly absorbed into the monolith of the Cape Wine and Distillers Group. The area of land has increased, too, enlarged by a series of acquisitions from Graue's modest 90-odd hectares to the impressive 1 000 hectares of today.

This land has recently become the subject of complex law making. In 1972 the Wine of Origin legislation was introduced, in terms of which individual farms were invited to apply for registration as officially designated Estates. Hitherto, the wines made from the vineyards around the Nederburg winery were incorporated as an integral part of the winery's production. In terms of the new law, however, the conflation of a local with a more widespread operation debarred Nederburg from claiming the status of an Estate – notwithstanding the fact that its cellars were among the most advanced in the country and its wines demonstrably of a superior quality.

The Nederburg concern responded by offering to separate itself, amoeba-like, into two operations, both to be run by

Günter Brözel. The Estate portion of the project was to be renamed Johann Graue, while the bulk of the wines were to continue under the Nederburg label.

To expedite this scheme a number of practical obstacles had to be overcome, chief among them being the problem of keeping the two wine-making operations separate while still under the same roof. Assurances that this could be done secured the go-ahead for the company, which duly produced the first of what was intended to be an extensive range of Johann Graue Estate wines. In the event, however, only six of these superb wines (now collector's items) had in fact appeared before a combination of political problems brought their production to a standstill three years later.

The question of the status of the Johann Graue Estate wines abides. In the meantime, the wine-loving public is more than content with a spectrum of wines from Nederburg which includes many of the country's classics, among them the famous Edelkeur, made with the help of *Botrytis cinerea*, otherwise known as 'noble rot'. In this instance the Nederburg wine makers were granted an indulgence by the Department of Agriculture. Commonly used in the making of natural dessert wines such as Trockenbeerenauslesen in Germany when it occurs on the grapes at harvest time, the mould attacks the fruit, reducing its moisture and greatly increasing the concentration of natural sugar. Thus it enabled a wine with a sugar content of as much as 200 grams a litre to be made – far above the legal limit as it applied at that time. Eventually granted special dispensation, the Nederburg wine makers added this magnificent sweet wine to their collection.

The genius of Günter Brözel was recognized in 1985 when he won the Robert Mondavi Trophy for the International Wine Maker of the Year at the Club Oenologique Internationale Wine and Spirit Competition held in London. He has won the Diners' Club Award on two occasions and was further honoured in 1986 for his outstanding contribution to

Wines made and marketed by Nederburg

Although Nederburg has its own vineyards, the bulk of its commercially available products are made from grapes bought from selected farms in the Paarl and Stellenbosch Districts. Details of the Nederburg vineyards are therefore not given. Cellar tours are available by arrangement.

Red wines: Paarl Cabernet Sauvignon, Edelrood and Baronne
White wines: Paarl Riesling, Rhine Riesling, Premier Grand Crû, Fonternel, Stein, Edeltropfen and Special Late Harvest
Sparkling wines: Premier Cuvée Brut, Cuvée Doux (for export only) and Kap Sekt
Rosé wines: Rosé and Rosé Sec
A Cabernet Blanc de Noir and a Nouvelle Light are also made.

Nederburg 'Private Bin' and Auction wines

Red wines: Cabernet Sauvignon, Shiraz, Pinotage, Private Bin R103 and Private Bin R115
White wines: Private Bin D207, Private Bin D212, Private Bin D229, Private Bin S333, Private Bin S312, Private Bin S311, Private Bin S354, Sauvignon Blanc, Paarl Riesling, Steen, Weisser Riesling, Bukettraube, Chardonnay, Kerner, Muscat de Frontignan, Riesling Late Harvest, Gewürztraminer, Edelkeur, Riesling Edelkeur, Bukettraube Noble Late Harvest, Weisser Riesling Special Late Harvest and Weisser Riesling Noble Late Harvest

Nederburg Limited Vintages

Red wines: Cabernet Sauvignon, Gamay Noir and Pinot Noir
White wines: Sauvignon Blanc, Wood Matured Paarl Riesling, Chenin Blanc, Bukettraube, Gewürztraminer and Steen Noble Late Harvest

the advancement and international recognition of the South African wine industry.

THE NEDERBURG AUCTION

Wine auctions have long been a feature in Europe, at places such as the Hospice de Beaune in France and Kloster Eberbach in Germany. London, too, sees regular auctions of rare wines, conducted by Sothebys, Christies and Bonhams.

On March 8, 1975, the first Nederburg Auction of South African wines was held, and though there had been auctions before, it was the first to draw extensive interest

locally and abroad. Since then, it has been held every year and has become a highlight of winelands' life. Presided over by the elegant figure of the well-known British wine-auctioneer, Patrick Grubb, the event has all the excitement that goes with competitive bidding and high prices. Although the amount of wine sold is less than 0,02 per cent of all wine marketed in South Africa, the return is high.

At the eighth Auction, in March 1982, for example, 4 567 cases (12 bottles in each) were sold at an average price of R161, and 24 half-bottles of Zonnebloem Cabernet 1965 fetched R6 150 – this was the highest price paid for a case of South African wine and works out at about R85 a glass. At the 1986 Auction, the turnover exceeded R1 million and the following year R1,5 million. In the last few years the average number of cases sold at each Auction has been 8 000.

One of those who has helped the Nederburg Auction to become one of the best-known wine auctions in the world is Sue Wardrop, who organized the Auction during the years 1983 to 1987. Sue has studied the management of wine auctions all over the world, attending, among others, those at the Hospice de Beaune and Kloster Eberbach, those held in California, and the famous auctions of London.

Every producer of wine in the country is invited to participate at the Auction and must submit their selection to a panel of judges who, in a blind tasting, select some 35 to 40 of South Africa's best wines to be auctioned alongside those of Nederburg.

Nowadays all the major wholesalers participate, except for the Bergkelder, which runs its own Wine Tender scheme (see page 176). Such names as Bellingham, Bertrams, Boschendal, Douglas Green and Laborie (KWV) are to be found in the Nederburg Auction catalogue. Over 45 Estates, Co-operatives and private cellars have participated to date. At the end of the day's proceedings a number of items are auctioned for charity. At the sixth auction in 1980, a half-bottle of 1791 Constantia wine changed hands in a good cause for R2 500, and in 1982 a Grande Fine Champagne Imperial Cognac of 1811 was purchased by Mr Bennie Goldberg for R16 000.

Mr and Mrs Goldberg have been the biggest buyers over the years and always bid very generously at the charity section. In 1986 they bid R8 500 for 3 bottles of Nederburg port, the only port ever made by Günter Brözel in his more than 30 years of wine making. In 1987 the Goldbergs bid the extremely generous sum of R20 000 for a half-bottle of Constantia, vintage *circa* 1790, donated by the retiring manager of the Auction, Sue Wardrop.

If these good prices spell good publicity both for Nederburg and for the buyers, there are other more important general credits for the Auction. It provides a showcase for the best of the local products as well as offering an incentive to local wine makers to aim for yet higher standards of quality. At the same time, overseas buyers are attracted to the Auction and thus to South Africa, and though they may buy relatively little at the Nederburg event (an average of about 10 per cent of the total), the amount is increasing and their visits help to forge links between the wine makers of the Cape and possible future markets for their wines in Europe and America. They also purchase other wines for export to their home countries while in South Africa, and so all in all the Nederburg Auction has a wider beneficial effect on the South African wine industry than merely the amount of money realised on the day.

Since 1975 the Nederburg Auction has been the premier event in the South African wine calendar, when several thousand guests, including dignitaries and journalists, gather to enjoy both the business and the fare. Here the auctioneer, Patrick Grubb (right), discusses a wine with David Hughes.

A bottle of grape juice accompanies the serious business of bidding at the Nederburg Auction.

Perdeberg Co-operative

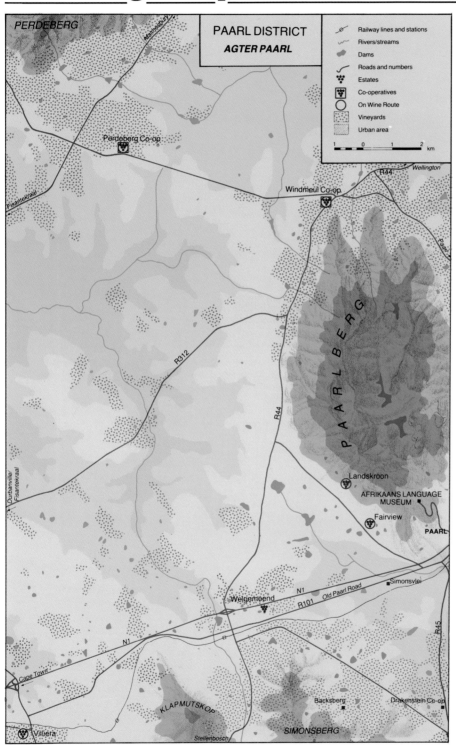

On 22 August 1941 a meeting was held in the vicinity of the Perdeberg (the *perde* (horses) were the zebra which once roamed the area) on the farm Vryguns, which belonged to Jan Rossouw. As a result of this meeting the Perdeberg Wine Farmers' Co-operative was formed, under the chairmanship of S.F. Dreyer. Jan Rossouw sold two hectares of Vryguns at a nominal price to provide the land on which to build a cellar, and, in 1942, it was ready to receive its first intake of 1 322 tonnes of grapes.

Pieter Dreyer, the chairman's brother, became the wine maker, while Jan Rossouw's brother, D.J. Rossouw, was manager. The functions of manager and wine maker were combined by the time Joseph Huskisson joined the Co-operative in 1956.

Joseph has had the privilege of working with experienced and respected wine makers. After finishing his schooling at the Paarl Gymnasium, he worked at Nederburg, where he trained under Arnold Graue for five years. In early 1956 he moved to the Bolandse Co-operative, where he gained the invaluable experience of handling large volumes of grapes. In November 1956 he joined the Perdeberg Co-operative.

Joseph Huskisson's dedication to quality has made Perdeberg a regular trophy and prize winner at the Cape Young Wine show. The Co-operative receives grapes from 55 member farmers, processing 14 000 tonnes annually. Only a small amount of its wine is bottled for the public, as most of the production is sold to merchants for blending into their better wines.

Perdeberg Co-operative

Wines bottled and marketed by the Perdeberg Co-operative

Red wines: Pinotage and Cinsaut
White wines: Chenin Blanc, Chenin Blanc Dry, Riesling, Late Vintage, Colombar and Muscat d'Alexandrie

A dessert wine, Cinsaut Liqueur, is also bottled and marketed by the Perdeberg Co-operative.

The Co-operative is open to the public on weekdays from 08h00 to 12h30 and from 14h00 to 17h00.

Simonsvlei Co-operative Wine Cellar

Formerly the domain of wine maker 'Oom Sarel' Rossouw, the Simonsvlei Co-operative was established in 1945. On hand as a young wine maker to supervise that first load, Sarel presided over every subsequent vintage at Simonsvlei for almost 40 years. He officially retired in 1981 but stayed on as administrator, with one of his sons, Johan, in charge of the cellar.

During his time with Simonsvlei, Sarel was not only mentor for many emerging wine makers, but was also the inspiration for a range of distinguished wines, including the Simonsvlei Cabernet Sauvignon of 1973, the first co-operative-made wine to receive Superior certification. Simonsvlei was also the first Co-operative to participate at the Nederburg Auction. Sarel's long career

received due recognition in 1981 when he was nominated 'Champion Wine Maker of the Year'; in fact Sarel has won 126 trophies in all at South African champion wine shows.

Kobus Rossouw took over from Johan at the end of 1985 and with his very first vintage became champion wine maker for the Paarl region, thus upholding the family's tradition, the Co-operative's prestige and the company's motto – 'Only the best'.

The cellar gathers about 17 000 tonnes of grapes grown in a wide area, stretching from the cool Wemmershoek and Klein Drakenstein, along Paarl and the Simonsberg to the gravel soil of Muldersvlei. As a result, Simonsvlei is able to produce quality wines of a wide variety year after year.

Simonsvlei Co-operative

Wines bottled and marketed by the Simonsvlei Co-operative

Red wines: Cabernet Sauvignon, Shiraz, Pinotage, Claret and Cinsaut
White wines: Riesling, Dry Steen, Chenin Blanc, Bukettraube, Grand Crû, Selected Dry White, Late Vintage, Rhine Riesling, Stein and Special Late Harvest

Three house wines are available (bottled, with screw-top caps): a Semi-Sweet White (Stein), a Grand Crû and a Blended Red (Claret).

A Rosé and a Red and a White Hanepoot are also made.

On the Paarl Wine Way, the cellar is open on weekdays from 08h30 to 12h30 and from 14h30 to 17h00; and on Saturdays from 08h30 to 12h00.

Simonsvlei Co-operative, where the wine makers have always been Rossouws.

Union Wine Limited

The Wellington-based firm of Union Wine Limited was established on 10 April 1946 in Graaff-Reinet by a group of farmers and businessmen headed by Mr J.C. van Rensburg. Its original name was Union Wine and Spirit Corporation. The first company on the platteland to be granted a listing on the Johannesburg Stock Exchange, it operated numerous outlets, both hotels and bottle stores. It soon developed into a flourishing concern and in 1956 the head office was moved from

Graaff-Reinet to Oudtshoorn, its headquarters for the next 15 years.

In 1966 Robertson Distillers utilized their considerable shareholding in Oude Meester Cellars to take over the control of Union Wine. Jan Pickard, who would later play a leading part in the development and growth of the company, was appointed chairman. Several more depots were opened, with Oudtshoorn the central distribution point, and more hotels and bottle stores were also acquired.

In 1967 the Germiston depot was opened to serve the Witwatersrand and with the acquisition of Stag Breweries in mid-1968, a strong distribution network in the Transvaal was established.

A further acquisition was that of Culemborg Wineries (Pty) Limited of Wellington, which already marketed the famous Bellingham range of wines, and on 1 January 1972 the head office of the greatly enlarged company was moved from Oudtshoorn to Wellington, to establish

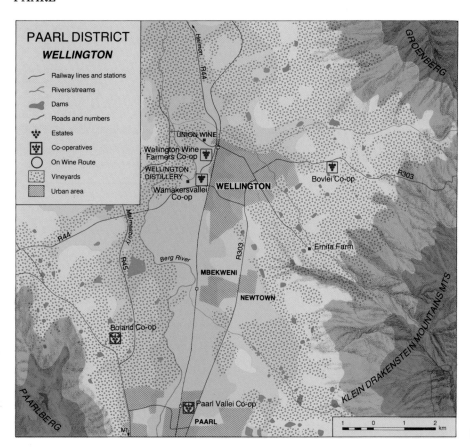

Wines distributed by Union Wine Limited

Culemborg Range

Red wines: Pinotage, Claret and Claret Light
White wines: Bijoux Blanc, Colombard, Grand Crû, Stein, Late Harvest, and Crystal Blanc Sec
The following dessert wines are also included in the range: Red and White Muscadel, Red and White Hanepoot and Soet Hanepoot.

Bellingham Range

Red wines: Cabernet Sauvignon, Pinotage and Shiraz
White wines: Bukettraube, Classic Thirteen, Grand Trinité, Johannisberger, Premier Grand Crû, Rhine Riesling, Riesling, Sauvignon Blanc, Special Late Harvest, Stein and Vin Gris
Rosé wines: Almeida Rosé and Rosé Sec
Sparkling wines: Premier Brut
A Blanc de Noir is also included in the range.

Other wines distributed by Union Wine include Golden Pride, Summerstein and Grand Provence.

closer ties and communication with the wine industry generally and the primary producers in particular. In 1973 another company, Picardi Hotels Limited, was formed, to control and administer the retail operations. Union Wine purchased a further 75 retail licences during 1979, thereby increasing the total to 97.

Today Union Wine Limited is one of the bigger liquor-producing companies, with bottling plants and branches throughout

the country, marketing products such as the Bellingham range of wines, Culemborg wines, Private Stock Brandy, Long John Whisky, and various liqueurs and sherries. The company is one of the few independents left in the industry, a status of which they are very proud and which has resulted in a fierce rivalry with the two opposition 'giants'. Selected cultivars best suited to the Franschhoek area are grown on the Bellingham Estate for marketing

under the Bellingham label, but the bulk of the total wine requirements is purchased from various farms throughout the Cape and blended in the company's own cellars. The appointment of Johan Schreuder to take charge of production in 1982 has introduced a new era of innovative wines of good quality, which are enthusiastically and energetically marketed by Henry Kempen and his team. (See also Bellingham Estate, page 215.)

Villiera

In 1975 Helmut Ratz, owner of an entertainment complex in Kärnten in Austria, arrived in South Africa accompanied by an experienced viticulturalist, Josef Krammer, with the object of purchasing a local wine farm from which they could make and export wine to Austria. After reviewing a number of possibilities in the Stellenbosch and Paarl

areas and making a close analysis of the soil and conditions, they finally chose the Estate of Villiera on the Stellenbosch side of the road to Paarl.

Once owned by the De Villiers family, from whom it took its name, it had hardly featured as a wine farm. There were no vineyards on the land at the time of purchase, but its sandy, deep-draining

soils promised well for the shy-bearing cultivars such as Cabernet Sauvignon, Merlot, Shiraz, Sauvignon Blanc, Gewürztraminer and Weisser Riesling, which Josef Krammer planted. At the same time the old Villiera cellar was modernized and redesigned, and a reception room and tasting parlour added.

Early in 1983, Helmut sold the thriving

Villiera Estate

Cultivars Planted	Size of Vineyards (Hectares)	Training Practice
Chenin Blanc	50,31	Bush vines, Perold and 3-wire vertical trellises
Cinsaut	9,50	Bush vines and one-wire trellis
Cabernet Sauvignon	12,17	
Sauvignon Blanc	10,74	
Pinot Noir	10,14	
Rhine Riesling	5,10	
Merlot	4,25	
Muscat Ottonel	3,67	3-wire vertical trellis
Gamay Noir	3,00	
Chardonnay	2,00	
Hárslevelü	1,50	
Morio Muscat	1,30	
Müller-Thurgau	1,00	
Gewürztraminer	4,20	
Shiraz	1,13	Perold trellis

Total area under vines in 1987: 120,2 ha
Irrigation: The vineyards of Villiera are irrigated when necessary.
Temperatures: Records are not kept.
Average annual rainfall: 750 mm
Stock: Rooted vines are purchased from a nursery.
Envisaged new cultivar: Cabernet Franc
First wines bottled under the Villiera Estate label: Steen and Dry Red (both in 1976)
Wines currently bottled under the Villiera Estate label: Operette, Sonnet, Gavotte (Blanc de Noir), Cabernet Sauvignon, Crû Monro, Crû Monro Blanc, Sauvignon Blanc, Rhine Riesling, Garonne (Special Late Harvest) and Tradition de Charles de Fére
Wood ageing: Wine is aged in wood on the Estate.
Capacity of the Villiera cellar: 8 000 hectolitres

Villiera is open to the public on weekdays from 08h30 to 17h00, and on Saturdays from 08h30 to 13h00. Terrace lunches are served from November until Easter.

Shaking the yeast down into the neck of each bottle of Tradition de Charles de Fere *is a daily activity for Villiera's cellarmaster, Jeff Grier.*

Estate to the Grier family, who owned a large poultry business. The enterprise is now run by Jeffrey Grier, as cellarmaster, and his cousin, Simon, who is the manager responsible for viticulture. In 1984 the family met Jean-Louis Denois, son of a champagne producer near Epernay. This association resulted in 'Tradition de Charles de Fere', a sparkling wine produced at Villiera by the *méthode champenoise* under the guidance of Jean-Louis.

To complement its wines, Villiera offers visitors free tastings and the opportunity to appreciate the culinary expertise of Cathy Grier, who was trained in London by Prue Leith. In summer, light luncheons are served on the terrace under the oaks.

Wamakersvallei Co-operative Winery

Wamakersvallei was originally known as Limietvallei, at one time an outpost of the Cape settlement. With the arrival of the French in the area in 1688 the name changed to 'Val du Charron', later translated by the Dutch to 'Wamakersvallei', meaning 'wagon maker's valley'. Whether wagons were ever made here is uncertain, but there is

no doubt that one of the first farms in the area belonged to a blacksmith, and it is not unlikely that he repaired wagons.

The Wamakersvallei Co-operative was formed by a number of discontented farmers, whose grape production was limited, as their main production was other types of fruit. They were not members of the long-established Bovlei or

Wellington Co-operatives and so delivered their grapes to the Sedgwick Wellington Distillery. Their discontent arose from the distillery's delayed handling of their produce – a delivery could take up an entire day.

In 1941 two farmers, by the names of Peterson and Jordaan, rallied together 45 others to form a co-operative winery and elected its first board of directors. A semi-constructed cellar was purchased and, once complete, it was ready to receive its first crop of approximately 2 000 tonnes in 1942.

Nowadays more than 10 000 tonnes of grapes, from 70 members, are pressed annually under the capable supervision of Chris Roux, who has been wine maker since 1975. The bulk of the wine is sold to the trade, only a small amount being retained for the members of the Co-operative.

Wamakersvallei Co-operative

Wines bottled and marketed by the Wamakersvallei Co-operative

Red wines: Pinotage
White wines: Premier Grand Crû, Late Vintage
  A Hanepoot Jerepigo is also made.

The Co-operative is open to the public on weekdays from 08h00 to 12h30 and from 14h00 to 17h30.

Welgemeend

Welgemeend Estate

Cultivars Planted	Size of Vineyards (Number of vines)	Training Practice
Cabernet Sauvignon	19 500	3-wire vertical trellis and bush vines
Merlot	11 500	
Grenache	3 400	Bush vines
Shiraz	2 800	
Pinotage	800	
Sauvignon Blanc*	400	
Cabernet Franc	6 500	3-wire vertical trellis
Malbec	1 700	
Petit Verdot	1 000	

*Sauvignon Blanc is for home consumption only.

Total area under vines in 1987: 13,5 ha
Irrigation: The vineyards of Welgemeend are not irrigated, although vertical spraying facilities and a catchment dam can be used during extra dry periods.
Temperatures: Average maximum 18 °C; average minimum 12 °C
Average annual rainfall: Approximately 585 mm
Stock: Parent stock is used for grafting; rooted vines are also purchased from a nursery.
First wines bottled under the Welgemeend Estate label: Amadé and Welgemeend (both 1979)
Wines currently bottled under the Welgemeend Estate label: Welgemeend, Amadé, Cabernet Sauvignon and Douelle
Wood ageing: Wine is aged in wood on the Estate.
Capacity of the Welgemeend cellar: 400 hectolitres

Welgemeend is open to the public on Saturday mornings from 09h30 to 12h00.

A 'cake' of pressed grape skins is removed from an old basket press at Welgemeend, where the owner and vigneron, Billy Hofmeyr (top), makes fine wines in the tradition of Bordeaux.

On the site where the Jan van Riebeeck High School in Cape Town now stands was once situated the last working vineyard within the city's boundaries. Its name was Welgemeend, it belonged to the Hofmeyr family, and when the well-known wine connoisseur and writer, W.A. (Billy) Hofmeyr, finally realized a life-long ambition of buying a wine farm of his own, this was the name he gave it.

The farm at Klapmuts which he chose in 1974, then named Monte Video, soon showed the imprint of his personal taste. A passionate aficionado of the noble wines of Bordeaux, he set about reorganizing the Estate's vineyards according to the traditional plantings in certain wine producing regions of France, the first of the South African Estates to do so. To this end he replaced the straggly and neglected

Hanepoot, Steen and Cinsaut vines with Cabernet Sauvignon, Cabernet Franc, Merlot, Petit Verdot, and Malbec, the cultivars that more often than not are those blended to make the elegant Clarets of Bordeaux. These plantings were later supplemented with Pinotage, Grenache and Shiraz. Some of the vines on Welgemeend are not trellised and this combined with soil type and no irrigation produces a low yield by South African standards. But this is by design, for Billy wants quality rather than quantity, and intends to limit his production to a very low six tonnes per hectare, as is the practice in Bordeaux. His present production is five and a half tonnes per hectare, as some 15 per cent of his vines are not fully mature, and he only uses grapes from vines which are at least seven years old.

During the replanting of his vineyards

Billy also devoted considerable energy and ingenuity to the task of putting together a wine-making cellar for his modest 16-hectare property. Equipment for the cellar came from a variety of sources, including the rubbish dump from which one item was rescued.

Some of his equipment may have been second-hand, but his enthusiasm was in mint condition. In 1979 it bore fruit in the first two wines produced on the Estate, the one being the appropriately named 'Welgemeend' and the other Amadé. Welgemeend is a classic Bordeaux blend of Cabernet Sauvignon, Merlot and Cabernet Franc. Amadé, akin to the Rhône wines, is a blend of Grenache, Shiraz and Pinotage, in the ratio of 5:4:1. Two later wines have been added to the range, a pure Cabernet Sauvignon and Douelle, a blend of equal proportions of Malbec and Cabernet Sauvignon.

Billy and his wife, Ursula, who is both farm and cellar manager, are a formidable team and with each successive vintage their wines have developed more of the character they are striving for.

Wellington
WYNBOERE CO-OPERATIVE

Founded in 1906, this Co-operative lost ground in its early years, to be formally re-established by a committee of 12 local farmers in 1934. Since then the membership has increased to 37 growers whose produce is made into good-quality wines by the wine maker, Gert Boerssen.

In the earlier years the Co-operative's entire production was delivered to merchants, but nowadays a proportion is bottled for sale to the public. On average over 10 000 tonnes are crushed annually, with the bulk made up of Steen and Cinsaut. Noble cultivars are becoming more important with a Cabernet being bottled from the 1984 vintage.

Wellington Co-operative

Wines bottled and marketed by the Wellington Co-operative

Red wines: Cinsaut
White wines: Chenin Blanc, Riesling, Stein, Late Harvest and Special Late Harvest
    A Hanepoot Jerepigo is also made.

Wellington Co-operative is open to the public on weekdays from 08h00 to 12h30 and from 14h00 to 17h00.

Windmeul CO-OPERATIVE WINE CELLARS

During the 1880s there were some 27 mills in the Paarl area, but only one of them was a windmill, situated at Agter Paarl. In 1927 the mill was broken down to a height of three metres, a roof constructed over the circular base and the building used as a farm store room. It still stands today, and one of the old mill stones can be found at the local primary school.

In 1944 a group of export table-grape farmers wanted to form a co-operative winery, in order to make use of those grapes not suitable for table use. They were unable to provide the minimum requirement of 1 500 tonnes needed to form a co-operative, and so several wine grape growers were invited to join in their venture. On 4 September 1944 the Windmeul Co-operative was registered and its 23 members undertook to deliver 1 700 tonnes of grapes. In 1946 the first crop was pressed in the newly-completed cellar.

By 1953 the Co-operative had established depots at Hopefield and Vredenberg to sell their bottled products. These depots were closed ten years later, however, when the control of the cellar changed from the table grape growers to a new board of predominantly wine farmers, heralding a change in style of management. After the closing of the depots, the production was sold to the wholesale merchants.

Another result of the new management was the appointment of the present wine maker at Windmeul, German-born Bernhard Lüttich. Among the innovations he introduced were an automatic off-loading system, a modern crusher, and juice separators. A novel cooling system for the fermentation and settling tanks was also introduced, the only one of its kind in South Africa, designed jointly by Lüttich, Dieter Thielhelm of the Stellenbosch Farmers' Winery, and Günter Brözel, a director of Windmeul.

In the late 1970s the Co-operative returned to the practice of bottling some of its prime production for sale to the public, but again this was stopped in 1984. At the time of this book going to press, the cellar is considering the reintroduction of bottling for sales to the public.

The rondavel in this vineyard is actually the base of the windmill which once stood on the farm Roelanda, and gave this winery its name.

SWARTLAND

The first mention of *Het Swartland* occurs in a report made in Willem Adriaan van der Stel's journal on August 26, 1701, which described a skirmish that had taken place four days earlier between a party of soldiers, led by Corporal Daniel Taus, of the Riebeek Kasteel outpost, and a group of Bushmen. It is a moot point why the land was thus called, for the soil in the areas is not black, but an explanation may be that the name is derived from the colour of the indigenous vegetation, which appears almost black at certain times of the year.

Whatever the source of the name, the land itself, open and undulating, proved fertile. For most of its history the district has been used for large-scale wheat farming, and this continues to be its main crop. As a wine-producing area the region is comparatively new, with the biggest expansion having taken place in the last decade and a half, concentrated mainly in the southern areas of Malmesbury, Darling and Riebeek.

The Swartland District is bounded on the south by the Durbanville and Paarl regions, on the east by the Berg River, and on the west by the Atlantic Ocean, whose cool breezes modify many of the micro-climates in the area. The generally low-lying landscape is interrupted by mountains at Perdeberg, Riebeek West and Riebeek Kasteel, and between Darling and Mamre.

The predominant soil type is Malmesbury Shale. Isolated granitic patches occur, while the soils in the south originate from Table Mountain Sandstone. Vineyards are cultivated on all three soil types, on deep Hutton and Clovelly as well as sandy Fernwood and Kroonstad forms. The low pH soils are deep ploughed, with lime and phosphate added to the subsoil.

Apart from the cool Saldanha area near the sea, this is a hot region and the rainfall is marginal, the average annual supply varying between approximately 450 and 600 millimetres, but with a low annual average of 242 millimetres in the vicinity of Malmesbury. The average summer temperatures range from 19,5 to 21 °C, depending on location.

Grown mostly in dry land conditions, the predominant cultivars include Palomino, Steen, Sémillon, Cinsaut, False Pedro, Clairette Blanche and port varieties.

SWARTLAND DISTRICT

Cape Town

The steadings and vineyards of Allesverloren, the sole wine Estate in the Swartland, at the foot of the Kasteelberg.

Allesverloren

Situated at the foot of the Kasteelberg between Riebeek Kasteel and Riebeek West, this Estate is now the property and the wine-making domain of Fanie Malan, a specialist in red table wine making.

Originally granted in 1704 by Willem Adriaan van der Stel to a widow named Cloete, the farm acquired its unusual name during the eighteenth century, when one of its owners returned from a church visit to Stellenbosch to find that his property had been wiped out in a Bushman raid, his cattle stolen and his buildings razed. The event received its bleak commemoration in the new name for the farm: 'All is lost'.

Daniel Francois Malan, the first of his family to farm at Allesverloren, arrived from the Wellington district in 1870. He found a farm where all was far from lost: 700 fertile hectares of wheatland rolled down from the Kasteelberg, whose summit gathered welcome rainclouds when the lower land lay dry. By this time there were already a few vineyards established on the

farm, and he made wine from these vines for local consumption in the wheatlands. His main claim to fame, however, was posthumous and lay outside the realm of the wine farmer: his elder son, also Daniel François Malan, took the long road from the farm to become a Minister of the Dutch Reformed Church, a Member of Parliament and the first Nationalist Prime Minister in 1948.

It was left to his younger son, Stephanus, to take over Allesverloren in 1904. He introduced a few new vines, but did little to develop the land beyond its traditional rôle as a wheat farm. In 1945 it was inherited by his two sons, who divided it between them, the elder, Daniel Francois, receiving the half on which the old homestead stood.

It was he who made Allesverloren into a wine farm. On his 500 hectares of land he set out to develop a red port and, assisted by advice and encouragement from Professor Theron and the Department of Viticulture at Stellenbosch University, he introduced a range of suitable cultivars.

Over a decade he established varieties which included Tinta Barocca, Malvasia Rey, Muscadel, Shiraz, Souzão and Tinta Roriz.

A clear identity for the farm had been created, and recognition of Daniel Malan's achievement came with prizes for his port wines in the mid-1950s – the Cape Wine Show trophy for the best port wine went to Allesverloren in both 1956 and 1957.

In 1961 family history was repeated when Daniel sold the farm to his two sons who divided it between them. The elder, who is the present wine maker of Allesverloren, Fanie Malan, chose the area with the homestead, while the younger Gerard took the larger but less promising sector.

The post-war years had seen changes in the market and in the demand for port wines. In the early 1960s port simply fell out of fashion. On his 200 hectares Fanie then concentrated on red wine production and extensive new plantings, mostly of red wine cultivars, took place. Some port

Fanie Malan, owner and wine maker of Allesverloren.

Allesverloren Estate

Cultivars Planted	Size of Vineyards (Number of vines)	Training Practice
Cabernet Sauvignon	100 000	
Sauvignon Blanc	60 000	
Tinta Barocca	57 000	
Pinot Gris	30 000	
Souzão	30 000	
Chenin Blanc	21 000	4-wire vertical
Chardonnay	20 000	trellis
Muscadel	20 000	
Merlot	10 000	
Ruby Cabernet	10 000	
Alicante Bouschet	7 000	
Pontac	4 000	

Total area under vines in 1987: 180 ha
Irrigation: The vineyards of Allesverloren are not irrigated.
Temperatures: Average maximum 28 °C; average minimum 10 °C
Average annual rainfall: 460 mm
Stock: About 50 per cent of the parent stock is used for grafting and rooted vines are purchased from a nursery.
First wines bottled under the Allesverloren Estate label: Tinta Barocca 1972 and Cabernet Sauvignon 1974
Wines currently bottled under the Allesverloren Estate label: Swartland Rood, Tinta Barocca, Cabernet Sauvignon and Shiraz. A port is also made. All Allesverloren wines are bottled by the Bergkelder.
Wood ageing: Wines are aged in wood at the Bergkelder.
Capacity of the Allesverloren cellar: 12 000 hectolitres

Visits to the Estate can be made only by appointment through the Bergkelder.

varieties, though, particularly Tinta Barocca, were retained. These port cultivars impart a unique character to the Allesverloren red wines in which they are used. Fanie's famous Swartland Rood, for example, is a blend of Shiraz, Cabernet Sauvignon and the port cultivar, Souzão. Three separate wines are made from each cultivar, matured separately and only then blended to make Swartland Rood.

In general the Swartland is hot and dry. Stretching down the slopes of the Kasteelberg, and with an altitude differential of more than 170 metres (from 130 to 300 metres above sea-level), however, Allesverloren has to cope with varying soils and micro-climates. Soils range from sandy alluvial loam to clay, and to other mixtures of clay and sand, with a pebbly, gravelly structure throughout. Rainfall also varies, with a difference of 200 millimetres a year between the upper and lower reaches of the mountain. This double set of variables of soil and climate necessitates care in the planning of vineyards and in the choice of cultivars. At a distance of 50 kilometres from the coast and therefore with little benefit from a cooling sea-breeze, with fertile soil and a mountain rainfall, the grapes here can reach a high sugar content of 30 ° Balling at harvest time.

Besides developing the vineyards and experimenting with new cultivars, Fanie Malan has made innovations in the cellar technology of Allesverloren.

The high quality of Allesverloren's red wines has been attested with the award of several Superior classifications over the years. At the 1985 South African Wine Show, Allesverloren Port was judged the champion fortified wine, and in the same year Fanie won the trophy as the champion Estate wine maker at the Stellenbosch wine show. At present all five of Allesverloren's wines, four natural wines and a port, are marketed under the Estate's label by the Bergkelder.

Mamreweg
CO-OPERATIVE

Situated near Darling in the west of the Swartland District, this Co-operative presses 13 000 tonnes of grapes each year from 50 member farmers within the newly delimited wine-making ward of Groenekloof. Established in 1948 under its first wine maker, Mr P.D. du Toit, the Mamreweg Co-operative is now run by its present wine maker and manager, Jan Neethling. Under his direction the winery has developed a number of quality wines, including a fine Cinsaut which carried off the championship trophy for Cinsaut at the Cape Championship Wine Show four times in the space of a decade.

Notwithstanding the success of the Cinsaut, the emphasis at Mamreweg is on white wines.

Mamreweg Co-operative

Wines bottled and marketed by the Mamreweg Co-operative

Red wines: Cinsaut, Pinotage, Tinta Barocca and Groenekloof Origin Claret
White wines: Groenekloof Chenin Blanc, Steinwyn, Grand Crû, Late Harvest and Blanc de Noir

The Mamreweg Co-operative is open to the public on weekdays from 09h00 to 12h30 and from 13h30 to 17h30.

Riebeek WINE FARMERS' CO-OPERATIVE

The name of Pieter Cruythoff, who on February 4, 1661, was the first white man to reach Riebeek Kasteel, was for many years commemorated on the wine labels of this Co-operative, founded in 1941, and now under the direction of wine maker Sias du Toit. With a healthy membership of 70 farmers with vineyards between Riebeek West and Malmesbury, the winery produces a range of wines under its own label. The Co-operative's wines are bottled by the Stellenbosse Bottelerings-koöperasie Beperk.

Because of the rather sparse population of wineries in the District, Swartland wines are included in the Stellenbosch Young Wine Show where Riebeek Co-operative has, over the years, been regularly successful. They were also trophy winners in 1986 for their Blanc de Noir at the South African Championship Show.

Riebeek Co-operative

Wines made and marketed by the Riebeek Co-operative

Red wines: Cabernet Sauvignon, Pinotage and Shiraz
White wines: Colombard, Chenin Blanc, Cape Riesling, Weisser Riesling, Premier Grand Crû, Late Harvest and Special Late Harvest

A Blanc de Noir, a Hanepoot Jerepigo, a Red Jerepigo and a Port are also made and marketed by the Riebeek Co-operative.

The Co-operative is open on weekdays from 07h30 to 12h30, and from 13h30 to 17h30.

Swartland Co-operative Winery

The award of a second prize at the 1972 International Wine Show in Budapest for a 1969 vintage Pinotage made by the Swartland Co-operative Winery first brought this cellar to public attention. But it had already been established for some 24 years: in April 1948 a group of 15 farmers in the Malmesbury area assembled at the old Malmesbury 'bioscope' to vote for the formation of the new winery. A month later a Board of Directors was elected, and the Co-operative was duly registered.

Four hectares of land were donated by the Chairman, Mr P.L. Loubser, taken from his farm, Doornkuil, three kilometres

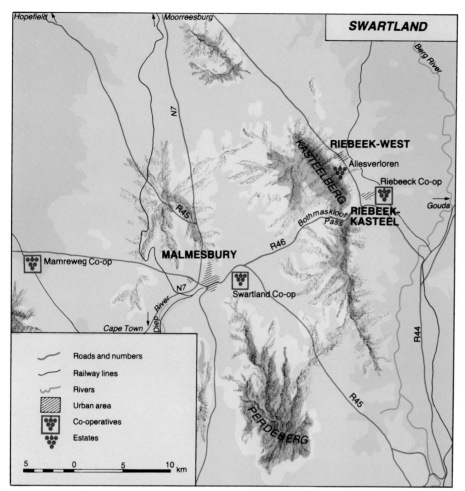

outside the town of Malmesbury. By 1950, when the winery's cellars were completed, the membership had grown to 48 farmers, who supplied 2 500 tonnes of grapes in the first year alone. The bulk of the wine made was white, with an emphasis upon Palomino, but including substantial quantities of Steen, Sémillon, and False Pedro. The red wine contribution in those early days was restricted to Cinsaut.

Since then the Swartland Co-operative has grown to almost double its original membership. At present 85 growers deliver some 20 000 tonnes of grapes at vintage time to the modern and streamlined wine-making plant which includes heat fermentation, or thermo-vinification, equipment to aid colour extraction in the making of increasing amounts of red wine.

This fairly hot, dry region with a low annual average rainfall of 500 millimetres falling mainly in the winter produces grapes high in sugar content. The Swartland winery's range includes a variety of sweet and semi-sweet, rich and full-bodied wines, both white and red – much of the red is supplied in bulk to the KWV, which uses it in the making of their export Roodeberg.

The first manager and wine maker was Nico Botha who held the post for over 30 years. He was assisted latterly as wine maker by Albie van Vuuren, who has now succeeded him as manager.

As the Swartland is included under Stellenbosch for the Young Wine Shows, the Co-operatives of the area compete with a great number of wineries at these shows and competition is stiff. It is no mean feat, therefore, to be the champion cellar. Swartland achieved that accolade twice, in 1985 and 1986. In 1986 it obtained no fewer than 10 gold medals at the South African Championship Young Wine Show.

The Co-operative sells a large range of 'good-value-for-money' wines and bottles considerable quantities for various retailers as 'own labels' and 'no-name brands'.

The Swartland is well respected for its wines, but is probably better known as one of the most extensive wheat-farming areas in South Africa. Albie van Vuuren (right) is manager of the Swartland Co-operative.

Swartland Co-operative

Wines bottled and marketed by the Swartland Co-operative

Red wines: Pinotage, Cinsaut, Dry Red, Tinta Barocca and Shiraz
White wines: Steen, Chenin Blanc, Late Vintage, Premier Grand Crû, Colombard, Select White, Special Late Harvest, Bukettraube, Grand Vin Blanc, Furmint, Blanc de Blanc, Hárslevelü and Riesling
   Fortified wines bottled by the Swartland Co-operative are: Red and White Jerepiko, Hanepoot and a Port.

The Swartland Co-operative is open to the public on weekdays from 08h00 to 13h00 and from14h00 to 17h00.

PIKETBERG

The first exploration of the area now known as Piketberg came about through a curious mercantile fantasy entertained by Jan van Riebeeck. During the fifteenth and sixteenth centuries Portuguese traders had established links with the legendary kingdom of Monomotapa, founded and expanded by kings Mutota and Matope to cover most of what is now southern Zimbabwe. The lure of the fabled gold of Monomotapa appears to have unsettled the otherwise sober mind of the Cape's first Commander, and in February, 1659, after what he referred to as 'protracted exhortation', he prevailed upon 'seven adventurers' to volunteer for an expedition to the realms of Monomotapa. The leader of this projected two thousand-kilometre hike was one Christiaan Janssen. His feelings on that February morning when he and his six fellows set out to intrude on the land of the Bushmen (the San), the Hottentots (the Khoi), the Kaapmans and the Chainouquas, can only be conjectured. At all events, whatever enthusiasm the party had mustered for their Commander's dream lasted no more than a hundred kilometres' march, and faded on the banks of the Great Berg River. They turned and trudged back to the Fort.

Van Riebeeck was not daunted. In 1660 he mounted a further expedition, this time under Jan Danckaert, which crossed the Swartland to ford the Great Berg River at Sonquasdrift, and penetrate the region now known as the Vier-en-Twintig Riviere. They made little advance on the earlier party's attempts to gather the gold of Africa, but left a description of this sun-baked land. It thronged with a variety of game, including rhinoceros, hippopotamus, lion and many kinds of buck. The land itself was reported as being 'fairly good soil for agriculture'.

In the next century this soil became tilled and settled. Much of the land was given over to wheat and fruit, but by the turn of the eighteenth century vineyards were also established in the region. The German physician and naturalist, Lichtenstein, in the course of a tour with the Commissioner-General, Jacob de Mist, in 1802, provided a brief but sharply focussed account of farming in the Vier-en-Twintig Riviere area. 'Wine, lemons, sweet-oranges and dried fruits,' he reported, 'are the principal produce of this place, as well as of the fertile district of the four and twenty rivers.' Of the farm Gelukwaard, which belonged to a farmer named Leiste, he wrote: 'The wine here is particularly good, and Mr Leiste has for some years turned his attention exceedingly to the culture of the vine, and the best mode of improving it; though he is well aware that to introduce the European manner of cultivating vines under the idea of improvement would probably be committing a great mistake. The best manner of cultivating them must indeed everywhere be principally dictated by the nature of the climate; the most important object here is to keep them clean from weeds, and in this the cultivators seldom fail. The three principal objects for obtaining good wine, plenty of slaves, ample buildings and stores of casks, are possessed by most of the colonists. Excellent Cape Madeira, and the Cape Pontac, as it is called, are the sorts which succeed best on this side of the country; the fine sweet Cape-wine is not so good here as to the east of Table Mountain.'

In spite of Lichtenstein's encouraging words, the Piketberg area, which covers the region between the Great Berg River to the south, the mountains of the Vier-en-Twintig Riviere on the east, and the Atlantic to the west, remains largely given over to wheat growing. Its modern vineyards are concentrated in the Piketberg and Porterville areas, as well as that of the Vier-en-Twintig Riviere. Here the soils are mostly deep and sandy with only a minimal production potential, and are normally ploughed to a depth of only about 500 millimetres before planting. Temperatures are high and the rainfall low, and intensive irrigation is needed in most vineyards. The average summer temperature is 21 to 22 °C, causing the grapes to ripen early. Rainfall across the whole district averages a meagre 175 millimetres a year, though it rises to 500 millimetres near the mountains.

Porterville
CO-OPERATIVE CELLAR COMPANY

Porterville Co-operative

Wines bottled and marketed by the Porterville Co-operative

Red wines: Pinotage
White wines: Premier Grand Crû, Blanc de Blanc, Sauvignon Blanc and Late Vintage
Fortified wines: Goue Hanepoot Jeropiko

The Co-operative is open to the public on weekdays from 08h30 to 13h00 and from 14h00 to 17h00, and on Saturdays from 08h30 to 12h00.

As the only co-operative winery in the Piketberg District, the Porterville cellars receive virtually the entire annual grape crop of the district. With a current membership of 120 farmers, mainly in the Porterville and Piketberg areas, it processes an impressive 13 500 tonnes a year, under the direction of its manager and wine maker, Klaas de Jongh, who is assisted by Bunny Rossouw.

Established in 1941, the Porterville Co-operative now concentrates mainly upon Chenin Blanc, Colombar and Sauvignon Blanc; improvements in quality in recent years have been reflected in a number of awards, including three gold medals at the South African Championship Wine Show. Only a fraction of the Co-operative's produce is bottled for sale to the public, the bulk being sold to the merchants.

TULBAGH

On a hot afternoon in February, 1658, a group of men reached the top of a mountain pass and looked down into the valley below. Of the 15 under Sergeant Jan van Herwaarden who had left the Fort at the Cape several days earlier, the majority had turned back, discouraged by dysentery (of which two of the party were to die before the end of the journey), the intense heat and no sign of cattle for which to barter. But Pieter Potter, the surveyor commissioned by Van Riebeeck to map and record the journey, and five others including two Hottentots (Khoi), had struggled on to the top of the steep pass. And there a magnificent view met their eyes.

It was an enormous rocky basin, completely enclosed by great mountains. In the distance a river threaded through the floor of the valley. But Potter was not impressed. He had expected to find verdant pastures like those of the Table Mountain area. But here in the shimmering midday heat the valley looked dry and infertile, in spite of the many trees along the river and in the kloofs of the mountains. Moreover, it appeared to be completely uninhabited. Seeing no sign of the Hottentots from whom they hoped to barter cattle, the party turned back and started on their homeward journey.

Potter and his companions were the first white men to look down into the Tulbagh basin, a vast mountain cul-de-sac enclosed on the north by the Winterhoek range, on the east by that of the Witzenberg, and on the west by the Oukloof and Elandskloof mountains, divided by the Roodezand pass up which Potter had climbed. The river he had glimpsed flows out of the valley to meet the Berg and was appropriately if unimaginatively named the Klein Berg River, the major source of water for the farms that lie in the valley today.

If Potter came, saw, and retreated, the next important visitor to the valley some 40 years later showed a more constructive interest in its possibilities. In November, 1699, Willem Adriaan van der Stel, the newly-arrived Governor of the Colony, eager to set his mark upon the rapidly expanding community, set out almost immediately after his arrival on a tour of inspection of the Stellenbosch and Drakenstein areas. By this time scattered farms had been established as far as what is now the Wellington area. Having inspected the already settled farming areas and searching for more land for allocation to the incoming flow of colonists, he moved on to explore further and on a cool, early summer's day he and his party broke through the narrow defile where the Klein Berg River leaves the valley of Tulbagh.

Impressed with his discovery, he celebrated it in gubernatorial fashion, by giving names to several of its outstanding landmarks. The great range of mountains to the east was to be called the Witzenberg, in honour of Nicolaas Witzen, burgermaster of Amsterdam. In contrast,

TULBAGH DISTRICT

Cape Town

The great basin of Het Land van Waveren, *the Tulbagh Valley, where many of South Africa's finest white wines are made.*

the range to the west over which he had just climbed became the Obiqua mountains: for they were a haunt of the Bushmen, and *obiqua*, meaning 'robbers', was what the Hottentots commonly called them. The valley itself he called 'The Land of Waveren', in honour of a well-known family of that name in Amsterdam.

Within a year or so the first pioneers were breaking the stony earth of the valley – at this stage, and for many years to come,

the land was used mainly for grazing sheep and cattle. The first farms here were on loan from the Dutch East India Company, but by 1720 eight had been granted freehold – four to Dutch settlers, and four to French Huguenots.

In 1743 a small church, described as 'a very humble and simple edifice', was built. Between it and its *pastorie* a row of about a dozen small houses was strung out, occupied mainly by traders and handicraft

workers who appeared to earn a solidly comfortable living from 40-odd families which had settled here by the end of the eighteenth century.

It is uncertain when wine making was first introduced to the valley. Given the climate and soil, as with the earlier established wine-making areas of Stellenbosch and Paarl, the vines must have made a natural complement to the wheat crop, particularly in stony areas where the wheat was hard to establish. No doubt the quantities made were small because of the difficulties of transportation to markets outside the valley, and most of it must have been consumed locally. Primitive stills made their appearance at this time, too, their rough brandy not only providing consolation at the end of a hard day in the sun but being used for medicinal purposes as well.

By the turn of the nineteenth century the 'Land of Waveren' had become a stable if not affluent community. It had also gained a measure of administrative independence, given official form in 1804 when the Commissioner-General issued a proclamation formally cutting the valley off from the Stellenbosch district and establishing it with a name and an identity of its own. The name he chose was that of an earlier and much-respected Governor, Ryk Tulbagh. From now on the valley would have charge of its own affairs, obviating the necessity for the long journey to Stellenbosch for such legal matters as powers of attorney, contracts and wills. In particular, it meant that the perpetual arguments over land, boundaries and water-rights which are apt to preoccupy farming communities could now take place on home ground.

The seat of the law in Tulbagh was the Drostdy, or local Magistrate's Court. In a piece of benign eccentricity the newly-established ward contrived to erect its new drostdy a full half-hour's walk from the village – perhaps in the hope that the walk would cool the citizens' ardour for litigation!

Self-sufficient and largely self-supporting, the valley passed quietly and unobtrusively into the twentieth century, with only an occasional tremor in the smooth passage of its years. One tremor, however, made the headlines. On September 29, 1969, the mountains spoke to the people of Tulbagh. In a matter of a few minutes, the greatest earthquake in recorded South African history split the old sun-baked village asunder. Hardly a house in the area was unaffected, while many, particularly in the oldest area of the main thoroughfare of Church Street, were brought to the ground.

The story of the rebuilding and restoration of Tulbagh is well known. Supervised by the architect, Gabriël Fagan, the reconstruction included the

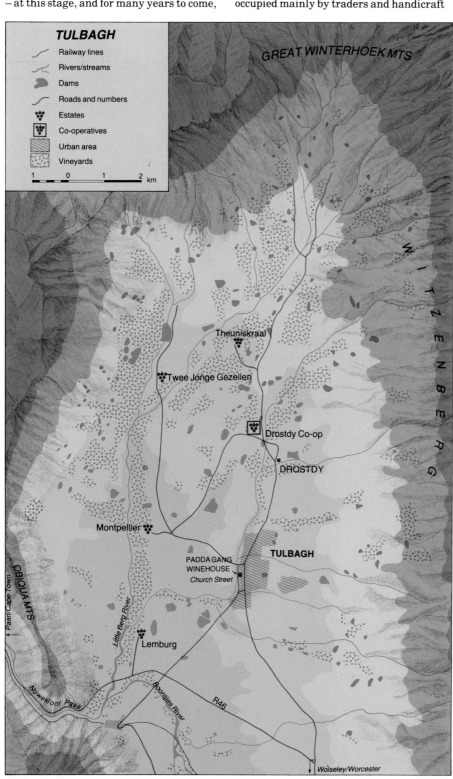

TULBAGH

Railway lines
Rivers/streams
Dams
Roads and numbers
Estates
Co-operatives
Urban area
Vineyards

1   0   1   2
km

GREAT WINTERHOEK MTS

WITZENBERG

Theuniskraal

Twee Jonge Gezellen

Drostdy Co-op

DROSTDY

Montpellier

TULBAGH

PADDA GANG WINEHOUSE
Church Street

Lemburg

OBIQUA MTS

Paarl/Cape Town

Little Berg River

Nuwekloof Pass

Boontjies River

R46

Wolseley/Worcester

incorporation of reinforcements as a guarantee against further tremors. With many of its houses now declared National Monuments, Tulbagh has been preserved as one of the most enchanting of the surviving early Cape villages and one which has remained almost entirely free of the encroachments of industrial civilization.

Much of the wheat-growing land of the early farmers has been taken over for fruit farming, but the most profitable form of agriculture is now wine farming, with an emphasis upon white wines. Compared with other wine-making Districts, Tulbagh is small – at present there are only four producing Estate farms and two Co-operatives in the area. Included with Paarl in the Boberg region, it is also the first of the true 'inland' areas: that is, the

generally mountainous areas at a remove from the cooling influence of the wind from the sea.

The soils of Tulbagh Valley vary considerably. Along the river banks, deep sand and loose stone cover a clay subsoil: an unpromising-sounding combination but one which has in fact proved generally fertile. The soils most represented are the low pH Hutton forms against the lower slopes, which require intensive additions of lime during soil preparation. The soils of the higher slopes also vary considerably, with mountain clay from a depth of one to as much as 2,5 metres, providing a seepage which acts as a natural, laid-on irrigation. The drawback of these mountain soils, and one which applies to much of the valley as a whole, is that the slopes carry more stone than soil, and the making of a vineyard

requires a preliminary removal of tonnes of stone – on one site vines were planted in earth which was still intractable after 30 000 tonnes of stone had been removed from ten hectares of land.

Within the district there are numerous micro-climates, represented by the different altitudes of the farming land. Temperatures vary greatly between winter and summer: those of summer range from an average 19 °C in the Winterhoek to 21 °C in the Wolseley area, while the winters are cold, with recurrent frost and snow on the higher mountains for up to two months of the year. Rainfall also varies from 750 millimetres in the Winterhoek to 450 millimetres in the Wolseley area, necessitating supplementary irrigation – mainly from the Klein Berg River – on most vineyards during the dry summers.

The Drostdy
CO-OPERATIVE WINE CELLAR

On April 30, 1906, a meeting took place at the old Drostdy outside the village of Tulbagh. A small gathering of six worried local wine farmers was convened under the leadership of Sir Meiring Beck, then Resident at the Drostdy. The subjects under discussion were the problems caused by over-production, the lack of marketing opportunities, and the generally chaotic state of the Cape wine industry as a whole.

At the conclusion of the meeting it was proposed that a co-operative wine cellar be built in the valley – Beck had been much impressed by the success of the co-operative system in Europe. The proposal was further approved in principle on May 14, when it was decided to erect a cellar which could handle an initial 500 to 1 000 tonnes of grapes a year. The basic function of the cellar was to receive grapes, process them, and sell the resultant natural wine to wholesalers. On July 17 the first Board of Directors was chosen, with Mr G. Euvrard, who had donated the property on which the Co-operative's cellar was to be built, as Chairman.

The building was completed, and the first crop of grapes taken in. The first wine to be sold was the 1907 vintage, for which E.K. Green and Company's offer of £5 5s a leaguer was accepted by the Directors. By 1908 the grape crop delivered to the cellar

had increased to 650 tonnes. In the same year a three-year contract with the merchants was signed and the company appointed Frank Myburgh, at the salary of £200 a year, as the Co-operative's wine maker. Within a few years his Witzenberg range of wines had become a feature of the cellar's produce.

In spite of the improved quality of the wine the times were difficult. In 1909 the Co-operative's members received no more than £1 10s for a tonne of grapes. By 1921 the situation had deteriorated to the extent that members were obliged to pay in their harvest. And in 1923, with no ready market for their produce, it was decided to let all the wine of the 1922 harvest drain away.

Against odds, the Drostdy Co-operative survived. In 1924 the Directors decided to market the Witzenberg wines themselves; the shareholders signed a bank security, and Mr P.F. Theron offered all his assets as security for the Co-operative's debts. At the same time a considerable sum was spent on advertising.

By 1928 a slow recovery had begun. The Drostdy cellars were by then supplying exports to England which later were extended to Sweden. In 1933 the KWV asked the Drostdy to produce Witzenberg wines for them for export to America,

having secured permission to trade under the name.

The Drostdy's first sparkling wine, known as Winterhoek, was being marketed by 1937. The outbreak of the Second World War, however, brought new problems for the exporters with a lack of shipping space and a premium on bottles – indeed, while the bottle shortage lasted, permission was granted to sell Witzenberg wines in tomato sauce bottles! In the 1940s, the Co-operative's range was enlarged to include sherry, liqueurs and brandy.

Drostdy Co-operative

Wines bottled and marketed by the Drostdy Co-operative

Red wine: Dry Red
White wines: Late Harvest, Grand Crû, Colombar and Riesling
A Blanc de Noir, a Red Jerepigo, a Hanepoot and a Port are also made and bottled by the Drostdy Co-operative.

The Co-operative is open to the public on weekdays from 08h00 to 12h30 and from 13h30 to 17h30, and on Saturdays from 08h30 to 12h00.

The maturation cellar at the Drostdy, the oldest co-operative winery in South Africa.

In 1964 the Distillers Corporation took over the marketing of the Co-operative's Witzenberg wines and their Drostdy sherry range. Today the co-operative cellar has 123 members, delivering some 14 000 tonnes of grapes annually to be made into wine under the supervision of the wine maker and manager, Jassie Coetzee, a legendary veteran of the winelands.

The original magistrate's office of the Drostdy is now used as the head office of the nearby wine cellar. In return, the Co-operative has undertaken to maintain the building, furnishing it as a museum with some fine eighteenth- and nineteenth-century antiques. In this tranquil enclave under the mountains the past and the present are in productive partnership.

Lemberg

In the Klein Berg River valley, at the foot of the Witzenberg, Winterhoek and Obiqua mountains, the Cape's smallest Estate, Lemberg, is the property of Jan and Janey Muller. In particular, its vineyards and cellar are the culmination of the life's ambition of Janey Muller, a rare case in South Africa of a woman wine maker responsible for the creation of her own style of wine.

Born and brought up in Cape Town, Janey Provan accompanied her father on wine-hunting tours of the Stellenbosch area after the opening of the first Wine Route there in the early 1970s. A passion for wine was kindled, together with a determination to become personally involved in its making. To this end while still in Standard Seven she sat down and fired off letters to all the farmers on the Wine Route, asking to be allowed to work on a farm during her school holidays, both to learn wine farming and to sharpen up her Afrikaans. A single encouraging answer to her pleas came from Attie Joubert of Koelenhof farm; he visited Janey's parents and arranged for her to work on his farm during the holidays until she matriculated.

During the next few years, at every opportunity, she worked at Koelenhof, gaining invaluable early experience 'from soil to glass'. At the same time it became clear that without a farming background formal academic weapons would be needed to fight her way into the winelands. She therefore enrolled for a four-year course under Professor Joël van Wyk at the University of Stellenbosch, eventually obtaining her BSc (Agric), majoring in viticulture, oenology and micro-biology.

The developments in this period were not all academic: while working as a tour guide with a local firm of bus-tour operators during her first university vacation she met a young law student named Jan Muller, a fellow Capetonian who was doing the same job. They were married in 1977 after Jan's graduation, by which time he had caught the infection of Janey's enthusiasm for her calling. Soon they began to look around for a small and inexpensive property to start a wine farm.

In late 1978 the Mullers bought a modest 13-hectare farm in the Tulbagh Valley. Then called Vergelegen, the Mullers changed the name to Lemberg, the German name for the Ukrainian town from which Jan's maternal family had emigrated to South Africa.

To gather extra experience and capital the couple worked in a variety of other places while taking their new farm in hand, in particular at Le Bonheur, where Jan learned much of the practice of viticulture from Le Bonheur's owner, Michael Woodhead. It was at Le Bonheur, too, that Janey met Gert van der Merwe of the Stellenbosch Estate of Lievland (see page 165). Gert was in search of a wine maker to be employed on an *ad hoc* basis; soon Janey found herself commuting wine maker between two Estates, her own and Lievland. At the same time, with increasing knowledge and confidence, Jan took on the running of the viticultural side of the Lemberg enterprise.

The Mullers, aware of the limitation in size of their land, have concentrated their efforts on the planting of high quality cultivars. Old blocks of Palomino, Cinsaut and Kanaan were cleared away, the soil was enriched with lime, and the land planted with Sauvignon Blanc and Hárslevelü, the latter being a Hungarian cultivar little known in South Africa but a vigorous grower and well suited to the low-lying terrain of Lemberg. Rootstocks have also been planted onto which the Mullers intend to graft Chardonnay.

Jan and Janey have been inspired by the traditional wine-making philosophy of the Old World, modelling Lemberg on the small chateau vineyards of Bordeaux and the 'boutique' vineyards of California. They feel that small ventures are at a distinct advantage, as the vintner can become more personally involved in the vineyard and its wines.

Traditional methods are employed in the care of the vineyards. Only natural fertilizers are used and the vineyards are never irrigated. By means of careful training and pruning, the crop yield is restricted to less than 40 hectolitres per hectare, allowing the grapes to ripen without stress and to reach optimum quality.

By South African standards the cellar at Lemberg is very small. It is fully equipped, however, with new stainless steel wine tanks and additional oak barriques, and a watchful eye has been cast upon it by Professor Chris Theron, now retired to his ancestral Tulbagh Valley, but still much involved in wine and its ways. Lemberg also boasts a tasting room for use by its patrons, and Christo Coetzee's original paintings of the Hommage label are on display there. (The Mullers decided to

Lemberg Estate		
Cultivars Planted	**Size of Vineyards** (Hectares)	**Training Practice**
Sauvignon Blanc	2	
Hárslevelü	2	4-wire vertical trellis
Chardonnay	1	

Total area under vines in 1987: 5 ha
Irrigation: The vineyards of Lemberg are not irrigated.
Temperatures: Records are not kept.
Rainfall: 500-550 mm
Stock: Vines propagated from parent stock.
Envisaged new cultivar: Pinot Noir
First wine bottled under the Lemberg Estate label: Sauvignon Blanc 1983
Wines currently bottled under the Lemberg Estate label: Lemberg Aimee (formerly Sauvignon Blanc), Vinum Arum, Hommage and Lemberg (formerly Hárslevelü)
Wood ageing: Wines are aged in wood on the Estate.
Capacity of the Lemberg cellar: 300 hectolitres

The Estate is open to the public by appointment only.

Lemberg, the smallest Estate, 'boasts' the smallest wine cellar in South Africa (above). This miniature winery, though, is fully equipped with stainless steel tanks and oak barriques, and in it Janey Muller (left) practices the art of making fine wines. She learned her wine making techniques from Attie Joubert at Koelenhof (the farm, not the Co-operative), from Professor Joël van Wyk at Stellenbosch University and from Michael Woodhead at Le Bonheur, and honed these skills at Lievland Estate and at Lemberg.

declare 1986 a 'vintage' year and to commemorate the limited supply of Sauvignon Blanc by naming it 'Hommage' and by commissioning the Tulbagh artist to create a special label, depicting the interrelation between wine and wood.)

With the help and encouragement of many people, coupled with a tenacity of purpose, the Mullers have found a small but secure place for themselves in the future of the winelands, and their wines have already acquired a loyal following.

Montpellier

The white wines in which this Estate specializes are now made in collaboration by two brothers, Jan and Hendrik Theron. Hendrik is in charge of the Montpellier vineyards and Jan responsible for the cellar operation. The modern history and development of Montpellier were largely the creation of the late De Wet Theron, father of the present wine makers.

The origins of Montpellier reach back from the thriving present of the Theron family to the early years of Tulbagh's history, and to the grant of a modest 50 morgen of fertile alluvial soil on the banks of the Klein Berg River. It was the first deed issued by the Landdrost of Drakenstein in 1714, signed by the then Governor of the Cape, Maurits Pasques de Chavonnes, and made to a Huguenot immigrant named Jean Joubert. A refugee from the Languedoc town of Montpellier, his birthplace, he named his new farm after it, and there built the first simple homestead, a three-room mud brick dwelling with a main room, a kitchen and a bedroom.

During the early years the farm was used exclusively for grazing cattle. Joubert

himself appears to have died without issue, for thereafter it passed into the hands of a widow, Susanna Gardé, who ran it till her death in 1771. In 1778 it was acquired by the first of the Theron family, Jan Theron, who enlarged and modified the house, adding the fine *holbol* gable, dated 1790.

During the nineteenth century, Montpellier saw a succession of different owners, who did not change its basic stock-farming character but expanded its grazing land to cover a substantial proportion of the valley – the extent of the present 600 hectares. In the early 1880s Montpellier again, and this time finally, became the property of the Theron family. The three brothers, Hendrik, Jan and Gawie Theron, bought it jointly and in 1884, De Wet Theron's grandfather, Hendrik, bought out his brothers to become sole owner.

The first making of wine at Montpellier dates from the last years of the nineteenth century. It was then that the original vineyards were laid out, from which modest leaguers of wine were made in 1926. But although a certain amount of wine, mostly from Sémillon, Cape Riesling

and Cinsaut grapes, was made prior to the Second World War, both the farm and its produce lacked distinction.

It was this quality which De Wet Theron sought to achieve when he inherited Montpellier in 1945. From the start he made radical changes in the structure of the farm, the most important being its conversion to the exclusive making of white wine. The old Cinsaut vines were uprooted and replaced with good white varieties. And, realizing that the commitment to white wine making would require a concomitant technology, he set about improving his cellar conditions and methods.

The crucial problem in this period before the introduction of cold fermentation was that of controlling the rate of white wine fermentation during the hot summers. Under the direction of cellar master Karl Werner, a system of cold fermentation was introduced and later modified to allow for fermentation in the absence of oxygen. Accent was also placed upon the careful choice of the right yeast cultures for specific wines.

The result of these innovations was a

Montpellier Estate

Cultivars Planted	Size of Vineyards (Hectares)	Training Practice
Chenin Blanc	23,26	
Weisser Riesling	20,05	
Colombar	14,61	
Sauvignon Blanc	8,71	
Clairette Blanche	8,66	
Hárslevelü	6,92	3-wire vertical
Roter Traminer	5,82	trellis
Bukettraube	5,15	
Cape Riesling	5,10	
Pinot Noir	4,04	
Pinot Gris	3,34	
Pinot Blanc	1,00	

Total area under vines in 1987: 110,46 ha
Irrigation: All Montpellier vineyards are irrigated.
Temperatures: Records are not kept.
Average annual rainfall: Records are not kept.
Stock: Parent stock used for grafting.
First wines bottled under the Montpellier Estate label: Riesling 1967 and Traminer 1971
Wines currently bottled under the Montpellier Estate label: Suzanne Gardé, Tuinwingerd, Weisser Riesling (1982 vintage) and Weisser Riesling Extra Dry
Wood ageing: Not practised.
Capacity of the Montpellier cellar: 7 000 hectolitres

Montpellier is not open to the public.

The late De Wet Theron of Montpellier.

spectacular improvement in the quality of the Montpellier wines, and in December, 1967, the first Montpellier white wine, a Cape Riesling, was made. Bottled and labelled by hand, this initial 1 000 bottles of Riesling was kept as an experimental product – as were the wines made in the following three vintages.

In 1968 Werner, having launched the new style of cellar technology on the Estate, went back to Geisenheim, and in the years since his departure the Therons have steadily confirmed the reputation of their fine white wines. In 1973 two Montpellier wines, the Montpellier Riesling and the Montpellier Gewürztraminer, were the first of their kinds to receive Superior classification from the Wine and Spirit Board.

The development of the cellar had been accompanied by attention to detail in many others areas. The Theron family has continued to improve the vineyards,

introducing new clones to enhance quality, among them clones of Chenin Blanc, and Rhine Riesling, which De Wet christened Tuinwingerd Riesling.

With the purchase of 17 adjoining properties over the years, Montpellier has grown to almost 600 hectares, of which 110 are devoted to vineyards. Harvested in 20-kilogram plastic lug-boxes to prevent undue crushing of the grapes, they are made into specific varietal wines and rarely blended – a central tenet of De Wet's code as a wine maker for he felt that blending leads to standardization of wines.

In the smooth progress of improvement of Montpellier wines only the year of the earthquake marked a hiatus. The September night which shook the valley brought down in ruins the beautiful old Cape Dutch homestead, built of the friable local mud-brick. Given the choice of rebuilding the homestead or of erecting a

new building, De Wet Theron elected to restore the first Jan Theron's ancestral home. The result is witness to the passion for good workmanship and fine finish which are themselves the hallmark of the Montpellier white wines.

In recent times Jan and Hendrik have decided not to seek certification of their wines. The very wines to which Montpellier owes its reputation, the cultivar wines, have now disappeared from its range, and have been replaced by wines such as Huiswyn, Dry White, Blanc de Blanc and Tuinwingerd. Use is being made of the names of former owners of the property: for instance Suzanne Gardé, the Estate's Blanc de Noir, has been named after the widow, Susanna Gardé, who owned the farm in the late 1700s. This is necessary as a wine which is not certified may not actually be called a Blanc de Noir, even if made in the usual Blanc de Noir manner.

Romansrivier

In the immediate post-Second World War years the rapid expansion of the wine industry in the Breede River area led to a heavy congestion at harvest time at the KWV depot in Worcester – farmers were allowed only two days in 14 on which to deliver their grapes. The founding of the Romansrivier Co-operative grew out of response to this crisis, and was initiated by two local farmers, H.F. Conradie and D.J. Viljoen. The winery was built in 1949 and the first crop, some 4 000 tonnes, delivered by the 18 founder members, was pressed in 1950.

Romansrivier Co-operative was, under the guidance of Monis of Paarl, one of the early users of cold fermentation and its wines were much sought after by wine merchants. The present wine maker is Olla Olivier who joined the Co-operative in

1974. Most of the wine produced at Romansrivier, made from an annual intake of about 12 000 tonnes of grapes received from 66 members, is sold in bulk to merchants. Although only part of the crop is bottled, the Co-operative provides an extensive range of products: some 20 different wines are bottled annually.

Olla Olivier's wines have an admirable record at young wine shows; his Colombar, in particular, is often white wine champion at the Worcester show and gold medal winner at the National show at Goodwood. Olla's success can be attributed partly to his excellent rapport with the farmers, as well as to his knowledge of their vineyards, enabling him to advise the farmers to harvest the grapes in exactly the condition he requires, providing the raw material he needs to produce his champion wines.

Romansrivier Co-operative

Wines bottled and marketed by the Romansrivier Co-operative

Red wines: Cabernet and Vino Rood
White wines: Riesling, Dry Colombard, Off-Dry Colombard, Colombard Late Harvest, Vin Blanc Special Reserve, Premier Grand Crû, Chenin Blanc, Stein, Late Harvest, Special Late Harvest, Dry Blanc de Noir, Off-Dry Blanc de Noir, Sauvignon Blanc and Off-Dry White

A Rosé and two fortified wines, a Port and a Hanepoot Soet, are also bottled and marketed by the Co-operative.

Romansrivier Co-operative is open to the public on weekdays from 08h30 to 12h00 and from 13h30 to 17h00, and on Saturdays from 08h30 to 10h00.

Theuniskraal

Kobus and Rennie Jordaan make the wine on this Estate at the northern end of the Tulbagh Valley between the twin shadows of the Obiqua and Witzenberg mountains. Since 1964, when they took over the

running of the farm, these two brothers have introduced cultivars such as Sémillon, Steen and Gewürztraminer. The one for which the Estate is famous, however, remains the Cape Riesling

introduced by their father, Andries Jordaan, in the late 1940s. It was with this Theuniskraal Riesling that the elder Jordaan achieved one of the great moments of local wine making with the

Kobus Jordaan (above) and his brother Rennie share the wine-making responsibility at Theuniskraal.

Theuniskraal Estate

Cultivars Planted	Size of Vineyards (Hectares)	Training Practice
Cape Riesling	40	
Steen	32	
Sauvignon Blanc	17	
Sémillon*	12	
Gewürztraminer	10	
Weisser Riesling	10	4-wire vertical trellising
Bukettraube	8	
Colombar	8	
Muscat Ottonel	6	
Pinot Gris	4	
Hárslevelü	3	

*Some Sémillon vineyards are 50 years old.

Total area under vines in 1987: 150 ha
Irrigation: The vineyards of Theuniskraal are irrigated.
Temperatures: Records are not kept.
Average annual rainfall: 750 – 1 000 mm
Stock: Parent stock is used for grafting; rooted vines are purchased from a nursery.
First wine bottled under the Theuniskraal Estate label: Riesling (about 1947)
Wines currently bottled under the Theuniskraal Estate label: Riesling, Sémillon and Gewürztraminer. All Theuniskraal wines are bottled by the Bergkelder.
Wood ageing: Wines are aged in wood at the Bergkelder.
Capacity of the Theuniskraal cellar: 14 000 hectolitres

Theuniskraal is open to the public by appointment only.

award of a gold medal at the Commonwealth Wine Show in 1950. This achievement was all the more striking in that Jordaan was a first-generation wine maker, with little or no knowledge of the craft before his mother's purchase of the farm in 1927.

Up till then, Theuniskraal's wine-making record had been generally undistinguished. First granted in 1714 to a Huguenot named Jacques Theron, it subsequently became part of the large property of La Rhône, which then covered a considerable area of the valley. After a number of intermediary owners, the farm came into the hands of a further scion of the abundant Theron family in 1818, by which time it had acquired its present name. Grapes were grown during the nineteenth century, but it was only in 1905 that a winery was built on the property.

The Jordaan family came from the Hex River Valley, where they had grown table grapes. Mrs Jordaan's intention in buying Theuniskraal was to launch her son on a wine-making career, for the Tulbagh Valley was already well known for its good white wines. When they moved onto their new farm the Jordaans found it planted with White French, Green Grape – now identified as Sémillon – and Cape Riesling. The young Jordaan's efforts to make wine from these crops were not at first a success. These were the years before the advent of cold fermentation, and although the problems of uncontrolled fermentation in white wines were recognized, as yet no viable solution had been found. It was at this point that the struggling wine maker received much assistance from Frank Myburgh of the Drostdy Co-operative, under whose expert guidance he made the farm's first blended wine. Named simply 'Theuniskraal', it was a sweet and delicate

blend of White French, Green Grape and Cape Riesling. It was an immediate success. But the wine which was to put the seal on this success was the Theuniskraal Riesling, a wine which, since its introduction in 1948, has remained the centre-piece of the farm's production.

The land at Theuniskraal is generally extremely stony but much of the soil is alluvial, fertile and well-drained. The present generation of Jordaans, Kobus and Rennie, use irrigation to balance the effects of the drainage and to boost production of their range of new white cultivars. These include Colombar, Pinot Gris, Hárslevelü and Bukettraube, as well as the spicy Gewürztraminer, with its elusive fragrance.

The three main wines made are Theuniskraal Riesling, Sémillon and Gewürztraminer. They are bottled and marketed in collaboration with the Bergkelder.

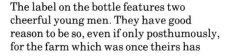

Twee Jonge Gezellen

The label on the bottle features two cheerful young men. They have good reason to be so, even if only posthumously, for the farm which was once theirs has

given them a little retrospective if anonymous immortality. The name of Twee Jonge Gezellen has become synonymous with the making of the finest

white wines, ranging from the famous Grand Prix 'TJ 39' to Schanderl.

Notwithstanding the presence of the two eighteenth-century bachelors on the label, the identity of these wines is very much bound up with the emergence of a modern wine-making family in the Tulbagh Valley – the Krones, currently represented in the Twee Jonge Gezellen vineyards and cellar by N.C. Krone and his son, Nicky. While the son has developed into a fine wine maker in his own right, the structure and style of the Estate has been the creation of his father.

The elder N.C. Krone is the maker *par excellence* of white wines. Every aspect of the process at Twee Jonge Gezellen bears the imprint of his personality and of the stringent standards which he has set both for himself and for those who work for him. A sense of the excitement and pleasure which comes from creative wine making based on these standards pervades the farm, from the owners to the cellar assistants to the workers in the fields. This is a family farm which is also a family in the extended sense.

In the long history of Twee Jonge Gezellen there have been many families and many generations. The initial grant of the land which includes the present Estate was made in 1710, when a considerable area to the north and west of the valley was leased by the Dutch East India Company to a Huguenot settler for the grazing of cattle. He named his farm 'La Rhône', and built the house which has been identified with the building known as the *bohuisie*, now restored as a guest-house. Among the unusual features of the homestead was its situation on a slope – the dynamics of mud-brick generally limited them to flat ground. Beside the adjacent cattle-kraal he also built a water-mill to grind wheat (destroyed by fire after the 1969 earthquake).

At some time in the early part of the eighteenth century the farm became the property of the two 'jonge gezellen', two Dutchmen who had been friends in Holland and, on leaving school, had decided to explore the Dutch colonies. One came ashore to live at the Cape, while his friend (their names have never been discovered) went on to Batavia. He returned a few years later and his arrival at the Cape co-incided with the first grants of land in the newly opened area of the *Land van Waveren*. They joined forces, blithely naming their farm 'Twee Jongegezellen', or 'Two Young Bachelors'

Apart from the intriguing choice of name, little is known of any further contribution they may have made to the farm's fortunes. But the thread of history is clearly picked up in 1745, when one of the early members of the Theron family gave the farm to his daughter (which in effect, meant to his newly acquired son-in-law, by the name of Du Preez) on the occasion of her marriage. The family line thus begun by the Du Preez couple has continued unbroken to the present, inheritance

Twee Jonge Gezellen Estate

Cultivars Planted	Size of Vineyards (Hectares)	Training Practice
Weisser Riesling	79	
Steen	60	
Frontignac	40	All the vines are
Sauvignon Blanc	30	trellised 1,65 m
Gewürztraminer	21	above the ground,
Sémillon	12	which is higher
Pinot Blanc	8	than usual; Perold
Sylvaner	7	trellises are used.
Chardonnay	6	
Furmint Nemes	6	

Total area under vines in 1987: 269 ha
Irrigation: The vineyards of Twee Jonge Gezellen can be irrigated if necessary.
Temperatures: Night temperatures are recorded; average temperature is 15 °C.
Average annual rainfall: 1 700 mm
Stock: Parent stock is used for grafting.
Envisaged new cultivars: Shiraz, Cabernet Sauvignon and Tinta Barocca
First wine bottled under the Twee Jonge Gezellen Estate label: TJ 39 (about 1955)
Wines currently bottled under the Twee Jonge Gezellen Estate label: TJ 39, TJ Light, Schanderl, Night Harvest and Engeltjepipi Special Late Harvest
Wood ageing: Wines are aged in wood on the Estate.
Capacity of the Twee Jonge Gezellen cellar: 23 000 hectolitres

Twee Jonge Gezellen is not open to the public, nor are wines for sale on the Estate. Private visits can be arranged by special appointment.

Twee Jonge Gezellen's wine-making team of N.C. Krone and his son Nicky.

The well-tended gardens and homestead complement the efficiency of the Twee Jonge Gezellen cellar where Nicky's wife, Mary (below) was responsible for the Estate's laboratory, a task now performed by Sakkie Moolman. Mary's young family is her main interest nowadays.

passing impartially, and most unusually, through both sons and daughters.

It was in this period that grapes were first grown and wine first made at Twee Jongegezellen. The wine was made under typically eighteenth-century conditions, being fermented in *velkuipe*, ox-hides filled with the wine and supported by four poles. All this early wine was distilled into brandy for easier transport over the old Roodezand Pass to the Cape. Until more sophisticated containers were available, the farm's wine was stored in calabashes.

On the established system of inheritance, the advent of an all-daughter family at Twee Jongegezellen offered golden opportunities to any other young 'gezellen' in the Tulbagh Valley; so when the Du Preez family in their turn failed to produce a male heir, a certain

Redelinghuys supplied the deficit. Several generations later a similar opportunity was taken by another member of the impressively prolific Theron family (by far the largest family in the valley), bringing them back to the land they had once owned.

With an eye for respectability, the Therons changed the name of the farm from 'Jongegezellen' to 'Jonge Gezellen', a minor surgery which transformed the 'bachelors' to 'companions' – to counter any impression that they might have been descended from bachelors, however enterprising. Christiaan Jacobus Theron, though a sturdy farmer, failed to produce a male heir, again leaving the field open for yet another young bachelor: in this case the first of the Krone family.

In addition to their other achievements, the Krones have produced an unbroken line of male heirs – with a solid sense of dynasty, all christened N.C. Krone – down to the present day. In 1916, the first N.C. Krone of Twee Jonge Gezellen married Christiaan Jacobus Theron's daughter, and bought the farm from his father-in-law.

If this was the young Krone's first contact with active farming, it was not his first with the world of wine. His father, also N.C. Krone, was a Dutch immigrant who on leaving school had spent 14 years in the wine and brandy trade in Holland before making his way to the Cape in 1869 to seek his fortune in the diamond fields. His impetus flagged somewhat on arrival, and when he reached the railhead at Worcester he decided to set up as a general dealer.

The father sold wine but the son was the first Krone to make it. In this period, in the early decades of the present century, the taste was for fortified wines; it is ironic that a farm now renowned for its white wines should first have made its mark with exports of red port, brandy and sherry.

But while the first N.C. Krone did much to consolidate wine making at Twee Jonge Gezellen, it was his son and namesake, the present N.C. Krone, who was to establish the farm firmly on the wine maker's map.

His career covers the major developments in modern South African wine making. He took over the running of the farm in 1939 after graduating from the University of Stellenbosch in viticulture and oenology, having already done practical work on it in 1936 during his university course, and he was well aware of its strengths and limitations.

The soils in this area of the valley vary considerably, from the fertile alluvial ground near the river to the rocky slopes of the Saronsberg whose bulk dominates the farm. At first glance they look unpromising, but they have a number of advantages for the wine maker which up till this point had not been exploited.

Beneath the stony surface is a substantial clay layer which retains moisture, even in the heat of summer. Together with this invisible supply goes a very visible supply of rain in the winter months, again one of the effects of the mountain's presence – Twee Jonge Gezellen has recorded up to 1 500 mm of rain in a season.

The winters here are cold but the summers are often scorchingly hot. Here again the mountain has a beneficial influence. The higher slopes receive the morning sun, but are shadowed from the fiercer heat of the late afternoon. They are also cooled in summer by the south-easter wind, which at this distance from the sea has spent most of its destructive force.

When the present N.C. Krone took over the farm, the bulk of the vineyards were concentrated on the alluvial soil close to the river. Many of their vines were of the port and sherry varieties, and the first area of development was that of the farm's sherries, still in demand up to the Second World War. In his first years on Twee Jonge Gezellen, 'N.C.' built up a reputation for the making of excellent flor sherries, made in one of the country's earliest soleras. At the same time he made detailed records of the progress of his vineyards from vintage to vintage. A student of Professor Theron of Stellenbosch University, he was aware of the need for a foundation of healthy vines and for controlled clone selection.

The most important move, however, was the development of the new vineyards on the mountain slopes. There is an old wine maker's adage which holds that 'the poorer the land, the better the grapes'. N.C.'s studies of his land had proved that vines grown closer to the mountain produced a higher quality wine and in the following years he steadily extended his vineyards to encroach on these slopes.

The labour involved in making these new plantings was prodigious. The Tulbagh Valley is stony at best, but here on the slopes of the Saronsberg the task of preparing the vineyards was more than usually difficult. On one 10-hectare site more than 30 000 tonnes of stone were removed, leaving ground which was still predominantly rocky.

On this inhospitable ground, with abundant irrigation and sunshine, the new noble white varieties which 'N.C.' introduced, the Cape Riesling, Sauvignon Blanc, Steen and Sémillon, flourished. And on the lower slopes of the original farm he replaced the old heavy-bearing White French and Green Grape stock with these new cultivars. At the same time he set about modifying and improving the Estate's cellar facilities, adapting them to the making of high-quality white wine. Doing away with the sherry-making solera, he began experimenting with methods of controlled fermentation of white wines, based on the concept of keeping the whole cellar at a uniformly cool temperature. One of the first of the Cape wine farmers to use the cold fermentation process in the mid-1950s, his enterprise paid off impressively in 1959, when his new wines made by this process won a decisive 13 first prizes at the Cape Wine Show – a success which persuaded many of the more sceptical white wine makers to invest in steel and cold water.

In an old wine-making community the family at Twee Jonge Gezellen retains a youthful sense of purpose. The immigrant Krones brought a new energy and character to the farm and its wines and in these developments 'N.C.' acknowledges the help of his wife, Vera, long a discriminating judge of her husband's wines. Moreover, the energy and vision of the older generation is still in evidence in the younger. In recent years, Nicky has taken an increasing share in the running of the Estate. His wife, Mary, was also involved in the family concern and used to run the laboratory and analyse the Estate's wines. These responsibilities have now been taken over by Sakkie Moolman, the cellar master, as Mary is kept too busy looking after her young children.

Nicky is a graduate of Elsenburg Agricultural College and of the famous Geisenheim Institute in Germany, and has explored new avenues in wine-making technology. In particular, he has experimented with the use of a wide range of imported yeasts, inoculating the must with up to six different yeasts, each of which, he maintains, adds an aspect to the character of the final wine. Awarded the trophy for the Champion Estate Wine Maker in 1979 and 1981 at the South African Championship Wine Show in recognition of his innovations, the latest 'N.C.' of the many N.C. Krones plans to develop further the noble cultivars on the Estate, and to expand the vineyards to yet higher reaches of the mountain. Nicky has also introduced night harvesting to the Estate, as the extreme heat in the Tulbagh Valley during the harvesting season can cause serious deterioration to the quality of the grapes. Another cause for concern has been the possible health hazard in the use of pesticides and weed-killers and Nicky has employed the services of some 4 000 ducks to rid the vines of snails, rather than using conventional methods. Each morning the ducks board a trailer for their ride to the vineyards and congregate again in the evening for the return trip.

Extreme heat in the Tulbagh Valley during the harvest can cause serious deterioration in the quality of grapes from the moment of picking to the time they reach the winery. To combat the problem, the Krones have developed a successful night-picking programme.

WORCESTER

In the early days of the Cape's history the main route through the great mountain barrier which stretches northwards from the Hottentots-Holland, Wemmershoek and Slanghoek mountains to the Groot Winterhoek mountains, lay through the Roodezand Pass into the valley of Tulbagh. From here the road gave access in the south-east to the wide valley of the Breede River.

In the course of the eighteenth century scattered farms and settlements grew up in this valley. Much of the land was used for grazing and remained otherwise undeveloped until the early nineteenth century when Lord Charles Somerset shifted the seat of the magistracy from Tulbagh to Worcester, near the banks of the Breede River – Tulbagh had been granted its own administrative independence in 1804 but slight damage to the old Drostdy during a storm in 1822 prompted the Governor to transfer the magistrate to new quarters.

The fortunes of the Breede River community improved but difficulties of access still limited development and it was only with the building of the Bain's Kloof Road, completed in 1853, that a viable commercial route was established between Cape Town and Worcester. By this time flourishing vineyards were settled in the area, and by the 1860s production compared favourably with that of the Stellenbosch and Paarl valleys. Much of the crop was dried for raisins, and this continued to be an important aspect of the local industry into the present century. But the decline in the demand for raisins after the Second World War persuaded

Snow-clad mountains, leaden skies and sodden vineyards paint a bleak winter landscape near Rawsonville in the Worcester District.

most of the farmers to convert to wine-grape growing, and in response to this change an extensive network of co-operative wineries sprang up – a total of some 32 across the whole Breede River Region.

The results of these developments have been spectacular. Approximately 25 per cent of the total national crop, grown on 18 120 hectares, is processed in the Worcester District, making it in terms of volume the most important of the wine-making districts of South Africa.

Geographically, the District is delimited mainly by mountain ranges, while the border on the eastern side is formed by a natural watershed with the Robertson area. There are a number of wards within the official Worcester District, reflecting a marked internal variation in soil types and micro-climates. Worcester and its surroundings form part of the Breede River catchment area, which is fed by a number of smaller rivers supplemented by the run-off from the winter snows in the mountains. The district includes the Hex River Valley which produces mainly table grapes for export.

In the Breede River, Botha, Slanghoek and Goudini areas the soils are sandy loams with a varying loose stone content and a fairly high, free water table: they often require artificial drainage during soil preparation. Other types include deep fertile alluvial soils along the river banks, and calcareous clayish soils which require intensive ripping during preparation.

Average summer temperatures range between 19 and 22 °C. Rainfall varies considerably, the annual average in the Slanghoek area to the west being approximately 1 500 millimetres, in contrast with a low 300 millimetres in the Nuy and Scherpenheuvel areas to the east.

Vineyards in the Worcester District are found mainly along river banks. Many of the farmers depend on the Brandvlei dam for irrigation, especially in the lower rainfall regions where all vineyards must be intensively irrigated. Where the rainfall is higher some vineyards are grown without, or with only supplementary, irrigation.

Cultivars grown in the region are Chenin Blanc, Cinsaut, Colombar, Palomino, Hanepoot, Chenel, Weldra, Raisin Blanc, Heroldrebe and Hàrslevelü which go to make mainly dry white wine, fortified sweet wine and a bulk of distilling wine for the making of brandy.

Aan-De-Doorns CO-OPERATIVE WINERY

Situated in the Aan-de-Doorns Ward of the Worcester District, this winery came into production in 1955. Some 48 member farmers in the District supply 15 000 tonnes of grapes at harvest time to Alwyn Mostert, the cellar's wine maker and manager.

Alwyn produces a range of approximately 10 wines, of which the Cabernet Sauvignon and the Chenin Blanc show consistently good quality. The Cabernet Sauvignon regularly receives the reserve champion award at the Worcester show, while the Chenin Blanc is often a gold medal winner at the national show at Goodwood. The Co-operative's sweet dessert wine, Muscat d'Alexandrie, has carried Superior certification on occasion.

Aufwaerts CO-OPERATIVE WINE CELLAR

Near Rawsonville in the Worcester District, the Aufwaerts winery was started as a family concern in 1974 and serves only three farms. The manager and wine maker is Anton Lachenicht and the chairman and secretary is W.T. Hanekom. The bulk of the Co-operative's production is sherry, sold to wholesale merchants, with only limited bottlings of table and dessert wines.

Badsberg CO-OPERATIVE WINE CELLAR

Badsberg was inaugurated in 1951 and wine making began the following year. Since then its wine maker, Lourens de Jongh, has achieved remarkable success with his Hanepoot: invariably carrying Superior certification, it has been a prolific award winner at both local and S.A. Championship shows. The Co-operative also produces a number of natural wines, but pride of place must surely go to Lourens's champion Hanepoot, a consistently excellent dessert wine.

Aan-de-Doorns Co-operative

Wines bottled and marketed by the Aan-de-Doorns Co-operative

Red wines: Cabernet Sauvignon, Pinotage, Vin Rouge and Dry Red
White wines: Chenin Blanc, Premier Grand Crû, Clairette Blanche, Late Harvest, Special Late Harvest, Sauvignon Blanc and Muscat d'Alexandrie
A Rosé and a Port are also bottled and marketed by Aan-de-Doorns Co-operative.

The Co-operative is open to the public on weekdays from 07h30 to 12h00 and from 13h00 to 17h00.

Aufwaerts Co-operative

Wines bottled and marketed by the Aufwaerts Co-operative

White wines: Aufwaerts White Table Wine and Hanepoot Jerepiko (dessert)

Aufwaerts Co-operative is open to the public but by appointment only.

Badsberg Co-operative

Wines bottled and marketed by the Badsberg Co-operative

White wines: Riesling, Servan Blanc, Chenin Blanc, Tafelwyn, Badlese, Stein and Hanepoot (dessert)

Badsberg Co-operative is open to the public on weekdays from 07h00 to 12h00 and from 13h00 to 17h00 (on Fridays it closes at 16h00).

Bergsig

The cellar on the huge Bergsig Estate.

Bergsig Estate

Cultivars Planted	Size of Vineyards (Hectares)	Training Practice
Chenin Blanc	150	
Hanepoot	60	
Colombar	40	
Cape Riesling	20	
Cabernet Sauvignon	10	
Cinsaut	10	Various trellising
Raisin Blanc	10	systems are used
Sauvignon Blanc	10	throughout the
Weisser Riesling	10	vineyards
Pinotage	7	
Gewürztraminer	5	
Furmint	4	
Fernão Pires	2	

Total area under vines in 1987: 338 ha
Irrigation: The vineyards of Bergsig are irrigated.
Temperatures: Average maximum 34 °C; average minimum 20 °C
Average annual rainfall: 690 – 720 mm
Stock: Rooted vines are purchased from a nursery.
Envisaged new cultivars: Chardonnay and Pinot Noir.
First wines bottled under the Bergsig Estate label: Cabernet Sauvignon, Colombard, Sweet Hanepoot and Chenin Blanc (all from the 1978 vintage).
Wines currently bottled under the Bergsig Estate label: Sauvignon Blanc, Cape Riesling, Weisser Riesling, Fernão Pires, Furmint, Bouquet Light, Colombard, Bukettraube Special Late Harvest, Chenin Blanc Special Late Harvest, Chenin Blanc Noble Late Harvest, Pinotage Blanc de Noir, Pinotage, Cabernet Sauvignon, Sweet Hanepoot and Port. Bergsig wines are bottled by the Breërivier Bottling Co-operative.
Wood ageing: Wines are aged in wood on the Estate.
Capacity of the Bergsig cellar: Some 3 500 tonnes of grapes are processed annually.

The Estate is open on weekdays from 08h00 to 12h00 and from 13h00 to 17h00, and on Saturdays from 09h00 to 12h30.

One of the largest wine Estates in the country, Bergsig in recent years has been developed by the Lategan family. Established as a wine-producing farm in the 1930s, it is now run by 'Prop' Lategan and his wine maker, Kas Huisamen, who grow an impressive range of cultivars, including Chenin Blanc, Colombar, Cape Riesling, Cinsaut and Cabernet Sauvignon, as well as more unusual varieties such as Fernão Pires, in 338 hectares of irrigated vineyards. Approximately two per cent of the total crop is bottled, while the rest is sold to wholesalers. A year after its emergence as an officially recognized Estate in 1978, Bergsig received its first Superior award for the 1979 Cabernet Sauvignon.

Since then the Estate has won a number of awards for its wines. In 1985 and 1986 Bergsig was awarded the accolade of Champion Estate at the Worcester Young Wine Show. At the same show a year later, the Bergsig Colombar was voted the best dry white wine, and the Estate was the joint winner with the Goudini Co-operative for the Pietman Hugo Trophy, a coveted award in the Worcester area.

Botha CO-OPERATIVE WINE CELLAR

The prolific Botha family in this area of the Breede River Valley gave a name both to the locality and to the small railway station on the line between Worcester and Wolseley – and also to the co-operative winery which was established here in July, 1948. Originally named the Botha's Halt Co-operative Wine Cellar, the wine cellar is now run by wine maker André Stoffberg,

his assistant, Johan Morkel, and the winery's secretary, Nel Bester.

Improvements in quality control in recent years have been matched by increases in production – the annual crop taken in is now 16 500 tonnes. Recent awards for this Co-operative's wines include those at the Worcester Show and the Cape Championship Wine Show.

Botha Co-operative

Wines bottled and marketed by the Botha Co-operative

Red wines: Cabernet Sauvignon and Pinotage
White wines: Weisser Riesling, Colombard, Chenin Blanc and Chenin Blanc Late Harvest
A Blanc de Noir, a Soet Hanepoot and a Port are also bottled and marketed by the Botha Co-operative.

The Co-operative is open to the public on weekdays from 08h30 to 12h30 and from 13h30 to 17h30, and on Saturdays from 10h00 to 12h00.

Brandvlei CO-OPERATIVE WINERY

The Co-operative was built in 1955 on five hectares of land donated by Danie de Wet from his farm Brandvlei. Extensions to the Brandvlei dam forced the winery to move to a new site in 1974. Here a new and improved modern cellar was constructed, much of its operation now being automated, which allows Booysen Maree, Brandvlei's general manager, and his wine maker, Theuns le Roux, to produce good quality wines.

The Brandvlei Co-operative's main claim to fame is its Chenel wine. In 1965

Danie van Tubbergh obtained a few cuttings from Professor Chris Orffer, who developed this Chenin Blanc/Trebbiano crossing, and planted them on his father's farm, Riverside, along the banks of the Breede River. Further plant material was propagated from these vines, and wine from the new cultivar was made commercially for the first time in 1978 at the Brandvlei Winery.

Brandvlei's bottled wine, however, accounts for only a small portion of production, the bulk being sold to the trade.

De Doorns CO-OPERATIVE WINE CELLAR

Pieter Hamman is the wine maker and manager of this winery, which is situated just outside De Doorns, in the Hex River Valley. Besides wines, the cellar also handles large quantities of export table grapes grown by the member farmers, who

now number 210. The first bottled wine under the De Doorns label came on the market in 1977. Nowadays about a dozen different wines, including sherry and port, are bottled annually by this Co-operative.

De Wet
CO-OPERATIVE WINE CELLAR

The De Wet Co-operative at the base of the pass leading through the mountains into the Hex River Valley has an interesting history in that it developed from being a packing co-operative for export grapes. Wine making began in 1946 and today is under the direction of Stephanus Kok. Export grapes remain a major aspect of the Co-operative's activities and some 200 000 cartons are packed each year.

Du Toit's Kloof CO-OPERATIVE WINE CELLAR

At the entrance to the Du Toit's Kloof Pass near Rawsonville, this winery began production in 1962 under the management of Ursus Schirmer. He was succeeded in 1979 by Ernst Gouws, who in turn was succeeded by the present wine maker, Philip Jordaan. Philip was formerly an assistant to Dassie Smith at Rooiberg, where he clearly received a good training as he has consistently won awards for his wines, as well as being reserve champion at the Worcester show. He produces a very good Cinsaut – an achievement which eludes many wine makers – as well as particularly good Bukettraube and Late Harvest wines.

Goudini
CO-OPERATIVE WINE CELLAR

The Goudini winery was established in the Rawsonville district in 1948. The manager and wine maker is Mr C.P. le Roux, who makes a range of red and white wines including Hanepoot which is marketed as Muscat d'Alexandrie and which was national champion in 1983. Since then it has been a regular gold medal winner. The Goudini Clairette Blanche took the prize as the best of its variety at the Cape Championship Wine Show for three successive years from 1977 to 1979: and the cellar's Colombard won the same award in 1979. Several wines are now marketed under the Goudini label – the winery's symbol on this label shows a honeycomb: 'goudini' is believed to be an old Bushman word for 'bitter honey'.

Harvesting in the Rawsonville area.

Groot Eiland Co-operative

Wines bottled and marketed by the Groot Eiland Co-operative

Red wine: Cinsaut
White wines: Premier Grand Crû, Chenin Blanc, Colombard, Semi-Sweet White Table Wine, Late Harvest Steen, Fernão Pires, Cape Riesling and Bukettraube
   A port and Hanepoot Soetwyn (dessert) are also bottled and marketed by the Groot Eiland Co-operative.

The Co-operative is open to the public on weekdays from 07h30 to 12h30 and from 14h00 to 17h00.

Groot Eiland
CO-OPERATIVE WINE CELLAR

This cellar was established near Rawsonville in December 1960 with an initial 14 members. The first crop of 5 295 tonnes of grapes was delivered in 1962 and the pressing was supervised by the newly-appointed wine maker and manager, Cecil Bredell, late of Santhagens in Stellenbosch. Now assisted by Marthinus Joubert, Bredell receives 8 000 tonnes of grapes each year from 15 member farmers; the emphasis is on white varieties, the most important being Hanepoot and Steen.

Lebensraum

Originally a part of the farm 'Het Groote Eiland', this Estate was given independent life in 1943. The present owner and fifth generation of his family to farm in this area is Philip Deetlefs, who has expanded the basic range of white wine grapes, once grown for raisin production, to include new varieties such as Weisser and Cape Riesling. Both the wine and the wine maker have won an impressive array of awards in recent years at the Breede River Valley Wine Show, now known as the Worcester Wine Show.

The vineyards of Worcester produce some 25 per cent of the total South African wine grape harvest.

Lebensraum Estate

Cultivars Planted	Size of Vineyards (Number of vines)	Training Practice
Hanepoot	158 655	
Chenin Blanc	139 010	
Sémillon	36 619	
Clairette Blanche	24 120	Bush vines
Pedro	15 420	
Colombar	10 794	
Weisser Riesling	9 204	
Cape Riesling	5 550	Vertical trellis

Total area under vines in 1987: 90 ha (10 ha still to be planted)
Irrigation: All the vineyards of Lebensraum are irrigated.
Temperatures: Average maximum 30 °C; average minimum not recorded.
Average annual rainfall: Approximately 650 mm
Stock: Rooted vines are purchased from a nursery.
First wines bottled under the Lebensraum Estate label: Stein 1978, Clairette Blanche 1978 and Soet Hanepoot Superior 1978
Wines currently bottled under the Lebensraum Estate label: Stein, Weisser Riesling, Cape Riesling and Soet Hanepoot (fortified wine)
Wood ageing: Not practised.
Capacity of the Lebensraum cellar: 9 600 hectolitres

Lebensraum is open to the public, by appointment, on weekdays between 14h00 and 18h00.

Louwshoek Voorsorg
CO-OPERATIVE WINE CELLAR

Grapes grown only in the Louwshoek and Voorsorg regions are used at this winery which has been in production since 1957. The Co-operative's wines have done well at the Breede River Wine Show; they are made under the supervision of wine maker and manager, Abel Carstens. The winery now markets seven wines under its own label

Louwshoek Voorsorg Co-operative

Wines bottled and marketed by the Louwshoek Voorsorg Co-operative

Red wine: Dry Red
White Wines: Chenin Blanc, Colombard, Riesling, Premier Grand Crû, Late Harvest and Muscat d'Alexandrie (dessert)

Louwshoek Voorsorg Co-operative is open to the public on weekdays from 07h00 to 17h00.

Merwida
CO-OPERATIVE WINE CELLAR

One of the dense concentration of Co-operatives in the Rawsonville district (whose ten Co-operatives here make it the highest producing area in the winelands), the Merwida Co-operative is also one of the few family concerns. After its formation in November, 1962, it was bought out by the Van der Merwe family, already majority shareholders in the company and owners of

Merwida Co-operative

Wines bottled and marketed by the Merwida Co-operative

Red wine: Dry Red
White wines: Riesling, Sweet Table Wine, Fernão Pires, Chenin Blanc and Soet Hanepoot (dessert)
   A Port is also bottled and marketed by the Co-operative.

The Co-operative is open to the public on weekdays from 07h30 to 12h00 and from 13h30 to 17h30.

Nuwehoop Co-operative

Wines bottled and marketed by the Nuwehoop Co-operative

Red wine: Cabernet Sauvignon
White wine: Chenin Blanc
   A Blanc de Noir and a Sweet Hanepoot are also bottled and marketed by the Nuwehoop Co-operative.

The Co-operative is open to the public on weekdays from 09h00 to 12h30 and from 13h00 to 17h00.

Nuy Co-operative

Wines bottled and marketed by the Nuy Co-operative

Red wine: Pinotage
White wines: Colombard, Colombard Effesoet, Steen, Chant de Nuy, Bukettraube, Riesling and Fernão Pires
   Two dessert wines, a Red and White Muscadel, are also bottled and marketed by the Nuy Co-operative.

The Co-operative is open to the public on weekdays from 08h30 to 12h00 and from 13h00 to 17h00.

much of the land in the vicinity. Now under the chairmanship of Schalk van der Merwe, the winery draws a wide range of grape varieties from some 700 hectares in the locality. Of the wines made by wine maker, Jacobus 'Wollie' Wolhuter, and his assistant, Sarel van Staden, eight are currently bottled under the Merwida label.

Nuwehoop
WINE CELLAR CO-OPERATIVE

Hennie Sieberhagen is the wine maker and manager of this cellar which was started in 1965 outside Rawsonville. Most of the Co-operative's wines are bottled for its members, although there are limited sales to the public at the cellar.

Nuy
WINE CELLAR CO-OPERATIVE

The Nuy Wine Cellar was inaugurated in 1963, with C.P. le Roux as its first manager and wine maker; he was succeeded in 1971 by the present incumbent, Wilhelm Linde. Situated on the uppermost part of the valley between the Slanghoek and Hex River mountains, the Co-operative has won awards both regionally and nationally for its wines, which are available only at the cellar and the 'Wynhuis' at the Kleinplasie Museum in Worcester.

Opstal Estate

Situated near Rawsonville in the Slanghoek Valley, this Estate, in its early years a large cattle farm, was first settled in the middle of the nineteenth century by 'Lang Jan' Rossouw. The name of its homestead, 'De opstal bij de fonteine' (the homestead by the spring), in due course became attached to the farm itself.

The former owner and wine maker, the late Attie Louw, planted a number of white varieties such as Clairette Blanche, Chenin Blanc and Colombar, as well as the red cultivar, Cabernet Sauvignon, on the upper slopes of the farm. The first wines bottled under Attie's guidance and the Estate's own label were a Chenin Blanc and a Volsoet Hanepoot in 1978.

Opstal is now run by Stanley Louw, the sixth generation of the Louw family. 1987 was a particularly good year for Stanley, as he was not only awarded medals, ranging from bronze to gold, for all his wines at the 1987 Worcester show but he also won the 1987 Vineyard Competition run by Stellenbosch Farmers' Winery (see page 55) for the best vineyard block of Steen. The overseas trip, which was the prize for the Vineyard Competition, enabled Stanley to visit the wine-growing countries of Europe and the Californian vineyards.

Opstal Estate

Cultivars Planted	Size of Vineyards (Hectares)	Training Practice
Chenin Blanc	36	
Hanepoot	16	
Colombard	14	
Clairette Blanche	10	
Sauvignon Blanc	5	One- and 3-wire vertical trellises
Cinsaut	3	
Cabernet Sauvignon	2	
Ferdinand de Lesseps	1	
Weisser Riesling	1	

Total area under vines in 1987: 88 ha
Irrigation: The Opstal vineyards are under computerized drip and micro-irrigation.
Temperatures: Records are not kept.
Average annual rainfall: Approximately 1 100 mm
Stock: Rooted vines are purchased from a nursery.
First wines bottled under the Opstal Estate label: Chenin Blanc and Volsoet Hanepoot (1978)
Wines currently bottled under the Opstal Estate label: Chenin Blanc, Chenin Blanc Semi-Sweet, Colombard, Droë Wit and Volsoet Hanepoot. Opstal wines are bottled by the Breërivier Bottling Co-operative.
Wood ageing: Not practised.
Capacity of the Opstal cellar: 10 000 hectolitres

Opstal Estate is open to the public for wine sales from 09h00 to 11h00 and 15h00 to 17h00. Cellar tours can be arranged by appointment.

Overhex Co-operative

Wines bottled and marketed by the Overhex Co-operative

White wines: Dry Colombard, Semi-Sweet Colombard, Dry White Table Wine and a Riesling

Overhex Co-operative is open to the public on weekdays from 07h30 to 12h45 and from 14h00 to 17h30 (the cellar closes at 17h00 on Fridays).

Overhex CO-OPERATIVE WINE CELLAR

The Overhex winery was started in 1963, with Doug Lawrie, an MSc graduate from the University of Cape Town, in charge of its design, construction and eventual wine making – this included the installation of the first Bucher separator to be used in a

local winery. Four gold medals were won by the cellar at the 1973 Cape Championship Wine Show and two years later Doug won the General Smuts Trophy for the best wine maker of the year. He has also won several gold medals at the Worcester show.

Slanghoek
CO-OPERATIVE WINE CELLAR

Stettyn
CO-OPERATIVE WINE CELLAR

Slanghoek Co-operative

Wines bottled and marketed by the Slanghoek Co-operative

Red wine: Pinotage
White wines: Chenin Blanc, Colombard, Riesling, Premier Grand Crû, Late Harvest and Soet Hanepoot

Slanghoek Co-operative is open to the public on weekdays from 07h00 to 08h30, 09h00 to 12h00 and from 13h30 to 17h30 (on Fridays the cellar closes at 16h30).

Tucked away in a valley of the Slanghoek mountains, this winery was formed in 1951, taking in its first crop of 3 000 tonnes of grapes in the following harvest. Izak (Bill) Pretorius was the wine maker at that first vintage; he still holds the post, though

since 1964 he has been assisted by Carel van Breda.

Since the early days both the membership and the crop received have increased dramatically: 36 farmers now supply the winery with nearly 18 000 tonnes of grapes annually. In spite of this bulk, however, the emphasis at Slanghoek has always been on the making of quality wines, and it has performed well at the regional wine shows; a number of the winery's products have been certified Superior, and the 1979 Colombar was sold at the Nederburg Auction.

Technical innovations have in part been responsible for this high quality. One example was the centrifugal pump developed by the Slanghoek wine makers in collaboration with Professor Joël van Wyk of Stellenbosch University; this gives a cleaner must than the pumps previously used.

On the road between Worcester and Villiersdorp, the Stettyn winery was started in 1964, the first wine being made the following year. The Co-operative has 18 members operating from 13 farms, who deliver an annual 4 000 tonnes of grapes; the cellar is supervised by wine maker and manager, Tienie Crous.

Stettyn Co-operative

Wines bottled and marketed by the Stettyn Co-operative

White wines: Dry Chenin Blanc and Colombard

The Co-operative is open to the public on weekdays from 08h00 to 17h00.

Waboomsrivier CO-OPERATIVE WINE CELLAR

The design of the wine labels of the Waboomsrivier Co-operative features the flower of *Protea arborea*, the 'waboom' from whose sturdy wood the local wagon wheels were made. Established in 1949, the Co-operative concentrated from the outset on the making of quality wines. An area of the farm Kleinberg was purchased as the site of the winery, which pressed its first crop of 4 148 tonnes in 1950.

In the post-war years capital was limited, and the initial 22 members of the Co-operative loaned their farm tractors to

the winery to power the cellar machinery until finance for electricity was available. But while electricity powered the machinery, much of the Co-operative's human energy and resources were supplied by its wine maker and manager, Mynhardus Cloete, whose career has spanned the full working life of the cellar. Born on a wine farm in the Somerset West area, he obtained a BSc in Agriculture under Professor Theron at the University of Stellenbosch, majoring in chemistry and Viticulture. After three years' experience

at the Stellenbosch Farmers' Winery, working under Bill Winshaw, he took up the post of wine maker at Waboomsrivier in December, 1949.

His subsequent career has been distinguished by fine wine making and a continued commitment to the founders' ingenuity and inventiveness. In 1956 he designed a drainer made of wood which improved the yield of free-run juice in white wine making. Twelve such drainers, soon known as the Cloete drainer or separator, were installed, and by 1958

Waboomsrivier Co-operative

Wines bottled and marketed by the Waboomsrivier Co-operative (Wagen Boom label)

Red wines: Cabernet Sauvignon, Cinsaut, Pinotage, Ruby Cabernet and Roodewagen
White wines: Riesling, Steen, Laatoes, Chenin Blanc Late Vintage and Hanepoot Late Vintage
Two dessert wines are also made: a Port and a Sweet Hanepoot Jerepigo.

The Co-operative is open to the public on weekdays from 08h00 to 17h00, and on Saturdays from 08h30 to 10h00.

virtually the entire crop at Waboomsrivier was processed through them. Other inventions developed by him included a special tank for the fermenting of quality red wines, and a quick-fermenter for the fermentation of husks for distilling. Some have been superseded, but in their time they helped to improve both quality and efficiency, and, as a result, Mynhardus has seen many of his wines awarded prizes at the local wine shows.

Harvest time requires very early rising on the part of the grape-pickers, as grapes are at their best when picked in the cool of dawn. Here pickers take a well-earned breakfast break. Right: Waboomsrivier Co-operative.

OVERBERG

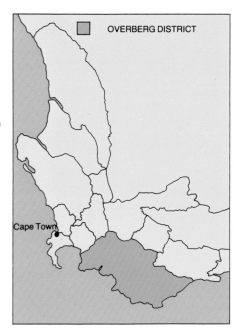

Previously known as the Caledon District, the Overberg District includes Villiersdorp, Caledon, Riviersonderend, Bredasdorp and Bot River. A mountainous region, it is mainly given over to wheat production, but vines are grown in the Villiersdorp and Bot River areas. The soil here is mainly of a sandy nature which makes for straightforward preparation and cultivation. The climate is cool, and the vines do not receive as many hours of sun as in other Districts because of the proximity of the mountains. Also, because of the coolness of the climate, the grapes ripen late in the season. The mean annual rainfall is high, at some 750 millimetres.

Hamilton Russell Vineyards

Hamilton Russell Vineyards are situated in the Hemel-en-Aarde Valley, behind the Raed-na-Gael mountains which form the backdrop to Hermanus. Approximately eight kilometres from the town, the vineyards fall under the Walker Bay Ward of the Overberg District. The concern is owned by a business executive, Timothy Hamilton-Russell, and its wine maker is Peter Finlayson.

Much of Hamilton-Russell's youth was spent in Constantia and it was there in the early 1950s that his interest in wine was nurtured. Later, while taking a degree at Oxford, he came into contact with French wines, particularly the red and white wines of Burgundy. He became convinced that excellent red and white wine could be produced from noble varieties such as Pinot Noir and Chardonnay in carefully selected cool areas of South Africa (although he regrets that the country does not extend a further 200 kilometres to the south which would temper its climate to that of central France.)

During a career in the firm of J. Walter Thompson in Johannesburg, Timothy nursed this ambition. Then, in 1974, it found practical form with the purchase of land in the Hemel-en-Aarde Valley.

The choice of land was carefully made, bearing in mind the kinds of wine he

Timothy Hamilton-Russell (right) and his wine maker, Peter Finlayson.

Hamilton Russell Vineyards

Cultivars Planted	Size of Vineyards (Hectares)	Training Practice
Pinot Noir	19	
Chardonnay	17	All cultivars grown
Sauvignon Blanc	3,5	on 3-wire vertical
Gewürztraminer	0,5	trellis

Total area under vines in 1987: 40 ha
Irrigation: The vineyards are irrigated only in times of drought.
Temperatures: Temperatures are recorded on a daily basis at two Government-registered weather stations. Seven years' weather data, interpreted according to the Winkler system, indicate 1 560 degree-days for the mountain vineyards and 1 620 degree-days for the valley vineyards.
Average annual rainfall: Approximately 750 mm.
Stock: Parent stock is used for grafting.
First wines bottled by the Hamilton Russell Vineyards: Blanc de Blanc and Grand Crû (under the Hemel-en-Aarde label), Grand Vin Blanc and Grand Vin Noir (under the Hamilton Russell label).
Wines currently bottled by the Hamilton Russell Vineyards: Chardonnay, Sauvignon Blanc, Grand Crû Noir, Pinot Noir and HRV Hemel-en-Aarde Valley Vin Blanc.
Wood ageing: Wines are aged in wood in the cellar.
Capacity of the Hamilton Russell Vineyard cellar: 2 600 hectolitres

The cellar of Hamilton Russell Vineyards is not open to the public, but private visits can be made by appointment.

The Hamilton Russell Vineyards cellar, designed to Peter Finlayson's specific requirements, nestles in the tranquil Hemel-en-Aarde Valley near Hermanus.

wanted to produce. He undertook a thorough study of a broad spectrum of different areas and micro-climates, before finally settling on the Hermanus area.

The great advantage of this area is the cool climate during the growing months. At latitude 34 ° 23′ South, as compared for instance to Constantia, at a latitude of 34 ° 02′ South, it has fewer than 3 000 degree-days of heat a year. During the summer months it is cooled by breezes off the sea, only five kilometres distant. The rainfall in the area is about 710 millimetres a year. The soil is primarily an arenaceous shale, part of the Bokkeveld Series. It varies in depth, but the average is about 600 millimetres.

In the year after purchase the first serious planting of vines began. In the following years approximately 20 000 vines were planted annually, with an emphasis upon two high-quality cultivars, Pinot Noir and Chardonnay. Small amounts of Sauvignon Blanc and Gewürztraminer have also been established.

While the vineyards were being planted a cellar was built in 1980, specifically designed to deal only with wines of high quality. Its capacity, therefore, is limited. Producing its first wine from the 1981 vintage, it now produces about 15 000 cases a year and is one of the smaller premium wine cellars in the country.

Peter Finlayson, the wine maker, who

graduated from Stellenbosch University in 1973 with a degree in oenology, first worked on his family's Estate, then known as Montagne. It has since reverted to its orginal name of Hartenberg (see page 155). In 1975 he studied at Geisenheim in Germany, returning the following year to become the wine maker at Montagne. After Montagne was acquired by Gilbeys and renamed Hartenberg, Peter worked at Boschendal, assisting Achim von Arnim before moving to the Hamilton Russell Vineyards in 1979, where one of his first tasks was to help in the design of the new cellar.

With his three top wines, the Grand Vin Noir, the Chardonnay and the Sauvignon Blanc, Peter deliberately – and successfully – strives for the Burgundy style. He regularly tours Burgundy, Bordeaux and California, and in particular exchanges ideas with the eminent French grower and shipper Prosper Maufoux of Santenay, Burgundy. All Hamilton Russell wines are wooded in oak from Burgundy and Limousin, for periods ranging from 12 months in the case of the 100 per cent Pinot Noir wine known as Grand Vin Noir, to three months in the case of the Sauvignon Blanc and two in the case of the Hemel-en-Aarde Valley Vin Blanc. The yields at Hamilton Russell Vineyards are deliberately low, the wines are among the Cape's very best, and their prices, not surprisingly, the highest in the country.

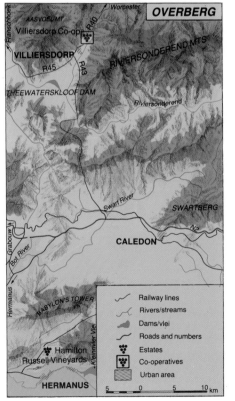

Villiersdorp MOSKONFYT AND FRUIT CO-OPERATIVE

Originally started in 1922 with the intention of concentrating on *moskonfyt* and processed fruits, the Villiersdorp Co-operative was expanded to include wine production in 1976, the first bottling taking place in 1978 under the wine maker, Chris van der Merwe. The winery's labels feature the old steam engine which originally provided power for the Co-operative and now stands outside the Victoria Street Building.

Nowadays the Co-operative markets its range of wines in screw-top bottles, as a convenience for its customers and to keep prices low.

Villiersdorp Co-operative

Wines bottled and marketed by the Villiersdorp Co-operative

Red Wine: Overberg Pinotage
White Wines: Overberg Chenin Blanc, Late Vintage, Grand Crû, Perlé and Overberg Colombar

The Villiersdorp Co-operative is open on weekdays from 08h00 to 13h00 and from 14h00 to 17h00, and on Saturdays from 08h00 to 11h00.

277

ROBERTSON

The first farmers in what is now the Robertson District arrived there at the beginning of the nineteenth century, extending the settlement of the Breede River Valley into its lower reaches. Here, on the wide expanses of wild grass, the pioneers herded sheep and cattle. Later in the century crops of lucerne were planted in the lime-rich soils as feed for the race-horses which began to be bred here. At the beginning of the present century the same feed was used for the ostriches whose tail feathers graced the hats of fashionable ladies in Europe – until the advent of the motor-car blew away the feathers along with the large hats they had adorned.

In this period little wine farming was seen in the area. As is so much of the Cape hinterland, it is a hot, dry region, and without irrigation the chance of survival for the vineyards was slender. Two factors changed this bleak prognosis. The first was the building of the Brandvlei dam at the turn of the century, providing a supplement to the Breede River which regularly runs dry in the heat of summer. The second was the advent of the cold fermentation process. For the first time in the post-Second World War years, controlled conditions allowed for the making of technically sound white wines. Recent decades have seen a marked expansion of the vineyards in response to this revolutionary innovation, and a proliferation of Estate cellars and co-operative wineries to cater for the expanded production.

Geographically, the Robertson District forms an extension of the Breede River Valley, and is bordered by mountains to the north and east – the Langeberg range dominates this stretch of the valley. The Breede River flows from west to east on its way to the sea and, as in the Worcester District, most of the vineyards are in proximity to it, ensuring an adequate supply of water.

There are two main types of soil here. One is a very fertile alluvial soil along the river banks which requires deep ploughing during preparation. The other is a fairly heavy calcareous, or lime-rich, soil with a high clay content that requires intensive ripping before planting. With adequate irrigation most soils in the area have a good production potential. The average annual rainfall is less than 400 millimetres. Average summer temperatures vary from 19 °C at De Hoop, Vinkrivier and McGregor, to 22 °C in other areas.

Agterkliphoogte
CO-OPERATIVE WINE CELLAR

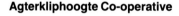

Situated in a dry and inhospitable area 28 kilometres from Robertson is the Agterkliphoogte winery. It was started in 1965 and by 1982 some 4 500 tonnes of grapes were being pressed here, of which 2 000 tonnes were Chenin Blanc and the balance was made up of Muscadel, Pinotage, Cabernet Sauvignon, Colombar and Raisin Blanc.

The present winemaker and manager is Helmard Hanekom. Of the 24 members, four draw water from the Le Chasseur Canals which run from Brandvlei Dam; the other 20 members rely on their own dams to collect the natural winter run-off from the mountains and thus supplement the insufficient and unpredictable rainfall.

Most of the wine made here is delivered in bulk to merchants, but some is bottled under the Agterkliphoogte label.

> **Agterkliphoogte Co-operative**
>
> **Wines bottled and marketed by the Agterkliphoogte Co-operative**
>
> **Red wine:** Muskadel
> **White wines:** Chenin Blanc and Colombard
>
> Agterkliphoogte Co-operative is open to the public on weekdays between 08h00 and 12h30 and between 13h30 and 17h00.

Ashton CO-OPERATIVE WINERY

This large Co-operative winery is situated on the Robertson side of Ashton, at the foot of the Langeberg. Inaugurated in 1962, the first wine-making season was in 1963, when the first 6 000 tonnes of grapes were crushed. Because many of the grapes delivered to the cellar were too low in sugar to allow good quality wine making, a grape juice concentrating plant was installed and its product exported (to the extent of 50 000 hectolitres annually).

The present wine maker is Tertius Siebrits and the Co-operative's current membership stands at 132, with an annual delivery of 20 400 tonnes of grapes of 22 different varieties. A consistent prize-winner at young wine shows, the winery bottles a substantial range of wines. All the wines, except the Cabernet Sauvignon, are now marketed in screw-top bottles in an endeavour to keep costs as low as possible.

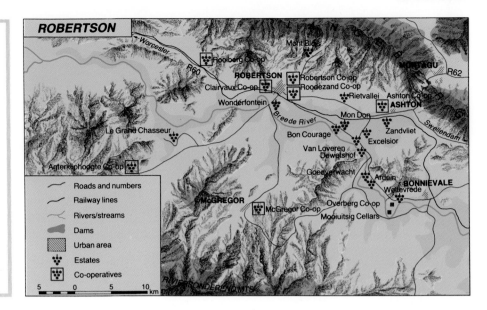

ROBERTSON

Ashton Co-operative

Wines bottled and marketed by the Ashton Co-operative

Red Wines: Dry Red, Cabernet Sauvignon and Red Muskadel

White Wines: Colombar, Chenin Blanc (dry), Riesling, Chenin Blanc (semi-sweet), Bukettraube, Late Harvest, Hanepoot, White Muskadel, Sauvignon Blanc and Gewürztraminer

The Co-operative is open to the public on weekdays from 08h00 to 13h30 and from 14h30 to 17h30. It is usually closed on Saturdays, except during the December school holidays when it is open from 08h00 to 12h00.

Bon Courage

Bon Courage is situated at the confluence of the Klaas Voogds and Breede rivers, about nine kilometres outside Robertson, and has been owned since the 1920s by the Bruwer family. The name 'Bon Courage' is a French translation of Goedemoed, the farm of which it was once a part. André Bruwer, the present owner and wine maker, took over the farm in 1965 and proclaimed it an Estate some 12 years later.

With the installation of cold fermentation equipment on his property in 1966, André began making dry white table wines, then a new development in this generally hot and dry region. Plantings of the traditional Steen and Muscadel were extended with a range of cultivars especially suited to dry wine making,

Bon Courage homestead

including Clairette Blanche, Colombar, Bukettraube, Sauvignon Blanc and Kerner.

The original cellar was redesigned by André in 1974 to allow for more modern methods of wine production. He started bottling his own wine in 1983 and soon established a good reputation for his wine-making skills. At the South African Wine Show in 1984 André was Champion Private Producer Winemaker and in 1985 and 1986 took the honours as Champion Estate Winemaker. In 1986 the Bon Courage Riesling was judged the best wine in its class at the same show and the Estate also won the trophy for the champion natural sweet white table wine.

Bon Courage has an interesting range of certified dry, off-dry, semi-sweet and dessert wines, which are on sale from the beautifully thatched and well-preserved Goedemoed homestead, built in 1818.

Bon Courage Estate

Cultivars Planted	Size of Vineyards (Hectares)	Training Practice
Muscadel Colombar Steen	90	
Bukettraube Clairette Blanche Colombar Gewürztraminer Kerner Merlot Pinot Noir Rhine Riesling Sauvignon Blanc Shiraz	30	Perold trellises

Total area under vines in 1987: 120 ha
Irrigation: All the vineyards of Bon Courage are irrigated.
Temperatures: Average maximum 25 °C; average minimum 16 °C
Rainfall: Approximately 300 mm
Stock: Rooted vines are purchased from a recognized nursery.
Envisaged new cultivars: Chardonnay, Auxerrois and Pinot Gris
First wines bottled under the Bon Courage Estate label: Colombar, Blanc de Noir and Kerner Late Harvest (all 1983 vintage)
Wines currently bottled under the Bon Courage Estate label: Blanc de Noir, Blanc Fumé, Bouquet Blanc, Colombar, Gewürztraminer Special Late Harvest, Kerner, Riesling, Rhine Riesling, Sauvignon Blanc and Red Jerepigo.
Wood ageing: Wines are aged in wood on the Estate.
Capacity of the Bon Courage cellar: 14 000 hectolitres

The Estate is open to the public from 09h00 to 17h00 on weekdays.

Clairvaux
CO-OPERATIVE WINE CELLAR

This winery, situated on the outskirts of the Robertson urban area, was developed from a private cellar owned by Rial Kloppers in the 1920s and was established as a Co-operative in 1963. The wine maker and manager, Kobus van der Merwe, makes a range of wines under the Clairvaux label from grapes received from the winery's 15 member farmers.

Clairvaux Co-operative

Wines bottled and marketed by the Clairvaux Co-operative

Red wine: Cabernet Sauvignon
White wines: Blanc de Clairvaux, Chenin Blanc Late Vintage and Special Late Harvest
    A Rosé and two fortified wines (Red and White Jerepigo) are also bottled and marketed by the Clairvaux Co-operative.

The Co-operative is open to the public on weekdays from 08h30 to 17h30 and on Saturdays from 08h30 to 13h00.

De Wetshof

In 1968, Johann de Wet, the owner of De Wetshof since 1952, sent his son, Danie, to the viticultural institute at Geisenheim in Germany, to acquire an up-to-date education in the ways of modern wine making. Two years later the younger De Wet arrived back at the family farm in the Robertson area to begin putting his new discoveries into action.

He had certain other advantages, besides a contemporary wine-maker's qualification. These included a father with many years of experience in his craft, and fertile land of good extent – recent expansion has brought it up to a present 165 hectares. De Wetshof boasts the country's highest lime content in its soils, giving a high fixed acid content to the wines made here. Besides a supply of

irrigation water from the Breede River, special climatic conditions help in the growing of high quality grapes: at night the cool sea air from the Agulhas coast mingles with the warmer air from the hinterland and causes a thick mist which blankets the land well into the following morning. Together with a heavy dewfall, this mist helps to protect the farm and its vineyards from the full ferocity of the sun.

On his return from Geisenheim, one of Danie's first moves was the installation of cold fermentation equipment, enabling him to begin making light, fragrant white table wines.

Hereafter, he began systematically to experiment with new cultivars and new clones of familiar varieties, while retaining old and trusted favourites such as the traditional Steen. New introductions by the mid-1970s included Rhine Riesling and Pinot Gris, as well as Sauvignon Blanc and Chardonnay – two clones of the latter were tried. Danie observed that the Chardonnay from the Champagne region gave a bigger crop under his particular conditions, but that its Burgundy counterpart gave better acids and sugar. Of these, the Rhine Riesling , Sauvignon Blanc and Chardonnay have proved the most successful. Other experiments include investigations into different kinds of oak for wood maturation of the Estate's red wines, though the traditional Limousin oak still came out ahead with a higher tannin content than Navarre or Balkan oaks.

All this energy and innovation soon paid visible dividends. The first farm in the Robertson District to be granted Estate status and the first Estate outside the Coastal Region to be awarded a Superior certification for its wine, De Wetshof carried off the champion wine prize at the Robertson Wine Show in 1973 for the De Wetshof Riesling, contrary to all expectations. It was followed by a Sauvignon Blanc, the first to be designated 'Superior' and the South African Champion white wine in 1984, and the Edeloes, a 'Superior' botrytis or noble rot wine. Released for the first time in 1980 (it is made only in years when there is a heavy dewfall), the latter is made from Riesling and Chenin Blanc grapes; the must for this wine is kept at a constant low temperature and is allowed to ferment for two to three months. The Estate also makes a wood-matured Chardonnay, the first of its kind in the country to achieve a 'Superior' classification. In 1987 this Chardonnay (from the 1985 vintage), containing 20 per cent Auxerrois, was judged the best wine at the world's most extensive wine and wine machinery exhibition in Bordeaux. Known as 'Vinexpo', this show coincides with a judging of wine held by the Oenological Department of the University of Bordeaux, and it was here that Danie de Wet's wine claimed highest honours.

De Wetshof Estate

Cultivars Planted	Size of Vineyards (Hectares)	Training Practice
Chardonnay	45	
Rhine Riesling	30	
Steen	30	
Sauvignon Blanc	28	
Cape Riesling	12	All cultivars are
Pinot Blanc		grown on 5-wire
Hárslevelü		vertical trellises
Morio Muscat		
Palomino	12	
Gewürztraminer		
White Muscadel		
Pinot Gris	8	

Total area under vines in 1987: 165 ha
Irrigation: All the vineyards of De Wetshof are irrigated.
Temperatures: Annual maximum 36 °C; annual minimum −6 °C
Average annual rainfall: Approximately 375 mm
Stock: Parent stock is used for grafting; rooted vines are purchased from Fleur du Cap.
First wines bottled under the De Wetshof Estate label: Steen Dry 1973, Steen (with 10 g sugar) 1974 and Riesling Dry 1974
Wines currently bottled under the De Wetshof Estate label: Sauvignon Blanc, Rhine Riesling, Chardonnay and Edeloes. All De Wetshof wines are bottled and marketed by the Bergkelder.
Wood ageing: Chardonnay and Sauvignon Blanc are aged in wood on the Estate.
Capacity of the De Wetshof cellar: 18 000 hectolitres

The De Wetshof Estate is open to the public by appointment only.

The new cellar at De Wetshof (above). The success of De Wetshof white wines in recent vintages, particularly Chardonnay, owes much to the innovative approach to wine making of Danie de Wet (left).

Excelsior

This Estate on the Kogmanskloof River is run as a partnership by the brothers Stephen and Freddie de Wet. As do many of the farmers in this lime-rich district, they divide their energies between the growing and making of wine and the breeding of aristocratic racehorses. In the case of Excelsior, the horse stud, vineyards and cellars are divided between the brothers: Stephen takes charge of the horses and the cellar, and Freddie is responsible for the vineyards, with their complex irrigation systems so necessary in this hot, dry region only partly modified by mists prevalent on summer mornings.

Traditionally, Muscadel varieties were grown here, and still are, but, to cater for the changes in public taste towards dry white wines, other cultivars have been planted during the last decade. These include Chenin Blanc, Sauvignon Blanc, Colombar and Trebbiano.

The view from the Excelsior homestead over the Kogmanskloof River. Irrigation is extensively used in this dry area.

Excelsior Estate

Cultivars Planted	Size of Vineyards (Hectares)	Training Practice
Sauvignon Blanc	46	
Colombar	37	
Red Muscadel	36	
Hanepoot	11	Extended Perold,
Steen	9	Factory and vertical
St Emilion	4	trellising are used.
White Muscadel	4	
Raisin Blanc	2	

Total area under vines in 1987: 149 ha
Irrigation: All the vineyards are irrigated.
Temperatures: Records are not kept.
Average annual rainfall: 250 mm
Stock: Rooted vines are purchased from a nursery.
First wines bottled under the Excelsior Estate label: Red and White Muscadel (both in 1977). Wine is no longer bottled on the Estate and is sold in bulk to the wine merchants.
Capacity of the Excelsior cellar: 16 000 hectolitres

Excelsior is not open to the public.

A mechanical grape-harvester at Le Grand Chasseur Estate. These amazing machines are still relatively rare in the Cape winelands.

Le Grand Chasseur

Until the early 1950s this farm on the Breede River near Robertson was mainly limited to the production of raisins and sultanas, with a moderate amount of sweet Hanepoot being supplied to the KWV for export.

Then, in 1950, Wouter de Vos de Wet inherited the family farm, and soon set about enlarging the existing vineyards. In the course of planning these new blocks in 1956, he ordered a supply of St Emilion vines. In good faith he planted the vines he received only to discover when they came to bearing that he had been given the then little-known variety of Colombar by mistake. With little idea of the potential of these new arrivals in his vineyard, Wouter approached the KWV for advice. Told to experiment with the making of sweet and semi-sweet wines of the kind long made in this region, he continued to cultivate his Colombar, and was soon followed by many of the local farmers.

In 1968 the discovery of the good wine capabilities of Colombar by Pon van Zyl of the local Robertson Co-operative resulted in further extensive plantings of the variety in this area.

Since those days Wouter, assisted since 1979 by his son, Albertus, has added further cultivars to his almost exclusively white grape vineyards. These include Steen, Clairette Blanche, Cape Riesling, Sauvignon Blanc and St Emilion, which go to the production of dry table wines.

Le Grand Chasseur Estate

Cultivars Planted	Size of Vineyards (Hectares)	Training Practice
Steen	38,05	
Colombar	30,70	
White Muscadel	9,64	
Clairette Blanche	7,73	
Sauvignon Blanc	7,02	Modified Perold
Cape Riesling	4,63	trellises
Palomino	2,39	
St Emilion	1,50	
Weisser Riesling	1,00	
Morio Muscat	0,92	

Total area under vines: 103,58 ha
Irrigation: All the vineyards of Le Grand Chasseur are irrigated.
Temperatures: Average maximum 30 °C; average minimum 6 °C
Average annual rainfall: Records are not kept.
Stock: Rooted vines are purchased from a nursery.
Envisaged new cultivar: Chardonnay
First wines bottled under the Le Grand Chasseur Estate label: Chenin Blanc, Colombar, Late Harvest and Cape Riesling 1984
Wines currently bottled under the Le Grand Chasseur Estate label: Sauvignon Blanc, Cape Riesling, Colombar and Late Harvest
Capacity of the Le Grand Chasseur cellar: 16 500 hectolitres

Limited quantities of Le Grand Chasseur wines are bottled. These are available at the Estate as well as at Brandewynsdraai during business hours. Visits to the Estate can be arranged by appointment.

McGregor CO-OPERATIVE WINERY

McGregor Winery is situated 18 kilometres from Robertson on the road to the beautiful historic town of McGregor, which is possibly the best preserved and most complete example of a mid-nineteenth century townscape in the Cape. The winery was started in 1948 and made its first wine in 1950. From 1972 till 1982 the wine maker here was Gielie Swiegers who showed his skills in producing a Steen and Colombar blend that was judged the overall champion white wine at the Breede River Valley Wine Show in 1972 and, the

following year, the overall champion white wine at the South African Championships at Goodwood. This was followed by a long list of award-winning wines, white, rosé and fortified.

Membership of the McGregor winery is now 46, providing a total grape crop of 7 200 tonnes a year, made into wine by Swiegers' successor, Carel van der Merwe. Most of the wine is sold in bulk to wholesalers, but an interesting range – including a botrytis wine, Edel Laat Oes – is now bottled under the cellar's label.

McGregor Co-operative

Wines bottled and marketed by the McGregor Co-operative

White wines: Blanc de Blanc, Colombard, Weisser Riesling, Edel Laat Oes and Late Harvest Steen

A Blanc de Noir and a Red Muscadel are also bottled and marketed by the McGregor Co-operative.

The Co-operative is open to the public on weekdays from 08h00 to 12h00 and from 13h00 to 17h00.

Mon Don

The name of this farm – it means 'My gift' – commemorates the transfer for a nominal sum of the property from Hannetjie Marais to her son, Pierre, the owner and wine maker since 1962. Since then Pierre has refurbished the near-derelict vineyards, making first sweet wines and sherry and then extending the range to include dry wines which he supplies to merchants. He has bottled small quantities of white wine, which he has released to the public under the Mon Don label. The Chardonnay is particularly good. Cultivars grown here now include Steen, Colombar, Clairette Blanche and Trebbiano, together with the Hungarian vine, Hárslevelü.

Mon Don Estate

Cultivars Planted	Size of Vineyards (Number of vines)	Training Practice
Colombard	81 308	
Chenin Blanc	77 796	
Clairette Blanche	21 162	All cultivars are
Trebbiano	10 600	grown on extended
Hárslevelü	9 800	trellises
Sauvignon Blanc	2 978	
Weisser Riesling	1 706	

Total area under vines in 1987: 66 ha
Irrigation: All the vineyards of Mon Don are irrigated.
Temperatures: Average maximum 28 °C; average minimum 14 °C
Average annual rainfall: 306 mm
Stock: Rooted vines are purchased from a nursery.
First wine bottled under the Mon Don Estate label: Colombard 1983
Wines currently bottled under the Mon Don Estate label: Blanc de Blanc and Late Harvest
Capacity of Mon Don cellar: 10 420 hectolitres

The Estate is open to the public on weekdays between 08h00 and 17h00 and by special appointment on Saturdays.

Mont Blois

Situated in the De Hoop Valley near Robertson, this farm was described in its original title deed as 'De Hoop in het Land van Waveren aan de Witter water'. By the 1880s it had been acquired by the Bruwer family, descendants of a Huguenot named Estienne Bruère who had come to the Cape from the French town of Blois in 1688. The name of De Hoop was retained by the Bruwer family until 1920, when it was changed to the present name in honour of their ancestor and his distant origins on the River Loire.

Mont Blois is now owned by Ernst Bruwer, who has added two further farms, La Fontaine and Sunshine, to create a substantial spread of some 3 500 hectares. Of these, about 165 hectares are under vines, including Steen, Colombar and Hanepoot. The range also includes Red and White Muscadel, and it is the wines from these which are the pride of the Estate and the main source of its renown.

The gravelly soil in this high, narrow valley – it is less than two kilometres across – is particularly suited to Muscadel grapes, which have been grown here by the Bruwers since the turn of the century. Fortified with pure spirit, these rich,

Mont Blois Estate

Cultivars Planted	Size of Vineyards (Hectares)	Training Practice
White Muscadel	40	
Red Muscadel	40	
Steen	20	
Sauvignon Blanc	16	
Colombar	11	Extended Perold
St Emilion	11	trellis
Weisser Riesling	10	
Chardonnay	8	
Hanepoot	7	
Pinot Noir	2	

Total area under vines in 1987: 165 ha
Irrigation: The vineyards of Mont Blois are irrigated.
Temperatures: Average maximum 27 °C, average minimum 12 °C
Average annual rainfall: Approximately 500 mm
Stock: Rooted vines are bought from a nursery.
Envisaged new cultivar: Gewürztraminer
First wine bottled under the Mont Blois Estate label: White Muscadel 1974
Wines currently bottled under the Mont Blois Estate label: White Muscadel, Weisser Riesling and Chardonnay. Mont Blois wines are bottled by the Bergkelder.
Wood ageing: Wines are aged in wood at the Bergkelder.
Capacity of the Mont Blois cellar: 16 000 hectolitres

Mont Blois is not open to the public.

luscious wines are made from late harvested grapes supported on the drip-irrigation which is carefully controlled. The Mont Blois White Muscadel has consistently received Superior

classification over the past decade as well as a formidable array of prizes; these include Championships over many years at both the Robertson and Breede River Young Wine Shows, numerous trophies

and gold medals at the South African Young Wine Championships, and gold medals every year since 1977 in the Club Oenologique International Wine and Spirit Competition.

Rietvallei

Muscadel is the only wine marketed by this Estate at Klaasvoogds under its own label. The present owner is Johnny Burger, the fifth generation of his family to own Rietvallei, which the family purchased in 1864. As have generations of his family before him, Johnny concentrates exclusively on the growing and making of Muscadel.

On leaving school in 1968 he served an apprenticeship under the elderly foreman of the farm, Jan Vytjie, and was well rewarded when his first wine was judged the South African Champion Muscadel. Although the cellar has been thoroughly modernized, the formula, or recipe, of Rietvallei's Muscadel, which was tacked on to the cellar door for many decades, has hardly changed. Johnny believes that part of the success of his excellent Muscadel, which frequently wins gold medals and always carries a Superior label, is due to the use of some grapes from vines which are over 70 years old.

Rietvallei Estate

Cultivars Planted	Size of Vineyards (Hectares)	Training Practice
Steen	43,09	
St Emilion	20,87	
Clairette Blanche	20,07	
Red Muscadel	17,04	3-wire vertical trellises are used for all cultivars. There are also, however, some 15 000 untrellised, bush vines.
Raisin Blanc	11,66	
Cinsaut	10,03	
Colombar	9,50	
Chardonnay	9,30	
Sauvignon Blanc	4,53	
Weisser Riesling	4,36	
Shiraz	2,03	
Pinotage	1,58	

The oldest vineyard at Rietvallei was planted in 1908. This Red Muscadel vineyard continues to produce the Estate's best wine.

Total area under vines in 1987: 154 ha
Irrigation: All Rietvallei vineyards are irrigated.
Temperatures: Records are not kept.
Average annual rainfall: Approximately 300 mm
Stock: Parent stock is used for grafting; rooted vines are purchased from a nursery.
First wine bottled under the Rietvallei Estate label: Red Muscadel in 1975
Wine currently bottled under the Rietvallei Estate label: Red Muscadel (bottled by the Bergkelder)
Wood ageing: Not practised.
Capacity of the Rietvallei cellar: 16 000 hectolitres

Rietvallei is not open to the public.

Winter pruning, the kortsnoei, *in a Robertson Vineyard.*

Robertson CO-OPERATIVE WINERY

Founded in 1941, this Co-operative has since become renowned for its Colombar wines. The introduction of this cultivar to the gamut of natural wines is intimately

bound up with the career of the Robertson winery's former wine maker and manager, Pon van Zyl, who turned a happy accident into a major development.

In 1954 a local farmer, Wouter de Wet, of the farm Le Grand Chasseur near Robertson, ordered a supply of Saint

The Robertson Co-operative 1 where the late Pon van Zyl 2 developed his renowned Colombar wine when he was manager and vigneron there.

Emilion vines from a nursery run by Wynand Viljoen at Ladismith in the Little Karoo. De Wet duly planted the vines with which he was supplied, but discovered when they came to bear that he had been given Colombar by mistake. Since, however, both vines were equally adapted to the making of rebate wine, he proceeded to press his vintage as usual. In the following years other farmers in the vicinity began to plant cuttings of Colombar, but it was left to Pon van Zyl to

recognize the real potential of this cultivar. Walking through the Robertson Co-operative's cellars in 1968, he was assailed by a heady perfume which he later compared to the scent of the koekemakranka flower (*Gethyllis spp.*) and at that moment he decided to make the Colombar into a good wine rather than a rebate wine for brandy.

It was an inspired move, and one which was to earn him a modest but secure place in the local wine makers' pantheon. The Robertson Co-operative's Colombar has become one of the area's finest wines, and a consistent prize-winner at wine shows. Its success has encouraged others to follow

suit to the extent that plantings of Colombar in the Cape vineyards now exceed 14 million vines.

Apart from the Colombar, a further 10 wines are now bottled under the guidance of the present wine maker, Mr B.H. Botha, who joined the winery in 1986. These include the first commercial wine made from a new cultivar, Therona Riesling, recently developed at the University of Stellenbosch and named after Professor C.J. Theron.

Roodezandt
CO-OPERATIVE WINERY

W.F. (Robbie) Roberts is the cellarmaster at this winery situated on Voortrekker Street in the town of Robertson. The Robertson Wards of Hoopsrivier and Le

The Roodezandt Co-operative in Robertson.

Chasseur are represented by the wine cellar's current 51 members, who deliver more than 17 500 tonnes of grapes a year.

Assisted by the wine maker, Christie Steytler, Robbie supervises the production of a range of wines under the Roodezandt label, many of which have won prizes in local and national shows. One of these, Le Grand Deluge Noble Late Harvest, has its origin, as the name suggests, in the devastating floods of 1981.

On Philip du Toit's farm, La Maison, at the confluence of the Breede and Vink rivers near Robertson, is a huge vineyard of Chenin Blanc, which disappeared under a metre of water when the rivers burst their banks. The flood waters subsided but the grapes were expected to rot and were given up for lost. Instead of 'vulgar' rot, however, noble rot developed and after careful nurturing a colossal crop for botrytis grapes of 20 tonnes was harvested. The challenge of turning these into a Noble Late Harvest was eagerly tackled by Robbie Roberts and his assistant, Christie Steytler, and resulted in the making of 104 hectolitres of Superior wine.

New cultivars, such as Sauvignon Blanc and Hárslevelü, have been planted to fit into the cellar's viticultural plan for the future. The cellar has moved into a new field of marketing, providing single-strength juice to the wine industry for the sweetening of table wine and the making of light-bodied wines. Furthermore, Robbie is going to great lengths to promote Muscadel to the wine-drinking public: he feels that the excellent Muscadels of the Robertson area go largely unnoticed by the public and he is willing to show visitors to the winery the different ways to serve these wines.

Rooiberg

Rooiberg Co-operative was established in 1964 by 11 farmers near Goree in the Robertson District, and now has 40 members contributing from individual farms under the guidance of the wine maker, Dassie Smith. A graduate of Stellenbosch University where he studied under Professor Chris Orffer, Dassie has placed Rooiberg firmly on the Co-operative map since he took over as wine maker in 1970. He has won an impressive array of wine awards within a few years, including the champion Cabernet Sauvignon at the Cape Wine Show in 1979; at the 1982 show Dassie was awarded, jointly with Sydney Back of Backsberg, the General Smuts Trophy for the best wine maker, and was champion wine maker in 1984. Rooiberg was champion Co-operative for the first time in 1978 and thereafter for three successive years in 1982, 1983 and 1984.

Drawing grapes from the Wards of Vinkrivier, Goree, Riverside and Eilandia, the modern and streamlined Rooiberg winery bottles a comprehensive selection of some 30 different, 'good-value-for-money' wines. Dassie introduced wood ageing of white wines to the Robertson area and now bottles a selection of oak-matured red and white wines. He also produces good Special Late Harvest and fortified wines.

Rooiberg Co-operative

Wines bottled and marketed by the Rooiberg Co-operative

Red wines: Cinsaut, Roodewyn, Pinotage, Cabernet Sauvignon, Selected Red Wine and Shiraz

White wines: Weisser Riesling, Oak Blended Sauvignon Blanc, Oak Matured Riesling, Vinkrivier Vintage Reserve, Vinkrivier Riesling, Vinkrivier Steen, Premier Grand Crû, Selected Dry White, Blanc Fumé, Vinkrivier Bukettraube, Vinkrivier Colombard, Vinkrivier Chenin Blanc, Late Vintage and Special Late Harvest

A Rosé, a Blanc de Noir and three fortified dessert wines (Hanepoot, Red and White Muskadel) are also bottled and marketed by the Rooiberg Co-operative.

The Co-operative is open to the public on weekdays from 08h30 to 18h30 and on Saturdays from 08h30 to 13h00.

Van Loveren

A tract of land on the banks of the Breede River, between Robertson and Bonnievale, was once a large farm called Goudmyn. This farm thrived during the ostrich boom, but eventually had to be divided amongst the nine offspring of the Potgieter family. In 1937 Nicholaas Retief purchased one of these 28-hectare sections of land for his son, Hennie, and the farm was known simply as 'Goudmyn F'.

Hennie's wife, Jean, a woman with a great sense of tradition, felt strongly about the lack of originality in the name and took it upon herself to lend something of her family heritage to the identity of their new farm. Mrs Retief was born a Van Zyl, a descendant of Guillaume van Zyl, who had arrived at the Cape in 1692, with his wife, Christina van Loveren. The new bride had brought her trousseau to the Cape in a beautiful Philippine mahogany kist, which today has pride of place in the Retief home. So cherished is this piece of furniture that Mrs Retief persuaded her husband to name their new farm 'Van Loveren'.

The Van Loveren cellar was one of the first to produce sweet wines, particularly Red Muscadel, for delivery to the Stellenbosch Farmers' Winery. This was the main activity at Van Loveren until 1977 when cold fermentation facilities were installed. This led to the planting of natural white wine varieties, including Colombar and Steen. In 1980 the Retiefs planted the Hungarian cultivar, Hárslevelü, and the Portuguese Fernão Pires, resulting, two years later, in the first wines from these cultivars to be launched in South Africa.

Van Loveren Estate.

Van Loveren

Cultivars Planted	Size of Vineyards (Hectares)	Training Practice
Chenin Blanc	10	
Colombar	10	
Sauvignon Blanc	10	
Chardonnay	6	
Hárslevelü	5	
Red Muscadel	5	
Raisin Blanc	4	
Fernão Pires	3	
White Muscadel	3	3-wire vertical trellis
Gewürztraminer	2,5	
Rhine Riesling	2,5	
Albatross	2	
Chenel	2	
Pinot Blanc	2	
Pinot Gris	2	
Cape Riesling	1,5	
Shiraz	1,5	

Total area under vines in 1987: 72 ha
Irrigation: The vineyards of Van Loveren are irrigated.
Temperatures: Average maximum 25 °C; average minimum 16 °C
Stock: Rooted vines are purchased from the KWV.
First wines bottled under the Van Loveren label: Premier Grand Crû, Hárslevelü and Fernão Pires (1982)
Wines currently bottled under the Van Loveren label: Hárslevelü, Fernão Pires, Pinot Gris, Rhine Riesling, Sauvignon Blanc, Blanc de Blanc, Premier Grand Crû, Selected Stein, Colombar, Blanc de Noir Muscat, Blanc de Noir Shiraz, Special Late Harvest and Noble Late Harvest
Wood ageing: Wines are aged in wood on the farm.
Capacity of the Van Loveren cellar: 12 000 hectolitres

Van Loveren is open to the public on weekdays from 10h00 to 17h00 (excluding lunch hours), and on Saturdays from 10h00 to 13h00.

At present Van Loveren consists of four farms which are run by the brothers Nico and Wynand Retief. The farm, Schoemanskloof, was purchased for Nico when he married in 1964. Prior to that Nico had studied at Elsenburg Agricultural College, where he was awarded a gold medal for his achievements. Wynand, after completing a B. Comm. degree at the University of Stellenbosch, had planned to enter the business world. He changed his mind, however, and purchased the farm, Jacobsdal, when he married in 1968. In 1980 a portion of the farm, Goededmoed, with its rich lime soils, was bought and in the same year the Van Loveren cellar was modernized to include only cement and fibreglass tanks. The total capacity of the cellar is 1 000 tonnes, although a new storage wing has been added in the hope of reaching the total pressing quota of 1 800 tonnes.

The brothers have been farming in partnership since the death of their father in 1982. Nico is the viticulturist and also manages the fruit and vegetable enterprises (there are approximately 35 hectares of fruit orchards and 5 hectares of vegetables) and Wynand, in spite of having no formal wine-making training, has taken on the role of Van Loveren's wine maker.

Although Van Loveren is known for its innovative Hárslevelü and Fernão Pires wines, its Blanc de Noirs have also gained recognition. The Blanc de Muscat in particular has been a class winner at the local Robertson wine show. The unusual perlé wine, Fernão Pires Crémante, in a bottle with screw-on 'pop' top is another innovation from the Van Loveren cellar and has been certified by the Wine and Spirit Board.

Weltevrede Estate

The Jonker family includes a number of the most influential wine personalities in the Robertson District, among them Lourens Jonker, owner and wine maker of the Weltevrede Estate.

The name Weltevrede can be translated as 'well-satisfied' and suggests the pleasure which three generations of the Jonker family have derived from farming alongside the Breede River. Situated just outside Robertson, Weltevrede provides a picturesque scene of green vineyards and lucerne fields, the wine cellars along the highway and the homestead with its fine garden, the whole set against the backdrop of the Langeberg.

On 30 August, 1912, Klaas Jonker, grandfather of the present owner, Lourens Jonker, acquired 280 hectares of shrub veld and named it Weltevrede. The land was divided into four parts, to be farmed by his four sons. The youngest son, Japie, commenced farming during 1933 on the part closest to Bonnievale and retained the name of the original farm, after his three brothers had renamed their farms.

Vines were planted on a small scale, and wine production commenced during the Depression, when, on occasion, taps had to be opened and the wine allowed to run out, disposing of a product for which no market existed. Japie persevered, however, and as more vines were planted, the cellars were extended. The wines, mainly sweet wine and sherries at that stage, were initially marketed by the barrel but eventually bottled and sold to the public until 1948, when Japie and his brother, Herman, started a wholesale liquor business. This partnership was terminated four years later, when Japie decided to concentrate

mainly on farming and wine was sold in bulk to various wholesalers.

After qualifying as a pilot in the South African Air Force, Japie's only son, Lourens, decided to follow in his father's footsteps. He studied viniculture at the University of Stellenbosch and, after graduating in 1961, he visited the wine-growing areas of California and Western Europe. In late 1962 he started farming with his father, devoting himself to wine

making. He was soon rewarded by winning various prizes at a number of wine shows. With Lourens in full control of the farm, Japie was able to devote more time to public service and, among other things, became a director of the KWV, an appointment Lourens was to take up nearly twenty years later.

After his father's death in 1969, Lourens acquired the neighbouring farm, Muscadel, from his uncle. Being an ardent

Weltevrede Estate

Cultivars Planted	Size of Vineyards (Number of vines)	Training Practice
Sauvignon Blanc	32 000	
Clairette Blanche	12 263	
Ugni Blanc	11 707	
Rhine Riesling	10 838	
Cape Riesling	8 455	
Gewürztraminer	7 850	
Kerner	5 688	Perold trellis
Raisin Blanc	5 265	
Chardonnay	3 000	
Therona	2 355	
Bukettraube	188	
Sylvaner	100	
Chenin Blanc	94 461	
Colombar	58 352	3-wire vertical
Muscat de Hambourg	20 015	trellis
Muscat de Frontignac	17 000	
Hanepoot	17 075	Bush vines
Red Muscadel*	40 744	Bush vines and 3-wire trellis

*The first vineyards were planted in 1926 and are still in good production.

Total area under vines in 1987: 100 ha (25 ha still to be planted)
Irrigation: All the vineyards of Weltevrede are irrigated.
Temperatures: Average maximum 25 °C; average minimum 20 °C
Average annual rainfall: Approximately 200 mm
Stock: Rooted vines are purchased from a nursery.
First wines bottled under the Weltevrede Estate label: Colombard 1975, Rooi Muskadel 1976 and Wit Muskadel 1976
Wines currently bottled under the Weltevrede Estate label: Cape Riesling, Privé, Sauvignon Blanc, Blanc Fumé, Blanc de Noir, Privé du Bois, Colombar, Rhine Riesling, Weltheimer, Gewürztraminer, Therona, Special Late Harvest, Noble Late Harvest and Chardonnay, Red Muscadel, White Muscadel and Muscat de Hambourg
Wood ageing: Wine is aged in wood on the Estate.
Capacity of the Weltevrede cellar: 16 000 hectolitres

Weltevreden Estate is open to the public on weekdays from 08h30 to 12h30 and from 14h00 to 17h00, and on Saturdays from 09h30 to 11h30. Cellar tours will be conducted on request.

supporter of the law for Wines of Origin, he consolidated the two farms and registered Weltevrede as an Estate with the Wine and Spirit Board during 1974. With the marketing of its first bottled Estate wine in 1976, which was the 1975 vintage Colombard, Weltevrede became the first Estate in the first Estate in the Breede River Valley to bottle and supply wine direct to the public. In 1977 the Estate marketed the first Red Muscadel sweet wine in the country. This wine is made by Tommy Loftus, who assists Lourens as wine maker. It was the champion muscat

fortified wine at the South African Wine Show in 1986.

During May, 1981, Lourens bought another neighbouring farm, Riversedge, and consolidated the entire 150 hectares as one Estate. This farm with its south-facing slope and gravelly soil is extremely suitable for the planting of classic cultivars. Each year more Rhine Riesling, Kerner, Gewürztraminer, Sauvignon Blanc and Chardonnay vines are planted.

Some 12 different wines are bottled annually at Weltevrede. Wine from selected grapes only is bottled and

marketed as Estate wine, and most of the good quality wine is supplied to wholesalers in bulk. Since 1979 experiments have been conducted with white wine in small French oak casks and the Weltevrede Privé du Bois, a wood-matured dry white blend of Colombar and Chenin Blanc, is enjoying wide recognition.

Apart from its wine, which has received many gold medals and other awards at local shows over the years, Weltevrede also boasts a fine Friesland herd, which supplies milk to the largest dairy in the country at Bonnievale.

Zandvliet

The nutritional value of the lime-rich, Karoo-type soils of this farm in the Ashton district makes it eminently suitable for the breeding of horses, and Zandvliet has long been famous for its thoroughbreds. The horse stud flourished under 'Paulie' de Wet, but since he took over the farm in 1947 there has been a parallel development of wine farming. His sons, Dan and Paul, now manage the stud farm and the vineyards respectively. Paul has adventurously introduced red wine cultivars to an area hitherto almost exclusively given over to semi-sweet white wines. The first of these varieties was a

Shiraz vine acquired from the Durbanville Estate of Meerendal, long a specialist in the making of fine, dry Shiraz wines. Although other varieties are planted here, including Red and White Muscadels, and other red wine plantings are planned for the future, the Zandvliet Shiraz remains to date the most important wine under the Estate's label. Some Pinot Noir has been produced since 1983 and its release is eagerly awaited.

The Shiraz is left in small wood for as long as Paul sees fit and thereafter it is transferred to large oak vats for approximately a year before bottling. Once

bottled it is left to mature for yet another year before being released.

The severe floods of 1981 wrought havoc among many of the low-lying vineyards along the banks of the Breede River. Zandvliet was particularly badly affected, with literally tonnes of topsoil being swept away by the flood waters. It has taken years for the De Wets, and others too, to restore their vineyards to their pre-deluge condition.

Since 1950 Zandvliet has won numerous awards on local shows and in 1980 won a Club Oenologique Gold Medal for the 1976 Zandvliet Shiraz.

'Paulie' de Wet, owner and wine maker of Zandvliet.

Zandvliet Estate

Cultivars Planted	Size of Vineyards (Hectares)	Training Practice
Steen		
Colombar	50	
Sauvignon Blanc		
Pinot Noir		3- and 4-wire
Cabernet Sauvignon	45	vertical trellises
Shiraz		
Muscadel	20	

Total area under vines in 1987: 115 ha
Irrigation: All the vineyards of Zandvliet are irrigated.
Temperatures: Average maximum 30 °C; average minimum 20 °C
Average annual rainfall: Approximately 200 mm
Stock: Parent stock is used for grafting; rooted vines are purchased from a nursery.
Envisaged new cultivar: Merlot
First wine bottled under the Zandvliet Estate label: Shiraz 1976
Wines currently bottled under the Zandvliet Estate label: Shiraz and Pinot Noir (bottled by the Bergkelder). Fortified wine is also bottled under the Zandvliet Estate label.
Wood ageing: Wine is aged in wood at the Bergkelder.
Capacity of the Zandvliet cellar: 12 000 hectolitres

Zandvliet is not open to the public.

SWELLENDAM

The massive Langeberg range sets the northern border to the Swellendam District, while the watershed formed by the extension of the Riversonderend mountains marks its southern limit. From west to east it reaches from Bonnievale to Suurbraak. The Breede River winds through the region to meet the Indian Ocean at Cape Infanta.

Apart from alluvial sandy soils along the river banks, the soils are fairly compact, somewhat saline and with a high clay content. They require intensive ripping during vineyard preparation, and provision for heavy drainage – the average annual rainfall is 600 millimetres, and the average summer temperature between 20 and 21 °C. Late frost can occur.

Bonnievale CO-OPERATIVE WINE CELLAR

Established in 1964, this cellar now has 60 members and presses a substantial 12 000 tonnes of grapes a year, of which 2 300 tonnes are Steen and 1 000 tonnes Colombar. Depending upon the vintage, 30 to 40 per cent of good wine is made by wine maker, Piet 'Kelder' Linde, and his assistant, Hannes Botha.

Jonkheer FARMERS' WINERY

Originally established in the early 1900s as an ostrich farm by the grandfather of the current chairman, Nicolaas Jonker, Jonkheer is in the very centre of Bonnievale. When the ostrich boom declined, the Jonkers changed to wine, planted their own vineyards and sold their products direct to the public.

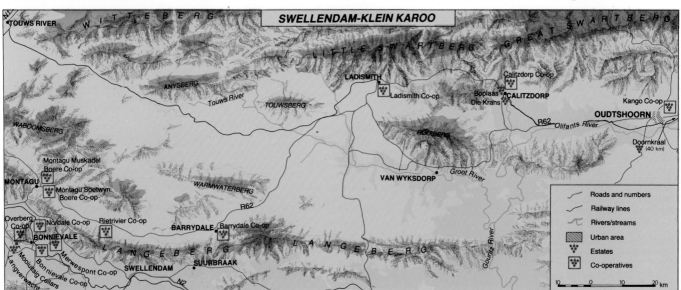

Jonkheer Co-operative

Wines bottled and marketed by the Jonkheer Co-operative

White wines: Bakenskop Riesling, Bakenskop Colombar, Bakenskop Grand Crû, Bakenskop Laat Oes, Edelweiss Stein and Edelstein Semi-Sweet

Dessert wines: Red and White Muscadel, Red and White Myrtella, Melita, Marsala, Red and White Muscadel Liqueur Wine, Red and White Malmsey and Medium Sweet Hanepoot

Sherries: Matador Sherry (Medium Cream, Medium Dry and Pale Dry) and Jonkheer Old Brown, Golden, Milk, Club and Full Cream Sherry

Ports: Jonkheer Old, White, Cape and Invalid Port

Jonkheer products are available to retailers only.

Business developed in the 1950s and in 1964 a bottling and distribution plant was established in De Aar. Various retail outlets were purchased in an arc from Mossel Bay, across the Klein Karoo and into the Great Karoo, as well as in Worcester and Bonnievale, from which to sell Jonkheer's wide range of wines.

Existing farms were replanted, then two more north of the Breede River were added to put some 260 hectares under irrigation. These supply less than 20 per cent of Jonkheer's needs with the remainder coming from Co-operatives ranging through from the area around Bonnievale to Du Toit's Kloof.

Langverwacht CO-OPERATIVE WINERY

Originally called the Boesmansrivier Co-operative, this winery was given its present name following objections from the Boesmansrivier Co-operative Cheese Factory. The cellar was designed by Pon van Zyl, formerly of the Robertson Co-operative, and built to receive the 1956 crop. Danie Kritzinger was appointed wine maker and manager in 1972. An annual crop of about 8 000 tonnes is supplied by the 37 members, no less than nine of whom are Wentzels.

The Co-operative's range of wines is certified as Boesmansrivier Wine of Origin; four natural wines and one fortified wine are produced.

Langverwacht Co-operative

Wines bottled and marketed by the Langverwacht Co-operative

White wines: Colombard Dry, Colombard Semi-Sweet, Late Harvest and Stein

A White Hanepoot Jerepigo is also bottled and marketed by the Langverwacht Co-operative.

The Co-operative is open to the public from 08h00 to 12h30 and from 13h00 to 17h00.

Merwespont CO-OPERATIVE WINERY

Situated on the road between Bonnievale and Swellendam, the Merwespont winery was formed in 1955, the building being completed in 1957. The main stress of production in the past has been on rebate wine for brandy distillation, but good wine now makes up about ten per cent of the winery's output, supervised by the wine maker, Dirk Cornelissen. This percentage should increase as other varieties are planted by the Co-operative's members, now numbering 60 and growing a combined annual crop of approximately 11 000 tonnes. A limited range of wines is available under the Merwespont label.

Merwespont Co-operative

Wines bottled and marketed by the Merwespont Co-operative

White wines: Colombard Effesoet, Chenin Blanc Dry and Late Vintage

The Merwespont Co-operative is open to the public on weekdays from 08h00 to 12h30 and from 13h30 to 17h00.

Mooiuitsig Wynkelders and Overberg Co-operative Winery

Mooiuitsig Co-operative

Wines bottled and marketed by the Mooiuitsig Co-operative

Red wines: Oude Rust Cabernet Sauvignon and Overberg Red Table Wine.
White wines: Oude Rust Riesling, Oude Rust Colombard, Oude Rust Chenin Blanc, Oude Rust Late Vintage, Rusthof Premier Grand Crû, Rusthof Stein, Overberg White Table Wine, Bonselect Semi-Sweet and Mooiuitsig Dry White.

Other wines include: Bonistein, Bonperlé and Clairvaux Mousseau.
Dessert wines: Oude Rust Red Muscadel, Oude Rust White Muscadel, Oude Rust Red Hanepoot, Oude Rust Red Malmsey, Oude Rust White Malmsey, Overberg Red Jerepigo, Overberg White Jerepigo, Bonwin Ruby Liqueur wine, Bonwin Golden Liqueur Wine, Muscana, Marsala, Mooiuitsig Sweet Hanepoot and Overberg Hanepoot.
Sherries: Monte Vista (Pale Dry, Medium Dry and Medium Cream).
Ports: Mooiuitsig Ports (Fine Old, Old Tawny, Old White, Cape and Invalid Port).

The Mooiuitsig Co-operative is open to the public on weekdays from 08h00 to 12h30 and from 13h00 to 17h30 (the Co-operative closes at 17h00 on Wednesdays and Fridays).

Mooiuitsig Wynkelders is a wholesale liquor concern, owned by the Jonker and Claassen families. Situated in the Breede River valley in the Bonnievale Ward, it markets a range of wines, many of which are made from grapes supplied to the Overberg Co-operative. This Co-operative, under the guidance of Boet Jonker, the managing director, comprises a complex of farms including Mooiuitsig, De Rust, Aan-De-Drift, Ardein and Rheenen. The winery itself was established in 1979. Chris Versfeld, the wine maker at both Overberg and Mooiuitsig, produces a range of some 40 wines, with an emphasis on sweeter wines, under a variety of labels including Mooiuitsig, Oude Rust, Bonwin, Monte Vista, Overberg and Rusthof.

Nordale
CO-OPERATIVE WINERY

Nordale Co-operative

Wines bottled and marketed by Nordale Co-operative

White wines: Steen, Colombard and Late Harvest
A Red Muscadel is also bottled and marketed by the Nordale Co-operative.

The Co-operative is open to the public on weekdays from 08h00 to 12h30 and from 13h30 to 17h00.

When it was first established in the early 1950s, this Co-operative's entire production was sold to the Castle Wine and Brandy Company for distillation. Rebate wine still accounts for 60 per cent of the winery's output, but since the introduction of cold fermentation in 1965 good wine production has been increased to its present 20 per cent of the total. Wine maker, Emile Schoch, currently bottles four of his quality wines under the Nordale label.

KLEIN-KAROO

In the town of Oudtshoorn a few examples still survive of the 'ostrich palaces', the ornately splendid Edwardian houses which sprang up here at the height of the ostrich feather boom at the beginning of the century. Besides that of *Struthio camelus*, other types of farming associated with the area include tobacco and, in recent years, an expanding wine production.

The Klein-Karoo District, narrow from north to south, stretches a considerable distance from west to east, running north of the Langeberg range from Montagu and eastwards through Barrydale, Ladismith and Calitzdorp to Oudtshoorn and De Hoop.

Because of inadequate supplies of irrigation water, vineyards are restricted to deep alluvial soils along the river banks, as well as to deep, red, clayish soils of a shale origin with a tendency to salinity and compaction. All must be extensively irrigated, for the climate here is dry to arid, with an average rainfall of less than 300 millimetres a year. The average summer temperatures vary between 20 and 22 °C, though in this inland region late frosts often occur during the winter.

Prominent co-operatives here include the Rietrivier Wine Cellar Co-operative, the Barrydale Co-operative Winery and Distillery (the only co-operative brandy distillery in the country), and the Kango Co-operative Tobacco and Wine Company – a rare case of two kinds of production under one roof.

Vineyards near Bonnievale against the blue massif of the Langeberg.

Barrydale CO-OPERATIVE WINERY AND DISTILLERY

The Barrydale Co-operative began life as a distillery in the early 1940s. However, it was soon found that the wine produced by the member farmers was not good enough to distil for fine brandy; for the 1942 season, therefore, wine-making facilities were provided at the distillery and the first 540 tonnes pressed. From then on wine making became a staple of the Co-operative's activities.

The wine maker and manager is Manfred van Heerden, who was appointed to the post in 1972. A total of 90 member farmers supply a crop of about 4 500 tonnes annually. A variety of grapes is received, but mostly Steen, Palomino, Colombar and Cinsaut. Limited bottling of wine for sale to the public takes place. Although brandy is distilled at Barrydale, it is not sold to the public but supplied to the KWV.

Boplaas

Situated on the outskirts of Calitzdorp and abutting the land of Die Krans from which it was subdivided in 1980, Boplaas Estate is run by Danie Nel and his son, Carel, with Leon Mostert as their cellar master. Danie and his brother, Chris, ran the original property of Die Krans until 1980, when they divided it. It had been in the Nel family since 1890, when it was purchased by their grandfather. Chris and his son, 'Boets', farmed the section which retained the name Die Krans, and Danie and Carel registered the remainder as a new Estate, Boplaas, on which they built a modern controlled-fermentation cellar in 1981, and restored an old cellar which they now use for maturing their wines.

Although the Calitzdorp area is generally warm to hot in summer, the nights are cool and a cool southerly wind from the sea, 80 kilometres away, prevails. These conditions are conducive to growing high-quality wine grapes and Carel and Danie concentrate on producing high-quality wines rather than on bulk wine making.

An extensive replanting programme was undertaken from 1979 onwards, during which most of the old bulk wine cultivars were uprooted. A representative range of cultivars, including Chenin Blanc, Sauvignon Blanc, Colombar, Cabernet Sauvignon, Merlot, Cabernet Franc, Shiraz, Pinotage, Tinta Barocca, Pinot Noir and White Muscadel, is now grown both on Boplaas and on the 35 hectares of

An enchanting winter view of Calitzdorp from the Boplaas Estate.

the nearby farm of Welgeluk, also owned by the Nel family.

Carel Nel has been experimenting with these various cultivars, and has come to the conclusion that the range of micro-climates and soil types on Boplaas is especially suited to the making of four types of wine in particular. Consequently, he gives special attention to his Port, which has won several gold medals at the South African Championship Wine Show, his Merlot, his wood-aged Blanc Fumé made from Sauvignon Blanc pressed at maximum ripeness, and his Boplaas Vonkel, a sparkling wine made by the *méthode champenoise* from Pinot Noir.

In 1986 Danie and Carel bought Ruiterbosch Mountain Vineyards in the Outeniqua mountains near Mossel Bay, which is probably the coolest wine farm in the country. Temperatures at this farm, from which one can see the sea, are generally even lower than those of the Constantia District. These conditions are ideal for the cultivation of certain varieties and the following cultivars have been planted: Chardonnay (six hectares), Pinot Noir (three hectares), Sauvignon Blanc (three hectares), and Weisser Riesling (two hectares).

Boplaas Estate

Cultivars Planted	Size of Vineyards (Hectares)
Steen	6
Colombar	4
Sauvignon Blanc	4
White Muscadel	4
Pinotage	2
Tinta Barocca	2
Cabernet Franc	1,5
Cabernet Sauvignon	1,5
Pinot Noir	1,5
Merlot	1
Weisser Riesling	1
Other cultivars	31,5

Total area under vines in 1987: 60 hectares
Wines currently bottled under the Boplaas Estate label: Sauvignon Blanc, Blanc Fumé, Vin Blanc, Late Harvest, Special Late Harvest, Sparkling Wine, Cabernet Sauvignon, Merlot, Tinta Barocca, Blanc de Noir, Rosé, White Muscadel, Sweet Hanepoot and a Port
Wood ageing: Wines are aged in wood on the Estate.

Boplaas Estate is open to the public on weekdays from 08h00 to 13h00 and on Saturday from 09h00 to 12h00.

Calitzdorp Co-operative

Wines bottled and marketed by the Calitzdorp Co-operative

Red wines: Pinotage and Rosetta
The Co-operative also bottles and markets a Blanc de Noir, Sherry and a number of dessert wines: Golden Jerepigo, White Jerepigo, Red Jerepigo, White Muscadel, Red Muscadel and a Sweet Hanepoot.

The Calitzdorp Co-operative is open to the public on weekdays from 08h00 to 17h30 and on Saturdays from 08h00 to 12h00.

Calitzdorp

FRUIT AND WINE CELLAR CO-OPERATIVE COMPANY

In 1928, 15 farmers founded the Calitzdorp Fruit Exporters Co-operative to export Hanepoot grapes. Ironically, not a single bunch was despatched abroad and in spite of its present name, fresh fruit plays no part in its activities. Wine production began during the Second World War and, after somewhat shaky fortunes in the first decades, the cellar was considerably modernized in the mid-1970s. The 106 member farmers supply over 3 000 tonnes of grapes annually. The main emphasis is upon Hanepoot, though White French, Steen, Colombar and Pinotage are also important – a champion red wine was made in 1978 from the Pinotage by the wine maker, James O'Kennedy.

The bulk of the wine goes to merchants, while the distilling wine is delivered to the KWV; a range of wines, mostly dessert wines, is bottled under the winery's own Buffelskroon label.

Die Krans

Situated in the picturesque valley of the Gamka River, on the edge of the town of Calitzdorp, the Estate of Die Krans was formerly part of a larger property owned and farmed by the brothers, Chris and Danie Nel, whose grandfather bought the farm in 1890. Brandy and sweet fortified wines were produced, some of which were exported to Britain. Ninety years later the land was divided, Chris and his son, 'Boets', retaining the 33,5 hectares of Die Krans, while Danie and his son, Carel, settled on the subdivision which was registered as the new Estate of Boplaas. In 1964 the present cellar was built and in

1979 Die Krans was registered as an Estate, the first in the Klein Karoo Region.

On Chris Nel's death in 1981, Boets took over the running of Die Krans and its wine making. The elder generation of the Nels had established a comprehensive range of cultivars, including Steen, Hanepoot and White Muscadel among the white varieties, and Pinotage, Tinta Barocca and Red Muscadel among the reds.

In 1985 the first Hárslevelü in the Region was bottled under the Estate's label and in 1986 the first Fernão Pires was bottled in the Klein Karoo, also from Die Krans. A dry red blend and a Tinta Barocca are wood-matured in new small French oak for at least six months, and the Estate's port for a year or more.

An array of prize-winning wines from Die Krans.

Die Krans Estate

Cultivars Planted	Size of Vineyards (Hectares)	Training Practice
Muscat d'Alexandrie	12	
Chenin Blanc	5	
White Muscadel	5	
Tinta Barocca	4	Most cultivars are
Colombard	2	on 2-wire vertical
Pinotage	2	trellises, while
Fernão Pires	1	vines on lower-lying
Gewürztraminer	1	ground are supported by
Hárslevelü	1	high-trellising.
Sauvignon Blanc	1	
Shiraz	1	

Total area under vines in 1987: 37 ha (2 ha are planted to table grapes)
Irrigation: All the vineyards of Die Krans are irrigated.
Temperature: Average maximum 25 °C; average minimum 10 °C
Average annual rainfall: Approximately 240 mm
Stock: Rooted vines are purchased from a nursery.
Envisaged new cultivar: Cabernet Sauvignon
First wines bottled under the Die Krans Estate label: Wit Muskadel, Pinotage, Tinta Barocca and port (all 1979) and Steen (no vintage date)
Wines currently bottled under the Die Krans Estate label: Chenin Blanc, Hárslevelü, Muscat d'Alexandrie, Stein, Fernão Pires, Pinotage Blanc de Noir, Chenin Blanc Special Late Harvest, Sauvignon Blanc, Shiraz, Dry Red, Pinotage and Tinta Barocca. A Sweet White Muscadel and a Port are also bottled and marketed by Die Krans.
Capacity of the Die Krans cellar: 9 000 hectolitres

Die Krans is open to the public on weekdays from 08h00 to 13h00 and from 14h00 to 17h00. On Saturdays the cellar is open from 09h00 to 12h00. Cellar tours, wine tasting and cheese lunches can be arranged throughout the year; during December cheese lunches are available every day from 12h00 to 14h00.

Die Poort

Nelis Jonker farmed with his father near Bonnievale for 15 years until, in 1957, he bought the undeveloped farm, Die Poort, on the banks of the Gouritz River. The farm is situated on the coastal side of the Langeberg at the spot where the river penetrates the mountain range, hence the name Die Poort. It was originally 120 hectares in extent but in 1960 Nelis purchased two adjoining farms across the river, Waterval and Die Hoek, thereby adding 82 hectares to the property. Nelis had found his father's Bonnievale farm too cramped, with almost every available square metre planted to vines. He revelled in the space at Die Poort and planned to introduce livestock as well as vines. He planted Hanepoot originally, as he had no KWV quota at the time and Hanepoot could be marketed as table grapes, and later, once the quota was obtained, would be acceptable for wine making. A quota was obtained in 1963, a cellar erected and the first grapes crushed. Meanwhile, Nelis had

Die Poort

Cultivars Planted	Size of Vineyards (Number of vines)	Training Practice
Colombar	13 000	Perold trellis
Hárslevelü	4 000	

Total area under vines in 1987: 45 ha
Irrigation: The vineyards of Die Poort are irrigated.
Temperatures: Records are not kept.
Average annual rainfall: Records are not kept.
Stock: Rooted vines are purchased from a nursery.
Envisaged new cultivar: Steen
First wine bottled under Die Poort label: Sweet Hanepoot (about 1971)
Wines currently bottled under Die Poort label: Rochelle Dry Red, Grand Crû, Steen, Blanc de Blanc, Fröhlich Stein, Late Vintage, Angelica and Hanepoot Semi-Sweet, Red Jerepigo, Red Muscadel, Rosé, Sherry and Special White Port
Wood-ageing: Wines are aged in wood on the farm.
Capacity of Die Poort cellar: 100 000 hectolitres

Die Poort is open to the public on weekdays from 08h00 to 17h30 and on Saturdays from 08h00 to 13h00.

established a Jersey herd and built a dairy on the farm, kept some 300 head of beef cattle and 1 000 head of Merino sheep.

Nowadays, however, the vineyards are the main source of income, although a good deal of lucerne is grown for sale. Farming with livestock at Die Poort has mostly been discontinued.

Prior to the flood of 1981, there were deep alluvial soils along the river, with rich, red soil away from the river up the slopes of the foothills of the Langeberg range, but with the flood most of the riverside vineyards were washed away. Those that were not were covered with new deposits of silt, up to 10 metres deep in places. New vineyards have since been

planted in these deposits on top of the old.

Most of the wine produced is fortified although small amounts of natural wine and distilling wine are produced. Some of the natural wine finds its way to the Reef and Cape Town markets but most of the production is sold through three 'farm depots'. These are Voorbrug, between Groot Brak River and George; Cooper Siding, between Albertinia and Mossel Bay; and Louterwater, near Joubertina.

The current wine maker, Anton Bredell, is a gentle giant of a man who, after graduating from Stellenbosch University, began his career at Windmeul Co-operative under the guidance of Bernhard Luttich.

The main cultivar grown is Colombar, but also grown are small quantities of Red and White Muscadel, Chenin Blanc, Muscat Humbro as well as Hárslevelü which Nelis and Anton pressed for the first time in 1987.

The farm does not produce enough grapes for the winery's needs and so grapes are bought in from the surrounding area, including Herbertsdale. Among the grapes bought in are Hanepoot, Raisin Blanc, Sémillon, Cinsaut and Palomino. In total some 2 500 tonnes are pressed annually. Many visitors to Mossel Bay and the Garden Route call at the winery, which is equipped with an attractive tasting room.

Doornkraal

The owner and wine maker of Doornkraal, Gerrit le Roux, took over the running of the farm in 1959 from his father, a Member of Parliament who combined parliamentary duties with farming in the Karoo. In the intervening decades Gerrit and his son, Piet, have expanded the vineyards and won prizes at the local shows for Doornkraal's sweet and fortified

wines. More recently they won a gold medal at the 1987 South African Wine Show in Goodwood for Doornkraal's Tinta Bianca, a Blanc de Noir wine, blended from Red Muscadel, Pinotage and Tinta Barocca. A dry white blend of Muscat Ottonel, Steen and Colombard is also available in limited quantities.

In an area where the annual rainfall is

some 100 millimetres, irrigation is supplied from the Stompdrift Dam on the nearby Olifants River, giving good crops in the fertile alluvial soils. Gerrit, a founder member of the Klein-Karoo Wine Trust, is particularly proud of his brightly coloured wine shop, which attracts many visitors on the road between De Rust and Oudtshoorn.

Kango

CO-OPERATIVE LIMITED

This company began life as a tobacco Co-operative in 1926. It was expanded in 1974, however, to take in the making of wine as well – many of the grape farmers in this area of the Klein-Karoo had traditionally delivered their grapes to the Union Wine Cellar at Oudtshoorn, an arrangement which ended in that year, leaving the farmers in urgent need of alternative facilities.

The winery section of the Kango Co-operative began production the following year, with 70 members, with both sections

of the enterprise under the former general manager, Mr P.K. Steyn. Since then the former wine maker, Pieter Conradie, has taken over as manager and the membership has increased to 86, supplying an annual 5 000 tonnes of grapes, the main cultivars being Palomino, Steen, Hanepoot, Muscadel and Colombar, together with some Pinotage and Tinta Barocca. The wine maker is Mr B.W. Myburgh. His wines have had a number of successes at the local wine shows, including a gold medal at Goodwood in

1979 for the Co-operative's Raisin Blanc. Some 11 wines now comprise the winery's marketed range – the 'Rijckshof' label depicts a now-demolished 'ostrich palace', Oliver Towers.

Ladismith CO-OPERATIVE WINERY AND DISTILLERY

This company began as a distillery in 1939. Then in the early 1970s its production was expanded to include wine, and modern equipment for cold fermentation was installed. In 1975 Alex Rossouw was appointed manager and wine maker. The Ladismith wines (the present range is three) are sold under the name Towerkop – 'Bewitched Mountain' – after the highest peak of the Klein Swartberg which towers behind the town and which legend claims was split asunder by a witch.

Ladismith Co-operative

Wines bottled and marketed by the Ladismith Co-operative

Red wine: Dry Red
White wines: Dry White and Stein

Ladismith Co-operative is open to the public on weekdays from 08h00 to 13h00 and from 14h00 to 17h00

Montagu MUSCADEL FARMERS' CO-OPERATIVE

The original intention of this Co-operative was to concentrate upon fortified Muscadel wines, other grapes not suitable for this purpose being sent to the KWV for distillation. In 1968, however the cellar was modified to produce dry natural wines, and in 1970 a further diversification took place when the winery began making concentrated grape juice for export to West Germany. Membership is now about 90, and each year these farmers deliver some 8 700 tonnes of grapes, made into wine under the supervision of Mr S.B. (Sonnie) Malan. The Co-operative's Volsoet Rooi Muskadel has an excellent show record; in 1980 it was the South African champion Muscat fortified wine and has been a regular trophy winner ever since. The cellar also produces good natural dry white wines.

Montagu Muscadel Farmers' Co-operative

Wines bottled and marketed by the Montagu Muscadel Farmers' Co-operative

White wines: Chenin Blanc, Colombar, Late Vintage and Sauvignon Blanc
   A Red Muscadel is also bottled and marketed by the Co-operative.

The Co-operative is open to the public on weekdays from 08h00 to 12h00 and from 13h00 to 17h00.

Rietrivier WINE CELLAR CO-OPERATIVE

Situated 20 kilometres east of Montagu on the road to Barrydale, the Rietrivier cellar was completed in 1967. Under the aegis of Piet Frick, wine maker and manager, the winery specializes in making top quality rebate wine for brandy production, for which it has won numerous prizes and trophies over the years, including the title of Champion Co-operative at the Klein Karoo Wine Show in 1983 and 1985. The 45 member farmers deliver an annual 4 000 tonnes of grapes. Besides making rebate wine, a range of table wines is now marketed under the Rietrivier label.

Rietrivier Co-operative

Wines bottled and marketed by the Rietrivier Co-operative

White wines: Chenin Blanc, Hárslevelü, Blanc de Blanc, Late Harvest, Stein and Colombar
   A Red Muscadel is also bottled and marketed by the Rietrivier Co-operative.

The Co-operative is open to the public on weekdays from 08h00 to 13h00 and from 14h00 to 17h00, and on Saturdays from 08h00 to 11h00.

Soetwynboere Co-operative

Wines bottled and marketed by the Soetwynboere Co-operative

White wines: Colombard, Chenin Blanc, Late Harvest, Stein and Grand Crû
   A Red Muscadel and a White Hanepoot are also bottled and marketed by the Soetwynboere Co-operative.

The Co-operative is open to the public on weekdays from 08h00 to 12h30 and from 13h30 to 17h00, and on Saturdays from 08h00 to 11h00.

Soetwynboere CO-OPERATIVE

Founded in 1941, the Soetwyn Co-operative was built under conditions of war-time shortage, and the original cellar had to be thatched for lack of any other roofing material. In 1953, Kenneth Knipe was appointed winery manager and wine maker, a position he still holds. Despite its name, the cellar also makes dry natural wines and excellent rebate wine for brandy production. The 54 members supply between 4 000 and 5 000 tonnes of grapes a year.

OLIFANTSRIVIER

By the middle of the nineteenth century vineyards were planted along the banks of the southern reaches of the Olifants River. The wine produced was mainly kept for local consumption, and included a percentage of dessert wine but the creative enthusiasm of most of the wine farmers was reserved for the making of brandy. These were palmy days for the brandy industry in the mountains, for permits for distilling wine were issued with cheerful abandon (the owner of the Matjiesrivier farm in the Cedarberg received a permit to distil the produce of a single vine!). Given such official encouragement the making of brandy flourished through to the 1920s, when the issue of distilling permits became the responsibility of the Department of Customs and Excise and the KWV. The resulting stringency cast a shadow over the distillers of the high valleys, and within a few years the healthy flow of brandy had dwindled to a trickle.

But while brandy is no longer so important along the Olifants River, a substantial amount of grapes is still grown here, processed in the six local Co-operatives.

The District reaches from Citrusdal in the south to Lutzville in the north, and includes the areas of Clanwilliam, Klawer, Vredendal and Koekenaap. It is a hot, dry part with the lowest rainfall near the sea. At Citrusdal and Clanwilliam, citrus and rooibos herbal tea farming predominate and the vineyards are largely concentrated to the north, along the Olifants River and between Trawal and Koekenaap, where they receive intensive irrigation from the Clanwilliam and Bulhoek dams.

Three soil types are mainly used for viticulture – the fertile soils near the rivers, medium potential red sandy soils, and high potential Karoo soils. On the mountain range between Clanwilliam and Graafwater the vineyards have an average rainfall of approximately 400 millimetres, and a summer temperature of 21 °C. In the Trawal and Koekenaap areas the annual rainfall at about 300 millimetres is appreciably lower and the winters are very mild. The vineyards here are planted on terraces to provide flood irrigation, and are intensively trellised to give active leaf surface, ripening heavy crops under cool micro-climate conditions in the shade of the leaves.

The slow-moving waters of the Olifants River are the life-blood of the vineyards of the District, providing much-needed irrigation during the hot months of the growing season.

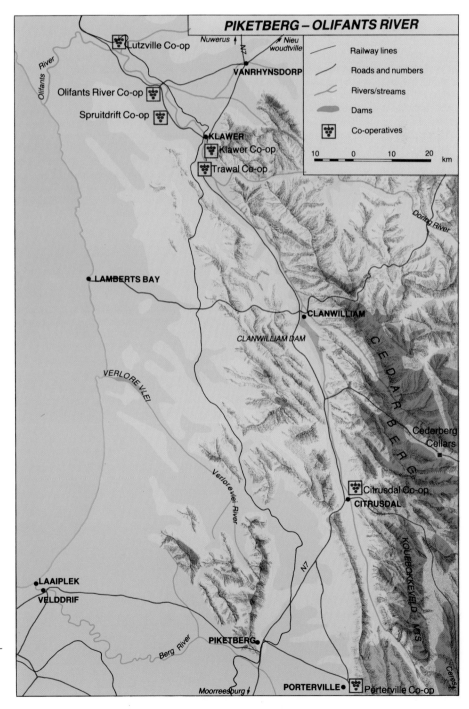

PIKETBERG – OLIFANTS RIVER

- Railway lines
- Roads and numbers
- Rivers/streams
- Dams
- Co-operatives

10   0   10   20 km

Lutzville Co-op
Nuwerus
Nieuwoudtville
VANRHYNSDORP
Olifants River Co-op
Spruitdrift Co-op
KLAWER
Klawer Co-op
Trawal Co-op
Doring River
LAMBERTS BAY
CLANWILLIAM
CLANWILLIAM DAM
CEDARBERG
VERLORE VLEI
Cederberg Cellars
Verlore vlei River
Citrusdal Co-op
CITRUSDAL
KOUEBOKKEVELD MTS
N7
LAAIPLEK
VELDDRIF
Berg River
PIKETBERG
Moorreesburg
PORTERVILLE
Porterville Co-op
Ceres

Cederberg Cellars

Overlooked by the Sneeuberg, the Tafelberg, and the Wolfberg Cracks in the Cedarberg mountains, this family-run winery is part of Dwarsrivier, the farm owned by David Josephus Nieuwoudt, universally known as 'Oom Pollie'. The running of the cellars, as well as the 18-hectare vineyard, is the responsibility of Pollie's son, Frikkie, while the remainder of the farm, comprising fruit orchards, livestock and tobacco, is in the charge of his elder brother, Ernst.

At a lofty 1 200 metres above sea-level, Dwarsrivier has a cool, mild climate for most of the year, with an annual rainfall of 450 to 500 mm. Much of the higher ground is stony, but the lower reaches have good, fertile red soils on which is grown a mix of Cabernet, Pinotage, Barlinka (a table grape), Riesling and Bukettraube.

Until 1964 there were no vines on Dwarsrivier. Then, following a suggestion by Attie Rabie of the Deciduous Fruit Board, Oom Pollie introduced a small block of Barlinka table grapes. With his modest vineyard doing well, he and Frikkie then built a small wine cellar, later enlarged at

Frikkie's insistence. Registered in 1973 as the Cederberg Cellars Company, they at first made only a small amount of 'boerewyn' from the Barlinka grapes.

Within a few years, however, they had increased their plantings with blocks of Cabernet and Pinotage, causing much local comment with their investment in these high quality red varieties in an area largely given to white wine production. It was a bold move, but it paid off, and with startling speed: the 1978 Cabernet made local history as, with its first entry in 1979 in the Olifants River Wine Show, it won the Distillers Corporation Trophy. In the same year this Cabernet also won the Gold Medal at the Cape Championship Wine Show. These successes were later emulated by the 1986 Cabernet.

Now firmly on the map of the Olifantsrivier District, Cederberg Cellars currently bottle Pinotage under their own label. One of the more recent labels is most attractive, featuring the 'Maltese Cross Rock' in the Cedarberg mountains. The wines can be bought on the farm, by postal order, or at retail outlets.

'Oom Pollie' Nieuwoudt of Cederberg Cellars.

Citrusdal CO-OPERATIVE WINE CELLAR

The first vintage of 783 tonnes was pressed at this cellar in 1958, under the supervision of Hermann Wolff. One of the winery's first products was a 'chianti' style of wine, a blend of Cinsaut and Grenache, which was the pride of the cellar for many years. Under the general managership of Hannes Ehlers production increased dramatically, and by the time he retired at the end of June 1987, the cellar was crushing between 8 000 and 9 000 tonnes, depending on the vintage.

The cellar is unique in the area in that it packs and sells almost its entire production in a range that varies with the year, but usually numbers some 15 to 20 natural wines, including a Riesling, a dry white wine and a semi-sweet Weisser Riesling. The cellar also produces about seven fortified wines and a range of 'standard' price wines that are highly competitive. The wines are sold at the cellar and at the Co-operative's own bottle store in Citrusdal.

The Citrusdal Co-operative Wine Cellar which bottles an extensive and varying range of wines.

Klawer CO-OPERATIVE WINE CELLAR

Klawer Co-operative

Wines bottled and marketed by the Klawer Co-operative

Red wines: Pinotage and Shiraz
White wines: Late Vintage, Special Late Vintage, Premier Grand Crû, Muscat Ottonel, Chenin Blanc, Colombar, Sauvignon Blanc and Hárslevelü
A Blanc de Noir is also bottled and marketed by the Co-operative as well as three dessert wines: Soet Hanepoot, Red Muskadel and Wit Muskadel.

The Klawer Co-operative is open to the public on weekdays from 08h30 to 12h30 and from 13h30 to 17h30.

One of the larger Co-operatives, the Klawer Wine Cellars receive some 20 000 tonnes of grapes annually from 80 members in the Vredendal and Klawer districts. The former wine maker and present manager, Piet Matthee, won a number of prizes for his wines, both in the local Olifants River Show and in the Cape Championship Wine Show – including the 1979 trophy for the champion fortified muscat-type wine. The present wine maker, Bob de Villiers, was awarded a gold medal for his Colombar at the Club Oenologique in London.

An impressive avenue of stainless steel tanks at the Klawer Co-operative.

Lutzville Co-operative

Wines bottled and marketed by the Lutzville Co-operative

White wines: Sauvignon Blanc, Emerald Riesling, Chenin Blanc (all under the Fleermuisklip label), Colombard, Bukettraube and Late Harvest (under the Lutzville Co-operative label)
A Sweet Hanepoot is also bottled and marketed by the Lutzville Co-operative.

The Co-operative is open to the public on weekdays from 08h00 to 17h00 and on Saturdays from 09h00 to 12h00.

Lutzville VINEYARDS CO-OPERATIVE

Established in 1962, this Co-operative receives 30 000 tonnes annually from 109 members in the Wards of Lutzville and Koekenaap. Most of the grapes are processed into rebate wine for brandy production and only the best grapes are reserved for the making of dry white wines. Lutzville Vineyards is under the management of Johan Theron and the wine maker is Gerhard van Deventer.

Part of the extensive irrigation scheme on the Olifants River near the Lutzville Co-operative.

Tank cleaning in the Spruitdrift winery.

Spruitdrift
CO-OPERATIVE WINE CELLAR

One of the younger Co-operatives in the Vredendal area, the Spruitdrift winery, which is quite spectacular in size, has the benefit of advanced cellar technology and equipment in the handling of its 20 000-tonne annual intake from 127 members. The former wine maker, Gielie Swiegers, made his name at McGregor Co-operative where he pioneered Cabernet Sauvignon and Noble Late Harvest wines. After Gielie's arrival at Spruitdrift the quality of the Co-operative's wines improved beyond recognition. Production was mainly from Palomino (45 per cent) and Hanepoot (40 per cent), with the balance coming from Steen, Grenache, Colombar and others. The present wine maker is Johan Rossouw, formerly wine maker at Simonsvlei Co-operative. Under his guidance a number of new cultivars have been planted; these include Gewürztraminer, Sauvignon Blanc, Fernão Pires, Hárslevelü and Ferdinand de Lesseps.

Spruitdrift Co-operative

Wines bottled and marketed by the Spruitdrift Co-operative

Red wines: Pinotage and Dry Red
White wines: Premier Grand Crû, Sauvignon Blanc, Hárslevelü, Late Harvest, Special Late Harvest, Chenin Blanc and Colombard
 Rosé, Blanc de Noir, Red Port and two dessert wines, Red Muscadel and White Hanepoot, are also bottled and marketed by the Co-operative.

The Spruitdrift Co-operative is open to the public on weekdays from 08h00 to 12h30 and from 14h00 to 17h30, and on Saturdays from 08h00 to 11h00.

Trawal
CO-OPERATIVE WINE CELLAR

Situated near Klawer, this Co-operative was started in 1969, and is currently run by J.P. (Kobus) Basson. All wine made here is supplied in bulk to the trade.

Vredendal CO-OPERATIVE WINE CELLARS

Modern stainless steel equipment gleams in the sun at the Vredendal Co-operative.

Formerly known as the Olifantsrivier Co-operative, this is the largest co-operative winery under one roof in the country and up to 50 000 tonnes of grapes, from 175 members, have been delivered to the Co-operative at harvest times. Situated in the village of Vredendal, it was established in 1948, and is run by Gielie Swiegers, who took over from Corrie de Kock when he retired in 1986. Gielie had spent four years at Spruitdrift Co-operative, and had previously made a name for himself at McGregor Co-operative.

Mostly white wine cultivars are grown in the Ward of Vredendal, among them Fernão Pires, Hárslevelü, Bukettraube, Sauvignon Blanc and Weisser Riesling, but some reds, such as Pinotage and Tinta Barocca, are also grown. Although much of the crop is turned into distilling wine, a range of light table wines and good quality single-cultivar wines is made. The

Vredendal Co-operative

Wines bottled and marketed by the Vredendal Co-operative

Red wines: Pinotage and Dry Red
White wines: Grand Crû, Hárslevelü, Fernão Pires, Bukettraube, Late Harvest, Special Late Harvest, Chenin Blanc and Sauvignon Blanc
 A Red Muscadel and a Sweet Hanepoot are also bottled and marketed by the Vredendal Co-operative.

The Co-operative is open to the public on weekdays from 08h30 to 12h30 and from 14h00 to 17h30, and on Saturdays from 08h00 to 12h00.

attractive emblem of the Co-operative is the Namaqua dove, symbolizing the peace ('vrede') of Vredendal, and the wine labels, depicting the area covered in spring blossoms, incorporate the Vredendal Municipality's coat of arms, which also features the Namaqua dove.

DOUGLAS

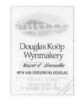

Originally part of the Orange River wine area, and sharing its generally hot, dry climate, the Douglas District was given separate Wine of Origin status in 1981.

Douglas
CO-OPERATIVE WINERY

Started in 1968, this winery now receives grapes from the Douglas, Prieska, and Hopetown areas. The intake comprises about 30 per cent Sultana grapes and 15 per cent each of Hanepoot and Palomino, with the balance being shared between Steen and Colombar. 'Pou' le Roux makes a

Douglas Co-operative

Wines bottled and marketed by the Douglas Co-operative

Red wine: Droë Rooi
White Wines: Colombard, Late Vintage, Stein, Soet Sultana and Soet Muscat d'Alexandrie
  A Rosé is also bottled and marketed by the Douglas Co-operative.

The Co-operative is open to the public on weekdays from 08h00 to 17h00, and cellar tours are conducted by appointment only.

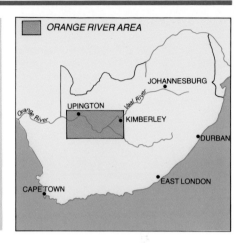

ORANGE RIVER AREA

range of wines bearing the Douglas label from a small percentage of the winery's

output, the bulk of the wine being sold to merchants.

ANDALUSIA

In 1933 the then Minister of Lands, Colonel Denys Reitz, announced the establishment of the Vaalharts Irrigation Scheme. Based on ideas put forward by Cecil Rhodes, for his own profit, as far back as 1881, the Minister hoped instead to settle farmers who were in hardship as a result of drought and economic depression. Developed at the confluence of the Vaal and Harts rivers, some 80 kilometres north of Kimberley, it has become one of the world's largest irrigation schemes.

The general produce of the scheme is handled by the Vaalharts Agricultural Co-operative. The growing of grapes has steadily increased, and with it the making of wine, to the extent that the area previously known as the Ward of Vaalharts was declared a District in its own right and renamed Andalusia. It has since reverted to the status of a Ward, but it does not fall under any Region or District.

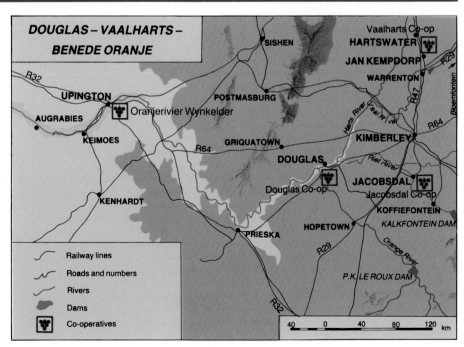

Jacobsdal WINE CELLAR CO-OPERATIVE

The Orange Free State's solitary co-operative winery, the Jacobsdal Wine Cellar, part of the South Western Transvaal Agricultural Co-operative, was started in 1974. Much of the setting up of the vineyards was overseen by the Viticultural and Oenological Research Institute, mostly from its Jan Kempdorp station, which advised on the most appropriate cultivars for this arid climate. The first wine was made from the 1977 vintage, under the supervision of the former wine maker, 'Bertie' Bruyns. The winery's produce is marketed under the Bloemdal label and the present wine maker is Jan Sieg.

Vaalharts FARMERS' CO-OPERATIVE

This modern, well-equipped cellar is the only Co-operative north of the Vaal River, and was started in 1977 under the aegis of the Vaalharts Agricultural Co-operative. The Vaalharts irrigation area is about 100 kilometres north of Kimberley in a shallow, wide valley between the Vaal and Harts rivers. It is the largest irrigation area in the southern hemisphere, drawing water via a complicated canal system from the Vaal River near Warrenton, and was started in 1933 during the Depression, when the State made irrigated farmland available to ex-soldiers. Today the area supports huge crops of wheat, maize, groundnuts, table grapes and wine grapes.

The Co-operative is situated near Hartswater, one of the two towns in the area, the other being Jan Kempdorp.

Roelof Maree is the manager of the cellar and also the wine maker, having previously been a wine blender with Distillers' Corporation, an assistant at the Franschhoek Co-operative and cellar manager at Frans Malan's Simonsig Estate. His assistant is Joshua du Toit. The Co-operative also has a viticulture adviser for the members, Koos Le Roux. Cultivars such as Colombar, Clairette Blanche, Chenel, Fernão Pires, Emerald Riesling and Erlihane have been planted on about 300 hectares of vineyards. The certified wines are marketed as Andalusia Wine of Origin while the uncertified range is marketed under the Overvaal label.

Jacobsdal Co-operative

Wines bottled and marketed by the Jacobsdal Co-operative

White wines: Late Harvest and Stein
A Rosé and two dessert wines, a Volsoet Sultana and a Volsoet Hanepoot, are also bottled and marketed by the Jacobsdal Co-operative.

The Co-operative is open to the public on weekdays from 09h00 to 13h00 and from 14h00 to 17h00, and on Saturdays from 09h00 to 12h00.

Vaalharts Co-operative

Wines bottled and marketed by the Vaalharts Co-operative

White wines: Overvaal Grand Crû, Overvaal Stein, Overvaal Late Harvest, Andalusia Colombard and Andalusia Chenel
Dessert wines: Overvaal Hanepoot, Andalusia Jerepiko and Andalusia Erlihane
An Overvaal Sherry is also bottled and marketed by the Vaalharts Co-operative.

The Co-operative is open to the public on weekdays from 08h00 to 17h00 and on Saturdays from 08h00 to 12h00.

BENEDE ORANJE

Centred around the town of Upington on the Lower Orange River, this very hot area is the most northerly of the country's wine-making regions. As with the Ward of Andalusia, it is based on a large-scale irrigation scheme along the banks of the river, and, like Andalusia, this Ward does not fall under any Region or District. The Benede Oranje vineyards extend between the Boegoeberg Dam and the Augrabies Falls, and yield heavy crops on deep, fertile soils.

Oranjerivier WYNKELDER

Established in 1965 with its headquarters at Upington, this Co-operative has branches along the Orange River at Groblershoop, Grootdrink, Kakamas and Keimoes. Under the general managership of Noel Mouton, the combine handles a massive 80 000 tonnes of grapes a year; of this a small amount goes to make the Co-operative's range of dry and sweet white wines.

Oranjerivier Co-operative

Wines bottled and marketed by the Oranjerivier Co-operative

Red wine: Pinotage
White wines: Grand Crû, Colombard, Stein and Late Harvest
A Rosé is also bottled and marketed by the Oranjerivier Co-operative, as well as a number of dessert wines: Effesoet Sultana, Dessert Hanepoot, Jerepigo and White Muscadel.

The Co-operative is open to the public on weekdays from 08h30 to 12h45 and from 14h00 to 17h00, and on Saturdays from 08h30 to 13h00.

Cape Independent Wine Maker's Guild

The Cape Independent Wine Maker's Guild was founded in 1983, at the instigation of Billy Hofmeyr of Welgemeend, with the aim of promoting the production, bottling and marketing of excellent wine by its members. An aim of the Guild is 'to contribute to the advancement of the quality of Cape wines by mutually developing the knowledge, capabilities and horizons of the members'. Members must be active wine makers themselves, and be prepared to share their knowledge and experience with each other and to learn from each other. They must be independent, that is, free of connection with wholesalers or co-operative groups. Their methods of promoting their wines include an annual auction, group export arrangements and general publicity. A small export venture has been started in Britain, where the wines are sold by mail order under the Guild label.

The Guild's annual auction is held at Sotheby's in Johannesburg and has become a highlight of the wine lover's year. In September 1987, for example, some 3 000 cases of wine from the cellars of 14 of the Guild's members were auctioned. All the bottles at each year's auction are individually numbered and display the Cape Independent Wine Maker's Guild label. Tastings of the wines to be auctioned in Johannesburg are held from about a week beforehand in all the main cities of the country, under the auspices of Sotheby's, and one does not need to be physically at the auction to be able to take part in the bidding – postal bids may be submitted. In addition, tastings of the wines to be auctioned are held at embassies all over the world and bids are received from every conceivable quarter. Features of the auction are the high prices fetched, and the relative youth of most of the wines. The Guild is scrupulous in satisfying itself, through rigorous self-scrutiny, that the wines on offer measure up to the best of wine-making standards. None of the wines offered is ever older than five years and all have been selected with a view to long life and good bottle maturation potential. The auctions generally take place in September and to date have been conducted by David Molyneux-Berry, Master of Wine, head of the wine department of Sotheby's, London.

Wine makers currently belonging to the Guild include Jannie Engelbrecht and Kevin Arnold of Rust-en-Vrede, Jan 'Boland' Coetzee of Vriesenhof, Pieter Ferreira of Clos Cabrière, Janey Muller of Lemberg, Braam van Velden of Overgaauw, Billy Hofmeyr of Welgemeend, Johan Malan of Simonsig, Neil Ellis of Zevenwacht, Etienne le Riche of Rustenberg and Schoongezicht, Jeff Grier of Villiera, Beyers Truter of Kanonkop, Walter Finlayson of Blaauwklippen, Peter Finlayson of Hamilton Russell Vineyards, Kurt Ammann of Rozendal and Achim von Arnim of Boschendal.

OTHER AUCTIONS

After the success of the annual Nederburg Auction and having been made aware of the need for wine collectors to be able to trade their wine legally, the Minister of Justice under whose department the Liquor Act was administered, announced when opening the fifth Nederburg Auction in 1979 that the law would be altered to allow auctions at which the consumer could participate. It took some years, however, until the law was changed accordingly.

Nowadays, regular auctions are held by the internationally renowned auction house, Sotheby Park Bernet of London, through Sotheby's of South Africa, by the Cape Independent Wine Makers' Guild, South African Vintage Wine Auctions (Julius Buchinsky) and others. The Durban Wine Centre has established the Durban Wine Auction and a whole host of charity auctions are regularly held throughout the country to raise money for various good causes.

AN APPROACH TO WINE

The practical art of the wine maker ends with the bottling of his wines. Their distribution to the public can then be through restaurants, hotels or bottle-stores, and in some cases direct. From this moment on, the wine becomes the creative province of the individual wine lover.

The relationship between wine and drinker may be simple or sophisticated. It may be a casual matter of the odd glass of wine over lunch, the occasional bottle with a good dinner, a passing but pleasurable acquaintance. Or it may be a deeper and fuller commitment. All aspects of wine and its culture, from its history to its growing and making, from its storage to its presentation, and above all, its tasting and appreciation, may become areas of exploration and delight in their own right. The pleasures of wine may thus be developed with knowledge and experience into something more complex, rewarding and enduring, a lifetime's pursuit.

As with art, music and literature, wine appreciation is a matter of aesthetics, for a wine too has properties of balance, harmony and complexity. And like art, there are no simple equations which exist for its evaluation; the way to understand it is through conscious effort.

Your first reaction to a wine is purely subjective – you like it or you don't and with continued wine-tasting experience you confirm or reverse your initial reaction. For example, a wine found undesirable may suddenly become quite pleasurable or a wine once praised may no longer have appeal.

Wine appreciation is a learned response comprising sensory pleasures, social custom and personal experience. Individual preferences and prejudices certainly increase the complexity of understanding wine but there is a rational basis for its appreciation which provides general aesthetic principles.

Price, region, producer and vintage all have a bearing on the quality of wine but it is the sensory attributes of the wine in the glass that are important and not the words on the label, the price, or the excellence of the advertising. The intelligent wine connoisseur develops sufficient sensory skill and aesthetic appreciation to be able to ignore with confidence both advertising agencies and 'wine snobs' who contend that expensive and imported products are automatically better and that wines from certain vineyards, producers, Estates or vintages are always superior. The expensive may be poor because it is too old or for other reasons, and every vineyard, producer and vintage has its failures.

Wine appreciation

The best way to increase your knowledge of wines is through wine-tasting gatherings where you can benefit from the expertise of others and share the group experience. Such events often seem discouraging for they can imply an over-zealous approach to serving wine or for setting rigid rules for the tasting of a variety of wines. This need not be so, however, and the following guiding principles will help you to gain confidence in wine-tasting, thereby adding immeasurably to your enjoyment of wine.

THE GLASS

A clear wine glass should be used – preferably one with a tulip-shaped bowl to capture and hold the bouquet. A coloured or distorted glass will make the assessment of a wine's clarity or colour impossible. The glass should be clean and then rinsed with a little of the wine to be tasted. Warm glasses or glasses recently rinsed in hot water are unsuitable since temperature plays a vital role in the evaluation of wine.

Pour the wine into the glass to a depth of 20 to 25 millimetres. This will be sufficient for you to swirl the wine so that it coats the maximum surface area inside the glass, thereby giving off a sufficient bouquet.

Hold the glass by the stem or base and not by the bowl so that the wine is not obscured by fingers or finger marks. This also prevents the bowl being warmed, which in turn would raise the temperature of the wine. Furthermore, the glass can be swirled with ease . . . and it also looks more professional!

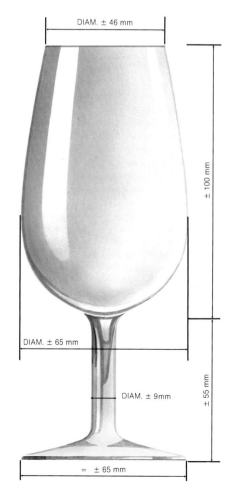

The ideal wine glass as recommended by the International Standards Organisation, but any clear glass with a 'tulip-shaped' bowl will hold the bouquet of the wine.

DIAM. ± 46 mm

± 100 mm

DIAM. ± 65 mm

DIAM. ± 9mm

± 55 mm

= ± 65 mm

THE WINE

Wine must have a lively, living appearance and not the flat, dull or lifeless look of a liquid that has been standing for too long. It should be bright and clear, although in many of the best red wines a sediment can be an indication of great quality.

Swirl the wine in the glass and note the 'tears' or 'legs' which form on the sides and run back into the wine. These are thought by some to show wines of high quality, although others contend that this is not necessarily so. Legs are a sure indication of high alcohol, however, as they form as a result of rapid evaporation of alcohol from the thin film of wine adhering to the sides of the glass. High sugar and/or glycerol levels could further enhance this effect.

Small bubbles may be seen inside a bottle of 'still' wine and these adhere to the wine glass at the edge of the wine after pouring. They are often a desirable characteristic, in fact people in Europe prefer wines with a slight 'sparkle'. Such bubbles can result from carbonic acid which dissolves in wine during the fermentation process and is eventually released as bubbles, a natural liveliness, when the wine is opened and served, or from the modern pressure filtering machine designed to ensure that wine reaches the consumer in peak condition.

The range of colours displayed by wines is very wide from the almost transparent steely tint of a delicate white through the soft pink of rosés and Blanc de Noir wines, to the deep rich red of the Cabernet Sauvignons and Pinot Noirs.

COLOUR

As you look at your wine, preferably against a white surface, note its gradations of colour. In a poorer wine probably only a few will be noticeable, but in a wine of quality whether young or old there will be many more. Bear this in mind during a 'blind tasting' when you might be asked to assess the quality of, or identify, a wine. Generally, white wines darken with age whilst red wines lighten but become browner in hue.

White wines range in colour from green tinged with yellow to dark amber, although table wines are usually pale greeny-yellow to straw-yellow; young wines are often paler. Those made from very ripe or late-harvest grapes are darker than those that do not ripen fully. Wines made from grapes grown in cool areas are usually lighter in colour, whilst grapes grown in warmer regions produce wines that are more gold than yellow.

When white wines are stored over a long period, whether in a bottle or a vat, they eventually turn amber or brown mainly as a result of oxidation. One can distinguish an oxidized wine from one that is well bottle-aged by appearance: oxidized whites have a brownish, misty look, while bottle-aged whites show yellowness rather than

brownness and don't lose their clarity. The process of browning and oxidizing is loosely called maderisation, as the wine thus affected tastes slightly like Madeira wine and is related to the presence of ethylic aldehyde in the wine. Such wines give off a caramel-type odour but they do not always deteriorate as a result. Crisp white wines made from Riesling and dry Steens generally lose quality but certain fortified wines can attain greatness through maderisation.

Although it is often held that white wines are better drunk young and fresh, a particularly good white wine will retain its freshness and vigour while maturing for five years or more.

Blanc de Noir wines have only the faintest blush of colour, a pale salmon pink variously described as 'onion skin' or 'Oeil de Perdrix', 'The Eye of the Partridge'.

Rosé wines made in South Africa should preferably be pink without traces of brown, orange or tan. Usually brown and tawny hues in rosés indicate that the wine has aged too long or has become oxidized. The great rosés of Tavel in France are the exception, however, as they are very definitely more orange than pink.

Red wines have a wide range of acceptable colours depending on vintage conditions, the age of the wine, the type of grape used and the style of wine making. Some very young reds may be purple-red, whilst others are more ruby and develop a tawny tint with age.

The colour of red wine is pH dependent: the lower the pH (or the higher the acid content), the more purple the colour of a young red wine; and the higher the pH (or the lower the acid content) the greater the tendency to have traces of yellow and/or orange intermingled with the purple.

As red wines mature their colour changes from ruby to a brick red. This change results from polymerisation or the linking together of pigment molecules. In a young wine these molecules occur singly, but as the wine matures they form chains. Sediment developing in very old wines (a bottle age of about 20 years) results when such chains become too heavy to remain suspended and collect at the lowest point of the bottle.

Other colours to note are those found in red wines which have either been over-matured in the bottle or which have become oxidized. With good bottle maturation of 20 to 30 years red wines tend to lose some colour but an oxidized wine turns a very dark brown-red and usually becomes cloudy. When nosing or smelling an oxidized wine a definite baked smell is apparent.

SMELL

A good sense of smell is essential for the proper appreciation of wine, not only because the nose perceives and recognizes various subtleties of bouquet and aroma but also because the sense of smell constitutes some 75 per cent of taste perception. Consequently, a person with little or no sense of smell cannot fully appreciate the subtle nuances of flavour and aroma.

Fortunately very few people have no olfactory sense, and with a little practice and concentration it is possible for most of us to develop this sense to the extent that wine appreciation becomes a joy. The biggest problem facing all wine lovers, experts and connoisseurs alike is that they find it very difficult to express their perceptions of various smell and taste sensations verbally, and each publication on wine seems to have evolved its own lengthy list of often meaningless terms, thus confusing the issue to an even greater extent.

How to smell or nose a wine. Swirl the wine in the bowl of the glass and then sniff it hard to assess the bouquet. The best method is to sniff the wine quickly, then remove the glass and sniff again after about 30 seconds. The first sniff, however, is all important and is often the basis of judgement. Try to memorise the smell by associating it with something personally experienced.

Wine odours (or smells) may be divided into two groups: bouquet and aroma; and the so-called off-odours.

Although bouquet is used generally when discussing the fragrance or smell of the wine, some experts maintain that the term is only correctly applicable to odours derived from the fermentation, processing, or maturation. The range of pleasant and desirable wine odours derived from the grape itself is called the aroma. Certain grape varieties when grown under optimum conditions, have characteristic aromas. The serious taster should develop a clear impression of these basic, easily identifiable varietal aromas so that when faced with an unknown wine sample he can at least identify the grape variety from which the wine was made.

Desirable odours include fruity, flowery, clean, perfumed, positive, spicy, depth , penetrating, heady, sweet, fine, fresh and piquant.

Undesirable odours include sulphur and those of bacteria, mousy, butyric,

acetic, oxidized, maderised, cooked or burnt, mouldy or musty, woody or oaky (if too pronounced), corked, corky, acidic, baked, dumb, little or poor, green, stemmy or stalky, yeasty and peppery.
All these terms are explained in the glossary (see page 324).

TASTE

In appreciating wine the ability to taste is considered less important than the ability to nose or smell, the reason being that taste usually serves to confirm information given by the nose. However, if the wine is poorly balanced in that it is too sweet, too bitter, too acid or too astringent, it will be rejected on taste though not necessarily on smell.

The nose plays an important role in wine appreciation not only for smelling the wine directly but also for tasting. To illustrate this, pinch the nostrils together to block out smell and then taste the wine – you will find that your taste sensitivity has diminished sharply. In fact, when smell is blocked out the only sensations perceived arise from the taste receptors on the tongue and the palate alone and these are sensitive only to the most basic taste elements.

The four primary tastes perceived by the tongue are sweetness (the tip), sourness or acidity (the upper edges and sides), bitterness and astringency (the back), and saltiness (the middle). Usually only sweetness, bitterness and sourness are important in tasting wines, but saltiness may be noticed in some very dry sherries. Although the taste buds are predominantly concentrated on the tongue, they are also spread throughout the mouth, albeit in lesser numbers. In fact the cheeks, palate and throat are most important in the assessment of wine as in addition to taste they are receptive to touch (important in judging the 'body' or 'weight' of a wine), pain (a wine or spirit too high in alcohol will produce a hot, burning sensation when nosed or swallowed), and temperature which greatly affects taste and smell.

How to taste wine. First take a sip, rinse your mouth with the wine, effectively cleaning out other tastes, then spit it out into the nearest spittoon. Take another sip and hold the wine in your mouth, rolling it around the tongue so that it reaches the sides and root of the tongue where the most delicate taste buds are situated. Try opening your lips as you roll the wine and draw in air through the mouth as this will help to release volatile ingredients and to draw them into the upper reaches of the olfactory system where they can be sensed. Then breathe out gently through the nose, swallow or spit out the wine and then assess it.

A good memory will help you relate past

tasting experiences to those you are presently acquiring. Notes, however, are a great aid to memory and should be made as you nose and taste the wine; notes made an hour or more later will never be as effective. Every time you taste a wine also consciously try to commit outstanding characteristics to memory.

After making your notes clear your palate by chewing a dry biscuit. While cheese has been traditionally associated with wine tastings it is discouraged when making a keen assessment since it may leave a flavour in the mouth which will affect subsequent tastings.

Sweetness is usually one of the easiest taste elements to detect but it ranges widely from the slightest hint of sweetness in off-dry wines to sweet (such as many late harvests) and very sweet (such as ports, marsalas and Muscat wines as well as highly prized botrytis wines). This quality is usually derived from natural glucose and fructose, traces of which sometimes remain in the wine after the fermentation process has been completed. Glycerol may also exert a minor influence in this respect.

Sweetness usually serves to improve the palatability (roundness or smoothness) of the wine and in this respect enhances the organoleptic harmony. When unbalanced in relation to acidity and astringency, sweetness can produce an undesirable flat sweetish taste. Tannins, compounds responsible for astringency of taste, reduce the detectable sweetness of a wine. In young red wines this effect is predominant but it also occurs to a lesser extent in whites. As red wines age the effect of tannins becomes less detectable and the wine softens. Astringency in wines is relatively easy to detect as it causes 'furry teeth' in a similar way to strong tea.

Sourness should not be confused with dryness. When all the sugar naturally present in grape juice has been converted to alcohol (and carbon dioxide) during fermentation, a dry wine is produced. Because virtually no sugar remains in such a wine it oftens seems sour or acidic to the novice taster.

Acidity is an essential element in the composition of wines; without it wine would be a completely undrinkable, flat, lifeless, brown liquid. Wines with a relatively high acid content usually have the best finish and are eminently suitable for maturation, but too much acid results

The Stellenbosch Young Wine Show is an extremely popular event on the South African wine taster's calendar and winning wines here go on to compete at the Cape Championship Wine Show at Goodwood. Pictured here is Kevin Arnold of Rust-en-Vrede Estate.

When nosing a wine, sniff deeply and quickly to draw the bouquet into the upper reaches of the olfactory system.

heat may cause extraction of tannins and other phenolic compounds from the skins during crushing, thereby resulting in a bitter and/or astringent flavour in the eventual wine.

Body is best described as the feel or 'weight' of a wine in the mouth. It is a result of the combined effect of both glycerol and ethyl alcohol. Wines of high ethyl alcohol and glycerol content are full in body (glycerol is a normal by-product of alcoholic fermentation).

Balance is that elusive quality in a wine that wine maker and connoisseur strive to produce and find respectively for a wine that achieves or has the potential to achieve complete harmony between all its components is a joy indeed. Tasted individually the various wine constituents may often be unpleasant but when found in perfect combination they produce wines with exquisite flavour and balance.

After-taste – or 'follow through', if pronounced, is usually the hallmark of a great wine and refers to the length of time the taste lingers on the palate. In a lesser quality wine the taste, although very pleasant while the wine is in the mouth, usually disappears immediately on swallowing.

As with nosing the wine the most difficult part of tasting is finding the words to express the sensations experienced. The following terms all have reasonably standard applications in the appreciation of wine and are explained in the glossary.

Desirable qualities include big, delicate, dry, elegant, fat, finish, fresh, finesse, luscious, implicitly sweet, medium dry, medium sweet, mellow, neutral, noble, meaty, nutty, ripe, rich, robust, silky, smooth, soft, supple, sweet and sparkling.

Undesirable qualities include acetic, astringent, bitter, coarse, common, cloying, earthy, dull, flat, green, hard, harsh, inky or metallic, mousy, off-taste, overripe, rough, severe, sharp, oxidized, sick, pricked, sour, tart, thin, tough, sour-sweet, sweetish, syrupy and unctuous.

in a hard, thin wine which is just as unpalatable as one with too little.

Fruit acids occurring naturally in grapes are, of course, also present in wine and include malic and tartaric acids which account for approximately 98 per cent of all the acid found in wine. Other such as succinic, lactic and minute quantities of acetic acid are natural by-products of fermentation.

Acids, which give the wine sharpness, keenness, and freshness, essentially have no taste but rather they produce a sensation which many people confuse with the effect of tannin. Tannin tends to be abrasive and is 'felt' on the top of the tongue, roof of the mouth and as a 'furriness' on the teeth. Acids on the other hand hit the tip of the tongue, then the sides and then dissipate.

Bitterness is often confused with astringency (a mouth-puckering sensation)

but with sufficient experience the two can be distinguished. Both result from the presence of polyphenolic compounds (tannins) which are most abundantly found in the stalks, skins and pips.

During red wine processing the skins and pips are left to ferment with the juice so that the colouring matter may be extracted from them. As a result, tannins are also extracted and therefore red wines usually have a marked degree of astringency. Unless excessive it usually indicates a wine of good maturing potential; with bottle ageing the tannin content actually decreases, resulting in a wine that is less astringent and therefore more palatable.

In making white wine it is usual to remove the stalks, skins and pips before fermentation and therefore bitterness and astringency are not usually found in white wines. However, if the grapes are harvested on a very hot day ($\pm$ 30 °C), the

Assessing wine

The ability to judge wines on their appearance, smell and taste varies from person to person. Some people are more naturally sensitive to colour differences than others. A person with good colour

sense will, for example, be able to discern the full spectrum of red wine colours – purple, ruby, red, red-brown, mahogany, tawny and amber-brown – while someone with a poor sense may only be able to

differentiate between purple, red and amber-brown.

To ensure that wine tasters use their natural colour sense to best advantage it is important that the correct lighting is used at a tasting. Natural daylight is best and tungsten or warm white fluorescent lighting is also acceptable, but blue fluorescent lighting gives red wine an unhealthy, dark, blue-black tinge.

As with colour, individual sensitivity to smell varies from person to person and even for the individual it varies during the day. People may not realize it, but they are at their freshest both mentally and physically in the morning, and for this reason many professional tastings are held at this time. Sensitivity to taste is also highest before a meal. To appreciate the wines with the appropriate food a light lunch may be served after the tasting.

Avoid highly spiced foods, however, as these distract the taste-buds and fruit, with its high acid content, does nothing to complement the acidity of wine.

There is little evidence that a smoker's tasting ability is inferior to that of a non-smoker, as many fairly heavy smokers are excellent tasters. However, some non-smokers are disturbed by the smell of tobacco smoke whilst judging wines and at a serious tasting the 'no smoking' rule should be strictly enforced. By the same token women should avoid wearing strong perfume or powder, while men should steer clear of powerfully scented deodorants and after-shave lotions. By attending to these

finer points one's natural sense of smell will not be distracted from the fragrant wine bouquets. Illness or accident may result in altered, diminished or lost sensory response; for example, don't waste time trying to taste wine if you have a streaming cold!

A further point is to help one's palate by tasting wines in the most appropriate order: dry before sweet, young before old and modest before fine. Whether red wines are tasted before whites depends on their relative 'weights'; light dry whites are better before fuller-bodied reds, but light, young red wine is probably better tasted before full-bodied, sweet white wines.

CONDUCTING A WINE-TASTING

Tasting, whether a simple affair with a few friends at your home or a grander more sophisticated event, can take many forms, from the comparison of different vintages, grape varieties, quality grades and wine-producing regions, to a comparison of wines at various stages of maturity. The relatively inexperienced taster, however, should restrict the scope of tasting, gradually attempting more 'sophisticated' or complicated tastings as experience is gained.

Whatever the level of sophistication of the tasting it becomes rather vague and unsatisfactory without a system of scoring the wines. There are a number of systems available, but the internationally accepted 20-point system is best understood and most widely used in South Africa.

In this point-scoring system a high score for an individual wine is 18 points out of a total of 20. A wine in this category would score full points on colour, and perhaps miss one point on the nose and one on the taste. The comment column may be used to exercise your descriptive powers. On this system, reasonable wines usually gain 11-13 points, rather good wines 14 or 15, excellent wines 16-18, while scores of 19 or 20 are reserved for masterpieces.

Remember the order in which wines should be tasted and guard against tasting too many wines; for the novice taster two to four wines are sufficient, with eight or nine being the maximum for someone reasonably experienced.

The number of people present at a tasting may vary from two upwards, but for a meaningful, yet manageable, home tasting 10 to 20 guests would be optimum.

Once you have decided how many people will attend the tasting you can calculate how much wine you will need. With a small number of people at a tutored tasting, one bottle will comfortably serve between 12 and 15 tasters. If it is a casual party, allow at least half-a-bottle for each

Wine tastings differ widely in purpose, from a relaxed introduction to the basics to the business of these professional buyers at the Nederburg Wine Auction.

Score Card

Taster		Date:			
NAME OF WINE	clarity and colour 3 +	nose 7 +	taste 10 =	total 20	comments

guest. Each glass should be filled to about a third as some of the bouquet will be lost if there is too little wine in the bowl. Use plastic wastebins for the taster to empty his glass before moving onto the next wine. It is not considered impolite to spit out a wine you do not like, or feel might impair your judgement as the alcohol takes effect. Many wine clubs provide fresh glasses for each wine to be tasted, but for the home tasting this is unnecessary and a few jugs of water for guests to rinse their glasses is adequate.

Early evening is probably the most convenient time for a wine tasting as tastebuds are sharpest just before a meal. Ask your guests to be prompt; it is surprising how long it takes to taste and talk about half-a-dozen wines, so allow about an hour and a half for discussion. At

a dinner party, a 'blind tasting' can be great fun and can be organized quite simply by slipping a paper sleeve over the bottle so that the label is covered. Try to guess the grape variety, vintage and wine-growing region. You can be certain of an animated discussion amongst your guests and some hilarity at the incorrect interpretations of flavour and bouquet!

Holding a wine tasting, even a modest event in your own home, takes careful planning, but the following check list should aid its smooth running:
- Compile a guest list.
- Inspect your cellar and stock up if necessary.
- Set a date and send out invitations.
- Check the availability of chairs, tables, glasses, corkscrews, paper napkins and spittoons (plastic buckets will suffice).

- Use white tablecloths, as coloured cloths affect colour judgement of the wine.
- Lighting will also affect colour judgement. Ordinary tungsten or warm white fluorescent lighting is best.
- Supply score cards, a list of the wines to be tasted, note-pads and pencils.
- Supply jugs of water for rinsing glasses.
- Have dry biscuits at hand for cleaning the palate between wines.
- Allow the wines to settle well in advance.
- Serve wines at the correct temperature: red wines approximately 16 °C; rosé and white wines approximately 10 °C. Chill white and rosé wines for not longer than two or three hours before tasting, as over-chilling can cause loss of flavour and aroma.

How to establish a wine-tasting club

Attending wine tastings from time to time is fun, but the knowledge gleaned will be limited. Your confidence in wine appreciation will grow far more quickly if you meet on a regular basis with a group of people who have a similar enthusiasm for wine. Most existing wine-tasting societies are unfortunately 'closed shops', as their membership is limited for practical reasons. A manageable number for a wine club is about 40 as no more than two bottles are needed for any one wine at a tasting (a bottle can provide 20 tastes).

In many instances the answer to the membership problem is to set up a wine circle of your own, together with a few friends. If it is well run, the word will soon spread and other enthusiasts will want to join. The aims of the club should be well set out. The Stellenbosch Wine Circle and the South African Society of Wine Tasters suggest that, broadly, these should

embrace providing a body wherein lovers of wine may meet to increase their knowledge and experience of wine and fostering increased knowledge and appreciation of the wines of South Africa.

There are many ways to realize these ambitions for your club: regular functions such as judging or tasting wines; gourmet meals; tours and visits to co-operatives, Estates, Stellenbosch Farmers' Winery and the KWV; lectures and discussions.

Like any other formal organization a wine-tasting society requires a constitution governing membership, meetings, finance, management and dissolution. As a rule of thumb subscriptions for members can range from as little as R15 to R200 a year.

Any society of a non-political or non-religious nature may have its name registered if the chosen name cannot be confused with another such society. Registration is not compulsory but it

affords the name legal protection. The Bureau of Heraldry imposes no rules or regulations on a society so registered. The imposition of rules remain the domestic concern of the society but the Bureau must be supplied with a copy of the constitution. Registration is accomplished by completing a formal application and upon paying a R35 registration fee.

If the society wishes to register the Afrikaans/English translation of its name, it may do so at the same time at no extra cost. Should such a request not be specifically made, only the name put forward in the application form will be registered.

No specific regulations apply to the registration of names other than the fee stipulation. The conditions that apply to the acceptance of a name are contained in the Law of Heraldry, No. 18 of 1962, as amended by Act 54 of 1969.

Wine societies

Wine societies are of long standing in Europe, particularly in France, where each of the more important wine-making districts has its own society or *confrérie*. Elaborate ceremonies attended by growers and shippers of wine, decked out in mediaeval costumes, are invariably followed by a vast, wine-laden banquet.

Without the mediaeval panoply, the

local South African wine societies have nevertheless proliferated in recent decades, making up in enthusiasm what they lack in history. They provide a vital link between the public at large and the producers, stimulating a heightened interest in the one and providing an indication of shifts in public taste to the other. A few lay the emphasis equally upon

food and wine but the majority concentrate on the wine itself, occasionally following their tastings with a meal. The following are among the oldest, most prominent and influential.

Les Tastevins du Cap
Les Tastevins du Cap was the inspiration of an immigrant Frenchman, Dr I.C. van

Oudenhove de St. Géry, who first visited the Cape as a young man in the late 1940s, then returned in 1958 to settle.

The first official assembly of *Les Tastevins* took place at their Spring Dinner of 1963. The 38 enthusiasts present elected themselves as the founder members of the group and the French Consul, Count Max de Montalembert, became the first Honorary President. General membership was restricted to 70 ordinary members who held regular monthly dinners. It was soon found, however, that a regular monthly banquet with all the trimmings was a burden even for dedicated gourmets and it was therefore decided to restrict the banquets to four a year.

Les Tastevins continues to flourish. Many of the original members came from France or from other European wine-making countries and over and above the generally convivial aims of the society persists a desire to promote goodwill between these countries and *'L'Afrique du Sud'*, with wine as the diplomatic language of these contacts.

The South African Society of Wine-Tasters

In the early 1970s a Cape Town advertising executive, Roger Sinclair, was transferred to Johannesburg. A long-standing member of the Cape Wine-Tasters Guild, Roger soon discovered that no wine society then existed in the Transvaal and promptly set about filling the gap. Thus, in 1972, was born the South African Society of Wine-Tasters, now one of the most energetic in the country and one particularly dear to expatriate *Kaapenaars* far from home.

Membership of the society was limited from the start to a maximum of 40, to retain as far as possible a personal approach and interaction in wine tastings, the meetings for which are held in members' homes. A further rule states that although food may be served after tastings it should be simple so that attention

remains focussed on the wine. An emphasis is placed on a knowledge of the technology of wine making, giving evaluation of the wines a certain professional rigour, a contrast to the looser descriptive approach used in many circles.

From its inception the society has set out to compensate for the apparent disadvantage of its distance from the creative life of the winelands. To ensure a flow of new ideas, each chairman may serve a maximum of three years. With the advent of the second chairman, Ian Johnson, the group began to expand its influence, in particular by inviting guest speakers from the Cape and from overseas. The third chairman, Peter Devereux, one of the founder members and one of South Africa's most respected wine writers, further publicised the aims of the society, holding large annual tastings in Lesotho and Swaziland, and in various game reserves. He, more than anyone, put the society on the map.

Durban Wine Society

With not a living grape in sight, surrounded on all sides by sugar-cane, mangoes and bananas, in the midst of a community with a deep traditional allegiance to the joys of beer, whisky, cane spirits and gin, the Durban Wine Society might appear at first blink to be little more than a cheerful anachronism. It flourishes, however, for since its inception in 1974 under its first chairman, Cas Dreyer, it has grown rapidly to its present membership of over 100. The society has its own cellar and holds well-attended wine tastings, with a monthly newsletter relaying members their scores in these tastings.

With the lengthening waiting-list for membership of the Durban Wine Society, some of the members have helped to start similar societies elsewhere in Durban and in Pietermaritzburg. All of these groups, aware of their distance from the vineyards of the Cape, make efforts to lure experts and wine makers to their meetings –

the costs being shared among the societies.

The International Wine and Food Society

This international organization was founded by the late André Simon and the Cape Town Branch enjoyed at least two visits from this 'grand old man' of the wine trade. The local chapter was inaugurated at 'Steenberg', then the home of Nico Louw, on February 9, 1947 and was one of the earliest branches to be formed outside the United Kingdom. In South Africa today, there are also active branches in Durban and Johannesburg, the latter being chaired by the energetic wine expert, Peter Devereux.

The Wine Tasters' Guild of South Africa

This society is probably the oldest in the country, having been established in 1938. It has a strong core of members in the southern suburbs of Cape Town.

Other well-known wine societies are the Grahamstown Wine Circle started by John and Lil Haigh of Rhodes University and Leon Reich of the Grand Hotel (famous for its wine cellar), The Bacchanalian Society, Johannesburgse Wynproewersgilde, Free State Wine Tasters' Guild, The Wine Swines, Stellenbosch Wynstudiekring and many others in centres large and small.

Encouragement is given to these societies, not only by the KWV and the Stellenbosch Farmers' Winery-controlled Cape Wine Academy, but also by 'Die Wynboer' – the official mouthpiece of the KWV and South Africa's only wine magazine – whose enthusiastic editor, Henry Hopkins, is generous in providing publicity to the various societies. From time to time he also publishes a complete list of the country's many wine clubs. Angela Lloyd organizes the annual Blaauwklippen Blending Competition and Colin and Helen Frith run an Inter-Club Quiz.

Setting up a home cellar

It is not necessary to have a huge underground room to begin keeping wine in your home. Most folk begin with a simple rack or cupboard fitted with shelves. A rack 450 mm wide and 180 mm high by 420 mm deep houses 12 bottles of any kind, whereas a shelf 320 mm high by 660 mm long will hold 7 x 4 Burgundies (red wine bottles) or 8 x 4 Hocks (white wine bottles). If you are handy at carpentry, build a unit containing a series

of classical wine 'bins' – diamond shaped pigeon holes big enough for 12 bottles placed horizontally. It is best to store your white wines on the lowest racks where it is coolest, for they are most affected by temperature.

In South Africa, even with insulation, it is too hot to use roof space without the installation of suitable air-conditioning. Other possibilities include the cubicle under the stairs, a built-in cupboard or the

unused space below the floor boards. With a little extra expenditure, a larger area can be made. For example, use the end wall of a garage and brick up about a metre in depth, providing a door for access – insulate walls and roof, if necessary install a small air-conditioning unit and you have the perfect cellar.

If your collection grows to more than 200 bottles you cannot rely on memory, so keep a cellar book. In this way you not only

As demonstrated here by the late Rufus Kenney, author and wine connoisseur, simple shelving is adequate for even the most extensive home cellar.

keep a record of what you put in and take out, it's also fun to look back at your own and your friends' comments. The vintage is not always indicated on a wine's label so write the year in your cellar book and on the label or carton when you buy it. Conventional cellar books have columns ruled for comments, but unless you have minute handwriting, these seldom allow enough space. A looseleaf book ruled with pages something like the example given is probably more satisfactory.

Guard against keeping wines for too long. Today many wines are made ready for drinking sooner. Taste them from time to time to see when they reach their peak,

and enjoy them when they are at their best.

Your cellar, storeroom or cupboard should be kept dark and have an even temperature of 10-12 °C. Without an air-conditioning unit you will probably not be able to maintain this temperature during the South African summer, but this is not necessarily cause for alarm; the temperature may rise to 20 °C without adversely affecting your wine, but the rise must be gradual and gentle. Higher temperatures speed up the maturing process, while at lower temperatures the wine ages better, but more slowly. A sharp increase or decrease in temperature will

kill the wine. Try to provide some ventilation; air movement will not harm your wine and it will prevent mustiness.

Bottles with patent screw caps can be stored upright, whereas bottles with corks should lie on their sides to keep the cork moist and swollen. If the cork dries it shrinks, allowing air into contact with the wine, thereby causing damage by oxidation. The bottles should be stored with their labels uppermost for easy reading without undue disturbance. Wines that throw a sediment should lie on their sides as the deposit then forms along the side of the bottle, simplifying its removal. When bottles are stored upside down the

Wine	Year	Quantity	Merchant	Date bought	Price paid	Date of drinking	Accompanying food	Guests	Tasting notes	Balance in stock

sediment then forms on the inside of the cork, making decanting difficult. Try to prevent vibration or excessive movement of bottles as this too can disturb the sediment and also damage the flavour.

Aside from having good wines to hand, the cellar has financial advantages as well. For example you are more likely to buy in bulk and wine purchased by the carton is usually cheaper than individually purchased bottles. Also, red wines mature in the bottle and increase in quality and value. For instance, 1984 was considered to be a particularly good vintage for local reds while 1976 is considered to be a good vintage for Cabernets in particular. But remember, good years can also produce some poor wines, and poor years some good wines, so judge each wine on its own merit rather than relying on vintage.

Today many wines are packed upside down in the carton to ensure that the cork stays wet, but even if the wine has been standing upright, it can still be acceptable. Before purchasing, check the fill heights. Well stored bottles should be as near as possible completely full, but some very old wines may have lower levels; here only experience helps in making a decision. The point is, once you have purchased the wine, you want to get the best value for your money. Increase your chances of enjoying good wines by storing them correctly.

Ageing wines

South Africans are often chided about drinking their wines too young and then concluding that they don't like red wines because they 'bite' too much. This is a gross misapprehension, resulting from drinking the right wine at the wrong time. For although vintage is not reputed to play a very important rôle in South African wines, knowing the vintage year is relevant to the ageing or maturing of wines in the bottle.

Traditionally South African red wines are full-bodied, needing ten or, if you can wait that long, 20 years of maturation. However, today there are an increasing number of light-bodied and some distinctly fruity red wines available on the market. These are either ready for immediate drinking or need far less maturation. Buy across the spectrum and choose a light red wine to drink through the year and at least two bottles a month of select red wines to put away. In this way you will soon build up your cellar and be in that enviable position of being able to match a memorable occasion with an equally memorable wine.

RED WINE
It is generally held that the older a red wine the better it gets.
Cabernets require about ten years or longer from vintage to reach their peak.
Pinotages may vary from three to nine years. For a typically young Pinotage taste with a flowery flavour keep the wine for three years, but if you prefer a more full-bodied bottle with mature character store it for five or six years more.
Shiraz wines are soft and drinkable after three years but with a further three years can mature to a very full-bodied roundness and softness.
Tinta Barocca does not require long bottle maturation so store it for three years and then drink it.
Cinsaut likewise reaches its peak at three years but can also mature for up to ten.

The ageing times related here are, however, no more than rules of thumb, the actual time will depend on how the wine was made and how it will be stored. Judging the optimum time for an individual wine comes only with experience.

WHITE WINES
White wines, unlike the reds, do not need long bottle maturation, in fact most of them should be drunk immediately. One can, however, drink a white wine anytime within one or two years from vintage, when the flavour is delicate, fruity and characteristically young and fresh. However, some wines, especially those that are semi-sweet, benefit from storing for some two to three years from vintage. Nederburg Edelkeur, the honey-sweet golden-hued wine, should be stored for ten years after vintage, according to Patrick Grubb, the wine auctioneer. In all, very few local dry white wines will benefit with age, notable exceptions being some dry Rieslings which need two or three years to reach full development.

CAPE VINTAGE GUIDE

Region/District	70	71	72	73	74	75	76	77	78	79	80	81	82
Coastal Region													
CONSTANTIA/DURBANVILLE	8	6	8	7	8	6	8	5	8	8	8	7	9
STELLENBOSCH	7	6	8	7	7	7	8	6	9	8	8	7	9
PAARL	8	7	9	7	8	6	8	6	8	8	8	7	9
TULBAGH	–	–	6	5	4	5	7	5	7	6	7	6	8
Breëriviervallei Region	–	–	6	5	4	5	7	5	7	6	7	5	7

– No records

The above table and following notes provide a guide to vintages in major wine-producing Regions and Districts. The ratings on a scale of 1-10 refer to quality overall, but are mainly influenced by red wines. Do not apply this guide rigidly as even in a poor year individual cellars may produce excellent wines.

1971 A large crop and at the time generally considered to be of average quality. Some of the reds have developed well with time, although many are now past their best.

1972 A hot, dry vintage and one that was acclaimed as being one of our greats – exceptional for reds and Cabernet Sauvignon in particular.

1973 A small crop in which downy mildew gave problems and rain affected the late-ripening reds. It is generally considered that the whites of this vintage were better than the reds, although some Cabernets developed well; most should have been drunk by now.

1974 A very dry year. The consistent warmth produced high sugars and 1974 is considered by many as the outstanding vintage of the decade for reds. In general the whites suffered, although some Steens proved exceptional. The overall crop was down in quantity owing to poor setting conditions in the spring. Broadly, 1974

Cabernets are showing well, although many have now reached their best and can be drunk.

1975 A fairly dry vintage with an exceptionally hot February that resulted in whites of very low acid; late rains tended to spoil the late-ripening reds, especially Cabernet. The largest crop since 1971.

1976 A long, cold winter with late rains and snow. The vintage took place in almost ideal conditions and all cultivars produced good quantity and quality. The reds are proving to be outstanding.

1977 A cool winter which was followed by a wet spring and poor berry set. The harvest was troubled with rain and extensive downy mildew damage resulted. The Cape Riesling crop was small but produced some excellent wines. High acids benefited whites and gave reds a very French character, although many lacked colour. Red cultivars are now showing well, though most will peak earlier than the 1974s and 1976s.

1978 Another cool wet winter followed by rains in March and April which kept sugars low. Considered overall to be a vintage of good quality.

1979 The driest and also warmest winter since 1926. February conditions were warm and wet and resulted in high incidence of botrytis which in some areas developed into noble rot. March was dry and cool so late-ripening reds showed rather well, and some have developed well, but most are not great.

1980 Overall a good vintage with some exciting wines. Hot dry weather gave sound grapes with good sugars, but low acids. Cabernets and Cabernet-based blends are beginning to show well.

1981 The year of the great flood at Laingsburg. This deluge did untold damage to many wine-making areas in the Robertson, Montagu and Bonnievale areas. The cool weather from flowering to pressing resulted in relatively higher fruit acids in all wines. There was large variation of quality within wine types with some exceptionally good white wines being produced. Red grapes tended to lack sugar and colour and the wines they produced are generally lighter than usual.

1982 The biggest crop ever with the quality areas of Stellenbosch, Paarl, Durbanville, Constantia being up by 20 per cent. Almost perfect climatic conditions, however, enabled superb wines to be made.

1983 The crop was up some five per cent on the record harvest of 1982 and it was a sound vintage, although the acid and sugar levels were generally lower than in 1982. Some exceptional wines were made, but overall 1983 does not match the great vintage of 1982. Certain cooler areas and slopes were exceptions; wines from such vineyards, as well as normal crop loads, are well balanced and developing better than expected.

1984 The 1984 vintage was disease-free but slightly down on 1983. It was preceded by one of the wettest winters in ten years. Late bud burst meant that the harvest began some ten days later than in 1983. A long, dry period from October to February resulted in some white varieties (such as Cape Riesling, Colombar and Steen, growing on shallow, sandy soils in the Coastal Region) ripening under stress. This gave high sugars but low acid which led to rather neutral wines. The reds, however, were magnificent, Cabernet being helped by some late rains. The late red cultivars produced excellent colour and a variety of red wine styles, which are ageing well.

1985 A greater range of style and variety of wine was produced from the 1985 vintage than ever before. The total crop was almost ten per cent down on 1984 and with a few notable exceptions whites were generally better than reds. Cool conditions and frequent rains during the ripening period produced grapes with good acid/sugar ratio. The 1985 season was probably one of the longest ever on record. The white wines are exceptionally fragrant with an ideal sugar/acid balance. The red wines have good flavour but are lighter than those of 1984.

1986 The hottest, driest summer for a couple of decades. In most areas the vintage started four weeks earlier than usual. The overall crop was down in quantity, the late-ripening Cabernet Sauvignon being most affected. Vintners were delighted with the quality of the grapes and expect some excellent wines as fruit acids were good in spite of the heat.

Should wine breathe?

Breathing is a strange term when applied to wine and even stranger ideas have developed around it. There are many different ideas on when to pull the cork from the bottle of wine and most people seem to have their own pet theory.

In 1974, a series of tastings took place where experienced tasters and wine drinkers tasted numerous samples of the same wine opened 24 hours, eight hours, one hour and just immediately before tasting. They also tasted the same wines that had been decanted at the same intervals before tasting.

At different sessions, different wines were used, ranging from very young Tassenberg, through young Cabernets to eight- and ten-year-old Cabernets; also included were eight-, ten- and 15-year-old

First Growth Bordeaux Chateau wines and a 12-year-old Burgundy.

It is unnecessary to list all the results here, but what immediately became apparent was that personal preference cropped up time and again. Eventually, after much analysis of the results, the following pattern of sorts emerged.

The older the wine, the less time is needed between cork pulling and tasting.
- These wines, whether local or French, were better when freshly opened than those opened many hours before, even though the latter were often still very good.
- There are always exceptions, but as a guideline wines 12 years and older need not be opened long before drinking – the most dramatic change takes place

within 20-40 minutes of decanting or pouring into the glass.
- A young red wine definitely improves with breathing and is less harsh.
- The best results with young wine are achieved by decanting.

BOTTLE BREATHING VERSUS DECANTING

The experiment referred to above, also showed that removing the cork an hour before tasting did not change the particular wine when compared with the same wine opened at the time of tasting. (When one considers the small surface area of wine exposed to the atmosphere in the neck of the bottle, it is not surprising that there is no detectable difference.) Also, those opened 8-24 hours before were, in most cases, not preferred to those opened immediately before tasting.

When it came to decanting, most of the older wines which had stood for longer were definitely scored down in comparison to the freshly opened wines. In many cases, however, younger wines which had been decanted 24 hours before were unanimously preferred to those opened at the tasting.

Since the abovementioned tests, it has been conclusively established that hours of aeration, or breathing, does not reduce tannins – in fact, the effect of air on wine is to diminish its bouquet and taste fairly rapidly. As with all aspects of wine appreciation, however, the effect of air on wine is the subject of often heated exchanges and in the final analysis your own experience is again the best measure.

Get to know your wine and determine with each what sort of timing suits you best when it comes to cork removal or decanting. To pull the cork some time before a meal or tasting simply for the convenience of not hassling with uncorking when it comes to the time of consumption, is just sensible – as already mentioned, no appreciable change takes place if this is done.

Serving wine

The protocol involved in serving wine raises many questions. Who should pour the wine after the host has poured the first round? Is it acceptable for a guest to pour or top up glasses? Is it acceptable for a woman, the hostess, to pour the wine in the absence of a male host or should she request a male guest to 'do the honours'? Much depends on the degree of formality or informality of the occasion. Considering the 'correct' procedure for the service of wine, whether in a private home or in a restaurant, will help you to decide what would be appropriate in your home.

At a restaurant the wine steward should present the bottle, prior to opening, on the right hand side of the host to ensure that it is in fact the wine he ordered and to allow the host to check the temperature.

Once the host has given his approval the steward will cut the capsule, remove the upper portion and wipe the bottle clean with a napkin. He will then gently pull the cork, once again wiping the lip of the bottle with a clean napkin to remove any small

particles of cork which might have adhered to it. All this should be done within the host's sight and a good wine steward will always present the cork for inspection. Care should also be taken not to shake the bottle and disturb any sediment which may be present.

Serving from the host's right the steward will pour about a third of a glass into the host's glass for approval, holding the bottle in his right hand. The steward gives the bottle a slight twist as he takes the bottle away from the glass to prevent dripping. Should a small piece of broken cork fall into the glass no fuss need be made as it does not affect the wine.

Once the wine has been approved the steward may proceed. Ladies will be served first, then the men and finally the host. The steward should remember that the glasses should only be two-thirds filled so that there is space for the aroma to collect above the wine. Once all the glasses have been charged the steward should place the bottle on the table to the right of the host.

A white or a sparkling wine which needs to be kept cool will be placed by the steward in an ice bucket within reach of the host. Red wines should be served at the temperature at which they are stored in the cellar, which should be approximately 16 °C. White wines should be served chilled to approximately 10 °C. When chilling white wine, it is better to put the bottle in the fridge only some two or three hours before you plan to serve it, to prevent overchilling, which can cause the wine to lose a great deal of its flavour and aroma. The best way to chill a wine quickly, is to put it into an ice bucket with a mixture of ice and cold water. This chills the wine evenly throughout the bottle, helping the wine to retain its delicacy of flavour.

In a private home where there is no steward the host should serve the wine, inviting the most appropriate guest to taste. This could be the guest of honour, the eldest person in the party, or simply the person on his left whose glass would be within easy pouring distance.

Wine and Food

The aim here is to indicate the basic rules and to encourage a sense of adventure in exploring the world of food and wine. There is no personal satisfaction in blindly following the opinions of others and once you know the rules and have gained a little experience it is time to bend, break and recreate them.

Sherries or other *apéritif* wines are traditionally served before the meal. However, any wine may be served provided consideration is given to those to be served with the meal. If you wish to get maximum benefit from your palate, observe the

following order: dry before sweet, young before old and white before red with the exception of full-bodied sweet white wines such as Nederburg Edelkeur which would be appropriate after red wine. Preserve your palate by nibbling a few nuts or plain chips and avoid very savoury and spicy snacks.

Often only one wine is served before and throughout the meal. If you are not familiar with your guests' tastes you are safer sticking to white wine.

For an all purpose wine for a light meal choose a Steen or Colombar; for a heavier

meal choose a more substantial Riesling or Gewürztraminer which will stand up to most meats. Sparkling wine is also fine with a light meal but few people will enjoy it throughout a very substantial meal. There are also certain foods which simply do not combine that well with wine but fortunately these are few in relation to the vast number which are enhanced by it. Wine lovers should avoid such foods or not serve wine with them at all. They include heavily pickled or garlic-flavoured foods and anything dressed wih vinegar or strongly flavoured mayonnaise. Eggs too

Although one probably learns most about wine at a formal tasting it undoubtedly gives great pleasure as a companion to a good meal. Cheese and wine make ideal partners, too, especially when enjoyed in the open in the heart of the Cape winelands.

tend to dull the palate and will make a light white wine taste strange. Sherry is traditionally served with soup. However, if the soup includes red wine or port in the making, serve the same wine. A fullish white wine makes an excellent accompaniment to fish-based soups.

With few exceptions white wine is generally served with fish and shellfish but your choice will be greatly influenced by sauces, stuffings and methods of cooking. A creamy sauce requires a delicate wine while strongly flavoured dressings necessitate a fuller bodied wine. If you wish to appreciate the true flavour of the wine and the fish, avoid lemon juice, Worcestershire sauce, tabasco and vinegar-based sauces. A delicate white wine is suitable with grilled or lightly fried fish but if the fish is fried in batter, or baked with additional flavouring, a medium-bodied fuller-flavoured wine is preferable.

It is generally assumed that white wines should be served with white meats and red wines with red meats. But this is an area where it is possible to be far more adventurous. For example, try to imagine the taste of a dish in advance by taking

into account factors such as herbs, spices, marinades, stuffings and sauces. Informal dishes such as casseroles, stews and pastas may be accompanied by informal wines. Save your good red wines for plain roasts of beef or lamb and enjoy everyday robust wines with garlic-flavoured pasta dishes and dishes strongly flavoured with herbs, mustard and spices. There are many ranges of jug wines which are meant to be drunk and enjoyed in this context.

White wine is commonly suggested as an accompaniment to poultry. However, chicken and turkey are usually roasted with strongly flavoured stuffings and served with a rich gravy and would be better partnered with red wine. Roast pork is rich and needs a fruity white wine high in acidity or a medium to full-bodied red.

When salads are served, keep the dressing simple. Lemon juice is preferable to vinegar and may be diluted with a little water and shaken up with five times the quantity of salad oil.

The French maintain the sensible tradition of serving cheese after the meat course so that the main wine of the meal may be finished off with the flattering

accompaniment of cheese. A good cheese board should include a hard cheese such as Cheddar, a full fat cheese such as Brie or Camembert, a cream cheese and a strongly-flavoured cheese like Roquefort to accompany assertive full-bodied red wines.

It is not essential to serve a wine with the sweet course of a meal. But if you do it must be sweeter than the dessert, and sweet sparkling wine is often most suitable. A dessert containing chocolate or a liqueur can be detrimental to the taste of wine. But as an alternative a delicious sweet marsala or Muscat dessert wine may be served with cheese.

Fresh fruit served with a dessert wine or port is a superb way of ending a meal and it is strange that this custom is little practised in South Africa where fruit is so abundant. There are however, a few fruits which do not combine with wine: citrus and pineapple tend to be too acid and bananas are not particularly complementary to wine. Grapes, apples, pears and plums are all excellent with dessert wines but peaches and nectarines are best of all! For ready reference a 'food and wine' checklist is included on page 322.

Choosing a corkscrew

We have all at some stage or another been faced with a stubborn cork or even worse, one that breaks or crumbles. But such embarrassments should be few and far

between especially if you have an efficient corkscrew. Today there are many and varied instruments for removing corks but the most effective and readily available are

the openers that employ the use of the screw process.

The ever important screw should be a perfect spiral, its point should be exactly in line with the spirals of the worm and should be sharp enough to penetrate the top of the cork easily. The threads should not be too sharp, however, as this tends to cut the cork in such a manner that when you pull, the greater part of the cork remains in the bottle and only a neat core is withdrawn.

The traditional corkscrew usually has a screw that is long enough to pierce the cork completely, so ensuring that the whole cork is withdrawn and the last half inch is not broken off and left snugly behind in the neck. When this happens the remaining piece of cork almost without fail drops back into the wine when you try to prise it out! The screw is fitted to a wooden handle for a good hearty but steady heave to remove the cork. The screw usually passes through the hand-grip and is flattened out on the upper side of the grip away from the bottle so that when pulling, the cork comes out of the bottle and not the screw out of the handle.

Many of the corkscrews supplied with 'bar kits' are not made in such a manner and after a very short period of use the screw pulls out of the handle. Rare indeed is the gift-type corkscrew that combines attractiveness with utility.

Some corkscrews operate on a lever principle and are very effective for easing stubborn corks. The common bootlever corkscrew is a good example but others which also save on muscle power include the 'cap' and the 'butterfly' or 'winged' corkscrews. Their only drawback is when the cork crumbles in the centre the screw cannot be repositioned as it is designed to operate on the centre of the cork. With the good old-fashioned corkscrew you can reposition it on some other part of the cork if the centre crumbles.

The best corkscrew of all, however, is the recently developed 'Screwpull' which justly lays claim to being the world's finest cork remover.

RECORKING

Opened natural wines can be kept for a short time if the unfinished bottles are properly resealed. But this is often easier said than done. Normally the end of the cork that has been in contact with the wine is moist and has swelled to the extent that it is impossible to force it back into the bottle. The other end of the cork is often still narrow enough to be used, but it may be contaminated where it has been in contact with the foil or lead capsule for example. But if this topmost portion is cut away with a sharp knife it can be effectively used to re-cork the bottle. This works purely as a temporary measure, however, as once opened the wine has been in contact with the atmosphere and even with refrigeration will not keep well. If you have a clean 250-ml bottle it is better to decant left-over wine into it as there will be less air space in the bottle and the screwcap is an excellent closure.

Pre-dinner drinks in perspective

Today the trend is towards relaxed informal entertainment. So why not ignore the 'What would you like to drink?' routine that keeps the host as busy as a bartender during peak hour in a city pub. If dinner is to be served buffet style set the same easy tone by offering guests one or two well-chosen drinks.

Open a bottle of sparkling wine or serve a mixed wine drink – cool and refreshing in summer – or hot and heartwarming in the winter. Sherry or one of the other apéritif wines can be served as an alternative in the winter and the wine to accompany the meal may also be enjoyed as a pre-dinner drink.

Hot spiced drinks are among the oldest

mixed wine drinks to come from the countries of northern Europe. Our winters may be short but they can certainly be sharp and a steaming wine bowl is just as welcome on a bitingly cold winter's night in the Transvaal and Free State, or on a wet, rainy night in the Cape. There are many versions of hot wine drinks: the German *glühwein* meaning the 'glowing wine'; the *julglogg* or Swedish 'Christmas wine'; and the English 'mulled' wine.

Hot wine drinks should be heated slowly to simmering but should never be allowed to boil as the alcohol evaporates rapidly at temperatures higher than 79 °C. The combination of spices called for in the recipe, can be held together in a little

muslin bag which is easy to retrieve from the drink before it is poured into the jug or bowl. A few whole spices can remain in the drink for decorative purposes. Sweetening by adding sugar and fruit juices may be adjusted according to your personal taste or that of your guests.

A punch bowl is very decorative for serving but a pyrex or some other sturdy jug is more practical, and a hot tray set on low is ideal for keeping the drink at a perfect temperature. Serve in tall, thick bottomed, cocktail glasses which should be gently warmed on the hot tray to avoid cracking. Hot wine drinks may be made well in advance and reheated when ready to serve.

Cooking with wine

The best cookbooks contain many recipes calling for the use of wine yet it seems some cooks underestimate the need for this ingredient. Wine is indeed a liquid seasoning as essential as the herbs, sauces and spices on the kitchen shelf. It is used to accent and improve food flavour and adds delicious new relish to ordinary food.

Fortunately, cooking with wine is not a precise operation. Instead you add to suit your taste. A general rule to follow,

however, is that where a recipe calls for water, milk or stock, and you think wine could improve the flavour, replace part of that liquid with wine. For instance, in preparing the can or packet of mushroom soup you buy – add a few spoonfuls of sherry to water you are directed to mix in.

When cooking with wine there are some useful hints to bear in mind. If a wine is not good enough to drink, it is not good enough for cooking. If sour and vinegary, it

will give the dish these qualities. Left-over wines can be kept for the kitchen but, as with other ingredients, the better the wine, the better the dish. Left-over table wine can be stored for cooking if a thin film of salad oil is poured over it in the bottle and then recorked. Remember that liquid lost through evaporation during cooking should be replaced with water, not wine. Wine added at this stage will alter the character of the dish.

The care of glasses

Before denouncing a wine for its stale or musty aroma check whether the wine is indeed the culprit, for such odours can originate from a glass which is not completely clean or has been incorrectly stored.

A fine residue forms on all glasses owing to a natural build-up of bacteria over a period of time. If this residue is detectable, in the form of a milky white film on the bowl or rim, the glasses are less than 'squeaky' clean and should be washed. However, even if not noticeable, this fine deposit can still cause a musty odour. If the glass is suspect, hold the rim to your mouth and breath out strongly into the glass. Any mustiness should 'come out' with the warmth and moistness of the breath; if not, wash the glass. Should the mustiness

persist the wine may well be at fault. Such blatant examination is obviously not possible in public and if you are at a friend's home it is even more of a problem and, unless willing to risk offending your host, you will have to suffer in silence. In a restaurant you are perfectly entitled to request a freshly washed, still-wet glass. At a wine tasting there is usually rinsing water available; if not, use wine. Swirl the liquid around the glass, pour it out and use a paper napkin or your handkerchief to remove any residue.

Wine lovers are frequently advised not to use dishwashing detergent when washing glasses. This is nonsense. The residue which builds up on a glass sticks like glue, and so do lipstick, salad oil and other food stains. Detergent is the only

way to render glasses 'squeaky clean', but be sure to rinse them well, removing all traces of detergent smell.

Most people, particularly restaurant owners, store wine glasses upside down. Unless they are hanging from the base so that air can circulate in the bowl, this is the worst possible way. By storing them upside down you are creating the very environment which is perfect for the development of musty odours. Right side up or hanging are the only ways and even then glasses will eventually acquire some musty scents, but it will happen far more slowly. Prevention is always better than cure, however, and, particularly if you are serving a fine wine, wash and dry your wine glasses before serving. It takes extra time but is worth the effort.

FOOD AND WINE CHECKLIST

Some wines, such as a good dry sparkling wine, partner almost any food successfully, and most people find it quite acceptable to drink the same wine throughout a meal. However, for those who prefer to match wine to food, the list below suggests types of wine which best complement certain dishes.

STARTERS
Antipasto/Hors d'Oeuvres: dry or medium white.
Artichokes: (Vinaigrette) light-bodied red or dry rosé; (Hollandaise) full-bodied dry white.
Asparagus: light dry white or rosé.
Avocado: (Vinaigrette) fino sherry; (Ritz) dry or medium white.
Bisques: full-bodied dry white.
Bouillabaisse: very dry white.
Caviar: sparkling wine.
Cheese Fondue: light reds.
Consommé: dry sherry.
Escargots: light red or rosé.
Grapefruit: medium sherry.
Ham (with melon): medium-bodied.
Herrings: dry white.
Melon: sweet fortified wine.
Minestrone: medium-bodied red or rosé.
Pasta: light reds.
Pâté: dry white or, in total contrast, a late harvest.
Prawns or shrimps: light-bodied dry white.
Salad: dry white.

Salami: spicy red or dry rosé.
Salmon, smoked: fruity white.
Soufflés: (fish) dry white; (cheese) medium-bodied red.
Terrine: as for pâté or sometimes light reds.

FISH DISHES
Haddock: full-bodied dry white.
Lobster or Crab: dry white or sparkling wine.
Line Fish: any dry or semi-sweet white (depending on the sauce if any).
Mussels: (Moules Marinière) fruity white.
Oysters: sparkling wine, sweet or dry.
Shellfish: as for line-fish.
Trout: delicate white.

MEAT DISHES
Beef (cold): medium to full-bodied red.
Roast or casserole: medium to full-bodied red.
Beef Stroganoff: spicy or full-bodied red.
Cassoulet: young red.
Chicken or Turkey (roast): dry white or smooth red.
Chili con carne: young red.
Chinese food: dry to medium white.
Coq au vin: robust red.
Curry (light): fruity robust white.
Curry (strong): sweet muscadel (well chilled).

Duck or Goose: full-bodied semi-sweet white or dry red.
Frankfurters: any semi-sweet white.
Game birds: good smooth reds.
Goulash: robust young reds.
Ham: young red or semi-sweet white.
Kidneys/liver: medium-bodied red.
Lamb: good, preferably well-aged, Cabernet or blended red.
Oxtail: rich strong red.
Paella: rosé or dry white.
Pork: fruity white, rosé or dry red.
Rabbit: young red.
Veal: smooth red.
Venison: your best red.

CHEESE
Port is good with all types of cheese but the following combinations are very complementary.
Cheddar, Gouda and Edam: any red or semi-sweet white.
Brie, Camembert and Bel Paese: best with reds – any one of your choice.
Blaukrantz, Roquefort and Danish Blue: any full red wine of your choice.
Goat's cheese: fortified dessert wine.

Finally, sweet dessert wines or sweet sparkling wines go well with puddings, confections, and fruit, while port is the ideal accompaniment to nuts.

HOT WINE DRINKS

Mulled white wine (12 servings)

1 litre fresh pineapple juice or a mixture of
    pineapple and orange juice
One 750 ml bottle of Premier Grand Crû
1 ml ground cloves
1 ml ground allspice
15 ml sugar
A pinch of salt

Combine all ingredients and heat slowly to
simmering. Decorate glasses with a
pineapple slice and serve hot.

Winter punch (6 servings)

1 large unpeeled orange
12 whole cloves
15 ml sugar
One 750 ml bottle light dry white wine
45 ml brandy

Press cloves into the skin of the orange.
Roast orange under the grill or over an
open fire until light brown. Cut orange into
slices; place in a saucepan. Add sugar and
warm for an instant. Add wine and brandy.
Bring to simmering and keep warm on a
hot tray ready to serve.

Winter warm-up (12 servings)

One 750 ml bottle medium cream sherry or
    moscato
1 litre fresh orange juice
5 ml ground cardamon

Combine ingredients, heat to simmering
and serve.

Mulled red wine (6 servings)

375 ml boiling water
125 ml sugar
½ lemon sliced
3 sticks cinnamon
3 whole cloves
One 750 ml bottle dry red wine
A sprinkling of grated nutmeg

Combine the boiling water, sugar, lemon,
cinnamon and cloves; stir until sugar
dissolves. Add wine and heat to
simmering. Do not boil. Strain or remove
muslin bag containing spices. Serve hot
with a sprinkling of nutmeg.

Hot spicy fruit drink (6 servings)

1 litre apple juice
2 whole cinnamon sticks
2 whole cloves
375 ml white muscadel

Combine ingredients and heat to
simmering. Serve topped with a thin slice
of lemon.

Port punch (8 servings)

One 750 ml bottle vintage port or moscato
45 ml sugar
3 ml mixed spice
½ grapefruit
1 lemon
250 ml water
125 ml raisins

Heat wine with sugar, spice and grapefruit
juice, lemon juice and rind, to simmering.
(Do not allow to boil.) Using the cup of
water, boil raisins slowly until soft. Add to
the wine mixture; do not strain. Serve in a
punch bowl.

GLOSSARY

Acetaldehyde The principal aldehyde of wine, occurring in amounts of up to about 100 parts per million. It is generated during the yeast fermentation of a must and contributes much to the bouquet and characteristic flavour of wine and the other alcoholic drinks distilled from it.

Acetic A vinegary smell, caused by the action of acetobacteria which spoil the wine if it is left in contact with air for extended periods of time. The taste of the wine is also affected by these bacteria.

Acetic acid A volatile acid present in virtually all table wines in small quantities. The legal limit varies from country to country but is usually less than 1,5 grams per litre; the flavour threshold is around 0,5 to 0,6 grams per litre. A wine described as volatile suffers from an excess of acetic acid.

Acidic Sharp taste from an excess of various acids which cause an imbalance in the wine.

Acids There are two kinds of organic acid which occur in wine. The first of these are the fruit acids or fixed acids. These are present both in the grape and in the wine and are indispensable to high quality wines. The principal acids of this type are tartaric acid and malic acid. Their ratio varies, depending upon the grape variety, the soil type, and the weather during growth and ripening and when the grapes are harvested. These acids play an essential rôle in the maturation of wine; better wines tend to be higher in acid content, and take longer to mature. If the wine contains too little acid it will taste insipid; too much and the result will taste sharp. The correct balance lends freshness and individuality to the wine.

The second type of acid is volatile acid. This is the acid of vinegar, acetic acid. It is not found in the grape but develops after alcoholic fermentation. In minute quantities it can be attractive, especially in red wines, but larger amounts represent substantial bacterial spoilage and a deterioration towards vinegar.

Aftertaste Appreciation of the aftertaste is the final stage of the ritual of tasting a wine and is important for its complete assessment. When a wine is swallowed new sensations are experienced by the taste-buds on the part of the tongue beneath the uvula and in the throat itself. These taste-buds are highly sensitive, and a wine which may have appeared sound through the colour, bouquet and tasting stages may carry a fault which is only revealed in the aftertaste.

Ageing The ageing or maturation of most wines is a continuous process from the time of fermentation, whether in vat, tank, cask or bottle. The rate of ageing varies; in general, white wines usually mature more quickly than red, but there are notable exceptions among whites, for example, Special Late Harvests and particularly Noble Late Harvests such as Nederburg Edelkeur.

Alcohol The alcohol present in wine and spirits is ethyl alcohol. This primary alcohol, or pure spirit, is a colourless liquid with a faint but pleasant smell; it is derived from the fermentation of sugar and has the formula CH_3CH_2OH. Ethyl alcohol is the only pure spirit which is safe to drink.

Alcoholic strength The strength of a wine depends upon the proportion of alcohol present which can be expressed in percentage by volume or as degrees Proof Spirit. In wine the range is usually from 8-14% by volume. Fortified wines are between 17 and 22% alcohol, and spirits are from 30-40% alcohol in general (in South Africa 43%) though some spirits can be purchased with a content of up to 80% volume.

Absolute alcohol is 100% by volume, which on the Sykes scale is 175,35 degrees Proof Spirit (PS). Similarly 100° PS is 57,1% by volume, while a wine of 21 PS has 12% alcohol by volume.

Comparative Alcoholic Strengths

By Volume	Proof Spirit Degrees
Pure alcohol – 100%	175,35° PS (75,35° over proof)
Gin, Brandy – if 43%	75,25° PS (25° under proof)
Liqueur – if 36%	63° PS (37° under proof)
Sherry – if 20%	35° PS (65° under proof)
Natural white wine – if 12%	21° PS (79° under proof)

Aldehydes A group of chemical compounds derived from dehydrogenated alcohols. There are many forms, such as acetaldehyde, which is produced from ethyl alcohol. *See separate entry on acetaldehyde.*

Alluvial soils These are soils which have been laid down by the action of rivers through the ages. Specific kinds of alluvial soils, known as Dundee soils, show alternating layers of different textures, commonly of silt and sand.

Ampelography The scientific study of the description and classification of the vine and the grape.

Anthocyanin A colouring pigment found in grape skins and playing an important part in both the colour and keeping qualities of a red wine.

Anthracnose *(Gloeosporium ampelophagum)* A vine disease. It appears on the leaves as small circular, greyish-black spots which are sometimes bordered by a yellow discoloration. The spots gradually enlarge, the middle portion often falling out. Sunken cankers form on the shoots till the bark is destroyed, the shoot becoming hard and black. Modern organic fungicides are used to control the disease.

Appearance The first step in wine appreciation which is the assessment of colour and clarity.

Appellation Controlée A system of laws which guarantees the authenticity of a wine with a given label, extending both to region, grape variety, methods of viticulture and (occasionally) methods of vinification. Wine of Origin is South African version.

Aroma To be distinguished from the bouquet. The aroma is the smell of the fresh ingredients of the grape, largely contained in its skin, which are carried through into the wine. A young wine will tend to have an aroma, but relatively little bouquet. As the wine ages and matures the aroma slowly diminishes while the bouquet increases. In a good wine there should be a nice balance of aroma and bouquet, and in judging a wine both qualities should be assessed.

Astringency Not to be confused with dryness, acidity or sourness. Some red wines make the mouth pucker – this depends on the amount of tannin absorbed by the wine from the skins, seeds and stalks of the grapes, as well as from the casks. A moderate astringency is desirable in many types of wine.

Baked A 'hot' earthy smell caused by burnt and shrivelled grapes due to excessive sunshine and little rainfall.

Balance A well-balanced wine is one which is completely harmonious and balanced in its make-up, with no quality overpronounced and with no striking deficiency in bouquet, flavour or aftertaste. If light it will be delicate, if full-bodied it will have a corresponding amount of flavour and character. Although the term praises the wine, it need not be a great wine but merely what it should be in type and class.

Balling *see also* Hydrometer. A measure of the concentration of sugar in grape juice or wine, named after the inventor of the saccharometer, the instrument with which this measurement is taken and which is calibrated in degrees Balling. The reading gives the grams of sugar in 100 grams of juice. As a rough rule-of-thumb, the Balling reading multiplied by 0,55 will give the wine's future alcoholic content; juice of 22° Balling, for example, should give a 12% alcohol content.

Bead The bubbles in sparkling wine. The smaller the beads and the longer they continue to rise in the glass, the better the quality of the wine. Bottle fermentation produces the smallest beads and the longest-lasting; carbonation produces the largest, which are also the quickest to disperse.

Bentonite This is a type of clay used as a clarifying or fining agent for the protein stabilization of wine. It is mined mainly in Wyoming in the USA, and when properly used has no effect on the bouquet and flavour of the wine.

Big A big wine is one which has more than the average amount of flavour and body, and is high in alcohol, tannin acidity and grape extract. It is not necessarily a term of distinction, since a wine thus described could be somewhat coarse and heavy.

Bin A repository for wines where they can be suitably stored, lying horizontally.

Bitter Usually an unpleasant taste detected on the palate, on the back of the tongue and in the aftertaste; however, it may be desirable in certain wines and vermouths.

Black-mould rot *(Aspergillus rot)* A vine disease; it is usually a secondary infection, following on botrytis rot.

Blanc The French word for 'white'.

Blanc de Blanc A French term used traditionally for champagne when it has been made only from white grapes, but now widely used for other wines as well.

Blanc de Noir This term, literally 'white from black', refers to wine made from red grapes. The skins, however, are removed at the time of pressing and thus they impart only the slightest blush to the wine. Blanc de Noir wine is lighter in colour than a rosé – it is a lovely salmon pink. There are some excellent Cabernet Sauvignon Blanc de Noirs available, but a blend of cultivars may also be used. Pinotage is probably the most commonly used grape at the moment. These wines should be drunk young and always served chilled.

Blending The art of mixing together wines or spirits to obtain a better product, or uniformity from year to year, to create a specific style of wine, or to enhance the final product by bringing together each element with its own outstanding feature, thus creating a masterpiece.

Bloom The waxy, water-resistant layer which forms on the outside of ripe grapes and in which yeast cells are found.

Body Used for a 'mouth-filling' wine of good substance which contains a high quantity of 'solid' matter or extract in solution. A wine lacking in body tends to be thin or watery-tasting.

Botrytis cinerea (Noble rot) This is a fungus disease which attacks ripe grapes under certain conditions of temperature and humidity. During the growth of the fungi, the mycelia penetrate the skin and in feeding to develop the botrytis growth extract moisture from the grapes, causing them to shrivel and to increase in relative sugar content. This phenomenon has been turned to good account by wine makers, who use 'noble rot' to make rich, sweet wines. The classic Sauternes, Trockenbeerenauslese and Tokay wines of Europe as well as the local Nederburg Edelkeur and various other noble late harvest wines are made from grapes affected by this co-operative fungus. If the fungus does not have optimum weather conditions it can rapidly turn to vulgar rot and absolutely ruin the harvest.

Bottle age Mellow development observed in the bouquet of a wine and in its smoothness across the palate.

Bottle sickness A temporary loss of flavour and bouquet usually found straight after bottling – it is caused by too much contact between air and wine at the bottling stage.

Bouquet The fragrance of the wine as it arises when first poured into the glass. Unlike the aroma, which is the wine's memory of the natural ingredients of the grape, the bouquet is specifically a product of the fermentation process and of the complex reactions of ageing and mellowing, both in the cask and in the bottle. Involving the subtle combinations of esters, tannins, alcohols and aldehydes, its assessment is an important part of the wine-tasting process.

Brandy A spirit distilled from wine and usually made anywhere that wine is made. The world's most celebrated brandy comes from Cognac in France where it is distilled in pot-stills; in South Africa the law requires that a minimum 30% of a brandy blend be distilled in pot-stills. Elsewhere the word is also used to refer to distillates from other fruits besides grapes – peaches, apples, pears and cherries, among others. In such cases the name of the brandy will be qualified by that of the fruit concerned.

Breathing *see also* Decanting. A wine is allowed to 'breathe' after it has been opened as contact with the air animates the bouquet and enhances its effect. This applies particularly to red wines. The wine must be decanted for this process to have its full effect; leaving the wine in the bottle after drawing the cork is a useless exercise. It is important to know which wines should be allowed to breathe, for not all benefit from the treatment. Overlong exposure to air, however, leads to oxidation. Very old wine should be drunk soon after

decanting, otherwise the wine can literally 'fall apart'.

Brut The French word for 'dry' as applied to wines, in particular to sparkling wines and dry champagnes with a sugar content of 1,5% or less.

Bung The 'cork' for a wine cask, usually made of wood, but can also be of earthenware, glass or other patent material.

Butt From the old French *bot*, this is a barrel or cask for holding approximately 400 litres of wine.

Butyric The smell of rancid butter or spoiled Camembert cheese.

Callus The woody outgrowth which develops and joins scion and rootstock in the formation of a graft.

Cane The mature shoot of the vine.

Cap During the fermentation of red grapes the carbon dioxide gas which is released during the reaction forms as bubbles around the solid matter of skins and pips in the must, lifting it to the surface. There it forms a floating layer known as a 'cap'. This has to be frequently roused or broken up so that contact between the skins and the liquid can be re-established.

Capsule The plastic or lead cap which protects the cork of bottled wines.

Caramel Burnt sugar added to spirits as colouring matter; it is tasteless and virtually odourless.

Carbonated wines These are sparkling wines in which the bubbles or carbon dioxide have been introduced under pressure.

Carbonic maceration Vinification without crushing grapes. Whole bunches are placed into pressure tanks and intercellular fermentation under oxygen-free conditions occurs. This process is used for Beaujolais Nouveau production.

Cask A wooden wine barrel, varying in capacity; it is usually made of oak and bound with steel hoops.

Cellar A suitable place (cool, quiet and away from direct sunlight) for the storage of wine, not necessarily underground.

Chambre To bring a wine to the temperature of the room in which it is to be drunk by letting it stand there for 24 hours or so.

Champagne The classic sparkling wine from the Pinot Noir and Chardonnay grapes, made by the *méthode Champenoise* to specific atmospheric pressures and sugar content. The 'singing wine' has its own separate mythology and the pop of champagne corks is a natural accompaniment to festive occasions. Champagne is a specific region of France and the term 'champagne' should only be used for the wines of this area. However, it is often used loosely to describe any sparkling wine.

Chaptalization *see* Sugaring.

Character As with many wine-tasting terms, this one is generated by human analogy. A wine of character is like a person of character: unique, individual, distinctive.

Clarity A wine must be attractive to the eye, clean and bright, not cloudy or dull.

Clean A wine smell without any foreign or off odours.

Clone Vegetatively reproduced plants from one superior parent plant.

Cloying Excessively sweet taste, usually that of a wine of low acidity.

Coarse A generally dismissive word for a badly made, low quality wine of rough texture.

Cold fermentation This is the general name for a number of related technical processes all having the same basic principle, that of cooling and so controlling, often with the use of refrigerated water, the fermenting must of white wine. Its use counteracts the effects of the high temperatures generated by fermentation when weather temperatures are such that they cannot cool the reaction.

Common A flat and dull taste – although a drinkable wine.

Cooked or burnt Wines which have been subjected either to a heating process to extract colour or to pasteurization.

Co-operative Any one of about 70 organizations in the local winelands, now producing about 85% of the South African good wine crop. The member-farmers deliver their grapes at harvest time to the Co-operative's winery, where they are made into wine. Some of this wine may be bottled under the Co-operative's own label, but in general the bulk is supplied to the KWV or to one of the large producing wholesalers.

Corked wine, corky wine, corkiness All meaning the same thing: microbial infection in the cork introduces a disagreeable smell and taste into the wine. This is fortunately a rare occurrence and if you sniff a cork after opening a bottle of wine and it smells of wine and not of dirty mould all is well.

Crisp Good acid; a clean and refreshing wine.

Crushing The first stage of the wine-making process, when the skins of the grapes are mechanically split to release the juice.

Crust Sediment precipitated on the inside of a bottle of wine, especially port, after long bottle maturation.

Cultivar Also called the varietal or variety of grape. One of the many different cultivated vine-types, each of which yields its own characteristic wine.

Cuvée Literally, the contents of a cask, generally applied to a specially prepared blend of wine.

Dead arm *(Phomopsis viticola)* This is a vine disease indicated by the formation of small cankers on the basal parts of the shoots and small black spots bordered with yellow on the leaves.

Decanting Slowly pouring a wine into a decanter sometimes enhances and releases the aroma and bouquet of a wine (see Breathing). The main reason for decanting is to separate a wine from its sediment and therefore care must be taken that any sediment in the wine is not disturbed during the operation (a light, traditionally a candle, under the neck of the bottle enables one to see if the sediment is moving).

Delicate Balance and charm in quality light wine.

Demijohn A wicker-covered wine container with a large body and small neck.

Deposit A sediment that is commonly precipitated from red wines during their normal development in the bottle and is completely harmless; it comprises pigment and tannin complexes. Some rich white wines might also form slight sediments which are usually made up of tartrate deposits.

Deposit The money one puts down on a jug! Refunded on return of the empty.

Depth Richness with many flavour nuances that linger in the mouth.

Dessert wine Wine to which a small amount of brandy or spirit has been added to arrest fermentation and to preserve the unfermented grape sugar which lends the wine its sweetness.

Dionysus The ancient Greek god of wine, vegetation and fertility, the son of Zeus and Semele. A happy traveller, he was later adopted by the Romans as Bacchus.

Distillation When wine is heated to a certain temperature the alcohol vaporizes with little or no vaporization of the water. In the process of distillation, the vapour is collected and cooled, condensing to form a colourless and, with high refining, almost odourless spirit.

Downy mildew *(Plasmopara viticola)* A vine disease which appears as a white downy mass of spores on the underside of the vine leaf. On the upper surface of the leaf an oily-looking spot appears; this is at first light yellow, but later turns a reddish colour. A white powdery covering may also appear on young bunches of grapes, causing them to shrivel and drop. The disease is treated with copper oxychloride and a variety of fungicides.

Dry wine A natural wine in which the grape sugar has been converted into alcohol during fermentation, leaving no fermentable sugars.

Dull Uninteresting and insipid, although drinkable.

Dumb The smell of an undeveloped wine which, however, has promise of quality.

Dundee soils *see* Alluvial soils

Duplex soils These soils exhibit a marked contrast of texture between topsoil and subsoil. A large proportion of the soils in the western Cape Coastal Region are made up of three local types of Duplex soils, the Kroonstad, Sterkspruit and Estcourt forms, which feature a relatively sandy topsoil over an underlying clay pan. In the Kroonstad form these two layers are separated by a further layer of *ouklip*, which is a rough, iron-bearing pan.

Earthy An earth-like taste but not necessarily derived from soil.

Egrappoir A machine for removing stalks and crushing grapes at the start of the wine-making process.

Elegant A description of a graceful and finely made wine which is well-balanced and shows special qualities and finesse.

Estate In terms of the Wine of Origin legislation, this is a wine farm which both grows its own grapes and makes wine from them in its own cellar. The wines are generally bottled on the Estate, although some Estate wines are bottled and matured by wholesalers.

Estcourt soils *see* Duplex soils

Esterification This is the production of esters in a wine. One of the reasons for the softening of a wine with age is the reduction of acidity by the process of esterification.

Esters Responsible for the aroma and bouquet of a wine, these are sweet-smelling compounds which derive from the fruit and from reactions between acids and ethyl alcohol during maturation.

Extract The soluble solids that are non-volatile and non-sugars.

Farewell A term used to describe the flavour as well as the length of time that the flavour remains in the mouth after swallowing the wine.

Fat A 'fat' wine is one showing considerable 'body' or substance when held in the mouth; it is usually high in glycerol and grape extract.

Feel The term used to describe the sensation that the wine gives in the mouth before swallowing.

Fermentation The chemical and biochemical reaction upon which all wine making is based. Derived from the Latin *fervere*, to boil, the word describes the process whereby sugar in the grape is transformed through the action of yeast into alcohol and gaseous carbon dioxide. Although fermentation has been observed since the dawn of history, it was thought to be a wholly spontaneous phenomenon until Pasteur showed in 1864 that it was the work of living organisms – more specifically of zymase, the enzyme of the naturally occurring yeasts found in the waxy 'bloom' on the surface of the grape. In most cellars and wineries today the reaction is carefully and scientifically controlled.

A further kind of fermentation can occur in respect of wines. This is secondary, or malo-lactic fermentation. Malic acid is a natural acid present in most fruit and vegetables. By the action of bacteria the malic acid which is contained in wine is converted into the milder lactic acid with the release of carbon dioxide gas. This happens without adverse effects provided it takes place before the wine is bottled; after bottling gasiness and off-odours may be formed in the bottle.

Fernwood soils *see* Structureless soils

Filtering In the wine-making process the wine is clarified prior to bottling by passing it through any one of many different types of filter.

Fine A general expression of superior quality – but probably the most over-used expression in the wine taster's vocabulary.

Finesse The breed, class or natural distinction which separates a wine from its more ordinary fellows. A wine lacking in finesse will be heavy and dull. A great wine is often one which is full-bodied, yet possesses an innate finesse.

Fining This is the traditional method of clarifying wine (called *collage* by French wine makers) known since Roman times, whereby certain substances are added to the wine after fermentation to precipitate insoluble suspended particles such as dead yeast cells. These gradually settle in the form of a sediment, or lees, on the bottom of the tank, leaving the wine clear and bright. Examples of fining agents used in the modern winery are bentonite, gelatine and, more traditionally, egg albumen. *See also* Isinglass.

Finish The term is sometimes used to describe how a wine 'finishes' in the mouth; in other words, the aftertaste. Finish can also refer to the final preparation of the wine before bottling, for example, polish filtration, sweetening with grape juice or sweet reserve, or final sulphur dioxide adjustment.

Fino The palest, lightest, most delicate, and generally the driest of sherries.

Firm A term usually applied to the finish of a wine, and denoting the impact of tannin and possibly acid.

Fixed acids *see* Acids

Flat Dull, insipid, often lacking acidity.

Flor This word, derived from the Spanish for 'flower', refers to a particular kind of yeast, *Saccharomyces beticus*, used especially in the making of sherry. Soon after fermentation it forms a white film or 'flower' on the surface of the must, covering a large surface area as the casks are only three-quarters full. The yeast multiplies rapidly under these conditions, covering the surface and separating the wine from the air as it gradually forms a layer which is up to 15 millimetres deep and resembles chunky cottage cheese. It has an important effect on the final bouquet and flavour of the sherry.

Flowery A term of praise when applied to the bouquet of certain cultivars, particularly used for white wines.

Fortification The addition of alcohol to wine to raise its strength. Port, sherry, Muscadel, Marsala and Madeira are examples of fortified wines.

Fruit(y) Descriptive of a wine with an aroma reminiscent of other fruits; either of a single fruit such as guava, apple or pineapple, or a combination. If the wine has the aroma of grapes then it is described as having a 'varietal' or 'grapey' nose.

Fruity can also indicate acidity and as such show a freshness of taste in young wines. This attribute is lost with age.

Free-run juice As opposed to the press-juice, this is the juice which is released at the start of the cellar process when the grapes are mechanically ruptured but not pressed.

Fresh Having natural vitality and youthful character.

Fruit acid *see* Acids

Full Refers to a wine of good body, possessing a heavy degree of substance.

Gewürz Spicy flavour or bouquet.

Glycerine A byproduct of fermentation which adds to the texture of a white wine.

Good wine This phase is used in South Africa not only to describe the wine, but to distinguish it from rebate wine, which is distilled for brandy. Because 'good wine' is good does not necessarily indicate that rebate wine is of poor quality; on the contrary, it must reach exacting standards before being accepted for brandy production.

Grafting Developed in answer to the phylloxera aphid, this is a technique in which a scion of the desired cultivar is allowed to form an organic union with a phylloxera-resistant rootstock. Various kinds of cuts – long-whip, short-whip, Jupiter and Omega are examples commonly used – have been evolved to ensure the best join at the interface of the two parts. Virtually all modern vineyards contain only grafted vines.

Grapey The grapes of certain vines – the Muscat and Concord grapes are examples – tend to transmit their special flavour to the wine; in general, though, a wine should taste like wine, not like fresh grapes.

Great An accolade: as a taster's term it should not be used lightly, but reserved for the most outstanding of the best wines, those without flaw, perfect in balance and possessing real character and distinction of their own.

Green Acid-type smell of the unripe, raw or young wine.

Hard Refers to an austere wine, lacking in suppleness. This is not necessarily a fault, since many excellent wines are hard in their youth. Time to age and mature is the answer to a hard wine.

Harsh A harsh wine is one in which 'hardness' is carried to an extreme and is usually accompanied by astringency. In red wines, providing other qualities are present, it can be an indication of youth and the harshness will disappear with time.

Hazy Often the first symptom of a 'sick' wine. A good wine should be clear and brilliant; a hazy wine may be reasonably clear initially but will soon develop the cloudiness of a poorly made product.

Heady High in alcohol – intoxicating.

Heavy A full-bodied wine without delicacy or distinction; it is an unfavourable word in general but less severe than 'coarse'.

Hectare Metric measure of area of 10 000 square metres or 2,471 acres.

Hectolitre Metric measure of volume equal to 100 litres and the equivalent of 22,3 British Imperial Gallons or 26,42 US Gallons.

Hock A general term used in nineteenth-century England for wines produced along the banks of the River Rhine – it is an abbreviation of the name of the town of Hochheim.

Honest No great attribute, but a good, clean, well-made wine.

Hot Not to be confused with 'hot' as in 'peppery'; this term is descriptive of some wines, usually dry wine of high alcohol content, made from grapes grown in very warm regions. It is often considered a negative quality and is sometimes associated with wines coloured, or those that appear to be coloured, with caramel.

Hot bottling Bottling wine immediately after pasteurization, while it is still hot; used mainly for inexpensive everyday wines

Husk The skin of the grape.

Hutton and Clovelly soils *see* Structureless soils

Hybrid A cross between an American and a European vine achieved by cross-pollination as opposed to grafting.

Hydrogen sulphide The smell of rotten eggs found in red wines resulting from the reduction of sulphur dioxide or elemental sulphur. Detectable in tiny quantities (one part per million); when bound into the wine it becomes mercaptan.

Hydrometer An instrument for measuring the specific gravity of a liquid, that is, its density relative to that of water. In wine making a hydrometer is used for measuring the sugar content of a must and the sugar and alcohol content of a wine. (See page 328.)

Implicitly sweet Apparent sweet taste from elements other than sugar, e.g. glycerol.

Inky or metallic A tinny or metallic taste

Hydrometer Graduations			
Specific Gravity	Degrees Baume	Degrees Twadell	Degrees Brix/Balling
1,005	0,7	1,0	1,3
1,010	1,4	2,0	2,5
1,015	2,1	3,0	3,8
1,075	10,0	15,0	18,5
1,080	10,7	16,0	19,8
1,085	11,3	17,0	20,8
1,090	11,9	18,0	22,0
1,095	12,5	19,0	23,0
1,100	13,1	20,0	24,2
1,105	13,7	21,0	25,3
1,110	14,3	22,0	26,4

derived from the presence of tannate of iron.

Isinglass Sometimes used by the wine maker as a fining agent to clear a hazy white wine. It is made from the swim bladder of fresh water fish, especially sturgeon, and is a form of gelatine.

Kroonstad soils *see* Duplex soils

Lactic acid *see also* Fermentation. A byproduct of fermentation and therefore present in wine in small quantities, lactic acid can also be formed as a result of malo-lactic fermentation.

Late Harvest, Special Late Harvest, Noble Late Harvest The term 'Late Harvest' is a specifically South African usage and refers to a sweetish, medium- to full-bodied white wine with sugar levels of more than 20 but less than 30 grams per litre. Special Late Harvest wines require a residual sugar content of between 20 and 50 grams a litre, obtained without the addition of any sweetening. Noble Late Harvest wines are made from grapes harvested at a sugar count of at least 28° Balling, and showing a residual sugar content after fermentation of more than 50 grams a litre. *See also* Sugar Level Laws.

Lathuis A 'shade-house', it houses the young vine at an interim stage in its progress from nursery to vineyard. The lathuis, made of vertical wooden slats set at intervals, allows the young rooted vines to receive sun and air but protects them from the force of the wind.

Leaguer One leaguer equalled slightly more than 577 litres, or 127 gallons. However, the traditional measure of Cape wine is now superceded by metrication.

Lees During fermentation and maturation wines deposit a heavy, coarse sediment of insoluble matter at the bottom of the tank; this residue or 'lees' is left behind when the wine is 'racked', an operation which is performed several times before the wine is bottled.

Legs Wine vernacular for the drops which appear on the side of the glass after the wine has been swirled.

Light The opposite of full-bodied or heavy.

Light wines are usually slightly lower in alcohol than full rich wines, and though they often possess grace and charm, rarely have the complexity of a great wine.

Lime The calcium oxide content of the soil is important to the growth of the vine in that it balances the acidity of the soil. It can occur naturally or can be artificially introduced to the vineyard where it is lacking.

Liqueur A strongly alcoholic liquor, sweetened and flavoured with aromatic extracts of fruit and plants, intended to be drunk after a meal.

Little or poor Hardly any bouquet or aroma in a wine lacking character or quality.

Lively When a wine stimulates the palate with a pleasant but not dominant acidity; a wine lacking in this quality tends to be flat or dead.

Long Denotes the capacity of the flavours of the wine to linger in the mouth and palate after the wine has been swallowed.

Luscious Soft, sweet, fruity, ripe and fat – all in balance with each other.

Maderization A condition of oxidation which afflicts white wine which has been kept for too long or held at too high a temperature. The wine turns a gold-brown colour, and acquires a characteristic 'baked' taste. It is a requirement of Madeira style wines, hence the name.

Malic acid *see* Acids

Malo-lactic fermentation *see* Fermentation

Maturation The process of ageing wine and spirits until they reach peak condition and are ready for drinking.

Measures (see Table)

Meaty Heavy, rich, almost chewable

Mealy bugs These are lice which form a sticky, shiny deposit on the bunches of grapes, making them unfit for normal wine-making purposes. The deposit attracts ants which protect the mealy bug from its natural enemy, the ladybird. Spraying the ants leaves a clear field for the ladybirds, providing a natural control on the mealy bugs.

Medium dry Containing traces of sugar but tasting predominantly dry.

Medium sweet Tasting quite sweet but not a dessert wine.

Mellow A rounded and well-matured wine.

Mercaptan Produced by ethyl mercaptan and ethyl sulphides in wine deriving from hydrogen sulphide and produced during the fermentation process. It manifests itself in a range of unpleasant odours ranging from burnt rubber to garlic, onion, gamy meat, stale cabbage and asparagus. While hydrogen sulphide can easily be removed, once mercaptan is formed it is much more difficult to eliminate.

Méthode champenoise The method of making sparkling wine employed in Champagne in which the all-important second fermentation takes place in the bottle in which the wine is ultimately sold. The method is being used more and more in the Cape.

Mildew *see* Downy mildew *and* Powdery mildew

Millerandage The occurrence of small and immature grapes among the normally developing grapes in the bunch.

Mispah *see* Shallow soils

Mouldy An unmistakable smell or taste caused by rotten grapes or unclean casks.

Mousse The froth or foam produced when perlé or sparkling wines are poured.

Mousy The smell of mouse droppings – a sign of bacteriological disease affecting only wine in cask.

Must Fermenting grape juice.

Measures	Metric	USA	Imperial
Half pint	284 ml	8 fl. oz	10 fl. oz
Pint	568 ml	16 fl. oz	20 fl. oz
Quart	1,136 litres	32 fl. oz	40 fl. oz (2 pints)
Gallon	4,546 litres	128 fl. oz	160 fl. oz (8 pints)
Half bottle wine	(37 cl)		13⅓ fl. oz
Bottle wine	(75 cl)		26⅔ fl. oz
One litre wine	(100 cl)		35½ fl. oz
Magnum	(1,5 litres)		2 bottles
Jeroboam	(3 litres)		4 bottles
Rehoboam (1 gallon)	(4,5 litres)		6 bottles
Methuselah	(6 litres)		8 bottles
Imperiale (as above)			
Salmanazar (2 gallons)	(9 litres)		12 bottles
Balthazar	(12 litres)		16 bottles
Nebuchadnezzar	(15 litres)		20 bottles
Hogshead varies from 46 gallons to 65 gallons (210 to 300 litres)			
Butt (Sherry)	(491 litres)		108 gallons
Pipe (Port)	(523 litres)		115 gallons
Pipe (Madeira)	(418 litres)		92 gallons
Pipe (Marsala)	(423 litres)		93 gallons
Tun	(955 litres)		210 gallons

(All cask sizes vary slightly as they are handmade)

Musty A musty odour and flavour, often the result of poor cellar techniques related to uncleanliness.

Natural wine As distinguished from fortified wine, this is wine to which no alcohol is added.

Nematodes Otherwise known as eelworms, these are microscopic worm-shaped pests which attack the roots of the vine, causing damage similar to that of phylloxera; unlike phylloxera, they prefer moist and sandy soils. Fumigation of the vineyard soil before new plantings and the use of resistant rootstock effectively control nematodes.

Neutral Having no positive or marked physical characteristics.

Noble Can be used when referring to wine or to certain grape varieties. A noble variety of grape is one capable of giving outstanding wine under optimum conditions and, within reason, good wine almost wherever it is planted. A noble wine is one that will be recognized as exceptional quality even by a novice wine drinker.

Noble rot *see* Botrytis cinerea

Nose Wine jargon for the aroma or bouquet of a wine. It can be average, good, excellent, disappointing or bad.

Nutty An aroma and flavour reminiscent of hazels and other nuts. The term is usually used in describing sherries.

Oak This is the preferred wood used for the casks and barrels in which wine is matured. All the finest red wines, most of the fortified wines and some white wines owe part of their quality to the flavour imparted by the oak.

Oaky An odour of oak apparent in wines aged too long in casks. It is desirable in fine red table wines but is unpleasant when excessive and especially so in white table wines.

Oenology The science of wine and wine making – that is, of the cellar as opposed to the vineyard, which is the province of viticulture.

Off The broadest and least specific term of disapproval which can be levelled at a wine; it is a permanent fault.

Off-taste An unclean foreign or tainted flavour.

Oïdium *see* Powdery mildew

Olfactory Pertaining to the sense of smell.

Oloroso One of the two basic types of Spanish sherry – Fino being the other. It has a recognizable and typical bouquet and is darker in colour than the Fino and fuller-bodied. Oloroso sherries are developed in 'soleras', but without the use of the flor yeasts which give the Finos their special character.

Organoleptic This term is gaining currency amoung wine tasters and refers to the ability to perceive a sensory stimulus, for example taste, touch and smell.

Overripe A raisin-like odour and taste.

Oxidized The smell is generally found in white table wines which have been in bottle for many years. This odour is usually accompanied by a darkening in colour.

Oxidation Various oxidative reactions occur at every stage in the life of the wine. Excessive oxidation, usually from prolonged contact with the air, causes browning of the wine and a marked and unpleasant flavour.

Ouklip *see* Duplex soils

Palate Technically, the roof of the mouth, though it can be used as a compliment to a wine taster who is said to have a 'good palate'.

Pasteurization This is a process of sterilizing wine (it is used for other commodities such as milk as well) by heating it to a temperature of about 80° C (185° F) for one minute; this destroys micro-organisms in the wine, making it micro-biologically stable. The treatment is not usually given to high quality wines, but to those destined for early consumption. A method known as 'flash' pasteurization is more commonly used in 'hot' bottling where the wine is raised to the required temperature only momentarily.

Penetrating A powerful content smell on the nostrils – indicating high alcohol and volatile esters formed from malic, acetic and tartaric acids.

Peppery A raw harshness – due to immature or unsettled compounds which have not yet intermingled.

Perlé, Perlant Somewhere between a still wine and a sparkling wine, this is one to which some bubbles of carbon dioxide have been introduced, giving it a slight effervescence.

Perfumed An aroma usually derived from the grape, e.g. Muscadel, Traminer.

Pétillant Originally used only by the French, this word is now used to describe wines which, like perlé wines, contain a little gas, causing a prickle in the mouth and giving them a slight lift. These wines may not have a pressure in excess of two atmospheres, while most have far less – in contrast to sparkling wines, including champagne, which contain a minimum of four atmospheres pressure.

pH This is a measure of the hydrogen-ion concentration of a liquid and records its relative degree (not the amount) of acidity or alkalinity. The neutral point is a pH of 7 (that of water); the higher the reading above 7 the greater the alkalinity, the lower the reading below 7 the greater the acidity. The optimum pH range for musts and wine is from 3,1 to 3,4 but some wines show an acid reading as 'high' as 2,7 and others as 'low' as 3,9.

Phylloxera (*Phylloxera vastatrix*, now sometimes classified as *Dactylasphaera vitifoliae*) An aphid or plant louse which attacks, at different stages of its life cycle, both the roots and branches of the vine which, unable to heal the lesions, succumbs to secondary infection. It originated in the eastern part of the United States where it lived on the local wild vines which were resistant to its predations. Released accidentally in Europe, it caused widespread destruction of the vineyards; this was followed by the devastation of the vineyards of the Cape. Most modern vines are grown on phylloxera-resistant rootstocks derived originally from the American indigenous vines; no permanent chemical control of phylloxera has yet been found.

Pipe A cask made of oak and tapered sharply towards the ends, it is used to mature port. It comes in varying sizes, the most common holding 522 litres; the standard Madeira pipe is considerably smaller. Those used in South Africa are imported from Europe.

Piquant Fresh, mouth-watering bouquet – a result of balanced acidity.

Plastering In sherry production this is the addition of calcium sulphate, or gypsum, to grapes before fermentation, increasing the total acidity and improving the colour and clarity of the resulting wine; it is a normal procedure in the making of sherry and certain other wines.

Polishing The final filtration of a wine before bottling.

Port A sweet, heavily fortified dessert wine. It originated in the region of Oporto, Portugal – hence the name – and some of the best port still comes from a delimited district in the upper Douro Valley in northern Portugal.

Positive A marked or noticeable fragrance, as opposed to 'little' or 'dumb'.

Powdery mildew (Oïdium) This vine ailment first made its appearance in the Cape vineyards in the 1850s. It is a form of fungus which appears on the lower surface of the leaf of the vine as small spots and on the upper surface as a white, powdery, cobweb-like growth. The grapes are its normal target, though the shoots may be affected as well. It causes mature berries to crack and dry up, opening the way to further micro-organism infections, such as *Botrytis cinerea*. It is controlled with sulphur and a number of other modern compounds.

Premier Grand Cru A term used in South Africa as a name for a class of blended dry wines. This wine should be as dry as vinification techniques allow.

Pungent Refers to a very aromatic wine with a high level of volatiles.

Punt Indentation at the base of a bottle originally introduced to strengthen the bottle.

Racking Drawing off or decanting clear must or wine after allowing the lees to settle.

Red wine Made by fermenting red grapes

in the presence of their skins so that the pigments in the skin can colour the wine. Red wines usually contain more tannin than whites and are often aged for a year or two in wooden barrels before being bottled.

Residual sugar All grapes contain sugar and it is the conversion of this sugar by yeast into alcohol and carbon dioxide that gives wine. If not all the sugar is converted and some remains behind in the wine, this portion is termed residual sugar.

Remuage An essential operation in the making of champagne, this is the slight shaking and turning of the bottles in their racks, or *pupitres*, so that the sediment is brought down against the cork. After this the neck of the bottle is frozen and the temporary stopper removed, bringing with it the sediment locked in ice, before the wine is made ready for sale.

Rhoicissus capensis An indigenous vine of the Cape, encountered by the early Dutch pioneers.

Rich A wine which has an abundance of bouquet and flavour. A symphony of fruitiness, flavour, alcohol and grape extract well blended together.

Ripe A mature wine ready for drinking.

Robust A tough wine – although full-bodied and well-rounded.

Rootstock One of a wide range of especially developed phylloxera-resistant vine-stocks onto which the scion of the fruiting cultivar is grafted.

Rosé A 'pink' wine. It is normally made on the same basis as a red wine, that is, by leaving the heavily pigmented skins of the red grapes in the fermenting must till sufficient colour is extracted. In a rosé wine the period of contact is much shorter than for a red wine, just enough to give the wine its characteristic tinge.

Rouge The French word for 'red'; used in most countries for a red wine.

Rough Lacking in finesse. A coarse, rough-edged wine, resulting from high tannin content, which is harsh and not particularly pleasant to drink.

Rounded Without a major defect, the wine is well-balanced and complete – never used to describe a poor wine. When described thus, a wine is not necessarily a wine of great quality.

Rubbery The most common manifestation of hydrogen sulphide in the form of mercaptan.

Saccharometer An instrument for measuring the sugar content of the grape juice or must; it is often calibrated in degrees Balling.

Saccharomyces A generic name for the various yeasts used for wine fermentation.

Sack Sir John Falstaff's favourite beverage was sack, the name by which sherry was known in Elizabethan England.

Scion A cutting of a vine cane bearing fertile buds, which is grafted onto the rootstock cultivar to become the fruiting part of the vine.

Sediment The deposit or precipitate of crystals and other solids which most red wines tend to throw as they are aged; it has no effect on the wine.

Severe Hard and probably immature.

Shallow soils These are soils which feature a layer of topsoil directly over rock. Otherwise known as 'Mispah', they are not normally suitable for grape-growing unless the underlying rock can be broken or ripped.

Sharp An unpleasant prickly acidic taste.

Sherry A fortified wine, originally from a specific delimited district in southern Spain round the town of Jerez de la Frontera, between Seville and Cadiz.

Short Lacking in finish. The aftertaste is with you very briefly, whereas in a really good wine it lingers.

Shy bearer A cultivar which produces a small crop of high quality grapes.

Semi-sweet A term used in South Africa to describe wines that have an excess of four grams per litre of residual sugar but not more than 30 grams. In practice wines so described normally have about 20 grams per litre and are usually white.

Sick Usually cloudy, with an unpleasant bouquet and an 'off' odour.

Silky Particularly smooth and fine-textured.

Skin The peel or outer covering of a grape, often called the 'husk'.

Smooth A soft texture without rough edges.

Snout beetle These are insects which eat young shoots, leaf petioles and young flower clusters, and, given the chance, can devour all the green parts of the plant. They spend the daylight hours in the soil or under the bark of the vines, coming out at night to eat. They are controlled with pesticides from October onwards.

Soft Not harsh, the acidity and tannin being well-balanced; however, this wine could still be flat and dull.

Soil series The classification of soil types based on texture and chemical composition.

Solera A system by which all quality sherries are matured and progressively blended in tiers of casks; the object is to produce wines of consistent quality from year to year.

Sound Without abnormal qualities or defects, in other words a well-made wine. After this general comment a taster would go into more detail of bouquet and other qualities, defining the wine in greater depth and precision.

Sour Not to be confused with dry, tart or astringent, this term is used to describe a wine that has been spoiled by acetic acid and is practically vinegar.

Sour rot (*Rhizopus* rot) Like black-mould rot, it is usually a secondary infection following an attack of botrytis rot. It is controlled with the use of rot-resistant varieties and with fungicides.

Sour-sweet Disagreeable taste associated with lactic bacteria development in fortified sweet wines.

Sparkling Carbon dioxide gas effervescence in wine.

Spicy Often used to describe a wine with an especially pronounced aroma or taste; Gewürztraminer is perhaps the best-known example with its herb-like smell.

Stabilisation The chilling of a white wine to near-freezing point to precipitate tartaric crystals.

Stalky The smell of damp twigs – resulting from too long contact of the must with grape stalks during wine making – undesirable in white wines, although sometimes desirable in reds.

Steely Extremely 'hard'.

Stein Should not be confused with the cultivar Steen and its wine, though Steen, otherwise known as Chenin Blanc, is normally the basis of the local Stein wines. The name applies specifically to the style in which the wine is made, being semi-sweet with over four grams of sugar per litre and usually between 12 and 20 grams, and with a fruity flavour.

Stemmy Fortunately not often found. This term would be used if a wine had acquired an unpalatable, harsh taste because of extracts released when skins and stalks are fermented in the must.

Sterkspruit soils *see* Duplex soils

Stretch A wine is said to stretch when, after the bottle has been opened, it takes up oxygen and develops its aroma and bouquet.

Structureless soils These are well-drained soils without restrictive layers in the subsoil which would impede growth. They are therefore generally suitable for grape-growing. Two important forms of structureless soils are found in the Cape, the Hutton and Clovelly and the Fernwood forms. Hutton and Clovelly are well-drained red and yellow soils, while Fernwood soils are deep, dry and sandy.

Sturdy Lacking the finesse of a robust wine.

Sugaring Called *Chaptalisation* by the French, this is the adding of sugar to must to bring the final alcohol content obtained by fermentation up to a determined level. It is forbidden in South Africa, California and Italy (where weather conditions normally give good sugar content to the grapes), but authorized in France and Germany. An exception is usually made for champagne and sparkling wines where the secondary fermentation is usually effected by the addition of refined sugar.

Sugar level laws
Regulations strictly define any claims made on a label to the wine's degree of dryness or sweetness:

Extra Dry
Residual sugar not more than 2,5 grams per litre.

Dry Wine
Residual sugar not more than 4,0 grams per litre.

Semi-Dry Wine
Residual sugar more than four but not more than 12 grams per litre (if more than nine the total acid content shall not be more than two grams per litre lower than the sugar content).

Semi-Sweet Wine
Residual sugar more than four but not more than 30 grams per litre (if sugar less than 12 grams per litre then the total acid content must be lower than for semi-dry wine).

Late Harvest
Residual sugar more than 20 but less than 30 grams per litre.

Special Late Harvest
Residual sugar more than 20 but less than 50 grams per litre.

Noble Late Harvest
Residual sugar more than 50 grams per litre.

Further requirements for Late Harvest wines are stated in the Government Gazette of December 19, 1980.

Late Harvest Wine
a. Shall be obtained by the complete or partial fermentation of must;
b. Shall not be fortified;
c. Shall have an alcoholic strength of at least 10 per cent alcohol by volume;
d. Shall have a residual sugar content, expressed as invert sugar of more than 20 grams per litre but less than 30 grams per litre, irrespective whether such residual sugar content has been obtained through the addition of sweet must or concentrated must to the wine concerned.

Special Late Harvest wine
a. Shall be produced from must of which the sugar content prior to fermentation is at least 22° Balling: provided that:
1. grapes of a sugar content of less than 21° Balling may not be pressed to obtain such must;
2. such must may not be concentrated (dehydrated);
3. no sweetening agent of any kind whatsoever may be added to such must;
b. Shall be obtained from partial alcoholic fermentation of such must;
c. Shall not be fortified;
d. Shall have an alcoholic strength of at least 10 per cent alcohol by volume;
e. Shall have a residual sugar content of more than 20 grams per litre but not more than 50 grams per litre: provided that such residual sugar content will be derived solely from the grapes from which such wine has been produced, and that no sweetening agent of any kind whatsoever may be added to such wine;
f. Shall have a sugar free extract of not less than 19 grams per litre;
g. Shall possess the character which is distinctive of wine which was produced from grapes which were harvested at a full-ripe stage.

Noble Late Harvest
a. Shall be produced from grapes of which the sugar content at the time of pressing thereof is at least 28° Balling;
b. Shall be obtained from the partial alcoholic fermentatin of the must of such grapes; provided that:
1. such must may not be concentrated (dehydrated);
2. no sweetening agent of any kind whatsoever may be added to such must;
c. Shall not be fortified;
d. Shall have a residual sugar content, expressed as invert sugar, provided that such residual sugar content shall be derived solely from the grapes from which such wine has been produced and that no sweetening agent of any kind whatsoever may be added to such wine;
e. Shall have a sugar free extract of not less than 30 grams per litre;
f. Shall have the character which is distinctive of wine which was produced from grapes that were harvested late.

Sulphur dioxide (SO₂) The use of sulphur to sterilize wine is almost as old as wine itself – in the *Iliad* Achilles fumigated his cup with sulphur before pouring a libation to Zeus. In the modern wine cellar small but effective amounts of sulphur dioxide are used as the standard sterilizing agent for casks and barrels. It is also extensively used in the vineyards to control vine disease. Compared to some European countries the sulphur level in South African wines is very low. For natural table wines the permitted maximum is 200 parts per million. This can be exceeded only in Noble Late Harvests.

Supple Easy to taste yet hard to define; a combination of juiciness; liveliness and good texture.

Sweet Honeyed or grapey sweet smell which is often affirmed in the tasting.

Sweetish Unpleasant sweet taste due to low fruit acid.

Syrupy Very sweet taste – usually low in ethanol.

Table wine A term usually applied to unfortified wine which is drunk with meals. It is normally between 10 and 12% alcohol by volume with a legal maximum in South Africa of 16% alcohol.

Tank carbonation A method of making sparkling wines. Syrup is added to the wine (to obtain the degree of sweetness required), which is then refrigerated. Carbon dioxide is passed through a porous 'candle' and dissolved in the wine as it circulates through the candle. It is then stored in pressurized tanks till the carbon dioxide is fully absorbed, before being filtered and bottled under pressure.

Tannin A group of organic compounds occurring in the bark, wood, roots and stems of many plants and fruits, including the grape. It is most pronounced in red wines which pick up tannin from the skins and pips during maturation in oak barrels.

Tart Sharp and tongue-curling from too much acidity and/or too much tannin.

Tastevin A flat, shallow, silver wine taster's cup that reflects light very effectively. It is widely used in Burgundy for sampling wines, especially young wines from the vat.

Tawny 1. Applied to wines which have turned from red to a brownish colour with maturation.
2. A type of port.

Temperature Wine is sensitive to the temperatures at which it is stored and served. A white wine served too warm is dull and unresponsive, while a red wine which is served too cold seems numbed, almost entirely lacking in bouquet.

Terpene An odourous component found in certain varieties including ageing Rhine Riesling and some Muscats.

Total Acidity (TA) This is the collective amount or volume of fruit and volatile acids in a wine and is usually expressed in this country as grams per litre.

Thin Describes a wine deficient in alcohol and body; it therefore tastes watery and is generally poor.

Tinge Refers to a wine slightly tinted by another colour. It is usually seen at the edge of the wine where wine and glass meet.

Tint A grade of colour: for example, a red wine may have a purple tint when young and a mahogany tint when aged.

Tired A wine which has been aged for too long in the bottle, but is not yet completely oxidized.

Topping 1. The refilling of casks or barrels of young wine to prevent ullage, or air space, between the wine and the bung.
2. The removal of the first 15 to 20 cm of young growing vine shoots, usually by hitting them off with a strong switch or thin stick. (See page 72.)

Tough A full-bodied but immature wine with an excess of tannin.

Training Encouraging a vine plant to grow in the direction most convenient for the farmer, for yield of grapes, for accessibility to the sun and the cooling wind and for convenience of harvesting; most vines are trained onto a trellis.

Trellising A wire-and-wood structure to support the vine through its productive life. A deciduous creeper, the vine takes well to trellising which both provides it with support, keeping it clear of the ground with its moisture and insects, and providing it with access to sun and air and ease of harvesting. The type of trellis used depends on many factors, including the type of soil.

Ullage The empty space above the liquid in an incompletely filled wine container, be it tank, cask or bottle.

Unctuous Cloying and overly sweet.

Unfortified wine A table wine produced naturally, without the addition of spirit.

Vaaljapie Traditionally the wine produced in the Cape for the vineyard labourers. It was usually of indefinite colour (vaal) and a mixture of all varieties. Often turbid.

Varietal *see* Cultivar

Variety *see* Cultivar

Velvety Smooth on the tongue owing to lower acidity and high glycerol content.

Vermouth A fortified herbal wine, dry or sweet, flavoured with aromatic herbs. Most wine-producing countries produce vermouth-type wines.

Vigneron The wine maker or grower of vines.

Vin gris A pale pink wine made, as with Blanc de Noirs, from red grapes. Not to be confused with the cultivar Pinot Gris.

Viniculture 'From soil to glass': a general term covering the whole science of the growing of wine grapes, the making of wine and the wine's preparation for marketing.

Vin ordinaire An inexpensive wine often sold by the glass or carafe. Taken to mean everyday wine, or house wine.

Vinosity The depth or degree to which a wine shows vinous qualities.

Vintage The word 'vintage' originally meant the gathering of the grapes, the gatherer being called the vintager. This meaning is retained but has a further connotation with reference to a vintage wine, which is one of a specific year or a specific gathering.

Vintner Strictly, a wine merchant; but the word is often and incorrectly applied to a wine maker as well.

Viscosity The resistance of wine to flow: light dry wines flow freely (low viscosity) while heavy, thick, sweet ports flow more deliberately and slowly (high viscosity).

Vitaceae The family to which all the genera, species and varieties of the grape vine belong.

Viticulture 'From soil to grapes': the science of grape-growing.

Vitis One of the 10 genera of the family Vitaceae.

Vitis vinifera The most important of the species of the *Vitis* genus, *Vitis vinifera* comprises several thousand varieties throughout the world.

Velkuipe A primitive container used for fermentation in the very early days of the Cape winelands, it consisted of an ox-hide suspended on four poles and filled with fermenting must.

Volatile acidity *see* Acids

Weeper One of a number of terms to describe the effect of wine seeping between the neck of the bottle and the cork. If the bottle has been 'weeping' unnoticed for some time and the level of the wine has dropped considerably, it should be checked for quality and, if acceptable, consumed forthwith; otherwise it should simply be recorked. If this is impossible remove the top of the capsule covering the cork and wipe the cork with a cloth that has been dipped in warm water. Allow it to dry and seal generously with melted candle wax.

Weight A term applied to the feel of the wine in the mouth.

Wine of Origin South African legislation controlling the division of the winelands area into official wine-making Districts, the granting of Estate status to certain farms, and the affixing of an official Wine of Origin seal to about 10% of wines marketed. It is for the producer to apply for the seal if he so wishes. Wines can also be submitted for a Superior rating or seal.

If a cultivar claim is made for a wine in terms of the Wine of Origin legislation it must comply with the provisions laid down by the Wine and Spirit Board. These have changed over the years and are summarized in the table at the foot of this page.

'Witblits' Otherwise known as Dop, White Lightning, Boerblits, Cape Smoke, or Kaapse Smaak. With a potent tradition of its own, Witblits was a rough local brandy which was made by distilling the wet mash of skins and pips left at the bottom of the tank when the fermented must had been run off at the end of the traditional wine-making process. Long outlawed (though the subject of defiant moonshining for many years), it is now making a tentative official come-back. The equivalent of the French 'Marc' and the Italian 'Grappa'.

Woody A table wine which has acquired a specific aroma and flavour from the cask; usually more noticeable in a young wine, it is a criticism if the woody character predominates.

Yeast Unicellular micro-organisms, some of which (*Saccharomyces cerevisiae*) bring about the fermentation of grape juice into the wine.

Yeasty Smelling of yeasts from fermentation.

Yield In viticultural terms, this is the production of a given area of vines, expressed in tonnes of grapes per hectare.

Young Recently bottled, and in the case of some white wine and more red wines, it has not yet reached its peak, but is still improving.

Minimum cultivar content of wine (*see also* Wine of Origin)

Name of cultivar	Date of harvesting	Percentage %
Cabernet Sauvignon Cabernet Franc Pinotage Shiraz Riesling Sylvaner	From September 1, 1973 to June 30, 1976 .... 30 From July 1, 1976 to June 30, 1983 .... 50 From July 1, 1983 75	
Palomino Chenin Blanc Cinsaut	Since September 1, 1973 75	
Muscat d'Alexandrie (White or Red Hanepoot) Muscadel (red or white)	From September 1, 1973 to December 31, 1977 .... 40 From January 1, 1978 to June 30, 1983 .... 50 From July 1, 1983 75	
All other approved vine cultivars	Since September 1, 1973 75	

In the case of Wine of Origin Superior, 100% cultivar was required until December 1977; it is now 75%.

In *all* instances each wine must be characteristic of wine derived from grapes of the cultivar concerned.

INDEX

Bibliography

Burger, J. and Deist, J. (ed.), © 1981.
    Wingerdbou in Suid-Afrika. Cape Town,
    Maskew Miller Limited.
Burman, Jose, 1979. *Wines of Constantia*.
    Cape Town, Human and Rousseau.
De Bosdari, C., 1966. *Wines of the Cape*. Cape
    Town, Balkema.
De Jongh, S. J., © 1981. *Encyclopedia of
    South African Wine*. 2nd ed., rev. and
    supplemented. Durban, Butterworths.
Hughes, David, 1988. South African Wine
    Buyers' Guide. Cape Town, Struik
    Publishers.
Johnson, H., 1977. *The World Atlas of Wine*.
    Enlarged and completely revised ed.
    London, Mitchell Beazley Publishers.

Knox, G., © 1982. *Estate Wines of South
    Africa*. 2nd ed., rev. and enlarged. Cape
    Town, David Philip.
KWV., 1975. *Wine: A Guide for Young People*.
    Paarl, KWV.
Leipoldt, C. Louis, 1952. *Three Hundred
    Years of Cape Wines*. Cape Town,
    Tafelberg.
Opperman, D. J. (ed.), 1968. *Spirit of the Vine*.
    Cape Town, Human and Rousseau.
Orffer, C. J. (ed.), 1979. *Wine Grape Cultivars
    in South Africa*. Cape Town, Human and
    Rousseau.
Perold, I. A., 1926. *Handboek oor Wynbou*.
    Stellenbosch, Pro Ecclesia.
Platter, J., 1988. *John Platter's Book of

South African Wines*. Stellenbosch, John
    and Erica Platter.
Pongrácz, Desiderius, P., 1978. *Practical
    Viticulture*. Cape Town, David Philip.
Rappoport, Simon. Contributions to *Wynboer*,
    April 1978 to May 1983.
Scholtz, Merwe (ed.), 1971. *Red Wine in South
    Africa*. Cape Town, Buren.
Simon, André (ed.), 1973. *Wines of the World*.
    New York, McGraw-Hill.
Simpson, Sally, undated. *Wine of Good Hope*.
    Cape Town, Saayman and Weber.
Van Zyl, D. J., 1975. *Kaapse Wyn en Brande-
    wyn 1795 – 1860*. Cape Town, H A U M.
Wynboer. official journal of KWV, published
    monthly. Paarl, KWV.